S0-AXQ-285

Mastering Symphony

NOT FOR RESALE

Mastering Symphony™

Douglas Cobb

Contributors:
Gena B. Cobb
Steven Cobb

Berkeley • Paris • Düsseldorf • London

Cover design: Stewart/Winner, Inc.
Design and layout: Lisa Amon
Photography: Guy Orcutt
          Mush Emmons

1-2-3 is a trademark of Lotus Development Corporation.
Compaq and Compaq Plus are trademarks of Compaq Computer Corporation.
dBASE II is a trademark of Ashton-Tate.
Epson MX-80, Epson FX-80, Epson FX-100, and Epson LQ-1500 are trademarks of Epson America, Inc.
Hercules Graphics Card is a trademark of Hercules Computer Technology.
IBM, IBM PC/XT, and IBM PC/AT are trademarks of International Business Machines Corporation.
Lotus is a trademark of Lotus Development Corporation.
MS-DOS is a trademark of Microsoft.
Plantronics Colorplus is a trademark of Plantronics Corporation.
SuperCalc is a trademark of Sorcim, Inc.
Symphony is a trademark of Lotus Development Corporation.
VisiCalc is a trademark of VisiCorp.
WordStar is a trademark of MicroPro, Inc.
Zenith Z-17 is a trademark of Zenith Computer Systems.

SYBEX is a registered trademark of SYBEX, Inc.

SYBEX is not affiliated with any manufacturer.

Every effort has been made to supply complete and accurate information. However, SYBEX assumes no responsibility for its use, nor for any infringements of patents or other rights of third parties which would result.

Copyright©1984 SYBEX Inc., 2344 Sixth Street, Berkeley, CA 94710. World rights reserved. No part of this publication may be stored in a retrieval system, transmitted, or reproduced in any way, including but not limited to photocopy, photograph, magnetic or other record, without the prior agreement and written permission of the publisher.

Library of Congress Card Number: 84-51746
ISBN 0-89588-244-2
Printed in the United States of America
20   19   18   17   16   15   14   13   12   11   10   9   8

To my father, Westray Stewart Cobb,
who keeps getting smarter as I get older

ACKNOWLEDGEMENTS

My most sincere thanks to all of the people who made this book possible:

Steven Cobb and Gena Cobb, who were so much more than just contributors

Barbara Gordon, editor, whose hard work allowed the deadline to be met and whose patience and good humor made even the tough moments bearable

The entire *Mastering Symphony* editorial and production team:
Bonnie Gruen, Valerie Robbins, Antonio Padial, Joel Kreisman, Rudolph Langer, Karl Ray, Bret Rohmer, Sarah Seaver, Chris Mockel, Barbara Wetzel, Ellen Campbell, Lisa Amon, Ingrid Owen, Cheryl Vega, Donna Scanlon, Dawn Amsberry, Laura Bennett, Rick Reid, Diane Hobbs, Liz Roberts, David Clark, and Anthony Horton

Rodnay Zaks, for committing the resources

Pam Masterson, who kept the ship afloat

Michelle Cobb, who wondered if she would ever see her husband again

John Rogers and Phil Terry, for keeping the wolves at bay

Chris Morgan, Steve Miller, Ezra Gotthiel, and Brian Stains of Lotus Development Corporation

Joe Campbell, author of *The RS-232 Solution,* published by SYBEX

Ed Harpring of CBM Computer Centers

Douglas Cobb
August 1984

TABLE OF CONTENTS

PART III: SERVICES

PART IV: GRAPHICS

PART VIII: ADVANCED TOPICS

PART
I

INTRODUCTION

CHAPTER ONE

ABOUT THIS BOOK

Early in 1983, Lotus Development Corporation introduced its first product: Lotus 1-2-3. Within a few months, 1-2-3 had zoomed to the top of the software bestseller charts, where it has remained for over a year. From January 1983 to July 1984, an unprecedented 400,000 copies of 1-2-3 were sold. Lotus 1-2-3 has been widely hailed as the most powerful and flexible program ever introduced for microcomputers.

Almost as soon as 1-2-3 was released, however, microcomputer users began to speculate about how Lotus would follow an act like 1-2-3. What would the new product be like? Could they duplicate the success of 1-2-3? Would the new product be merely an upgrade from 1-2-3, or would it be an entirely new program?

Finally, in February 1984, Lotus announced its 1-2-3 encore: Symphony. Although Symphony is in some ways similar to 1-2-3, it is in every way a dramatic improvement over that program. Not only does Symphony significantly improve on the advanced electronic spreadsheet, graphics, and data base management capabilities that made Lotus 1-2-3 so popular; the program also includes an excellent word processor and telecommunications capability, and a sophisticated programming language. The whole package is tied together with a windowing system that is as advanced as any on the market (and some that are not yet available). Symphony offers an unprecedented level of power and sophistication to the microcomputer user. The difference between the two programs is so great that it is probably better to think of Symphony as an entirely new program than as an upgraded version of 1-2-3.

WHAT IS SYMPHONY?

At heart, Symphony, like 1-2-3, is an electronic spreadsheet. The Symphony spreadsheet is the latest step in the evolution of the electronic spreadsheet that began in 1978 with VisiCalc and continued with the development of the so-called second- and third-generation spreadsheets such as 1-2-3.

In fact, Symphony probably offers the most powerful and flexible electronic spreadsheet currently available for microcomputers. The Symphony spreadsheet is bigger, faster, and offers more commands and functions that any other electronic spreadsheet. Even if Symphony were only a spreadsheet program, it would be worth its $695 price.

But Symphony's abilities don't stop with the electronic spreadsheet. Symphony is a program that combines a spreadsheet with graphics, word processing, data base management, and data communications, plus an advanced windowing capability and an advanced command language, into one comprehensive, integrated package.

Because Symphony is so comprehensive, it appeals to many different types of computer users, from accountants, financial analysts, and engineers to small business people and farmers. Symphony probably has a wider appeal than any other microcomputer software program.

LEARNING SYMPHONY

The name Symphony is appropriate for the newest program from Lotus Development Corporation. If you've ever heard an orchestra perform a symphony, you know how complex a symphony can be. The composer must blend the string, brass, woodwind, and percussion instruments that make up an orchestra to create a harmony. The Symphony program is like a musical symphony in that it integrates several different types of software into one harmonious (or nearly harmonious) whole.

With all of Symphony's power and flexibility comes a great deal of complexity. Symphony is not an easy program to learn. In fact, some observers claim that Symphony may be too complex for the average PC user, and may be have too much power for the current generation of personal computers. I don't believe these claims. Although it will take you some time to learn Symphony, the program is by no means too complex for the average computer user to master.

Patience is one of the keys to learning Symphony. There is simply too much to learn for you to expect to master Symphony in a few days or even a few weeks. In fact, you'll probably never memorize all of Symphony's commands, functions, and other features. There is just too much to hold in your head at one time.

However, if you are like most Symphony users, you'll find that for most of your applications you will need to use only a relatively small part of Symphony's capabilities. It is this part of the program's overall capabilities that you should strive to master. The longer you use Symphony, the more you'll learn about the program. Eventually, you'll try out nearly everything. At first, though, it's better to learn a little piece at a time, picking up the basics before going on to the fine points.

Because Symphony is at heart a spreadsheet, and because most Symphony users work with the spreadsheet far more than any other application, I recommend that you begin learning about Symphony by mastering the spreadsheet. Former 1-2-3 users will find the Symphony spreadsheet familiar and easy to work with from the very start. Many of Symphony's commands are identical to those contained in 1-2-3. But even Symphony users with no prior computing experience should find the spreadsheet easy to learn.

Once you have learned about the Symphony spreadsheet, you'll be ready to move on to more advanced topics, such as windowing, and to the other elements of Symphony—word processing, graphics, data base management, and data communications. The concepts that you master while learning the Symphony spreadsheet will help make the other parts of the program much easier to understand.

Mastering Symphony is a tutorial that will help you learn about Symphony. We begin with the basics, such as entering information into the worksheet, and build to the advanced topics, such as the Symphony Command Language. At every point along the way, the book provides examples that demonstrate the concepts explained in the text. We also look behind the concepts to help you understand not only the how but the why of each command, function, and setting. As you can see, *Mastering Symphony* is a thick book. We have tried to keep the book accurate and comprehensive while making it easy to read and understand. The number of pages in this book is a reflection of the complexity and depth of Symphony itself.

Mastering Symphony is also a reference guide that will aid you long after you have mastered Symphony's fundamentals. The book includes tips and techniques that will help you as you move on to Symphony's more advanced concepts.

If you have experience with 1-2-3 but are now working with Symphony, you'll appreciate the book's coverage of Symphony's new features, such as the word processor, the communications capability, and the form capability of the data base management feature. Where applicable, *Mastering Symphony* draws attention to differences between 1-2-3 and Symphony.

AN OVERVIEW OF THE BOOK

Mastering Symphony is divided into eight parts: Introduction, The Spreadsheet, Services, Graphics, Word Processing, Data Base Management, Communications, and Advanced Topics. We've attempted to present the topics in this book in a logical order. Because many of the concepts interrelate, however, there are places where we present one concept in the process of explaining another. If you come across a concept that isn't clear to you, use the index to find more about it in another part of the book.

Chapter 2, "Getting Started with Symphony," tells you what hardware is needed to use Symphony and how to install Symphony to take full advantage of your hardware. This chapter also introduces you to the Symphony worksheet and provides a tour of the Symphony video display and keyboard.

Chapters 3 through 8 cover Symphony's spreadsheet capabilities. Because Symphony is fundamentally a spreadsheet program, this is the largest section of the book. In Chapter 3, "Introducing the Symphony Spreadsheet," you'll learn how to move around on the worksheet and how to enter labels, numbers, and formulas into it. This chapter also covers the SHEET Settings command, which gives you control over some of the basic characteristics of the Symphony spreadsheet.

Chapter 4 is the longest chapter of the book for a good reason—it introduces you to Symphony's numerous and powerful spreadsheet functions. You'll learn about Symphony's mathematical, financial, engineering, text, and other functions. This chapter not only explains how to use the functions but also provides examples that clearly illustrate their power.

Chapter 5, "Formats," demonstrates how Symphony's Format command can clarify and improve the appearance of your spreadsheet. Chapter 6 covers Symphony's date and time functions. In this chapter you'll learn how Symphony keeps the time and how you can use Symphony's time and date capabilities in your spreadsheets.

In Chapter 7 we present Symphony's cut-and-paste commands. These commands allow you to move blocks of information about on the sheet, to insert and delete rows and columns from the worksheet, and to erase ranges of entries. You won't have to work very long with a spreadsheet before you find these commands extremely useful.

Chapter 8 explains Symphony's seven range commands. These commands are powerful because they allow you to deal with many cells at a single time. Among other things, these commands allow you to fill a range of cells with a series of numbers, to assign a name to a range of cells, to change the alignment of a series of labels, and to create a special "what-if" table that can help you perform sensitivity analyses.

Part 3 covers the three main commands on Symphony's Services menu: Print, File, and Windows. You have to have a good grasp of these commands before you can really do much with Symphony. Chapter 9, "Printing," offers a detailed description of the commands and settings that allow you to print your worksheets. You'll also find yourself referring to this chapter when you're printing documents and data base reports. Chapter 10, "Files," shows you how to save and retrieve your Symphony worksheets. Chapter 11, "Windows," explains the basic concepts of creating and modifying windows. This chapter is extremely important, because the real power of Symphony's integrated package lies in being able to manipulate the various parts of the program through the windows.

The fourth section of *Mastering Symphony* shows you how to build, view, and print graphs. Chapter 12, "Creating Graphs," covers all of Symphony's graphics commands and demonstrates all six of Symphony's graph types. Chapter 13, "Graph Windows," teaches you how to create and use graph windows. Once you know how to do this, you can display several different graphs on the screen of your computer at one time. Chapter 14, "Printing Graphs," covers the Lotus PrintGraph program. It tells you how to print those charts and graphs you're always being asked for, and it gives you some tips on how to make the most of their appearance.

Part 5, "Word Processing," explains Symphony's DOC environment. Chapter 15 shows you how to create and edit a document in Symphony. This chapter also explains the basics of formatting a document. Chapter 16 takes you further with editing and formatting, explaining format lines and format settings sheets. "Printing Documents," Chapter 17, builds on the concepts explained in Chapter 9 to teach you how to print the memos, letters, and reports you create with the Symphony word processor. The last chapter in this section, "Advanced Word Processing Topics," explains DOC windows in detail and discusses the relationship between Symphony's SHEET and DOC environments.

Part 6 covers Symphony's data base management capabilities. In Chapter 19 you'll learn what a Symphony data base is and how a data base can be created. This chapter also introduces you to Symphony's FORM window type. Chapter 20 shows you how to use the capabilities a FORM window provides to select records from and sort a Symphony data base.

Chapter 21 shows you how to work with data bases within a SHEET window. It explains the SHEET Query command, which allows you to find, delete, and extract information that you store in a data base. This chapter also covers Symphony's special data base statistical functions.

Chapter 22, "Advanced Data Base Topics," explains Symphony's report printing capability. This chapter shows you how to print address labels and how to merge names and addresses from a Symphony data base into a letter created within the DOC environment.

From there we move on to Part 7 of the book, which covers Symphony's exciting data communications capability. The first chapter in this section explains many of the concepts and terms that you must understand to use the COMM environment. Chapter 24, "Symphony Communications Basics," is a command-by-command summary of the most important COMM environment commands.

"Getting On-line with Symphony," Chapter 25, shows you how to use Symphony to send and receive information over the telephone lines. This chapter tells you how to use Symphony to transmit a range from the worksheet to another computer, how to capture information transmitted by another computer into the worksheet, and how to send and receive disk-based files.

Chapter 26, "A Sample Communications Session," is a detailed, command-by-command guide to communicating with another computer using Symphony. Chapter 27, "Advanced Communications Topics," covers some of the fine points of using Symphony's COMM environment.

Part 8, "Advanced Concepts," introduces you to the Symphony Command Language and add-in programs. It also shows you how the {Services} Configuration command can be used to alter some of Symphony's basic default settings.

Chapter 28, "Macros and the Symphony Command Language," introduces you to Symphony's built-in programming language. The first half of this chapter shows you how to create and run a macro and provides a few pointers that should help you become more proficient at creating macros. The last part of this chapter explains each of the commands in the Symphony Command Language. Along the way, we create and demonstrate some sample macros.

Chapter 29, "Add-in Programs," explains the concepts of add-in applications and covers the two applications that are provided with Symphony: DOS.APP and TUT.APP. This chapter also speculates on possible future add-ins for Symphony. Chapter 30, "Configuring Symphony," explains the {Services} Configuration command in detail.

Now that I've sketched the outline of the book, you should have a good idea of the structure of Symphony. Where you start depends on how much experience you already have with Symphony or 1-2-3. If you have already mastered the basic concepts and feel familiar with the Symphony spreadsheet, you might want to scan Chapter 3 through 8 and begin reading seriously with Chapter 9. If, on the other hand, you are just starting out with Symphony, you'll probably want to begin with Chapter 2, "Getting Started with Symphony."

CHAPTER TWO

GETTING STARTED WITH SYMPHONY

This chapter tells you what you need to know to start using Symphony. You'll learn what hardware is required to use Symphony, how to install Symphony for your particular computer system, and how to load Symphony into your computer. You'll also take a tour of the worksheet and learn about the Symphony screen and the keyboard.

HARDWARE NEEDS

Before you can use Symphony, you must have the proper computer hardware, including the right kind of computer, at least 320K of RAM, one double-sided disk drive, and a video display. To take full advantage of all of Symphony's capabilities, you also need additional RAM, another disk drive, a graphics monitor, a graphics printer, a letter-quality printer, and a modem.

Right now, Symphony will run only on the IBM PC, the PC/XT, and a handful of computers that are compatible with the IBM models, such as the Compaq and Compaq Plus. Eventually, Symphony will be available for other computers, including the IBM PC/AT, the DEC Rainbow, the Zenith Z-100, and others.

You also need PC-DOS version 2.0 (or later) or an equivalent version of MS-DOS. The Symphony program files take up so much room on a disk that *they will not fit* on the 320K-capacity disks created by the PC-DOS 1.1 Format command. If you have not yet upgraded to DOS 2.0, you'll have to do so before you attempt to use Symphony.

RAM Requirements

Symphony is a very large program. The main Symphony file, SYMPHONY.CMP, occupies more than 237K bytes on the Symphony program disk. When you use Symphony, this entire file, as well as a number of smaller Symphony files and three DOS files (IBMBIO.COM, IBMDOS.COM, and COMMAND.COM), are loaded into your computer's memory. The result is that some 293K bytes of RAM are needed just to *load* Symphony into your computer. Because you need at least a few more bytes to use the program, the minimum amount of RAM required to use Symphony is 320K.

This minimum configuration, however, leaves only 19K bytes of RAM free for you to use. In general, you'll need far more than the minimum amount of memory to make effective use of Symphony. In Chapter 3 we discuss how Symphony uses memory and how much memory you need to use the program. For now, it's enough to say that the more memory you have, the better off you are.

Disk Drives

To use Symphony, your computer must have at least one double-sided, double-density (DS/DD) floppy disk drive. However, to install the program, you need *two* double-sided, double-density disk drives or one hard disk and one double-sided, double-density disk drive.

Because you need two drives to install Symphony, and because Symphony is easier to use if you have two disk drives, I recommend the two-drive configuration. All but the most basic IBM and Compaq models have two disk drives anyway, so this recommendation shouldn't cause you any hardship.

The Monitor

The type of monitor (video display) you choose has a major effect on the way you use Symphony. If you use a standard IBM monochrome display (or the equivalent) with a monochrome display controller card, your screen will not display the graphs Symphony is capable of producing.

If, however, your IBM monochrome display is attached to a special monochrome graphics controller card (such as the Hercules card) instead of the standard IBM monochrome display card, you will be able to view graphics on your monochrome display. Likewise, if you have a non-IBM monochrome graphics monitor (such as a Zenith Z-19) attached to an IBM color/graphics display adapter (or its equivalent), you'll be able to view one-color graphs.

If you have a color monitor and a color/graphics display adapter, you'll see your graphs in living color. A color monitor is the only video display that allows you to take full advantage of Symphony's graphics capabilities.

Printers

You may also wish to connect one or more printers to your computer to take advantage of Symphony's text- and graph-printing capabilities. If your printer can generate graphs, you'll be able to use Symphony's PrintGraph program to produce hardcopy graphics. Likewise, if you choose a letter-quality printer, you'll be able to use Symphony's word processing capabilities to create letter-perfect correspondence and reports.

If you are really serious about your graphs, you might consider a plotter. Plotters are expensive and their only use is printing graphs, but they make your graphs look fantastic.

Printers and plotters are strictly optional pieces of hardware. However, I recommend that you purchase at least a simple dot-matrix printer (preferably one that can generate graphics) before starting to work with Symphony.

Modems

You need a modem to use Symphony's COMM window to connect with other computers or information services. At the time of publication, Symphony supported only three modems: The Hayes Smartmodem 1200, the Hayes Smartmodem 300, and the Popcom X100.

SOFTWARE—THE SYMPHONY DISKS

Before you install Symphony, get a few preliminaries out of the way. First, open up the plastic case containing the Symphony disks. You will find, among other things, a pouch containing the six disks that hold Symphony and all of its related programs:

> Install program disk
> Install Library disk
> Symphony program disk
> PrintGraph program disk
> Help and Tutorial disk
> Tutorial Lessons disk

You use the first two disks, Install and Install Library, only when you install Symphony. The Symphony program disk contains Symphony itself; you load Symphony into your computer from this disk. If you have a graphics printer, you can use the PrintGraph program to print your graphs. The final two disks, the Help and Tutorial disk and the Tutorial Lessons disk, help beginners learn how to use Symphony.

Before using Symphony, you must prepare the six Symphony disks for use. There are three basic steps in this process. First, you should make copies of all of the Symphony disks, either onto other floppy disks or onto a hard disk. Second, if you are not using a hard disk system, you should make the Symphony disk bootable by copying DOS onto it. Third, you need to "customize" Symphony to your hardware when you install the program. Installation is the most critical and time-consuming of these three steps.

Copying the Disks

Before doing anything else, make copies of each of the six Symphony disks. To copy the disks, you must first format six blank disks using the DOS Format command. Next, use the DOS Diskcopy command to make copies of the original disks. After you copy the disks, store all six copies in a safe place as backups for your original disks.

Although you can make a copy of the original Symphony program disk, you cannot use a copy of the disk to load Symphony into your computer. The original Symphony program disk is formatted by Lotus in a special way. When Symphony is loaded into your computer, it checks the disk from which it is being loaded to see if that disk has the special format. If the disk does not have the special format, the load will be aborted.

Since the special format cannot be copied, you will not be able to load Symphony from any of the copies you create with Diskcopy or Copy. However, since the Help and Tutorial disk uses the same special formatting as the Symphony program disk, you can make the Help and Tutorial disk into a working backup of the Symphony program disk if you wish. (According to the licensing agreement, this process should be used only to replace a lost or damaged original Symphony program disk.) To back up your program disk in this way, first erase all of the files on the Help and Tutorial disk (be sure that you have created a working copy of this disk before you erase the files). When the files are erased, use the Copy command to copy all of the Symphony program files onto the Help and Tutorial disk. Presto! You've created another working copy of Symphony.

If you have a hard disk system, you should copy all six disks directly onto the hard disk. You may want to use the DOS 2.0 MKDIR command to create a special directory for the Symphony program files. This directory can be given a name like C:\Symphony\Programs. Be sure to copy all six disks into the same directory of your hard disk.

When you finish copying the files onto the hard disk, store all of the Symphony disks, with the exception of the Symphony program disk, in a safe place. Even though the Symphony program files are on the hard disk, Symphony requires that you place the specially formatted original Symphony program disk in drive A whenever you load Symphony.

Making the Symphony Program Disk Bootable

If your computer has two floppy disk drives, you might want to make the Symphony program disk bootable by copying DOS onto it. To make this disk bootable, simply insert your DOS disk into drive A and your original Symphony program disk into drive B. Issue the command **Sys B:** to transfer part of DOS onto your Symphony disk. Next, use the Copy command to transfer the file COMMAND.COM to the Symphony program disk.

With these preliminaries out of the way, you can proceed to install Symphony to match your particular hardware.

INSTALLING SYMPHONY

You cannot use Symphony as it comes from the box. Before you can use it, you must run the Install program to configure Symphony for use with your particular hardware. You might view the install process as an inconvenience, since it takes a bit of time to install Symphony. Actually, the time required to install the program is a small price to pay for the ability to use Symphony with a variety of computers, printers, plotters, video displays, and modems.

Each time you load Symphony, it looks for a Driver Set file that tells it how to communicate with the particular computer, text printer, graphics printer, video display, and modem you are using. This file also provides some other operating parameters. Installation is the process of choosing individual drivers, each of which tells Symphony how to use a particular piece of hardware, combining these drivers into a file called a Driver Set, and copying that Driver Set onto the Symphony disks. In essence, the Install process customizes Symphony for your particular computer system.

Lotus has prepared a whole library of drivers that tell Symphony how to use a variety of different pieces of hardware. You can pick and choose from this library during installation.

The Install Program

Before beginning the installation process, take a few minutes to make a list of the hardware you will use when you work with Symphony. You need to note the manufacturer and model number of the following items:

1. Your video monitor and video controller card
2. Your text printer (if any)
3. Your graphics printer (if any)
4. Your modem (if any)
5. Your asynchronous communications port (if any)

During installation, Symphony asks you to specify the make and model of the hardware that makes up your computer system so that it can select the drivers that allow it to run on your system. If you don't have some of these pieces of hardware, don't worry. Of these five selections, only the specification of a video monitor and controller card is mandatory.

With this list in hand, boot your system so that the DOS prompt appears on the screen, then insert the Install program disk in drive A (if you have a two-drive system) or make the directory containing the six Symphony disks current (if you have a hard disk system). Next, type **Install** and press **[Enter]**.

Next Symphony instructs you to remove the Install program disk from drive A, insert the Install Library disk, and press any key. This makes the library of possible drivers stored on the Install Library disk accessible to the Install program. If you have a hard disk system and have copied the Install Library disk into the same directory as the Install program disk, your computer performs this step automatically.

After reading the Install Library disk for a few seconds, the Install program gives you some basic instructions and the choice of pressing the **[Space bar]** to continue or {**Help**} to access more detailed instructions. If you press the **[Space bar]** you see the following menu:

```
            MAIN MENU
    1   Installation: Create a driver set
    2   Display selections in a driver set
    3   List names of driver sets
    4   Change selections in a driver set
    5   Exit Install program
```

To create your first Driver Set, choose option 1. When you make this selection, the Install program displays another screen, which gives a basic outline of the steps in the Install process. Read this message if you wish, and press the **[Space bar]** to move to the next step.

Adding Drivers to the Master Library

Next, the Install program asks you if you wish to add extra drivers to the master library. As we noted above, Lotus has provided a number of drivers that tell Symphony how to use many different kinds of printers, monitors, and modems. These drivers are all a part of the master library on the Install library disk. In all likelihood, the drivers for your hardware are already a part of the master library, so you will probably never use this command. To pass it by, simply press the **[Space bar].**

However, you might have a printer, modem, or other hardware device for which Lotus has not yet prepared a driver. In this case, you need to add a special driver prepared by the company that manufactures the hardware device or by a another third party, to the master library. If Symphony does not presently support your hardware, contact Lotus or the manufacturer of the hardware to inquire whether special drivers are available for your equipment.

Naming the Driver Set File

Next, Symphony asks you to supply a name for the Driver Set you are creating. You can choose the default name, Lotus, just by pressing the **[Space bar],** or you can type a name of your choosing in response to the prompt. The name you select can be up to eight characters long and should not include a file name extension. Unless you plan to create several different driver sets, we recommend that you use the default name, Lotus.

Selecting a Video Controller Card

After you select a name for the driver set, the Install program moves on to the selection of the video display driver. This driver tells Symphony what kind of video display you will be using. This driver is mandatory, so you must select one of the choices offered.

Symphony offers 14 text and graphic display options that cover most possible IBM PC, IBM portable, and Compaq portable video controller card possibilities, including the use of the Hercules and Plantronics cards. These 14 choices are listed on five separate screens. To scroll forward through these screens, press the **[Space bar]**. To go back, press **[Esc]**.

From this list, select the display option that matches your hardware configuration most closely. If you have a monochrome display attached to a standard monochrome display adapter card, select choice 1. Remember that when you make this choice, you cannot view Symphony graphs on the screen.

If you have a graphics-capable monitor and a graphics adapter board in your computer, the choice for this driver is a bit trickier. You'll have to decide whether you want

Symphony to operate in the shared mode or the toggle mode. In the shared mode Symphony allows you to view graphs and text on the screen at the same time, but with some sacrifice of text quality and speed. The toggle mode, by contrast, gives improved text clarity but does not allow text and graphics to appear on the screen at the same time. Unless you have a pressing need to view text and graphs on the screen at the same time, I strongly recommend that you choose one of the toggle mode options.

If you are fortunate enough to have *both* a color graphics monitor and a text monitor, you can choose option 5, which lets Symphony operate in the dual mode. When in the dual mode, Symphony lets you view graphs on one screen and text on another.

Select your choice by typing the appropriate number (1–14) and pressing **[Enter]**. The Install program records this choice and moves on to the next step. If you change your mind about the choice after pressing **[Enter],** simply press **[Esc]** to jump back to the beginning of this step and then type a new number. Your new choice overrides the old one. Pressing **[Enter]** again moves you to the next step.

Selecting a Text Printer

The second step, selecting a text printer driver, is optional. If you have a text printer or a combined text/graphics printer, you will want to make a selection in this step. If you do not have a text or combined printer, press the **[Space bar]** to move to the next option.

To make a selection, type **Y** followed by **[Enter].** You can use the [Space bar] to scroll through the 33 printer options supported by Symphony. Since most Symphony users have only one printer, the choice of a text printer driver is usually straightforward. If you have both a letter-quality printer and a graphics printer, install the letter-quality printer as your text printer.

When you decide which option is right for you, type the number that matches your printer and press **[Enter].** After you make a selection, the Install program displays the screen listing the choices, marks your selection with an asterisk (*), and asks you to confirm this choice by pressing [Enter]. To change this choice, simply type a new number and press **[Enter].** You can also type the original number preceded by a minus sign (−) to erase the original selection without replacing it.

If your text printer is not listed, call Lotus or your printer manufacturer to see if a special driver is available for your printer.

Selecting a Graphics Printer Driver

The next step is selecting a graphics printer driver. This optional step is similar to selecting a text printer driver. If you have a dedicated graphics printer or a combined text/graphics printer, type **Y [Enter]** to display the 54 possible graphics printer driver choices. Again, use the [Space bar] to scroll through the four screens and find the correct driver for your system.

You will notice that there are several selections for some of the printers in the list. For example, the Install program offers four choices for the Epson MX-100 printer: density 1, density 2, density 3, and density 4. Density defines the number of passes that the printer head makes over each character and thus affects the darkness of the print. Choosing a density of 3 or 4 results in darker, more attractive graphs, but it also increases the time required to print a graph.

The graphics printer driver selection is unique in that Symphony allows you to specify more than one graphics device driver in a single driver set. For example, you could tell Symphony to include drivers for both an Epson FX-100 printer and an HP7175 plotter in a single driver set. In a later chapter, you'll see that the PrintGraph program allows you to choose which of the selected graphics devices you want to use before you print a graph.

Selecting a Modem

The next step is selecting a modem. To use the communications abilities afforded by Symphony's COMM windows, make a selection in this step. If you do not plan to use Symphony for communications, press the [Space bar] to move to the next step.

Symphony lets you choose only one of two modem drivers: the Hayes Smartmodem (1200 or 300) and the Popcom X100. If you have another brand of modem that is compatible with one of these popular models, you can use your modem by choosing the compatible driver set. If your modem is not compatible with either of these choices, contact the modem manufacturer to see if a special driver is available.

Selecting an Asynchronous Communications Port

If you select a modem driver, you also need to specify an asynchronous communications port driver. Because many computers have more than one serial board, you must specify into which one you will plug your modem. The two choices are COM1 8250 and COM2 8250. The 1 or 2 specifies the board you are using, if your computer has multiple boards. The 8250 specifies the standard chip used in most PC serial boards.

In the vast majority of cases, COM1 8250 is the appropriate choice. If you are not sure which choice to make, ask your dealer for help.

Selecting a Collating Driver

The final Install program selection, the collating driver, is mandatory. This driver determines the general rule Symphony follows when sorting entries in a data base in response to the Query Record-Sort command. Symphony gives you only two choices for this driver: Numbers First or Numbers Last. If you choose Numbers First, Symphony sorts entries so that those beginning with numbers appear before those beginning with letters. The Numbers Last choice does just the opposite. See the chapters on data base management for a further discussion of the function of a text collating driver.

Saving Your Driver Selections

After you specify these drivers, the Install program pulls each one from the Install Library and combines them into a Driver Set file, using the name you specified in the first step of this process. If you use a hard disk system, you need to save this file in the same directory where you saved the rest of the Symphony files. If you use a two-drive system, you must copy this Driver Set file onto three of the Symphony disks: the Symphony program disk, the PrintGraph disk, and the Install program disk. In this way, Symphony can access the Driver Set file(s) you created.

If you use a two-drive system, leave the Install Library disk in drive A and insert the Symphony program disk in drive B. Then type the path specification for Symphony program disk (in this case, **b:**) and press **[Enter]**. Symphony compiles the drivers you selected and saves them as FILENAME.SET on the Symphony program disk. When this is finished, do the same for the PrintGraph and Install program disks. Now you are ready to use Symphony on your computer system.

Installation Notes

In addition to the optional and mandatory drivers you selected in the preceding steps, the Driver Set file contains some other drivers you don't choose. Symphony automatically specifies these drivers because there is only one option for each.

To view a listing of all the drivers in the Driver Set file, including these "no-option" drivers, select option 2 from the Install program main menu. A sample listing might look like this:

TYPE	DESCRIPTION
Text Display	COMPAQ display
Graph Display	IBM or COMPAQ, high resolution, toggle
Keyboard	IBM or COMPAQ
Printer Port	IBM or COMPAQ
Graph Printer	Epson LQ-1500, density 2
Async Port	COM1 8250
Modem	Hayes Smartmodem
Protocol	X-Modem (Christensen or Modem-7)
Translation	IBM or COMPAQ
Text Printer	Epson FX, RX, and JX series
Collating	Numbers First

Notice that Symphony has included Keyboard, Printer Port, Protocol, and Translation drivers in the set. These are the "no-option" drivers supplied by the Install program. The keyboard and printer port drivers simply tell Symphony that an IBM-compatible computer is being used. The protocol driver determines the method Symphony uses to send or receive files from a COMM window. Symphony uses the translation driver to match the characters you use to the Lotus International Character Set.

At this point, you may wish to choose option 1 from the menu once again to create another Driver Set file so that you can use Symphony with different pieces of hardware. For instance, if you have an IBM PC at work and a COMPAQ at home, you would want to create two driver sets so that you can use one copy of Symphony on both computers.

There is enough room on the Symphony program disk for only two or three different Driver Set files (if you have made the disk bootable). If you want to create additional files, you must save all of your Driver Set files on a separate disk, selectively copying them to the Symphony program disk under the name LOTUS.SET for each application, so that only one Driver Set file exists on the Symphony program disk at one time.

Alternatively, you can choose menu option 4 to edit the selections in a driver set. Editing a driver set is very similar to creating one. To exit the Install program, simply choose option 5. At this point, you will return to the A > prompt of the operating system.

Now that you have copied the Symphony disks, selected drivers, created Driver Set files, and copied those files onto the necessary Symphony disks, you are ready to load Symphony.

LOADING SYMPHONY

Now that Symphony has been installed to match your computer's hardware, you are finally ready to use the program. The way you go about loading Symphony depends on the kind of computer you are using and where you decide to store Symphony.

There are two main ways to load Symphony into your computer. You can either use the Lotus Access System or load Symphony directly from DOS. In the following paragraphs we explore these methods of loading Symphony.

Loading through the Access System

The usual way to enter Symphony is to first load the Lotus Access System into your computer and then select Symphony from the Access System menu.

If you have made the Symphony disk bootable by copying DOS onto the Symphony program disk, you can enter the Lotus Access System simply by booting your computer using this disk. The Symphony program disk includes an autoexec file that automatically loads the Access System into your computer when you boot with the Symphony program disk. To do this, insert the bootable Symphony program disk in drive A of your computer and turn the computer on. (If your computer is already on, press [Ctrl] [Alt] [Del] simultaneously to boot the operating system.) In either case, drive A comes to life, the computer beeps, and DOS asks you to supply the current date and time. You can either enter the current date and time or press **[Enter]** to skip this step. However, many of Symphony's date-related functions (such as @NOW) will not work properly if you do not supply the current date and time.

At this point, DOS automatically loads the file ACCESS.COM, which contains the Lotus Access System. The top of your screen looks like Figure 2.1.

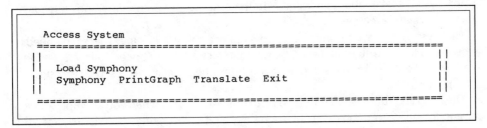

```
    Access System
    =================================================================  | |
  | |                                                                  | |
  | |   Load Symphony                                                  | |
  | |   Symphony   PrintGraph   Translate   Exit                       | |
  | |                                                                  | |
    =================================================================
```

Figure 2.1

Choosing Symphony from this menu loads Symphony into your computer. The other options allow you to access the PrintGraph program, with which you print graphs created on Symphony, or the Translate utility, which converts non-Symphony files (such as VisiCalc and dBASE II files) into the Symphony worksheet file format. The Exit option allows you to return to DOS.

Loading Symphony Directly from DOS

Alternatively, you can bypass the Access System altogether by typing **Symphony** instead of Access in response to the DOS prompt. Because this method is faster than using the Access System, I prefer it. To load Symphony directly on a two-drive system, simply boot the system, insert the Symphony program disk in drive A, type **Symphony** next to the DOS prompt, and press **[Enter]**. If your computer has a hard disk, you must first go to the directory that contains Symphony and then type **Symphony** next to the DOS prompt. Remember that even when you load Symphony from a hard disk subdirectory the original Symphony program disk must be in drive A.

Specifying Alternate Driver Sets

As we mentioned previously, when you load Symphony into your computer, Symphony looks for the Driver Set file named LOTUS.SET unless you specify a different file. To specify another driver set, simply type the name of that set following the word Access or Symphony you load the program. For example, if you wish to use an alternate driver set named COMPAQ.SET, you would type the following after the DOS prompt:

       A>symphony compaq

or

       A>access compaq

These commands instruct Symphony to use the drivers contained in COMPAQ.SET to communicate with the various pieces of hardware in the system.

Entering Symphony

After you choose Symphony from the Access System menu or type Symphony next to the DOS prompt and press [Enter], your computer begins reading the Symphony program files from the Symphony program disk. Since Symphony is such a large program (238K bytes), it takes about 35 seconds to load. At the end of this time, the "title page" shown in Figure 2.2 appears.

The message that Symphony gives here is unnecessarily confusing. There is no need to insert the Help and Tutorial disk at this time; in fact, you don't need to insert the Help and Tutorial disk until you want to use Symphony's help facility, accessed by pressing the {Help} key.

The Help and Tutorial disk must also be in the system drive when you attempt to attach an add-in application. You need not insert this disk, however, until you wish to attach the application. (For more on add-in applications, see Chapter 29.)

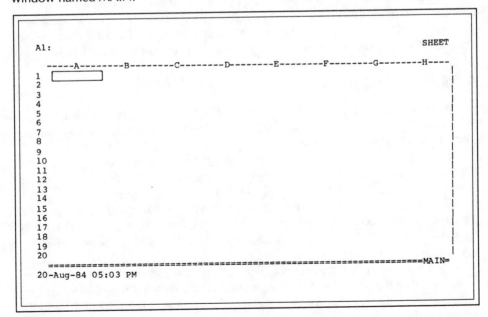

```
        ----------------------------------
        |            S Y M P H O N Y            |
        |                                       |
        | Copyright (C)  1982, 1983, 1984 |
        |   Lotus Development Corporation  |
        |        All Rights Reserved         |
        |           10000200-4181647         |
        |             Release 1.00            |
        ----------------------------------
      To make the following Symphony features available, replace
    the Symphony program disk with the Help and Tutorial disk.  Press
    [Enter] to begin.


        * On-Line Help Facility        (SYMPHONY.HLP)
        * Symphony Electronic Tutorial  (TUTORIAL.APP)
        * Add-In Applications               (.APP)
        * Stored Telecommunications Settings  (.CCF)
        * Automatically-Loaded Worksheet    (.WRK)
```

Figure 2.2

A SYMPHONY OVERVIEW

Once the title page is displayed, you need only press **[Enter]** to bring the Symphony worksheet into view. When you first load Symphony, your screen looks something like Figure 2.3. This figure shows the Symphony worksheet as viewed through the SHEET window named MAIN.

```
 A1:                                                             SHEET

      -----A---------B---------C---------D--------E--------F--------G--------H---
   1  [               ]
   2
   3
   4
   5
   6
   7
   8
   9
  10
  11
  12
  13
  14
  15
  16
  17
  18
  19
  20                                                             =====MAIN=
      =================================================================
      20-Aug-84 05:03 PM
```

Figure 2.3

Notice the row number on the left edge of the window in Figure 2.3 and the column letters along the top edge of the figure. Letters and numbers like these identify the rows and columns that make up the worksheet.

The basic workspace in Symphony is a giant spreadsheet with 8192 rows and 256 columns. Every row in the worksheet has a number and every column has a letter. The intersection of each row and column is called a cell. Cells are identified by their column-row coordinates. For example, the intersection of column A and row 1 is cell A1. The cell at the intersection of row 100 and column Z is cell Z100.

Cells are the basic building blocks of the Symphony SHEET mode. Each cell is a separate worksheet location into which you can enter information.

A little math reveals that the 256-column by 8192-row Symphony worksheet has over two million cells. Before you begin to dream of modeling the entire United States economy on a single Symphony spreadsheet, however, I should warn you that the memory places a heavy restriction on the number of cells you can fill.

The Concept of Windows

Your 8192-by-256 worksheet would be 171 feet long and 21 feet wide if it were made of paper and if each cell were ¼ inch tall and 1 inch wide. Thus, the Symphony worksheet is much too large to view on the screen at one time. The rows and columns you can see through the window MAIN represent only a tiny fraction of the entire worksheet. The window MAIN is like a porthole looking onto a limited portion of the worksheet. To view other parts of the worksheet, you must move the window around.

You can illustrate the concept of a window by cutting a small square hole in a piece of cardboard and placing the cardboard on this page. At any one time, you can see only a small portion of the page through the square. By moving the cardboard around on the page, however, you can eventually read the whole page through that small hole.

A Look Around the Screen

Notice the rectangle in cell A1 in Figure 2.3. This rectangle is called the *cell pointer*. You can think of the cell pointer as the point of a pencil because you use it to write information into the worksheet.

The cell pointer always occupies only one cell in the worksheet. The cell in which the cell pointer is currently positioned is called the *current cell* or the *active cell*. You can make entries to the worksheet from the keyboard only in the current cell.

You can determine which cell is the active cell simply by looking at the location of the cell pointer in the worksheet or by reading the cell reference in the upper-left corner of the screen. Notice that the upper-left corner of Figure 2.3 shows the reference A1, which indicates that the cell pointer is in cell A1.

The first two lines on the screen, including the line that contains the active cell reference, are called the *control panel*. The control panel is very important in Symphony. First, as you learned in the previous paragraph, the location of the cell pointer and the contents of the active cell are displayed in the control panel. In addition, whenever you issue a command in Symphony, the menu for that command will appear in the control panel.

There are a few other items of interest in the screen in Figure 2.3. First, notice the word SHEET in the upper-right corner of the screen. This word indicates that Symphony is currently in the SHEET mode. Symphony has many other modes, which we'll cover in more detail later in this book. The mode indicator always tells you which of its many modes Symphony is in. Since Symphony behaves differently in different modes, this indicator is very important.

Also notice the date and time in the lower-left corner of the screen in Figure 2.3. Symphony always displays the date and time in this part of the screen as a convenience to the user.

THE SYMPHONY KEYBOARD

Like its predecessor, 1-2-3, Symphony makes full use of the keyboard of the IBM and Compaq personal computers. Although the functions of specific keys are explained in detail in later chapters dealing with Symphony's various operating environments, let's take a brief look at the basic layout of the keyboard and each key's basic functions.

From the Symphony user's point of view, the computer keyboard is divided into three parts. The ten tan-colored keys on the left edge of the keyboard are Symphony's special function keys. The four columns of keys (white and tan) at the right edge of the keyboard contain the numeric keypad and cursor-movement keys. The keys between these two sectors are similar to those of a standard typewriter.

The "Typewriter" Keys

The middle part of the keyboard contains the letters, numbers, punctuation marks, and mathematical symbols found on standard typewriter keyboards. Most of these keys are white, although the keys on the right and left edges of this sector are tan. Most of these keys are simply used to enter numbers, letters, or punctuation marks into the Symphony worksheet.

Several keys in the middle section of the keyboard serve special purposes in Symphony. Look first at the left side of this section. The [Esc] key, located in the upper-left corner of the keyboard, is Symphony's all-purpose "backup" key. For example, the [Esc] key can be used to exit from a menu that you have entered in error, or to erase a part of an entry you are making in a cell. In fact, whenever you get lost or confused in Symphony, you can nearly always get back to familiar territory by pressing [Esc] several times. You will use the [Esc] key a great deal in Symphony.

The key immediately under the [Esc] key is [Tab]. This key has different functions in different Symphony windows. For instance, in a word processing (DOC) window, this key works like a regular tab key on a typewriter. However, when you issue a SHEET or DOC command, the [Tab] key helps define the range the command should apply to.

The last special key on the left is [Alt]. This key is used in conjunction with the letter keys to invoke Symphony Command Language programs. Additionally, this key accesses the "alternate" function of some of the ten special function keys at the left edge of the keyboard.

Now look at the right side of the middle section. The [Enter] key, referred to by the Symphony manuals as the [Return] key, is located at the right edge and marked with a crooked arrow. The [Enter] key has many different applications in Symphony. For example, this key is used to "lock in" the entries you make to cells in the Symphony worksheet, to select options from Symphony command menus, and to insert blank lines in a word processing document.

The Numeric Pad and Cursor-Movement Keys

The second keyboard section encompasses the four columns of keys on the extreme right of the keyboard. Basically, these keys control the movement of the cursor or cell pointer in each of the Symphony operating environments. Alternatively, they provide a convenient way to enter numbers into the Symphony worksheet. (These keys have slightly different functions in each of Symphony's different windows. The functions of these keys as they apply to each window type are explored in the appropriate chapters of this book.)

The function of the numeric keypad is controlled by the [Num Lock] key. Normally, pressing any of the keys marked with both numbers and arrows causes the cell pointer to move around the worksheet. If you press [Num Lock], however, the keypad is "shifted" and you can use these keys to enter numbers into the worksheet.

The white [Del] key has different functions in different windows, but it basically serves to erase the character under the cursor or cell pointer. The [Ins] also wears two hats in Symphony. When used in the word processing environment, [Ins] toggles back and forth between the Overwrite mode and the Insert mode. When used in a FORM window, [Ins] enters records into a Symphony data base.

The Special Key Convention

In this book, we always enclose the name of a special key in brackets. Whenever you see a key in brackets—for example, [Del], [Enter], or [Esc]—you know that we are referring to one of the important special keys on the computer keyboard.

The Function Keys

The ten function keys, labeled F1 through F10, are at the extreme left edge of the keyboard. These keys control 23 special Symphony functions. Packing 23 functions into only ten keys is a difficult task, and the results are a bit confusing. Although we explain each of these keys in detail in the appropriate chapters of this book, let's look at the basic layout of these Symphony function keys.

In the back pocket of the plastic case that holds the Symphony disks, you will find a curved plastic template that fits around the ten function keys. Notice that this template is divided into ten squares, labeled with the names of one or more of Symphony's 23 special functions. Observe that some of the functions are written on a tan background at the bottom or middle of each square, while others are written on a shaded background at the top of each square. Further, notice that some of the function labels have black letters and some have blue or red letters. Also, some of the red and black functions are on a tan background, while some are on a shaded background. Let's try to make some sense out of this confusing mess!

To begin, let's take a look at what the shading means. You access the functions written in the shaded upper portion of each of the ten squares by pressing [Alt] and that function key simultaneously. You invoke the functions written on the light tan background at the bottom of each square by simply pressing that key. As you can see, you must press [Alt] to use 10 of the 23 Symphony functions.

The Black Functions

The color of each function label denotes which windows that function applies to. As a rule, the functions written in black are usable in all five Symphony window types: SHEET (a spreadsheet), DOC (word processing), FORM (data base management), GRAPH (graphics), and COMM (communications). These "universal" function keys are listed in Table 2.1.

Key	Press	Function
{Help}	[F1]	Accesses the Symphony help facility
{Compose}	[Alt][F1]	Allows you to create special characters contained in the Lotus International Character Set
{Goto}	[F5]	Moves cursor to selected location in a spreadsheet, document, or data base
{Window}	[F6]	Switches you to another window
{Zoom}	[Alt][F6]	Enlarges a window to full screen
{Calc}	[F8]	Recalculates the worksheet
{Draw}	[Alt][F8]	"Recalculates" the contents of all windows
{Services}	[F9]	Displays the {Services} menu
{Switch}	[Alt][F9]	Returns window to previous type
{Menu}	[F10]	Displays the menu for the current window
{Type}	[Alt][F10]	Changes the window type

Table 2.1

Three of the black function keys relate to the creation and execution of macros. These keys are primarily used in SHEET windows but can be used in any environment. These three keys and their functions are shown in Table 2.2.

Key	Press	Function
{User}	[F7]	Invokes a macro
{Learn}	[Alt][F5]	Records your keystrokes to create a macro
{Step}	[Alt][F7]	Causes a macro to execute one step at a time (used for debugging)

Table 2.2

The Red Functions

The red function keys apply only to DOC windows. These six keys affect word processing features, as shown in Table 2.3. These functions are covered in greater detail in the word processing chapters (Chapters 15–18).

Key	Press	Function
{Justify}	[F2]	Justifies the margins of the current paragraph
{Where}	[Alt][F2]	Displays the page and line location of cursor as determined by the Print settings
{Indent}	[F3]	Indents an entire paragraph
{Split}	[Alt][F3]	Splits a line of text
{Erase}	[F4]	Erases a specified block of text
{Center}	[Alt][F4]	Centers a line of text

Table 2.3

The Blue Functions

The remaining three special functions are printed in blue on the function key template. These functions are the leftovers and don't strictly apply to one window type or another. The {Edit} function allows you to revise the entry in a cell of the worksheet (the SHEET window) or in an Entry form (a FORM window) without having to erase that entry totally. This key is of no use in the COMM, DOC, or GRAPH environments.

The {Abs} function provides an easy way to change a cell reference in a cell of the worksheet or in an Entry form to an absolute reference. (Absolute references are discussed in Chapter 3 and again in Chapter 7.) Again, this function serves a purpose only in SHEET or FORM windows.

The {Capture} function applies only to COMM windows. This key allows you to capture into the worksheet information which is received from another computer across the telephone line. This function is not useful in any other environment.

The Function Key Convention

In this book, we enclose the names of Symphony's function keys in braces. Whenever you see a word in braces—for instance, {Menu}—you know that you should press one of the function keys on your keyboard. If you use an IBM PC and see the word {Menu}, press [F10].

COMMANDS

Commands are the tools Symphony provides for manipulating the worksheet. Symphony includes commands that allow you to print the contents of the worksheet, save the worksheet to disk and retrieve it for later use, edit the contents of the worksheet, and much more.

One potential source of confusion for new Symphony users is its dual menu configuration. Most software has only one main menu; additional menus appear when you make a selection from the main one. The menu system of 1-2-3 works this way. In Symphony, however, there are several different "main" menus. In fact, in Symphony one menu controls the global characteristics of the program, and five separate menus control each of the program's five environments.

As confusing as this may seem at first, don't let it intimidate you. The menu structure is really very logical. It works this way: The first Symphony menu is Services. You activate this menu by pressing the {Services} key. The Services menu looks like this:

Window   File   Print   Configuration   Application   Settings   New   Exit

As you can see, the choices on the Services menu control capabilites that overlap the five environments. Print, for example, lets you print information stored in the worksheet, whether that information is viewed through a DOC, SHEET, or other type of window. Similarly, File lets you save the contents of the worksheet to disk.

You will use five of the commands on this menu—Window, File, Print, New, and Exit—far more than the other three. This book devotes a chapter apiece to the Window, File, and Print commands. New and Exit are covered in the second section following this one. For now, I suggest that you ignore the Configuration, Application, and Settings commands. We'll cover them near the end of the book.

Command Basics

All of Symphony's menus work in the same way. To make a choice from a menu, you can either point to the desired choice with the ← and → keys, or you can type just the first character of the name of the desired command. For example, to issue the {Services} File command, you first type **[F9].** This brings the Services menu into view. From this menu, you could select the File option by typing F or by pointing to the File command in the menu and pressing **[Enter].**

Beginning users usually find it easier to point to the choices. As you become more experienced, however, you'll find that typing certain command sequences becomes automatic.

In this book, when we tell you to issue a command, we show you the full command and boldface the first letter in the command. By boldfacing the first letter in a command, we remind you that you need to type only that letter to issue the command. For example, the command for hiding a window is **{Services} W**indow **H**ide. Notice that the W and H are boldfaced. To issue this command you would type

        [F10] W H

Don't forget, however, that you can also select a command by pointing if you find that method more convenient. For this reason, we give the entire name of the command instead of just the first initial.

New and Exit

The New command erases the entire worksheet and restores all settings in the worksheet to their defaults. New is a powerful command. Unless you have used the {Services} File Save command to save the contents of the worksheet into a disk file, everything in the worksheet will be lost for good.

Fortunately, before Symphony erases the entire worksheet, it asks you a simple question:

> **Erase all data from all windows and create a new worksheet?**
> **Yes   No**

This safety step gives you a chance to cancel the command before the worksheet is erased. If you choose No, the command will be canceled and you'll be returned to the SHEET mode. If you choose Yes, the entire worksheet will be erased instantly.

The {Services} Exit command is even more destructive. Not only does {Services} Exit erase the entire worksheet; it also "turns off" Symphony and returns you to DOS. As with the New command, however, Symphony includes a safety step in the Exit command. When you issue the Exit command, Symphony displays the prompt:

> **End Symphony Session? (Select "No" if your work isn't saved)**
> **Yes   No**

If you want to exit from Symphony, choose Yes. Otherwise, select No from this menu to remain in Symphony.

If you load Symphony using the Access System, you will be returned to the access system menu when you issue the Exit command. Otherwise, Symphony will dump you straight out into DOS.

By the way, did you notice that when you issued the commands {Services} New and {Services} Exit, the Mode indicator at the upper right corner of the screen changed from SHEET to MENU? As you learned earlier in the chapter, the Mode indicator always provides a clue to what's happening in the program. When you issue any command, the Mode indicator changes to MENU.

Also, did you notice that when you issued these commands the Date and Time legend in the lower-left corner of the screen was replaced with the name of the command you selected? Whenever you issue a command, Symphony will display the name or names of the command in the lower-left corner of the screen. When you get into some of Symphony's more sophisticated commands, this legend can help you figure out exactly where you are in Symphony.

The Environment Menus

There are five "main" menus in Symphony, one for each of the program's five environments. You access each of these menus through the {Menu} key. The menu that pops up when you press {Menu} is determined by the type of the current window. If you are in a SHEET window, the spreadsheet menu appears when you press {Menu}. If you are in a DOC window, pressing {Menu} brings up the word processing menu.

As you learn more about Symphony, you will notice that some commands (such as Copy) appear on several different menus. For the most part, commands in different environments with similar or identical names work in much the same way. There are a few exceptions to this rule, but in general, once you've learned one or two of Symphony's menus, the remaining ones will be clear to you.

SYMPHONY'S HELP FACILITY

Just like its predecessor, 1-2-3, Symphony has an excellent on-line help facility. The help screens are stored on the Symphony Help and Tutorial disk. While you are using Symphony, you probably will want to keep this disk in drive A at all times. Simply pressing the {Help} key tells Symphony to search the Help and Tutorial disk for the help screen that matches the program's current condition. For instance, if you press {Help} while you are entering information into a FORM window, Symphony displays information about how to enter information into a data base through a FORM window.

The help facility is extensively cross-referenced, allowing you to choose a related topic from the menu presented on each Help screen. Alternatively, you may wish to choose a topic from the Help menu, which references 32 topics, as shown below:

@Functions	Macro Keywords
Arithmetic	Operators Macros
Cell Entries	Numeric Display Formats
Command Language	Pointer Movement Keys
Communications	Print Attributes
Compose Character	Sequences Printing Your Work
Configuring	the System Ranges
Customer Support	Saving Your Work
Databases	Security
File Commands	Services Menu
Formulas	Settings Sheets
Graphs	Special Keys
How to Use Help	Spreadsheet Operations
Key Location	Guide Strings
Leaving Symphony	Windows
Macro Key Names	Word Processing

I strongly recommend that you use Symphony's help facility as a ready reference as you are learning to use Symphony.

Now that you have installed Symphony, loaded the program into your computer, and briefly toured the screen and the keyboard, you are ready to begin using the program. In the next chapter, you'll learn more about the Symphony spreadsheet: how to move the cell pointer around the spreadsheet, how to enter information into the spreadsheet, and how to change some of the basic spreadsheet settings.

PART
II

THE SPREADSHEET

CHAPTER THREE

INTRODUCING THE SYMPHONY SPREADSHEET

Symphony is the best electronic spreadsheet available for a personal computer. No other program—not even 1-2-3—offers as much spreadsheeting power as Symphony. The Symphony spreadsheet is bigger than than any of its competitors, faster than most, and offers more functions and commands than any other spreadsheet. If you want a great spreadsheet, Symphony is an excellent choice.

In this section of the book you'll learn all about the Symphony spreadsheet. This chapter is an introduction to Symphony's spreadsheeting capabilities. You'll learn how to move the cell pointer about the worksheet; how to enter numbers, labels, and formulas in the worksheet; and how to edit those entries. We'll show you how Symphony uses memory and how you can conserve memory when working with the program. You'll also learn about Symphony's SHEET Settings command, which controls several of the most basic characteristics of the Symphony spreadsheet, including the window defaults, titles, and the method of recalculation.

THE SHEET WINDOW

Figure 3.1 shows a basic blank SHEET window called MAIN. For the first couple hundred pages of this book, we'll be looking at Symphony only through this window. In the previous chapter, you were introduced to the concept of a SHEET window. You learned about the size of the worksheet, columns and rows, cells, and the cell pointer. In this chapter we'll expand on those basic concepts.

MOVING THE CELL POINTER

Symphony offers many different ways to move the cell pointer around the worksheet. The simplest tools for moving the cursor are the arrow keys on the numeric keypad. These four keys (↑, →, ↓, and ←) move the cell pointer one cell in each direction.

For example, if you press → when the cell pointer is in cell A1, the cell pointer moves to cell B1. If you then press ↓, the cell pointer moves to cell B2. If you then press ←, the cell pointer moves to cell A2. Finally, pressing ↑ from here moves the cell pointer back to cell A1.

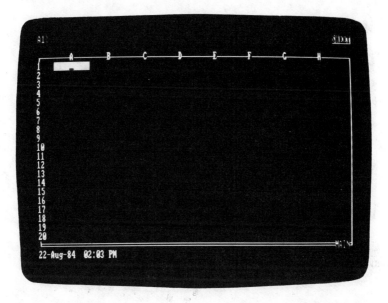

Figure 3.1

If you press ↑ or ← from cell A1, Symphony beeps, which means that you have tried to move the cell pointer to a position outside the boundaries of the worksheet. Symphony will never allow you to move the cursor up from row 1, right from column IV, left from column A, or down from row 8192.

[Pg Up] and [Pg Dn]

The [Pg Up] and [Pg Dn] keys move the cursor one full screen (20 rows) at a time. For example, if you press **[Pg Dn]** with the cell pointer in cell A1, the screen will look like Figure 3.2. Notice that the cell pointer is now in cell A21.

If you look back at Figure 3.1, you'll see that row 20 was the last row visible through the window MAIN. When you pressed [Pg Dn], MAIN shifted down 20 lines to view a new portion of the worksheet. If you press **[Pg Up]** from the position shown in Figure 3.2, the cell pointer immediately jumps back to cell A1, and the screen looks once again like Figure 3.1.

Big Right and Big Left

Now press **[Ctrl]** and → at the same time. The cell pointer jumps to cell I1, and the worksheet looks like Figure 3.3. Pressing [Ctrl]→ always moves the cell pointer one full screen (72 spaces) to the right.

With the cell pointer in cell I1, press **[Ctrl]←**. Symphony moves the cell pointer to cell A1, and the screen once again looks like Figure 3.1. Pressing [Ctrl]← always moves the cell pointer 72 spaces (one full screen) to the left.

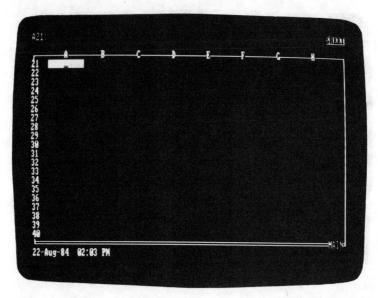

Figure 3.2

Lotus calls the [Ctrl]→ and [Ctrl]← combinations "Big Right" and "Big Left," but I like to refer to these combinations by naming both keystrokes.

[End] and [Home]

Symphony offers a number of other keys that help you move the cell pointer. For example, with the cell pointer in cell A1, press **[End]** and ↓ at the same time. The cell pointer jumps instantly to cell A8192, and the worksheet now looks like Figure 3.4. Now press **[End]**→. The cell pointer jumps to cell IV8192—the last cell in the worksheet.

As you can see, the [End] key, when used in conjunction with one of the arrow keys, causes the cell pointer to jump great distances. In effect, the [End] key acts as an accelerator for the arrow keys.

The specific rule that governs the [End] key is this: When used with an arrow key, the [End] key causes the cell pointer to move in the indicated direction to the next boundary between cells containing entries and empty cells. Since we haven't made any entries into the worksheet yet, this concept may be a little confusing. Don't worry if it doesn't make sense to you right now; we'll talk about the [End] key in more detail in Chapter 7.

With the cell pointer in cell IV8192, press **[Home]**. Instantly, the cell pointer jumps to cell A1. The [Home] key is a real timesaver, since there are many occasions when you'll want to return to cell A1 from a remote location in the worksheet.

The [Scroll Lock] Key

With the cell pointer in cell A1, press → several times until the cell pointer is in column H. Now press → again. Notice how column A disappears from the left edge of the window and column I appears at the right edge. In other words, the cell pointer seems to

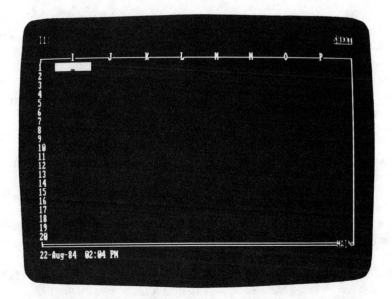

Figure 3.3

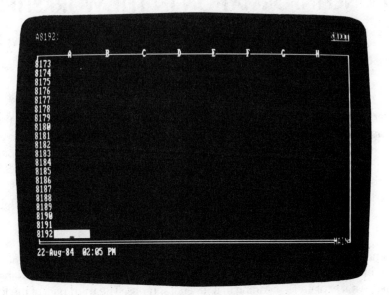

Figure 3.4

"drag" the window across the worksheet. If you press → again, the cell pointer moves to cell J1, column B disappears from the left edge of the screen, and column J comes into view at the right edge.

Now press [**Home**] to move the cell pointer back to cell A1 and then → to move it to cell C1. When the cell pointer is in C1, press [**Scroll Lock**]. Notice the legend Scroll that appears at the bottom of the screen.

Now press → again. This time the window shifts one column to the right, with column A disappearing from the left edge and column I appearing at the right edge, even though the cell pointer remains in column C. If you press the → key again, the window shifts to the right again, even though the cell pointer does not move from cell C1.

Of course, the [Scroll Lock] key can also be used in conjunction with the ↑ and ↓ keys. If you were to position the cell pointer in cell C3, press [**Scroll Lock**], and then press ↓, the cell pointer would remain in cell C3, but row 1 would disappear from the top of the screen and row 21 would come into view at the bottom.

To summarize, [Scroll Lock] causes the arrow keys to move the screen rather than the cell pointer. When you press → with [Scroll Lock] active, the cell pointer remains fixed in its current location, but the entire screen shifts one column to the right. Similarly, pressing ↓ with [Scroll Lock] active causes the cell pointer to remain fixed in its current location while the screen shifts down one row.

[Scroll Lock] is like [Caps Lock]; once you press it, it stays active until you press it again. If you use the [Scroll Lock] feature, be sure to turn it off when you are finished.

ENTERING INFORMATION IN THE WORKSHEET

You can enter two different kinds of information into a cell in the Symphony worksheet: labels and values. As you would expect, labels are simple text entries. Values fall into three categories: simple numbers, formulas, and string values.

Labels and Numbers

To enter a label in a cell, simply move the cell pointer to that cell and enter the label. For example, to enter the label "Abcdefgh" in cell B5, move the cell pointer to that cell with the arrow keys and type the label. When you are finished typing the label, press [**Enter**] to store the entry in cell B5. The worksheet will now look like Figure 3.5. As you can see, the label you typed has been entered into cell B5.

Notice the legend that appears in the control panel at the top of the screen in Figure 3.5:

    B5: 'Abcdefgh

This legend tells you several things. The first part of the legend, B5:, tells you that the cell pointer is in cell B5. The apostrophe between the B5: and the actual label is a label-prefix character; we'll explain its meaning in a few paragraphs. The third part of the legend is the label itself.

Now move the cursor to cell C2 and enter the number 100. When you press [**Enter**] to store the entry in cell C2, the worksheet will look like Figure 3.6. Notice the display in the control panel:

    C2: 100

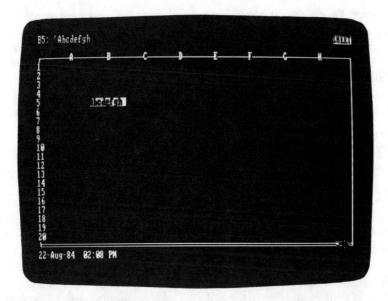

Figure 3.5

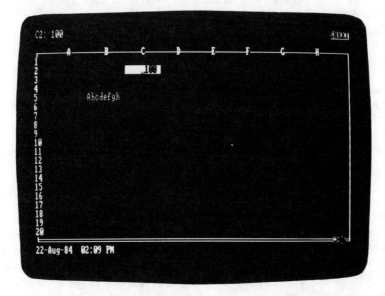

Figure 3.6

How did Symphony know that the entry you made to cell B5 was a label but that the entry in cell C2 was a value? The program took its cue from the first character you typed in entering the label. Because the entry in cell B5 started with a letter, Symphony assumed (correctly) that the entry was a label. Similarly, Symphony assumed the entry in cell C2 was a value because the first character in that entry was a numeral. In general, Symphony assumes that any entry that begins with the characters 0 to 9, +, −, $,), #, ., or @ is a value. All other entries are considered labels.

Although this convention works pretty well, it isn't always correct. For example, if you tried to enter the label "1234 Any Street" into a cell, Symphony would assume that the entry was a value because the first character in the entry is a number. Since you want this entry to be a label, you need to find a way to tell Symphony that this entry is a label.

Label Prefixes

A *label prefix* is a special character that precedes all label entries in Symphony. Label prefixes serve two purposes. First, they tell Symphony how to align labels in cells. Second, they allow you to enter phrases like "1234 Any Street" as labels.

For example, to enter the label "1234 Any Street" into cell A10, you would move the cell pointer to that cell and type **'1234 Any Street.** Notice that the first character you typed was the apostrophe, which is one of Symphony's label prefixes. Any time you begin an entry with a label prefix, Symphony will treat that entry as a label.

Symphony offers four label prefixes: ', ", ^, and \. (A fifth prefix, ¦, is used by Symphony to mark special lines in a SHEET window; we will not discuss it here.) The apostrophe causes text to align flush left in the cell. The double-quote prefix causes Symphony to align the label at the right edge of the cell. The carat (^) tells Symphony to center the label in the cell if there is sufficient room. Finally, the blackslash (\) tells Symphony to repeat the label until you reach the edge of the cell. Figure 3.7 shows the effect of each of the label prefixes on the simple label ABC.

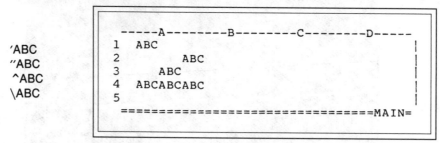

'ABC
"ABC
^ABC
\ABC

```
     -----A--------B--------C--------D-----
  1    ABC                                 |
  2            ABC                         |
  3         ABC                            |
  4    ABCABCABC                           |
  5                                        |
     ===============================MAIN=
```

Figure 3.7

You don't need to begin all of your labels with label prefixes. Symphony interprets all entries that begin with a letter as labels, so all you need to do to enter a label that begins with a letter is type the label itself. Symphony automatically supplies a label prefix for all labels that you enter in this way. The default label prefix is the apostrophe, so most of the time when you enter a label without specifying a prefix the label will end up flush left in the column. Later in this chapter, when we talk about the SHEET Settings commands, we'll show you how to change the default label-prefix character.

Overlapping Labels

Notice that the label you entered in cell A10 seems to overlap the edge of the cell. Symphony will always allow a label that is too wide to fit in one column to overlap into the next column, provided the adjacent cell does not contain any information. Don't let this ability confuse you, however. Even though the label appears to overlap into cell B10, the entire label is actually entered in cell A10.

If you move the cell pointer to cell B10 and enter the number 100, the worksheet should look like Figure 3.8 once you press **[Enter]**. The long label in cell A10 no longer overlaps into cell B10, because Symphony will not allow a label to overlap into a cell that contains an entry.

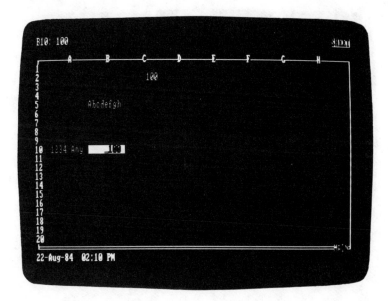

Figure 3.8

Locking in Your Entries

Let's make one more simple entry to the worksheet. Move the cell pointer to cell D10 and enter the number 1000. This time, instead of pressing [Enter] after you type the number, just press →. Notice that the cell pointer jumps to cell E10 and the number 1000 appears in cell D10. If you press ← to move back to cell D10, the control panel will look like this:

> D10: 1000

You can always use one of the cursor-movement keys (including the [Pg Up] and [Pg Dn] keys) instead of the [Enter] key to store an entry in a cell.

Formulas

If Symphony only allowed you to enter numbers and labels into cells in the worksheet, the program would not be very useful. Symphony's real power lies in allowing you to enter formulas in the worksheet that refer to other cells.

For example, suppose you enter the formula

D15: +C2

in cell D15 and press **[Enter].** Your worksheet will now look like Figure 3.9. Notice that cell D15 has assumed the value in cell C2. In a way, cell D15 is now linked to cell C2; whenever the value in cell C2 changes, the value in cell D15 will also change.

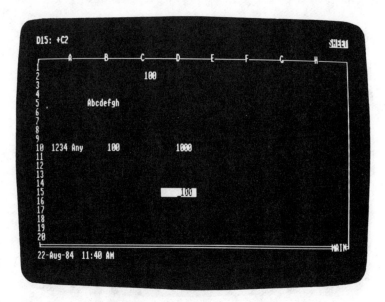

Figure 3.9

For example, suppose you move the cell pointer to cell C2 and enter the number 1. Instantly, the value in cell D15 also changes to 1. If you change the entry in cell C2 to 500, cell D15 assumes that value.

Notice that the entry in cell D15, +C2, begins with a plus symbol. If you had entered the formula as C2, Symphony would have assumed the entry was a label because the first character in the entry is a letter. Whenever the first term of an entry is a cell reference, you must precede the cell reference with a plus sign.

Notice that cell D15 displays the *result* of the formula +C2, not the formula itself. This concept is a tricky one for some new Symphony users. You should remember that Symphony always displays the result of a formula, not the formula itself, in the worksheet. However, when you position the cell pointer in cell D15, the top line of the control panel looks like this:

D15: +C2

Notice that the control panel displays the actual contents of the cell rather than the result of those contents.

More Complex Formulas

Of course, Symphony lets you build formulas that are more complex than the simple one shown above. For example, suppose you move to cell A20 and enter the formula

> A20: +C2+B10

After you press **[Enter]** cell A20 displays the value 600, which is the sum of the value in cell C2, 500, and the value in cell B10, 100. This is a simple addition formula.

Since this formula refers to two cells, its value will change if you change the value in either of those cells. For example, if you enter the number 200 in cell B10, the value in cell A20 will change to 700. If you then enter the value 100 in cell C2, A20 will change to 300.

Symphony also allows you to build formulas that combine numbers and cell references. For example, the formula

> G1: +B10+100

adds 100 to the current value of cell B10 and displays the result in cell G1. In the worksheet shown in Figure 3.10, this function has the value 300.

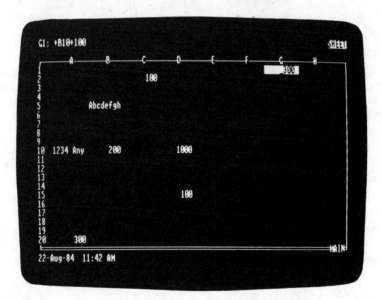

Figure 3.10

In fact, a formula can even refer to another formula. For example, if you enter the formula

> C10: +D15+G1

in cell C10, that cell will display the number 400. If you change the entry in cell B10, which is referred to by the formula in cell G1 and thus is referred to indirectly by the formula in cell C10, both the value of cell G1 and the value of cell C10 will change.

Mathematical Operators

Symphony offers mathematical operators for addition ($+$), subtraction ($-$), multiplication ($*$), division ($/$), and exponentiation ($\wedge$). For example, the formula

H1: +C2/100

would display the value 1 in cell H1. The formula

H2: +C2*5

would return the value 500 in cell H2.

Symphony allows you to construct functions that are far more complex than the simple examples we've considered so far. These complex formulas can (and usually do) use several of Symphony's mathematical operators. For example, the formula

H3: +C2*5/100

multiplies the value in cell C2 by 5 and then divides that result by 100.

When you build formulas that combine several of Symphony's operators, you must keep in mind the precedence of the operators. The word *precedence* simply refers to the order in which Symphony performs the calculations in a complex equation. In the previous example, the precedence of operation is multiply first, then divide.

But suppose you enter the formula

H4: +C2+5/100

in cell H4. The result of this formula, 100.05, may not be what you expected. In computing the value of this formula, Symphony first divided 5 by 100 and then added the result, .05, to the value in cell C2, 100. In other words, the precedence of operation in this example is division first, addition second.

It isn't always easy to determine exactly how Symphony will evaluate a given formula. Fortunately, you can always overcome the built-in operator precedence by enclosing parts of the formula in parentheses. I recommend that you always use parentheses in your formulas to tell Symphony exactly the order in which you want the elements of the formula to be evaluated.

The following list shows several different formulas, each one of which uses parentheses differently. Notice that although all of the formulas use the same numbers, the results are completely different.

3+5/15+1*100	103.333
(3+5)/15+1*100	100.533
3+5/(15+1)*100	34.25
(3+5)/(15+1)*100	50
(3+5)/(15+1*100)	.069565
(((3+5)/15)+1)*100	153.333

Whenever you include parentheses in your formulas, you must be sure that the number of opening parentheses matches the number of closing parentheses.

Pointing

Up to now we have been defining formulas simply by typing the coordinates of the cell or cells to which we want the formula to refer. Symphony offers a better way to create these references, however—pointing. In Symphony, you can use the arrow keys while defining a formula to point to the cell to which you want to refer. For example, suppose you want to enter the formula

    H5: +C2

in cell H5. Obviously, you can just move the cell pointer to cell H5 and type the reference to cell C2.

Alternatively, you can move the cell pointer to cell H5, type a plus sign, and then press ←. Notice that the cell pointer moves one space to the left and that the control panel now reads

    G5:   POINT
    +G5

Notice that the Mode indicator in the upper-right corner of the screen now says POINT. Now move the cell pointer to cell C2 by pressing ← four more times and ↑ three times. When the cell pointer is positioned on cell C2, the control panel will look like this:

    C2: 100   POINT
    +C2

Now press **[Enter]**. Instantly, the cell pointer jumps back to cell H5. Notice that the number 100 is displayed in cell H5 and that the control panel reads

    H5: +C2

In this simple example, you have defined a cell reference by pointing to the selected cell. Although in this example you created only a simple one-cell reference, you can also use the POINT mode to create longer and more complex formulas. For example, suppose you want to enter the formula

    H6: (H1 + H2)/H3

in cell H6. To create this formula, move the cell pointer to cell H6, type (, and press ↑ five times to position the cell pointer on cell H1. Now press **+**. Notice that the cell pointer jumps back to cell H6 and that the control panel now reads

    H6:   POINT
    (H1 +

Now press ↑ four times to position the cell pointer on cell H2 and press) and /. The cell pointer again returns to cell H6 and the control panel changes to

    H6:   POINT
    (H1 + H2)/

Finally, move the cell pointer to cell H3 and press **[Enter]**. The number 100.2 should appear in cell H6, and the control panel should show that cell H6 contains the formula

    H6: (H1 + H2)/H3

Once you are in the POINT mode, you can only "lock in" a formula by pressing [Enter]. If you try to lock in the formula by pressing an arrow key, Symphony will simply assume that you want to point to another cell.

Symphony will not allow you to lock in an incorrect formula. For example, if you try to press [Enter] when the control panel looks like this, Symphony beeps and does not allow the entry to be locked in:

```
H6:
(H1 + H2)/
```

Before Symphony will accept this entry, you either have to complete the formula or use the [Backspace] key to get rid of the hanging /.

If you make an error while pointing, you can correct it by pressing [Esc] or [Backspace]. For example, suppose that in the previous example you made an error while entering the formula so that the control panel looked like this:

```
H6:
(H1 + H3)/
```

To correct this error, just press [Backspace] enough times to erase the error. The control panel should now look like this:

```
H6:
(H1 +
```

Now use the arrow keys to point to the correct cell and continue to define the formula.

The POINT mode is one of Symphony's most useful features. (Although in the examples it would probably be easier just to type the formulas, in other cases you will find it much easier to point.) In addition to offering a convenient way to enter formulas into the worksheet, the POINT mode can also be used to designate the range to which a function or a command should apply. We'll cover those uses for the POINT mode in a later chapter.

Absolute, relative, and mixed references   The cell references shown in the previous examples are a special kind of reference called a relative reference. Symphony also allows you to define absolute references to other cells. Absolute references are identified by placing a dollar sign ($) in front of both the column letter and the row number in the reference. For example, $A$1 is an absolute reference to cell A1.

The {ABS} key allows you to define absolute and mixed references very quickly while you point to the cell references in a formula. For example, suppose you want to define the absolute reference

```
H7: +$C$2
```

in cell H7. To enter this formula, type + and then point to cell C2. When the cell pointer is positioned on cell C2, the control panel will look like this:

```
C2:
+ C2                                                      POINT
```

Now press {Abs}. The control panel display instantly changes to

C2:   **POINT**
+ $C$2

You could press [Enter] at this point to lock in this absolute reference. Alternatively, you could press {Abs} again to change the entry to a mixed reference. If you pressed {Abs} again, the control panel would look like this:

C2:   **POINT**
+ C$2

Pressing {Abs} again would change the control panel display to

C2:   **POINT**
+ $C2

A final press would change the reference back to a relative reference (C2).

The importance of absolute, relative, and mixed cell references will become clear when you learn about the Copy command in Chapter 7. These references are explained in more detail in that chapter.

Functions

A function is a special kind of formula that performs the work of a long or complex formula. For example, the @SUM function can be used to total the numbers in any range. The @SUM function

@SUM(A1 . . A15)

can take the place of the formula

+ A1 + A2 + A3 + A4 + A5 + A6 + A7 + A8 + A9 + A10 + A11 + A12 + A13 + A14 + A15

Symphony offers more functions than any other spreadsheet program. Functions are covered in detail in Chapter 4.

String Values

One of the biggest improvements of Symphony over 1-2-3 is in the program's ability to manipulate labels stored in the worksheet. In fact, you can use labels in almost all the same ways as you can use numbers.

For example, suppose you enter the formula

A11: + A10

in cell A11. Notice that this formula refers to cell A10, which contains a label. When you press enter, the worksheet should look like Figure 3.11. The formula in cell A11 has assumed the "value" of the label in cell A10. Because this kind of formula treats a label (or a string of text) as a value, we call it a string value.

Concatenation

Symphony offers a special operator, &, which can be used to concatenate, or string together, several different string values. For example, if you move the cell pointer to cell

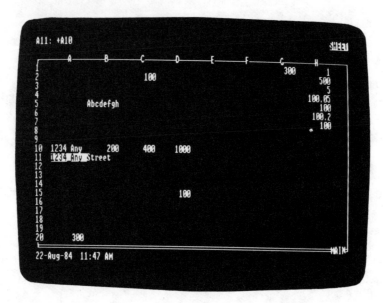

Figure 3.11

F10 and enter the formula

      F10: +A10&+B5

the worksheet would look like Figure 3.12. Notice that cell F10 appears to contain the label

      1234 Any StreetAbcdefghi

The formula in cell F10 has concatenated the two labels in cells A10 and B5 into one string value.

    Although the string value created in the previous example is meaningless, there are some important uses for the concatenation operator in Symphony. For example, suppose cell A1 in a worksheet contains the first name of a customer, Debbie, and cell A2 contains her last name, Jones. If you enter the string value

      A3: +A1&" "&+A2

in cell A3, that cell will display the long string value

      Debbie Jones

Notice that the formula in cell A3 uses the concatenation operator twice. This formula includes a *literal string*—a simple space enclosed in quotes. This space separates the two halves of the string value.

    The main rule to remember about including literal strings in your string values is that they must always be enclosed in double quotes. In other words, Symphony will not understand the strings

      A3: +A1& &+A2
      A3: +A1&' 'A2

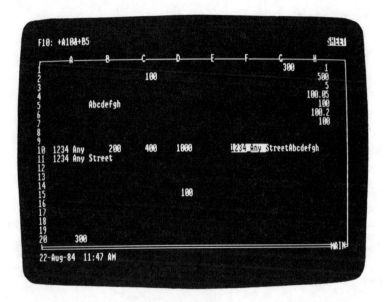

Figure 3.12

EDITING THE CONTENTS OF A CELL

You have already seen the easiest way to change the entry in a cell: simply type the new entry over the old. But Symphony allows you to make less drastic changes to cell entries as well. You can use the {Edit} key to edit the contents of any cell in the worksheet.

For example, suppose that you want to change the entry in cell A10 from 1234 Any Street to 1235 Any Street. To make this change, move the cell pointer to cell A10 and press {**Edit**}. Symphony immediately displays the contents of the cell, followed by a small cursor (an underline character), on the edit line of the control panel:

    A10: '1234 Any Street
    '1234 Any Street_

If you press ←, the cursor will move backward through the label. After you've pressed ← 12 times, the line will look like this:

    A10: '1234 Any Street
    '1234 Any Street

Now press [**Del**]. The display on the edit line will now be

    A10: '1234 Any Street
    '123_ Any Street

Finally, type the numeral **5** and press [**Enter**]. The label in cell A10 is now

    A10: '1235 Any Street

Let's look at an example of editing a formula. Suppose you want to change the formula in cell H6 from

        H6: (H1 + H2)/H3

to

        H6: (H1 + H2)/100

To make this change, move the cell pointer to cell H6 and press {**Edit**}. The control panel will now look like this:

        H6: (H1 + H2)/H3
        (H1 + H2)/H3_

Now press [**Backspace**] twice. The control panel will now look like this:

        H6: (H1 + H2)/H3
        (H1 + H2)/_

Finally, type the new divisor—100—and press [**Enter**]. The formula is now changed.

You can also edit cells containing numbers with the {Edit} key. In most cases, it is easier to retype a simple value than to edit that entry.

HOW SYMPHONY USES MEMORY

In the second chapter, you learned that Symphony requires a great deal of memory to function. In fact, your PC must have at least 320K bytes of RAM just to load Symphony. To use the program effectively, your computer must have far more than this minimum. Because an understanding of memory is so important in using Symphony, we'll go into the topic in detail now.

As you might expect, every entry you make to the Symphony worksheet uses memory. However, some entries use a lot more memory than others. For example, the entry

        A1: 1

uses only a tiny amount of memory (about two bytes) but the entry

        A1: 'This is a very long label stored in cell A1.

uses quite a bit more. The difference in the memory used by these two entries is due primarily to the length of the entries. In general, you'll be able to enter more short entries than long entries in a worksheet, given the same amount of RAM.

However, memory management in Symphony isn't as simple as keeping your entries brief. Whenever you make an entry in the Symphony worksheet, Symphony allocates a few bytes to every cell above and to the left of the cell in which the entry was made. For example, if you enter the number 100 in cell C10, Symphony uses a few bytes to store the number 100 itself, but it also allocates a few bytes to cells A1, A2, A3, B1, B2, and so on. The result is that the simple entry in cell C10 eats up quite a bit of memory.

The same thing happens if you make an entry in cell A25 and another entry in cell G1. In this case, Symphony allocates a few bytes to every cell in the rectangular area A1 . .

G25. Since there are 175 cells in this range, these two entries can be very costly in terms of memory.

To push this concept to the limit, move the cell pointer to cell IV8192 (the lower-left corner of the worksheet) and attempt to enter the number 1. When you press [Enter], Symphony will beep and deliver the message "Memory Full". This error occurs because Symphony has tried to allocate a few bytes to every cell above and to the left of cell IV8192, the bottom-right cell in the worksheet. This means that Symphony has tried to allocate a few bytes to *every cell* in the worksheet. Since the worksheet contains over 2,000,000 cells, Symphony would need over 4,000,000 bytes of RAM to accommodate an entry in cell IV8192!

The Active Area

The range of cells from A1 to the last cell to which Symphony has allocated any bytes is called the active area of the worksheet. In the first example, the active area is A1 . . C10. In the second example, the active area is A1 . . G25. As you can see, the active area is always a rectangle.

The last cell in the active area isn't always a cell that contains an entry. In the above example, the active area spans the range from A1 . . G25, even though the only entries in the sheet are in A25 and G1. You can have *only* empty cells in the active area if you use the {Menu} Format command to assign a special format to the range A1 . . Z100 in a blank worksheet. Symphony expands the active area to cover the entire formatted range, even the though the worksheet contains no entries.

You can determine the dimensions of the active area in any worksheet by pressing **[End]** followed by **[Home]**. This combination of keystrokes causes the cell pointer to jump to the last cell in the active area. In the example where you made entries in cells A25 and G1, pressing [End][Home] causes the cell pointer to jump to cell G25.

Since Symphony allocates bytes to every cell in the active area, the best strategy for managing the use of memory in Symphony is to keep the active area as small as possible. Keep your entries as close to cell A1 as possible, and avoid blank rows and columns above and to the right of cells that contain entries.

The second example above is a good illustration of this concept. In that example, we made two entries to a worksheet, one in cell G1 and the other in cell A25. These entries expanded the active area to A1 . . G25 and caused Symphony to allocate RAM to 173 empty cells. If, on the other hand, these entries had been made in cells A1 and A2, no memory would have been allocated to blank cells.

Of course, there are times when you will want to include blank rows and columns in the active area for formatting or other purposes. As long as your computer has sufficient memory, these blank cells should not cause a problem. But when you are creating a really large model that pushes the limits of your memory and every byte counts, you'll want to remember this rule.

Keeping Track of Available Memory

The quickest way to find out how much memory is available in your system at any time is to issue the {**Services**} **S**ettings command. The settings sheet that is controlled by this command includes a display like this:

Memory Available: 74123 of 80096 Bytes (93%)

You'll probably get in the habit of checking this settings sheet from time to time when working in Symphony, especially when you're working with a large worksheet. If you forget to check, however, Symphony will warn you if your available memory is low. When the amount of free memory falls below 5 percent of the total available memory, the message "Mem" will appear in inverse video at the bottom of the display. For example, if your computer has 320K of RAM memory, your total available memory after loading Symphony is only about 19K. If the free memory falls below 5 percent of 19K, or about 1000 bytes, the "Mem" message will appear.

If you ignore the "Mem" message and continue to work in Symphony, eventually you'll run out of memory. When this happens, the message "Memory full" will appear in the lower-left corner of the worksheet. At this point, you must either reduce the size of the current worksheet and thus free up some memory or terminate the current session by saving the worksheet, issuing the New command, and starting over in a blank workspace. In Chapter 10 we'll show you how the File Xtract command can be used to overcome memory-full errors.

If there is one common bond that unites all Symphony users, it is that none of them feel that they have quite enough memory to do everything they'd like to do with the program. Their complaint highlights the progress in the microcomputer industry in the last five years. My first computer was an Apple II+ with 48K of memory. When VisiCalc was loaded into the machine, only about 16K of free space remained for creating a worksheet. At the time, 16K seemed like an adequate amount of memory for most applications. Today, however, Symphony users with 640K of total memory and over 300K of memory for their worksheets find that amount too limiting. Spreadsheets, like gases and the federal bureaucracy, seem to expand to fill the available space.

Reminiscing aside—if you use Symphony, you'll need to monitor memory carefully, especially if your system has just 320K to 384K of main memory. The following table shows approximately how much available memory you'll have after loading Symphony if you have a certain amount of total RAM.

Total System Memory	Available Memory
320	19
384	80
448	144
512	208
576	272
640	336

My advice is that you should get as much memory as you can possibly afford. You're likely to encounter memory limitations eventually even with 640K of RAM, so if you have less than that amount you'll almost certainly be limited. The price of RAM memory has fallen dramatically in the past few years, so 640K won't put a huge dent in your pocketbook. If you can possibly afford it, we recommend that you buy the maximum.

COMMANDS

As you learned in Chapter 2, Symphony offers a large number of commands that allow you to do everything from printing the worksheet to copying a range of cell entries. The {Services} menu includes those commands, like Print and File, that apply to two or more of Symphony's environments. Pressing this key always causes Symphony to display the same menu. The menu that appears when you press the {Menu} key, on the other hand, depends on the type of window you are in when the key is pressed. {Menu} controls those commands that apply to only one of Symphony's five environments (SHEET, DOC, FORM, GRAPH, and COMM).

THE SHEET MENU

If you press {Menu} from within a SHEET window, the following menu appears:

Copy Move Erase Insert Delete Width Format Range Graph Query Settings Quit

We'll call the first six commands on this menu cut-and-paste commands because they take the place of the scissors and glue you used to use to edit a paper spreadsheet. These commands are covered in Chapter 7. The Format command lets you format the contents of a cell in a variety of ways. This command is explained in Chapter 5. The Range commands are discussed in Chapter 8. The Graph command, which allows you to create and preview graphs, is covered in Chapters 12 and 13. Query, Symphony's data base command, is covered in Chapters 21 and 22. The Settings command is covered in the next section.

If you are a former 1-2-3 user, you may wonder why Lotus has decided not to use the trusty "/" key to activate commands in Symphony. In fact, they have not abandoned this key completely. When you are working in a SHEET window, the / key and the {Menu} key have the same function. However, in all of the other environments, you must press {Menu} to activate the command menu. Because / substitutes for {Menu} only in the SHEET environment, we use {Menu} throughout this book to activate Symphony's command menus.

THE SHEET SETTINGS COMMAND

The only command we'll explain in this chapter is {Menu} Settings. The {Menu} Settings command gives you control over some of the most basic default settings for a SHEET window. When you issue this command, the menu and settings sheet shown in Figure 3.13 appear on the screen.

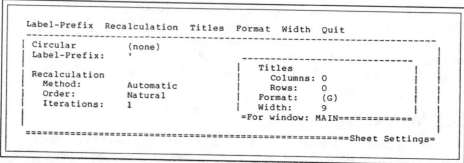

```
Label-Prefix  Recalculation  Titles  Format  Width  Quit
-------------------------------------------------------------------
| Circular            (none)
| Label-Prefix:       '
|                                   -----------------------------------
| Recalculation                     | Titles
|   Method:           Automatic     |   Columns:  0
|   Order:            Natural        |   Rows:     0
|   Iterations:       1             |   Format:    (G)
|                                   |   Width:     9
|                                   =For window: MAIN=============
|
| ============================================================Sheet Settings=
```

Figure 3.13

This command is in fact a bit of a hybrid, since its Recalculation option affects the entire workspace, while the other options (Label-Prefix, Title, Format, and Width) affect only the settings in the current window. Since for the next few chapters you'll be working in only one window, you shouldn't worry about this distinction for now. We'll cover it again in Chapter 11, where we show you how to create multiple windows.

Before we cover the SHEET Settings command in detail, we'll detour to consider the concept of settings sheets in general. A settings sheet is a form that shows the current configuration of a certain part of Symphony. Settings sheets are always related to a set of commands that control the status of each item in the settings sheet.

When you issue a command that controls a settings sheet, the settings sheet will replace the current contents of the screen. As you issue commands, the settings in the sheet will change. This makes it possible to quickly determine the status of any item in the sheet. The sheet remains in view until you exit from the command that controls the sheet.

Settings sheets take a bit of getting used to (in part because there are so many of them and they all look alike), but they are really very handy. If you are a former 1-2-3 user, you know how difficult it was to determine the exact status of all the settings that affected a certain 1-2-3 operation. In Symphony, all of the settings are instantly visible on settings sheets.

The Window Defaults

Every SHEET window has three important default settings: The default label prefix, the default column width, and the default cell format. These settings are important because they affect how your entries look as you enter them into the worksheet.

Label Prefix

Earlier in this chapter you learned that every label entry has a label prefix. However, you also learned that you don't need to supply a label prefix every time you make a label entry. As long as the label begins with a letter, you can just type the actual label; Symphony automatically supplies a label prefix. For example, if you move the cell pointer to cell A1, type **ABCDEF**, and press **[Enter]**, cell A1 will contain the label entry

A1: 'ABCDEF

Notice that the label prefix ' has been inserted by Symphony in front of the label you typed. Remember that the label prefix is visible only in the control panel; it is not displayed in cell A1.

The Label-Prefix option on the SHEET Settings menu controls the label prefix that Symphony automatically supplies when you enter labels in this way. The default for this setting is ', the flush-left label prefix.

To change the default label prefix, select **L**abel-Prefix from the Settings menu and select the desired alignment: Left, Center, or Right. If you choose **C**enter, the default label prefix changes to ^; if you choose **R**ight, it becomes ".

It is important that you understand that changing the default label prefix has no effect whatsoever on label entries that are already in the worksheet. Only labels entered after the Label-Prefix setting is changed will assume the new default prefix. To change the alignment of existing entries, you must use the **R**ange **L**abel-Alignment command, which is explained in Chapter 8.

Width

The Width option in the SHEET Settings menu allows you to choose the width of the columns in the current window. The standard default column width is 9, but you can change this setting to be as small as 1 and as large as 240. To change the Width setting, issue the {Menu} Settings command and select the Width option. Symphony displays the prompt

Default column width: 9

The number 9 in this prompt indicates that 9 is the current default setting. If you had previously changed the default column width, the current width would appear in the prompt.

There are two ways to change this setting. First, you can simply type a number that represents the new width. For example, to change the default width to 12, you would simply type **12** next to Symphony's prompt and then press **[Enter].**

Alternatively, you can use the ← and → keys to "point" to the desired width. Suppose you want to increase the default column width to 12 using this method. When Symphony pauses for you to specify the new width, simply press → three times. Notice that the width of all the visible columns increases each time you press →. When the columns are all 12 characters wide, press **[Enter]** to lock in the width.

Just as the → key can be used to widen a column, ← can be used to decrease the default width. For example, if after increasing the default column width to 12 you decide you want to return it to 9, you need only issue the {Menu} Settings Width command, press ← three times, and press [Enter].

Because the maximum width of a window in Symphony is 75 characters, you probably won't find much use for a default column width greater than 75. If you choose a larger width—for example, 100 characters—Symphony will override your setting to display the column in the current window. Similarly, you probably won't use a default column width smaller than two or three characters very often, since it is difficult to display numeric entries in very narrow columns.

Symphony also offers the {Menu} Width command, which allows you to change the width of a single column. This command is discussed in Chapter 7 with the cut-and-paste commands.

Format

The Format option on the SHEET Settings menu lets you control the default format that is assigned to the numeric entries in your worksheet. The default Format setting is General, which means that numbers are displayed more or less as they are entered. By choosing a different format, such as Currency, Percentage, or Scientific, you can force Symphony to display your numeric entries in a variety of ways. Formats are covered in detail in Chapter 5.

A Complaint

Unfortunately, there is no way in Symphony to "permanently" change the default settings in the SHEET settings sheet. In other words, the default column width is always 9 when you first load Symphony into your computer, the default format is General, and the default label prefix is '. If you like some other combination of default settings—for example, Format Currency, Width 11, Prefix "—then you must manually change these settings every time you begin creating a new worksheet.

Titles

The {Menu} Settings Titles command allows you to "lock" certain rows and columns onto the screen so that they are always visible, no matter where the cell pointer is located in the worksheet. Former 1-2-3 users will recognize this command as being very similar to the 1-2-3 /Worksheet Titles command. Suppose you've created a spreadsheet that fills the range of cells from A1 to Z100. In columns A and B you've entered some labels that identify the contents of each row in the worksheet, and in rows 1, 2, and 3 you've entered headers that identify the contents of each column. The upper-left corner of such a worksheet is shown in Figure 3.14.

With the cell pointer in cell A1, press ↓. The screen will now look like Figure 3.15. Similarly, if you press [Ctrl]→ with the cell pointer in cell A1, the screen will look like Figure 3.16.

Notice that in Figure 3.15 the labels in rows 1 to 4 disappeared from view when the cell pointer was moved to cell A21. Similarly, when the cell pointer was moved to cell I1, the labels in columns A and B disappeared from view. Since these labels help you to remember the contents of each row and column in the worksheet, not being able to see them except when the cell pointer is in certain parts of the worksheet is a problem. Fortunately, the {Menu} Settings Titles command can help you overcome this problem.

When you issue the Titles command Symphony displays the following menu:

Both Horizontal Vertical Clear

```
    -----A--------B--------C--------D--------E--------F--------G--------H-------
 1  A Small Midwestern Company
 2  1984 Business Plan
 3                               Jan-84    Feb-84    Mar-84    Apr-84   May-84
 4                               ------    ------    ------    ------   ------
 5  Sales
 6    Product 1                 $10,943   $12,132   $12,723   $13,004  $12,876
 7    Product 2                 $13,567   $13,628   $13,749   $13,892  $14,541
 8    Product 3                 $32,704   $34,582   $35,114   $37,910  $38,021
 9    Product 4                 $52,187   $52,366   $52,387   $50,813  $48,530
10    Product 5                 $12,563   $12,592   $12,612   $12,900  $13,033
11    Product 6                 $23,109   $21,019   $20,340   $21,982  $22,086
12    Product 7                 $19,043   $19,051   $19,184   $19,850  $20,129
13    Product 8                 $21,870   $21,879   $21,896   $22,821  $21,965
14    Product 9                 $78,401   $86,180   $92,352  $100,912  $98,123
15    Product 10                $40,963   $40,985   $41,065   $43,986  $45,122
16                              ------    ------    ------    ------   ------
17  Total Sales               $305,350  $314,414  $321,422  $338,070 $324,426
18
19  Cost of Goods Sold
20    Product 1                  $3,830    $4,246    $4,454    $4,886   $5,417
    =================================================================MAIN=
```

Figure 3.14

```
    -----A--------B--------C--------D--------E--------F--------G--------H-------
21    Product 2                  $6,105    $6,132    $6,187    $6,231   $6,281
22    Product 3                 $17,987   $19,020   $19,313   $20,170  $20,783
23    Product 4                 $18,787   $18,852   $18,859   $19,006  $19,078
24    Product 5                  $5,025    $5,037    $5,045    $5,083   $5,093
25    Product 6                  $9,013    $8,197    $7,932    $7,454   $6,979
26    Product 7                  $9,522    $9,526    $9,592    $9,642   $9,675
27    Product 8                 $10,935   $10,940   $10,948   $10,955  $11,028
28    Product 9                 $33,712   $37,058   $39,711   $41,508  $44,864
29    Product 10                $24,578   $24,591   $24,639   $24,876  $24,936
30                              ------    ------    ------    ------   ------
31  Total Cost of Goods Sold  $139,494  $143,599  $146,680  $149,811 $154,134
32
33  Gross Margin
34    Product 1                  $7,113    $7,886    $8,270    $9,075  $10,058
35    Product 2                  $7,462    $7,495    $7,562    $7,615   $7,677
36    Product 3                 $14,717   $15,562   $15,801   $16,503  $17,005
37    Product 4                 $33,400   $33,514   $33,528   $33,788  $33,917
38    Product 5                  $7,538    $7,555    $7,567    $7,625   $7,639
39    Product 6                 $14,096   $12,822   $12,407   $11,658  $10,915
40    Product 7                  $9,522    $9,526    $9,592    $9,642   $9,675
    =================================================================MAIN=
```

Figure 3.15

The Horizontal option allows you to lock one or more rows onto the screen, and the Vertical option allows you to do the same with one or more columns. Both allow you to define both a horizontal and a vertical title range at one time. Clear resets any titles you have previously defined.

Suppose you want to use the Titles command to lock rows 1, 2, 3, and 4 onto the screen. To do this, you must move the cell pointer to any cell in row 5 and issue the {**Menu**} **S**ettings **T**itles **H**orizontal command. As soon as you issue this command, Symphony "locks" the first four rows onto the screen. If, after issuing the command, you press [Pg Dn], the screen will look like Figure 3.17.

```
     ----I--------J--------K--------L--------M--------N--------O--------P-----
  1                                                                           |
  2                                                                           |
  3    Jun-84   Jul-84   Aug-84   Sep-84   Oct-84   Nov-84   Dec-84           |
  4    ------   ------   ------   ------   ------   ------   ------           |
  5                                                                           |
  6   $18,406  $18,493  $21,622  $22,636  $25,138  $26,948  $28,139          |
  7   $14,057  $14,194  $14,218  $14,348  $14,480  $14,486  $14,503          |
  8   $40,878  $44,410  $47,060  $49,077  $50,958  $55,687  $59,238          |
  9   $53,316  $53,754  $53,778  $54,127  $54,207  $54,252  $54,761          |
 10   $12,773  $12,804  $12,825  $12,865  $12,946  $13,009  $13,122          |
 11   $16,904  $15,697  $15,111  $14,475  $13,206  $13,118  $12,276          |
 12   $19,501  $19,571  $19,655  $19,715  $19,747  $19,759  $19,933          |
 13   $22,183  $22,304  $22,462  $22,583  $22,645  $22,747  $22,813          |
 14  $112,565 $120,784 $125,891 $131,001 $139,768 $143,216 $149,465          |
 15   $41,883  $42,059  $42,111  $42,361  $42,438  $42,450  $42,470          |
 16   ------   ------   ------   ------   ------   ------   ------           |
 17  $352,467 $364,069 $374,732 $383,188 $395,534 $405,672 $416,719          |
 18                                                                           |
 19                                                                           |
 20    $6,442   $6,473   $7,568   $7,923   $8,798   $9,432   $9,849          |
     ===========================================================================MAIN=
```

Figure 3.16

```
     ----A--------B--------C--------D--------E--------F--------G--------H-------
  1  A Small Midwestern Company                                               |
  2  1984 Business Plan                                                       |
  3                                                                           |
  4                        Jan-84   Feb-84   Mar-84   Apr-84   May-84         |
     ------   ------   ------   ------   ------   
 21    Product 2          $6,105   $6,132   $6,187   $6,231   $6,281         |
 22    Product 3         $17,987  $19,020  $19,313  $20,170  $20,783         |
 23    Product 4         $18,787  $18,852  $18,859  $19,006  $19,078         |
 24    Product 5          $5,025   $5,037   $5,045   $5,083   $5,093         |
 25    Product 6          $9,013   $8,197   $7,932   $7,454   $6,979         |
 26    Product 7          $9,522   $9,526   $9,592   $9,642   $9,675         |
 27    Product 8         $10,935  $10,940  $10,948  $10,955  $11,028         |
 28    Product 9         $33,712  $37,058  $39,711  $41,508  $44,864         |
 29    Product 10        $24,578  $24,591  $24,639  $24,876  $24,936         |
 30                       ------   ------   ------   ------   ------          |
 31  Total Cost of Goods Sold $139,494 $143,599 $146,680 $149,811 $154,134    |
 32                                                                           |
 33  Gross Margin                                                            |
 34    Product 1          $7,113   $7,886   $8,270   $9,075  $10,058         |
 35    Product 2          $7,462   $7,495   $7,562   $7,615   $7,677         |
 36    Product 3         $14,717  $15,562  $15,801  $16,503  $17,005         |
     ===========================================================================MAIN=
```

Figure 3.17

Notice the row numbers at the left edge of this figure. The top of the screen shows rows 1, 2, 3, and 4—the rows you designated as titles—but the row right after 4 is 21. By designating rows 1 through 4 as title rows, you have "locked" those rows onto the screen. Wherever the cell pointer is in the worksheet, rows 1, 2, 3, and 4 will be visible at the top of the screen.

Suppose on the other hand that you want to lock columns A and B onto the screen. To do this, you must position the cell pointer in any cell in column C and issue the {**Menu**} **S**ettings **T**itles **V**ertical command. As soon as the command is issued, Symphony designates columns A and B as a 2-column vertical title. (By the way, Symphony also erases the horizontal title settings as soon as the Titles Vertical command is issued.) Now if you press [Ctrl]→ with the cell pointer in column C, the screen will look like Figure 3.18. Notice that in this figure the labels in columns A and B are visible even though the first column of information you can see is column I.

```
     -----A--------B--------I--------J--------K--------L--------M--------N-----
  1  A Small Midwestern
  2  1984 Business Plan
  3                          Jun-84    Jul-84    Aug-84    Sep-84    Oct-84    Nov-84
  4                          ------    ------    ------    ------    ------    ------
  5    Sales
  6      Product 1          $18,406   $18,493   $21,622   $22,636   $25,138   $26,948
  7      Product 2          $14,057   $14,194   $14,218   $14,348   $14,480   $14,486
  8      Product 3          $40,878   $44,410   $47,060   $49,077   $50,958   $55,687
  9      Product 4          $53,316   $53,754   $53,778   $54,127   $54,207   $54,252
 10      Product 5          $12,773   $12,804   $12,825   $12,865   $12,946   $13,009
 11      Product 6          $16,904   $15,697   $15,111   $14,475   $13,206   $13,118
 12      Product 7          $19,501   $19,571   $19,655   $19,715   $19,747   $19,759
 13      Product 8          $22,183   $22,304   $22,462   $22,583   $22,645   $22,747
 14      Product 9         $112,565  $120,784  $125,891  $131,001  $139,768  $143,216
 15      Product 10         $41,883   $42,059   $42,111   $42,361   $42,438   $42,450
 16                         ------    ------    ------    ------    ------    ------
 17    Total Sales         $352,467  $364,069  $374,732  $383,188  $395,534  $405,672
 18
 19  Cost of Goods Sold
 20    Product 1            $6,442    $6,473    $7,568    $7,923    $8,798    $9,432
     ==========================================================================MAIN=
```

Figure 3.18

Finally, let's consider the Both option. When you use Both, Symphony sets up both a vertical and a horizontal title range. Before you issue the command, you must move the cell pointer to the cell in the row below the last row in the planned horizontal range and in the column to the right of the last column in the planned vertical range. In this example, you would move the cell pointer to cell C5. After positioning the cell pointer, simply issue the **S**ettings **T**itles **B**oth command. Both columns A and B and rows 1 through 4 would be locked onto the screen. If you move the cell pointer to cell I21, the screen will look like Figure 3.19.

Symphony automatically creates a title range based on the location of the cell pointer when you issue the Titles command. If you are designating a vertical title range, Symphony assumes that the range should cover all columns to the left of the current column. Similarly, if you are designating a horizontal range, Symphony assumes that the range should include all rows above the row the cell pointer is in when the command is issued. For this reason, Symphony will not allow you to designate a vertical range when the cell pointer is in column A or a horizontal range when the cell pointer is in row 1. As you can see, titles can be very beneficial when you are working on a large spreadsheet. However, titles also have some limitations that are worth considering. The most important of these is that when you designate a title range, you effectively lock the cell pointer out of that range. For example, if you set up a vertical title range that includes columns A and B, you will not be able to scroll the cell pointer into those columns using the arrow keys. (The only exception to this rule is that you can move the cell pointer into the title range when Symphony is in the POINT mode.)

```
   -----A---------B--------I---------J---------K---------L---------M---------N----
 1  A Small Midwestern
 2  1984 Business Plan
 3                       Jun-84    Jul-84    Aug-84    Sep-84    Oct-84    Nov-84 |
 4                       ------    ------    ------    ------    ------    ------ |
21    Product 2          $6,442    $6,473    $7,568    $7,923    $8,798    $9,432 |
22    Product 3          $6,326    $6,387    $6,398    $6,456    $6,516    $6,519 |
23    Product 4         $22,483   $24,426   $25,883   $26,992   $28,027   $30,628 |
24    Product 5         $19,194   $19,351   $19,360   $19,486   $19,515   $19,531 |
25    Product 6          $5,109    $5,121    $5,130    $5,146    $5,178    $5,204 |
26    Product 7          $6,592    $6,122    $5,893    $5,645    $5,150    $5,116 |
27    Product 8          $9,750    $9,785    $9,827    $9,857    $9,873    $9,879 |
28    Product 9         $48,403   $51,937   $54,133   $56,331   $60,100   $61,583 |
29    Product 10        $25,130   $25,235   $25,266   $25,416   $25,463   $25,470 |
30                       ------    ------    ------    ------    ------    ------ |
31  Total Sales       $160,521  $165,990  $170,690  $174,544  $179,944  $184,735 |
32                                                                               |
33  Gross Margin                                                                 |
34    Product 1         $11,964   $12,020   $14,054   $14,714   $16,340   $17,516 |
35    Product 2          $7,731    $7,807    $7,820    $7,891    $7,964    $7,967 |
36    Product 3         $18,395   $19,985   $21,177   $22,085   $22,931   $25,059 |
   =======================================================================MAIN=
```

Figure 3.19

If you need to move the cell pointer into the title range (say to edit a label in column A), you can use the {Goto} key to jump into the title range. However, you should expect to see strange things on your screen when you use {Goto} in this way. If, for example, you had designated Both titles with the cell pointer in cell C5 and then you press {Goto} followed by **A1,** the screen will look like Figure 3.20. Notice that rows 1 through 4 and columns A and B both appear twice on this screen.

Recalculation

Recalculation is the word used to describe Symphony's computation of the formulas in a worksheet. The {Menu} Settings Recalculation command gives you quite a bit of control over the method Symphony uses to recalculate the worksheet and the timing of recalculation.

Symphony offers two methods of recalculation: Manual and Automatic. When recalculation is Automatic (the default), Symphony recalculates the entire worksheet every time you make an entry in a cell or issue a spreadsheet command. If you've worked with Symphony for any time at all, you've probably noticed that the program seems to pause each time you make an entry in a cell. These pauses occur because Symphony is recalculating the worksheet.

Although these pauses are hardly noticeable in a small spreadsheet, they can become an irritation when you are working with a large worksheet. In fact, it is possible to create a sheet that requires several seconds to recalculate. If you're using the Automatic method of recalculation in that sheet, you have to wait several seconds after making every cell entry. These delays can make the task of building such a worksheet unbearable.

```
    -----A--------B--------A--------B--------C--------D--------E--------F-----
 1  A Small MidwesternA Small Midwestern Company                              |
 2  1984 Business Plan1984 Business Plan                                      |
 3                                         Jan-84    Feb-84    Mar-84         |
 4                                         ------    ------    ------         |
 1  A Small MidwesternA Small Midwestern Company                             |
 2  1984 Business Plan1984 Business Plan                                      |
 3                                         Jan-84    Feb-84    Mar-84         |
 4                                         ------    ------    ------         |
 5  Sales               Sales                                                 |
 6    Product 1           Product 1        $10,943   $12,132   $12,723        |
 7    Product 2           Product 2        $13,567   $13,628   $13,749        |
 8    Product 3           Product 3        $32,704   $34,582   $35,114        |
 9    Product 4           Product 4        $52,187   $52,366   $52,387        |
10    Product 5           Product 5        $12,563   $12,592   $12,612        |
11    Product 6           Product 6        $23,109   $21,019   $20,340        |
12    Product 7           Product 7        $19,043   $19,051   $19,184        |
13    Product 8           Product 8        $21,870   $21,879   $21,896        |
14    Product 9           Product 9        $78,401   $86,180   $92,352        |
15    Product 10          Product 10       $40,963   $40,985   $41,065        |
16                                         ------    ------    ------         |
    ==========================================================================MAIN=
```

Figure 3.20

Fortunately, Lotus designed Symphony so that you can "turn off" Automatic recalculation by selecting the Manual method. When the Manual method is selected, the spreadsheet will not recalculate until you press the {Calc} key.

If you set the recalculation method to Manual and make a change to the worksheet, the legend "Calc" will appear at the bottom of the screen. This legend will remain on the screen until you press {Calc} to recalculate the worksheet.

I nearly always set recalculation to Manual when working with any but the smallest spreadsheets. This lets me work without waiting for the sheet to recalculate after every entry. When I'm ready to recalculate the sheet, I just press {Calc}.

The Order of Recalculation

One of the problems that faces the designer of an electronic spreadsheet like Symphony is deciding the order in which the program recalculates the worksheet. There are several different recalculation-order conventions, each of which has advantages and disadvantages.

Symphony offers row-by-row, column-by-column, natural-order, and iterative recalculation. Natural-order recalculation is Symphony's default calculation order.

Row-by-row order means that recalculation begins in the upper-left corner of the worksheet (cell A1) and progresses cell by cell across row 1, then row 2, and so on until the entire worksheet is recomputed.

For example, if you use the **R**ecalculation **O**rder command to change the order of calculation in a worksheet to **R**ow-by-**R**ow and then press {**Calc**}, cell A1 will be computed first, followed by cell B1, then cell C1, D1, and so on until all of row 1 has been recalculated. Next row 2 will be computed, beginning with cell A2, followed by row 3, row 4, and so on until the whole sheet is computed.

Column-by-column recalculation is very similar to row-by-row recalculation, except that it computes the sheet one column at a time instead of one row at a time. If you press

{**Calc**} with the order set to **Column-by-Column**, Symphony first computes cell A1, then cell A2, then cell A3, and so on.

Forward References

Unfortunately, under certain conditions both the row-by-row and column-by-column methods fail to correctly recompute the worksheet. This occurs whenever the worksheet contains a *forward reference:* a cell that derives its value from another cell that lies below or to the right of the first cell in the worksheet. As an example of a forward reference, assume that you want to recompute the worksheet in Figure 3.21 using the row-by-row order.

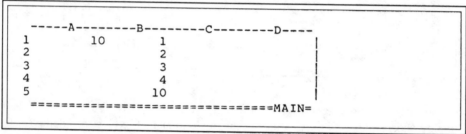

Figure 3.21

Cell A1 in this worksheet contains the formula

    A1: +B5

Cell B5 contains the formula

    B5: @SUM(B1 .. B4)

Suppose that before recalculating the sheet, you change the number in B1 from 1 to 100. Now recalculate the worksheet. Figure 3.22 shows the worksheet after the recalculation is completed.

```
     -----A---------B---------C---------D----
  1       10        100                     |
  2                   2                      |
  3                   3                      |
  4                   4                      |
  5                 109                      |
     =============================MAIN=
```

Figure 3.22

Notice that the value in cell A1, 10, does not equal the total in cell B5, 109, even though cell A1 refers directly to cell B5. This error occurs because when the worksheet was recalculated, cell A1 was calculated before cell B5. When A1 was recalculated,

Symphony gave it the value 10, the current value of cell B5. Symphony then went on to recalculate the cells in row 1, then row 2, then row 3, and so on until cell B5 was recalculated. Only when the recalculation reached cell B5 did the change in cell B1 register in B5. If we were to recalculate the worksheet again without making any changes, cells A1 and B5 would agree, but after one pass the worksheet contains a substantial error.

This type of reference is called a forward reference because one cell (A1 in the example) refers forward along the recalculation line to another cell (B5) for its value. Since A5 will always be computed before B5, there is a chance that A5 will not accurately reflect the value of B5. In this simple example, it is easy to see that there is a problem. In more complicated worksheets, however, forward references aren't so easy to spot.

Natural-order recalculation is designed to overcome this limitation of the linear recalculation orders (row-by-row and column-by-column). In natural-order recalculation, Symphony computes any cells on which a particular cell depends before computing that particular cell. Taken to the extreme, this means that Symphony begins recalculating the worksheet with the most fundamental cells in the worksheet—those cells that must be computed first if the remaining cells are to be accurately computed.

You might think of natural-order recalculation as proceeding up an inverted pyramid, where the cells on every level depend on the cells on the previous level. The few cells at the apex are the most fundamental, so Symphony computes these cells first, followed by cells on the second tier, and so on until the worksheet is completely calulated.

Natural-order recalculation is totally dependent on the structure of the worksheet being recalculated. Symphony automatically determines which cells must be recalculated first—the user does not have to do anything except press the {Calc} key.

Natural order is the default recalculation order. In nearly every case, you will want to leave the Recalculation Order set at Natural, since there is very little to gain from using one of the other methods. (In fact, I believe that the row-by-row and column-by-column methods are included in Symphony primarily for use by those who plan to import VisiCalc worksheets into Symphony.)

Circular References

The second type of recalculation error occurs when there is a circular reference. This means that two cells in a worksheet are either directly or indirectly dependent on each other. Natural-order recalculation alone is not capable of solving the problems that arise from circular references.

Figure 3.23 shows an example of a circular reference. Cell A1 contains the formula

> A1: .5 * A3

Cell A2 contains the value 100. Cell A3 contains the formula

> A3: +A1 + A2

These formulas display the value 0 in cell A1 and the value 100 in cell A3, even though the formula in cell A1 refers directly to cell A3. Notice the "Circ" indicator at the bottom of the figure. This legend is Symphony's way of telling you that a circular reference exists in this worksheet.

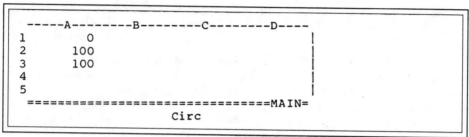

```
   -----A---------B---------C---------D----
1         0                                  |
2        100                                 |
3        100                                 |
4                                            |
5                                            |
   ==============================MAIN=
                    Circ
```

Figure 3.23

To correctly calculate a worksheet that contains a circular reference, you must recalculate the worksheet several times in a row. Assume for a moment that Recalculation is set to Manual and the Order is Natural. The following table shows how the values in cells A1 and A3 change each time you press {**Calc**}.

A1	A2	A3
0	100	100
50	100	150
75	100	175
87.5	100	187.5
93.75	100	193.75
96.875	100	196.875
98.375	100	198.375
99.375	100	199.375
99.6875	100	199.6875

As you can see, the values in cells A1 and A3 get closer and closer to the correct values after every recalculation. For example, although A1 is supposed to be equal to one-half of A3, after one recalculation A1 is only 33 percent of A3. After 5 recalculations, however, A1 is 49.2 percent of A3. Each time you recalculate the sheet, A1 gets closer and closer to 50 percent of A3.

Fortunately, Symphony is capable of performing this kind of iterative recalculation automatically. If you select the Iterations option from the Settings Recalculation menu, Symphony prompts you to supply a number between 1 and 50. The number you enter in response to this prompt determines the number of times Symphony will recalculate the spreadsheet *each* time you press {Calc}. For example, if you specify the number 8 in response to Symphony's prompt and then press {**Calc**}, Symphony will recalculate the sheet eight times in a row, duplicating the manual process you went through a few paragraphs back.

Iterative recalculation has a couple of disadvantages. First, if you choose an iteration count over 10 or so (or even less in very large worksheet) Symphony requires a great deal of time to complete the recalculation. For example, if the worksheet itself requires 3 seconds to recalculate, Symphony will need 45 seconds to complete 15 iterations. It is always a good idea to choose the Manual method of recalculation whenever you specify an iteration count.

Certain types of circular references cannot be resolved even by iterative recalculation. For example, a set of references like

    A1: +A3
    A2: 100
    A3: +A1+A2

cannot be resolved in 50, 100, or even 1000 iterations. The value in cell A1 will never be equal to the value in cell A3. (Try it and see what I mean.)

Although there are times when you will deliberately build a circular reference into a worksheet, the appearance of the "Circ" indicator usually means that you have made an error in defining a cell. If this happens to you, you'll need to find the circular reference and correct it.

One of the biggest complaints of 1-2-3 users is that the program offers no clue as to the location of circular references in the worksheet, but merely informs the user that such a reference exists. This problem is compounded by the fact that if you have changed the Recalculation method setting to Manual, the Circ indicator does not appear on the screen until you press {Calc}, which may be hours after the reference was created.

Fortunately, Symphony rectifies this problem. If the Circ indicator appears while you are working with Symphony, you need only look at the SHEET settings sheet to determine the location of the circular reference. Once you know where the reference is, it is easy to correct.

In this chapter you've learned all of the basic concepts that you'll need to begin using the Symphony spreadsheet. You now know how to move the cell pointer around the worksheet, how to enter labels, numbers, and formulas into the worksheet, and how to edit entries you've already made. In the following chapters, you'll use these basic skills as you learn more about the Symphony spreadsheet.

CHAPTER FOUR
SPREADSHEET FUNCTIONS

Functions are Symphony's way of simplifying complex formulas. You can think of functions as a kind of shorthand that simplifies computations that would be very difficult, sometimes nearly impossible, to express as formulas. Some functions perform routine mathematics; others allow you to perform complex operations, like net present value, quickly and simply.

Functions generally have two parts: a *function name* and one or more *arguments*. Function names always begin with the symbol @, followed by an abbreviation that describes what the function does. The @ symbol lets Symphony distinguish a function from a label. The argument usually consists of one or more numbers or cell or range references. For example, in the function

@SUM(A1 . . A3)

@SUM is the function name and (A1 . . A3) is the argument. As you might expect, this function computes the sum, or total, of the numbers in cells A1, A2, and A3. If this function were used in the spreadsheet in Figure 4.1, the result would be 15.

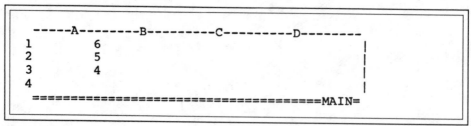

Figure 4.1

Another simple function is

@AVG(1,5,10)

The name of this function is @AVG. The argument is (1,5,10). This function computes the average of the numbers in the argument, in this case, 5.3333.

ARGUMENTS

Notice that the arguments in the two functions shown above are enclosed in parentheses. Almost every Symphony function refers to an argument that is enclosed in parentheses. The argument of a function can consist of either numbers or cell references, or both. The function

@SUM(A1 . . A3)

uses an argument that refers to three cells, while the argument in the function

@AVG(1,5,10)

contains numbers. Both are perfectly acceptable to Symphony. You can also use a range name as the argument in a function. For example, if the name TEST had been assigned to the range A1 . . A10, the function

@SUM(TEST)

is equivalent to the function

@SUM(A1 . . A10)

In fact, if you have created the range name TEST, and you enter the function @SUM(A1 . . A10) into a cell, Symphony automatically transforms it into the function @SUM(TEST).

You can even mix cell references, formulas, and range names in a function. For example, the function

@MOD(A1,5)

computes the remainder of the division of the number in cell A1 by 5. This kind of mixed function can be very useful in certain situations, such as when you want to compare the result of a computation with a constant.

There are a couple of important rules to remember about functions and arguments. In general, functions are designed to operate only on ranges containing values (which includes, of course, numbers, functions, and formulas). They completely ignore blank cells and usually assign a value of 0 to cells containing labels. Thus if cells A1 and A2 contained labels, the value of @SUM(A1 . . A2) would be 0, and the value of @COUNT (A1 . . A2) would be 2. If A1 and A2 were blank, the value of @COUNT(A1 . . A2) would be 0. We'll consider this quirk of functions in detail in a few pages.

Compound Functions

Of course, functions can be far more complicated than the simple examples shown above. In fact, the argument of a function can be another function. For example, the following is a legal 1-2-3 function:

@MOD(@LOOKUP(@COUNT(A1 . . A6),H1 . . J15,2),@AVG(A20 . . D20))

This is an example of a compound function—a large function that combines several subsidiary functions.

WHY USE FUNCTIONS?

Functions are useful because they can save you a great deal of time and effort. For example, consider the worksheet in Figure 4.2.

```
-----A--------B---------C---------D--------
1          123                                    |
2          234                                    |
3          345                                    |
4          456                                    |
5          567                                    |
6          678                                    |
7          789                                    |
8          987                                    |
9          876                                    |
10         765                                    |
11         654                                    |
12       ------                                   |
13                                                |
14                                                |
===========================================MAIN=
```

Figure 4.2

Suppose you want to compute the total of the numbers in the cells in the range A1 to A11. One way to compute this total would be to enter the formula

A13: +A1 + A2 + A3 + A4 + A5 + A6 + A7 + A8 + A9 + A10 + A11

in cell A13. If we use a function, however, this formula can be shortened to

A13: @SUM(A1 .. A11)

which is quite a bit easier to write.

An even stronger illustration can be made with the Symphony's net present value function, @NPV. Suppose you want to compute the net present value of the numbers in cells A1 to D1 (see Figure 4.3). One way to compute this value would be to enter the formula

A3: (A1/(1 + .15)) + (B1/(1 + .15) ^2) + (C1/(1 + .15) ^3) + (D1/(1 + .15) ^4)

in cell A3. Not so simple, is it? Thanks to the @NPV function, however, we can simplify this function to

A3: @NPV(.15,A1 .. D1)

MATHEMATICAL FUNCTIONS

Math functions are the simplest Symphony functions. The Symphony math functions are @SQRT, @SUM, @ABS, @ROUND, @INT, @EXP, @MOD, and @RAND.

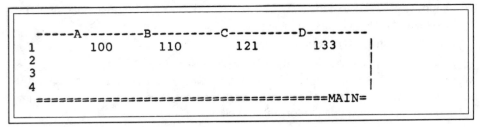

Figure 4.3

@SQRT

The @SQRT function computes the square root of a number. For example, the function

> @SQRT(100)

returns the value 10. If the value is negative, the function yields the @ERR message.

@SUM

The @SUM function is used to compute the total of a series of numbers. Usually this function is used to compute quickly the sum of all numbers in a specific range. The @SUM function shown above is an example of this sort of use. However, the argument of an @SUM function does not have to be a range. @SUM can be used to total a series of individual cells, as in the function

> @SUM(A1,A3,A16)

The numbers to be added can even be entered as constants, as in the function

> @SUM(1,3,7)

These last two methods, however, are not much better than using a formula to compute the total. For example, the first function could be restated as

> +A1+A3+A16

which is just as easy to write as the function.

The Advantages of @SUM

Many times when you create a Symphony worksheet, you'll need to make changes to the basic sheet. If you use the @SUM function to compute your totals, those changes will be easier to make.

For example, consider the worksheet in Figure 4.4. Cell A13 in this worksheet contains the formula

> A13: +A1+A2+A3+A4+A5+A6+A7+A8+A9+A10+A11

Now suppose you want to add a new row to this worksheet just before what is now row 9. Move the cursor to cell A9 and issue the command

{**Menu**} Insert Row [Enter]

After the new row is in place, enter the number 1000 in the new cell A9. The worksheet will now look like Figure 4.5. Notice that the total in what is now cell A14 is still 6474. The number 1000 in cell A9 has not been included in the total. If we want to include this new cell in the total, we must edit the formula in cell A14.

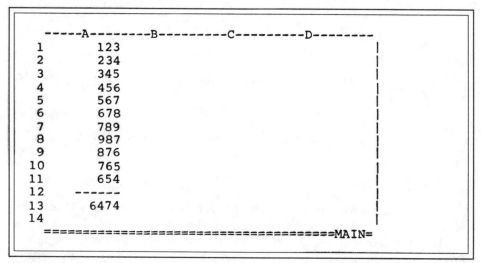

Figure 4.4

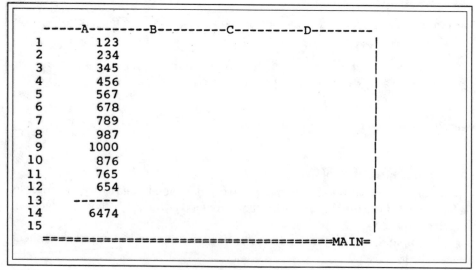

Figure 4.5

If we had used the @SUM function

A13: @SUM(A1 . . A12)

in cell A13 in Figure 4.4 instead of the formula, we wouldn't have this problem. After the row was inserted, the function would look like this:

A14: @SUM(A1 . . A13)

and the correct total, 7474, would be displayed in cell A14 in Figure 4.5. This occurs because Symphony always adjusts cell ranges when rows or columns are inserted or deleted.

A Special Tip

Notice that the function used in the above example,

A13: @SUM(A1 . . A12)

includes cell A12, which contains the dashes underlining the numbers to be totaled. This is done to make it possible to add a new line at the end of the range of numbers. If we used the Insert Row command to insert a row just before row 12 in Figure 4.4, the formula in what is now cell A14 would change to

A14: @SUM(A1 . . A13)

If the @SUM function in cell A13 in Figure 4.4 had spanned only the cells including numbers (A1 . . A11), adding the row above row 12 would not expand the range, and the function would have to be edited.

Because the @SUM function is used so much, this tip can save you a great deal of time. It's a good idea to get in the habit of including an extra line or column in your @SUM ranges whenever you can.

The Rounding Functions: @ROUND and @INT

@INT and @ROUND are two functions that can be used to eliminate unwanted decimal places from numbers. @INT converts a decimal number into a integer with no decimal places. @ROUND allows the user to specify how many decimals should be included in a number.

@ROUND

The form of the @ROUND function is

@ROUND(number or cell reference,number of decimal places)

The number of decimal places can be any integer between 16 and − 16. Table 4.1 shows several examples of the @ROUND function.

The @ROUND function follows the same rules you memorized when you learned to round in the third grade: Digits smaller than 5 are rounded down; digits equal to or larger than 5 are rounded up; and never round from a rounded number. (For example, @ROUND(14.4445,2) equals 14.44, not 14.45, even though @ROUND(14.4445,3) equals 14.445). Notice that specifying a negative rounding factor causes rounding to the left of the decimal place.

Function	Value
@ROUND(114.4567,3)	114.457
@ROUND(114.4567,2)	114.46
@ROUND(114.4567,1)	114.5
@ROUND(114.4567,0)	114
@ROUND(114.4567, − 1)	110
@ROUND(114.4567, − 2)	100

Table 4.1

Confusing @ROUND with Format Fixed

Many Symphony users are confused by the difference between the @ROUND function and the Format Fixed command. At first, these two features seem to accomplish the same thing. But there is an important difference—Format Fixed affects only the way in which a number is *displayed*, while @ROUND actually changes the number. For example, if we used the Format Fixed command to force the number 123.001 to be displayed with two decimal places, the result would be 123.00. However, 123.00 is only the *display*; the actual value in the cell is still 123.001. Adding .004 to this number would result in the display 123.01 and a value in the cell of 123.005.

On the other hand, if we enclosed the number 123.001 in the function

   @ROUND(123.001,2)

both the display and the number being displayed would be 123.00. Adding .004 to this function would result in a value of 123.004 and a display of 123.00.

The Format Fixed command can lead to problems in certain situations. Consider this example:

Values in cells	Formatted with Format Fixed 2
100.025	100.03
100.025	100.03
200.050	200.05

The formatted numbers appear not to add correctly, even though the math is correct. Fortunately, this problem can be corrected by using @ROUND on the two addends:

Values in cells	As Displayed
@ROUND(100.025,2)	100.03
@ROUND(100.025,2)	100.03
200.06	200.06

Thanks to the @ROUND functions, the numbers now appear to add correctly. (Notice, however, that the result is now technically incorrect—100.025 + 100.025 equals 200.05, not 200.06. In most situations, the advantage of a display that appears to total correctly is more important than the results in the least significant digit.)

@INT

@INT is similar to @ROUND in that both functions eliminate unwanted decimal places from a number. However, unlike @ROUND, which actually "rounds off" numbers, @INT merely truncates all decimals in a number.

The form of the @INT function is

@INT(number or cell reference)

The function @INT(123.001) produces a value of 123, as does the function @INT(123.999). It is important to remember that the @INT function and the @ROUND(number,0) functions are not equivalent. @ROUND(123.001,0) is 123, but @ROUND(123.999,0) is 124.

@ABS

@ABS returns the absolute value of a number. The form of the function is

@ABS(number or cell reference)

If the number or value in the argument is positive, the @ABS function will have no effect. If, on the other hand, the argument is negative, the function will convert the number in the argument into its positive equivalent. For example, @ABS(− 55) is 55. @ABS(55) is simply 55.

@MOD

@MOD is a clever function that was used for the first time in an electronic spreadsheet by the 1-2-3 program. @MOD computes the difference that results from the integer division of two numbers. The form of the function is

@MOD(dividend,divisor)

The dividend is the number to be divided by the divisor. For example, in the formula 7/3, 7 is the dividend and 3 is the divisor.

We find that the grade-school phrase for division, "X goes into Y," makes it easy to remember the order of the arguments in the @MOD function. Since 3 "goes into" 7 two times with a remainder of 1, the function @MOD(7,3) has the value 1.

Whenever the dividend in an @MOD function is smaller than the divisor, the function returns the dividend. For example, the function @MOD(3,7) returns the value 3, since 7 "goes into" 3 zero times with a remainder of 3.

Because Symphony considers division by 0 impossible, if you try to use 0 as the divisor in an @MOD function, the function will return the @ERR message. Notice that this can occur if you use a reference to a blank cell as the divisor.

The @MOD function is one of Symphony's most useful functions. For example, suppose you are the inventory manager at a toy-store chain with 13 retail outlets. You have 735 "Indiana Jones and the Temple of Doom" action figures to distribute to the stores. If you distribute the toys evenly, how many will be left over? Using the function @MOD(735,13) it is easy to find the answer, 7.

In Chapter 6, which covers Symphony's date functions, we'll show another very important use of @MOD.

@RAND

The @RAND function allows Symphony to generate random numbers. @RAND is one of the few Symphony functions that does not take an argument.

The @RAND function returns a random number between 0 and 1. The value of the @RAND function changes every time you recalculate the worksheet. If recalculation is in the automatic mode, the value of any @RAND function in the worksheet will change every time you make an entry in any cell in the worksheet.

Although Symphony's random number generator is adequately random for most applications, you might be interested to know that Symphony calculates the same @RAND values in the same order in every work session. In other words, the first time you enter the @RAND function in a worksheet after loading Symphony, it returns the value .147506. The second @RAND function in each session returns the value .414100.

@RAND has several important uses. Monte Carlo simulation, an advanced method of forecasting, uses random numbers. Thanks to the @RAND function, Symphony can do Monte Carlo simulation.

STATISTICAL FUNCTIONS

The second main group of functions in Symphony, statistical functions, allows you to compute statistics on ranges of cells. The statistical functions are @MAX, @MIN, @COUNT, @AVG, @STD, and @VAR.

Statistics are tools that can be used to understand a set of data. Just like height, weight, and hair color are used to describe a person, statistics are used to describe a collection of data. Some statistics describe the limits of a data set. Others describe the arrangement of the numbers within those limits.

If you were going to analyze a set of numbers, you might begin by figuring out how many numbers are in the set. You might also examine the set to determine the largest and smallest numbers. Next, you might compute the average of the set, and if you were especially diligent, you might compute the variance and standard deviation. Symphony includes functions that can compute all of these statistics automatically.

The Simple Statistics: @MIN, @MAX, @AVG, and @COUNT

The first four statistical functions, @MIN, @MAX, @AVG, and @COUNT, compute simple statistics about a range. @MIN and @MAX return the minimum and maximum values of a range of cells. In the worksheet shown in Figure 4.6, cell B7 contains the function @MAX(A1 . . C5), and cell B8 contains the function @MIN(A1 . . C5).

@MAX and @MIN always assign the value 0 to a label and ignore blank cells. For example, if cell A3 in the example was changed to a blank cell, as shown in Figure 4.7, the function @MIN(A1 . . C5) would return the value 21, since cell A3 would be ignored. If a label was entered in cell A3, @MIN(A1 . . C5) would revert to 0, since the label has the value 0.

```
    -----A---------B----------C----------D---------
1        100        115        34                  |
2         78       1341       155                  |
3          0         21       781                  |
4        121        318        77                  |
5       2416         71       560                  |
6                                                  |
7   Maximum        2416                            |
8   Minimum           0                            |
9                                                  |
    ===================================MAIN=
```

Figure 4.6

```
    -----A---------B----------C----------D--------
1        100        115        34                 |
2         78       1341       155                 |
3                    21       781                 |
4        121        318        77                 |
5       2416         71       560                 |
6                                                 |
7   Maximum        2416                           |
8   Minimum          21                           |
9                                                 |
    ===================================MAIN=
```

Figure 4.7

@AVG

The @AVG function computes the arithmetic mean of a range of numbers. The arithmetic mean is commonly called the average, or just the mean. The form of the function is

> @AVG(range)

In Figure 4.6, the function @AVG(A1 .. C5) has a value of 412.533. This value is computed by dividing the sum of the numbers in the range (6188) by the number of entries in the range (15).

You need to be particularly careful about the contents of your range when using the @AVG function. For example, since cell A3 in Figure 4.7 is blank, the value of @AVG(A1 .. C5) is 442. Why the change? Since functions ignore blank cells, cell A3 is now being ignored. This changes the number of elements to be averaged from 15 to 14. Although the total of the range, 6188, has not changed, the average is now calculated by the formula 6188/14.

Now suppose we enter a label in cell A3. Can you guess what happens to the value of @AVG(A1 .. C5)? Since functions recognize labels in the argument range, and assign the value 0 to each label, the value of the @AVG function is once again 412.533.

Like most other functions, the argument for an @AVG function can be a range name. If the range A1 . . C5 in Figure 4.6 were given the name RANGE, the function @AVG(RANGE) would return the value 412.533.

The arithmetic mean computed by @AVG should not be confused with the other statistics that describe the central point of a group of numbers: the median and the mode. The median is defined as the number that exactly divides the group—half of the items in the group are greater than the median and half are less. The mode of a group of numbers is that number which occurs most often. Not all data sets have a meaningful mode. Unfortunately, Symphony does not have functions that will compute the median or the mode.

@COUNT

@COUNT returns the number of nonblank cells in the argument range. In the worksheet shown in Figure 4.8, the function @COUNT(A1. .A3) has the value 3. If A4 is blank, the function @COUNT(A1. .A4) has a value of 3. Since A5 contains a label, @COUNT(A1. .A5) returns the value 4.

```
     -----A---------B---------C---------D--------
1            101                                |
2           2396                                |
3            705                                |
4                                               |
5      Testing                                  |
6                                               |
7                                               |
     ==================================MAIN=
```

Figure 4.8

@COUNT is one of the few functions that is never used with a numeric argument. The argument for @COUNT always refers to a range of cell references. If you think about it for a second, you'll see that this makes sense. Of what value is the function @COUNT(1,2,3,4)? The answer, 4, is obvious from inspection. @COUNT only makes sense when used with a range of cell references.

@COUNT peculiarities   Those Symphony users who have converted to the program from 1-2-3 may know that the @COUNT function in 1-2-3 had some strange characteristics. These characteristics are unfortunately carried over to Symphony. For example, whenever the @COUNT function is used with a one-cell argument, the function always returns the value 1. This occurs even if the cell is blank. For example, if cell A1 is blank, the function @COUNT(A1) returns the value 1. But if B1 is also blank, the function @COUNT(A1 . . B1) has the value 0. Similarly, the function @COUNT(A1,B1) is 2, since both blank cells are considered separately.

This peculiarity is especially troublesome when @COUNT is used in a macro program. We'll examine that problem in the chapter that covers the Symphony Command Language.

Sophisticated Statistics: @STD and @VAR

Symphony offers two other important statistical functions: @STD and @VAR. These two functions compute the standard deviation and the variance of a series of numbers, respectively. Both functions measure the dispersion of a group of numbers. (The standard deviation equals the variance squared, so the two measures are very closely related.) In general, about 68% of the data items in a normally distributed data set will be within one standard deviation of the mean. A high standard deviation indicates that the data set is widely disbursed, while a small standard deviation indicates a tight grouping.

To illustrate these functions, consider the worksheet shown in Figure 4.9. This worksheet shows the daily sales for a small business across a 10-day period. The average daily sales is computed in cell D2 using the formula

D2: @AVG(B2 . . B11)

The variance is computed in cell D3 with the formula

D3: @VAR(B2 . . B11)

and the standard deviation is computed with the function

D4: @STD(B2 . . B11)

```
    -----A---------B----------C---------D--------
 1     Day       Sales                            |
 2       1      $12,743   Mean         12298.9    |
 3       2       $9,748   Variance     7514571.   |
 4       3      $13,900   Std Dev      2741.271   |
 5       4      $11,722                           |
 6       5      $10,652                           |
 7       6       $9,211                           |
 8       7      $15,901                           |
 9       8      $17,453                           |
10       9       $8,657                           |
11      10      $13,002                           |
12                                                |
    ==========================================MAIN=
```

Figure 4.9

The standard deviation of this data set—2741.271—indicates that roughly 68% of the days fall between $9557.628 and $15,040.17, or between the mean minus one standard deviation and the mean plus one standard deviation.

Data Base Statistical Functions

Data base statistical functions are a special subset of Symphony's statistical functions. Data base statistical functions allow you to compute statistics like count, mean, and standard deviation on the records stored in a data base. Data base statistical functions will be covered in the section of this book on Symphony's data base.

FINANCIAL FUNCTIONS

If, like many Symphony users, you will be using the program's spreadsheet primarily for financial calculations, you will almost certainly use Symphony's financial functions. Financial functions allow you to perform financial computations, like net present value, without needing to use a long or complex formula. The Symphony financial functions are @PV, @FV, @PMT, @NPV, and @IRR.

@PV

The @PV function computes the present value of a constant stream of payments. Such a constant stream of payments is technically called an *ordinary annuity.*

To compute the present value of an ordinary annuity, you need to know the term of the annuity (the number of payments you will receive), the amount of each payment, and the interest rate that will be used to compute the present value. This interest rate is called the discount rate. The form of the @PV function is

@PV(payment,discount rate,term)

The term and the payment amount of an annuity are facts, so these two elements are easy to plunk into the function. You must choose the correct discount rate, however. Selecting the discount rate can be tricky. To understand the concept of discount rates better, let's take a look at the whole concept of present value.

The Concept of Present Value

Why do we compute present value, anyway? Consider this example. Suppose someone offered to give you $1.05 one year from today in exchange for $1 today. Would you take the deal? Probably not. If you invested the $1 in a money market account at an annual rate of 8%, you would have $1.08 in one year. All other things being equal, wouldn't you rather have $1.08 than $1.05?

Another way to analyze this problem is to compute the present value of the deal you were offered. Since you know that you will receive one payment of $1.05, you know the payment in this annuity is $1.05 and the term is one year.

Now you must decide on a discount rate. Since you know that you can earn 8% in a money market account, you might choose 8% as your discount rate. By choosing this rate, you are in effect saying, "I require this investment to achieve a return of at least 8% before it will interest me." The rate becomes a hurdle over which the investment must leap before it will be attractive to you. For this reason, the discount rate is sometimes called the hurdle rate.

Now compute the present value. Since we have Symphony at our disposal, we'll use the program instead of computing the present value by hand. Enter the function

A1: @PV(1.05,.08,1)

in cell A1 of a blank worksheet. This function returns the value .9722, the present value of this simple ordinary annuity. Since the present value of this annuity, .9722, is less than one, the price you have to pay for the annuity, this is not a very attractive investment. Another way of saying this is that the present value of the investment is less than the cost of the investment.

Naturally, most annuities have a term of many years and a payment of more than one dollar. And the discount rate is rarely as simple to compute as in this example. However, the basic principles from this example apply to all present value calculations. (If you want to learn more about the concept of present value, I recommend the book *Techniques of Financial Analysis* by Erich Helfert, published by Richard Irwin, Inc.)

Let's look at one other example. Suppose someone offered to sell you an annuity that would pay you $1000 per year for 5 years. The annuity costs $3000. You want to know whether the annuity is a good investment or not.

The worksheet in Figure 4.10 is set up to solve this problem. Cell B5 contains the function

B5: @PV(B1,B2,B3)

Where B1 contains the payment, B2 contains the chosen discount rate, and B3 contains the term of the annuity. This function returns the value 3790.787, so the present value of the annuity is $3,790.787. Since the present value of the annuity exceeds the cost of the annuity, this is probably a good investment.

```
     -----A--------B---------C---------D--------
  1 Payment:       1000                          |
  2 Rate:           10%                          |
  3 Term:            5                           |
  4                                              |
  5 PV:          3790.787                        |
  6                                              |
  7                                              |
    ======================================--MAIN=
```

Figure 4.10

A Word of Caution

Be sure that the discount rate you choose matches the spacing of the payments in the annuity. For example, suppose you want to compute the present value of an annuity that will pay you $100 per month for 24 months. Suppose further that your hurdle rate is 15%. Since the payments in this annuity are spaced one month apart, to properly compute this present value, you'll need to convert 15%, which is an annual rate, to a monthly rate. To do this, simply divide by 12. The result, 1.25%, is the correct monthly discount rate.

Also be aware that the @PV function assumes that the first payment occurs at the end of the first period and thus should be discounted. For example, the function

@PV(100,.15,1)

assumes that you would receive a $100 payment one year from today. The present value of this payment is $86.96.

@NPV

The @NPV function differs from the @PV function in that @PV computes the present value of an even stream of cash flows, while @NPV computes the present value of an uneven stream of payments. The form of the @NPV function is

@NPV(rate,range containing payments)

To illustrate the @NPV function, consider the worksheet in Figure 4.11. The function

@NPV(B3,B1 .. D1)

computes the present value of the three payments in cells B1, C1, and D1 at the rate of 15%. The result, 3318.81, is the present value of this stream of payments.

```
    -----A--------B---------C----------D--------
  1 Payments      1000      1500       2000    |
  2                                             |
  3 Rate          15%                           |
  4                                             |
  5                                             |
    ====================================MAIN=
```

Figure 4.11

When you use the @NPV function, you'll usually want to include the outflow as well as the inflows in the range to be operated on. Consider the worksheet in Figure 4.12. The function

@NPV(B3,B1 .. E1)

```
    -----A--------B---------C----------D---------E--------
  1 Payments     -2000     1000       1500      2000    |
  2                                                      |
  3 Rate          15%                                    |
  4                                                      |
  5                                                      |
    ============================================MAIN=
```

Figure 4.12

computes the net present value of the stream of payments in cells B1 to E1. Cell B1 contains a negative amount, which represents an outflow, or the amount required to earn the three inflows in cells C1 to E1. The result, 1146.79, is the *net* present value of the investment. Since this number is greater than 0, this is an attractive investment.

Notice that the @NPV function requires that you list each payment separately, while @PV simply requires that you enter the payment once in the functions. This is because @NPV allows you to compute the present value of an *uneven* stream of payments, which means that you must list each payment individually.

As with the @PV function, it is important to be sure that the spacing of your payments and your discount rate agree. It is also important to remember that the @NPV function assumes that the first payment occurs at the end of the first period.

@PMT

If you know the present value, the interest rate, and the term of a loan, and you want to compute the payment, you should use the @PMT function. The form of @PMT is

> @PMT(principal,interest rate,term)

@PMT is very closely related to the @PV function. If you use the words *present value* instead of *principal* in the equation above, you can see that the formula for @PMT is very close to that for @PV, except that @PV solves for the present value, or principal, and @PMT solves for the payment.

To see how @PMT works, consider this example. You want to buy a new house and plan to finance $65,000 of the purchase price. If the current annual interest rate for mortgages is 14%, then what will the monthly payment be? Figure 4.13 shows a worksheet set up to solve this problem.

```
    -----A--------B---------C---------D--------
  1 Principal:   60,000                         |
  2 Interest:     1.167%                         |
  3 Term:            360                         |
  4                                              |
  5 Payment:    $711.11                          |
    =====================================MAIN=
```

Figure 4.13

Cell B5 contains the function

> B5: @PMT(B1,B2,B3)

Notice that the interest rate in cell B2 equals the annual rate, 14%, divided by 12. Notice also that the term is stated in months. The value in cell B5 represents the monthly payment that will fully amortize the mortgage.

This simple model offers a chance to demonstrate an important modeling technique. Whenever possible, we try to make our assumptions *explicit* rather than implicit. By this we mean that each assumption is entered in a separate cell instead of being lumped together in the formula.

Since we made the assumption explicit in this case, we can easily modify the model to compute the payment at an annual rate of 15% by entering the formula .15/12 in cell B2. If the assumptions were implicit, we would have to edit cell B5 to change the formula.

@FV

@FV computes the future value of a stream of payments. @FV is essentially the opposite of @PV. The form of the function is

@FV(payment,interest rate,term)

Future value is a concept that can be used to compute the amount of money you'll have at some point in the future if you periodically invest a constant amount. One common use for @FV is to figure out how much your IRA will be worth some day. For example, suppose you decided to invest $4000 per year in an IRA. You assume that the market rate of interest will average 10% in the future. Since you are now 25 and expect to retire at 65, the term of this computation is 40 years. The function

@FV(4000,.1,40)

computes the value of your investment 40 years in the future—$1,770,370.

@IRR

The final financial function, @IRR, is used to compute the internal rate of return on an investment. An investment's internal rate of return is that rate which causes the net present value of the outflows and inflows of an investment to equal 0. To put it a different way, the internal rate of return is the discount rate that causes the present value of the inflows to equal the present value of the outflows.

Like net present value, internal rate of return is a technique that is used to measure the attractiveness of an investment. Internal rate of return is really very closely related to net present value. Remember, we said that an attractive investment was one that, when discounted at the appropriate hurdle rate, would yield a net present value greater than 0. Turn that equation around, and you see that a discount rate higher than the hurdle rate is necessary to generate a net present value of 0. This means that an attractive investment is one where the discount rate required to yield a net present value of 0—the internal rate of return—is higher than the hurdle rate.

The form of the @IRR function is

@IRR(guess,range of cash flows)

The "guess" is simply an approximation of the internal rate of return provided by the user and used by Symphony as a starting point in the iterative process of solving the function. The guess must be between 0 and 1. As long as the guess is reasonably close to the IRR (say, within 50 percentage points), Symphony will perform the needed iterations almost instantly.

To understand how this function works, consider the following example. Suppose you invested $100,000 in a building that you expect will generate $30,000 per year in rental income for 3 years and then will be sold for $125,000. The worksheet in Figure 4.14 is set up to handle this problem.

```
    -----A--------B---------C---------D---------E---------F-----
  1 Payments   -100,000    30,000    30,000    30,000    125,000 |
  2                                                               |
  3 IRR:         29.18%                                           |
  4                                                               |
  5                                                               |
    ===========================================================MAIN=
```

Figure 4.14

Cell B3 contains the function

   B3: @IRR(.14,B1 .. F1)

In this example we selected .14 as our "guess" at the IRR. The fact that this guess is far from accurate is not important. Symphony figured the correct IRR, .2918, in an instant.

There are some IRR functions that are beyond Symphony's capabilities. For example, some sets of inflows can have two different internal rates of return. Symphony cannot solve these problems. In general, if Symphony cannot reach the correct IRR within .0000001 second after 20 iterations, @ERR is returned.

ENGINEERING FUNCTIONS

Symphony includes a number of geometric functions that appeal primarily to engineers and scientists who use the program. If your main uses of the Symphony spreadsheet are financial, you probably won't have much use for these functions. The engineering functions are @PI, @LN, @LOG, @EXP, @COS, @SIN, @TAN, @ACOS, @ASIN, @ATAN, and @ATAN2.

@PI

@PI is one of few Symphony functions that doesn't take an argument. The function @PI always returns the value of the constant pi, accurate to 15 decimal places, or 3.141592653589794.

@LOG

@LOG computes the base 10 logarithm of the number or cell reference in the argument. The form of the function is

   @LOG(number or cell reference)

For example, the function @LOG(10) returns the value 1.

The argument for the @LOG function must be positive. A negative argument, or an argument of 0, causes @LOG to return the @ERR message.

@LN

@LN computes the natural, or base e, logarithm, of the number or cell reference in the argument. This function has the form

    @LN(number or cell reference)

The function @LN(4) returns the value 1.3862. The argument must be positive or @LN returns @ERR.

@EXP

The @EXP function computes the value of the constant e (about 2.71828) raised to the power specified by the function's argument. For example, @EXP(2) returns the value 7.389, or 2.71828 times 2.71828.

@EXP is the inverse of the @LN function. For example, the function @LN(@EXP(10)) returns the value 10.

Like most functions, the argument for @EXP can be either a number or a cell reference. If cell A100 contains the number 4, the function @EXP(A100) returns the value 54.598, or 2.71828 times 2.71828 times 2.71828 times 2.71828.

The Trigonometric Functions

Symphony offers functions that compute the basic trigonometric functions—the sine, cosine, and tangent, and the arc functions—arctangent, arcsine, and arcosine.

The functions @SIN, @COS, and @TAN compute the sine, cosine, and the tangent of the number or cell reference in the argument. Symphony interprets the argument as a radian angle.

You may not be familiar with radians. Like degrees, radians are a way to measure the size of an angle. Radians are convenient because they are based on the constant pi. For example, a right angle, which measures 90 degrees, can also be stated as pi/2, or approximately 1.57 radians. 360 degrees is equivalent to pi × 2, or 6.2831 radians. Radians can be converted to degrees using the formula

    180/pi × angle measure in radians

The functions @ASIN, @ACOS, and @ATAN compute the arcsine, arcosine, and arctangent of the value in the argument. Symphony interprets the argument as a sine, cosine, or tangent. These functions return a number that represents the radian measure of an angle. @ATAN(2) computes the four-quadrant arctangent of the tangent described in the argument.

These functions can be remembered with the phrase "the angle whose." For example, the function @ASIN(1) can be read, "the angle whose sine is 1." It returns the value 1.57 radians, or 90 degrees. The function @ACOS(0) can be read, "the angle whose cosine is 0," and it returns the value 1.57 radians.

The argument for @ACOS and @ASIN must be greater than or equal to − 1 and less than or equal to 1. Any value outside of this range will cause the function to return the @ERR message.

SPECIAL FUNCTIONS

While most of Symphony's functions are simplifications of complex formulas that would be awkward to enter in "longhand," Symphony's special functions perform tasks that simply cannot be done with a formula. Included in this group are @CHOOSE, @VLOOKUP, @HLOOKUP, @INDEX, @COLS, @ROWS, @CELL, and @CELLPOINTER.

@CHOOSE

@CHOOSE is a function that Symphony and 1-2-3 borrowed from VisiCalc. @CHOOSE allows the user to store a list of values or labels in a cell and retrieve items from that list using key numbers. The form of @CHOOSE is

@CHOOSE(offset,item 0,item 1,item 2, . . . ,item n)

The value of an @CHOOSE function is the element of the list that corresponds to the offset value. The offset value must always be positive and must be greater than or equal to 0. For example, the function

@CHOOSE(2,10,20,30,40,50)

returns the value 30 because 30 holds the second position in the list. Don't let the method used to number the items in the data list confuse you. @CHOOSE considers the first item in the list to have an offset of 0, the second item to have an offset of 1, and so on. An offset of 0 always selects the first data item in the list, and an offset of 1 always selects the second item.

Some other Symphony functions, including @VLOOKUP, @HLOOKUP, and the data base functions, use the same convention for numbering offsets. We'll cover those functions in later sections.

If the offset value in an @CHOOSE function is greater than the number of data items in the list minus one, the function returns the @ERR message. For example, the function

@CHOOSE(3,1,2,3)

will not work because the offset, 3, exceeds the offset of the last data item. If the offset is not an integer, Symphony uses only the integer part. For example, the offset 3.99 is equivalent to the offset 3.

As with other Symphony functions, the items in the data list can be numbers, cell references, formulas, or functions. The data items in an @CHOOSE function can even be labels. Any labels in the argument must be enclosed in double quotes. Symphony users who have upgraded from 1-2-3 will recognize this as a major change between the two programs.

For example, the function

@CHOOSE(2,"A","B","C")

would return the string value C. You can even mix strings and numbers in the argument.

Putting @CHOOSE to Work

@CHOOSE can be used in a number of interesting ways. Suppose your business has three different billing areas for different types of jobs. These rates could be called 1, 2, and 3. Now suppose you want to create a cash flow forecast for your business, and you want to create a single formula that automatically selects the correct rate for a given job. Figure 4.15 shows a simple version of such a worksheet.

```
    -----A---------B----------C----------D----------E-----
 1   Job                    Rate                              |
 2   Number    Hours        Code        Rate       Total      |
 3    101       10           1            30         300       |
 4    115        2           2            50         100       |
 5    127        4           1            30         120       |
 6    132        7           1            30         210       |
 7    134        3           3            75         225       |
 8                                                             |
    ==================================================MAIN=
```

Figure 4.15

The cells in column D each contain an @CHOOSE function that returns the proper rate based on the rate codes in column C. For example, cell D5 contains the formula

   D5: @CHOOSE(C5 – 1,30,50,75)

Since C5 contains the number 1, the @CHOOSE function returns the data item with an offset of 1 – 1, or 0, so the function returns the value 30.

@CHOOSE functions can also be used in conjuction with Symphony's lookup functions to create lookup tables that alter themselves automatically. This kind of hybrid table can be used in depreciation analysis and income tax worksheets.

@VLOOKUP and @HLOOKUP

@VLOOKUP and @HLOOKUP are variations on a very powerful function first used in VisiCalc. @VLOOKUP and @HLOOKUP are both table lookup functions. In other words, they "look up" a value or a label from a table based on the value of a key.

Both of these functions require that a table, called a lookup table, exists in the worksheet. This table must contain at least two partial rows and two partial columns. @HLOOKUP operates on a table that is arranged horizontally, while @VLOOKUP operates on a vertical table. Otherwise, the two functions are identical.

The forms of the two lookup functions are

   @VLOOKUP(key,table range,offset)
   @HLOOKUP(key,table range,offset)

As with the @CHOOSE function, the *key* is the number or cell reference that is used to access one of the values or labels stored in the table. The *table range* is a rectangular area that contains at least two partial rows (for @HLOOKUP) or two partial columns (for @VLOOKUP).

Lookup Tables

In a vertical table, the first partial column of the table range contains the index values that are used to locate the values in the table. The table range must include at least one other column, adjacent to the first, which contains the data that will be looked up. In a horizontal table, the index values are located in the first row of the table. The remaining rows in the range are used to store the values or labels to be looked up.

When we say that a table is horizontal or vertical, what we are really doing is giving Symphony a hint about the location of the index values in the table. If the index values are located in the left-most column of the table, then we say that it is a vertical table and use the @VLOOKUP function. If the index values are located at the top of the table, then we say the table is horizontal and we use the @HLOOKUP function. @VLOOKUP always expects to find the index values in the left-most column of the table range and @HLOOKUP always expects to find those values in the top row of the range.

The *offset* tells the lookup function which column or row of the lookup table contains the data to be looked up. The column or row containing the index values has an offset of 0. The first data row or column has an offset of 1. The offset value must always be positive and must never be greater than the number of rows or columns in the table minus 1. That is, if a vertical table is three columns wide, the offset cannot be greater than 2. Any offset value that does not meet these rules will cause the function to return an @ERR message.

Figure 4.16 shows a simple vertical lookup table. In this simple table, column A contains the index values. Notice that the values in this column are arranged in ascending numeric order. Any value (including negative values) may be used as an index in lookup table, provided the index values in a lookup table are always in ascending order. No index value can be repeated in the same table.

The vertical lookup table in Figure 4.17 will not work properly because the index values in column A are not in ascending order. Similarly, the horizontal table in Figure 4.18 will not function properly because one index value, 5, appears twice in row 2.

Column B in Figure 4.17 and rows 3 and 4 in Figure 4.18 contain data. This information is not arranged in any particular order.

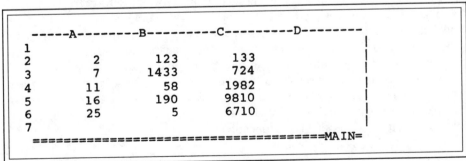

Figure 4.16

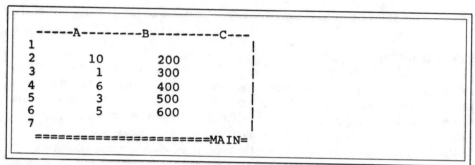

Figure 4.17

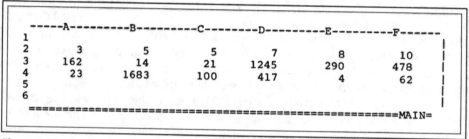

Figure 4.18

@VLOOKUP

To access the table in Figure 4.16, you would use the @VLOOKUP function. For example, the function

@VLOOKUP(7,A2 . . C6,2)

would return the value 724. The function works by first locating the table range and then the column containing the index values—in this case, column A. Next, the function scans the index values in column A to find the greatest index value that is less than or equal to the key value in the function. In the example, since 7, the second index value, is equal to 7, the key value, the function knows to look in row 3 for the correct data.

Finally, the function uses the offset to determine which column in the offset range should be probed for the data. In this case, the offset is 2, which means column C contains the desired data (remember, the column containing the index values has an offset of 0). The function returns the number in row 3, column C—724.

As you might expect, the key value in a lookup function can be a value or a cell reference. The table range can be indicated by using cell references or a range name. For example, if we assigned the name TABLE to the range A2 . . C6 in Figure 4.16, and we entered the number 7 in cell A1, the function

@VLOOKUP(A1,TABLE,2)

would be identical to our previous example.

Since the lookup functions look for the greatest index value that is less than or equal to the key value, and not for an exact match between index value and the key value, the function

$$@VLOOKUP(8,A2 . . C6,2)$$

would also return the value 724. Similarly, the function

$$@VLOOKUP(15,A2 . . C6,2)$$

would return the value 1982. Why? Because the index value that corresponds to 1982, 11, is the greatest index value in the table that is less than the key value, 15.

If all of the index values in the assigned table range are greater than the key value, the function will return the @ERR message. If all of the index values are less than the key value, the function will return the data value with the proper offset which corresponds to the last (greatest) index value. For example, in Figure 4.16, the function

$$@VLOOKUP(1000,A2 . . C6,2)$$

returns the value 6710, the value corresponding to the largest index number in the table.

What happens if the offset in a lookup function is 0? Take, for example, the function

$$@VLOOKUP(7,A2 . . C6,0)$$

This function returns the value 7, since the function's key value, 7, selects the row corresponding to the index value 7. The offset of 0 causes the function to return the number stored in the first column of the table in the indicated row.

Remember also that an offset that is greater than the number of columns or rows in the table minus one will result in an error message. For example, the function

$$@VLOOKUP(7,A2 . . C6,3)$$

will not work with the table in Figure 4.16, because the table range only allows for two columns of data. Mismatched offsets and table ranges are one of the most frequent causes of errors when working with lookup tables. Always be sure your offset and your table range agree.

HLOOKUP

The horizontal lookup function, @HLOOKUP, is virtually identical to the vertical lookup function, except that it is used to access tables that are laid out horizontally. All of the rules that apply to vertical tables and @VLOOKUP also apply to horizontal tables and @HLOOKUP.

Let's examine one example of @HLOOKUP at work. The worksheet in Figure 4.19 shows an acceptable horizontal lookup table. The function

$$@HLOOKUP(15,A2 . . D5,3)$$

would return the value 33 from this table, since 15, the key value, equals 15, the index value in column B, and since the offset, 3, tells the function to look in the third data row of the table for the correct item.

Looking back for a moment, notice that the table in Figure 4.16 can be either a vertical or a horizontal table. If we decided it was a horizontal table, then the values in the range

```
    -----A---------B---------C---------D-----
1
2        5         15         75        1000  |
3       21         17        105           5  |
4      122          3         17         984  |
5       12         33         45          90  |
6
    =================================MAIN=
```

Figure 4.19

A2 to C2 would become the index values, and the values in rows 3, 4, 5, and 6 would be the data values. An @HLOOKUP function like @HLOOKUP(10,A2 . . C6,3) would be used to access this table. Of course, not all tables can be changed from horizontal to vertical as quickly as can this one.

Text Lookup

In 1-2-3, Symphony's predecessor, the lookup functions could only be used to look up values. Text had a value of 0. Fortunately, Symphony's lookup functions do not have this limitation. Look at the vertical lookup table in Figure 4.20.

```
    -----A---------B---------C---------D--------
1        1    John Smith                          |
2        2    Tracy Jones                         |
3        3    David Brown                         |
4        4    Mike Williams                       |
5        5    Susan Johnson                       |
6                                                 |
7                                                 |
    ==================================MAIN==
```

Figure 4.20

The function

   @VLOOKUP(3,A1 . . B5,1)

returns the label David Brown from this table.

This new capability makes lookup tables far more useful. In fact, Symphony's lookup functions are so powerful that many simple data base applications can be handled perfectly well by these functions, without the need to create and manage a data base.

Symphony's ability to use text in lookup tables goes a step further. Not only can the data items in a table be text strings; the keys in the first column or row of the table can be strings as well. For example, the table in Figure 4.21 is another acceptable vertical lookup table.

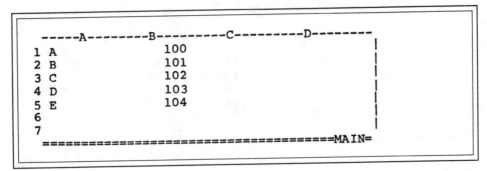

Figure 4.21

The function

@VLOOKUP("A",A1 . . B5,1)

returns the value 100 from this table.

There are some special rules to remember if you use text strings as the keys in your lookup tables. First, as in the example, the key argument in the function must be enclosed in double quotes. For example, the function

@VLOOKUP(A,A1 . . B5,1)

returns the @ERR message.

Second, when you use text as the lookup key, Symphony searches the key column in the table for a string that exactly matches the string in the argument. The two strings must agree in all regards. For example, the string TEST does not match test, and the string A does not match a. If no exact match is found, the function returns an @ERR message. Remember that numeric lookups don't require an exact match.

Finally, if you specify an offset of 0 in a string lookup, Symphony will not return a label, but will return a number that indicates how far down (in vertical tables) or across (in horizontal tables) Symphony traveled to find the matching string value. If no match is found, the result is @ERR.

@INDEX

@INDEX is one of Symphony's new functions. Like @CHOOSE, @HLOOKUP, and @VLOOKUP, @INDEX is a simple date base function. The form of the function is

@INDEX(range,column,row)

Where range represents the location of the index table, and column and row describe the column and row coordinates of the particular cell being referenced.

Like @HLOOKUP and @VLOOKUP, @INDEX requires that you set up and identify a special rectangular area in the worksheet, called an index table. An index table is a rectangular range spanning at least two rows and two columns. Typically index tables are much larger. Figure 4.22 shows an example of a simple index table.

This table is in fact a portion of the ACRS Cost Recovery Table for Real Property. The numbers in row one represent the month in which an asset was placed in service.

```
    -----A---------B---------C---------D---------E-------
 1                 1         2         3         4    |
 2         1       .12       .11       .10       .09  |
 3         2       .10       .10       .11       .11  |
 4         3       .09       .09       .09       .09  |
 5         4       .08       .08       .08       .08  |
 6         5       .07       .07       .07       .07  |
 7                                                    |
    ================================================MAIN=
```

Figure 4.22

The numbers in column A represent the years in the life of the asset. (The complete table would cover 15 rows and 12 columns.)

Suppose we entered the month the asset was placed in service in cell Z1, the purchase price of the asset in cell Z2, and the current year in the life of the asset in cell Z3. We could then use the formula

Z4: +Z2 × @INDEX(A1 . . E6,Z1,Z3)

to compute the current year's depreciation. Assuming that cell Z1 was equal to 2 and cell Z3 was equal to 4, the @INDEX function would return the value .08, the number in the second column and the fourth row of the index table.

Notice that row 1 is the 0th row in the table and column A is the 0th column. In this regard the @INDEX function parallels the @CHOOSE, @VLOOKUP, and @HLOOKUP functions.

Cursor Location Functions

Among Symphony's special functions is a new group of functions that can return information about the worksheet or a single cell. These functions are @COLS, @ROWS, @CELL, and @CELLPOINTER.

@COLS and @ROWS

Two of the most useful of these new functions are @COLS and @ROWS. These functions return the number of columns and the number of rows in a range. The forms of the functions are

@COLS(range)
@ROWS(range)

Let's look at these functions at work. The function

@COLS(A1 . . G17)

returns the value 7, since there are 7 columns in this range. The function

@ROWS(A1 . . G17)

returns 17, because there are 17 rows in the range.

If the argument of an @ROWS or @COLS function is a single cell, or a range name describing a single cell, the function will return the @ERR message. For example, the function

@ROWS(A1)

returns @ERR. However, if the argument is a range containing only one cell, the function returns the value 1. For example, the function

@ROWS(A1 . . A1)

equals 1.

If these functions seem trivial, it is because in this example we've used simple cell reference range designations in the arguments. The real value of these functions comes when they are used within macros and when they are applied to named ranges.

As you will see in a later chapter, there are certain advantages to using range names instead of cell references to describe ranges. However, it can be difficult to determine the exact dimensions of a named range. @COLS and @ROWS can also be used with macros to quickly determine just how wide or deep a range name is. There are times when it is necessary for a macro to "know" just how large a range is before a command is issued. For example, if the name TEST is assigned to the range A1 . . G17, the function

@ROWS(TEST)

still returns the value 17.

@CELL and @CELLPOINTER

The other special functions are @CELL and @CELLPOINTER. These functions allow Symphony to enter information about the attributes of one cell in another cell. When the information has been entered in the worksheet, it can be used by Symphony in calculations and logical functions. The forms of these functions are

@CELL("code",range)
@CELLPOINTER("code")

@CELL and @CELLPOINTER are identical except that @CELLPOINTER returns the status of the cell occupied by the cell pointer the last time the worksheet was calculated, while @CELL can return information on any cell in the worksheet. The code argument is a one-word expression, always enclosed in double quotes, that tells the function exactly what you want to know about a given cell.

Although the @CELL function returns information about a particular cell, the range argument must be in the form of a range. For example, to obtain information about cell A1, you would specify the range A1 . . A1. If the range argument describes a multi-cell range, then @CELL returns the desired information about the upper-left cell in the range. For example, if you use the range A1 . . C5 in an @CELL function, the function returns information about cell A1. If you use a single cell as the range argument, the function returns the @ERR message.

As with most functions, the range argument in the @CELL function can also be a range name. If a named range that describes more than one cell is used, the function returns the requested attribute for the upper-left cell in the named range.

There are seven codes that can be used with the @CELL and @CELLPOINTER functions: "Address", "Row", "Column", "Width", "Prefix", "Format", and "Type". Symphony does not care whether the codes are written in upper- or lowercase.

The first three codes, "Address", "Row", and "Column", return the absolute address, row location, or column location of the cell reference in the argument. For example,

> @CELL("Row",A1 .. A1)

returns the value 1, the row number of cell A1. The "Row" option can return any number between 1 and 8192. Similarly,

> @CELL("Column",A1)

returns the value 1, the function's designation for column A. The "Column" code always returns a number instead of a column letter. Since there are 256 columns in the Symphony workspace, the "Column" option can return any integer between 1 and 256. Finally, the function

> @CELL("Address",A1)

returns $A$1 in the cell containing the function. The "Address" always returns the absolute reference of the cell in the range.

The "Width" code instructs the function to return the width of the column containing the cell in the argument. For example, if column A had been formatted to be 11 characters wide (using the {**Menu**} **W**idth **S**et command), the function

> @CELL("Width",A1)

returns the value 11. We will see in Chapter 7 that the same column can have two widths in two different windows. This means that the same @COL("Width",range) function can have two different values in two different windows.

The code "Prefix" causes the @CELL and @CELLPOINTER functions to return the label prefix of the label in the argument cell. For example, if cell A1 contains the label 'Smith, the function

> @CELL("Prefix",A1)

returns the label prefix character '. The other possible results are ^ (for centered labels), " (for right-justified labels), \ (for repeating labels), and ¦ (for hidden comment labels). If the cell being referred to is blank, or contains a number or a formula, the function returns a blank.

The code "Type" causes the function to return l if the cell in the argument contains a label, v if the cell contains a value, or b if the cell is blank. For example, if cell A1 contains a label, the function

> @CELL("Type",A1)

returns the letter l. If A1 contains a value, the same function returns a v. If the cell is blank, the "Type" code causes the function to return a b.

The "Format" option returns the format that has been assigned to the cell. For example, if cell A1 has been assigned the Currency format with two decimal places, the function

> @CELL("Format", A1)

returns the code C2. Table 4.2 shows the possible results when the "Format" option is used in the @CELL function.

Result	Format
C0 to C15	Currency, 0 to 15 decimals
F0 to F15	Fixed, 0 to 15 decimals
%0 to %15	Percentage, 0 to 15 decimals
S0 to S15	Scientific, 0 to 15 decimals
P0 to P15	Punctuated, 0 to 15 decimals
D1 to D5	Date formats 1 to 5
T1 to T4	Time format 1 to 4
L	Literal
H	Hidden

Table 4.2

These codes are identical to the codes used in the control panel to indicate a cell's format. If no special format has been assigned to the cell being tested, the function returns the result G, for General.

@CELLPOINTER is identical to @CELL except that it returns the requested information about the cell in which the cell pointer was positioned the last time the worksheet was calculated. For example, if the cell pointer was positioned in cell A1 when the worksheet was last calculated, the @CELLPOINTER function returns the requested attribute of cell A1. @CELLPOINTER will continue to return information about cell A1 until the worksheet is recalculated with the cell pointer in a different cell. If recalculation is set to Manual, the cell *currently* occupied by the cell pointer may not be the cell referred to by @CELLPOINTER.

Like many of Symphony's other new functions, the @CELL and @CELLPOINTER functions are most frequently used within macros to test the condition of a given cell. For example, suppose you were writing a macro that used range names instead of cell references. Imagine further that at some point you needed to determine the upper-left cell reference of one of these ranges, named TEST. You could use the function

> @CELL("Address",TEST)

to return the coordinates of the upper-left corner of the named range. These functions will be very helpful to those Symphony users who create sophisticated macro programs with the Symphony Command Language.

ERROR FUNCTIONS

Symphony includes two functions that indicate the presence of an error in the spreadsheet. These functions, @ERR and @NA, are unusual in that Symphony can insert them into the worksheet in response to a faulty function or formula without the need for action on the part of the user.

If a cell in your worksheet contains either an @ERR or an @NA function, every cell in the worksheet that depends on the cell containing the function also displays the message. This can make it tricky to locate the ultimate source of the problem.

An @ERR message can occur for any number of reasons. The most common is division by 0. Anytime you enter a formula in the worksheet that forces Symphony to divide by 0, an @ERR message will be returned in the cell containing the formula.

You may encounter the division-by-zero error frequently when you are first setting up a worksheet. It occurs when you enter a formula like

   C5: +A5/D5

in a cell, without yet having made an entry in cell D5. Since Symphony assigns the value 0 to a blank cell, this formula will produce division by zero until you put a number in cell D5.

Another frequent cause of errors is the deletion of a row or column from the worksheet. Suppose, for example, that you had entered the formula

   E5: +A5+B5+C5+D5

in cell E5. Now imagine that you used the /Delete Column command to delete column B from the worksheet. Once this command was completed, the formula in cell E5 would read

   D5: +A5+ERR+B5+C5

and cell D5 would display the @ERR message. Unfortunately, there is no way to recover from this type of error short of reentering the formula that has been affected by the deletion. If there were a large number of references to the deleted cells in the worksheet, you would have quite a repair job on your hands.

By the way, this problem is another reason the @SUM function is generally preferable to a long addition formula. If we had used the function

   E5: @SUM(A5 . . D5)

in cell E5, deleting the column would not create an error. After the column was deleted, the function would read

   D5: @SUM(A5 . . C5)

The @SUM function will usually prevent errors resulting from deletions of rows and columns.

There are times when you'll want to enter an @ERR function in the worksheet. For example, suppose you had created a worksheet in which the cells in column E depended on the cells in columns C and D. You wish to place a limit on the allowable inputs in column D.

One way to accomplish this would be to create an {IF} macro that tested each input to column D to be sure that it met the limitations. Another way would be to enter a formula like

E5: @IF(D5<.66*B5,@ERR,C5*D5)

in all of the cells in column E. This formula says: If the value in cell D5 is less than 66% of the value in cell B5, enter an @ERR message in this cell. Otherwise, enter the result of D5 times C5 in cell E5.

@NA

@NA is an infrequently used function that serves as a placeholder in the worksheet. Suppose your worksheet requires a particular input, but you are not yet certain of the value of that input. If you enter the function @NA in that cell, Symphony displays NA in that cell and in every other cell in the worksheet that depends on that one.

Most Symphony users don't find much use for the @NA function. There just aren't many times when you need a placeholder like @NA in most spreadsheets.

LOGICAL FUNCTIONS

Symphony and 1-2-3 both offer the logical, or conditional, function @IF. @IF allows the user to create conditional tests into cells. The form of the @IF function is

@IF(condition,true value,false value)

The *condition* is an equation that compares two numbers, functions, formulas, or labels. The following are examples of some acceptable conditions:

A1 = 5
C5 > 3
(D17-3) < 0
@SUM(A1 .. A7) = 5
A1 = "Male"
@RIGHT(A1,5) = "ABCDE"

Logical Operators

Every condition must include one or more logical operators. Logical operators define the relationship between the terms of the condition. For example, in the condition A1 = 5, " = " is the logical operator. Following is a list of Symphony's logical operators and their definitions.

Operator	Definition
=	equals
>	greater than
<	less than
> =	greater than or equal to
< =	less than or equal to
< >	not equal to

If you think about it for a second you'll realize that any condition that contains a logical operator must be either true or false. For example, the statement A1 = 5 will be true if cell A1 contains the number 5 or a formula whose value is 5, and it will be false if A1 contains anything else. For this reason, every condition is a test.

Simple Conditions

Symphony's @IF function has the ability to determine whether a given condition is true or false. If the condition is true, the function returns the *true value*. If the function is false, the *false value* is returned. For example, consider the function

>   A2: @IF(A1 = 5,1,2)

If cell A1 has the value 5, the condition is true and cell A2 displays the value 1. Otherwise, cell A2 contains the value 2. Similarly, the function

>   C5: @IF(B3 > 12,A1,A2)

returns the contents of cell A1 if the value in cell B3 is greater than 12. Otherwise, the value in cell A2 is returned.

The function

>   D8: @IF(A7 < >B7,@SUM(D1 . . D7,0)

can be translated: If the contents of cell A7 do not equal the contents of cell B7, return the sum of the range D1 . . D7. Otherwise, return the value 0.

Using Labels in Conditionals

One big improvement of Symphony over 1-2-3 is the new program's ability to include labels as well as values in conditional functions. A label or string function can be used in the condition or in either the true value or false value. For example, the function

>   C5: @IF(B5 = 1,"Male","Female")

returns the label Male in cell C5 if cell B5 has a value of 1, and the label Female if B5 has any other value.

There are a couple of rules governing the use of text in a conditional. First, if a literal text string is used in the function, the text must be enclosed in double quotes. For example, the function

>   C5: @IF(B5 = 1,Male,Female)

is not acceptable to Symphony. You can also include text in a conditional function by using a cell reference. For example, if cell A1 contains the label Male and cell A2 the label Female, the function

>   C5: @IF(B5 = 1,A1,A2)

is acceptable and is identical to

>   C5: @IF(B5 = 1,"Male","Female")

One clever use of Symphony's new "labels-in-conditionals" capability is the use of a space instead of a 0 as the false value in an @IF function. For example, in the function

D5: @IF(C5 = D1,B5," ")

if C5 equals D1, D5 assumes the value of cell B5. Otherwise, a space will be entered in the cell, giving it the appearance of being blank.

You can also use a label in the condition. For example, the function

G7: @IF(E7 = "Exempt",0,.0677)

tests the contents of cell E7. If E7 contains the label Exempt (the quotes are included to satisfy the requirements of the function), cell G7 assumes the value 0; otherwise, cell G7 takes the value .0677.

Complex Operators

Symphony also offers three complex logical operators that allow you to create more sophisticated logical functions. These operators are #AND#, #OR#, and #NOT#.

As you might expect, the complex logical operators allow you to combine conditions formed with simple operators into compound conditions. For example, using the #AND# operator would allow you to create the function

A5: @IF(A1 = 5#AND#A2 = 10,3,5)

This function says: If the value in cell A1 equals 5 *and* the value in cell A2 equals 10, return the number 3. Otherwise, return the number 5. Similarly, the function

A5: @IF(A1 = 5#OR#A2 = 10,3,5)

reads this way: If the value in cell A1 is 5 *or* the value in cell A2 is 10, return the value 3; otherwise, return the value 5.

Although these two functions look alike, they are vastly different in meaning. The compound condition in the first function, which uses #AND#, will be true only if both halves of the condition are true. The compound condition in the second function will be true if either half is true.

The final complex operator is #NOT#. This operator is used to negate a condition. For example, the function

@IF(#NOT#A1 = 5,3,5)

is essentially the same as

@IF(A1 < >5,3,5)

and is similar to

@IF(A1 = 5,5,3)

Because these other forms require fewer characters and are easier to understand, you'll usually use them instead of the #NOT# operator.

Sometimes you'll want to create a compound condition, both parts of which refer to the same cell. The function

@IF(A1 <3#AND#A1 > − 3,100,0)

is an example of such a function. Notice that the reference to cell A1 is repeated in both halves of the condition. Many Symphony users have a tendency to want to abbreviate this kind of condition. For example, they would try to write the example above as

@IF(A1 <3#AND# > −3,100,0)

omitting the second cell reference. If you make this mistake, Symphony will not accept the entry.

Nested Conditionals

There are times when a complex logical problem cannot be handled with even complex operators. In this case, you can use *nested conditional* statements to solve the problem. The function

@IF(A1 >5,15,@IF(A1 >0,10,@IF(A5 = 1,5,0)))

is an example of such a function. This example reads like this: If A1 is greater than 5, return 15; otherwise, If A1 is greater than 0, return 10; otherwise, If A5 equals 1, return 5; otherwise, return 0. This function uses three separate conditional functions to create a kind of "logical selection process." If the first condition is false, the function considers the second; if that is also false, the third is analyzed.

You can string together as many logical functions as you want, provided the formula length does not exceed Symphony's single cell limit of 240 characters. Be sure, though, that you have a closing parenthesis for every function in the formula. For example, notice that the example above ends with three closing parentheses—one for each of the three @IF functions. If you don't include enough parentheses, or if the parentheses are in the wrong spot, Symphony will not allow you to enter the function into the worksheet.

Special Conditional Functions

Symphony offers four special conditional functions: @ISERR, @ISNA, @ISVALUE, and @ISSTRING.

These functions are all designed to be used as conditional statements within @IF statements. These functions test the value of a cell to determine whether it contains a particular value or, in the case of @ISSTRING, a label. Like all conditionals, these functions are either true or false. They return the true or false value depending on whether the cell has the contents you're searching for. For example, the function

@ISERR(A1)

will be true if cell A1 contains @ERR, and it will be false if A1 does not contain an error.

Trapping Errors

@ISERR and @ISNA allow you to test the value of a cell to determine whether it contains the @ERR or @NA function. These functions are designed to "block" unneeded ERR or NA messages, preventing them from filtering through the sheet.

@ISERR is frequently used to block errors that sometimes arise due to division by zero. (We'll talk about this problem more later in the chapter.) For example, the function

A3: @IF(@ISERR(A1/A2),0,A1/A2)

tests the result of the division A1/A2. If that division returns @ERR, the condition is true and the value 0 is returned by the @IF function. If A1/A2 does not result in an error, the @ISERR condition is false and the @IF statement returns the result of the division A1/A2.

@ISNA is used in the same way to trap @NA functions. For example, the function

A2: @IF(@ISNA(A1),1,2)

returns 1 if cell A1 contains the function @NA and 2 if the cell contains any other value.

Label or Value?

The @ISSTRING and @ISVALUE functions can be used to determine whether a cell contains a label or a value. Like @ISERR and @ISNA, these conditional functions are true if the cell being tested contains the proper type of entry and are false if the cell contains a different type of entry or is blank. For example, if cell A1 contains the label "This old man," the function

@IF(@ISSTRING(A1),1,2)

returns the value 1, since @ISSTRING(A1) is true. If A1 contained a value or was blank, @ISSTRING(A1) would be false and the @IF function would return the value 2.

As you might expect, @ISVALUE is used to determine whether a cell contains a value. If A1 contains the value 1 (or any other value, including a function or a formula), the conditional function @ISVALUE(A1) is true. If A1 contained a label or was blank, then @ISVALUE(A1) would be false.

Notice that although @ISSTRING and @ISVALUE are nearly opposite, they both will be false if the cell being tested is blank. So a false reading from @ISVALUE does not mean that a cell necessarily contains a label and a false value from @ISSTRING does not mean that a cell contains a value.

@ISSTRING and @ISVALUE are most frequently used as conditional tests in conjunction with the Symphony Command Language command {IF}.

TEXT FUNCTIONS

Symphony's text functions are one of the most important differences between the program and its predecessor, 1-2-3. Text functions allow Symphony to perform many of the same operations on cells containing text as it can on cells containing numbers. In addition, text functions allow you to manipulate words and phrases in some interesting ways. Symphony's text functions are @UPPER, @LOWER, @PROPER, @CODE, @CHAR, @LENGTH, @TRIM, @CLEAN, @LEFT, @RIGHT, @MID, @FIND, @EXACT, @REPEAT, and @REPLACE.

Changing Case: @UPPER, @LOWER, and @PROPER

Symphony includes three functions—@UPPER, @LOWER, and @PROPER—that can be used to change the case of all or part of the letters in a label. This capability is particularly useful when you want to transform a label into a standard form for comparison to the items in a data base.

@UPPER transforms all of the letters in a label into uppercase. For example, the function

> @UPPER("john jones")

would return the label JOHN JONES.

Remember that the argument of a label function can be either a label enclosed in double quotes or a reference to a cell containing a label.

@LOWER is the opposite of the @UPPER function. @LOWER transforms all of the characters in a string into lowercase. For example, the function

> @LOWER("JOHN JONES")

would return the label john jones.

The third case function, @PROPER, changes only the first letter in every word in a label into uppercase. For example, the function

> @PROPER("john jones")

would return the label John Jones.

These functions have several common characteristics. First, they have no effect on numeric labels (labels made up of numeric characters). For example, the function

> @UPPER("1234")

would simply return the numeric label 1234. On the other hand, all of these functions return @ERR if you use a value in the argument. For example, if cell A12 contained the number 13, the function

> @LOWER(A1)

would return an @ERR message.

Working with ASCII

All computers use a code to represent the numbers and letters you see on the screen. The most commonly used code in the world of personal computers is called ASCII, or American Standard for Character Information Interchange. ASCII assigns a three-digit code to every letter, numeral, and punctuation mark. For example, the letter a is represented by the ASCII code 97. The numeral 1 is represented by the code 49. The ASCII codes from 0 to 32 are used to represent special characters that do not appear on the screen, like Control-G (bell) and Escape. The standard ASCII character set uses the numbers between 0 and 127.

Although all computers use the ASCII codes from 0 to 127 in the same way, the codes between 127 and 255 (called the "upper 128" codes) are not standardized. Many computers, including the IBM PC, use these additional codes to represent special graphics characters. In Symphony, these upper 128 codes are used to represent characters used in foreign alphabets and other special symbols, like the British pound sign. The Symphony international character set is discussed at more length in a later chapter.

Symphony includes two functions that can convert a character into its ASCII equivalent or an ASCII code into a character. The function

@CODE(string)

will return the ASCII value of the first character in the string. For example, the function

@CODE("This old man")

would return the value 84, the ASCII code for the letter T.

The function @CHAR(value) can be used to convert a three-digit ASCII value into a character. For example, the function

@CHAR(115)

returns the letter s (lowercase), whose ASCII code is 115. The argument in an @CHAR function can be any number between 1 and 255; any value outside this range returns @ERR.

Some computers cannot display every character in the Symphony international character set. If your computer cannot display the character that results from an @CHAR function, Symphony substitutes a character similar to the one it cannot display, or it displays the character ∎ .

The @ASCII and @CHAR functions will probably be most useful to heavy users of the Symphony Command Language.

The Substring Functions

Symphony includes several functions that can be used to break a string down into smaller parts. For example, there may be a time when you need to break a string like "John Smith" into two strings: "John" and "Smith".

Symphony includes several functions that allow you to operate on strings or portions of strings (called substrings) in this way. The forms of these functions are as follows:

@LENGTH(string)
@TRIM(string)
@CLEAN(string)
@LEFT(string,X characters)
@RIGHT(string,X characters)
@MID(string,X,Y)
@FIND(string 1,string 2,offset)
@REPLACE(string 1,offset,X characters,string 2)
@EXACT(string 1,string 2)
@REPEAT(string,X times)

@LENGTH

The simplest string function is @LENGTH. This function returns the length of the string in the argument. As with the other string functions, the argument can be either a label enclosed in double quotes or a reference to a label cell. For example, the function

@LENGTH("Tom and Jerry")

would return the value 13, the number of characters in the string. If cell A1 contained the label "Tom and Jerry", the function

> @LENGTH(A1)

would also return 13.

@LENGTH can be very useful in testing labels to make sure they conform to length restrictions. For example, suppose you want to write a Symphony Command Language program that gets a set of labels from the keyboard and stores them in a data base. The first field of the data base is 15 characters wide, and you want to be sure that no label wider than 15 characters is entered in this field. Your program could contain the lines

> {GETLABEL Enter a Label: ,INPUT}
> {IF @LENGTH(INPUT)>15}{BRANCH AA150} ~

The first line requests the user to enter a label and stores that label in the cell that has been named INPUT. The second line tests the length of the string in INPUT; if the string is longer than 15 characters, the macro continues to process at cell AA150, which we'll assume contains a code that requests the user to reenter the label.

If a cell containing a value is used in the argument of @LENGTH, the @ERR message is returned.

@TRIM and @CLEAN

@TRIM and @CLEAN are two new Symphony functions that let you remove unwanted characters from labels. The @TRIM function is designed to remove preceding and trailing spaces from a label. The function has the form

> @TRIM(string)

Suppose cell A1 contained the label

> A1:'   This is a string

This string has five leading spaces and (we'll assume) ten trailing spaces. If we enter the function

> A2: @TRIM(A1)

in cell A2, the string in cell A2 will have no leading or trailing spaces.

Like @LENGTH, @TRIM will probably be used most heavily by those who are programming with the Symphony Command Language. @TRIM can be used in a program to "slim down" a label that has been entered from the keyboard or stored in a cell for use in a different part of the worksheet.

@TRIM can also be used to convert a long left-justified label created in the DOC mode into a simple left-justified label. For example, suppose cell A1 contains the label

> A1:' Functions

then the function

> A2: @TRIM(A1)

would return the label Functions, without leading or trailing spaces.

@CLEAN is used to strip control codes from labels. (Control codes are ASCII codes below 32). The DOC environment uses control codes to represent special characters in documents, like the indentation at the beginning of paragraphs and the hard carriage return at the end of every line. Control codes are also sometimes included in text received through the COMM mode, and can be included in text strings imported into the worksheet with File Import.

Although control codes create visible characters in DOC windows, these codes cannot be displayed in SHEET windows. For this reason, you may want to remove control codes from labels before working with them in the SHEET environment.

@LEFT, @RIGHT, and @MID

Symphony includes three functions that will extract a substring from a string. @LEFT allows the user to create a substring that consists of the left-most characters in the string. @RIGHT returns a substring containing the right-most characters in the string. @MID can extract a substring from any part of the string.

The forms of @RIGHT and @LEFT are virtually identical:

> @RIGHT(string,X)
> @LEFT(string,X)

The term X in both functions tells the function how many characters should be in the substring. For example, the function

> @LEFT("abcdefghi",3)

would return the substring abc, the three left-most characters in the string. The function

> @LEFT("abcdefghi",5)

would extract the string abcde. Similarly, the function

> @RIGHT("abcdefghi",2)

would return the two right-most characters in the string, hi.

The X term of the @LEFT and @RIGHT functions must be greater than or equal to 0. If the X term is equal to or greater than the total number of characters in the string, the entire string will be returned.

@MID is slightly more complicated than @LEFT and @RIGHT. The form of this function is

> @MID(string,X,Y)

where X is the position of the character at which you wish the substring to begin, and Y is the length of the string. For example, the function

> @MID("abcdefghi",3,1)

would return the single character d. (Remember that a is in position 0 in this string, so d is in position 3.) The function

> @MID("abcdefghi",5,3)

would return fgh.

The X and Y terms in the @MID function should both be equal to or greater than 0. An X term of 0 makes the @MID function functionally identical to the @LEFT function. If the X term is greater than the length of the string, the function will return a blank.

A Y term of 0 causes the function to return 0 characters, or a blank. Normally, the Y term will be less than or equal to the total length of the string; however, the Y argument can be as large as you wish. A Y argument that exceeds the total length of the string tells Symphony to return the remainder of the string. Thus the function

@MID("abcdefghi",3,400)

would return the string defghi.

@FIND

@FIND is a new Symphony function which can be used to pinpoint the start of one text string within a longer string. The form of the function is

@FIND(string 1,string 2,offset)

The function tells Symphony to find string 1 within string 2, beginning with the offset specified in string 2. For example, the function

@FIND("b","abc",0)

tells Symphony to locate the character b in the string abc, beginning the search at the start of the string abc. This function returns the value 1, the location of b in abc. Remember that Symphony likes to count beginning with 0, so a is located in position 0 and b is in position 1.

The offset term is included to make it possible to find multiple occurrences of a string within a longer string. For example, the character b occurs three times in the string abcabcabc. The function

A10: @FIND("b","abcabcabc",0)

returns 1, the location of the first b. The function

A11: @FIND("b","abcabcabc",A10 + 1)

returns 4, the location of the second b. The second function uses the result of the first function in cell A10, plus 1, as its offset term. This tells the function to begin looking for the second b at the end of the first b. The location of the third b is returned with the function

A12: @FIND("b","abcabcabc",A11 + 1)

@REPLACE

The @REPLACE function is the most complicated of the string functions. @REPLACE allows you to substitute one string for a portion of another string. The form of the function is

@REPLACE(string 1,offset,X,string 2)

The function deletes X characters beginning at the offset in string 1, and substitutes string 2 into string 1 at the offset position. For example, the function

@REPLACE("This old man",5,7,"young man")

returns the string This young man. The function deleted 7 characters beginning with offset position 5 (the letter o) and replaced them with the string "young man".

The number of letters to be deleted must not exceed the number of letters in the string between the offset and the end. For example, in the function above, an X term of 9 would have generated an @ERR message. If the number of characters to be deleted (the X argument) is 0, the function will insert the replacement string at the location specified by the offset.

If the replacement string is blank (the string ""), @REPLACE just deletes the original string from the total string.

@EXACT

The @EXACT function compares two strings to determine if they match. If the two strings match exactly, the function returns the value TRUE; otherwise, the function returns the value FALSE. If one of the cells referred to by the @EXACT function contains a value, the function returns the @ERR message.

@EXACT is usually used as a conditional test in a logical function. The function

@EXACT("ABCDE","ABCDE")

is TRUE, so the function

@IF(@EXACT("ABCDE","ABCDE"),5,10)

returns the value 5. Similarly, if cell A1 contains the label ABCDE, the function

@EXACT("ABCDE",A1)

is TRUE. Remember that the strings must match exactly. The string abcde does not match ABCDE; nor does ABCD match ABCDE.

@EXACT is very similar to the logical operator = . The difference is that @EXACT insists on an exact match between the two strings, while = can tolerate differences in case. For example, the function

@EXACT("ABCD","abcd")

is FALSE, but the conditional

"ABCD" = "abcd"

is TRUE.

@REPEAT

@REPEAT is designed to quickly duplicate a string within a single cell. The form of the function is

@REPEAT(string,X)

where X is the number of times you want the string to be repeated. For example, the function

@REPEAT("abc",3)

would return the label abcabcabc. @REPEAT is virtually identical to the repeating label prefix \. The main difference between the two is that \ always repeats the label enough times to fill the column width exactly. @REPEAT repeats the label only as many times as you specify with the X argument.

Using the String Functions

Symphony's string functions clearly have a great deal of power. But you may not be sure about how to put that power to work for you. Following are a couple of examples of uses for the string functions.

Using @LEFT

Suppose you have set up a name and address data base in Symphony and have also written a macro that will print address labels for you from the list. One problem is that your data base can accept names of unlimited length, but you can print only 20 characters on a line of your mailing labels. You could use the @LEFT function to trim each name down to the maximum 20 characters before printing.

@LEFT could also be used with @EXACT to test a string input from the keyboard against some predetermined string. For example, suppose you input the string ABCDE into cell A1. Cell A2 might contain the function

A2: @IF(@EXACT("ABC",@LEFT(A1,3)),1,0)

Since the three left-most characters in the string in A1 match the string ABC, this function will return the value 1. If another label had been entered in cell A1, the function would return the value 0.

Using @FIND and @RIGHT together

Suppose you've created a simple data base that holds the names and addresses of your clients. The Name field contains both the first and last names of the clients—for example, John Smith. You need to break out only the last name of each client.

Assume that you copy the name John Smith from the data base to cell A10. Now enter the function

A11: @RIGHT(A10,@FIND(" ",A10,0) + 1)

in cell A11. This cell now displays only the last name, Smith. The function says: Extract the right-most characters from the string in cell A10, beginning one character to the right of the space in the label in A10. The location of the space is determined by the @FIND function. We add 1 to the result of the @FIND function, because we want the @RIGHT function to begin with the first character in the last name, not with the space.

SPECIAL TEXT AND VALUE FUNCTIONS

Symphony includes four more functions—@STRING, @VALUE, @S, and @N—that perform special operations on cells containing text or values.

The @STRING and @VALUE functions allow you to change a numeric label into a value or a value into a numeric label. The functions have the forms

@STRING(value,number of decimal places)
@VALUE(numeric label)

@STRING transforms a value into a numeric string. As with most Symphony functions, the argument for @STRING can be any value: a number, a function, or a formula. The second part of the argument specifies the number of decimal places to be included in the string. For example, the function

A5: @STRING(55,0)

transforms the number 55 into the numeric string 55.

Although the number 55 and the numeric string 55 look the same, Symphony treats them very differently. First, the number 55 can be used in a formula, while the numeric string 55 cannot. Second, assuming that the default label justification is in effect, the numeric string 55 will be left justified, while the value 55 will be right justified.

@STRING is even more useful when a cell address is used in the argument. For example, if cell A1 contains the number 15, the function

@STRING(A1,0)

returns the numeric string 15. If, however, you change the value in cell A1 to 10 and recalculate the worksheet, the numeric string also changes.

Notice that the @STRING function is quite a bit more powerful than the old 1-2-3 technique for transforming a value into a numeric string. In 1-2-3, a number could be transformed into a label by inserting a label prefix in front of the number. This method had two disadvantages. First, it could be used only on a pure number. Trying to transform the result of a function like @SUM(A1 . . A5) into a label would result in the label

'@SUM(A1 . . A5)

The @STRING function, on the other hand, returns a numeric label representing the result of the @SUM function. Second, as we saw above, the @STRING function creates a dynamic label that changes as the underlying value changes.

@VALUE changes a numeric string into a value. In effect, @VALUE is the opposite of @STRING. Consider this example. Suppose cell A1 contained the numeric label

A1: '12345

The function

@VALUE(A1)

would return the value of this numeric string, 12345. If the label in cell A1 was "9 1/2", the function would return the value 9.5. If cell A1 contained the label "12300", then the function would return the value 12300.

If the argument is a value or refers to a cell containing a value, the @VALUE function will have no effect. For example, @VALUE(12) is simply 12.

@N and @S

The @N and @S functions return the value of the cell in the upper-left corner of a range. @S is used if the range contains labels; @N is used to return numeric values.

@N and @S can both operate on a single cell. However, the argument of both functions must always be in the form of a range. For example, the function

@N(A1 . . A1)

would return the value in cell A1. Since the simple formula

    +A1

has the same impact, you may wonder why this function is so important. One value of the function is that it can return the value of just one cell in a range. For example, the function

    @N(A1 . . C5)

would also return the value in cell A1, since cell A1 is the upper-left cell in the range.

Another use of this function is to protect against the @ERR messages that arise when you accidentally add two cells together, one containing a label and the other a value. For example, the formula

    +A1 +A2

returns @ERR if A2 contains a label. However, since like all functions @N assigns the value 0 to a string, the function @N(A2) has the value 0, and the formula

    +A1 + @N(A2)

does not return @ERR. If you are not sure whether a cell being referred to by a formula contains a value or a label, you can use @N in the function as an insurance policy against errors.

@S operates on cells that contain text. If cell A1 contained the label Test, the function

    @S(A1 . . A1)

returns the string Test. If A1 contained the number 1, or was blank, the function would return a blank string.

Symphony offers more functions than any other electronic spreadsheet or integrated program. There are five major categories of functions in Symphony: mathematical functions, financial functions, engineering functions, special functions, and text functions. If you feel a bit overwhelmed, don't worry. Learn the functions as you need them. Soon you'll master all of them.

CHAPTER FIVE
FORMATS

Formats

Formats control the way the contents of cells in the Symphony worksheet are displayed. Every spreadsheet window has a default format. In addition to this default format, Symphony allows you to assign special formats to any cell or range in the worksheet. In fact, Symphony offers more cell formats than any previous electronic spreadsheet.

THE DEFAULT FORMAT

Every cell in a given window assumes the window's default format unless the user assigns a special format to that cell. The *default* format is the General format. Unless you specifically change the default format in a window (we'll discuss that process at the end of the chapter), that window will have the General format.

In the General format, values are displayed "as is." If the value has four decimals, the display has four decimals. If the value is negative, the display includes a minus sign.

There are a couple of special cases of the General format that must be considered. First, General always eliminates trailing zeros to the right of the decimal place. For example, the number 123.98000 is displayed in the General format as 123.98. However, the number 123.98001 is displayed "as is": 123.98001.

Second, the General format automatically shifts into Scientific format numbers that are too long to be displayed in the column width provided. For example, the number 123000000000 would be displayed as 1.23E11 in the General format. Typically, this transformation only occurs with very large values. However, very small numbers can also be too wide to be displayed in standard-width columns. For example, the number .00000000123 would be displayed as 1.23E – 10 in the General format.

SPECIAL CELL FORMATS

If you want some cells in a window to have one format but others to have a different format, you'll need to use Symphony's {**Menu**} Format command. The Format command is used to assign special (nondefault) formats to individual cells or ranges in a window.

Assigning Special Cell Formats

Special cell formats are selected by issuing the Format command from the spreadsheet menu and choosing the desired format from the menu. The Format command is selected by pressing {**Menu**} or the / key from within a SHEET window and then selecting Format from the main menu. The Format menu looks like this:

Currency Punctuated Fixed % General Date Time Scientific Other Reset

Selecting Other moves you to a second menu that offers these choices:

Bar-Graph Literal Hidden

After the desired format is selected, Symphony prompts you for a range to which the format should be applied. This range may be any rectangular group of cells, from a single cell to the whole workspace.

For example, imagine that you had built the simple worksheet in Figure 5.1. Suppose you wanted to assign cell A1 the Punctuated format. Move the cell pointer to cell A1 and issue the Format command by typing {**Menu**} Format. Next, select the **P**unctuated format from the Format menu. Symphony now prompts you with the message

Number of decimal places: 2

Many of Symphony's formats, including Punctuated, Fixed, % (Percentage), and Currency, require that the user specify the number of decimal places that should appear in the formatted number. The default number of decimal places in all of these formats is two. If you do indeed want two decimal places in the cells being formatted, then you need only press [Enter]. If you want a different number of decimals, you must type the desired number before pressing [Enter]. For purposes of this example, we'll assume that the default was accepted.

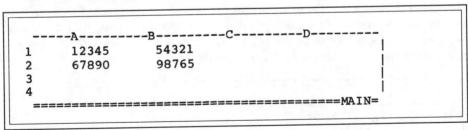

Figure 5.1

Next, Symphony prompts you for the range to be formatted with the message

Enter range to format: A1 .. A1

Notice that, as with the other spreadsheet commands, Symphony automatically provides a guess at the correct format range. As always, we have the choice of accepting this range by pressing [**Enter**] or typing or pointing to another range. In this case we would accept the program's guess by pressing **[Enter]**, and the worksheet would be changed to look like Figure 5.2.

```
    -----A---------B---------C---------D---------
 1  12,345.00       54321                            |
 2     67890        98765                            |
 3                                                   |
 4                                                   |
    ====================================MAIN=
```

Figure 5.2

By specifying a different range, we could have formatted any range of cells on the sheet. For example, the range A1 . . B2 would have changed the sheet to look like Figure 5.3.

```
    -----A---------B---------C---------D---------
 1  12,345.00   54,321.00                            |
 2  67,890.00   98,765.00                            |
 3                                                   |
 4                                                   |
    ====================================MAIN=
```

Figure 5.3

GENERAL RULES ABOUT FORMATS

There are some general rules that you should remember about Symphony's formats. First, remember that formats are associated with cells, not with the contents of a cell. For example, if you erase a value in a cell that has been assigned one of the Symphony formats, and then enter a new value into that cell, that new entry will have the format of the previous value. For example, in the worksheet in Figure 5.4, cell A1 has been assigned the Punctuated format with two decimal places.

```
    -----A---------B---------C---------D---------
 1  3,456.78                                         |
 2                                                   |
 3                                                   |
    ====================================MAIN=
```

Figure 5.4

If we type the number 8765 over the current contents of cell A1, the worksheet will look like Figure 5.5. Notice that the new number has assumed the Punctuated format.

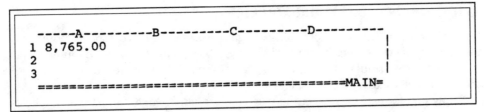

Figure 5.5

The second rule to remember is that if you copy the contents of a cell that has been formatted, the format is copied with the contents. In other words, all of the destination cells will have the same format as the original.

One of the easily avoidable errors beginning users make is to copy a formula or function *before* the cell containing that formula has been formatted. If you first format the cell, then copy its contents, you'll avoid having to repeat the formatting operation.

The third thing to keep in mind is that you can change the width of an entry by changing its format. For example, if you enter the number 12345 in a cell and then assign that cell the Currency 2 format, it will be displayed as $12,345.00. The formatted version is 10 characters wide—too wide to fit in a standard-width Symphony column. The problem is even worse if the number is − 12345. The formatted version of this number is ($12,345.00), which is 12 characters wide.

Symphony always displays as a series of asterisks any number too wide to fit in a given column as a result of user formatting. Figure 5.6 shows a worksheet that contains several cells whose contents, when formatted, are too wide to be displayed.

The simplest way to solve this problem is to use the {**Menu**} **W**idth **S**et command to widen the columns containing the wide entries. Figure 5.7 shows the same worksheet with columns A and B widened to 12 characters.

```
    -----A---------B---------C---------D---------
  1 ********                                       |
  2            ********                             |
  3 ********                                        |
  4                                                 |
    ====================================MAIN=
```

Figure 5.6

```
    -------A-----------B----------C---------D--------
  1   $123,345.00                                     |
  2                 $245,124.00                        |
  3    $1,237,909                                       |
  4                                                     |
    ====================================MAIN=
```

Figure 5.7

What You See and What You Get

There is probably nothing that confuses beginning users of all spreadsheets more than the concept of cell contents versus cell displays. We've already discussed this concept as it relates to formulas and functions (see Chapter 3). A related problem is the concept of cell values and cell displays.

Simply put, formats only affect the way cells are *displayed*. A format has no effect whatsoever on the contents of a cell. For example, suppose that cell A6 in a worksheet contains the formula

A6: @SUM(A1 . . A5)/12345678

and that the current value of this formula is exactly 12.346187490123417 when computed to 15 decimal places (Symphony's maximum accuracy). Now suppose that you formatted this cell using the {**Menu**} Format Currency 2 command. Cell A6 will now look like this:

$12.35

But it *still contains the same value as before*—12.346187490123417. Remember, formats affect only the way in which Symphony *displays* the contents of cells, not the contents of the cells themselves.

THE FORMATS

Former 1-2-3 users who have converted to Symphony will recognize most of Symphony's formats. However, Symphony adds two new formats—Time and Hidden—and has given new names, like Bar-Graph and Literal, to some of 1-2-3's functions. Table 5.1 shows the names of Symphony's formats and their 1-2-3 equivalents.

Symphony	1-2-3
Currency	Currency
Punctuated	, (Comma)
Fixed	Fixed
General	General
%	Percentage
Date	Date
Time	
Scientific	Scientific
Bar-Graph	+ / −
Literal	Text
Hidden	

Table 5.1

Currency

The Currency format displays numbers with a dollar sign ($) and commas between the hundreds and thousands, thousands and millions, and so on. Negative numbers appear in parentheses. The user can choose to display the numbers with any number of decimal places from 0 to 15.

For example, suppose you had entered the number 123456789.235 in cell A1 and then assigned the Currency format with two decimal places to that cell. The result would be

$123,456,789.24

Table 5.2 shows the result of applying the Currency format with different numbers of decimal places to several numbers.

Value	Decimal Places	Display
12345	2	$12,345.00
12345.67	0	$12,346
12345.9889	3	$12,345.989
1234567890	2	$1,234,567,890.00
− 12345.67	2	($12,345.67)

Table 5.2

Symphony's Currency format is virtually identical to 1-2-3's version of the same format. The main difference is that the Symphony international character set gives you more flexibility by making it possible to create Currency formats for foreign currencies like yen and pounds. This technique is explained in Chapter 30, Configuring Symphony.

Punctuated

Former 1-2-3 users will recognize that Symphony's Punctuated format is similar to 1-2-3's Comma (,) format. As we saw above, the Punctuated format causes numbers to be displayed with commas between every third digit and the specified number of decimal places. Table 5.3 shows several numbers formatted with the Punctuated format. Notice that the Punctuated format *does not* display negative numbers in parentheses, but retains the standard minus sign (−).

Value	Decimal Places	Display
12345	2	12,345.00
12345.67	0	12,346
12345.9889	3	12,345.989
1234567890	2	1,234,567,890.00
− 12345.67	2	− 12,345.67

Table 5.3

As with the Currency format, your numbers will look a bit different if you have specified an international Punctuated format. (International Punctuated formats are explained in Chapter 30, Configuring Symphony.) In that event, the commas and decimals will be reversed. For example, the formatted number

123,456,789.123

would be

123.456.789,123

General

The General option of the Format command is used to assign the General format to a particular cell or range. As explained above, the General format displays the contents of cells "as is," except that very large and very small numbers are displayed as exponents.

Since the General format is the default worksheet format, you may wonder when the Format General command would be used. Remember, though, that you can change the default format for any window. You might, for example, change the default format in a given worksheet to Currency with two decimal places. This would cause every cell in that window that had not been given a special format to be displayed in the Currency format. If there were no Format General command, there would be no way to force a few of the cells in this window to assume the General format.

% (Percentage)

Since many financial and statistical applications for Symphony require the use of percentages, Symphony includes a special format, %, that causes numbers to be displayed with a trailing percentage sign. The user is required to specify the number of decimal places that should be displayed.

The only tricky aspect of the % format is that it appears to multiply the value being formatted by 100 before displaying it. For example, the number .25 would be displayed as 25% and the number 25 would be displayed as 2500% using the % format. In fact, the percentage format simply substitutes the percentage sign (%) for the decimal point in numbers. Since .25 and 25% are two different ways of expressing exactly the same value, you wouldn't think this format would lead to confusion. Neverthless, I still find myself occasionally entering 25 instead of .25 for a percentage. Be sure to remember that the percentage format always creates a display equivalent to the actual contents of the cell, so percentages must be entered as decimals.

Fixed

The Fixed format is one of the most frequently used of the Symphony formats. Fixed allows you to specify the number of decimal places Symphony should display. Otherwise, the format is identical to the General format.

Table 5.4 shows several numbers and their appearance with several different numbers of decimal places.

Number	Decimal Places	Appearance
1.23456	0	1
1.23456	1	1.2
1.23456	2	1.23
1.23456	4	1.2345
1.23456	6	1.234560

Table 5.4

The Fixed format is frequently used to force values, for which decimal values would not make sense, to be displayed as integers. For example, suppose you were calculating the average number of employees at three companies in the same industry. Assume that the average is 105.25. Since fractional people are hard to come by, you might assign the Fixed format with zero decimal places to the cell containing this value. Using the Fixed 0 format, 105.25 is displayed as 105.

Hidden

The Hidden format can be used to hide the contents of a cell or range. The effect of this format depends on the current status of the Services Settings Security command, which allows you to lock and unlock the worksheet. (This command is covered in Chapter 8, Range Commands.)

A cell formatted with Hidden will appear to be blank. However, when the worksheet is unlocked and the cell pointer is positioned on that cell, the contents of the cell appear in the control panel. For example, in the worksheet shown in Figure 5.8, cell A4 contains the formula

> A4: @SUM(A1 . . A3)

and cell A5 contains the formula

> A5: +A4

```
  ------A----------B----------C----------D--------
1         100                                       |
2         200                                       |
3         300                                       |
4         600                                       |
5         600                                       |
6                                                   |
  ================================================MAIN=
```

Figure 5.8

If you assign the Hidden format to cell A4 with the {**Menu**} **F**ormat **O**ther **H**idden command, the worksheet will look like Figure 5.9.

```
  ------A----------B----------C----------D--------
1         100                                       |
2         200                                       |
3         300                                       |
4                                                   |
5         600                                       |
6                                                   |
  ================================================MAIN=
```

Figure 5.9

Cell A4 seems to be blank. Remember, though, that the cell only *appears* to be blank. The cell still contains the formula that computes the sum of cells A1 to A3. The formula in this cell will continue to be affected by any changes to other cells in the worksheet. For example, if we change the entry in cell A1 from 100 to 1000 and recalculate, the worksheet will look like Figure 5.10. Notice that the value in cell A5, which refers to cell A4, has changed to 1500, proving that the value in cell A4 has also changed.

```
    -----A---------B---------C---------D---------
 1      1000                                     |
 2       200                                     |
 3       300                                     |
 4                                               |
 5      1500                                     |
 6                                               |
    =====================================MAIN=
```

Figure 5.10

Since the worksheet is unlocked, if we move the cell pointer to cell A4, the control panel displays the contents of that cell, as shown in Figure 5.11.

```
 A4:  (H)  @SUM(A1..A3)

    -----A---------B---------C---------D---------
 1      1000                                     |
 2       200                                     |
 3       300                                     |
 4   [          ]                                |
 5      1500                                     |
 6                                               |
    =====================================MAIN=
```

Figure 5.11

If, on the other hand, the worksheet is locked, the control panel will be blank when the cell pointer is positioned over the hidden cell. Together, the Hidden format and the {**Services**} Setting Security Locked command combine to completely hide your proprietary information.

The Hidden format can be used to hide proprietary assumptions, data, or formulas that must be entered in a worksheet other people will see. In an extreme case you could use the Hidden format to hide an entire lookup table or data base. You'll probably find some clever uses for the Hidden format that Lotus never anticipated.

Literal

The Literal format is used to display the actual contents of a cell containing a formula or function, instead of the value that results from that formula or function. For instance, in the worksheet in Figure 5.12, cell A4 is formatted with Literal.

```
  -----A---------B---------C---------D---------
1      1000                                    |
2       200                                    |
3       300                                    |
4 @SUM(A1..                                    |
5      1500                                    |
6                                              |
  =====================================MAIN=
```

Figure 5.12

Notice that cell A4 now displays the function we entered in the cell, and not the result of that function, the value 1500. Even though cell A4 is displayed as a label, the function is still computed by Symphony. The proof of this is the value in cell A5, 1500, which is equal to the value of the function in cell A4. Remember—formats affect *only* the appearance of a cell, not the contents of that cell.

Because the function in the example is longer than the column is wide, Symphony truncates the function. The Literal command is the only exception to the rule that the contents of a cell which are formatted too wide to be displayed in the column width provided are displayed as a series of asterisks.

The Literal format is often used to avoid confusion in the worksheet. We'll see an example of this when we look at the Range commands in Chapter 8.

The Literal format can also be used when debugging a worksheet. If you believe that there is a formula error somewhere in the worksheet, you can format all or a part of the sheet with Literal and examine each formula.

One problem with this technique is that the Literal format truncates all formulas too wide to be displayed in the provided column's width. Since all but the simplest formulas are wider than Symphony's standard column width (nine characters), you'll probably need to use the Width command to widen some columns before using the Literal format to debug the worksheet.

Bar-Graph

Most Symphony users are familiar with the program's Graph command and Graph windows. Many users are not aware, however, that Symphony offers another type of graph—the Bar-Graph format. Symphony's Bar-Graph format is a carry-over from 1-2-3 (where it was called the + / − format), and before that from the VisiCalc program, where it was the only type of graphics offered. Although graphs created by the Bar-Graph format are not as sophisticated as Symphony's other graphs, they can be very useful for certain purposes.

The Bar-Graph format displays positive numbers as a series of + symbols and negative numbers as a string of − symbols. Cells with the value 0 are displayed as a single period. For example, if we formatted cells A1 to A5 in the worksheet in Figure 5.13 with the Bar-Graph format, the resulting spreadsheet would look like Figure 5.14.

```
-----A---------B---------C---------D----------
1          3                                  |
2         -2                                  |
3          0                                  |
4        -11                                  |
5          6                                  |
6                                             |
7                                             |
==========================================MAIN=
```

Figure 5.13

```
-----A---------B---------C---------D---------
1 +++                                        |
2 --                                         |
3 .                                          |
4 *********                                  |
5 ++++++                                      |
6                                            |
7                                            |
=========================================MAIN=
```

Figure 5.14

There are a couple of important limitations to this format. First, as with the other Symphony formats, if the column containing an entry is too narrow to display that entry in the chosen format, the cell displays a series of asterisks. Cell A4 in Figure 5.14 is an example of this problem. This is especially limiting with the Bar-Graph format, because the required width of the column increases directly with the magnitude of the value in the cell. For example, a column width of 11 is required to display a cell with the value 11 in Bar-Graph format. A column width of 99 is required to display the value 99 in Bar-Graph form.

Obviously, it is impractical to display numbers greater than about 50 in Bar-Graph format. The column widths required to display such numbers are impractical. One way to overcome this problem is to divide every value you want to format this way by some constant before formatting. For example, in Figure 5.15, cells B1 to B5 are all defined by dividing the equivalent value in column A by 100. For example, cell B2 contains the formula

B2: +A2/100

The cells in column B are also formatted with Bar-Graph. By dividing by 100 we have reduced the numbers enough to be practically displayed in Bar-Graph format while preserving the relative magnitude of the numbers.

```
-----A---------B---------C---------D---------
1        300 +++                               |
2        700 ++++++                            |
3        200 ++                                |
4        100 +                                 |
5        220 ++                                |
6                                              |
7                                              |
=====================================MAIN=
```

Figure 5.15

Another limitation of the Bar-Graph format is that it cannot accurately display fractional numbers. All numbers are truncated to integers before being displayed in Bar-Graph format.

Here's a practical example of the Bar-Graph format. Figure 5.16 shows a very simple worksheet that plots several of the tasks that are involved in writing a book.

```
--------A-----------B-------C-------D----E----F----G----H----I----J----
1                                 Week of:                              |
2 Task          Start    End      6/11 6/18 6/25  7/1  7/8 7/15 7/22    |
3 Outline        6/11    6/11     ++++++                                |
4 Write          6/18    6/25          ++++++++++                       |
5 Edit           7/1     7/15                    +++++++++++++++        |
6 Print          7/22    7/22                                   +++++++|
7                                                                       |
=============================================================MAIN=
```

Figure 5.16

The cells in the range D3 . . J6 contain formulas that compare the Start and End dates in columns B and C with the "Week of" numbers in row 2. For example, cell D3 contains the formula

D3: (B) @IF(B3 < = D2#AND#C3 > = D2,6,"")

This function says: If the value in cell B3 is less than or equal to the value in cell D2, *and* the value in cell C3 is greater than or equal to the value in cell D2, enter the value 6 in cell D3; otherwise, put a space in cell D3.

Since cells D3 to J6 are formatted with Bar-Graph, those cells for which the @IF function is true will appear as a string of six plus signs. Those cells for which @IF is false will remain blank. The result is a GANTT chart that shows the duration of each task and the order of the tasks in the job. (By the way, this is an excellent example of a complex conditional function.)

Scientific

The Scientific format is used to display large numbers in exponential, or scientific, notation. When a cell is assigned the Scientific format, the value in that cell is displayed as a decimal number between 1 and 10 with an exponent. For example, the number 123456789 would look like

1.23456789E + 8

in the Scientific format. Like many other Symphony formats, Scientific requires the user to specify the number of decimal places to be displayed. The number can be between 0 and 15. In this example, we assumed that 8 decimals had been requested. (A column 15 characters wide would be required to display this number.)

This number may be confusing, but it really makes quite a bit of sense if you understand the notation E+ 8. E+ 8 should be read "10 to the 8th power." 10 to the 8th equals

$$10 \times 10 \times 10 \times 10 \times 10 \times 10 \times 10 \times 10$$

or 100000000. Multiplying this number by 1.2345678 equals 12345678, our original number.

Very small numbers can also be expressed in exponential notation. For example, the number .000000001 could be expressed as 1.0E – 10. In this example, E – 10 should be read as "10 to the – 10th power." Since a negative exponent is used to signal division, 10 to the – 10th equals

$$10/10/10/10/10/10/10/10/10/10$$

or .0000000001. Table 5.5 shows several numbers and the form in which they would be displayed using the Scientific format. This format is most often used by scientists, engineers, and other Symphony users who commonly deal with very large numbers.

Number	Decimal Places	Display
12345	0	1E+ 4
12345	1	1.2E+ 4
12345	3	1.235E+ 4
123456789	3	1.235E+ 8
.000001234	2	1.23E – 7

Table 5.5

Time and Date

Two of Symphony's formats, Time and Date, are used specifically to format cells containing date or time functions. We will look at these functions in Chapter 6.

Reset

The Reset option on the Format menu cancels the special format that you have assigned to a range. The cells in the affected range will revert to the default format for the window.

Reset is very useful for quickly reversing any formats you have created. However, you don't need to use Reset to change the format of a cell. You can always simply assign a new format to any cell or range in the worksheet. For example, if cell A1 in a worksheet had been assigned the Currency format with two decimal places, and you wanted to change the format of this cell to Punctuated with zero decimal places, you would simply move the cell pointer to cell A1 and issue the command {**Menu**} Format **P**unctuated **0** [**Enter**]. The Currency format would be changed to the Punctuated format automatically. There is no need to use the Reset option to make this kind of change.

CHANGING THE DEFAULT FORMAT

Remember that every SHEET window has a default format that is assigned to any cell not given a special format. The default format is General. However, there may be times when you'll want to specify a different default format for one of your windows. Suppose, for example, that one SHEET window was going to contain nothing but currency entries. If you changed the default format for this window to Currency with two decimal places, you could save yourself a lot of wasted effort in formatting the cells individually.

The command to change the default format is {**Menu**} **S**ettings **F**ormat. When you issue this command, the following menu appears:

Currency Punctuated Fixed % General Date Time Scientific Other

As you can see, this menu is identical to Symphony's {Menu} Format command. In fact, the Settings Format command offers exactly the same options as the Format command, except that the Settings Format command affects the entire window.

Remember that a special format always overrides the window default format. This is true even if you change the default format. For example, if you used the {**Menu**} **S**ettings **F**ormat command to change the default format in a window to Currency with **2** decimal places, and then assigned the General format to cell A1, cell A1 would be displayed in the General format.

As you can see, Symphony's ability to format cells in a number of different ways is one of the program's most useful features. You should take the time to become familiar with the formats, and then get in the habit of using them to give your worksheets the best possible appearance.

CHAPTER SIX
DATE AND TIME FUNCTIONS

Before Lotus 1-2-3, most spreadsheets did not offer a simple way to enter dates into the worksheet. Dates either had to be entered as labels, which could not be used in mathematical functions, or as awkward decimal numbers, which were almost as hard to use.

1-2-3 was the first important spreadsheet to offer date functions, and this was a major step forward. However, many users felt that 1-2-3's date functions didn't go far enough—for one thing, 1-2-3 didn't include time functions.

Symphony has most of the same date functions that were introduced in 1-2-3. In addition, Symphony offers time functions that allow you to enter time information in the worksheet. Symphony also offers a couple of new string-to-value functions that can convert a label into a date or time value.

TIME AND DATE BASICS

The basic unit of time in Symphony is a day. All dates are represented in Symphony as an integer representing the number of days that have elapsed since the base date. Thus January 1, 1900 is stored as the number 1. December 31, 1984 is represented by the number 31047, the number of days between that date and December 31, 1899.

Symphony represents hours, minutes, and seconds as fractional days. Time values can exist independently of dates, or they can be a part of a date. For example, the fraction .23418 represents the time 5:37:13 AM, while the number 30125.1567 represents the date/time combination 3:45:39 AM June 23, 1982.

FUNCTIONS AND FORMATS

You may be thinking that the numbers Symphony uses to store dates and times don't look much like dates or times and are nearly impossible to understand. For this reason, Symphony includes two sets of tools for working with dates and times—a set of functions that allow you to enter dates and times in a comprehensible format, and a set of formats that display the dates in a variety of useful forms. This means that entering dates and times in the Symphony worksheet is a two-step process. The first step involves the use of a function; the second step requires you to format the cell or cells containing the function. It's important not to get confused about these two steps.

The first step is to enter a time or date function into a cell. For example, suppose you wanted to enter the date May 15, 1984 in cell A1 in a worksheet. You would simply position the pointer on cell A1 and type the function

   @DATE(84,5,15)

After this function is entered, cell A1 displays the number 30817. This represents the number of days between the date you entered—May 15, 1984—and Symphony's base date—December 31, 1899.

One thing to watch for is confusing the order of the terms in the @DATE function. Symphony requires you to enter the dates in YY-MM-DD format, but it displays full dates in the DD-MMM-YY or MM-DD-YY form. Just remember that you must enter the terms in the @DATE function in order of descending magnitude. Years, the largest unit, are entered first, followed by the month term and finally the day term.

The second step is to format cell A1 to display the date in a comprehensible way. Symphony offers five different formats for dates. To format a date cell, type **{Menu}** **F**ormat **D**ate from within a spreadsheet window. Next, select the date format you wish from the date-format menu:

   1 (DD-MMM-YY) 2 (DD-MMM) 3 (MMM-YY) 4 (Full Intn'l) 5 (Partial Intn'l)

The following list shows the result of formatting our date with each of Symphony's date formats:

1 (DD-MMM-YY)	15-May-84
2 (DD-MMM)	15-May
3 (MMM-YY)	May-84
4 (Full Intn'l) (MM/DD/YY)	05/15/84
5 (Partial Intn'l)(MM/YY)	05/84

There is one problem with date format 1. A date formatted in this way cannot be displayed in Symphony's standard-width column. To display a date formatted in this way, you must use Symphony's {Menu} Width Set command to widen the column containing the date to 10 characters.

Fortunately, date format 4, the full international format, delivers the same amount of information as date format 1, and it will fit in a standard-width column. The addition of this format is one of Symphony's major improvements over 1-2-3.

CREATING A SERIES OF DATES

There are many times when you'll want to enter a series of evenly spaced dates in a worksheet at one time. For example, when you create a cash projection, you may want to create a set of headers, with one header for each month in the projection. At other times you may want to enter a series of dates that must be evenly spaced to the day.

To enter a series of monthly dates, enter the first date using the @DATE function. Suppose you entered the function

   B2: @DATE(84,1,1)

in cell B2 of the worksheet in Figure 6.1. Cell B2 will now have the value 30682, Symphony's representation of the date January 1, 1984. Now move the cursor one cell to the right and enter the formula

   C2: +B2+31

Adding 31 days to the date January 1, 1984 results in the value 30713. If a similar formula,

   D2: +C2+31

is entered in cell D2, that cell will contain the number 30744, Symphony's representation for the date March 3, 1984. You can use the Copy command to project this formula across as many cells in row 2 as you wish. The resulting worksheet will look like Figure 6.1.

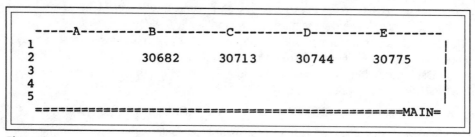

Figure 6.1

After you enter the number in cells B2, C2, D2, and so on, you can use the {**Menu**} **F**ormat **D**ate command to assign date format 3 (MMM-YY) to these cells. Figure 6.2 shows the worksheet after these cells have been formatted.

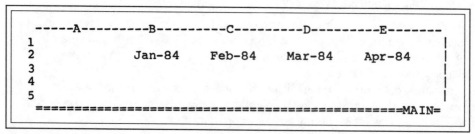

Figure 6.2

Since the formula adds 31 to each date, eventually you'll accumulate enough extra days to skip a month. However, this will occur only after about 50 months, which is more than most projections require. If you do have a problem, you might want to change the formula to use a fractional number, such as 30.7, instead of 31.

Now suppose you take out a mortgage on a new property that requires you to make monthly payments on the seventh of each month. You want to build a schedule that shows the date of each payment. Obviously, the method shown above, which uses 31 or 30.7 as the monthly skip factor, is not precise enough for this requirement. You need a method of incrementing dates that is accurate to the day, regardless of the month or year. Assuming cell B2 contains your starting date, enter this formula:

B3: +B2 + @CHOOSE(@MONTH(B2) − 1,31,@IF(@MOD(@YEAR(B2),4) = 0
#AND#@YEAR(B2) < >100,29,28),31,30,31,30,31,30,31,30,31)

This formula uses the @MONTH function to determine the month term of the previous date (the one in cell B2). Depending on this value, the formula selects the proper number of days to properly increment the date. This formula can be copied down column B into as many cells as you wish, and it will always deliver the correct dates.

KEEPING TIME IN SYMPHONY

Entering times is also a simple two-step process. The basic function used to enter times is @TIME(HH,MM,SS), where HH is hours, MM is minutes, and SS is seconds. For example, the function

@TIME(12,32,00)

represents the time 12:32:00 PM.

The hours portion of the @TIME function can be a bit tricky. Hours are entered using the military 24-hour clock convention. Thus 1 AM is 01 hours, 2 PM is 14 hours, and 11 PM is 23 hours. Especially tricky are times between 12 midnight and 1 AM. For example, the time 12:32:00 AM would be entered as

@TIME(00,32,00)

Symphony offers four formats for times. To format a date cell, issue the Format command by typing {**Menu**} **F**ormat and then selecting the **T**ime option. The following list shows the time function

@TIME(14,40,15)

as it would appear under each format.

1 (HH:MM:NN AM/PM)	2:40:15 PM
2 (HH:MM AM/PM)	2:40 PM
3 (Full Intn'l) HH:MM:SS	14:40:15
4 (Partial Intn'l) HH:MM	14:40

Time format 1 has the same limitation as date format 1—it won't fit in a standard-width column. Once again, however, the full international format can be used to deliver the same information in a standard-width column. Remember, though, that time format 3 uses the 24-hour military convention for displaying dates. The time 2:40:15 PM would thus be displayed as 14:40:15. If you're not familiar with this convention, it can be a little confusing.

One of the disadvantages of Symphony's time functions is that while the clock is based on a sixty-minute hour and a sixty-second minute, Symphony's functions depend on base-ten fractional representations for minutes and seconds. Thus, thirty minutes is .020833 days. Ten minutes is .006944 days. This can be very confusing. Table 6.1 should help, however. It shows the decimal equivalents for most of the minutes and seconds.

	Hours	Minutes	Seconds
1	0.04167	0.00069	0.00001
2	0.08333	0.00139	0.00002
3	0.12500	0.00208	0.00003
4	0.16667	0.00278	0.00005
5	0.20833	0.00347	0.00006
6	0.25000	0.00417	0.00007
7	0.29167	0.00486	0.00008
8	0.33333	0.00556	0.00009
9	0.37500	0.00625	0.00010
10	0.41667	0.00694	0.00012
11	0.45833	0.00764	0.00013
12	0.50000	0.00833	0.00014
13	0.54167	0.00903	0.00015
14	0.58333	0.00972	0.00016
15	0.62500	0.01042	0.00017
16	0.66667	0.01111	0.00019
17	0.70833	0.01181	0.00020
18	0.75000	0.01250	0.00021
19	0.79167	0.01319	0.00022
20	0.83333	0.01389	0.00023
21	0.87500	0.01458	0.00024
22	0.91667	0.01528	0.00025
23	0.95833	0.01597	0.00027
24	1.00000	0.01667	0.00028
25		0.01736	0.00029
30		0.02083	0.00035
35		0.02431	0.00041
40		0.02778	0.00046
45		0.03125	0.00052
50		0.03472	0.00058
55		0.03819	0.00064
60		0.04167	0.00069

Table 6.1

It is important to remember that Symphony's basic unit of time is a day. It is easy to become confused about this when working with Symphony's @TIME function. For example, you might think that the function

A2: @TIME(12,12,00) + 1

is equivalent to the function

A2: @TIME(13,12,00)

or

A2: @TIME(12,12,01)

but adding 1 to the function increments it by a *day*, not an hour or a second.

@NOW

Symphony includes a special function, @NOW, which allows you to enter the current DOS system date into the worksheet. (1-2-3 users take note: @NOW replaces the familiar @TODAY function.) @NOW is one of the few functions that does not have an argument. To enter the current date into the worksheet, simply move the cursor to the desired cell and enter the function @NOW.

The @NOW function depends on DOS for its value. DOS has the ability to remember the current date and time. You must update the current date and time each time you boot DOS by using the DOS commands DATE and TIME. Fortunately, Lotus has made it easy to remember to enter the correct date and time by including the DATE and TIME commands in an AUTOEXEC file on every Symphony disk. The AUTOEXEC file runs every time you boot DOS and automatically offers the opportunity to enter the date and time.

Each time a worksheet containing the @NOW function is loaded into memory, the function looks to DOS for the current date. From that point on, @NOW is updated every time the worksheet is recalculated. Remember that if you do not specify a date and time when you boot DOS, the date will default to January 1, 1980 and the time to 12:00:01 AM, which means that the @NOW function will not return the current date and time. If you are in the habit of not entering the system date and time when you boot DOS, and you want to use the @NOW function, you might consider buying a battery-powered clock for your computer. The clock makes sure that DOS always has the correct date and time.

After the function has been entered, you probably will want to format the cell in one of the date or time formats. Unfortunately, Symphony gives you the choice of formatting a cell containing @NOW using either a time format or a date format, but offers no hybrid time/date format. That is, you could display a cell containing an @NOW function to look like 15-May-84 or 12:32:05 PM, but there is no way to format a cell containing @NOW to look like

15-May-84 12:32:05 PM

SECONDARY DATE FUNCTIONS

In addition to the main time and date functions, @DATE, @TIME, and @NOW, Symphony offers a secondary set of functions that allow you to extract any term from a time or date. The secondary date functions are

@YEAR(cell reference or number)
@MONTH(cell reference or number)
@DAY(cell reference or number)

These functions allow you to "break down" a date in integer form into its components. For example, suppose you had entered the function

@DATE(84,12,1)

into cell A1 in a worksheet. The function

@YEAR(A1)

would return 84, the year portion of the date. The secondary date function

@MONTH(A1)

would return 12, the month portion of the date in cell A1. Finally, the function

@DAY(A1)

would return the value 1, the day portion of the date.

Obviously, you can discover the day, month, and year terms of the function @DATE(84,12,1) simply by inspection. As you might expect, the secondary date functions are used more often to extract month and day information from the results of date arithmetic. For example, suppose cell A1 contained the formula

A1: @DATE(84,12,1) + (123 + (100/12))

Can you tell by looking at this formula the month value of the resulting date? Probably not. But the function

A2: @MONTH(A1)

will give you the answer—4—instantly. One of the limitations of the @DAY and @MONTH functions is that they return the number, not the name, of the month term of a date. The number 4, which stands for the month of April, is not as easy to understand as the name of the month.

As you might expect, Symphony offers a way around this problem. First you create a lookup table like that in Figure 6.3.

Now change the function in cell A2 to

A2: @VLOOKUP(@MONTH(A1),AA1 . . AB12,1)

Now the function will return the label April instead of the number 4.

SECONDARY TIME FUNCTIONS

In addition to Symphony's secondary date functions, the program also offers secondary time functions. These functions are

@HOUR(cell reference or number)
@MIN(cell reference or number)
@SEC(cell reference or number)

```
     -----AA---------AB---------AC-----
 1          1  January            |
 2          2  February           |
 3          3  March              |
 4          4  April              |
 5          5  May                |
 6          6  June               |
 7          7  July               |
 8          8  August             |
 9          9  September          |
10         10  October            |
11         11  November           |
12         12  December           |
     ============================MAIN=
```

Figure 6.3

Like the secondary date functions, these functions allow you to extract one or more of the components of a time. For example, if cell A1 contained the formula

>   A1: @TIME(12,15,36)

the function

>   A2: @SEC(A1)

would return the value 36. As before, it is unlikely that you would want to use the secondary date functions just to extract the hours, minutes, or seconds portion of a simple @TIME function. These functions are more useful when they refer to a complicated time formula.

@DATEVALUE AND @TIMEVALUE

Symphony offers two new functions—@DATEVALUE and @TIMEVALUE—that can be used to translate a text string in the form of a date or a time into a date or time value. For example, suppose you had the string

>   A1: '15-Dec-84

in cell A1. The function

>   A2: @DATEVALUE(A1)

would return the value 31031, which is Symphony's representation of the date December 15, 1984. The function would also return 31031 if cell A1 contained the label

>   A1: '12/15/84

Similarly, if cell A1 contained the label

>   A1: '12:15:17 AM

the function

>   A2: @TIMEVALUE(A1)

would return the value .010613, Symphony's representation of 12:15:17 AM.

These functions are most frequently used to translate dates and times that have been imported into Symphony from other programs, particularly dBASE II. They make it possible to import these dates as labels and then translate them into values that can be used by Symphony for date arithmetic.

Symphony's Date and Time functions are among the program's most useful features. You'll probably find yourself using the @DATE function in many of your worksheets, and you'll likely find some special uses for @TIME. The most important thing to remember is that these functions are available and should be used whenever you want to enter a date or time into the worksheet.

CHAPTER SEVEN

CUT-AND-PASTE COMMANDS

Among the most useful Symphony commands are Erase, Insert, Delete, Move, Copy, and Width. These commands are collectively called *cut-and-paste* commands, because they are Symphony's equivalent to the scissors and glue required to make changes to a paper spreadsheet. The cut-and-paste commands are all found on the main SHEET environment menu, which is accessed by pressing {**Menu**} from within a SHEET window. The SHEET menu looks like this:

Copy Move Erase Insert Delete Width Format Range Graph Query Settings

Symphony's cut-and-paste commands make it easy to change the layout of your worksheet by adding or deleting rows or columns; erasing portions of the worksheet; copying or moving the contents of one range into another range; or changing the width of one or more columns in the worksheet.

ERASE

The simplest of Symphony's cut-and-paste commands is Erase. As the name suggests, Erase is used to erase portions of the worksheet. In fact, using this command is very much like using a pencil eraser on a paper spreadsheet.

Those Symphony users who have upgraded from 1-2-3 will recognize that Symphony's Erase command is very similar to 1-2-3's /Range Erase command.

Let's examine this command at work. Suppose you had built the simple spreadsheet in Figure 7.1, and that the cell pointer is located in cell A1. Issue the {**Menu**} Erase command. Symphony displays the prompt

Range to erase: A1 . . A1

which includes a "guess" at the correct range to be erased. The guess is simply the address of the cell that contains the cell pointer. If the cell pointer had been on cell Z100, the prompt would have looked like this:

Range to erase: Z100 . . Z100

As you'll see over and over again throughout the book, Symphony nearly always offers a guess at the correct range for commands.

```
    -----A---------B---------C---------D--------
  1       123       987       111                |
  2       234       876       222                |
  3       345       765       333                |
  4       456       654       444                |
  5       567       543       555                |
  6       678       432       666                |
  7       789       321       777                |
    ===================================MAIN=
```

Figure 7.1

There are three ways to specify the range to erase in response to Symphony's prompt. First, if the range is to be a single cell and if the cell pointer is on that cell, you can indicate the Erase range simply by pressing **[Enter]**. This is possible because Symphony automatically supplies the cell address of the cell pointer as a part of the prompt.

If you used this method and pressed **[Enter]** with the cell pointer on cell A1, the worksheet would look like Figure 7.2. Notice that cell A1, which used to contain the number 123, is now empty.

```
    -----A---------B---------C---------D--------
  1                 987       111                |
  2       234       876       222                |
  3       345       765       333                |
  4       456       654       444                |
  5       567       543       555                |
  6       678       432       666                |
  7       789       321       777                |
    ===================================MAIN=
```

Figure 7.2

It is important to understand that the Erase command completely eliminates the contents of the cells being erased. Unless the spreadsheet was saved to disk before the Erase command was issued, there is no way to recover the contents of erased cells other than retyping them from the keyboard.

In this example, the contents of cell A1 have been completely erased. If you wanted to restore the worksheet to its original condition, you could move the cell pointer to cell A1 and type the number 123—no great task. But what if cell A1 contained a complex formula? Or what if you had erased 100 cells instead of 1? The moral is that you should always be careful when using the Erase command.

The Erase command erases only the *contents* of a cell or range. If a special format has been assigned to the range, that format will remain even after the contents of the range are erased. For example, suppose cell A1 in Figure 7.1 had been assigned the Fixed format with zero decimal places. Suppose further that after erasing this cell you decided to enter the number 1234.123 in cell A1. The worksheet would now look like Figure 7.3.

```
-----A---------B---------C---------D--------
1        1234         987       111                   |
2         234         876       222                   |
3         345         765       333                   |
4         456         654       444                   |
5         567         543       555                   |
6         678         432       666                   |
7         789         321       777                   |
================================================MAIN=
```

Figure 7.3

Other Ways to Specify the Erase Range

In the example above we assumed that the cell pointer was on the cell we wanted to erase. If it isn't, or if the range you wish to erase is larger than one cell, you can type the coordinates of the Erase range in response to the prompt.

For example, if the cell pointer is in cell Z100 when you issue the {**Menu**} Erase command, the prompt looks like this:

Range to erase: Z100 . . Z100

To erase cell A1, just type **A1**. Notice that as soon as you begin typing the correct range, Symphony's "guess" range disappears from the control panel and the prompt changes to

Range to erase: A

If you finish typing the cell address A1 and press **[Enter]**, Symphony erases cell A1, and the worksheet looks like the one in Figure 7.2. Similarly, if you want to erase the range A1 . . C1, you can type these coordinates in response to the prompt.

After you enter the correct range and press **[Enter]**, the worksheet looks like the one in Figure 7.4. Notice that the cell pointer is still in cell A5.

If the range being erased has a name, you can use that name instead of the cell coordinates to specify the Erase range. For example, if cell A1 is named FIRST, typing **FIRST** in

```
     -----A---------B---------C---------D--------
 1                                                |
 2        234        876        222               |
 3        345        765        333               |
 4        456        654        444               |
 5        567        543       [555]              |
 6        678        432        666               |
 7        789        321        777               |
     ======================================MAIN=
```

Figure 7.4

response to Symphony's Erase prompt has exactly the same effect as typing A1. Range names will be covered in more detail in Chapter 8, which discusses Symphony's Range commands.

The POINT Mode

The third method of specifying the range in a command is by *pointing*. Pointing is the easiest way to specify ranges larger than one cell. The POINT mode allows you to use the cell-pointer movement keys to literally point to the cells that define the range you want to erase (or move or copy, as you'll learn in a few pages).

For example, assume that you want to erase the range A1 . . C1 in Figure 7.1. As before, you move the cell pointer to cell A1 and issue the {**Menu**} Erase command. The prompt now looks like this:

Range to erase: A1 . . A1

Now press the → key. Notice that the cell pointer expands to cover both cells A1 and B1, that the mode indicator in the upper-right corner of the screen changes to POINT, and that the prompt changes to

Range to erase: A1 . . B1

Press → again. As you might expect, the cell pointer now covers cells A1, B1, and C1, and the prompt is now

Range to erase: A1 . . C1

Now all you need to do to erase the range is press [**Enter**]. After the command is completed, the worksheet looks like the one in Figure 7.4, except that the cell pointer is in cell A1.

Pointing from a Remote Location

Suppose the cell pointer is in cell A3 when you issue the {**Menu**} Erase command. The prompt looks like this:

Range to erase: A3 . . A3

If you press the → key now, the prompt changes to

> Range to erase: A3 . . B3

Notice that the first part of the range definition, A3, does not change when you press the → key. In other words, this part of the range definition is *anchored,* and, as things stand, cannot be changed.

Fortunately, Symphony offers a way to free this anchored cell reference. Assume that you have issued the {**Menu**} Erase command and that the prompt looks like this:

> Range to erase: A3 . . A3

Press [**Esc**]. Pressing this key "unanchors" the range guess provided by Symphony and changes the prompt to

> Range to erase: A3

Now press the ↑ key. The cell pointer moves to cell A2, and the prompt changes to

> Range to erase: A2

Now press ↑ again. The cell pointer moves to cell A1, and the prompt changes to

> Range to erase: A1

Now press the period key. This "reanchors" the first half of the range and changes the prompt to

> Range to erase: A1 . . A1

Notice that although you pressed the period key only once, the prompt includes two periods. Symphony always displays two periods between the two cells referenced in a range definition, but you need type only one period. Symphony automatically provides the second one.

Finally, press → twice. The cell pointer expands to cover cells A1, A2, and A3, and the prompt changes to

> Range to erase: A1 . . A3

After the command has run, the worksheet looks just like the one in Figure 7.4, except that the cell pointer is now positioned in cell A3. Remember that the cell pointer was in cell A3 when you first issued the Erase command. When you use the POINT mode in a command, the cell pointer always returns to the cell it was in when the command was issued.

Pointing Comments

Given the simple range in our example, it would have been easier to define the erase range by typing A1 . . A3. But pointing to the range has several important advantages over typing the range. First, pointing is very intuitive. Defining a range is as simple as pointing with the cell pointer to its limits. In a sense the Symphony POINT mode is an alternative to the mouse and other new pointing devices that are now in vogue.

Second, pointing does not require that you know the limits of the range on which you wish to operate. For example, suppose you want to erase a range that extends across row 5 from column A to the last column in the active worksheet, but you don't know exactly which column that is. By pointing, you can define the range while you are hunting for the proper column.

Third, in many cases pointing is faster than typing—especially for slow typists. This is particularly true if you take advantage of Symphony's special cell-pointer movement keys, like [End], to speed the cell pointer around the worksheet.

Using [End] in the POINT Mode

Go back to the example in Figure 7.1. The cell pointer is in cell A1, and you've issued the {**Menu**} Erase command, so the prompt looks like this:

Range to erase: A1 .. A1

We want to erase the range A1 .. A3. In an earlier example, we pressed → twice to point out the range A1 .. A3. But there is a faster way. If you press [**End**] and → simultaneously, the cell pointer jumps directly to cell A3, and the prompt changes to

Range to erase: A1 .. A3

The [End] key's importance increases as your ranges get larger and larger. For example, if you want to point to the Erase range A1 .. Z1, using [End] saves 25 key strokes.

Using the Period in the POINT Mode

Figure 7.5 shows a window that displays only 4 rows and 3 columns of a spreadsheet. Suppose you want to erase the range A1 .. E6 in this worksheet.

```
   -----A---------B---------C-----
1          123       987       111 |
2          234       876       222 |
3          345       765       333 |
4          456       654       444 |
   =========================Main=
```

Figure 7.5

By now, the steps in this process should be familiar. First, move the cell pointer to cell A1 and issue the {**Menu**} Erase command. Next, point to the range you wish to erase by pressing [**End**] → and then [**End**] ↓. The window now looks like the one in Figure 7.6.

The window has shifted to show the lower-right corner of the indicated range, which is helpful. But because the window is so small, we can't see the upper-left part of the range. In fact, it isn't possible to see the entire range in this window at one time. In some situations this might make it difficult to know exactly what has been included in the range. Although our example uses a small window, the same problem can occur with full-screen windows.

There is a way around this problem, however. Starting with the window shown in Figure 7.6, press the period key. The worksheet should now look like the one in Figure 7.7.

```
     -----C----------D----------E-----
  3         333        777   CCC          |
  4         444        666   DDD          |
  5         555        555   EEE          |
  6         666        444   FFF          |
     ========================MAIN=
```

Figure 7.6

```
     -----A----------B----------C-----
  3         345        765        333 |
  4         456        654        444 |
  5         567        543        555 |
  6         678        432        666 |
     ==========================MAIN=
```

Figure 7.7

The window has shifted to bring the lower-left corner of the range into view. The prompt in the control panel has also changed to

   Range to erase: E1 . . A6

Now press the period key again. The worksheet should look like Figure 7.5 again, and the prompt should read

   Range to erase: E6 . . A1

If you press the period key once more, the worksheet will look like Figure 7.8 and the prompt will be

   Range to erase: A6 . . E1

Suppose we wanted to change the range to A2 . . E6. With the sheet in the position shown in Figure 7.8, just press ↓. The cell pointer shrinks to exclude row 1 and the prompt changes to

   Range to erase: E2 . . A6

This technique can be very valuable when you are working with ranges that exceed the size of the window. By using the period key, you can review the corners of any range and, if you wish, change the dimensions of the range. You'll probably find the period key particularly useful in defining Print Source Ranges, which are almost always larger than the current window.

Summing Up the POINT Mode

Just because we've used the Erase command to illustrate the POINT mode and the other techniques of designating command ranges, don't assume that these techniques

```
    -----C----------D----------E-----
1        111        999   AAA        |
2        222        888   BBB        |
3        333        777   CCC        |
4        444        666   DDD        |
        =========================MAIN=
```

Figure 7.8

are limited to working with the Erase command. For example, as you'll see throughout this book, the POINT mode can be used in almost any situation where Symphony asks you to supply a range. You can POINT to the ranges for the other cut-and-paste commands, the Range commands, the Print command, the Query commands, and even functions. You should use the POINT mode whenever you can. It is almost always the easiest way to define multicell ranges.

Using [Esc] to Correct Errors

As with all of Symphony's commands, the [Esc] key can be used to recover from mistakes you make in specifying the range to be erased. [Esc] throws Symphony into reverse, so that each time you press [Esc] you move one step backward in a command. For example, suppose that when trying to erase cell A1 you accidentally type A4 as the range to erase. The control panel looks like this:

Range to erase: A4

If you press **[Esc]** once, the prompt looks like this:

Range to erase:

Assuming that the cell pointer was originally in cell A5, pressing [Esc] again changes the prompt to

Range to erase: A5 . . A5

At this point you could type the correct cell reference, A1. If you press **[ESC]** once more, the prompt looks like this:

Range to erase: A5

You could also designate the erase range from here by pointing to cell A1. Pressing **[Esc]** once more returns you to the SHEET menu.

As with the POINT mode, the usefulness of the [Esc] key is not limited to the Erase command. You can use the [Esc] key in much the same way to "back up" through any Symphony command. In fact, one trick for escaping from any confusing position in Symphony is to press **[Esc]** several times in a row. No matter what the problem, pressing **[Esc]** several times returns you to a clean worksheet.

INSERT AND DELETE

The Symphony SHEET environment includes two commands that take the pain out of adding and deleting ranges from a spreadsheet: Insert and Delete. Former 1-2-3 users, take note: these commands are nearly identical to the 1-2-3 commands /Worksheet Insert and /Worksheet Delete. Even Symphony users who have never seen 1-2-3 will find that these commands are very simple to learn to use.

Inserting Rows and Columns

Suppose you have created the worksheet shown in Figure 7.9. Just when you're finished, your boss tells you about product 5, your company's newest offering, which he wants you to include in the forecast. If you were working with a paper spreadsheet, you'd either break out your eraser or you'd simply start over. With Symphony, though, there's a better way.

```
      -----A---------B----------C----------D------
  1 SALES FORECAST                                |
  2               Jan-84      Feb-84      Mar-84   |
  3 Product 1    $10,983     $13,821     $15,944   |
  4 Product 2     $7,620      $8,218      $9,413   |
  5 Product 3     $8,341     $10,499      $9,890   |
  6 Product 4     $2,145      $2,082      $2,115   |
  7                ------      ------      ------   |
  8              $29,089     $34,620     $37,362   |
  9
      =====================================MAIN=
```

Figure 7.9

First, move the cell pointer to cell A7. Now issue the {**Menu**} Insert command. The following menu is displayed:

Columns Rows Global

Select the Global option by pressing **G** or by moving the menu cursor to Global and pressing **[Enter]**. Now Symphony offers you another choice: Column or Row. Since we want to add another row to the worksheet, we'll select the **R**ow option.

Finally, Symphony prompts you to supply the range where the new row(s) should be inserted. As with the other cut-and-paste commands, Symphony guesses the correct range based on the current location of the cell pointer. Because the cell pointer in our example is positioned on A7, Symphony automatically supplies the range A7 . . A7. Since we want to enter the new row just above row 7, we can approve Symphony's guess by pressing **[Enter]**. When the command is finished, the worksheet looks like Figure 7.10.

```
    -----A---------B---------C---------D------
 1  SALES FORECAST                                    |
 2            Jan-84      Feb-84      Mar-84           |
 3  Product 1 $10,983    $13,821     $15,944           |
 4  Product 2  $7,620     $8,218      $9,413           |
 5  Product 3  $8,341    $10,499      $9,890           |
 6  Product 4  $2,145     $2,082      $2,115           |
 7                                                     |
 8            -------    -------     -------           |
 9            $29,089    $34,620     $37,362           |
10                                                     |
    ================================MAIN=
```

Figure 7.10

The cells in row 8 of the original spreadsheet contained formulas that totaled the cells in each column of the worksheet. For example, cell B8 contained the formula

   B8: (C0) @SUM(B3 . . B7)

In the worksheet in Figure 7.10, these formulas have been pushed down to row 9 by the Insert command. The formula in cell B9 is now

   B9: (C0) @SUM(B3 . . B8)

Notice that the sum range in this function has been stretched to include the added row. The Insert command always adjusts any ranges to include the rows or columns being inserted.

In addition to modifying cell references in formulas, as demonstrated above, the Insert command also adjusts range names, graph ranges, data ranges, and other ranges in the worksheet. For example, suppose the range name TEST has been assigned to the range A1 . . A8 in the original worksheet. After the new row is inserted, the name TEST describes the range A1 . . A9.

We could just as easily have selected another Insert range by typing another cell reference from the keyboard or by pointing to another range. For example, to insert a row above row 5, we could have typed the cell reference A5. The cell pointer does not *have* to be located at the position where you want to insert the row(s) or column(s), but designating the Insert range will be easier if it is.

Inserting Multiple Rows

If you want to insert five new rows into the example spreadsheet, issue the {**Menu**} Insert Global Row command and specify the Insert range A7 . . A11. Five new rows are inserted in the worksheet, and the contents of what was row 7 are now in row 12. The worksheet looks like Figure 7.11. As before, the formulas in what was row 8 are adjusted as the new rows are inserted.

You may wonder what would happen if you supplied the range A7 . . G11 in response to the Insert command. In fact, this range is functionally identical to A7 . . A11, B7 . . B11,

```
      -----A---------B---------C---------D------
   1   SALES FORECAST                            |
   2              Jan-84      Feb-84     Mar-84   |
   3   Product 1  $10,983    $13,821    $15,944   |
   4   Product 2   $7,620     $8,218     $9,413   |
   5   Product 3   $8,341    $10,499     $9,890   |
   6   Product 4   $2,145     $2,082     $2,115   |
   7                                             |
   8                                             |
   9                                             |
  10                                             |
  11                                             |
  12             ------     ------     ------    |
  13             $29,089    $34,620    $37,362    |
  14                                             |
      ===================================MAIN=
```

Figure 7.11

A7 . . Z11, or any other range that includes cells in rows 7 through 11. The Insert Global Row command does not use the column portion of the range reference. Similarly, the ranges A1 . . C1, A5 . . C5, and A1 . . C100 are all identical to the Insert Global Column command. All of these ranges cause three new columns to be added to the worksheet to the left of column A.

Inserting Columns

Suppose you decide that you need to add a new column to the left of column B in the example shown in Figure 7.9. This column will contain the December 1983 results. Move the cell pointer to cell B1 and issue the {**Menu**} Insert command. When the Insert menu appears, select the **G**lobal option and then the **C**olumn option. Now Symphony prompts you with its guess at the correct Insert range, B1 . . B1. As in our first example, the range provided by Symphony is exactly the range you want to insert, so you can make the insertion by pressing [**Enter**] and accepting Symphony's offered range. (Remember, the cell pointer doesn't have to be located at the point where you want to insert the new columns when the command is issued. You can position the cell pointer anywhere on the spreadsheet and type or point to any range.) When the command is finished, the worksheet looks like the one in Figure 7.12.

A Few Rules

There are a couple of simple rules to remember when using the Insert command. First, rows are always inserted above the first row in the specified range. Columns are added to the left of the first column in the specified range. Inserted rows and columns assume the default format and width of the window in which they appear.

Inserting columns or rows "pushes" the rows or columns already in the sheet down or to the right. In our examples, inserting one row at row 7 pushed the contents of rows 7 and 8 down one row, and inserting one column pushed the contents of columns B, C, D,

```
   -----A---------B---------C---------D---------E-----
                                                       |
 1  SALES FORECAST                                     |
 2                        Jan-84      Feb-84    Mar-84  |
 3  Product 1            $10,983     $13,821   $15,944  |
 4  Product 2             $7,620      $8,218    $9,413  |
 5  Product 3             $8,341     $10,499    $9,890  |
 6  Product 4             $2,145      $2,082    $2,115  |
 7                        ------      ------    ------  |
 8                       $29,089     $34,620   $37,362  |
 9                                                      |
10                                                      |
   ==============================================MAIN=
```

Figure 7.12

and so on one column to the right. In general, if inserting the number of rows or columns specified pushes cells containing data off the worksheet (that is, beyond column IV or below row 8192), the error message

> Worksheet full

is returned. In practice this is very unlikely, since very few worksheets extend to the bottom or the right edge of the worksheet.

Deleting Rows and Columns

Symphony makes it as easy to delete rows and columns from the worksheet as it is to add them. Going back to our first example (in Figure 7.9), suppose your boss told you that product 4 was being discontinued and should be removed from the plan.

Begin by moving the cell pointer to cell A6 (you don't have to do this, but it makes the command easier). Now issue the {**Menu**} **D**elete **G**lobal **R**ow command. As always, Symphony offers its guess at the range to be deleted:

> Range of rows to delete: A6 . . A6

Since the cell pointer is in row 6, the row you want to delete, you need only press [**Enter**] to activate the command. After the command has run, the worksheet looks like the one in Figure 7.13.

As you might expect, the Delete command works like the Insert command in reverse. For example, the formulas in row 8 (before the deletion) are adjusted to reflect the deleted row. The function in cell C8

> C8: @SUM(C3 . . C7)

is changed to

> C7: @SUM(C3 . . C6)

The Delete command automatically adjusts all ranges, including function arguments, graph ranges, and named ranges.

```
-----A---------B---------C---------D------
 1 SALES FORECAST                               |
 2            Jan-84      Feb-84      Mar-84     |
 3 Product 1  $10,983     $13,821     $15,944    |
 4 Product 2  $7,620      $8,218      $9,413     |
 5 Product 3  $8,341      $10,499     $9,890     |
 6            ------      ------      ------     |
 7            $26,944     $32,538     $35,247    |
 8                                              |
   =====================================MAIN=
```

Figure 7.13

There is one problem that can occur with Delete that is not a problem with the Insert command. Suppose that the formula in cell C8 prior to the deletion was

C8: @SUM(C3 . . C6)

The only difference between this function and the one above is that this one does not include row 7, which contains only a series of dashes. Since the dashes have a value of 0, these two formulas return the same value.

Now suppose you delete row 6. Since cells in this row are used to define the sum ranges in the formulas in row 8, deleting this row also destroys the range references in these formulas. When the deletion is complete, the formula in what is now cell C7 is

C7: @SUM(ERR)

This is a simple example of an important Symphony principle. Whenever you delete a row or column that contains cells used to define a range (in a formula or otherwise), the range is destroyed. You can do a lot of damage in a hurry with the Delete command—be very careful when you use it.

Remember that when you insert a row you shove the rows below the inserted row down, and when you insert a column you shove the columns to the right of the added column to the right. Conversely, deleting a row pulls all of the rows below the deleted rows up one row and adds a new blank row at the bottom of the worksheet. Deleting a column pulls all of the columns to the right of the deleted column to the left and adds a new blank column at the right edge of the worksheet.

Naturally, it is possible to delete more than one row or column at a time. For example, suppose your boss told you to delete both products 3 and 4 from the worksheet in Figure 7.9. You would issue the {**Menu**} **D**elete **G**lobal **R**ow command and specify range A5 . . A6 as the range to delete. When the command is complete, the worksheet looks like the one in Figure 7.14.

The range A5 . . A6 was only one of the possible range designations that could be used to delete rows 5 and 6. For example, the ranges B5 . . B6, Z5 . . Z6, and A5 . . Z6 would all delete rows 5 and 6 from the worksheet.

Naturally, the Delete command can also be used to remove columns from the worksheet. For example, suppose you want to delete column B from the worksheet in Figure

```
     -----A---------B---------C---------D------   |
  1  SALES  FORECAST                               |
  2              Jan-84       Feb-84       Mar-84   |
  3  Product  1   $10,983     $13,821     $15,944   |
  4  Product  2    $7,620      $8,218      $9,413   |
  5             -------      -------      -------    |
  6              $18,603     $22,039     $25,357    |
  7  ==================================MAIN=
```

Figure 7.14

7.12. To delete this column, simply position the cell pointer in cell B1 and issue the {**Menu**} Delete **G**lobal **C**olumn command. Symphony asks you for the range to delete and supplies the "guess" B1 . . B1. To accept Symphony's offering, simply press [**Enter**]. When the command is finished, the worksheet looks once again like it did in Figure 7.9.

Delete and Erase

Some Symphony users are confused about the difference between the Erase command and the Delete command. It might help to think of the difference in this way. Erasing a portion of the spreadsheet is analogous to erasing a portion of a paper spreadsheet. Once you are finished erasing, the information that was on that part of the paper is gone, but the actual dimensions of the paper haven't changed.

Deleting, on the other hand, is like using scissors to remove a few rows or columns from the spreadsheet. This not only erases the information stored in those rows or columns but also removes the rows and columns themselves from the worksheet. Any information stored in rows or columns below or to the right of the deleted areas is "pulled up" to replace the deleted space.

It is important that you realize that Delete does not change the dimensions of the workspace. When you delete a row or column, Symphony automatically replaces the deleted area with an empty row or column at the edge of the worksheet.

MOVE

The Move command allows you to move the contents of one cell or range to another cell or range. Let's look at how this function works. Suppose you have entered the label

> A1: 'Ann Brown Ford

in cell A1 in a worksheet, as shown in Figure 7.15.

Now suppose you want that label in cell A3 instead of cell A1. First, issue the {**Menu**} **M**ove command. Symphony presents you with a prompt:

> Range to move FROM: A1 . . A1

The FROM range is the range that contains the label or value you want to move. This range can be as small as a single cell or as large as you wish. In our example, the FROM

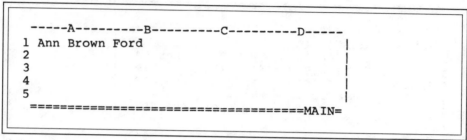

```
     -----A---------B---------C---------D-----
   1 Ann Brown Ford                              |
   2                                             |
   3                                             |
   4                                             |
   5                                             |
     ==================================MAIN=
```

Figure 7.15

range is A1, which appears in the prompt. Again, Symphony automatically supplies the address of the cell pointer as the FROM range. If the cell pointer had been on cell Z100, the prompt would have looked like this:

Range to move FROM: Z100 . . Z100

As we saw above in the discussion of the Erase command, there are three ways to specify the FROM range in response to Symphony's prompt. First, if the FROM range is to be a single cell and if cell pointer is on that cell, you can indicate the range simply by pressing [Enter]. Second, you can type the coordinates of the FROM range in response to the prompt. Third, you can *point* to the FROM range using Symphony's POINT mode. As you learned earlier in the chapter, pointing is usually the best way to designate a multicell range.

After you have specified the FROM range, Symphony prompts you for the range to which you want to move the contents of the FROM range. Assuming the cell pointer is located on cell A1, the control panel looks like this:

Range to move TO: A1

The TO range can be specified using any of the three methods that can be used to indicate the FROM range. If the cell pointer happens to be on the TO range cell, the TO range can be specified by pressing **[Enter]**. Otherwise you can type it or point to it.

In our example, the TO range is the single cell A3. To enter this address, type the new address, **A3**, and press **[Enter].** As soon as you enter this address in response to Symphony's prompt, the worksheet is changed to look like the one in Figure 7.16.

```
     -----A---------B---------C---------D-----
   1                                           |
   2                                           |
   3 Ann Brown Ford                            |
   4                                           |
   5                                           |
     ==================================MAIN=
```

Figure 7.16

There are a couple of important points to keep in mind when using the Move command. First, the Move command erases the contents, if there are any, of all cells in the TO range as it operates. Be very careful that you don't accidentally destroy important entries in the TO range when moving cells.

Second, the Move command leaves blank cells in the FROM range. The command moves not only the contents of a cell or range, but also any formats or names assigned to that range. In our example, after the Move command is finished, cell A1 is blank.

Third, remember that you don't have to have the cell pointer positioned on the FROM or TO ranges when you issue the {**Menu**} Move command (or any other command, for that matter), although it is convenient to do so. You can easily point to or type the coordinates of the FROM and TO ranges.

Adjusting Cell References

Like the other cut-and-paste commands, Move automatically adjusts cell references to cells that are moved by the command. For example, if cell A1 contained the formula

> A1: +A3/4

and you moved the contents of cell A3 from A3 to A4, the formula in cell A1 would be changed to

> A1: +A4/4

On the other hand, suppose that cell A3 contained the formula

> A3: +A1+A2

After this formula was moved from A3 to A4, the formula would still be

> A4: +A1+A2

This formula was not adjusted. Remember—the Move command never adjusts the formulas in the *cells being moved,* but always adjusts formulas that *refer* to the cells being moved.

A Warning to VisiCalc Users

If you are an experienced VisiCalc user, you may have noticed a couple of differences between Symphony's Move command and VisiCalc's version of the same command. Since these differences can lead to some major problems, they are worth discussing briefly.

First, VisiCalc's /Move command automatically inserts a row or column in the worksheet to make room for the row or column being moved. As we have seen, Symphony simply overlays the range being moved on the TO range and erases the previous contents of the TO range. If you use Symphony's Move command and expect it to behave like VisiCalc's, you may be in for a big surprise. (Interestingly, the DOC environment Move command is more like VisiCalc's, as you'll see in a later section.)

Second, VisiCalc's /Move command could only move a single entire row or column at a time. Symphony's version of the command can move any sized range, from a single cell to a rectangular range to a full row or column. Don't let Symphony's flexibility confuse you.

Move Command Cautions

The Move command can lead to big problems. If you move a cell or a range onto a cell that serves as the limit for a range reference in a function or a formula elsewhere in the worksheet, that function will return the @ERR message.

For example, if cell B5 contains the formula

A5: @SUM(A1 . . A4)

and you move the contents of cell B1 to cell A1, the formula in cell A5 is now changed to

A5: @SUM(ERR)

The error occurs because cell A1, one of the anchors of the @SUM range, was overwritten by the Move command, destroying the @SUM range.

You can also unknowingly alter the definition of a function or formula by using the Move command. For example, if cell A5 contains the formula

A5: +A1+A2+A3

and you move the contents of cell A2 to cell B2, this formula changes to

A5: +A1+B2+A3

These mistakes are very easy to make. For example, suppose you've built the advertising plan spreadsheet shown in Figure 7.17. You decide that the ad in *A Big, Fat Magazine* should be delayed one month, so you move the number in cell B3 to cell C3. The formula in cell B7, however, is now

B7: +C3+B4+B5

and the formula in cell C7 is now

C7: +ERR+C4+C5

which is most definitely not what you want! Instead of using the Move command to make this change, you should use the Copy command to copy the contents of B3 into C3. You could then erase the contents of B3 with the Erase command.

COPY

Symphony's Copy command allows you to duplicate the contents of a range in another part of the worksheet. The range being copied can be a single cell, a partial row or column, a rectangular range, or any other legitimate Symphony range, and it can contain numbers, functions, formulas, labels, and even blank cells.

Many Symphony users are confused by the Copy command, probably because there are several variations on the basic Copy command and several conditions that affect the way the command works. We'll examine all of these points in detail.

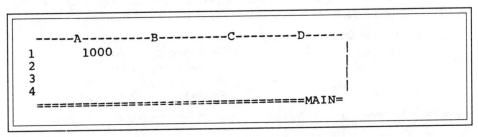

```
     ----------A-------------B---------C---------D-----
  1                      Jan-85     Feb-85    Mar-85 |
  2                                                  |
  3  A Big, Fat Magazine  $10,000             $10,000 |
  4  A Snobbish Weekly               $6,000           |
  5  A New Magazine        $3,500    $3,500    $3,500 |
  6                        -------   -------   ------- |
  7  Total                $13,500    $9,500   $13,500 |
  8                                                   |
     =======================================MAIN=
```

Figure 7.17

The simplest form of the Copy command is to copy the contents of a single cell to another cell. Suppose you want to move the number in cell A1 in the spreadsheet in Figure 7.18 to cell A2.

```
     -----A----------B---------C--------D-----
  1       1000                                 |
  2                                            |
  3                                            |
  4                                            |
     ============================MAIN=
```

Figure 7.18

First, you would issue the {**Menu**} **C**opy command. Assuming the cell pointer is in cell A1, Symphony prompts us with the message

Range to copy FROM: A1 . . A1

This prompt is very similar to the {Menu} Move prompt. Notice that Symphony automatically enters the current address of the cell pointer as a tentative FROM range, just as it does with the Move command.

As with the other Symphony cut-and-paste commands, there are three ways to specify the TO and FROM ranges for the Copy command: pressing [Enter] (which requires the FROM range to be a single cell and the cell pointer to be on that cell), typing, and pointing. In this case, we can simply press [Enter].

Next we must select the TO range. Once again, Symphony prompts us for a response:

Range to copy TO: A1

Once again, Symphony offers A1 as the TO range. This time, however, we can't use Symphony's help. The proper TO range is A2, which we specify by typing **A2** and then pressing **[Enter]**. As soon as we press [Enter], Symphony copies the contents of A1 to A2, and the worksheet looks like Figure 7.19. Notice that the Copy command, unlike the Move command, leaves the contents of the FROM range in place.

```
  -----A---------B---------C--------D-----
1         1000                              |
2         1000                              |
3                                           |
4                                           |
  ===================================MAIN=
```

Figure 7.19

The second form of the Copy command is to copy from a single cell into a range of cells. Starting from Figure 7.18, assume that you want to copy the contents of cell A1 into cells B1 to D1. Begin by typing {**Menu**} **C**opy and then specify the FROM range, which is again A1.

Next we must specify the TO range. In this example, the TO range is B1 . . D1. As before, you can either type the correct range or point it out using the POINT mode. To point to the range, point to cell B1 and press the period key. Finally, point to cell D1 and press [**Enter**]. At each stage, the TO prompt in the control panel looks like this:

Issue {**Menu**} Copy command	Range to copy FROM: A1 . . A1
Press [**Enter**]	Range to copy TO: A1
Point to cell B1	Range to copy TO: B1
Press .	Range to copy TO: B1 . . B1
Point to cell D1	Range to copy TO: B1 . . D1

After the TO range is specified, Symphony copies the contents of cell A1 into cells B1, C1, and D1, as shown in Figure 7.20.

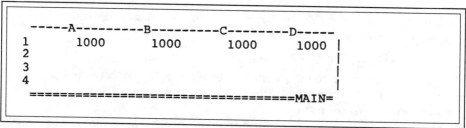

```
  -----A---------B---------C--------D-----
1       1000      1000      1000      1000 |
2                                          |
3                                          |
4                                          |
  ===================================MAIN=
```

Figure 7.20

The final form of the Copy command is to copy from a range of cells into another range of cells. Beginning with the worksheet in Figure 7.20, suppose we wanted to copy the contents of the range A1 . . D1 into the range A2 . . D2. As before, begin by issuing the {**Menu**} **C**opy command and specifying the FROM range—in this case, A1 . . D1. Assuming that the cell pointer was in cell A1 when the command was issued, we could point to the range by pressing [**End**] → and [**Enter**]. The FROM range prompt in the control panel would look like this at each step along the way:

Issue {**Menu**} **C**opy command Range to copy FROM: A1 . . A1
Press [**End**] { {**Right Arrow33** Range to copy FROM: A1 . . D1

Next we must specify the TO range. In our example, the TO range is the single cell A2. Were you expecting it to be A2 .. D2? When performing a range-to-range copy, the TO range is designated by specifying only the first cell in the range being copied to. Although the range A2 .. D2 seems to make more sense, it is incorrect. The TO range must be designated with the single cell reference A2. Symphony infers the remainder of the destination from this single-cell reference.

If you think about it for a minute, you'll realize that this single-cell reference actually makes sense. Since the range you are copying FROM is a four-cell partial row, the range you are copying TO must also be four-cell partial row. Given that the TO range must be a four-cell partial row, you need only provide the left-most cell in that range to adequately define the range. For example, there is only one four-cell partial row that begins at A2— A2 .. D2. Similarly, if you specified the TO range as Z10, the only possible destination for this command would be Z10 .. AC10. After the command is finished, the worksheet will look like Figure 7.21.

```
    -----A---------B---------C--------D-----
1        1000        1000        1000        1000 |
2        1000        1000        1000        1000 |
3                                                 |
4                                                 |
    =================================MAIN=
```

Figure 7.21

Suppose we want to copy from the range A1 .. D1 into the range A2 .. D5. As in the previous example, the FROM range is A1 .. D1, but can you guess the correct TO range? Given that we're copying a four-cell partial row into four 4-cell partial rows (A2 .. D2, A3 .. D3, A4 .. D4, A5 .. D5), we need only provide the beginning cell of each of these partial rows to adequately define the TO range. The correct TO range is thus A2 .. A5. This range would create a worksheet that looks like Figure 7.22.

Notice that the results shown in Figure 7.22 could also be generated by copying from A1 .. D1 to A2, then from A1 .. D1 to A3, then from A1 .. D1 to A4, and so on. In effect,

```
    -----A---------B---------C--------D-----
1        1000        1000        1000        1000 |
2        1000        1000        1000        1000 |
3        1000        1000        1000        1000 |
4        1000        1000        1000        1000 |
5        1000        1000        1000        1000 |
    =================================MAIN=
```

Figure 7.22

copying from A1 . . D1 to A2 . . A5 combines these four individual Copy commands into one command. The TO range in the combined copy operation is the composite of the four TO ranges in the separate operations; that is, A2 . . A5 is the composite of A2, A3, A4, and A5, the TO ranges of the individual Copy commands.

Suppose you want to copy the two-row range in Figure 7.21 (A1 . . D2) into the range A4 . . D5. In this case, we are copying a range containing two 4-cell partial rows. Since the destination area also contains two 4-cell partial rows, you only need one cell to define the range: A4. If you issue the {**Menu**} Copy command with A1 . . D2 as the FROM range and A4 as the TO range, the resulting worksheet looks like Figure 7.23.

```
  -----A---------B---------C---------D-----
1      1000      1000      1000      1000  |
2      1000      1000      1000      1000  |
3                                          |
4      1000      1000      1000      1000  |
5      1000      1000      1000      1000  |
=================================MAIN=
```

Figure 7.23

Let's look at one final example. Suppose you want to copy the contents of the range A1 . . A2 in Figure 7.19 into the range B1 . . D2. In this case, the FROM range is A1 . . A2, and the TO range is the partial row B1 . . D1. When the command is completed, the worksheet looks like Figure 7.24.

```
  -----A---------B---------C---------D-----
1      1000      1000      1000      1000  |
2      1000      1000      1000      1000  |
3                                          |
4                                          |
5                                          |
  =================================MAIN=
```

Figure 7.24

Overlapping FROM and TO Ranges

Look back a few pages to Figure 7.18. Suppose you want to fill the range A1 . . D5 with the contents of cell A1. To do this, issue the {Menu} Copy command and specify the FROM range as the single cell A1. Now designate the TO range: A1 . . D5. The resulting worksheet looks like Figure 7.25.

Notice that the FROM and TO ranges in this example overlap. Symphony has no problem with overlapping FROM and TO ranges in the Copy command. However, sometimes the result of a Copy command with overlapping ranges won't be what you expected, especially if the FROM range contains formulas.

```
    -----A---------B---------C---------D-----
1        1000      1000      1000      1000|
2        1000      1000      1000      1000|
3        1000      1000      1000      1000|
4        1000      1000      1000      1000|
5        1000      1000      1000      1000|
    ==================================MAIN=
```

Figure 7.25

Copying Formulas and Functions

In the worksheet shown in Figure 7.26, cell B5 contains the function

B5: @SUM(B1..B4)

```
    -----A---------B---------C---------D------
1                  1000      2000      3000    |
2                  2000      3000      4000    |
3                  3000      4000      5000    |
4                  ------    ------    ------  |
5                  6000                        |
6                                              |
    ===================================MAIN=
```

Figure 7.26

Suppose you want to total columns C and D using a similar function. One way to enter the proper formulas into cells C5 and D5 would be to move the cell pointer to each of those cells and enter the proper @SUM function from the keyboard. Since you only need to enter two formulas, this is a fairly simple task. But suppose you want to enter a similar formula in every column from E to AZ. We could spend hours entering each of these formulas.

Thanks to Symphony's Copy command, however, there is an easier way. You could issue the {**Menu**} Copy command, specifying B5 as the FROM range and C5 . . D5 as the TO range. The resulting worksheet would look like Figure 7.27.

Cell C5 in this worksheet contains the function

C5: @SUM(C1 . . C4)

and cell D5 contains the function

D5: @SUM(D1 . . D4)

The references to cells B1 and B4 in the original formula were shifted as the formula was copied into cells C5 and D5. For example, when the formula from B5 was copied into C5, the references to B1 and B4 changed to C1 and C4.

```
-----A---------B---------C---------D------
1                1000      2000      3000  |
2                2000      3000      4000  |
3                3000      4000      5000  |
4              ------    ------    ------  |
5                6000      9000     12000  |
6                                          |
=====================================MAIN=
```

Figure 7.27

Relative and Absolute References

As we saw in the introductory chapters, Symphony offers two different types of cell addresses: relative and absolute. Understanding the differences between the two is critical to understanding the process of copying formulas and functions.

Relative References

In the formula used in the previous example,

>   B5: @SUM(B1 . . B4)

the references to cells B1 and B4 are *relative references*. Relative references change as they are copied across the worksheet so that they always operate on the same relative cells, no matter where the formula is located in the worksheet.

It might help you to think about relative references like this. The function

>   B5: @SUM(B1 . . B4)

totals the four cells immediately above the cell containing the function. When this function is copied, the resulting function(s) always totals the four cells above the cell containing the function. So if the function is copied to cell F10, the result is the function

>   F10: @SUM(F6 . . F9)

and if it is copied to cell Z100, the result is

>   Z100: @SUM(Z96 . . Z99)

Notice that although each formula is different, each one totals the four cells directly above the cell containing the formula. These functions are thus relatively the same.

Absolute References

The second type of cell reference in Symphony is an absolute reference. Absolute references are indicated by placing dollar signs ($) before the row and column coordinates of the cell address. For example, the function

>   B5: @SUM($B$1 . . $B$4)

is the absolute equivalent of the relative function shown in the example above.

Suppose we want to copy this absolute reference from cell B5 in Figure 7.26 into cells C5 and D5. We could issue the {**Menu**} Copy command, specifying **B5** as the FROM range and **C5 .. D5** as the TO range. When the copy is completed, the worksheet looks like Figure 7.28.

```
    -----A---------B---------C---------D------
1                   1000      2000      3000  |
2                   2000      3000      4000  |
3                   3000      4000      5000  |
4                  ------    ------    ------ |
5                   6000      6000      6000  |
6                                             |
    ==================================MAIN=
```

Figure 7.28

The number 6000 appears in cells C5 and D5 because the formulas in those cells still refer to the range B1 .. B4. For example, the formula in cell C5 is

C5:@SUM($B$1 .. $B$4)

The reference $B$1 .. $B$4 is called absolute because it always refers to the same absolute cells, no matter where it is copied in the worksheet. If we copy this function to cell F10, the result would be

F10: @SUM($B$1 .. $B$4)

and if we copy the same function to cell Z100, the result would be the same:

Z100: @SUM($B$1 .. $B$4)

When to use absolute references   In the example above, the desired result was achieved by using a relative reference in cell B5. There are plenty of cases, however, when an absolute reference must be used. For example, suppose you had set up the simple worksheet in Figure 7.29.

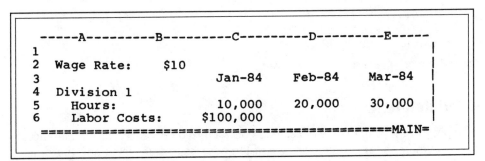

```
    -----A---------B---------C---------D---------E-----
1                                                       |
2  Wage Rate:     $10                                   |
3                            Jan-84     Feb-84    Mar-84 |
4  Division 1                                            |
5     Hours:               10,000     20,000    30,000  |
6     Labor Costs:    $100,000                           |
    ==================================================MAIN=
```

Figure 7.29

Cell C6 in this worksheet contains the formula

C6: (C0) +C5*$B$2

The first half of this formula, +C5, is a relative reference to cell C5. The second half, $B$2, is an absolute reference to cell B2. If we copy the contents of C6 into cells D6 and E6, the worksheet looks like Figure 7.30.

```
-----A---------B---------C---------D---------E-----
1                                                    |
2   Wage Rate:     $10                               |
3                       Jan-84    Feb-84    Mar-84    |
4   Division 1                                        |
5     Hours:            10,000    20,000    30,000    |
6     Labor Costs:    $100,000  $200,000  $300,000    |
=============================================MAIN=
```

Figure 7.30

Cells D6 and E6 contain the formulas

D6: (C0) +D5*$B$2
E6: (C0) +E5*$B$2

which are exactly what we want. The first term in the formulas is relative and thus changes as the formula is copied. The second term, however, is absolute, so it continues to refer specifically to cell B2.

By the way, notice that when we copied the function from cell C6 to cells D6 to E6, the format assigned to cell C6 was automatically assigned to those cells. In fact, the Copy command always transfers any format assigned to cells in the FROM range to the cells in the TO range.

Suppose we add a second division to the first example, changing the worksheet to look like Figure 7.31. Let's copy the formulas from the range C6 . . E6 to the range C10 . . E10. Remember, we need to give Symphony only one cell reference, C10, to identify the TO range. When the copy is complete, the worksheet looks like Figure 7.32, and cells C10, D10, and E10 contain the formulas

C10: (C0) +C9*$B$2
D10: (C0) +D9*$B$2
E10: (C0) +E9*$B$2

Again, this worksheet is just what we want.

Mixed References

Symphony offers a third type of cell reference: a mixed reference. Mixed references are used when one of the coordinates of the address remains fixed and the other changes. For example, consider the worksheet shown in Figure 7.33.

```
    -----A---------B---------C---------D---------E----
 1                                                        |
 2   Wage Rate:     $10                                   |
 3                          Jan-84     Feb-84     Mar-84  |
 4   Division 1                                           |
 5     Hours:               10,000     20,000     30,000  |
 6     Labor Costs:       $100,000   $200,000   $300,000  |
 7                                                        |
 8   Division 2                                           |
 9     Hours:                5,000     10,000     10,000  |
10     Labor Costs:                                       |
11   ===========================================MAIN=
```

Figure 7.31

```
    -----A---------B---------C---------D---------E----
 1                                                        |
 2   Wage Rate:     $10                                   |
 3                          Jan-84     Feb-84     Mar-84  |
 4   Division 1                                           |
 5     Hours:               10,000     20,000     30,000  |
 6     Labor Costs:       $100,000   $200,000   $300,000  |
 7                                                        |
 8   Division 2                                           |
 9     Hours:                5,000     10,000     10,000  |
10     Labor Costs:        $50,000   $100,000   $100,000  |
11   ===========================================MAIN=
```

Figure 7.32

The formula in cell C6 uses a *mixed* reference:

    C6: (C0) + $B4 * C5

Notice that there is a dollar sign in front of the reference to column B in this formula but no dollar sign in front of the row number. When we copy the formula, the column portion of the reference is held constant and the row references are changed. Because the reference to each cell is partly absolute and partly relative, the reference is called mixed.

If we copy the formula from cell C6 into cells D6 and E6, the worksheet looks like Figure 7.34 and the formulas in cells D6 and E6 are

    D6: (C0) + $B4 * D5
    E6: (C0) + $B4 * E5

```
     -----A---------B---------C---------D---------E-----
 1                                                      |
 2                      Jan-84     Feb-84     Mar-84    |
 3   Division 1                                         |
 4     Wage Rate:   $10                                 |
 5     Hours:               10,000     20,000     30,000|
 6     Labor Costs:    $100,000                         |
 7                                                      |
 8   Division 2                                         |
 9     Wage Rage:   $12                                 |
10     Hours:                5,000     10,000     10,000|
11     Labor Costs:                                     |
12                                                      |
     ===================================================MAIN=
```

Figure 7.33

```
     -----A---------B---------C---------D---------E-----
 1                                                      |
 2                      Jan-84     Feb-84     Mar-84    |
 3   Division 1                                         |
 4     Wage Rate:   $10                                 |
 5     Hours:               10,000     20,000     30,000|
 6     Labor Costs:    $100,000   $200,000   $300,000   |
 7                                                      |
 8   Division 2                                         |
 9     Wage Rate:   $12                                 |
10     Hours:                5,000     10,000     10,000|
11     Labor Costs:                                     |
12                                                      |
     ===================================================MAIN=
```

Figure 7.34

Notice that the reference to cell B4 remains constant as this formula is copied into the range D6 . . E6. You may think that an absolute reference would work as well in this case. If we go one more step, however, you'll see the reason for using mixed references.

Suppose you wanted to copy the formulas from cells C6 to E6 into the range C11 . . E11. After this command is complete, the worksheet looks like Figure 7.35.

Cells C11, D11, and E11 in this worksheet contain the formulas

> C11: (C0) +$B9*C10
> D11: (C0) +$B9*D10
> E11: (C0) +$B9*E10

When the formulas were copied, the reference to column B remained constant, but the reference to row 4 changed.

```
    -----A---------B---------C---------D---------E-----
 1                                                      |
 2                       Jan-84     Feb-84     Mar-84   |
 3   Division 1                                         |
 4      Wage Rate:   $10                                |
 5      Hours:                10,000     20,000     30,000 |
 6      Labor Costs:        $100,000   $200,000   $300,000 |
 7                                                      |
 8   Division 2                                         |
 9      Wage Rate:   $12                                |
10      Hours:                 5,000     10,000     10,000 |
11      Labor Costs:         $60,000   $120,000   $120,000 |
12                                                      |
     ===========================================MAIN=
```

Figure 7.35

It is sometimes difficult to decide exactly which of the three types of reference should be used in a particular situation. The hardest choice is between absolute and mixed references. About the only way to decide which type to use is to carefully examine the situation. If you want each instance of a formula or function to refer to exactly the same cell, use an absolute reference. If you want either the row or the column portion to remain the same, but you want the other element to vary, then a mixed reference should be used.

If you ever get puzzling results from a Copy command, you should check immediately to be sure that the formulas created by the Copy command are in fact the formulas you want.

WIDTH

The default column width in Symphony is nine characters. There are many times, however, when you'll need to use narrower or wider columns for various purposes. For example, you might need to widen a column to 20 characters or more to contain a long label in the worksheet or a long field in a data base. On the other hand, you might want to narrow a column to be only three or four characters wide so that it requires less space on the screen.

The {Menu} Width command allows you to adjust the width of the columns in your Symphony worksheet. For example, suppose you have created the simple worksheet shown in Figure 7.36.

Column A in this worksheet is currently nine characters wide—Symphony's default column width. Cells A1, A3, A4, and A5 contain labels that are wider than column A. As you learned in Chapter 2, Symphony allows a long label to overlap the edges of the column, provided the adjacent cell or cells do not contain an entry. For example, notice how the label in cell A1 overlaps into cell B1, which is empty.

```
    -----A--------B---------C---------D--------
  1 Sales Forecast                             |
  2                                            |
  3              1984       1985       1986     |
  4 Testing E $150,000  $175,000  $200,000     |
  5 Electrica $100,000  $100,000  $100,000     |
  6 Other Pro  $50,000   $45,000   $25,000     |
  7                                            |
    ====================================MAIN=
```

Figure 7.36

However, because cells B4, B5, and B6 contain value entries, the labels in cells A4, A5, and A6 are partially hidden. Since you want to be able to view these labels in their entirety, you decide to widen column A.

Begin by moving the cell pointer to cell A1. With most of the other cut-and-paste commands, this first step is a convenience. With the Width command, however, it is essential that the cell pointer be positioned in the column you want to widen or narrow.

Next, issue the {**Menu**} **W**idth command. This command offers two options: you can either set or reset the width of the column. In this example, you would select the **Set** option. Symphony asks you to supply the desired width for the current column with the prompt

>Column width: 9

The number 9 in this prompt represents the current column width.

There are two ways to specify the new width for a column in response to Symphony's prompt. First, you can simply type the new width. For example, if you wanted to widen the column to 20 characters, you would type **20** and press **[Enter]**. After the command is complete, the worksheet looks like Figure 7.37.

Alternatively, you could use the → key to expand the column one character at a time. Each time you press →, column A becomes one character wider. To widen the column to 20 characters, press → 11 times and then press **[Enter]**. The resulting worksheet also looks like Figure 7.37.

```
    ------------A--------------B---------C---------D--------
  1 Sales Forecast                                         |
  2                                                        |
  3                        1984       1985       1986       |
  4 Testing Equipment    $150,000  $175,000  $200,000       |
  5 Electrical Products  $100,000  $100,000  $100,000       |
  6 Other Products        $50,000   $45,000   $25,000       |
  7                                                        |
    ==========================================================MAIN=
```

Figure 7.37

Suppose you had pressed → 12 times instead of 11, widening column A to 21 characters. If you catch the mistake before you press [Enter], you can reduce the column width simply by pressing ←. After the column width is adjusted, press [Enter] to lock in the change.

If you discover the error after you've pressed [Enter], reissue the {**Menu**} Width command, select the **S**et option, press ← once, and press **[Enter]**.

If you press [Esc] at any time while specifying a new column width, Symphony immediately returns the column to its beginning width and returns you to the Width menu. For example, if you issue the {**Menu**} Width command in the example in Figure 7.36, press → 5 times, and then press [Esc], column A will remain 9 characters wide. If column A had been 11 characters wide before you issued the command, it would return to 11 characters after you pressed [Esc].

In general, it is better to make big changes in column widths by typing the width number rather than by pointing. However, when you want to fine tune the width of a column, or when you aren't sure exactly how wide a column should be, pointing is the only way to go.

Narrowing Columns

Of course, you can also use the Width command to narrow a column. The command sequence for narrowing a column is the same as it is for widening. Just move the cell pointer to the column whose width you want to change, issue the {Menu} Width Set command, and specify the new column width. Both the typing and pointing methods can be used define the new column width. To narrow a column in the POINT mode, just press ←.

Another Example

As you learned in Chapter 5, one of the problems with some of Symphony's cell formats is that they can sometimes make the contents of a cell too wide to be displayed in a standard-width column. For example, if we assign the Currency format with 2 decimal places to the range B4 . . D6 in Figure 7.37, the worksheet looks like Figure 7.38.

```
      -----------A-------------B--------C--------D--------
    1 Sales Forecast                                      |
    2                                                     |
    3                     1984      1985      1986        |
    4 Testing Equipment   *************************       |
    5 Electrical Products*************************        |
    6 Other Products      *************************        |
    7                                                     |
      ======================================================MAIN=
```

Figure 7.38

Obviously, the asterisks in this worksheet don't tell you much. To make the sheet intelligible, you need to widen columns B, C, and D to at least 12 characters. Begin by positioning the cell pointer in column B and issuing the {**Menu**} **W**idth **S**et command. When Symphony asks you how wide the column should be, type **12** and press **[Enter]**. The worksheet should now look like Figure 7.39.

```
     -----------A-------------B--------C--------D--------
   1 Sales Forecast                                      |
   2                                                     |
   3                    1984        1985       1986       |
   4 Testing Equipment  $150,000.00*****************      |
   5 Electrical Products$100,000.00*****************      |
   6 Other Products      $50,000.00*****************      |
   7                                                     |
     ===================================================MAIN=
```

Figure 7.39

Changing the Default Column Width

The Width command is useful for widening or narrowing one column at a time. But because it affects only one column, the Width command is not up to the task of widening or narrowing many columns. Even in the previous example, you would need to repeat the Width command three times to widen all of the columns.

Fortunately, Symphony offers a command that changes the default column width in a window: {Menu} Settings Width. This command is used to widen or narrow all of the columns in the worksheet at once. For example, suppose you wanted to widen columns B, C, and D in the worksheet in Figure 7.39 simultaneously. You could issue the {Menu} Settings Width command and specify 12 as the new default column width. After you type **Q**uit to exit from the settings menu, the worksheet looks like Figure 7.40.

```
     -----------A---------------B-----------C-----------D------
   1 Sales Forecast                                           |
   2                                                          |
   3                    1984         1985        1986          |
   4 Testing Equipment  $150,000.00 $175,000.00 $200,000.00   |
   5 Electrical Products $100,000.00 $100,000.00 $100,000.00   |
   6 Other Products       $50,000.00  $45,000.00  $25,000.00   |
   7                                                          |
     ================================================MAIN=
```

Figure 7.40

Notice that column A, which was previously assigned a specific width, is not affected by the Settings Width command. In this regard, Settings Width is like the Format command. Remember that the global format for a worksheet does not affect any cell with a specific cell format. Similarly, the Settings Width command does not affect any column that has been given a special width.

If, however, we move the cell pointer to cell A1 and issue the {Menu} Width Rest command, column A would assume the default column width—12 characters—not the width it had before it was widened to 20 characters. Figure 7.41 shows the worksheet after this command.

```
    ------A-----------B-----------C-----------D-------
  1 Sales Forecast                                     |
  2                                                     |
  3                 1984        1985        1986        |
  4 Testing Equi$150,000.00 $175,000.00 $200,000.00    |
  5 Electrical P$100,000.00 $100,000.00 $100,000.00    |
  6 Other Produc $50,000.00  $45,000.00  $25,000.00    |
  7                                                     |
    =========================================≈≈MAIN=
```

Figure 7.41

Windows and Column Widths

One of the most confusing aspects of the Width command is that it affects only the width of the column containing the cell pointer *within the current window*. If your worksheet has only one window, your columns will always have the same width. But if your worksheet has several windows, it is possible for the same column to have different widths in different windows. We'll discuss this characteristic of the Width command in Chapter 11, Windows.

CHAPTER EIGHT
RANGE COMMANDS

Symphony, like 1-2-3, has a special set of commands that operate on ranges of cells. In Symphony, the Range command includes options that let you name a range of cells; transpose the entries in a row, column, or rectangular range; copy the values represented by a range of formulas into another range; change the alignment of a set of labels; protect the entries in a range from accidental change; fill a range of cells with evenly spaced values; and create "distribution" and "what-if" tables.

Symphony's Range command is a part of the SHEET environment command menu. The Range menu shown below is activated by issuing the {**Menu**} **R**ange command from within a SHEET window:

Name Transpose Values Label-Alignment Protect Fill Distribution What-If

As you can see, the Range menu is one of Symphony's longest; so long, in fact, that there was no room left for the Quit option common to other Symphony menus. Because there is no Quit option, you must press [Esc] to exit from the Range menu.

Although most of the Symphony Range commands have equivalents in 1-2-3, many of these commands have new names in Symphony. Table 8.1 shows each of Symphony's Range commands and the equivalent commands in 1-2-3.

Symphony Range Command	1-2-3 Equivalent
Range Name	/Range Name
Range Transpose	
Range Values	
Range Label-Alignment	/Range Label
Range Protect	/Range Protect
Range Fill	/Data Fill
Range What-If	/Data Table
Range Distribution	/Data Distribution

Table 8.1

TRANSPOSE AND VALUES

Transpose

Let's begin by looking at the two range commands in Symphony that do not have parallels in 1-2-3: Range Transpose and Range Values. These two commands were added to Symphony in response to the suggestions of 1-2-3 users. The Transpose command converts a row of value or label entries into a column of entries or a column of entries into a row. This command covers the one case that the Move and Copy commands cannot handle, and it makes more sense to think of it as a subset of the Copy command.

Let's look at a simple example of the Range Transpose command. Suppose you have created the simple one-column worksheet shown in Figure 8.1.

```
    -----A---------B---------C---------D---------E------
1                                                         |
2 Quarter 1                                               |
3 Quarter 2                                               |
4 Quarter 3                                               |
5 Quarter 4                                               |
6                                                         |
    =================================================MAIN=
```

Figure 8.1

Now suppose you decide to change the layout of the worksheet so that the labels that are now in the range A2 . . A5 appear in the range B1 . . E1 instead. Move the cell pointer to cell A2 and issue the {**Menu**} **R**ange **T**ranspose command. Symphony begins by prompting you for the range to copy from. Since we want to copy the entries in the range A2 . . A5, this will be our FROM range. As usual, you can type the range coordinates or point to them. Next, Symphony asks for the range to copy to. In this example, the TO range is the single cell B2.

Once the TO range is designated, Symphony transposes the entries in the FROM to the TO range. The worksheet will look like the one in Figure 8.2.

```
    -----A---------B---------C---------D---------E------
1              Quarter 1 Quarter 2 Quarter 3 Quarter 4  |
2 Quarter 1                                              |
3 Quarter 2                                              |
4 Quarter 3                                              |
5 Quarter 4                                              |
6                                                        |
    =================================================MAIN=
```

Figure 8.2

As you can see, the Transpose command copied each entry in the FROM range into the TO range. The first cell in the FROM range, A2, was copied to cell B1; the second cell in the FROM range, A3, was copied to cell C1; and so on. Notice that the Transpose command did not erase the contents of the FROM range.

Notice also that the TO range is only a single cell, B1. Since the FROM range is a partial column, the Transpose command assumes that the TO range has to be a partial row. Given that the range has to be row, the single cell B1 is sufficient to define the range B1 . . E1.

If the FROM range in a Range Transpose command is a partial row, the TO range has to be a partial column. Again, a single cell is sufficient to define this range. For example, if the FROM range is B1 . . E1, and you want the new entries to occupy cells A2 to A5, the TO range would be A2.

Transposing Formulas

Transposing values is just like transposing labels, but transposing cells containing formulas can be tricky. For example, suppose you've created the worksheet shown in Figure 8.3, and you want to transpose the entries from the range A3 . . A6 into the range B2 . . E2.

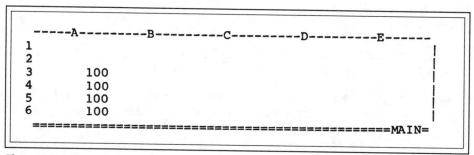

Figure 8.3

Cell A3 in this worksheet contains the number 100. The remaining cells in this column, however, contain cell references. For example, cell A4 contains the formula

        A4: +A3

and cell A6 contains the formula

        A6: +A5

Now let's transpose this range. Issue the {**Menu**} **R**ange **T**ranspose command, specifying A3 . . A6 as the FROM range and B2 as the TO range. When the command is completed, the worksheet will look like the one in Figure 8.4.

The value in cell A3, 100, seems to have been transposed correctly. But the entries in cells C2 to E2 don't seem to be correct. For example, cell C2 contains the reference

        C2: +C1

You would think that cell C2 should refer to cell B2 because you transposed a vertical

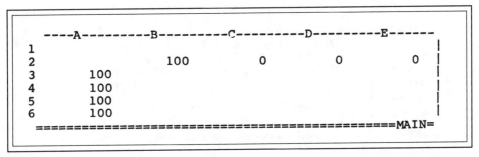

```
    ----A---------B---------C---------D---------E------
1                                                      |
2                    100         0         0         0 |
3         100                                          |
4         100                                          |
5         100                                          |
6         100                                          |
    ========================================MAIN=
```

Figure 8.4

range, in which each cell referred to the cell immediately above itself, into a horizontal range. Wouldn't it make sense for each cell in the horizontal range to refer to the cell immediately to its left?

The answer lies in understanding the nature of the Transpose command. A single Transpose command is really a combination of many individual Copy commands. For example, the transposition in our example can be thought of as four Copy commands linked together: Copy FROM A3 TO B2; Copy FROM A4 TO C2; Copy FROM A5 TO D2; and Copy FROM A6 TO E2.

Let's examine one of these Copy operations, for example, FROM A4 TO C2. Cell A4 contains a relative cell reference, +A3. This reference tells Symphony that the value in cell A4 should be equal to the value in the cell immediately above A4. This reference is copied to cell C2 as

   C2: +C1

As you can see, Symphony assumes that the value in C2 should be equal to the value in the cell immediately above C2. Since cell C1 is blank, cell C2 has a value of 0.

It's too bad Lotus didn't design the Transpose command so that the cell references in the transposed ranges are adjusted according to the way the Transpose command operates. But since they didn't, all I can do is offer a caution: you should be very careful when transposing ranges of cells that contain formulas. It is difficult to know exactly how the Copy command will affect each reference in a formula.

A More Complex Example

Suppose you create the worksheet shown in Figure 8.5. This worksheet shows the sales data for three products for the first two quarters of 1984. When completed, it will show the quarterly sales for each product throughout the year.

Now suppose you want to transpose this table so that the product names appear in column A and the quarter numbers appear in row 1. Begin by saving the worksheet; the Range Transpose command is tricky and can be destructive, so you want to be sure that you have a copy of your important worksheets before you start transposing rows and columns.

Now issue the {**Menu**} **R**ange **T**ranspose command. Symphony begins by prompting you for the range to copy from. Since we want to transpose the entire table, the FROM range is A1 .. D5. Next, Symphony asks for the range to copy to. Use the single cell A6 as

```
     -----A---------B---------C---------D------
1                 Product 1 Product 2 Product 3  |
2 Quarter  1    $10,984    $12,329   $16,971    |
3 Quarter  2    $15,727    $11,982   $16,034    |
4 Quarter  3                                    |
5 Quarter  4                                    |
6                                               |
7                                               |
     =================================MAIN=
```

Figure 8.5

the TO range in this example. After the TO range is specified, Symphony tranposes the rows and columns in this range, and the worksheet looks like the one in Figure 8.6.

To complete the transposition, erase the range A1 . . D5, and then copy the new table from the range A6 . . E9 to the single cell A1. The worksheet will now look like the one in Figure 8.7.

Notice that once again the TO range in this example was a single cell. In fact, the TO range in a Range Transpose command is *always* a single cell. Think about it this way: the

```
      -----A---------B---------C---------D---------E------
1                  Product 1 Product 2 Product 3           |
2 Quarter  1    $10,984    $12,329   $16,971               |
3 Quarter  2    $15,727    $11,982   $16,034               |
4 Quarter  3                                               |
5 Quarter  4                                               |
6               Quarter 1 Quarter 2 Quarter 3 Quarter 4    |
7 Product  1    $10,984    $15,727                         |
8 Product  2    $12,329    $11,982                         |
9 Product  3    $16,971    $16,034                         |
10                                                         |
11                                                         |
      ===================================================MAIN=
```

Figure 8.6

```
      -----A---------B---------C---------D---------E------
1               Quarter 1 Quarter 2 Quarter 3 Quarter 4    |
2 Product  1    $10,984    $15,727                         |
3 Product  2    $12,329    $11,982                         |
4 Product  3    $16,971    $16,034                         |
5                                                          |
6                                                          |
      ===================================================MAIN=
```

Figure 8.7

TO range of the Transpose command is the point about which Symphony "pivots" the cells in the FROM range. For example, in our sample worksheet cell A6 was the TO range. When Symphony copied the rectangular range A1 . . D5 to this range, cells A2 and B1 switched places; cells A3 and C1 switched places; and so on. The entire range "pivoted" around cell A6.

Notice also that we did not transpose the rectangular range directly upon itself, but instead we first transposed it into a different part of the worksheet and then copied it back into the original location. If we had transposed the range directly on itself by specifying the TO range A1, some of the cells would have been transposed correctly but others would have been erased because Symphony transposes certain cells in the FROM range before others. If the TO range and the FROM range overlap, the cells that are transposed first overwrite cells that will be transposed later, destroying the original values in those cells. As a general rule, you should not transpose a rectangular range onto itself.

Values

Symphony's other new Range command is Range Values. Range Values transforms a set of formulas into their current values while copying them to a different location in the worksheet. Like Range Transpose, this command really belongs in the Copy command.

To illustrate the function of Range Values, suppose you want to transform the formulas in range B4 . . E4 in the worksheet in Figure 8.8 into their current values. Each of these cells contains a simple @SUM function. For example, cell B4 contains the formula

        B4: @SUM(B1 . . B3)

```
    -----A---------B---------C---------D---------E------
1                1000      2000      3000      4000     |
2                2000      3000      4000      5000     |
3                -----     -----     -----     -----    |
4                3000      5000      7000      9000     |
5                                                       |
6                                                       |
    ==================================================MAIN=
```

Figure 8.8

Begin by issuing the {**Menu**} **R**ange **V**alues command. Symphony prompts you first for the FROM range—in the example, B4 . . D4—and then the TO range—B5. When the command is completed, the worksheet will look like Figure 8.9.

Cells B5 to E5 contain simple values. For example, the entry in cell B5 is

        B5: 3000

and the entry in cell E5 is

        E5: 9000

```
    -----A---------B---------C---------D---------E------
  1                1000      2000      3000      4000    |
  2                2000      3000      4000      5000    |
  3                -----     -----     -----     -----   |
  4                3000      5000      7000      9000    |
  5                3000      5000      7000      9000    |
  6                                                      |
    =====================================================MAIN=
```

Figure 8.9

You can also copy a range onto itself with Range Values. For example, suppose the TO range in the above example had been B4. When the command was completed, the worksheet would have looked like Figure 8.10. The @SUM formulas in cells B4 to E4 in this worksheet have been replaced with simple values. For example, cell B4 contains the entry

> B4: 3000

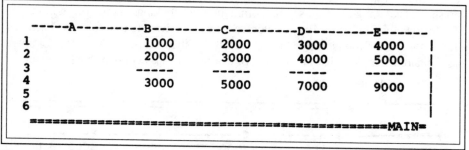

Figure 8.10

Copying a range onto itself with Range Values is a good way to "freeze" the values of certain formulas. Be careful with this command, however; when you copy a range onto itself with Range Values, the original contents of the range will be lost.

If the FROM range you provide contains numbers or labels, Range Values behaves exactly like the Copy command. For example, suppose you've created the worksheet shown in Figure 8.11.

Now you issue the Range Values command, specifying A1 . . A4 as the FROM range and B1 as the TO range. The resulting worksheet looks like the one in Figure 8.12. As you can see, Range Values simply copied the entries in the range A1 . . A4 into the range B1 . . B4.

A Fine Point

It seems to me that the Range Values and Range Transpose commands are misnamed and misplaced. Range Values should be a subcommand of the Copy command called

```
     -----A----------B----------C-----
   1  AAA                               |
   2  BBB                               |
   3  CCC                               |
   4  DDD                               |
   5                                    |
   6                                    |
      ===========================MAIN=
```

Figure 8.11

```
     -----A----------B----------C-----
   1  AAA          AAA                  |
   2  BBB          BBB                  |
   3  CCC          CCC                  |
   4  DDD          DDD                  |
   5                                    |
   6                                    |
      ===========================MAIN=
```

Figure 8.12

Copy Values, and Range Transpose should be a subcommand of the Copy command called Copy Transpose. I think it would make more sense if there were a submenu behind the Copy command that looked like this:

As-Entered   Values   Text   Transpose

The As-Entered option would copy cells in the usual way. The Values option would replace the Range Values command and the Transpose option would replace the Range Transpose command. Copy Text would replace the Print Destination Range command, which we'll cover in a later chapter. In fact, as we will discuss in a later chapter, there are several other commands that really belong in the Copy menu but are instead spread thoughout the program.

FILL

Range Fill is Symphony's equivalent of 1-2-3's /Data Fill command. Since the Fill command had nothing to do with 1-2-3's data base functions anyway, it is just as well that Lotus moved the command to the Range menu in Symphony.

Range Fill allows you to fill a range of cells with a set of evenly spaced numbers. You provide the range to be filled, the value to be entered in the first cell in the range, an interval, and, if you wish, a maximum value for the range. Symphony does the rest automatically.

For example, suppose you want to create a list of all the even numbers between 1 and 100 in column A. You could enter these numbers by hand, or you could create a formula and use the Copy command, but the fastest way to create this list is with Range Fill.

To create this list with Fill, issue the {**Menu**} **R**ange **F**ill command. Symphony prompts you first for the Fill range, the range in which you want Symphony to enter your series of numbers. In our example, the Fill range is A1 .. A50. Of course, you can either type or point to this range. As with most range and cut-and-paste commands, the range is easier to designate if you move the cell pointer to the first cell in the range before you issue the Fill command, and then you use the POINT mode to complete the range.

Next, Symphony asks you to provide a Start value. Since we want to include only even numbers in our list, the Start value is 2. The third required input is the Step value. This number determines the interval between each number in the list. Because we want our list to proceed by twos (2, 4, 6, and so on), the Step value in the example will also be 2. Be aware that although our Start and Step values are the same in this example, these two numbers can be and usually are different.

The Step value can be a number of any size, including tiny decimal numbers, but it is always a constant. That is, the interval between every number in the final list will be the same. There is no way to use Range Fill to create a list of numbers with varying intervals.

Finally, Symphony asks you to provide the Stop value. The Stop value places an upper limit on the values in the list. In the example, the Stop value would be 100. The default Stop value is 8191. Figure 8.13 shows a portion of the completed worksheet.

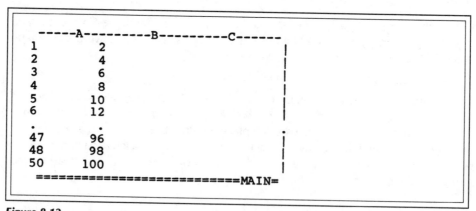

Figure 8.13

Fill Notes

The Start, Step, and Stop values in a Range Fill operation can be negative as well as positive. For example, if you issue the Range Fill command specifying the range A1 .. A5 as the Fill range, − 100 as the Start value, and 10 as the Step value, you'll create the worksheet shown in Figure 8.14.

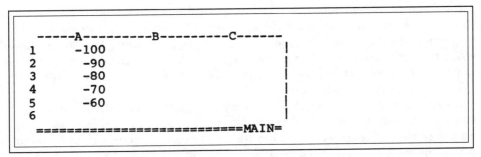

```
    -----A----------B---------C------
 1       -100                           |
 2        -90                           |
 3        -80                           |
 4        -70                           |
 5        -60                           |
 6                                      |
    =========================MAIN=
```

Figure 8.14

Although the Fill Range is usually a single row or column, it can be a rectangular range as well. If you use the Start value and Step value in the previous example and set the Fill range to A1 .. C5, you'll create the worksheet shown in Figure 8.15.

```
    -----A----------B---------C------
 1       -100        -50         0     |
 2        -90        -40        10     |
 3        -80        -30        20     |
 4        -70        -20        30     |
 5        -60        -10        40     |
 6                                     |
    =========================MAIN=
```

Figure 8.15

You can supply a cell reference or a function for any of the three values (Start, Step, and Stop) used by Range Fill. However, Symphony will convert the reference or function to a constant value before it uses it in the command. For example, suppose the function @SUM(A1 .. A3) currently has the value 4. If you use this function as the Step value in a Range Fill operation, the interval between each pair of numbers in the list is 4. If you repeat the Range Fill command, you will see that Symphony uses the constant 4 (the current value of the function), not the function itself, as the Step value. After computing the current value of the function, Symphony forgets the function altogether.

There are cases, though, where you'll want to use a function with the Range Fill command. For example, suppose you want to create a list of the dates between June 1, 1984 and July 1, 1984. You can use the Range Fill command to create this list. Your Start value would be the function @DATE(84,6,1), your Step value would be 1, and the Stop value would be @DATE(84,6,30). Although Symphony converts the functions into constants before it fills the range, the result is a list of Symphony's date representations for the desired dates: 30834, 30863, and so on.

Although you can use numbers, functions, and cell references in defining the Range Fill values, none of the values in the Range Fill command can be a string.

The Fill range and the Stop value can be thought of as two independent braking systems for the Range Fill command. If the Stop value is low enough that a number in the range equals the Stop value before the end of the Fill range is reached, the Fill command will stop and the remaining cells in the Fill range will be blank. If, on the other hand, the Stop value is so large that the entire Fill range is filled before the numbers equal the Stop value, the Stop value will have no effect.

The real advantage of the Stop value is that it eliminates the need to define your Fill range precisely when you're creating long lists of numbers. For example, suppose you want to create a list of 100 numbers, 1 to 100, that extend across the worksheet beginning in column A. Quick—what should the last column in the range be to create a list of exactly 100 numbers? You probably don't know. But if you set the range to extend to column EA (which you're sure leaves enough room) and then set the Stop value at 100, the Range Fill command will stop when the Stop value is reached. The extra cells in the Fill range are simply ignored.

NAME

Range Name is one of the most useful and important commands in Symphony. Range Name makes it possible to assign plain language names to cells and ranges in your worksheet. These names can be used in place of Symphony's conventional cell references (A1, B5, A1 .. B5, and so on) in functions, formulas, and commands.

When you issue the Range Name command, the following menu appears:

> Create   Delete   Labels   Reset   Table

If you are a former user of 1-2-3, this menu should look very familiar. Only one command, Table, is new to Symphony. The others are directly related to 1-2-3's /Range Name command.

Range Name Basics

There are a few simple rules that govern the use of range names. First, a range name can be up to 15 characters long, and it can contain any letter or number. Your range names should not include spaces. If you want to join two words into a single name, attach them with the underscore character (for example, JAN_SALES). Punctuation marks like the comma, semicolon, and period should not be used in range names. Symphony does not distinguish between upper- and lowercase letters in range names. For example, the names ABDCE, ABcdE, and abcde are the same to Symphony.

You should never create a range name that looks like a cell reference. For example, never create a range name like A1, B12, or PR12. Although these names are "legal," they lead to unbelievable confusion.

A given range name can only be used once in a worksheet. If you have assigned a range name to one range in a sheet, and then you assign the same name to a different range, Symphony will remember only the second use of the name.

A range name can apply to any rectangular range from a single cell up to the entire worksheet. Frequently your range names will apply to one cell only. When you create range names that apply to rectangular ranges, Symphony remembers the named range by the address of the upper-left and lower-right corners of the range.

Some Symphony commands and functions expect the user to supply a single cell in response to a prompt. If you supply these commands with a range name that applies to a rectangular range, the command or function will operate on the upper-left cell in that named range. For example, the {Goto} key displays the prompt

> Address to go to:

and expects the user to provide the address of the cell to which the cell pointer should jump. If you supply a range name that applies to a rectangular range in response to this prompt, the cell pointer will jump to the cell in the upper-left corner of the named range.

Creating Range Names

There are two ways to create a named range in Symphony. You can use the Create command, which asks you to provide a name and a range and then pairs the two; or you can use the Labels command, which uses labels that you have entered in the worksheet to name adjacent cells.

Create

Usually range names are created with the Range Name Create command. Range Name Create lets you assign any name to any cell in the worksheet.

For example, suppose you have created the worksheet shown in Figure 8.16 and you want to assign the name PROD1 to the range B2 . . E2. Move the cell pointer to cell B2 and issue the {**Menu**} **R**ange **N**ame **C**reate command. Symphony displays the prompt

> Range name:

```
  ------A---------B----------C----------D----------E---------F--+---
1                Quarter 1 Quarter 2 Quarter 3 Quarter 4
2 Product 1      $10,000   $15,000   $17,000   $19,000     $61,000
3 Product 2      $12,000   $11,000   $11,000   $13,000
4 Product 3      $16,000   $16,000   $17,000   $16,000
5
6                                                              ===MAIN=
  =====================================================================
```

Figure 8.16

Since you want to use the name PROD1, type this label next to the prompt and press **[Enter]**. If you make a mistake while typing the name, just press **[Backspace]** to erase the error and type the rest of the name.

Next, Symphony prompts for the range to be named:

> Range name: PROD1   Specify range: B2

Because the cell pointer was on cell B2 when you issued the Range Name Create command, Symphony offers B2 as its "guess" at the range to be named. If you wanted to name this one cell, you would just press **[Enter]**. But because you want the range name to apply to several cells, you need to specify the entire range for Symphony. As with every other command that requires you to specify a range, Range Name lets you designate the proper range either by typing or by pointing. Since the correct range in the example is B2 . . E2, it is more efficient to point. Once the range is properly defined, press **[Enter]**. Symphony automatically assigns the name PROD1 to the range B2 . . E2.

Cell F2 in the above worksheet contains the formula

> F2: (C0) @SUM(B2 . . E2)

When the range name PROD1 is assigned to the range B2 . . E2, however, this formula automatically changes to

> F2: (C0) @SUM(PROD1)

You could similarly name the ranges B3 . . E3 and B4 . . E4 in this worksheet PROD2 and PROD3. You could then enter formulas in cells F3 and F4 that use these names to total the ranges. For example, suppose you want to create a formula that totals the entries in cells B3 to E3. Move the cell pointer to cell F3 and enter the formula

> F3: @SUM(PROD2)

As you can see, the range name PROD2 is completely interchangeable with the conventional range designation B3 . . E3.

You might also want to name the range B2 . . E4 (the entire sales forecast) SALES. To name this range, issue the {**Menu**} **R**ange Name Create command, specifying SALES as the name to use and B2 . . E4 as the range to be named. You could then enter the formula

> F5: (C0) @SUM(SALES)

in cell F5. This formula would compute the total sales for all three products across the four quarters. Figure 8.17 shows the worksheet after all of these steps are completed.

```
    ------A---------B---------C---------D---------E---------F-----
 1                Quarter 1 Quarter 2 Quarter 3 Quarter 4            |
 2 Product 1      $10,000   $15,000   $17,000   $19,000   $61,000   |
 3 Product 2      $12,000   $11,000   $11,000   $13,000   $47,000   |
 4 Product 3      $16,000   $16,000   $17,000   $16,000   $65,000   |
 5                                                        $173,000  |
 6                                                                  |
 7                                                                  |
    ================================================================MAIN=
```

Figure 8.17

Editing range names   Range Name Create is also used to edit a range name that already exists in the worksheet. For example, suppose you create a name called TOTAL to apply to the range F2 . . F3 in Figure 8.16. After creating the name, you decide that you want it to cover the range F2 . . F4. To make this change, issue the **R**ange Name Create command. Notice that Symphony provides a list of all the names in the current worksheet in addition to the prompt

Range Name:
PROD1 PROD2 PROD3 SALES TOTAL

Because you want to modify the range name TOTAL, you select this name by typing it or by pointing to it and pressing **[Enter].** Symphony responds by displaying the range currently assigned that name, as shown in Figure 8.18.

```
     ------A----------B----------C----------D----------E----------F-----
  1             Quarter 1 Quarter 2 Quarter 3 Quarter 4                |
  2 Product  1    $10,000   $15,000   $17,000   $19,000    $61,000  |
  3 Product  2    $12,000   $11,000   $11,000   $13,000    $47,000  |
  4 Product  3    $16,000   $16,000   $17,000   $16,000    $65,000  |
  5                                                        $173,000 |
  6                                                                  |
     ===========================================================MAIN=
```

Figure 8.18

To expand the range from F2 . . F3 to F2 . . F4, just press ↓ and **[Enter].** The range name TOTAL now applies to the range F2 . . F4.

Labels

Suppose you have created the worksheet shown in Figure 8.19, which contains the total sales for each of five salespeople for the year 1984. Now suppose that you want to give each cell in the range B3 to B7 the name of the appropriate salesperson so that other formulas in the worksheet could refer to the cells by name rather than by cell reference. You could, of course, use the {Menu} Range Name Create command to name each of these cells individually. But you could save some time by using the Range Name Labels command to name each cell in column B with the label stored in the same row in column A.

```
     -----A----------B----------C------
  1            1984 Sales              |
  2                                    |
  3 Tom          $832,612              |
  4 Dick       $1,217,098              |
  5 Harry      $1,618,311              |
  6 Helen      $2,092,198              |
  7 Jane         $926,530              |
  8                                    |
     ============================MAIN=
```

Figure 8.19

To name these cells, move the cell pointer to cell A3 and issue the {**Menu**} **R**ange Name Label command. Symphony presents the following menu:

> Right   Left   Up   Down

Since you want to assign the names in cells A3 to A7 to the cells immediately to their right, select the Right option from this menu. In other situations, you might use one of the other options. For example, the Down option can be used to assign the first cell in each field of a data base the name of the field titles (we'll discuss this more in a later chapter).

Next, Symphony asks you to provide the range containing the labels you want to use as range names. In the example, this range is A3 . . A7. After this range is designated, press [**Enter**] to activate the command. When the command is completed, every cell in the range B3 . . B7 is named. The name assigned to each cell matches the label in the same row in column A. Thus cell B3 has the name Tom and cell B6 has the name Helen.

Be sure you understand that Range Name Labels can only be used to name the cells in a single column or row immediately adjacent to the column or row your labels are assigned to. In other words, you could not have used the Range Name Labels command to name the range B3 . . E3 in Figure 8.16. One of the most common uses for the Range Name Labels command is to name macros. We'll look at this technique for naming macros in Chapter 28.

Deleting Range Names

Occasionally you'll want to delete a range name from a worksheet. The Range Name Delete command makes this task very simple. When you issue the Range Name Delete command, Symphony prompts you to provide the name you want to delete and lists all the range names in the worksheet. For example,

> Name to delete:
> TEST   SALES   PROD1   PROD2   PROD3

If the worksheet contains more than eight names, you won't be able to see all of them at one time. In that case, press {**Menu**} or {**Services**} to display a complete list of the range names on the screen.

You can specify the name you want to delete by pointing to it or by typing it. If the name you type doesn't exist in the worksheet, Symphony will beep and return the error message "Name does not exist."

As soon as you select the name to be deleted and press [**Enter**], Symphony deletes the name. Unlike some of Symphony's other destructive commands, Range Name Delete gives no warning before deleting the selected name.

If the range name that you've deleted was used by any formulas, the range name will be replaced in these formulas by the cell address for the previously named range. For example, suppose that the name PROD1 applies to the range B2 . . E2 and that cell F2 contains the formula

> F2: (C0) @SUM(PROD1)

If the name PROD1 is deleted, this formula changes to

> F2: (C0) @SUM(B2 . . E2)

It's a good idea to delete a range name before you assign it to a different cell. For example, suppose you have assigned the name TEST to cell A1. Cell A2 contains the formula

> A2: + TEST/100

Now suppose you use Range Name Create to reassign the name TEST to cell B1. The formula in cell A2 still reads

> A2: + TEST/100

but TEST now refers to cell B1 instead of cell A1. Although the formula looks the same, its meaning has changed completely.

   You can avoid this problem if you use Range Name Delete to erase the name TEST before you reassign it to cell B1. Then when you issue Range Name Delete the formula in cell A2 changes to

> A2: + A1/100

Now the name TEST can be assigned to B1 without affecting the formula in cell A2.

Reset

   If you want to delete all of the range names in the current worksheet in one fell swoop, you can use the Range Name Reset command. When you issue this command, Symphony gives you one chance to reconsider:

> Reset all range names in worksheet?
> No   Yes

If you select Yes, every range name in the worksheet is deleted instantly. Any range names used in formulas will be replaced with standard cell references.

Table

   The Range Name Table command lets you create a table in the worksheet that lists all of the range names in that worksheet and the coordinates of the ranges to which those names apply. For example, Suppose your worksheet contains the following range names: PROD1, PROD2, PROD3, SALES, and TOTAL. You want to list these names in the worksheet.

   First, issue the {**Menu**} **R**ange **N**ame **T**able command. Symphony prompts you for the location of the table with the message

> Location for table: I1..I1

The I1 in the prompt assumes the cell pointer was in cell I1 when the command was issued. Like most other Symphony commands, Range Name Table tries to help out by "guessing" at the desired location for the table. If you want the table to appear at cell I1, you can accept Symphony's guess by pressing [Enter]. Otherwise, enter a new location by typing or pointing to a cell.

Assuming that you accept Symphony's prompt and press **[Enter]** to activate the command, the worksheet will look like Figure 8.20. Notice that the address used to identify the table location became the upper-left corner of the table. The range names themselves appear in alphabetical order in column I, the first column in the table, and the address that corresponds to each name appears in column J.

```
    -----I-------J----------K--------L--------
1  PROD1   B2..E2                           |
2  PROD2   B3..E3                           |
3  PROD3   B4..E4                           |
4  SALES   B2..E4                           |
5  TOTAL   F2..F4                           |
6                                           |
7                                           |
   ==================================MAIN=
```

Figure 8.20

If the range I1 . . J5 had contained any cell entries before you issued the Range Name Table command, these entries would have been destroyed by the table. Be careful! Range Name Table doesn't give any warning before it erases a part of your worksheet.

The Range Name Table command can be very handy to help document your worksheet. For example, if your worksheet contains a Range Name Table, this table will appear on the printed version of the worksheet. This printed guide to the range names can help you explain the worksheet to other users or reacquaint yourself with the sheet after a long absence.

Remember that range name tables are not dynamic; that is, once you create a table, it is fixed and will not reflect any additions or deletions of range names or any changes to existing names. If you want to keep the table up to date, you must reissue the Range Name Table command.

Why Use Range Names?

Because Symphony already provides a perfectly satisfactory way of designating ranges in commands, functions, and formulas, you may wonder about the real value of range names. In fact, range names are one of Symphony's most valuable features.

Range names are most obviously useful for transforming perplexing cell references into easy-to-understand, plain-language names. For example, in Figure 8.16 we named the range B2 . . E2 PROD1. This name is far more understandable than the reference alone.

Range names are also crucial to the Symphony Command Language. First, all macros created by the Symphony Command Language must be given a name. This range name is then used to activate the macro. In addition, range names are the preferred method for referring to cells from within a macro. We'll cover this concept in more detail in Chapter 28.

Range names can also help out when you're in Symphony's COMM environment. As you'll learn in a later chaper, Symphony's COMM mode allows you to capture information from another computer through the telephone line into a range in the worksheet. If you name this range CAPTURE, you can easily jump to the captured material just by pressing {Goto} CAPTURE.

Range Name Notes

Suppose you create two range names that apply to the same range in a worksheet. For example, suppose you assign the range name SECOND to the range B2 . . E2 in the worksheet in Figure 8.16. Remember that this range already has the name PROD1. Now suppose you issue the Range Name Create command to change the range covered by SECOND from B2 . . E2 to B2 . . E4. If you now issue the Range Name Create command and specify PROD1 as the range to be changed, you'll see that the range for PROD1 has already changed to B2 . . E4. Any time you create two or more range names that apply to the same range, and then change the range of one of the names, the range of the other also changes. However, deleting one of a pair of synonymous range names does not delete the other one.

You also need to be careful when you move cells around on a worksheet that contains range names. You can change the definition of a range name or even delete the name with the Move command. For example, suppose you issue the Move command in the worksheet in Figure 8.17. Specify cell B2 as the FROM range and cell A7 as the TO range. Remember that cell B2 is one of the cells that defines the range names PROD1 (B2 . . E2) and SALES (B2 . . E4). After the Move command is completed, the worksheet will look like the one in Figure 8.21.

```
    -----A----------B----------C----------D----------E----------F-----
1                Quarter 1 Quarter 2 Quarter 3 Quarter 4             |
2 Product 1                $15,000   $17,000   $19,000   $173,000  |
3 Product 2      $12,000   $11,000   $11,000   $13,000   $47,000   |
4 Product 3      $16,000   $16,000   $17,000   $16,000   $65,000   |
5                                                        $75,000   |
6                                                                  |
7   $10,000                                                        |
    ======================================================MAIN=
```

Figure 8.21

Notice that the totals in cells F2 and F5 have changed as a result of the move and are no longer correct. A look at the ranges covered by the names PROD1 and SALES reveals the reason: PROD1 now applies to the range A7 . . E2, and the name SALES now covers the range A7 . . E4. As you can see, moving cell B2, which served as one of the range markers for these two range names, changed the ranges themselves. Whenever you move a cell that serves as an anchor for a range name, the range changes.

Now suppose you issue the Move command again, this time specifying the FROM range as B3 and the TO range as A7. When the command is finished, the worksheet will look like the one in Figure 8.22.

```
    -----A---------B---------C---------D---------E---------F-----
1                 Quarter 1 Quarter 2 Quarter 3 Quarter 4         |
2 Product 1                 $15,000   $17,000   $19,000      ERR  |
3 Product 2                 $11,000   $11,000   $13,000  $102,000 |
4 Product 3       $16,000   $16,000   $17,000   $16,000   $65,000 |
5                                                            ERR  |
6                                                                 |
7   $12,000                                                       |
    ========================================================MAIN=
```

Figure 8.22

As you can see, things are really messed up now. The range names PROD1, PROD2, and SALES have all been affected by this second move. Range name PROD2 now covers the range A7 . . E3, so the @SUM formula in cell F3 now totals the cells in this range. Range names PROD1 and SALES, however, have been destroyed. The formulas in cells F2 and F5 are now

F2: (C2) @SUM(ERR)
F3: (C2) @SUM(ERR)

When you moved cell B3 to A7, you destroyed the anchor for these two range names, and thus destroyed the ranges themselves. Whenever you move one cell onto a cell that serves as one of the definitions for a range name, the range will be destroyed.

The Insert and Delete commands affect named ranges in the same way. Deleting a row or column that contains the anchor cell for a named range will destroy the range. For example, deleting row 4 from the worksheet in Figure 8.17 makes the worksheet look like Figure 8.23 and destroys the definition of the range name SALES.

Similarly, because all of the range names in Figure 8.17 depend on a cell in column B, deleting column B from the worksheet will destroy all of the ranges in the sheet.

Inserting or deleting a row or column in the middle of a named range does not destroy the range definition, but it does modify the size of the range. For example, inserting a

```
    -----A---------B---------C---------D---------E---------F-----
1                 Quarter 1 Quarter 2 Quarter 3 Quarter 4         |
2 Product 1       $10,000   $15,000   $17,000   $19,000   $61,000 |
3 Product 2       $12,000   $11,000   $11,000   $13,000   $47,000 |
4                                                                 |
5                                                            ERR  |
    ========================================================MAIN=
```

Figure 8.23

row above row 4 in Figure 8.17 makes the worksheet look like Figure 8.24 and changes the definition of the named range SALES from B2 . . F4 to B2 . . F5.

```
    -----A---------B---------C---------D---------E---------F------
1               Quarter 1 Quarter 2 Quarter 3 Quarter 4          |
2 Product 1     $10,000   $15,000   $17,000   $19,000   $61,000  |
3 Product 2     $12,000   $11,000   $11,000   $13,000   $47,000  |
4                                                                |
5 Product 3     $16,000   $16,000   $17,000   $16,000   $65,000  |
6                                                       $173,000 |
7                                                                |
    =================================================MAIN=
```

Figure 8.24

These examples should help you understand the effects of the cut-and-paste commands on a named range. If you want a quick reference on this subject, refer to Table 8.2, which summarizes the effects of Symphony's cut-and-paste commands on a named range.

Range: A1 . . C5
Range Name: TEST

Command	New Range	Name Intact?
Move A1 to A15	A15 . . C5	Yes
Move A2 to A15	A1 . . C5	Yes
Move A15 to A1	Range destroyed	No
Insert row above 1	A2 . . C6	Yes
Insert row above 5	A1 . . C6	Yes
Insert row above 7	A1 . . C5	Yes
Insert column B	A1 . . D5	Yes
Insert column D	A1 . . C5	Yes
Delete row 1	Range destroyed	No
Delete row 4	A1 . . C4	Yes
Delete row 7	A1 . . C5	Yes
Erase A1	A1 . . C5	Yes
Copy A15 to A1	A1 . . C5	Yes
Copy A1 to A15	A1 . . C5	Yes

Table 8.2

LABEL-ALIGNMENT

As you learned in Chapter 1, Symphony offers four different label prefix characters: ', ", ^, and \. The label prefix character you choose when entering a label determines the appearance of that label in the worksheet. Table 8.3 shows the effect of each label-prefix character.

Label Prefix	Alignment
'	Left
"	Right
^	Centered
\	Repeating

Table 8.3

```
---------A-----------B----
1 A label                  |
2         A label          |
3      A label             |
4 A labelA label           |
==========================
```

Most of the time when you enter a label you won't consciously choose a label prefix. Instead, you'll just type the label and let Symphony supply the prefix. The label prefix Symphony uses is determined by the label-prefix setting in the SHEET settings sheet. The standard label prefix is ', but this can be changed using the SHEET {Menu} Settings command.

There are times when you'll want to change the alignment of a label after it has been entered in the worksheet. For example, suppose you enter the headers shown in row 2 of the worksheet in Figure 8.25 using Symphony's default label prefix, '. Notice that all of the labels are left aligned.

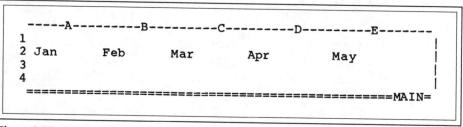

Figure 8.25

Now you want to change the alignment of these labels from left to center. First, move the cell pointer to cell A2 and issue the Range Label-Alignment command. The following menu appears:

       Left   Center   Right

Since you want to center the labels, select the Center option. Next, Symphony displays the prompt

       Range of labels: A2 . . A2

Since you want to change the alignment of the labels in the range A2 . . E2, you should use the → key to extend the provided range to A2 . . E2, and then press [Enter]. This command changes the alignment of these labels to that shown in Figure 8.26.

The Label-Alignment command works only on cells that contain labels. Cells containing values are not affected by this command. In fact, there is no way to change the alignment of a value in Symphony—one of the program's biggest weaknesses.

Another rule to keep in mind is that Range Label-Alignment cannot be used to format cells in anticipation of entering labels in those cells. For example, suppose cell A2 in a

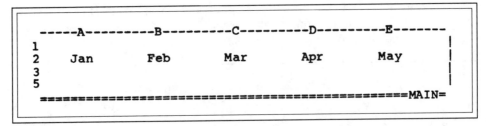

```
    -----A----------B----------C----------D----------E-------
  1                                                           |
  2    Jan         Feb         Mar         Apr         May     |
  3                                                           |
  5                                                           |
      ========================================================MAIN=
```

Figure 8.26

worksheet is blank. Now suppose you issue the Label-Alignment command, select the Center option, and specify A2 as the range to align.

Now enter the label WXYZ in cell A2. Assuming that the default label prefix was ' (left), the label is entered left aligned, as shown in Figure 8.27. The Label-Alignment command had no effect on the blank cell A2. Once the label has been entered, though, you can issue the Range Label-Alignment command to center it.

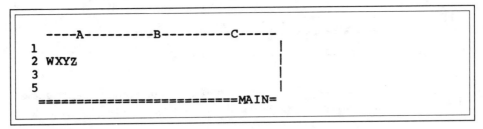

```
    ----A----------B----------C-----
  1                                 |
  2  WXYZ                           |
  3                                 |
  5                                 |
     ==========================MAIN=
```

Figure 8.27

The only way to enter a label with a prefix other than the default is to type the prefix as you enter the label. For example, to center the label WXYZ in the above example without using the Range Label-Alignment command, you could enter the label as ^WXYZ.

If you plan to enter a large number of right-justified or centered labels, you might consider changing the default label prefix setting with the {Menu} Settings Label-Prefix command.

DISTRIBUTION

You can use Symphony's Range Distribution command to create frequency distributions in your Symphony worksheets. A frequency distribution is a special table that shows how many items from a group fall into a series of predefined groups. For example, you might create a frequency distribution that groups the high temperatures for each day in a year into several groups: below 0, 1 degree to 32 degrees, 32 degrees to 50 degrees, 50 degrees to 80 degrees, and over 80 degrees. Such a frequency distribution would take a long time to compose by hand. Fortunately, the Range Distribution command can create a frequency distribution automatically.

Consider the following example. Suppose you are teaching a course in introductory accounting at a local college. You have just given a test to your students. The results of the exam are shown in column A in Figure 8.28.

```
 -----A----------B----------C----------D------
1       95          F          60                 |
2       82          D          70                 |
3       67          C          80                 |
4       85          B          90                 |
5       91          A         100                 |
6       72                                         |
7       70                                         |
8       73                                         |
9       82                                         |
10      96                                         |
11      44                                         |
12      72                                         |
13      89                                         |
14      92                                         |
15      83                                         |
 ===========================================MAIN=
```

Figure 8.28

In column B of this worksheet, we have entered the five common letter grades. Column C shows the cut-off points for each grade: 0 to 60 is an F, 61 to 70 is a D, 71 to 80 a C, and so on.

We want Symphony to tell us how many students earned each grade. To make this computation, issue the Range Distribution command. Symphony asks you to provide two ranges: The Data range and the Bin range. The Data range is the range containing the data set you want to analyze. In this example, the Data range is A1 . . A15. The Bin range is the range containing the numbers that define the "bins" into which you want to group the numbers.

As soon as the Bin range is defined, Symphony computes the number of items from the Data range that belong in each part of the Bin range and enters these counts in the range D1 . . D6. The completed distribution table is shown in Figure 8.29.

This frequency distribution tells us that only one student earned a grade between 0 and 60, two students earned a grade between 61 and 70, three students earned marks between 71 and 80, and so on.

There are a couple of points to remember about Range Distribution. First, notice that the numbers in the Bin range are arranged in ascending numeric order. This arrangement is required—the Bin range must always be a partial column containing a set of numbers in ascending numeric order. You cannot create a horizontal frequency distribution table in Symphony.

Also notice that Symphony assumes the existence of a bin in row 6, even though the Bin range extended only to cell C5 and no number was entered in cell C6. This last bin

```
-----A---------- -B----------C-----------D------
 1       95           F          60          1  |
 2       82           D          70          2  |
 3       67           C          80          3  |
 4       85           B          90          5  |
 5       91           A         100          4  |
 6       72                                  0  |
 7       70                                     |
 8       73                                     |
 9       82                                     |
10       96                                     |
11       44                                     |
12       72                                     |
13       89                                     |
14       92                                     |
15       83                                     |
       ===================================MAIN=
```

Figure 8.29

shows the number of entries in the table that fall above the last number in the Bin range. For example, the number in cell D6 in the example represents the number of students that scored greater than 100 on the exam. Since no student scored higher than 100, this range has a value of 0. All Symphony range distribution tables will have an extra bin that displays the number of items in the Data range that are greater than the last number in the Bin range.

Once you've defined a Data range and a Bin range, Symphony will remember these range definitions until you deliberately reset them. This means that you can repeat the same Range Distribution computation over and over by just typing {**Menu**} **R**ange **D**istribution [**Enter**] [**Enter**].

The results of a Range Distribution command are frequently used to create a bar or line graph. For example, we could use Symphony's Graph command to build the graph shown in Figure 8.30 from the results of our sample range distribution.

WHAT-IF

When you were first learning algebra, you were required to solve equations that involved two variables, X and Y. One of the ways to solve this kind of equation is to build a simple table that shows the value of Y for several different values of X. For example, suppose you want to solve the equation

$$2X + 4 = Y$$

You might build a table like this:

```
                    X
     1  2  3  4  5  6  7  8  9 10
 Y
```

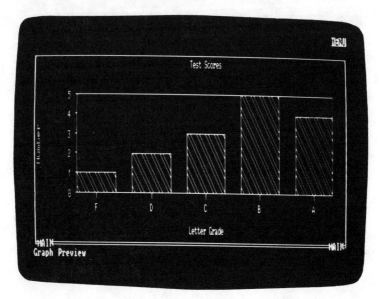

Figure 8.30

After building the table, you would solve the equation for each of the listed X values and then enter those values in the table. The completed table would look like this:

	X									
	1	2	3	4	5	6	7	8	9	10
Y	6	8	10	12	14	16	18	20	22	24

Symphony includes the Range What-If command to let you build such a table in the Symphony worksheet. Range What-If is powerful command because once you've defined the equation and the variables you want to test, Symphony automatically does all of the calculations for you. (Former 1-2-3 users will recognize the Range What-If command as the equivalent of the 1-2-3 /Data Table command.)

Suppose, for example, that you wanted to compute the amount of money you will be able to withdraw from your IRA 25 years from today. Since the future value of an IRA depends heavily on the average annual interest rate across the life of the IRA, you decide to compute the future value using several different interest rates. Begin by entering the rates you want to test in cells A3 to A7 in a worksheet, as shown in Figure 8.31. We'll call this the entry range, or variable range, for the what-if table.

Next, enter the formula

> **B2: @FV(2000,A1,25)**

in cell B2. We'll call this the master formula for the what-if table. This formula uses Symphony's @FV function, which computes the future value of a constant stream of payments, given an interest rate and a term. In the above formula, the annual payment is $2000 and the term is 25 years. The interest rate argument consists of a reference to cell

```
     -----A----------B----------C----------D-----
   1                                               |
   2                                               |
   3     5.00%                                      |
   4     7.50%                                      |
   5    10.00%                                      |
   6    12.50%                                      |
   7    15.00%                                      |
   8                                               |
       ===========================================MAIN=
```

Figure 8.31

A1. Because A1 is blank, the function will return the @ERR message. If you're wondering why this formula refers to a blank cell, keep reading—there is a reason for it.

Now that the entry values and the formula have been specified, you're ready to issue the {**Menu**} **R**ange **W**hat-If command. Since this will be a one-variable what-if table, choose 1-Way from the first What-If menu. Next, Symphony prompts you for the table range, which in this example is A2 . . B7. Notice that the range includes both the interest rates in column A (the "variables") and the equation in cell B2.

After the table range is defined, Symphony asks you to provide the location of the Input cell. In general, the Input cell should be a blank cell that is referred to, directly or indirectly, by the formula in the what-if table. In our example, the Input cell is A1. Remember that the interest rate term in the function in cell B2 refers to cell A1.

To understand the meaning of the Input cell, you must understand how Symphony processes a what-if table. When you issue the Range What-If command, Symphony automatically substitutes the values from the entry range, one by one, into the Input cell. Each time a value is entered in the Input cell, Symphony recalculates the worksheet. Because the master formula in the table refers to the Input cell, the value of this formula will be different after each substitution. Symphony records these different results in the what-if table, each result next to the variable from which it resulted. All of this happens too quickly to be seen.

In the example, the values in the entry range A3 . . A7 are substituted, one by one, into the Input cell, A1. As each value is substituted into this cell, the worksheet is recalculated. Because the interest rate term of the function in cell B2 refers to cell A1, the value of this formula is different for each different value in cell A1. Symphony records the value of the function after each substitution and recalculation in the what-if table.

For example, when you issue the Range What-If command in the example, Symphony substitutes the value .05 (5%) into cell A1 and recalculates the worksheet. Using .05 as the interest rate in the function

    B2: @FV(2000,A1,25)

results in the value $95,454, the future value of a stream of $2000 payments over 25 years at an annual interest rate of 5%. Since the value $95,454 is the result generated by the rate 5%, Symphony enters $95,454 in the what-if table in cell B3, next to the variable 5%.

Next, Symphony substitutes the value .75 (7.5%) into cell A1 and recalculates the worksheet. Given an annual interest rate of 7.5%, the function in cell B2 returns the value $135,956. Symphony enters this value in cell B4, next to the rate 7.5.

Symphony continues to substitute, recalculate, and store numbers until it reaches the end of the table. The resulting worksheet looks like the one in Figure 8.32.

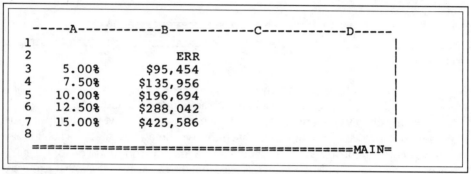

```
    -----A-----------B-----------C-----------D-----
  1                                                    |
  2                       ERR                          |
  3      5.00%        $95,454                          |
  4      7.50%       $135,956                          |
  5     10.00%       $196,694                          |
  6     12.50%       $288,042                          |
  7     15.00%       $425,586                          |
  8                                                    |
    ============================================MAIN=
```

Figure 8.32

The values in the range B3 . . B7 represent the value of the @FV function at each of the interest rates in column A. In essence, this table takes the place of five separate calculations.

Building a Table with Two Equations

Suppose that both you and your spouse work, qualifying you for an annual IRA contribution of $4000. You therefore want to compute the future value of the IRA assuming an annual contribution of $4000 at each of the interest rates in the range A3 . . A7. Fortunately, you don't have to build a separate table to make this computation. Symphony allows you to modify the basic what-if table to perform both of these calculations at once.

First, move the cell pointer to cell C2 and enter the formula

C2: @FV(4000,A1,25)

This function is identical to the one in cell B2 except that the payment term argument has been changed from 2000 to 4000. Notice that this second equation also refers to the Input cell A1.

Now issue the {**Menu**} Range What-If 1-Way command. When prompting you for the table range, Symphony automatically highlights the range specified in the previous What-If operation. As with many other commands, Symphony "remembers" the table range and the Input cell of a Range What-If command until you deliberately change those settings or until you exit from Symphony. Since you used the table range A2 . . B7 in the last example, this range is highlighted.

You want to change the table range for this What-If operation to A2 . . C7. You can make this change by pressing → once when Symphony displays the old range and then pressing **[Enter]**. Next, Symphony asks you to provide the Input cell. Again, the program highlights the previously defined Input cell. Since you want to use this cell again, you need only press **[Enter]**.

As soon as the Input cell is defined, Symphony begins to substitute the interest rates in the range A3 . . A7 into cell A1. After each substitution, Symphony recalculates the sheet, generating a new result for both equations in the table. These results are entered in the table, as shown in Figure 8.33.

```
   -----A----------- --B----------- -C----------- -D-----
1                                                        |
2                       ERR            ERR              |
3      5.00%         $95,454        $190,908           |
4      7.50%        $135,956        $271,911           |
5     10.00%        $196,694        $393,388           |
6     12.50%        $288,042        $576,083           |
7     15.00%        $425,586        $851,172           |
8                                                       |
    ============================================MAIN=
```

Figure 8.33

Provided your computer has sufficient memory, a one-variable what-if table can have as many as 255 different equations. However, each equation that you add to the table increases the time required to recompute the table. If the table has more than a few equations or more than a few variables, the table could require several minutes to recompute.

A Third Example

Suppose you had built the worksheet shown in Figure 8.34. This worksheet shows a simple profit-and-loss statement for a company. The terms CGS, GM, and Op Exp are abbreviations for the accounting terms Cost of Goods Sold, Gross Margin, and Operating Expenses. The following list shows the formulas and values contained in each cell in this worksheet:

B2: −B1*.45
B4: +B1+B2
B5: −5000
B7: +B4+B5

Suppose you want to compute the net income that will result from each of three different sales figures: $10,000, $12,000, and $15,000. You perform this test by entering each of these values in cell B1 manually, recomputing the worksheet, and recording the results by hand on paper or in another part of the worksheet. Alternatively, you could use the Range What-If command to test all three values automatically and record the results in a table.

Begin by entering the three values you want to test in cells D2, D3, and D4. These three cells are the entry range for this table. Next, enter the simple formula

     E1: +B7

in cell E1. This will be the table's master formula. Figure 8.35 shows the worksheet with the entry range and the master formula defined.

```
------A----------B-----------C---------D-----
1 Sales                                         |
2 CGS            ($0.00)                         |
3                -------                         |
4 GM             ($0.00)                         |
5 Op Exp  ($5,000.00)                            |
6                ----------                      |
7 Net     ($5,000.00)                            |
=========================================MAIN=
```

Figure 8.34

```
------A----------B-----------C---------D---------E-----
1 Sales                                         ($5,000)|
2 CGS            ($0.00)                $15,000          |
3                -------                $12,000          |
4 GM             ($0.00)                $10,000          |
5 Op Exp  ($5,000.00)                                    |
6                ----------                              |
7 Net     ($5,000.00)                                    |
===========================================================MAIN=
```

Figure 8.35

Now issue the **Range What-If** command. Since the example table is a one-variable table, select option **1-Way.** The table range in this example is D1 . . E4. As before, notice that this range includes the master formula and the entry range. Specify cell B1 as the Input cell.

When the command operates, each of the three values in the range D2 . . D4 is substituted into the Input cell. As each value is substituted, the worksheet is recalculated. Since the net income in cell B7 is indirectly related to the value in cell B1, each entry value results in a different net income. Each of these results is recorded in the what-if table.

For example, the value $15,000 is substituted into cell B1 and the worksheet is recalculated. Given the formulas in cells B2 and B4, and the value in cell B5, sales of $15,000 must result in a net income of $3,250. Symphony enters this value in cell E2, under the master formula and next to the entry value $15,000. After the table has processed this first variable, the number $12,000 is substituted into cell B1 and the cycle continues. After all three input values have been processed, the table looks like Figure 8.36.

```
  -----A----------B-----------C---------D---------E-----
1 Sales                                          ($5,000)|
2 CGS              ($0.00)              $15,000    $3,250 |
3                 -------               $12,000    $1,600 |
4 GM               ($0.00)              $10,000      $500 |
5 Op Exp  ($5,000.00)                                    |
6                 -----------                            |
7 Net     ($5,000.00)                                    |
  =============================================-=====MAIN=
```

Figure 8.36

This example demonstrates several important characteristics of what-if tables. First, notice that the master formula in this table does not refer directly to the Input cell. Instead, the master formula refers to cell B7, which indirectly refers to the Input cell B2. It is not necessary for the master formula in a what-if table to refer directly to the Input cell; it can refer to it indirectly.

Second, notice that the results in the range E2 . . E4 are formatted to display as currency with no decimal places. There is no magic to this format; we simply used the Format Currency 0 command to assign the format to these cells before the table was created. You can assign any format at all to the entry range, result range, and master formula in a what-if table.

Third, notice the value in cell E1 in Figure 8.36, ($5,000). This value represents the "null substitution" result of the table's master formula. In other words, ($5,000) is the result of the formula when no value has been substituted into the Input cell.

In this and many other cases, the "null substitution" value of the master formula is meaningless and can be confusing. For this reason, many Symphony users assign the Other Literal format to the cell containing the master formula of their what-if tables. If we used the {**Menu**} Format Other Literal command to change the format of cell E1 in the example, the worksheet would look like Figure 8.37. Alternatively, you could use the Format Other Hidden command to completely hide the formula in cell E1.

A fourth important thing to notice about this table is that the numbers in the range D2 to D4 are in descending order. If you look back to Figure 8.33, you'll see that the values in the entry range in the first table were in ascending order. In fact, the numbers in the entry ranges can be in any order you wish, including no particular order at all.

Repeating the Command

Suppose that after testing the three values in the previous example you decide to test three different values: $12,500, $13,000, and $13,500. To make this change, simply enter the new values in cells D2, D3, and D4 and issue the **R**ange **W**hat-If **1**-Way command.

```
     -----A----------B-----------C----------D----------E-----
   1 Sales                                            +B7      |
   2 CGS            ($0.00)                  $15,000   $3,250  |
   3                -------                  $12,000   $1,600  |
   4 GM             ($0.00)                  $10,000     $500  |
   5 Op Exp  ($5,000.00)                                       |
   6                -----------                                |
   7 Net      ($5,000.00)                                      |
     ==========================================================MAIN=
```

Figure 8.37

Notice that Symphony "guesses" that the range and the Input cell for this What-If operation match those you defined previously. For example, Symphony assumes that the Input cell for this table is B1 since B1 was the Input cell in the previous operation. Similarly, Symphony assumes that D1 . . E4 will be the range for this new table.

Since you want to use the same Input cell and range in this What-If operation, you need only press **[Enter]** twice to accept Symphony's guesses. Of course, you could have changed the location of the Input cell or the size of the range if you had wanted to simply by pointing with the cursor keys.

As soon as you press **[Enter]** the second time, Symphony begins to process the values in the entry range. As before, the values in the entry range are substituted one by one into cell B1, the worksheet is recalculated, and the results of the formula are entered in the result range. Figure 8.38 shows the completed table.

```
     -----A----------B-----------C----------D----------E-----
   1 Sales                                            +B7      |
   2 CGS            ($0.00)                  $12,500   $1,875  |
   3                -------                  $13,000   $2,125  |
   4 GM             ($0.00)                  $13,500   $2,425  |
   5 Op Exp  ($5,000.00)                                       |
   6                -----------                                |
   7 Net      ($5,000.00)                                      |
     ==========================================================MAIN=
```

Figure 8.38

Former users of 1-2-3 may recall that in 1-2-3 it was even easier to repeat a data table operation. Once a 1-2-3 data table was defined, you had only to press {Table} to recompute it. Unfortunately, Symphony does not offer a {Table} key, so you must repeat the Range What-If command every time you want to recompute a what-if table.

A Two-Variable Table

Going back to the first example, suppose you are considering holding onto your IRA investment for a few extra years, and you want to test the effect of this on the net amount in the IRA. You could use a two-variable what-if table to make this computation. The form of the two-variable what-if table is somewhat different than the form of the one-variable table. Still, the theory behind both tables is the same.

A two-variable what-if table can also be compared to tables you used to build in school. As you became more comfortable with algebra, you probably were asked to solve equations that involved two variables. For example, you might have been required to solve an equation like this:

$$4X + 2Y = Z$$

To solve this equation, you might have built a table that computed the result of the equation at several different values of X and Y. Figure 8.39 shows such a table. This simple table is very similar to a Symphony two-variable what-if table.

		X				
		1	2	3	4	5
	1	6	10	14	18	22
	2	8	12	16	20	24
Y	3	10	14	18	22	26
	4	12	16	20	24	28
	5	14	18	22	26	29

Figure 8.39

To create the example two-variable what-if table, enter the interest rates you want to test in cells A3 . . A7 in a blank worksheet. Next, enter the different terms you want to test in the range B2 . . D2. Now move to cell A2 and enter the formula

A2: @FV(2000,A1,B1)

This formula computes the future value of the IRA assuming a constant annual contribution of $2000, the interest rate in cell A1, and the term variable in cell B1. Since A1 and B1 are currently blank, this function would return the @ERR message.

Figure 8.40 shows the worksheet with both the interest rates and the term variables in place. Notice that the layout of this two-variable table is somewhat different than the layout of a one-variable table. First, this table includes two entry ranges: A3 . . A7 and B2 . . D2. These two ranges contain the two sets of values that you want to test.

Second, notice that the master formula in this two-variable table is in the first column of the table. In the one-variable table, the master formula was in the second column of the table. Because of the location of the master formula in two-variable tables, these tables cannot have more than one master formula.

To compute the table, issue the Range What-If command and choose option 2. Symphony prompts you to supply the table range, which in this case is A2 . . D7. Notice that the range includes all values in both entry ranges. Next, Symphony asks you to provide the two Input cells required in a two-variable table. You may have already guessed that the Input cells for this table will be A1 and B1. Specifically, Input cell 1 is A1 and Input cell 2 is B1.

```
     -----A-----------B-----------C-----------D-----
  1                                                  |
  2        ERR          25            28          30 |
  3       5.00%                                       |
  4       7.50%                                       |
  5      10.00%                                       |
  6      12.50%                                       |
  7      15.00%                                       |
  8                                                  |
     ==========================================MAIN=
```

Figure 8.40

After the necessary cells and ranges are defined, Symphony begins to compute the table. As with the one-variable table, processing a two-variable table is a three-step process: Symphony substitutes the values from the entry ranges into the Input cells, recalculates the worksheet, and enters the results of each calculation in the table. In a two-variable table, however, the substitutions occur two at a time.

For example, when Symphony begins processing this table, it first substitutes the value .05 (5%) into cell A1 and the value 25 into cell B1. Then Symphony recalculates the worksheet. Because the master formula uses the value in cell A1 as its interest-rate argument and the value in cell B1 as the term argument, the result of this recalculation is the future value of an even stream of $2000 payments across 25 years at an annual rate of 5%, $95,454. This result is entered in cell B3, below the term variable 25 and next to the term variable 5%.

Eventually, Symphony evaluates all of the combinations of terms and interest rates. The final table will look like the one in Figure 8.41.

```
     -----A-----------B-----------C-----------D------
  1                                                   |
  2        ERR          25            28          30  |
  3       5.00%      $95,454      $116,805     $132,878 |
  4       7.50%     $135,956      $175,359     $206,799 |
  5      10.00%     $196,694      $268,420     $328,988 |
  6      12.50%     $288,042      $416,903     $531,893 |
  7      15.00%     $425,586      $654,208     $869,490 |
  8                                                   |
     ===========================================MAIN=
```

Figure 8.41

Notice that even a simple two-variable table like this one contains 15 different combinations of interest rates and terms. Since the entire worksheet is recalculated once for each combination, and since one recalculation of even a moderate-sized sheet can take a few seconds, even a small what-if table may require a noticeable amount of time to recalculate. Large tables can take several minutes (in extreme cases, hours) to recalculate.

Range What-If is an extremely useful command. Unfortunately, many Symphony users avoid the command because they don't understand it. Now that you've seen how Range What-If works, you should able to find uses for this command in many of your spreadsheets.

PROTECT

Range Protect is one of the commands offered by Symphony that lets you secure your worksheet. The Range Protect command works with the {Services} Settings Global-Protection command and the {Services} Settings Security command to prevent changes to certain cells in the worksheet.

The Range Protect command offers two options: Allow-Changes and Prevent-Changes. Every cell in the worksheet has one of these two attributes. When Symphony is first loaded into your computer, every cell has the Prevent-Changes attribute.

The effectiveness of the Range Protect attributes is controlled by the {Services} Settings Global-Protection command. If Global-Protection is set to Yes, every cell that has the Prevent-Changes attribute will be protected. However, if Global-Protection is No, all cells can be changed, including those with the Range Protect Prevent-Changes attribute.

The relationship between the Global-Protection and the Range Protect commands is best illustrated by analogy. Imagine that you have a room in your house that contains hundreds of lamps. Each lamp has its own on-off switch. In addition, there is a wall switch that controls the electrical current to every outlet in the room. If the wall switch is on, you can use the switches on each lamp to control the amount of light in the room. However, if the wall switch is off, it doesn't matter whether the individual lamps are on or off—the room will be dark because no power is flowing to the lamps.

You can think about the {Services} Settings Global-Protection command as being like the wall switch in your make-believe room. If Global-Protection is set to No, no cells in the worksheet will be protected. Even cells with the Prevent-Changes attribute can be changed, since no "protection juice" is flowing to those cells. On the other hand, when the Global-Protection command is set to Yes, all cells with the Prevent-Changes attribute will be protected.

What Does Protection Do?

When the Global-Protection setting is Yes, Symphony will not allow you to make any change to a cell that has the Prevent-Changes attribute. You will not be able to edit, format, or enter a new label, value, or formula into a protected cell. You will also not be allowed to delete a row or column that contains one or more protected cells.

If you attempt to change a protected cell, Symphony responds with the message "Protected cell". Before you'll be able to alter the cell, you must either use the Range Protect command to assign the Allow-Changes attribute to the cell or change the Global-Protection setting to No.

Using Range Protect

When you first load Symphony into your computer, every cell in the worksheet is protected. In other words, the Range Protect attribute for every cell is Prevent-Changes. But the default Global-Protection setting is also No. This means that although each cell is set up to be protected, the protection "master switch" is turned off.

Because every cell has the Prevent-Changes attribute when Symphony is first loaded, issuing the {**Services**} Settings Global-Protection command prevents you from being able to make changes to any cell in the worksheet. However, you will rarely create a worksheet in which you really want all of the cells to be protected. Usually you'll need at least a few unprotected cells for data entry.

Because nearly every worksheet should contain a few unprotected cells, you'll probably want to use the Range Protect command to assign the Allow-Changes attribute to these cells immediately after you issue the {**Services**} Settings Global-Protection command. (In fact, the Range Protect command would more accurately be called Range Unprotect, since it is usually used to permit changes in cells.)

An "A" will appear in the control panel next to the cell reference when you position the cell pointer on a cell that has the Allow-Changes attribute. For example, if you have assigned the Allow-Changes attribute to cell A1, the control panel will look like this when the cell pointer is on cell A1:

A1: A

If cell A1 contained the number 100, formatted to display as currency with two decimal places, the control panel display would be

A1: A (C2) 100

Remember: you can always make changes to any cell that has the Allow-Changes attribute. Cells that have the Prevent-Changes attribute, on the other hand, can only be changed when Global-Protection is set to No.

{Services} Settings Security

The {Services} Settings Security command allows you to "lock" the worksheet. The protection settings in a locked worksheet cannot be changed until the user supplies a password.

To lock a spreadsheet, issue the {**Services**} Settings Security Lock command. Symphony prompts you to supply the password you want to use to lock this worksheet. The password can be up to 80 characters long and may contain any alphabetic, numeric, or punctuation character. The password may also include spaces.

Once a worksheet has been locked, Symphony will not allow the user to issue either the Range Protect command or the {Services} Settings Global-Protection command. If you try to issue either command, Symphony will return the message "worksheet is locked". In other words, locking the worksheet prevents you from changing the protection status of any cell.

To unlock the worksheet, issue the {**Services**} Settings Security Unlock command and type the appropriate password. If you type the wrong password, Symphony will respond with the message "Incorrect password". The password you type must match the locking password *exactly.* For example, the strings Cessna, CESSNA, and cessan will not match the password cessna.

Be careful when choosing a password. If you forget the password you used to lock a worksheet, you will not be able to unlock the worksheet again. In fact, the potential for loss with the Security command is so great that it is a good idea to keep *unlocked* versions of all your locked worksheets as an insurance policy. Should you ever forget a password, these backups will keep you from having to recreate the worksheet from scratch.

Hidden Cells

The {Services} Settings Security command has one more important impact on your worksheet. In Chapter 5 you saw that the Hidden format tells Symphony not to display the value or label in a cell. You also learned that you could determine the contents of a hidden cell by moving the cell pointer to that cell and looking at the contents display in the control panel.

For example, suppose cell A1 in a worksheet contains the label ABCDEF. Even if cell A1 had been assigned the Hidden format and thus was not visible on the worksheet, if you moved the cell pointer to that cell, you could view its contents in the control panel:

> A1: (H) 'ABCDEF

When you lock the worksheet with {Services} Settings Security, however, even the contents display in the control panel is suppressed. Only the cell address and the format code (H) will be displayed:

> A1: (H)

In other words, in a locked worksheet there is no way to determine the contents of a hidden cell. Before you can examine the contents of the cell, you must issue the {Services} Settings Security Unlock command to unlock the worksheet.

An Example

Let's consider a brief example of the Range Protect, Global-Protection, and Security commands. Although this example is trivially simple, it demonstrates all the important concepts of protection.

Suppose you have built the simple worksheet shown in Figure 8.42. You want to protect cell A5 in this worksheet, which contains the formula

> A5: @SUM(A1 . . A4)

Begin by issuing the {**Services**} **S**ettings **G**lobal-Protection **Y**es command. As you have learned, this command "turns on" protection in every cell that has the Prevent-Changes attribute. Since the default attribute for all cells in the worksheet is Prevent-Changes, setting Global-Protection to Yes will prevent you from changing any cell in the worksheet. For example, if you moved the cell pointer to cell A1 and tried to enter the number 200, Symphony would beep and display the error message "Protected cell".

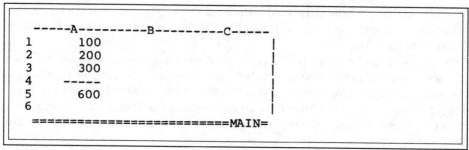

```
      -----A----------B----------C-----
   1         100                        |
   2         200                        |
   3         300                        |
   4         -----                      |
   5         600                        |
   6                                    |
      ===========================MAIN=
```

Figure 8.42

Since you only want cell A5 to be protected, you must use the Range Protect command to assign the Allow-Changes attribute to cells A1, A2, and A3. When you issue the Range Protect command, Symphony presents the menu

Allow-Changes Prevent-Changes

Since you want to permit changes in the range A1 . . A3, choose the **A**llow-Changes option. Then, Symphony prompts you for the range to which you want to assign this attribute. As with all other Symphony commands, you can designate the proper range by typing it or by pointing to it. Once the range is specified, press [Enter].

Now cells A1, A2, and A3 are unprotected. If you move the cell pointer to cell A1, the control panel displays the contents of the cell along with an A for Allow-Changes:

A1: A 100

If you enter the number 200 in cell A1, the worksheet will look like Figure 8.43. But if you try to make a change to the formula in cell A5, Symphony will return the message "Protected cell".

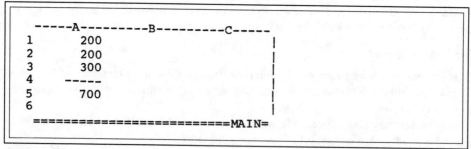

```
      -----A----------B----------C-----
   1         200                        |
   2         200                        |
   3         300                        |
   4         -----                      |
   5         700                        |
   6                                    |
      ===========================MAIN=
```

Figure 8.43

Note that all of the cells in this worksheet except A1, A2, and A3 are still protected. If you move the cell pointer to cell C1 and try to enter the label AAAAA, Symphony will respond with the "Protected cell" message. You can only change cells to which you have specifically assigned the Allow-Changes attribute. All other cells, including empty cells, are protected.

Now suppose you want to lock the worksheet. Issue the {**Services**} **S**ettings **S**ecurity

Lock command and enter the password you want to use for this worksheet. Be sure to choose a password that you are sure to remember later. For now, let's use the password PIPER to lock this sheet.

Now try to issue the **{Services}** **S**ettings **G**lobal-Protection **N**o command to suppress protection. When the command is issued, Symphony returns the message "Worksheet is locked". The same thing will happen if you try to use **{Menu}** **R**ange **P**rotect to change the attribute of a given cell. Until you issue the **{Services}** **S**ettings Security **U**nlock command and supply the correct password, you will not be able to change the protection status of any cell in the worksheet.

PART
III

SERVICES

CHAPTER NINE
PRINTING

The Print command allows Symphony users to create printed copies of their worksheets, documents, and data bases. Symphony's Print command allows you to control the printer from within Symphony, to print a range of the worksheet to the printer or to a special .PRN file on the disk, to adjust the length and margins on your printed page, to add headers and footers to your reports, and to format your reports in a variety of ways. Symphony even lets you build several different sets of Print specifications in each worksheet so that you can print different types of reports instantly. Because it offers so much flexibility, the Print command has perhaps the most complex menu structure in Symphony.

Because graphs use characters other than the standard letters, numbers, and punctuation marks, Symphony's Print command cannot be used to print graphs. But Symphony includes the PrintGraph program, which is designed to print the graphs you build in Symphony. PrintGraph is covered in Chapter 14.

Ex-1-2-3 users should have no trouble with Symphony's Print command. Except for a few changes in the names of some commands and a little rearranging of the command structure, Symphony's Print command is virtually identical to that command in 1-2-3.

The Print command is one of the options on the {Services} menu. When you issue the {**Services**} **P**rint command, the following menu appears:

> Go Line-Advance Page-Advance Align Settings Quit

The Align, Line-Advance, and Page-Advance commands allow you to control the printer directly from within Symphony. Go tells Symphony to begin printing, and thus should be issued only after all of the proper settings have been specified. The Settings option controls the parameters that determine what is printed, where it is printed, and what form the printed report will have.

SETTINGS

The Settings command controls most of the settings needed to print a report, including the range to be printed, the destination of the printed report, and the various print options. When the {**Services**} **P**rint **S**ettings command is issued, the menu and settings sheet shown in Figure 9.1 appears on the screen.

```
Page  Source  Destination  Init-String  Margins  Other   Name  Quit
---------------------------------------------------------------------
|Page                        Source:                                |
|  Length:        66         Destination: Printer                   |
|  Spacing:       1          Init-String:                           |
|  Number                    Margins          Other                 |
|    Print-Number 1            Left:     4     Space Compression:  No|
|    Start-Page   1            Right:    76    Attributes:        Yes|
|    End-Page     999          Top:      2     Format: As-Displayed  |
|  Breaks:        Yes          Bottom:   2     Top-Labels:           |
|  Wait:          No                           Left-Labels:          |
|  Header:                                                           |
|  Footer:                                                           |
|=============================================Print Settings: MAIN=|
```

Figure 9.1

The settings in the sheet in Figure 9.1 represent Symphony's defaults for each of the options. These defaults are stored in the file SYMPHONY.CNF. Each time you load Symphony into your computer or use the {**Services**} **P**rint **S**ettings **N**ame **I**nitial-Settings command, the program automatically reads the default settings for Margins, Page Length, Init-String, and Wait, which are stored in SYMPHONY.CNF, into the Print Settings sheet.

You can modify some of the default Print settings with the {**Services**} **C**onfiguration **P**rint command. This command is covered in Chapter 30. If you are just starting out with Symphony, we recommend you leave the settings as they are for a while. After you gain more experience with the program, you'll be better prepared to select default settings that meet your needs.

Only two settings are required to print a report: Source and Destination. In fact, Source is only required for printing spreadsheets. In the DOC mode, Symphony automatically supplies the print range. Since these two settings are required, we'll cover them first before moving on to the optional commands.

Source

Whenever you print a report from the SHEET environment, you must specify a Source for the information to be printed. As the name suggests, Source specifies the location in the worksheet of the information you want to print. The Source menu offers three options:

Range Database Cancel

In most cases, you'll be printing from a range in the worksheet. If you are printing a spreadsheet, the range is specified by pointing to the upper-left and lower-right corners of the range to be printed.

For example, suppose you have created a large financial projection worksheet, and now you want to print the entire projection. The projection occupies the range A1 . .

AC450 in this worksheet. To specify this range, you would issue the {**Services**} **Print Settings Source R**ange command. Assuming that the cell pointer was in cell A1 when the command was issued, Symphony would display the prompt

Range to Print: A1

Since A1 is the upper-left corner of the range you wish to print, you would press the period key to anchor this corner and then point to cell AC450, the lower-right corner of the range. If AC450 is the lower-right cell in the entire active spreadsheet, you can move the cell pointer there quickly by pressing [**End**][**Home**].

If the cell pointer had been in a cell other than A1 when the **Print Settings R**ange command was issued, you would have to press [**Home**] to move the cell pointer to cell A1 before specifying the rest of the range.

Of course, the range to be printed can be smaller than the entire spreadsheet. In fact, there are many times when you'll want to print only part of a large spreadsheet. For example, suppose our large example sheet included a summary section that occupied the range A1 . . I20. If you wanted to print just this part of the spreadsheet, your Source Range would be A1 . . I20.

All of the cell pointer movement tricks you learned in earlier chapters, like using [End][Home] to jump to the bottom of the active region of the worksheet, pressing [End] → to move long distances to the right, or using the period key to change the anchored corner of a range, can be used in defining the print range. Since you usually need to move the cell pointer a long way to designate the print range, these tricks can save a great deal of time.

If you are printing from the DOC environment, Symphony automatically assumes that you want to print the entire document shown in the current DOC window. If you do indeed want to print the entire window, you don't need to specify a Source. But if you want to print less than the entire document, you will need to specify a Source Range. (Printing in the DOC mode is covered in detail in Chapter 17.)

The Database option links the Print command to the data base report settings you specified using the Query Report command. The result will be a special data base report sent to the destination you specify with the Destination command. Be aware, however, that you can print a data base just like any other part of the worksheet without using the Report settings. To create a simple printed report from a data base, just specify a Source Range that includes the portion of worksheet occupied by your data base. This range will be printed just like any other worksheet range.

Symphony's Report capabilities are discussed in detail in Chapter 22.

As with most other Symphony commands, the program remembers the Range or Database report name you specify until you either erase it or exit from Symphony. This means that you can print the same range or data base report several times without having to respecify the Source. If you want to erase the Source—perhaps because you want to change from printing a data base report to printing a range from the worksheet—you can issue the **Source C**ancel command. This option causes Symphony to forget the current Source setting. Before you print again you'll need to respecify a Source Range.

Destination

The second required Print setting—and the only one that is required every time you print—is Destination. The Destination setting tells Symphony where you want the report to end up. The obvious destination, and the choice you'll probably use most often, is the printer, but Symphony also allows you to "print" the report to a disk file or to a range in the current worksheet. The {**Services**} **P**rint **S**ettings **D**estination menu looks like this:

> Printer File Range Erase Cancel

Choosing Printer causes your report to be printed to the printer. This is the default setting, which means that if you don't supply an alternate destination, Symphony prints to the printer.

Obviously, the Printer option assumes that a printer is attached to your computer. The relationship between the Print command and the Printer Destination command is determined by the choices you made while installing Symphony and by the settings you have specified with the {**Services**} **C**onfiguration **P**rint command, which is covered in Chapter 30.

The File and Range options are used to "print" your report to a disk file or to a range in the worksheet. We'll skip these commands for now and return to them after we've examined Symphony's other Print settings.

COMMANDS THAT CONTROL THE PRINTER

Once you've defined the proper Source and Destination for your report, you're nearly ready to print. However, if the Destination is Printer, you may want to adjust the printer before printing. Symphony offers three commands—Align, Line-Advance, and Page-Advance—that allow you to control the printer directly from within Symphony.

As the name indicates, Line-Advance causes the paper in the printer to advance one line. Similarly, Page-Advance issues a top-of-form command to the printer, causing the paper in the printer to move forward to the next page break.

Align is a bit trickier. The Align command is designed to make sure that the page breaks issued by Symphony while printing a report occur at the actual boundaries between sheets of paper, instead of in the middle of pages.

When you issue the **A**lign command, Symphony's page and line counters are returned to 0. This means that Symphony assumes the paper in the printer is in the starting position, with the print head on the first line of a sheet of paper. Symphony uses the Align command (and Length, which we'll cover in a page or two) to determine where page breaks should occur in the printed report.

Setting the initial alignment is easy. Simply position the paper in the printer so that the print head is at the top of a sheet of paper. Now issue the Align command, which puts Symphony in synch with the paper. Assuming the Length setting is correct, the page breaks issued by Symphony should match the physical boundaries between the pages.

(Since some printers have their own ideas about the location of the top of form, it isn't a bad idea to align your printer at the same time you align Symphony. The top-of-form setting on most printers can be reset by turning the printer off and then back on.)

Setting the alignment is easy, but keeping it set can be difficult. For example, suppose you have everything set up correctly, with Symphony and the paper aligned, and then you print a report. Since the last page of the report is only 20 lines long, the printer stops in mid-page after printing the last line. You use the *printer's* page-feed command to eject two sheets of paper.

The paper is now at the starting position. Symphony has no way of knowing this, however, and thus assumes the print head is still where it was when printing stopped— about the middle of the page. If you begin to print, Symphony will print about 46 lines (since 20 + 46 equals 66, the default page length) and then issue a page break in the middle of the page.

The moral to this story is this: once you've aligned Symphony, *leave the printer alone!* If you need to advance the paper in the printer, Use *Symphony's* Page-Advance or Line-Advance commands; don't use the printer's commands. If you must adjust the printer manually (for example, if you are printing on single-sheet paper and must insert a new sheet after each page is printed), be sure to realign Symphony before doing any more printing.

PRINTING THE REPORT

Once you have specified a Source and a Destination, and adjusted the printer, you're ready to print. The Go command on the Print menu instructs Symphony to begin printing from the Source to the Destination. In our previous example, Symphony would begin to print the range A1 . . AC450 to the printer.

TROUBLESHOOTING

If you press Go and nothing happens, you should check both Symphony and the printer for possible problems. First, have you defined a Source range and a Destination range? If the settings are correct, is the printer properly attached to your computer, plugged in, and turned on? If your printer has an "On-line" switch, is that switch in the On position? In other words, is the printer ready to receive data? If the answer to any of these questions is no, the report will not print.

Curiously, if something is wrong with the printer when you press Go, even though nothing appears on the paper, Symphony assumes that it is printing. This quirk can lead to problems with Symphony's alignment. For example, suppose you attempt print a 20-line report to a printer that is off line. As we have said, nothing appears on the printer. Symphony, however, assumes that 20 lines have been printed. Although the paper in the printer has not moved, and thus is still in the starting position, Symphony thinks that 20 lines have gone by. If you then attempt to print without realigning Symphony, the program will print about 46 lines and issue a page break (in mid-page). To avoid this kind of problem, be sure to realign Symphony if you have a printer problem during printing.

STOPPING THE PRINTER

You can stop the printing of a report at any time by pressing **[Ctrl][Break]**. Symphony immediately stops printing, although it may be a few seconds before you can issue any commands. Most printers will stop printing within a few seconds. Some printers, however, have a large print buffer and will continue to print for as much as a minute after you press **[Ctrl][Break].** Turning the printer off and back on usually erases the buffer and stops the printing.

If you stop the printing of a report in this way, be sure to realign Symphony before you begin printing again.

THE PRINT OPTIONS

The remaining options on the Settings menu control the optional print settings, including the physical dimensions of the page on which the report will be printed, the report margins, and many other optional settings.

Page

The Page command controls the physical dimensions of the page on which Symphony will print. Once again, there is a rather full menu located behind this command:

Length Spacing Number Breaks Wait Header Footer Quit

Length is used to set the length of the printed page. The default setting for Length is 66 lines per page, but you can change Length to any integer number between 20 and 100.

When Symphony prints a report, it automatically issues page breaks after printing the number of lines specified by Length. For example, if Length is set to 66, Symphony will issue a page break each time 66 lines have been printed. If the Length is set to 100, Symphony will issue page breaks after every 100 lines.

Since most printers automatically print 6 lines per inch, the default setting of 66 lines is perfect for printing on 11-inch-long paper. You usually won't change Length unless you change either the number of lines being printed per inch (using an Init-String or a switch on the printer) or use longer or shorter paper.

For example, suppose you decide to print a long report with 8 lines per inch instead of the usual 6. If you are using an Epson FX-80, FX-100, or LQ-1500 printer, you make this change by specifying the Init-String \027\048. (We'll cover Init-Strings in a few pages). You can now fit 88 lines on each 11-inch page, so you'll probably want to increase the Length setting to 88. If you don't increase the Length, Symphony will print 66 lines on the page; but since 8 lines are being printed per inch, only about two-thirds of the paper will be used before a page break is issued.

With some printers, it is important that the printer and Symphony agree about the lengths of the pages being printed. Since the default page length settings for most printers is 66 lines per page, just as in Symphony, there is usually no problem. But suppose you change the page length in Symphony to 100, but leave the printer set to 66. With some printers, you'll get multiple page breaks: one after 66 lines when the printer thinks the end-of-page has been reached, another 34 lines later, generated by Symphony after 100 lines are printed, and so on. To avoid this problem, make sure your printer and Symphony agree about the length of the pages being printed.

The relationship between the Length setting and the number of rows from the worksheet that are printed on each page can be very confusing. The Length setting determines the *entire* length of the page to be printed, including top and bottom margins and the space allocated for headers and footers. For example, if the Length setting is 66, the top and bottom margins are set to 2 (the default), and the header and footer lines are not disabled, only 56 lines of information will appear on each 66-line page. However, if you set the top and bottom margins to 0 and use the **P**rinter **S**ettings **B**reaks command to disable the header and footer lines, a full 66 lines will be printed.

The Breaks command is similar to 1-2-3's Print Options Other Unformatted command. When Breaks is set to No, Symphony ignores page breaks (and headers and footers) when printing reports. Breaks is automatically set to No by the **P**rint **S**ettings **M**argins **N**o-Margins command, which also sets all margins to 0.

If you are printing on individual sheets of paper (like your company's letterhead) instead of on continuous-form computer paper, you want to use the **P**age **W**ait option. Wait forces Symphony to pause after printing each page in a multipage report. The pause gives you time to insert a new sheet of paper into the printer before printing each new page.

Spacing

The **P**rint **S**ettings **P**age **S**pacing command controls the number of linefeeds Symphony issues after printing each line in a report. If Spacing is set to 1 (the default), Symphony sends one linefeed to the printer after each printed line, resulting in a single-spaced report. A setting of 2 creates a double-spaced report; a blank line is inserted between each printed line. Similarly, a setting of 3 causes two blank lines to be inserted between each printed line, resulting in a triple-spaced report. Figure 9.2 shows examples of single-, double-, and triple-spaced printing.

When printing a document, the Print Settings Page Spacing command is overridden by the DOC Format Spacing setting. So if you have specified double spacing for your document using the DOC {menu} Format Spacing command, the document will be double spaced, even if the Print Settings Page Spacing command is set to 1.

Margins

The Margins command gives you the ability to adjust the top, bottom, left, and right

```
This is a line printed by Symphony
This is another line printed by Symphony

This is a third line printed by Symphony


This is a fourth line printed by Symphony
```

Figure 9.2

margins that Symphony uses when printing your reports. Here is the Margins menu:

Left Right Top Bottom Initial-Margins No-Margins Quit

The first four options control each of the four margins: Left, Right, Top, and Bottom. The default settings for these four margins are as follows:

	Default	Range
Top	2	0–10
Bottom	2	0–10
Left	4	0–240
Right	76	0–240

The Left and Right margin settings are straightforward. The left margin is an absolute offset. In other words, a left margin of 4 inserts four blank spaces at the start of each line, causing the first character to be printed in the fifth space of every line. The right margin specifies the total number of characters in the printed line, including the left margin. The number of characters of text on a line is thus equal to the right margin minus the left margin. For example, in the default settings, where the right margin is 76 and the left margin is 4, the line length is 72 characters.

Symphony's concepts of Top and Bottom margins can be a bit confusing, since the program inserts several different kinds of lines at the top of reports. Symphony begins every page with the top margin. Next it prints the header, if any is provided, or a blank line if no header has been specified, and then two more blank lines. Thus five blank lines will appear at the top of every page in a report that is printed with a Top margin of 2 and the standard header lines. The same thing happens at the bottom of the page. After the last line of text is printed, Symphony prints two blank lines, the footer line, and then the bottom margin. Each page in a report with a Bottom margin of 2 and the standard footer lines will thus end with five blank lines. If this confuses you, join the crowd; we wonder why Lotus made these settings so complex.

The Initial-Margins command returns the margins to the default settings—usually Left 4, Right 76, Top 2, and Bottom 2. This command is useful for quickly resetting the margins after printing a report that used special margin settings.

Remember that the default margin settings are controlled by the SYMPHONY.CNF file, which can be altered with the {Services} Configuration Print command. For example, you could use this command to change the default Top margin to 5 and the default Right margin to 80. In this event, issuing the Margins Initial-Margins command would return the margins in the current settings sheet to the default values you've specified: Left 4, Right 80, Top 5, and Bottom 2.

The No-Margins option sets the left, top, and bottom margins to 0; the right margin to 240; the Page Spacing setting to 1; and the Page Breaks setting to No. Remember that Page Breaks controls not only Symphony's automatic page breaks but also the printing of headers and footers. This means that when you select No-Margins you turn off not only the top and bottom margins but also the three header and three footer lines. No-Margins really does what it says: it gets rid of all the marginal blank space on your printed reports.

No-Margins is especially handy when you want the page Length and the number of text lines printed on the page to match. If the page Length is 66 lines and No-Margins is

Yes, the printed page will include exactly 66 lines of text or numbers from the worksheet. No-Margins is also useful when printing to disk or to a range, as we'll see in a few pages.

PRINTING LARGE REPORTS

Many times your worksheets will be too large to print on a single sheet of paper. Symphony has some special rules for printing large reports. The following examples will help you understand those rules.

First, suppose you have built a worksheet that is 50 rows deep and spans columns A through M. If the columns are each nine characters wide, the worksheet has a total width of 117 characters. Assuming that your printer has a standard line width of 80 characters, and that you do not use an Init-String to select a compressed print mode, there is no way to print this report on a single page. When Symphony prints this report, it divides it into two pages: the first containing the 72 left-most characters (or eight columns, A through H) and the second containing the remaining five columns. Figure 9.3 diagrams the division of the report into two pages.

```
    -----A---- / ----H-----          -----I---- / ----M-----
   1                          |      1                          |
   2                          |      2                          |
   3        Page one          |      3        Page two          |
   •                          •      •                          •
   •                          •      •                          •
   •                          •      •                          •
  48                          |     48                          |
  49                          |     49                          |
  50                          |     50                          |
    ------------------------         ------------------------
```

Figure 9.3

Suppose the worksheet you wanted to print was not only 117 characters wide but also 78 rows deep. Since the standard page length in Symphony is 66 lines, minus 10 lines for the top and bottom margins and the header and footer lines, only 56 lines of the report can fit on a single page. In this situation, Symphony splits the report into four pages as follows:

Page one	rows 1 to 56	columns A through H
Page two	rows 57 to 78	columns A through H
Page three	rows 1 to 56	columns I through M
Page four	rows 57 to 78	columns I through M

This division is illustrated in Figure 9.4.

With some printers it might be possible to fit the entire 117-character-wide by 78-row-deep report on one page. If your narrow-carriage printer can produce compressed characters (more than the standard 80 characters per line) and can squeeze 8 lines

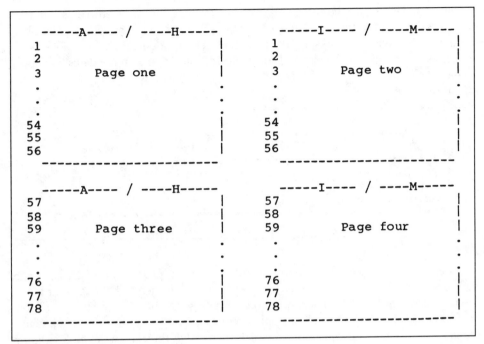

Figure 9.4

per inch instead of the usual 6, you're in luck. All you need to do is send the proper Init-Strings to the printer before printing the report.

For example, the Init-String to produce compressed print on our Epson LQ-1500 printer is \015, and the code to force 8 lines per inch is \027\048. If we sent these two control codes to the printer prior to printing the report, the result would be a single-page report that includes all 13 columns and 78 rows of the worksheet.

These same principles apply to printers with a standard line length of 132 characters. Suppose, for example, that you want to print a worksheet that is 78 rows deep and extends from column A to column T—a total width of 20 columns or 180 characters. If you printed this worksheet on a wide-carriage printer with no special Init-Strings, the printed report would be split into four pages.

Wide-carriage printers can usually handle reports up to 240 characters wide (the maximum Right margin in Symphony) and 88 lines deep if compressed print is used. If your printer supports these special features, you can squeeze a worksheet with 28 nine-character columns and 78 rows on a single page.

Labeling Reports Printed on Several Pages

In the preceding section we saw that Symphony automatically divides reports that are too large to fit on a single page into several parts. This is a neat trick, since it saves you the trouble of "fitting" your reports to the page size when you print.

Still, this ability of Symphony to break reports into pages can cause problems. Suppose the worksheet illustrated in Figure 9.4 contains a company's annual financial plan. Columns A and B in this worksheet contains the labels that identify each row: Total Sales, Expenses, Accounts Receivable, and so on. Rows 1 and 2 contain the dates that apply to each column: Jan-84, Feb-84, Mar-84, etc. Figure 9.5 shows the upper-left corner of this worksheet.

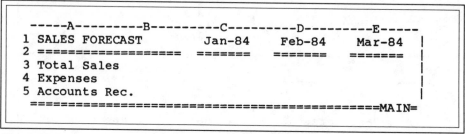

Figure 9.5

When Symphony prints the report, columns A and B appear only on pages one and three, and rows 1 and 2 only on pages one and two. This means that page four in the printed report includes absolutely no identifying labels. The numbers on this page seem to float aimlessly. Page two includes only row labels, so there is no way to tell which column of numbers corresponds to which date. Page three contains only column headers and no row labels.

Obviously, this report would be hard to read. What we need is a way to include the appropriate row labels and column headers from the worksheet on all four pages of the report. Fortunately, Symphony's Print Other Top-Labels and Left-Labels commands allow us to do just that.

The Top-Labels and Left-Labels commands are used to designate certain rows and columns that will appear on every sheet in the finished report. In our example, to be sure that the proper column headers were included on all four pages, we would move the cell pointer to cell A1 and issue the {**Services**} **P**rint **S**ettings **O**ther **T**op-Labels command. Symphony would prompt us with the message

    Range of Label Rows: A1

Since we want rows 1 and 2 to appear on each page of our report, we would press the period key (.) and point down one cell to set the Top-Labels range to A1 . . A2. Similarly, to define the Left-Labels you would issue the **O**ther **L**eft-Labels command and specify the range A1 . . B1. (These commands are the equivalent of 1-2-3's /Print Options Other Borders command.)

Be sure that you understand that we could have used the range A1 . . Z2 or B1 . . G2 to designate the Top-Labels range, and the range A1 . . B15 or A500 . . B501 to designate the Left-Labels. When defining the Top-Labels, Symphony is only interested in the row coordinates of the cells used to define the range, so any range that covers rows 1 and 2 will do. Similarly, when defining the Left-Labels, Symphony is looking for column designations only, so any range spanning columns A and B will do. In this regard, specifying the Top-Labels and Left-Labels is similar to specifying a Delete or Insert range.

There is one more thing we must do before printing this report. Since columns A and B and rows 1 and 2 will automatically be printed on each page of the report, we need to remove these rows and columns from the Source range. The new Source range for the report is C3 . . M78. When the report is printed, each page will include the appropriate column headers and row labels.

If we did not change the Source range, columns A and B and rows 1 and 2 would be printed *twice* on page one: once as a part of the Labels ranges and then again as a part of the Source range. Similarly, rows 1 and 2 would appear twice on page two, and columns A and B would appear twice on page three.

In the example, the Top-Labels range included two rows and the Left-Labels range included two columns. These ranges can include as many rows or columns as you wish, however. Frequently, we use six or seven rows as Top-Labels and four or five columns as Left-Labels. Your ability to use wide Left-Labels depends on the width of your report and your printer; wide Left-Labels work best on wide-carriage printers and those that can do compressed print.

There is one thing to be careful of when using the Top-Labels and Left-Labels. Suppose in our example you had moved the cell pointer to cell A1 and issued the **P**rint **S**ettings **O**ther **T**op-Labels command. The prompt

Range of Label Rows: A1

would appear on the screen. Now suppose you decided not to use a Top-Label. You must press **[Esc]**—not [Enter]—to exit this menu. If you press [Enter], Symphony assumes you want to use a one-row Top-Label, and it will print this row on each page of your report.

If you think you might have accidentally specified a one-row or one-column label range, you can issue the **P**rint **S**ettings **O**ther **N**o-Labels command. This command erases any Top-Labels or Left-Labels you have specified.

HEADERS AND FOOTERS

A header is a special line of text that you can print at the top of every page of a report. Similarly, a footer is a line of text you can print at the bottom of every page. The Print Settings Page Header and Footer commands let you specify the headers and footers you want to include in your reports.

For example, suppose you want the title "Any Company 1984 Financial Forecast" to appear at the top of every page in a multipage report. Just select the **{Services}** **P**rint **S**ettings **P**age **H**eader command and enter that line in response to Symphony's prompt. When the report is printed, the title

Any Company 1984 Financial Forecast

appears at the top of every page.

In the default mode, Symphony reserves three lines at the top of every page of your report for the header and three lines at the bottom for the footer. In both cases, only one line is used to print the actual header or footer text. The other two lines are provided for spacing; they separate the header or footer from the body of the report. These three lines are reserved; that is, they will be printed as blank lines even if you don't want a header or footer.

Remember that the six lines reserved for the header and footer are in addition to the top and bottom margins. Since the defaults for both the top margin and the bottom margin are two lines, in the default mode your reports will have five lines at the top and bottom.

If you do not plan to use a header or footer in printing a report, and you want to reclaim the three lines Symphony reserves for headers and footers, you can set the **Print Settings Page B**reaks command to No. When Breaks is set to **No**, Symphony does not print headers or footers and does not include space for headers and footers at the tops and bottoms of your pages.

The maximum length of the header and footer lines in a report is the same as the line length for the report, and it is computed by subtracting the Left margin setting from the Right margin setting. In the default configuration, where the left margin is 4 and the right margin is 76, the header and footer can be 72 characters long.

Symphony reserves several characters for special uses in headers and footers. The vertical bar (|) is used to divide the header or footer into left-justified, centered, and right-justified sections. For example, the header

Any Company|1984 Financial Forecast|Company Confidential

would be printed like this:

Any Company   1984 Financial Forecast   Company Confidential

To skip one of the three positions (left, center, or right), just position two bars next to each other in the header. For example, the header

Any Company 1984 Financial Forecast||Company Confidential

would be printed like this:

Any Company 1984 Financial Forecast   Company Confidential

and the header

|Any Company 1984 Financial Forecast

like this:

Any Company 1984 Financial Forecast

If you include the @ symbol in a header or footer, Symphony prints the current date in that header or footer. Similarly, the symbol # instructs Symphony to print the current page number in the header. For example, assuming that the current date was December 31, 1983, the header

Report Date: @|1984 Financial Forecast|Page: #

would be printed on the first page of the report as

Report Date: 12/31/83   1984 Financial Forecast   Page: 1

The format for the date is determined by the default setting for date format 4 (full international). Unless you change this default with the {Services} Configuration Other International Date command, date format 4 is MM/DD/YY.

CONTROLLING PAGE NUMBERS

The Number option on the Settings Page menu offers the following options:

Print-Number Start-Page End-Page

The first option, Print-Number, controls the number printed by Symphony the first time it encounters the # symbol in printing a report. The default setting is 1, meaning that Symphony usually numbers the pages in a report beginning with 1. Most of the time you'll use this default setting.

However, there are cases when the ability to start with a different number can come in handy. For example, suppose that you wanted to print a report that included three pages of text and three pages of financial data. Because of the way you designed the worksheet, the two sections will be printed in two different print operations. However, you want all of the pages in the report to be numbered consecutively. You begin by printing the three pages of text. Next you want to print the financial information. Since the next consecutive page number is 4, you would use the **Print Settings Page Number Print-**Number command to set the starting page number to 4 before printing the financial data. When the printing is complete, the pages in the report would be properly numbered from 1 to 6.

Start-Page and End-Page

The other two options on the Print Settings Number menu serve a completely different purpose. Start-Page and End-Page let you print a portion of a large Source range. These commands are most frequently used when printing from the DOC mode, but they can also be used when printing spreadsheets or data base reports. Remember that in the DOC mode you are not required to provide a Source range. Symphony simply assumes you want to print the entire document unless you specifically define a smaller range. The Start-Page and End-Page commands allow you to print a portion of the document without forcing you to define a specific Source range.

Start-Page prompts for the page in the report where printing should begin. End-Page asks you to provide the number of the last page to be printed. For example, suppose your total Source range was A1 . . I1245, but you wanted to print just the first page of this report. By setting the Start-Page to 1 and the End-Page to 1, you would instruct Symphony to print only the first page.

Of course, you can use Start-Page and End-Page to print any part of a long Source range—not just the first page. The default setting for Start-Page is 1, but you can set Start-Page to any number from 1 to 999. Similarly, the default End-Page setting is 999, but you can vary this setting between 1 and 999. Remember that the End-Page setting has no effect unless it is less than the total number of pages in the report. For example, an End-

Page setting of 25 would have no effect on a 10-page report. However, a setting of 10 would stop the printing of a 25-page Source range after the tenth page.

Don't be confused about the relationship between these options and the Source range setting. Start-Page and End-Page cannot be used to define the Source range for a report, but only to select a part of an already-defined Source range for printing. The problem with the Start-Page and End-Page commands is that it is difficult to determine exactly how many lines from your worksheet will appear on each page of a report. If the default page Length, Top, and Bottom margins are in effect and the Breaks setting is Yes, each page in a report will include 56 rows of text from the worksheet. In this situation, setting Start-Page to 2 instructs Symphony to begin printing with row 57 in the worksheet. However, if the No-Margins setting is Yes, the top and bottom margins are suppressed and 66 lines of text will be included on each page of the report. In this case, Symphony will begin printing the second page at line 67.

In a DOC window, pressing the {Where} key returns the current location of the cursor as a page and line, based on the current Page Length setting. {Where} is a handy tool to use when printing partial reports. Unfortunately, {Where} only works in DOC windows.

In general, the Start-Page and End-Page commands are most useful when printing reports that include manual page break commands. The Page command on the DOC menu is used to insert these breaks in the worksheet. Since manual page breaks force Symphony to divide the report into recognizable page sections, the effects of Start-Page and End-Page are easier to gauge.

CONTROLLING YOUR PRINTER'S SPECIAL FEATURES

The typical dot-matrix printer is set up to print 6 lines per inch, 66 lines per page, and either 80 or 132 characters per line (depending on the width of the printer's carriage). However, many printers have the ability to print more lines per inch or more characters per line. Some printers can even print in special typefaces like italic or boldface. In most cases, you can control these options by sending a special control code, or setup code, to the printer before you begin printing.

The {**Services**} **P**rint **S**ettings **I**nit-String command lets you specify a control code sequence of up to 39 characters. This sequence is transmitted to your printer each time you issue the Go command. The characters in this control string are not printed; instead, they deliver your instructions about character width, lines-per-inch, and so forth to the printer.

Most printer control codes consist of either the [Esc] or [Ctrl] key plus a letter. For example, the code to make an Epson printer print condensed characters is [Ctrl] O. Symphony gives you two ways to write this code: \O or \015. In the first form (which we'll call the literal form), Symphony assumes that the \ represents the [Ctrl] key, and the letter O is interpreted literally. In the second form, the actual three-digit ASCII code for [Ctrl] O, 015, is sent to the printer. In this form, the \ is simply a delimiter that marks the beginning of the code.

Only printer control codes that begin with [Ctrl] can be written in the literal form (for example, \O). If the code begins with [Esc], you must use the ASCII convention. For example, the code that selects double-strike printing on an Epson printer is [Esc] G. This code can only be written one way in a Symphony Init-String: \027\071. The ASCII code for [Esc] is 027 and the ASCII code for G is 071. The \ characters serve as delimiters.

Because many of the codes I use to control my Epson LQ-1500 printer require the [Esc] key, I've fallen into the habit of always using the ASCII code convention in my Init-Strings.

You can string together as many printer control codes as you wish in your Init-String, provided the length of the entire Init-String does not exceed 39 characters. For example, the Init-String

> \015\027\071\027\048

would cause an Epson printer to print condensed characters (\015), double struck (\027\071) with 8 lines per inch (\027\048). Notice that the [Esc] character code 027 was repeated before both the double-strike and line-per-inch codes. Also notice that all of the codes include a 0. These zeros serve as placeholders in the three-digit code and are required.

Occasionally a code requires a trailing character, like 1 or 0. For example, the code \027\0871 causes an Epson LQ-1500 to print expanded (wide) characters, and the code \027\0870 stops expanded print. Notice that the additional characters are simply appended to the end of the Init-String.

The following list shows the codes that activate the most popular special features on the Epson family of printers.

Compressed print	\015
8 lines per inch	\027\048
Expanded print	\027\0871
Underline	\027\0451
Boldface	\027\069
Double strike	\027\071
Italic	\027\052

Unfortunately, there are nearly as many control code sets as there are printers. Nearly every printer manufacturer uses a different set of codes to activate the special features of their printers (although in most cases the same codes are used by all printers made by a given manufacturer). For this reason, the Epson codes we've used in the examples and in the table may or may not work with your printer.

Most printer manuals include a list of the control codes for that printer. Be sure that the codes listed in the manual are ASCII codes, and not hexadecimal (base 16) or octal (base 8). If your manual does not give the codes in ASCII, you can convert the octal or hex codes into ASCII. The PC-DOS manual includes an ASCII/hex/octal translation table that lets you do just this.

Embedded Init-Strings

One interesting new feature of Symphony is the program's ability to read Init-Strings that are "buried" in the spreadsheet or document being printed. For example, suppose you were about to print the worksheet shown in Figure 9.6. You want the headers in row 2 to be underlined in the printed report.

```
   -----A---------B---------C---------D--------
 1                                              |
 2            Jan        Feb        Mar          |
 3                                              |
 4  Product 1  $1,234    $2,345    $3,456        |
 5  Product 2  $2,345    $3,456    $4,567        |
 6  Product 3  $3,456    $4,567    $5,678        |
 7  Product 4  $4,567    $5,678    $6,789        |
 8                                              |
   ====================================MAIN=
```

Figure 9.6

First you would move the cell pointer to cell A1 and enter the label

      A1: ¦¦\027\0451

Now move to cell A3 and enter the label

      A3:¦¦\027\0450

The code \027\045 is the underline control code for an Epson LQ-1500 printer. If the \027\045 is followed by a 1, underlining is turned on. If the code is followed by a 0, underlining is turned off.

Now issue the {**Services**} **P**rint **S**ettings **S**ource **R**ange command, designating the range A1 . . D7 as the Source range. Since we're printing to the printer, you don't need to designate a Destination. Now issue the **G**o command from the Print menu. When printed, this worksheet will look like Figure 9.7.

```
   --------------  Jan      Feb      Mar
   Product 1    $1,234    $2,345    $3,456
   Product 2    $2,345    $3,456    $4,567
   Product 3    $3,456    $4,567    $5,678
   Product 4    $4,567    $5,678    $6.789
```

Figure 9.7

There are a couple of important points to remember about embedded Init-Strings. First, notice that each printer control code was entered in a separate row. This is required; there is no way to enter this kind of printer control code on the same line as text. Second, notice that Symphony ignored the lines containing the codes when printing the worksheet. If you remember that the ¦ label prefix is used to mark comments, and that cells that use this label prefix are *never* printed, you'll understand why these codes are not printed. Third, look at how Symphony underlined all of row 2, including blank spaces and even the left margin characters, when printing. This is probably not what you wanted; chances are you wanted to underline only the text strings in cells B2, C2, and D2, not the spaces or the margins.

This example shows that embedded Init-Strings, while very clever and useful, have some problems. Specifically, embedded init-strings can only format an entire row at a time, and they require that you include special rows in your worksheet just for these strings. Because of these limitations, you'll probably not find embedded Init-Strings very useful.

Word Processing Format Codes

As you'll see in the chapters on word processing, Symphony offers a special set of commands that let you boldface, underline, superscript, subscript, and italicize a character, word, line, paragraph, or entire document. These special print format commands do not just apply to the DOC environment, however; they can also be used to format text in the spreadsheet. Fortunately, these format codes overcome many of the limitations of the embedded Init-Strings, and they can be used for many of the same purposes.

The command that activates a special print format is [Ctrl] B. You can think of the B as standing for beginning. The [Ctrl] B string is followed by the single character that designates the special format you wish to use—for example, U for underline, B for boldface, etc. (A complete list of these codes is included in the word processing chapters.) The command to cancel special formatting is [Ctrl] E (the E stands for end).

For example, suppose you wanted to underline the labels in row 2 of the example worksheet shown above. Move the cell pointer to cell A2 and type [Ctrl]BU. Did you see that when you typed [Ctrl]B, Symphony entered a solid triangle in cell A1? This triangle is the visual indication that you have given a "begin special format" command. This triangle should always be followed by one of Symphony's special format codes: U, B, etc.

Next, move to cell E2 and type [CTRL] E. Notice that Symphony enters an inverted solid triangle in this cell. This triangle is the symbol for the "end special format" command. Notice also that no format code accompanies the end marker.

Now print the worksheet. (Be sure to change the Source range to A1 . . E7 to include the code in cell E1.) When printed, the worksheet will look like Figure 9.8.

	Jan	Feb	Mar
Product 1	$1,234	$2,345	$3,456
Product 2	$2,345	$3,456	$4,567
Product 3	$3,456	$4,567	$5,678
Product 4	$4,567	$5,678	$6,789

Figure 9.8

The printout in this figure is close to what we want, but it still has a few problems. Each label in row 2 has been shifted two spaces to the left. This occurred because Symphony ignores the two-character (▲U) format code in cell A1 when counting the spaces in row 2. Thus Symphony thinks row 2 has two fewer spaces than the other rows in the worksheet, and it shifts the contents of that row two spaces to the left. This peculiarity is irritating, but it can be overcome by shifting each label two spaces to the right (by adding two spaces each in cells B2, C2, and D2) before printing. Making this change will cause the worksheet to look like Figure 9.9 and the printed report to look like Figure 9.10.

```
    -----A--------B---------C---------D--------E-----
  1                                                   |
  2 ▲U            Jan        Feb        Mar ▼          |
  3                                                   |
  4 Product 1     $1,234     $2,345     $3,456         |
  5 Product 2     $2,345     $3,456     $4,567         |
  6 Product 3     $3,456     $4,567     $5,678         |
  7 Product 4     $4,567     $5,678     $6,789         |
  8                                                   |
    ===========================================MAIN=
```

Figure 9.9

```
              Jan      Feb      Mar
  Product 1   $1,234   $2,345   $3,456
  Product 2   $2,345   $3,456   $4,567
  Product 3   $3,456   $4,567   $5,678
  Product 4   $4,567   $5,678   $6,789
```

Figure 9.10

The special format codes can also be included directly in the cells with each label. For example, we could retype the contents of cell B2 in the example as

> B2: ▲U Jan▼

Remember that Symphony always ignores the two-character special format code when counting the number of characters to print on a line, so you'll need to shift the label two spaces to the right to guarantee proper alignment.

Suppressing the Format Codes

The Print Other Attributes command can be used to suppress the effect of the special format codes inserted in your documents or spreadsheets. If the Attributes setting is No, the format codes will be suppressed and the report will be printed as though no format codes were included. Note, however, that Symphony continues to ignore the codes when counting the number of spaces on each line, and thus will properly align your labels.

I strongly prefer the word processing format codes over the imbedded Init-Strings for inserting special printer control codes in my spreadsheets. In fact, the only time I use imbedded Init-Strings is to insert a control code that isn't part of Symphony's DOC format code library (like compressed print, \015). In this event, there is no choice but to use the imbedded Init-Strings.

FORMULAS OR NUMBERS

There are times when you'll want to prepare a "listing" of a Symphony worksheet as a reference to the actual contents of each cell. If you want to create such a listing, select the Cell-Formulas option of the Print Settings Other Format command before you print. The resulting report lists the formula, value, or label stored in each cell in the worksheet, one cell to each line in the report, starting with cell A1 and finishing with the bottom right cell in the worksheet. This listing will also show the format, if any, that you've assigned to each cell. In fact, you may notice that the listings produced by the Cell-Formulas command are exactly the same as the cell definitions that appear in the control panel when you position the cell pointer on a cell.

Although the Cell-Formulas command is very handy, it lacks several important features. For example, the listing does not include the worksheet's range names, graph settings, data base ranges, or other "behind the scenes" information. If you want a more comprehensive listing, you'll need to use one of the special Symphony documentation programs, like DocuCalc, that are on the market.

The default setting for Print Settings Other Format, As-Displayed, prints the cells as they appear in the worksheet.

CREATING MULTIPLE PRINT SETTINGS SHEETS

Suppose you have created a worksheet that has two distinct parts: a spreadsheet 13 columns wide and 500 rows long and a document. The Print settings used to print these two parts of the worksheet are completely different, so you want to create two separate Print settings sheets in the worksheet and toggle between them to print the different parts of the worksheet.

Fortunately, Symphony's Print Settings Name command lets you create, use, and delete print setting sheets. You can create an unlimited number of settings sheets in a single worksheet. Symphony keeps a record of all the sheets you have created and remembers the settings that correspond to each name.

The Print Settings Name menu looks like this:

Use Create Delete Previous Next Initial-Settings Reset Quit

(This menu is identical to that presented by the Graph 1st-Settings Name command, which we will cover in Chapter 13.)

The default Print settings sheet name is MAIN. Because you want to create a new settings sheet but want to preserve the work you've done so far, you need to create a new settings sheet. To create a new sheet, issue the **Print Settings Name Create** command. Symphony then asks you to provide the new name for this settings sheet and would display a list of all the named settings sheets on the default directory. Since we are assuming that the current worksheet has only one settings sheet, only the name MAIN would appear.

To create a new settings sheet, simply type the new name—SECOND—and press [Enter]. Symphony immediately changes the name of the current settings sheet to SECOND. Of course, SECOND is just a sample name. You can specify any character string of up to 15 characters for your settings sheet names.

Let's review what happened here. When you issued the Create command, Symphony "created" a new Print settings sheet named SECOND. This new settings sheet is an exact clone of the settings sheet MAIN. SECOND is now the active Print settings sheet. MAIN is now in the background, so you can make changes to SECOND without effecting MAIN in any way. Why did Symphony create SECOND as an exact clone of MAIN? Simply because MAIN was the current Print settings sheet at the time you issued the Create command.

Throughout Symphony, the Name Create command is like a photocopier that produces an exact duplicate of the current settings sheet. The only difference between the photocopy and the original is that they have different names. The copy becomes the active settings sheet and can be manipulated by Symphony's Print commands. The original settings sheet is "filed" in Symphony's list of Print settings sheet names.

Resetting the Current Settings

Typically, you wouldn't keep two copies of exactly the same Print settings sheet. For example, once you had created the new settings sheet called SECOND, you would usually reset or edit the settings in this sheet and then create a new set of Print settings. After this new settings sheet was defined, you might create a new window called THIRD, and further modify the settings to create yet another sheet.

If you want to completely erase the settings in SECOND, you would issue the **Name Initial-Settings** command. Be careful! As soon as you issue this command, the settings in SECOND, including the Source, Destination, and all optional settings, are restored to the defaults.

Using a Settings Sheet

You can retrieve a settings sheet at any time simply by using the Print Settings Name Use command and supplying the name of the settings sheet you want to use. You can select the settings sheet by pointing to the correct name in the list provided by Symphony or by typing the name of the sheet you want to use.

For example, suppose that you wanted to retrieve the settings sheet MAIN. Simply issue the Settings Name Use command and select MAIN from the list of names offered by Symphony. When this command is issued, MAIN becomes the active settings sheet. SECOND is now in the background, waiting for future use. Any Print commands you give affect MAIN.

You can also retrieve a settings sheet with the Settings Name Previous or Next commands. These commands simply step through the settings sheet names in the current worksheet one at a time. Previous moves you back to the sheet just before the current sheet in Symphony's list; Next moves you forward to the next sheet in the list.

Creating a Library of Print Settings Sheets

Since Print settings sheets include all of the settings required to print a worksheet, once you've used a sheet you need only issue the Align and Go commands to print a report. You can probably imagine how much time this can save in a worksheet with several different sections, each of which requires a separate set of print parameters.

One of the nicest features of Symphony's DOC mode is that it is immediately available to you while you are working in the spreadsheet. For example, if you are working on a financial report and suddenly remember a memo you need to write, you need only create a DOC window with the {**Services**} **W**indow command and start writing.

The DOC mode can be even more useful if your worksheet contains a Print settings sheet that contains the settings you use to print memos and letters. If such a settings sheet exists, you need only issue the {**Services**} **P**rint **S**ettings **N**ame **U**se command, choose the correct settings sheet, and type **A**lign and **G**o to begin printing.

Deleting a Settings Sheet

The Print Settings Name Delete command is used to delete a settings sheet. This command differs from the Intial-Settings command in that Intial-Settings blanks a settings sheet without destroying the sheet itself. Name Delete, on the other hand, actually destroys the settings sheet. After the Name Delete command is issued, both the settings and the settings sheet are gone. If, for example, you used Name Delete on the sheet SECOND, the name SECOND would disappear from the list of named settings sheets.

The Name Delete command can be used to delete any settings sheet in Symphony's list of sheets except the active settings sheet. If you try to delete the active settings sheet, Symphony will display the error message

Cannot delete current settings sheet

If you want to delete all the Print settings sheets in the current worksheet at once, issue the **P**rint **S**ettings **N**ame **R**eset command. Symphony asks

Reset all catalogued settings?
No Yes

If you select the Yes option, all the settings sheets in the worksheet except MAIN will be destroyed, and MAIN will be reset to the default settings. Selecting No returns you to the Print menu.

PRINTING SPECIAL CHARACTERS

Depending on the type of printer you use to print, you may experience problems if your worksheet contains "special" characters like £ or {{ ¥ }}. Many printers are not capable of printing these characters and thus use a substitute character or character string to represent these special characters. Since these subtitutes can be confusing, we suggest that you avoid printing special characters if your printer cannot represent these characters.

SPECIAL DESTINATIONS

Although you'll usually use the Print command to print to a printer, the command also offers options that allow you to print to a file or to a range in the worksheet.

Printing to a File

The {Services} Print Settings Destination File command causes your report to be printed to a special disk file called a print file. Because the default file name extension for print files is .PRN, these files are sometimes called .PRN files.

Print files are different from worksheet files. Print files created by Symphony are a special kind of DOS file called ASCII text files. In an ASCII text file, the character codes in the file represent actual letters, numbers, and punctuation marks, not program instructions or "special" characters. Because they lack the required instructions and special characters, print files cannot be retrieved by the File Retrieve command. They can, however, be loaded into the worksheet with the File Import command. (See Chapter 10 for more on File Import.)

Using the Destination File Command

When you issue the Destination File command, Symphony prompts you for the name of the file to print the worksheet into and provides you with a list of the .PRN files on the directory. (If you press {Menu}, this list fills the screen.) You can choose any name you like for the file, provided the name doesn't violate any of DOS's file name rules. If you don't supply a file name extension, Symphony automatically provides the .PRN extension. You can, of course, supply any extension you desire.

If you select a file name that already exists on the current directory, Symphony appends the new version of the file to the old file when you press Go. This is the only situation in which Symphony will append the new file to the old. Usually the old file is simply erased.

You'll usually want to choose No-Margins before printing to a file. This will prevent the file from including meaningless margins and page breaks.

The actual characters stored in the file depend on the current character code translation table. Provided the default translation table is in effect (it will be unless you have used the {Services} Configuration File-Translation command to change it), the characters in the file will match the characters in the worksheet.

Space Compression

Space Compression is a special setting usually used only when printing a worksheet to a file. When Space Compression is on, Symphony converts sequences of spaces into tabs. If you are printing a spreadsheet, where one tab equals eight columns (usually 72 characters), Space Compression converts any eight consecutive spaces into one tab.

When printing a document, the number of spaces that must appear consecutively to be converted to a tab depends on the current Tab setting in the DOC settings sheet. For example, if the Tab setting is 5, then any group of 5 spaces will be converted into a tab.

The Space Compression command helps conserve space in your print files. Since a space and a tab are both represented by single-character ASCII codes, trading 72 spaces for a tab frees 71 bytes of disk space.

Why Use Destination File?

The Destination File setting is a carry-over from 1-2-3 (the equivalent command in that program was /Print File). In 1-2-3, the /Print File command was used to create files that could be read by word processors and certain other types of programs. 1-2-3's Print File capability thus made it possible to merge data from 1-2-3 worksheets into reports that were created with external word processors.

In Symphony, however, there is little need to transfer a worksheet to an external word processor. Instead, you can integrate the spreadsheet into a document created with Symphony's internal DOC mode. For this reason, the Destination File option is probably not going to be used very much by most Symphony users. However, if you have a word processor that you love and intend to continue to use, and you want to include parts of your Symphony worksheets in documents, you'll be able to do it with Destination File.

Printing to a Range

The Range option on the {Services} Print Settings Destination menu instructs Symphony to print one range of the current worksheet into another range in the worksheet. Each line in the source range is entered as a left-justified label in the left-most column of the To range. In other words, printing to a range creates a DOC-mode-compatible version of the information from the source range in the To range. In fact, the primary use of the Range command is to transfer information between Symphony's SHEET and DOC environments.

Since the contents of the source range are transmitted as a set of long, left-justified labels, the To range in a Print-to-Range operation can be a single column. If you print to a range that already contains cell entries, these entries will be overwritten by the report. For example, if the To range was A1 . . A100, any values, labels, or formulas in that range will be overwritten by the report. However, since the destination range is only a single column (in the example, column A), any entries in columns B, C, D, and so on will not be erased.

As when you print to the disk, you'll probably want to choose **No-Margins** before you print to a range. This will suppress unnecessary page breaks, margins, and headers and footers. If you don't suppress these options, the To range must include enough rows to accommodate at least the top margin and header lines in addition to the text. In the default configuration, these options will require five extra lines.

If you do not include enough rows in the destination range for the entire report plus any margins and headers or footers, Symphony prints as much of the report as it can into the destination range and then returns the error message

Print text range full

To recover from this error, simply use the Print Settings Destination Range command to enlarge the target range.

The Destination Cancel command erases the current destination setting. If you have been printing to a range and wish to begin printing to a different range, you should use Destination Cancel to destroy the old range definition before specifying the new range.

Suppose you decide to print the contents of row 2 in Figure 9.11 to the range A3. Assuming that Print Settings Margins No-Margins is set to Yes, the destination range in this example is the single cell A3. When the print operation is completed, the worksheet resembles Figure 9.12 and the contents of cell A3 are

A3: 'Sales $234,125 $276,109 $251,420

```
    -----A---------B---------C---------D---------E-----
 1                                                     |
 2 Sales       $234,125  $276,109  $251,420            |
 3                                                     |
 4                                                     |
   ======================================================MAIN=
```

Figure 9.11

```
    -----A---------B---------C---------D---------E-----
 1                                                     |
 2 Sales       $234,125  $276,109  $251,420            |
 3 Sales       $234,125  $276,109  $251,420            |
 4                                                     |
   ======================================================MAIN=
```

Figure 9.12

A Fine Point

I have a real philosophic difference with Lotus about where the "print to disk" and "print to range" commands should fall in Symphony's command structure. I feel that the Destination File command should really be called File Save Text or File Save ASCII, since it is conceptually closer to a File command than a Print command. Similarly, the Destination Range command should be a subset of the Copy command, Copy Text, since it effectively tells Symphony to convert one range in the worksheet to ASCII while copying it to another part of the worksheet. The current placement of these commands is awkward and confusing.

I'm not holding my breath waiting for Lotus to make these changes, however. They seem firmly committed to leaving the menu stucture as is. But in remembering the actual effect of both of these commands, it might help you to think of them as File Save Text and Copy Text.

If you feel a bit overwhelmed by the variety of printing options Symphony offers, don't worry. Most of the time you'll use only the most basic commands to print. Take your time learning the options and eventually you'll master the entire Print command.

CHAPTER TEN
FILES

As you use Symphony, you are likely to create many different worksheets. Some may contain only a single document or a simple spreadsheet; others may combine spreadsheets, documents, graphics, and data bases into a complex financial model.

However, although you'll create many worksheets, Symphony has only one large workspace, so only one of your worksheets can be active (in the workspace) at one time. This leaves only two alternatives: either Symphony provides a way to store worksheets that are not in use outside of the workspace, or you must recreate your worksheets each time you want to use them.

Fortunately, Symphony includes commands that allow you to save your worksheets to disk files and to retrieve these files for future use. Symphony's File commands are the tools you'll use to exchange worksheets (and other types of information) between Symphony and your disks.

FILE BASICS

When working with files, Symphony interacts closely with your computer's version of Microsoft's Disk Operating System (MS-DOS). For this reason, an understanding of some of the basic concepts of MS-DOS is required. The following discussion of MS-DOS should give you enough background to understand Symphony's File commands. If you want more information about MS-DOS, I recommend that you read *The MS-DOS User's Guide* by Chris DeVoney, published by Que Corporation.

Whenever you use Symphony's File commands, you'll need to supply the program with the name of the file or files you want to work with. In DOS, all files have a name. A file name can be up to eight characters long with an optional three-character extension. The name and the extension are separated by a period. The file name and the extension can use any of the following alphanumeric characters:

        0 to 9
        A to Z
        $ % # @ ! & ' ` ( ) - ^ _ ~

File names cannot include spaces, asterisks (*), colons (:), periods (.), commas (,), or any other character not shown above. Table 10.1 shows several legal and illegal file names.

Legal	Illegal
REPORT	REPORTCARD
REPORT.TXT	REPORT.TEXT
SPREAD.WRK	83,4:PLN.WRK
ABCDEFGH.IJK	ABC*DEFG.IJK
84PLAN	84.PLAN.WRK
84_BUGDT.WRK	84 BUDGET.WRK

Table 10.1

Symphony uses certain file name extensions to identify the different types of files the program uses. The .WRK extension indicates a worksheet file. Graphs can be saved in files with the extension .PIC. Other Symphony file types are .PRN (the result of printing a worksheet to the disk), .CNF (a configuration file), .CTF (a character-translation file, which is used only in the communications environment), and .APP (an add-in application file).

By definition, all files are stored on disks. Most computers on which Symphony will run have either two floppy disk drives or one floppy disk drive and one high-capacity hard disk drive. In PC-DOS version 2.0 the floppy drives are usually given the drive specifiers A: and B:, and the hard disk is usually C: (and sometimes also D:).

The main directory on any disk is called the root directory. The root directory is automatically created by Symphony when you format a disk. The root directory on a disk is designated by the drive specifier (A:, B:, C:, etc.) followed by a backslash. For example, the root directory of the disk in drive A is A:\.

PC-DOS 2.0 also makes it possible to divide the root directory on a disk into subdirectories. Although you can create subdirectories on any disk, usually only hard disk drives are divided into subdirectories. The purpose of these subdirectories is to divide the hundreds or even thousands of files that can accumulate on a hard disk into manageable related groups of files.

For example, you might set up four subdirectories on your hard disk called UTILITY, SYMPHONY, BASIC, and DBASE. All files that related to Symphony, including program files (Symphony.Exe), .WRK files, .PIC files, and .PRN files, would be stored in this directory. You could subdivide the directory SYMPHONY by creating another subdirectory, DATA, which would include only data files. DATA could be divided further into WRK, PICTURES, and PRINT, each of which would contain only a specific type of file.

The full file designation for the file TEST.WRK, which is stored in the WRK subdirectory of the DATA subdirectory of SYMPHONY, would be

C:SYMPHONY\DATA\WRK\TEST.WRK

In a simpler case, if TEST.WRK was stored on the root (main directory) of drive A, the complete file designation would be

A:\TEST.WRK

Notice that backslashes (\) divide the various parts of these two file designations. You can also use a slash (/) to divide the parts of the file designation.

THE FILE COMMANDS

The File commands allow you to save worksheet files on disk, to retrieve those files into the workspace, to extract portions of worksheets into disk files, to combine a disk file with an active worksheet, to erase files, and to obtain information about the status of your directories and your files. The File command is one of the options on the {Services} menu. When you press {**Services**} File, the following menu appears:

Save Retrieve Combine Xtract Erase Bytes List Table Import Directory

If you are an ex-1-2-3 user, this menu probably looks pretty familiar. The commands on the Symphony File menu are very similar to their 1-2-3 counterparts.

Saving Files

The Symphony worksheet that you see on the screen of your computer "exists" in your computer's RAM memory. Everything you type from the keyboard while you use Symphony, as well as everything you see in the worksheet—spreadsheets, data bases, documents, graphs, macros—is stored in RAM.

RAM memory is sometimes called volatile memory, because when your computer is deprived of electrical power, any information stored in RAM is instantly and irretrievably lost. If the contents of RAM happen to be a worksheet that you've been working on for several hours, and the power is suddenly turned off—on purpose, by accident, or by act of God—your worksheet will be lost.

The {Services} New Yes command has a similar effect. This command does not erase the entire contents of RAM—just the part that contains your worksheet. Whenever you issue the New command, the contents of the worksheet you have in RAM are completely erased.

When you save a worksheet you create a more or less permanent version of the worksheet in a disk file. This file provides a parking place where the worksheet can be stored until you need to use it again. It also preserves the contents of the worksheet from being erased accidentally.

Before you can save a file, you must insert a formatted disk into the default disk drive, A:\. If you do not have a formatted disk handy, the DOS.APP application program will let you exit from Symphony, format a disk, and then return to the program without losing your worksheet. If you try to save a worksheet onto an unformatted disk, Symphony will return the error message Data Error. If you see this message, press [Esc] and start over with a formatted disk.

To save the file, issue the {**Services**} File Save command. Assuming that you are saving this worksheet for the first time, you'll need to give Symphony a name for the file. Symphony will prompt you for the name with the message

Save file name: A:

The A:\ in the prompt is Symphony's default drive and directory specifier. If you want to save your file on the root directory of drive A:\, simply type the name you want to use to describe this file.

You can choose any name you want for your new file, as long as the name is not more than eight characters long and does not contain any illegal characters. If you do not provide an extension for the file name, Symphony automatically gives the file the suffix .WRK (for worksheet). You can create your own extension if you wish; however, as we'll see when we cover the File Retrieve command, there are advantages to using the standard extension.

Suppose you choose to save your file under the name TEST. Assuming that there is not already a file by the name TEST.WRK on the default directory, Symphony will save the file as soon as you type the name and press [Enter]. While the file is being saved, the mode indicator in the upper-right corner of the screen will say WAIT. When the file is saved, Symphony will return you to the File menu.

If there is already a file called TEST.WRK on the directory, Symphony displays the message

> **A file with that name already exists—replace it?**
> **No   Yes**

If you want to save the new file under the same name as the old file, you can do so by selecting Yes. You might make this choice if the TEST.WRK that is already on the disk is an old version of the current worksheet, or if the old TEST.WRK is not a file you need to keep. Be careful, however—when you select Yes, the new worksheet will be saved and the old file will be destroyed. Once the old file is overwritten, there is no way it can be recovered, unless a copy exists on another disk.

If, on the other hand, you do not want to overwrite the old file, you should select No. If you still want to save the file, you can issue the {**Services**} File **S**ave command again, this time selecting a different name for the current worksheet.

Suppose you have already saved and retrieved the worksheet TEST.WRK several times, and now you want to save it again. When you issue the {**Services**} File **S**ave command, Symphony will prompt you with the message

> **Save file name: A:\TEST.WRK**

Symphony always "guesses" that you will save a file under the same name that was used to retrieve the file, and that you will save it to the same drive and directory. If you want to go with Symphony's "choices," just press **[Enter].** The program then delivers this prompt:

> **A file with that name already exists—replace it?**
> **No   Yes**

Since you accepted Symphony's "guess" in the previous step, you'll probably select the Yes option at this point and overwrite the old version of the file. This serves as an extra level of security against accidentally overwriting a file you want to retain.

As you become more skilled with Symphony, you will probably get into the habit of accepting the offered file name by pressing [Enter] Yes very quickly. There are times when being skilled with a program can lead to trouble—like when you accidentally save a new version of a file over an old version because you flew through the Save command too quickly. The moral? Always move slowly and carefully when saving files.

If you want to save the file under a different name, press [Esc] to erase the old name and directory designation and then type the name under which you want to save this worksheet—for example, B:\SECOND—and press [Enter]. When this command is completed, Symphony will save the worksheet under the name SECOND.

Rather than delete the old name, you could edit it. For example, if you wanted to save the worksheet under the name TEST2.WRK, you would press ← five times, type a 2, and then press [Enter]. Since the name TEST2.WRK is different from TEST.WRK, both the new and the old versions of the worksheet would be saved.

Disk-Full Errors

If you are saving a very large worksheet, or if the disk you are saving to is already nearly full, there is a chance the disk will become full as you are saving the current file. If this occurs, Symphony will beep and display the message

Disk full error

at the bottom of the screen. You must press [Esc] to acknowledge the error and return to the READY mode.

Disk-full errors almost never occur on systems with hard disks. If you are using a hard disk, the chances of obtaining a disk-full error are pretty small. However, if you use floppy disks, you're sure to encounter this error from time to time.

When you encounter a disk-full error, you can do several things to try to save the file. First, check the size of the worksheet you are trying to save with the {Services} Settings command. Next, check the amount of space available on the disk with the {Services} File Bytes command. Compare these numbers to see how much work there is to do before you can save the file.

If the worksheet file is much larger than the available space on the disk (25,000 bytes or more), you'll probably need to either delete one or more files from the disk or save the file on a new disk. The {Services} File Erase command (covered later in this chapter) can be used to delete files. If you choose to use a new disk, and you have a formatted disk handy, simply remove the old disk from the drive and insert the new disk in its place.

If you do not have any formatted disks, you could use the DOS.APP add-in application to exit Symphony, format a disk, and then return to Symphony without losing any of your work. The DOS.APP program and the other add-ins are covered in Chapter 29.

If the worksheet is only slightly larger than the available disk space, you might try to shrink the worksheet slightly. The best way to shrink the sheet is to use the File Xtract command to save only the active portion of the worksheet, excluding memory-wasting unnecessary rows and columns (File Xtract will be covered later in this chapter).

If the worksheet you are saving is larger than about 360K bytes, it will not fit on a standard floppy disk under any circumstances. In this event, you can either shrink the worksheet or save it in two separate pieces with the File Xtract command.

A word of warning—when Symphony begins to save a file, it first deletes any file with the same name on the current directory. If, after deleting the old file, Symphony then runs out of space on the disk before the worksheet is completely saved, neither the new nor the old version of the file will exist on disk. If Symphony cannot save the worksheet (after you have taken steps to increase the available disk space or shrink the size of the model being saved), you will have lost that worksheet.

Changing the Directory

In the default configuration, Symphony assumes that all files are stored in the root directory on drive A. However, Symphony provides two different ways to change this setting.

Temporarily changing the default directory   The File Directory command allows you to temporarily change the default directory. For example, suppose you have a computer with two floppy disk drives. The default directory is A:\. During the current Symphony session, however, you will be retrieving files from disk drive B, so you want to change the default directory to B:\.

To make this change, just issue the {**Services**} File Directory command. When Symphony displays the current default directory, press [ESC] and type B:\ [Enter]. Presto! The default drive is now B.

These changes to the default directory are temporary; that is, they remain in effect only until you exit from Symphony. The permanent default is controlled by the setting in the SYMPHONY.CNF file, which can only be changed with the {**Services**} Configuration command.

Permanently changing the default directory   If your computer system has more than one disk drive, you'll probably want to permanently change the default directory when you configure Symphony for your system. For example, suppose your computer system has two disk drives. You plan to use drive A for your Symphony program disk and the Help disk and drive B for your data files. To change the default directory to B, issue the {**Settings**} Configuration File command. Press **[Esc]** to blank the current default setting, and then enter the new directory, **B:\.** Press **[Enter]** to lock in this choice.

If, instead of two floppy disk drives, your computer system has a hard disk, you'll probably want Symphony to save your files on a directory on the hard disk. Suppose you want to store your data files on the directory C:Symphony\Files\. Just issue the {**Services**} Configuration File command, press **[Esc],** and enter **C:Symphony\Files** as the default directory.

Remember that the changes you make with {Settings} Configuration are only temporary unless you use the {**Settings**} Configuration Update command to rewrite the SYMPHONY.CNF configuration file. If you make the changes permanent, each time you issue a File command, Symphony automatically looks for your data files on the new default directory.

Don't forget that the default directory is merely an aid in using the File commands. You are not by any means restricted to using the default directory. If you want to save a file on a directory other than the default, or if you want to retrieve a file from another directory, you need only replace the default supplied by Symphony with the directory you want to use at the time you issue the File Save or File Retrieve command.

For example, suppose you are creating a special version of one of your worksheets, called TAXES.WKS, for use by one of your business associates. When you finish modifying the worksheet, you want to save it on a floppy disk in drive A. The default directory on your system is C:Symphony\Files\. When you issue the {**Services**} File **S**ave command, Symphony responds with the prompt

> Save file name: C:Symphony\Files\TAXES.WKS

Since you want to save the file to drive A, Symphony's guess must be changed. Press **[Home]** to move the cursor in the control panel to the C in the file designation. Now press **[Del]** to erase the entire directory designation so that the prompt looks like this:

> Save file name: TAXES.WKS

Now type A:\ and press **[Enter]**. The file will now be saved on drive A.

Instead of using [Del] to erase the drive designation, you could have pressed **[Esc]** to erase the entire file name and directory designation, and then retyped both the directory and the file name.

Saving Graphs

When you save a worksheet that contains graphs, the graphs are automatically saved. When you retrieve that worksheet, the graph settings sheets will be retrieved as well. In other words, you don't need to do anything special to save graphs.

However, there is a command, Graph Image-Save, that can be used to save a graph into a special .PIC file. .PIC files exist only to allow graphs to be transferred between Symphony, where they are created, and PrintGraph, the special program that prints graphs. These files have no other purpose; in fact, there is not even a way to retrieve a .PIC file into Symphony.

.PIC files are discussed in Chapter 12, which explains Symphony's graphics capabilites, and in Chapter 14, which covers the PrintGraph program.

Retrieving Your Worksheets

Carrying on with our example, suppose that after saving TEST.WRK to directory B:\, you want to recall the file into Symphony to make a few changes. (We'll assume that the default directory is now B:\.) The command to load a file into Symphony is {**Services**} File **R**etrieve. When you issue this command, the control panel looks like this:

> Name of file to retrieve: B:\ * .wrk
> TEST.WRK   SECOND.WRK   THIRD.WRK

The first line of this display prompts you to supply a file name to retrieve. The prompt includes the default directory designation B:\ and the wild-card file name *.wrk. The asterisk in this name serves as a wild card, meaning that this file name matches every file name on the directory that ends with .WRK. Symphony uses this to retrieve a list of all the .WRK files on the directory. This list is displayed in the second line of the control panel. Notice that the list includes our sample file name TEST.WRK as well as two other file names.

You can the select the file you wish to retrieve in one of two ways. First, you simply point to the name of the file you want to retrieve and press [Enter]. Alternatively, you could just type the name of the file you want to retrieve. As soon as you start typing, the wild-card name ∗.wrk disappears and the name you type appears next to the directory designation. If you don't supply an extension when you type the file name, Symphony assumes the file has the .WRK extension.

It is clearly more efficient to select the file to be retrieved by pointing than by typing. You can now see why I recommend that you always save your worksheets with the standard .WRK extension. If you don't use this extension, your files won't appear in the list, and you won't be able to select them by pointing.

If the default directory contains more than five files, the one-line listing the control panel will not show the names of all files on the directory at once. In this event, you can press {Services} or {Menu} to switch from a one-line display to a full-screen display of the available files. Figure 10.1 shows such a display. Notice that in this mode the name, creation date and time, and size of the file being pointed to appears in the control panel.

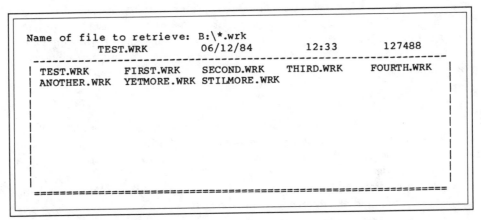

Figure 10.1

Once you have reviewed the entire list, you can press {Menu} or {Services} again to return to the single-line display. You can, of course, point to the files in the full-screen list. If you select a file in this way, the file list disappears when you press [Enter].

Symphony automatically assumes that the file you want to retrieve is located on the default directory. Of course, you can retrieve a file from a directory other than the default. For example, suppose you have changed the default directory to C:SYMPHONY\FILES\. Suppose further that a business associate has sent you a floppy disk containing a new worksheet. You want to load the worksheet, named BUDGET.WRK, into Symphony directly from the floppy disk. You would issue the {Services} File Retrieve command. When the prompt

Retrieve File Name: C:SYMPHONY\FILES\ * .wrk
TEST.WRK   SECOND.WRK   ANOTHER.WRK

appears, press **[Esc]** twice to erase the wild-card file name and the directory designation. Now simply type the full specification of the file you want to retrieve—**A:\BUDGET**—and press **[Enter]**.

File Retrieve automatically erases the worksheet you have in RAM before it begins to load the new file. This makes Retrieve a potentially devastating command. For example, if you have filled the workspace with a spreadsheet and neglect to save that sheet before you retrieve another one, your work will be destroyed by the Retrieve command. Always be sure that you've saved the contents of the worksheet before you issue the {**Services**} File **R**etrieve command.

Memory-Full Errors

If the file you are loading was created on a computer that had more memory than the computer you are currently using, it is possible that the file will be too large to fit into the available memory. If the file is too large, Symphony delivers the message

Memory Full

If you see this message, press **[Esc]** to return to the worksheet. Notice that Symphony has retrieved as much of the file as would fit in the available memory. Sometimes enough of the file is retrieved that you can easily trim out some memory-wasting entries and reconstruct the missing parts of the worksheet. However, if a large part of the worksheet is missing, there isn't much you can do to recover except find a machine with more memory.

Erasing a File

There are times when you'll want to erase one of your worksheet files from within Symphony. For example, you might erase an unimportant file to make room on a disk to save the current worksheet. Or you might erase an old file that was superceded by a new version of a different file.

The File Erase command lets you erase files from within Symphony. When you issue the File Erase command, the following menu appears:

Worksheet Print Graph Other

When you select one of these options, Symphony displays a list of all the files of that type on the current directory and prompts you to supply the name of the file you want to erase. For example, selecting Worksheet displays a list of the files on the directory with the extension .WRK. The Other option displays the names of all files on the current directory.

Unless you have a very large number of files on the current directory, it's usually wise to select the Other option, since it permits you to view more file names. For example, if the default directory is B:\, selecting the Other option causes the control panel to look something like this:

Name of file to erase: B:\ * . *
TEST.WRK SECOND.WRK GRAPH.PIC REPORT.PRN THIRD.WRK OTHER.TXT

Notice that this list contains .WRK files, a .PRN file, a .PIC file, and even a .TXT file created by another program. If we had selected one of the other options, fewer file names would be visible. For example, if we had selected the Worksheet option, the prompt would be

> Name of file to erase: B:\ * .wrk
> TEST.WRK   SECOND.WRK   THIRD.WRK

You can select the name of the file you wish to erase by pointing to the appropriate name in the list or by typing a name. As with the other Symphony file commands, if the list of file names is too long to view in the control panel, you can press {**Menu**} or {**Services**} to fill the screen with the list. If you use the Erase Other option as we have suggested, you'll probably want to take advantage of this full-screen display capability.

In the above example, if you wanted to delete the file called TEST.WRK, you would point to that choice on the list and press [Enter]. Symphony would then display the question

> Are you sure you want to erase this file?
> No   Yes

If you want to Erase the file, select the Yes option. Otherwise, press [**Enter**] or No to abort the Erase operation.

You can also use File Erase to erase files from a directory other than the default. For example, if you want to delete a file named TESTER.WRK from directory A:\, you would press [**Esc**] twice to erase Symphony's B:\ *.* prompt, and type the name of the file you want to erase:

> Name of file to erase: A:\TESTER.WRK

Notice that we included the extension .WRK when specifying the file to be erased. Since we selected the Other option from the File Erase menu, Symphony requires that we provide the full name, including extension, of the file we want to erase.

Be careful when you use File Erase. Once you erase a file, it's gone for good. Unless you have another copy of the file on a different directory, or one of the special utility programs designed to recover lost files, you will be out of luck.

File Xtract

The File Xtract command is used to save portions of worksheets into separate .WRK files. This command makes it possible to extract an important table, formula, or data base from a worksheet into its own .WRK file. This file can then be retrieved into Symphony or merged into another worksheet with the File Combine command.

File Xtract has two options: Formulas and Values. The Formulas option saves the extracted file as a standard worksheet—labels are saved as labels, numbers as numbers, and formulas as formulas. The Values option, on the other hand, converts all formulas into a simple number as it extracts the file. For example, suppose you have created a worksheet that contains the formula

A5: + A6

Let's assume that the current value of this formula is 15. If we extracted this cell into a separate worksheet file using the Values option, the contents of cell A5 would be saved as 15, not +A6.

Using File Xtract Formulas

File Xtract formulas can be very handy in overcoming memory-full errors. For example, suppose you have received a memory-full error while building a large worksheet. The bottom-right corner of the part of the worksheet you are using is Z100; however, when you press **[End][Home],** the cursor jumps to cell AC125, indicating that you have 3 empty columns and 25 empty rows in the worksheet. Although these rows contain no information, they are considered by Symphony to be a part of the active worksheet, and thus eat up valuable memory.

The File Xtract command can be used to eliminate these unwanted rows and columns. To eliminate these cells from our example worksheet, we would issue the {Services} File Xtract Formulas command and specify the range to be saved as A1 . . Z100. This command causes Symphony to save only the part of the worksheet you are really using. The unwanted cells are left behind.

As soon as the partial file is saved, retrieve it into the worksheet and issue the {Services} Settings command. The memory indicator should show that at least a few thousand bytes have been recovered.

For a general discussion of memory management, see Chapter 3.

The Values Option

The Values option of the File Xtract command can also be used to create a "frozen" version of a worksheet. For example, suppose you had created a worksheet that contained a large number of functions and formulas. You want to create a version of this worksheet that "locks" all of the formulas and functions in the sheet at their current values. You could do this by issuing the File Xtract Values command and specifying the entire active worksheet as the range to be extracted. The resulting file would contain the current values for all of the formulas and functions in the worksheet, but not the formulas and functions themselves.

File Xtract Problems

There are several problems that can result from using Xtract. For example, it is possible to extract a portion of a file that includes formulas with references to the part of the file that was left behind. When this partial file is retrieved into the worksheet, cells containing these references will contain inaccurate answers or @ERR messages.

File Xtract leaves behind any range names that are not wholly included in the range being extracted. For example, if the name TEST applies to the range A1 . . E1, and you extract the range A1 . . C3, the resulting file will not include this range name. However, the extracted file will include all of the graph settings sheets that were a part of the main worksheet. If the ranges in the graph settings sheets refer to cells outside the extracted range, though, the graph will not be correct when it is retrieved.

File Combine

The File Combine command is used to combine, or consolidate, one worksheet or portion of a worksheet with another. File Combine is extremely useful for transferring information between worksheets or for consolidating two or more related worksheets into one summary sheet. File Xtract and File Combine can be used together to overcome disk-full errors, as well.

File Combine differs from File Retrieve in that File Retrieve erases the entire worksheet before retrieving the selected file, while File Combine overlays the contents of the file on the current contents of the worksheet. The file being combined is loaded into the worksheet at the current cell pointer location. In other words, the upper-left cell in the file will be overlayed on the cell containing the cell pointer.

The File Combine command is rather complex; there are four levels of instructions behind this one command. When the command is issued, Symphony presents the user with three choices:

Copy Add Subtract

These options determine exactly how the file being combined interacts with the information already in the worksheet. The Copy option causes the file being combined to overwrite the contents of the worksheet. The Add option adds any values in the file being combined to the values in the corresponding cells in the current worksheet. Conversely, the Subtract option subtracts the values in the file being combined from the values in the corresponding cells in the current worksheet. Both the Add and the Subtract options ignore cells in the current worksheet that contain formulas or labels.

After you select one of these options, Symphony gives you the choice

Entire-File Named-Area

If you select the Entire-File option, the entire file whose name you provide will be combined into the current worksheet. The upper-left corner (cell A1) of the file being combined will be combined into the cell containing the cell pointer when the command is issued. The rest of the file will be loaded into cells B1, A2, B2, and so on.

The Named-Area option, on the other hand, combines only a named range from the specified file into the worksheet. This range can be as small as a single cell or as large as the entire worksheet (although it is more likely to be small than large). The upper-left corner of the named range will be combined into the cell containing the cell pointer at the time the command was issued. As you might expect, the Named-Area option requires that the range you intend to combine has already been given a name. If the range has not been named, the combine operation will not be successful.

The third option offered by the File Combine command is

Ignore Read

This choice lets you tell Symphony whether any range names and line-marker names in the source worksheet should be combined into the current worksheet. Ignore tells the program to combine the file or named range without the range names; Read includes these names in the new worksheet.

This command overcomes one of the more troublesome problems with the 1-2-3 File Combine command. In 1-2-3, File Combine automatically stripped any range names from the source file before combining it into the worksheet. This was done to prevent conflicts between range names in the current worksheet and range names in the source file. If both files contained the same name, the name in the worksheet would be destroyed by the file being combined. For example, suppose the name TEST had been assigned to cell A1 in the current worksheet and to cell A2 in the file being combined. When the combine operation was completed, the name TEST would be assigned to cell A2 only.

Unlike 1-2-3, Symphony lets you decide whether you want to combine range names. If you select the Ignore option, all range and line-marker names in the source file will be ignored by Symphony and will not be combined into the worksheet. If you choose the Read option, Symphony will include these names when it combines the file into the worksheet.

The choice between Read and Ignore is not always easy. As a general rule, you're probably better selecting Ignore to make sure no conflicts develop. Ignore is almost always the right selection for Combine Add and Combine Subtract, and usually gives the best results with Combine Copy. But if the file you're combining with Combine Copy and the worksheet you're combining it with contain range names that conflict, while selecting Ignore will prevent the names in the worksheet from being destroyed, it will also leave behind any names in the file. If these names are critical to that file, choosing Ignore could lead to problems.

About the only time you're certain to want to use the Read option is when you use Combine to restore a worksheet that you split into two pieces while saving. In this case, both parts of the worksheet may contain important range names.

Finally, File Combine asks whether you want to combine the formulas or only the current values of those formulas from the source file into the worksheet. The Values/Formulas choice applies only to Combine Copy, since Symphony always uses Values with Combine Add and Combine Subtract. This command is the converse of the File Xtract Formulas or Values command.

As with the Ignore/Read command, deciding whether to combine formulas or values is not always easy. Most of the time you'll want to include the formulas from the file into the worksheet. Occasionally, though, you might want to "freeze" the values of some formulas with the Values option as you combine them into the worksheet. If you are combining a data set that contains only values and labels, either option will do the trick.

File Combine Examples

Let's look at a few Combine examples, beginning with the Copy option. Suppose you've created the worksheet shown in Figure 10.2 and have saved that sheet into the file TEST.WRK. This worksheet shows the sales for Division 1 of a company for the first three months of 1984.

The cells in row 9 of this worksheet contain formulas that total each column. For example, cell C9 contains the formula

C9: (C2) @SUM(C3 . . C8)

```
    -----A---------B---------C---------D---------E------
  1 Division 1                                              |
  2 Sales Forecast       Jan-84     Feb-84     Mar-84       |
  3 Product 1            $15,000    $17,000    $19,000       |
  4 Product 2            $22,000    $20,000    $17,000       |
  5 Product 3            $18,000    $18,000    $18,000       |
  6 Product 4                                               |
  7 Product 5            $18,000    $18,000    $18,000       |
  8                      -------    -------    -------       |
  9    Total Sales       $67,000    $70,000    $70,000       |
    ==========================================MAIN=
```

Figure 10.2

Notice that row 6 in the worksheet is blank. We're assuming that Division 1 doesn't sell any Product 4. You'll see why in a few pages.

After issuing the {**Services**} **N**ew command, you build a new worksheet as shown in Figure 10.3. This worksheet contains the 1984 cash flow budget for the same division.

```
    -----A---------B---------C---------D---------E------
  1 Division 1                                              |
  2 Cash Flow Budget     Jan-84     Feb-84     Mar-84       |
  3                                                         |
  4 Total Sales                                             |
  5                                                         |
  6 Collections                                             |
  7    0-30 Days                                            |
  8    30-60 Days                                           |
    ==========================================MAIN=
```

Figure 10.3

We want to combine only the range C9 . . E9 from the file TEST.WRK into the cash flow forecast. Assuming we had named the range C9 . . E9 in TEST.WRK Sales_Tot before saving the file, we could move the cell pointer to cell C4 in the worksheet in Figure 10.3 and issue the **F**ile **C**ombine **C**opy **N**amed-Area **I**gnore **V**alues command, specifying Sales_Tot as the range to be combined. If everything works properly, the worksheet will look like Figure 10.4.

The cells in row 4 of the consolidated worksheet now contain the values from cells C9, D9, and E9 of TEST.WRK. For example, cell C4 contains the value

   C4: (C2) 67000

Notice that only the current value of the formula in cell C9 has been translated. This occurred because we used the Values option when combining.

The Add option   Now go back to Figure 10.2. Suppose the company in the example

```
     ------A----------B----------C----------D----------E-----
   1 Division 1                                                |
   2 Cash Flow Budget      Jan-84      Feb-84      Mar-84       |
   3                                                           |
   4 Total Sales          $67,000     $70,000     $70,000      |
   5                                                           |
   6 Collections                                               |
   7     0-30 Days                                             |
   8     30-60 Days                                            |
     ===============================================MAIN=
```

Figure 10.4

had two divisions, and top management wanted to prepare a consolidated sales fore-cast. Figure 10.5 shows a worksheet that is set up for the consolidation. The sales figures for Division 2 of this company are already in the worksheet.

```
     -----A----------B----------C----------D----------E------
   1 Division 2                                                |
   2 Sales Forecast        Jan-84      Feb-84      Mar-84       |
   3 Product 1            $13,000     $15,000     $12,000       |
   4 Product 2            $27,000     $21,000     $20,000       |
   5 Product 3            $20,000     $29,000     $19,000       |
   6 Product 4            $10,000     $11,000     $21,000       |
   7 Product 5                                                  |
   8                      -------     -------     -------       |
   9    Total Sales       $70,000     $76,000     $72,000       |
     ================================================MAIN=
```

Figure 10.5

Now we want to consolidate TEST.WRK into this worksheet. Begin by positioning the cell pointer on cell A1 and issuing the **File Combine Add Entire-File Ignore** command, specifying TEST.WRK as the file to be combined. After the files are combined, the worksheet should look like Figure 10.6.

Notice that the Combine Add command has added every value in TEST.WRK to the values in the worksheet. For example, January 1984 sales of Product 1 for Division 1 were $13,000 and for Division 2 were $15,000, and cell C2 in the consolidated worksheet contains the value $28,000.

Since row 6 in TEST.WRK was blank, row 6 in the consolidated worksheet contains only the Product 4 sales data for Division 2. Similarly, row 7 in the worksheet contains the sales figures for Product 5 from Division 1 only. In both of these cases, the Combine Add command assigned the value 0 to all the blank cells, then added 0 to the value in the corresponding cell of the other worksheet.

```
     -----A----------B----------C----------D----------E------
   1 Consolidated                                            |
   2 Sales Forecast        Jan-84     Feb-84     Mar-84      |
   3 Product 1            $28,000    $32,000    $31,000      |
   4 Product 2            $49,000    $41,000    $37,000      |
   5 Product 3            $38,000    $47,000    $37,000      |
   6 Product 4            $10,000    $11,000    $21,000      |
   7 Product 5            $12,000    $15,000    $16,000      |
   8                      --------   --------   --------     |
   9    Total Sales      $137,000   $146,000   $142,000      |
     ===================================================MAIN=
```

Figure 10.6

You should also be aware that Combine Add does not affect any cells containing labels or formulas. For example, the label in cell A1 in the worksheet remained Consolidated even after the combination was completed. Similarly, the formulas in row 9 of the worksheet were unaffected by the combination.

Recombining large files   Suppose you created a huge worksheet that spanned the range A1 . . BK2500 in your worksheet. When you tried to save this file, you found that the worksheet was too big to save on a single disk, so you used the **File X–tract F**ormulas command to break the file into two smaller pieces before saving. The first file, called PART1.WRK, includes the range A1 . . BK1250, and the second, called PART2.WRK, the range A1251 . . BK2500. These two files were saved on separate disks.

Now you want to reconstruct your model in the worksheet. You can load PART1.WRK into the workspace with the **File R**etrieve command. After this section is in place, replace the disk containing PART1.WRK with the disk containing PART2.WRK, move the cell pointer to cell A1251 and issue the **File C**ombine **C**opy **E**ntire-File **R**ead **F**ormulas command. After a few seconds, both parts of the model will be in the worksheet. All of the formulas, range names, graphs, and other settings in the original model will be included in the reconstructed model.

The Other File Commands

Symphony includes several other File commands that help manage files and directories. The first is **File B**ytes. **File B**ytes tells you the number of bytes of usable space that remain on the default disk. This command is handy for helping judge whether a worksheet can be saved in the available disk space. As long as the size of the worksheet (which can be read from the {Services} Settings sheet) is less than the available disk space, the current worksheet can be saved on the disk without any problems.

The **File L**ist command displays a list of the files on the disk. You can choose to list all the files on a disk or just the Worksheet files, Graph Files (.PIC), or Print files (.PRN).

Figure 10.7 shows a list of all the files on a floppy disk. The form of the list created by this command is identical to the list we saw when we pressed {**Services**} or {**Menu**} from within the File Erase Other command. Notice that this list includes not only Symphony files, but also files created by other programs (.TXT files) and DOS files (.COM and .EXE files).

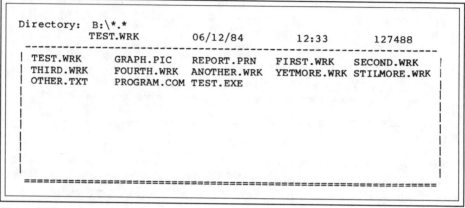

```
 Directory:  B:\*.*
             TEST.WRK           06/12/84          12:33          127488
 ------------------------------------------------------------------------
 I  TEST.WRK      GRAPH.PIC    REPORT.PRN   FIRST.WRK    SECOND.WRK    I
 I  THIRD.WRK     FOURTH.WRK   ANOTHER.WRK  YETMORE.WRK  STILMORE.WRK  I
 I  OTHER.TXT     PROGRAM.COM  TEST.EXE                                I
 I                                                                     I
 I                                                                     I
 I                                                                     I
 I                                                                     I
 I                                                                     I
 I                                                                     I
 I                                                                     I
 ========================================================================
```

Figure 10.7

The second line of the control panel in Figure 10.7 shows the name, creation date and time, and size of the file on which the pointer is positioned. If you point to a different file name, this display will show the same information for that file. Although you can point to the file names in this list, you cannot retrieve, erase, or otherwise access a file from within the List commmand.

EXCHANGING INFORMATION WITH OTHER PROGRAMS

Symphony has the ability to exchange information with other programs, including word processors, data base managers, and spreadsheets. In some cases, Symphony can read the files created by another program; in other cases, Symphony can also create files that can be read by another program. Symphony's file transfer capabilities are found in several different parts of the program, including the File command, the Print command, and the special Translation program.

1-2-3 Files

You can load your old 1-2-3 files directly into Symphony by using Symphony's File Retrieve command. If your 1-2-3 file is a basic spreadsheet, the translation should proceed without a hitch. Symphony can read and understand all of 1-2-3's functions and formulas.

However, because File Retrieve defaults to seeking files with a .WRK extension, you'll probably want to rename all of your 1-2-3 files so that they have the extension .WRK before you attempt to retrieve them. If you do not rename the files, you will not be able to see the names of the files when you issue the File Retrieve command from Symphony.

Remember that you cannot retrieve a Symphony .WRK file into 1-2-3. If you expect that you will want to use 1-2-3 to work on a file that has been transferred to Symphony, be sure to keep a 1-2-3 version of the file.

1-2-3 Data Bases

Data bases should also be translated accurately. Remember, though, that Symphony's data base capability goes well beyond 1-2-3's. For example, Symphony allows you to define default values and validity tests for data base fields. Your translated data bases will not have these special features. In addition, your translated 1-2-3 data bases will not be associated with any FORM window. If you want to work on the data base through a FORM window, you'll need to create one in Symphony.

1-2-3 Graphs

Any graphs (both named and unnamed) in your 1-2-3 worksheet are lost when the file is loaded into Symphony. Apparently, Symphony's sophisticated graph capabilities cannot handle 1-2-3's simple graphs. If your worksheets contain more than a few important graphs, this inability of Symphony to read 1-2-3 graphs will be a major irritation.

1-2-3 Macros

Any macros in your 1-2-3 file will be retrieved intact. Even the macro name will be retrieved into Symphony. However, the chances are very good that you will not be able to execute this macro in Symphony. First, the Symphony Command Language uses a completely different set of commands from 1-2-3's macro language. 1-2-3's macro commands, like /XQ and /XG, are meaningless to Symphony.

You probably won't have much better luck with macros that use standard 1-2-3 commands (like /Worksheet Format and /Data Query). Although there is a great deal of similarity between the menu structures of 1-2-3 and Symphony, they are different enough that 1-2-3 macros will probably not achieve the correct results in Symphony.

If your 1-2-3 macro is fairly simple, you might be able to modify it slightly to work in Symphony. One way to modify the macro would be to use a Symphony DOC environment's search and replace capabilities. For example, you could use the search and replace command to replace every occurrence of /FR in a macro with {Menu}FR.

Working with Text Files

The first of Symphony's file transfer commands is File Import. File Import makes it possible to load an ASCII text file into the Symphony worksheet.

ASCII text files are a special kind of DOS file. The .PRN files created by printing a worksheet to the disk are an example of an ASCII file. Most word processors create ASCII files. The .DBF data base files created by dBASE II are a special form of text file.

Suppose you have written a text file with a word processor that you want to import into Symphony. Move the cell pointer to the upper-left corner of the range you'll want the file to occupy (in a blank sheet, this will usually be cell A1), and issue the {**Services**} File Import command.

File Import has two options: Text and Structured. The Text option treats the file being imported as a series of long labels. Each line in the file is imported as a left-aligned label containing the text and numbers in that line. After one line is read into the worksheet, Symphony skips down one row and reads the next line as a left-aligned label, then skips down again, and so on. The result is a single column of long labels. If the text file has 10 lines, the worksheet will be 10 rows deep.

The Text option has a couple of limitations. First, the text file cannot contain any line longer than 240 characters. You might think that this is not a problem, since most text files have 80 or fewer characters per line. However, Symphony treats every paragraph in a WordStar file as a line in a normal text file. Since most WordStar paragraphs are more than 240 characters long, Symphony cannot import most WordStar documents and will display

Input line too long (240 characters max)

if you try.

Another limitation of the Import Text command becomes evident when noncharacter ASCII codes show up in your text files. The files of some word processing programs, like WordStar, include characters that lie outside the standard ASCII character range of 32 to 127. Although these character codes are not displayed in WordStar, when they are imported into Symphony they are passed through the current character code translation table and displayed as strange characters in your worksheet. (For more on importing WordStar files, see Chapter 18.)

The Structured option, on the other hand, treats the file being imported as a matrix of cell entries. This option only imports numbers, and text enclosed in quotes, into the file. For example, suppose you had created a text file with a BASIC program that included these two lines:

```
"John Smith" 1234 Woodbourne Rd. "Louisville, KY" 40205
"Bob Williams" 101 Main Street "Shepardsville, KY" 40111
```

(By the way, you can "look at" any text file type by typing

TYPE FILENAME

next to the DOS prompt (A> or C>). This command will "type" the file named FILENAME on the screen. The file will scroll line by line, until the end of file is reached or until you type [Ctrl] C.)

Suppose that we moved the cell pointer to cell A1 and issued the **{Services}** File Import command, supplying the name of the ASCII file. When imported into Symphony, these two lines will look like Figure 10.8.

Notice that any text that was enclosed in quotes in the ASCII file is imported as a left-justified label. For example, cell A1 contains the label

A1: 'John Smith

Columns A and C in this worksheet have been widened to accommodate the long labels. If these columns had not been widened, Symphony would have truncated these long labels as much as necessary to fit into the available space.

```
     ------A------------B--------------C-------------D------
   1 John Smith        1234  Louisville, KY        40205   |
   2 Bob Williams       101  Shepardsville, KY     40111   |
   3                                                       |
   4                                                       |
     =================================================MAIN=
```

Figure 10.8

Notice that the text strings in both lines that were not enclosed in quotes were not imported into the file. For example, the string Woodbourne Rd. was not imported.

Any numbers in the ASCII file are imported as numeric cell entries. For example, cell B1 in the worksheet contains the value

> B1: 1234

and cell D1 contains the value

> D1: 40205

If the ASCII file had included any numbers enclosed in quotes, these numbers would have been imported as numeric labels.

Because the Import Structured option makes a mess of files that don't conform exactly to its rules, this option is not usually used to import files like the one in our example. Typically, you would only use Import Structured to import files that include only numbers or that have been specially configured so that all text in the file is enclosed in quotes.

Blank Lines in the ASCII File

Anytime you import a file into the worksheet, the imported file overwrites the cell entries in the worksheet. However, Symphony will skip blank lines when importing the file. Any information in the row of the worksheet where the blank line would have been imported will not be overwritten. For example, imagine that you had created a text file that looked like this:

> This is the first line of the text file
>
> This is the third line of the text file

and you planned to import this file into the worksheet in Figure 10.9. First you would move the cell pointer to cell A1 and issue the {**Services**} File Import Text command. The resulting worksheet would look like Figure 10.10.

As you can see, the first and third lines in the text file overwrote the first and third lines in the worksheet. However, the second line of the file, which was blank, did not affect the second line of the worksheet.

Exporting an ASCII file

Symphony can both read and write ASCII text files. This means that you can export a file from Symphony that can be read by many word processors and some data management and graphics programs. The command for creating an ASCII text file from Symphony is not one of Symphony's File commands, however, but a special form of the

```
     ----A---------B---------C---------D------
   1 This is the first line of a worksheet      |
   2 This is the second line of the worksheet |
   3 This is the third line of the worksheet   |
   4                                            |
   5                                            |
     ====================================MAIN=
```

Figure 10.9

```
     ----A---------B---------C---------D------
   1 This is the first line of the text file   |
   2 This is the second line of the worksheet |
   3 This is the third line of text file       |
   4                                            |
   5                                            |
     ====================================MAIN=
```

Figure 10.10

{Services} Print command. In effect, to create an ASCII text file from Symphony, you "print" the contents of the worksheet to the disk. The {Services} Print Settings Destination File command is covered in detail in Chapter 9.

Reading and Writing Files Using the Translate Utility

The Lotus Access System offers four options: Symphony, PrintGraph, Translate, and Quit. The Translate utility programs are stored on the Install program disk and can be accessed either through the Access System or by placing the Install program disk in the active drive and typing Translate next to the DOS prompt (usually A > or C >). The Translate utility offers programs that make it possible to translate VisiCalc and dBASE II files into Symphony files.

The Translate menu looks like this:

VC to WRK   DIF to WRK   WRK to DIF   DBF to WRK   WRK to DBF Exit

The first part of each option describes the type of file you want to translate; the second part describes the type of file you want to create. For example, the VC to WRK option translates a VisiCalc .VC file into a Symphony .WRK file. The DBF to WRK option translates a dBASE II .DBF file into a Symphony .WRK file.

When you make a selection, Symphony prompts you for the path name (directory) that contains the file you want to translate. When you supply this directory name to Symphony, a list of the files of the specified type appears on the screen.

Translating VisiCalc Files

The VC to WRK option on the Translate Menu lets you translate a VisiCalc worksheet file into a Symphony .WRK file. If you have been using VisiCalc and have now moved up to Symphony, this utility will allow you to transfer your files.

Suppose, for example, that you want to translate some VisiCalc files into Symphony files, and that the VisiCalc files are stored on directory C:\VisiCalc\Files. You would specify this directory in response to Symphony's prompt, and Symphony would display a list of the files of the specified type stored on that directory. You would select one of these files by pointing to its name with the cursor and pressing **[Space]** and **[Enter].**

Finally, Symphony would prompt you to choose the directory where you want the translated file to be saved. For example, you might specify the directory C:\Symphony\Files\WRK\. Once the directory is specified, Symphony will begin to translate the file. The file name for the translated file will match the name of the old file, except that the extension will be changed to match the new file type. If the VisiCalc file being translated were named SECOND.VC, the translated Symphony file would be saved under the name SECOND.WRK.

If a file named SECOND.WRK already exists on the directory C:\Symphony\Files\WRK, it will be overwritten by the new file. Be careful! Symphony doesn't give any warning before it erases a file in this way. Be sure to check your current directory for conflicting file names before you translate.

Although the VC to WRK translation utility works well, it has a couple of limitations. VC to WRK cannot translate VisiCalc's @CHOOSE, @NOT, @AND, and @OR functions. When VC to WRK finds these functions in a VisiCalc file, it returns a formula error message and converts the function into a label. Once the file is translated, you can modify these functions using Symphony's {Edit} capability.

Another potential problem is the way VC to WRK interprets some of VisiCalc's cell formats. In VisiCalc, the $ format causes a number to be displayed with two decimal places. This format is frequently used to display currency amounts, but it is also used at times to display percentages and other values. When VC to WRK encounters a cell with the VisiCalc $ format, it translates this format into Symphony's Currency 2 format. If you want the cell to be displayed as a currency amount, everything is fine. But if the the cell contains a percentage or other value, you'll need to reformat the cell.

Translating to and from dBASE II

The Translation utility also makes it possible to translate your Symphony data bases into dBASE II .DBF files and to translate dBASE II .DBF files into Symphony's .WRK format. For example, suppose you have built a data base in Symphony that you want to translate to dBASE II. When you select the WRK to DBF option from the translate menu, Symphony asks if you want to translate the entire worksheet or only a named range.

If your Symphony data base is a part of a worksheet that contains other information (like documents or spreadsheet entries), or if your Symphony data base begins anywhere other than cell A1, you'll want to translate only the portion of the worksheet that actually contains the data base. The portion of the worksheet you want to translate must have been named before you saved the worksheet.

The named range must include at least the field names at the top of your Symphony data base. If only the row containing these names is included in the range, the WRK to DBF option first translates that row and then continues to process until it reaches a blank row.

None of the peripheral information that accompanies some Symphony data bases, like FORM windows or data base definitions, can be translated into dBASE II.

There are some things to keep in mind while translating worksheets into .DBF files. First, since a dBASE II file can have a maximum of only 64 fields, the Symphony data base you translate can have no more than 64 fields. In addition, the field names in your Symphony data base must be valid dBASE II field names. A dBASE II field name can be up to 10 characters long and may only contain letters, numbers, and imbedded colons. A dBASE II file name must also begin with a letter. Spaces and punctuation marks other than the colon are not allowed.

The length of each field in the .DBF file created by WRK to DBF is determined by the width of the column containing that field in the Symphony worksheet. For example, if the field TEST were located in column G, which was three characters wide, the field TEST in the .DBF file would be three characters wide.

The number of decimals in each numeric field in the .DBF file is determined by the format of the first cell in that field in the Symphony file. For example, if the first cell under the header TEST contained the number

G3: 100.23

in the General format, then the field TEST would have two decimal places. If cell G3 contained the same number, 100.23, but was formatted to Fixed with zero decimal places, the field TEST in the dBASE file would have zero decimal places.

You may occasionally want to translate a dBASE II file into .WRK format. The DBF to WRK option on the translate menu makes it possible to create a Symphony data base containing the same fields and the same data as a dBASE II file. The field definitions of a translated dBASE II file will appear in row 1 of the new worksheet, beginning in column A. The records will appear in rows 2, 3, and so on.

There are also some peculiarities that come into play when you translate a dBASE II file into Symphony. First, remember that the maximum number of records in a Symphony data base is about 8000. If your dBASE II file is larger than this limit, you will not be able to translate the entire file into Symphony at one time. You can, of course, divide the dBASE II file into two or more smaller files before you attempt to translate.

Second, the width of each field in the Symphony data base is determined by the width of the same field in the dBASE II file. If your dBASE II file contains some narrow fields, you may not be able to view the field name or contents of the field in Symphony without expanding the column width.

Third, the Translate utility might have difficulty translating the logical fields (if there are any) in your dBASE II files. In dBASE II, the letters Y and T are interchangeable symbols for logical true, and the symbols N and F are interchangeable symbols for logical false. The Translate utility, however, only recognizes T for true and F for false. Logical fields containing N or Y will not be translated correctly.

Why translate from dBASE II to Symphony? Although dBASE II is one of the most powerful data base managers available for microcomputers, and is excellent for managing large files (up to 64,000 records per file), it is not as fast as Symphony when it comes to sorting and finding individual records. dBASE II also lacks Symphony's graphics capabilities. This means that there may be times when you want to transfer a dBASE II file, or a part of a large file, into Symphony.

Conversely, while Symphony is very fast and is capable of creating graphs from the data in a data base, it can accommodate a maximum of about 8000 records, and in most situations the number is even smaller than that. Symphony also lacks some of the special data base management commands offered by dBASE II. For this reason, you may want to use Symphony as an input/output system for a large dBASE Ii data base.

Transferring DIF Files

The Data Interchange Format (DIF) was invented by Software Arts, the creators of VisiCalc, to provide a standard file format for exchanging information between programs. VisiCalc was one of the first programs that could read and write DIF files. In the old days (1982 and earlier), DIF was about the only way to transfer information from a spreadsheet to a graphics program or other external software. The age of integrated software has reduced the importance of DIF, but it is still used to transfer files between some programs.

The DIF to WRK and WRK to DIF options on the Translate menu make it possible for Symphony to read and write DIF files. If you use a special graphics program that uses DIF files, you can use the WRK to DIF option to send data from Symphony to your graphics program.

CHAPTER ELEVEN
WINDOWS

Probably the biggest single improvement of Symphony over 1-2-3 is Symphony's windowing capability. You have probably heard the term "windowing" used, but you may not be sure of its meaning. Simply put, windowing describes the ability of some advanced programs to divide the screen display of your computer into two or more windows. Depending on the design of the windowing program, you can view several different programs or several different parts of the same program at the same time through different windows.

Symphony allows you to divide the screen display into a theoretically unlimited number of windows. Symphony offers five separate types of windows: SHEET, DOC, GRAPH, COMM, and FORM. Each of these window types corresponds to one of Symphony's five environments.

Windows really serve two separate purposes in Symphony. First, you can create a number of different SHEET or DOC windows that view different parts of the workspace at the same time. At this level, Symphony's windowing capabilities are similar to but more advanced than 1-2-3's /Worksheet Window commands.

The other use of windows in Symphony is to access the different features of the program—such as word processing, communications, and graphics. Each of Symphony's five different types of windows is associated with a special set of Symphony capabilities and commands. For example, when you work with Symphony through a SHEET window, you have access to the spreadsheet commands covered in the previous chapters. Similarly, DOC windows allow you access to Symphony's word processing commands. Each window type offers a different view of the Symphony worksheet and causes Symphony to behave differently.

The most familiar window type is a SHEET window. When viewed through a SHEET window, Symphony behaves very much like 1-2-3 or any other sophisticated electronic spreadsheet. Up to this point in the book, we have been working in a single SHEET window called MAIN. How can you tell that MAIN is a SHEET window? First, the prompt in the upper-right corner of the screen says SHEET. Second, the window borders include the row numbers and column letters that distinguish a spreadsheet.

If you are like most Symphony users, at first you'll do most of your work with Symphony through a SHEET window. Even if you don't use Symphony's other window types (DOC, GRAPH, COMM, and FORM) very much, you'll still want to learn about windows, since you'll probably find times when two or more SHEET windows will be helpful.

CREATING A WINDOW

Let's walk through a simple example of creating a window. Suppose you are looking at the screen through the SHEET window MAIN and you want to create a second SHEET window called SECOND. To create this window, issue the {**Services**} **W**indow command. The following menu appears:

Use Create Delete Layout Hide Isolate Expose Pane Settings Quit

To create a new window, issue the Create command. At this point Symphony prompts you for a name for the new window. All windows in Symphony have names. A window name can be up to 15 characters long and may contain any alphabetic or numeric characters, spaces, and punctuation marks.

Notice that when Symphony prompts you for the name of the new window it also supplies you with a list of the names of the windows already in the worksheet. Since this worksheet has only one window, only one name—MAIN—appears in the list. Symphony automatically assigns the name MAIN to the first window in a worksheet.

Unlike most of Symphony's commands that display a list of names (for example, Range Name), you cannot choose the name for the new window from the list provided by the Create command. If you try to select a name that has already been assigned to a window in the worksheet—MAIN, for example—Symphony will respond with the error message "Name already exists". In other words, the list of window names provided by the Window Create command shows you the names that you *cannot* use for the current window.

To name the new window, simply type the desired name next to Symphony's prompt and press [Enter]. Since we want the name of the new window in the example to be SECOND, type SECOND and press [Enter]. By the way, Symphony does not distinguish between upper- and lowercase in window names, so the names second, Second, and SECOND are equivalent.

Next, Symphony prompts you for the type of the new window with a menu that looks like this:

SHEET DOC GRAPH FORM COMM

The five choices in this menu correspond to the five types of windows in Symphony. Since you want to create a SHEET window, select the SHEET option from the menu. (As with other Symphony commands, you can select SHEET by typing the first letter, **S,** or by pointing to the name SHEET with the cursor and pressing **[Enter].**)

After you specify the window type, Symphony displays the entire current window in inverse video (white, green, or amber background instead of black background) and pauses while you specify the size and location on the screen for the new window. The message "Identify window area" appears while Symphony is waiting.

If you wish, you can use the cursor-movement keys and the period to change the location and size of the new window. We'll discuss the creation of partial-screen windows in a few pages. For now, just press **[Enter]** to create a full-screen window. After you have specified the size and location for the new window, the menu and settings sheet in Figure 11.1 will be displayed.

```
 Name   Type   Restrict   Borders   Auto-Display   Quit
 -------------------------------------------------------------
| Name:           SECOND                                       |
| Type:           SHEET                                        |
| Restrict:       A1..IV8192                                   |
| Borders:        Standard                                     |
| Auto-Display:   Yes                                          |
|                                                              |
 =========================================Window Settings=
```

Figure 11.1

This is the Window Settings menu. Symphony automatically gives you a chance to alter the default settings for a new window after you create it. Right now, though, we don't want to change any of these settings, so just press [Esc] or issue the Quit command. (We'll cover these settings in more detail later in the chapter.) That's it! The new window is now created. If everything went right, your screen should now look like Figure 11.2.

You might wonder what has happened to the window MAIN, because SECOND is the only window visible in Figure 11.2. In fact, MAIN is "behind" SECOND. Only one full-screen window can be visible at a time in Symphony. Whenever you have more than one full-screen window in a worksheet, only one of those windows will be visible.

You can think about the windows in a given worksheet like a stack of papers. If all of the papers are 8½ by 11, you'll only be able to see the top paper in the stack. To view the other sheets, you must "shuffle" through the stack one sheet at a time.

SHUFFLING THE STACK

Symphony offers two commands that "shuffle" the windows that exist in a worksheet. First, you can move the cell pointer from one window to the next by pressing the {Window} key. Technically, pressing the {Window} key just causes the cell pointer to

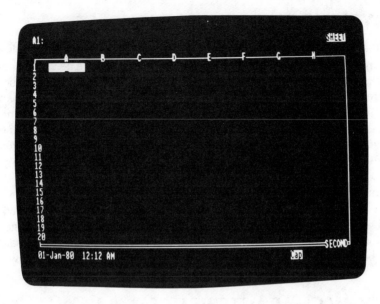

Figure 11.2

jump from one window to the next; however, if your worksheet contains only full-size windows, the effect of the command is to move the "top" window to the bottom of the stack, bringing the second window into view. In our sample worksheet, pressing {Window} when the cell pointer was in the window SECOND moves MAIN to the top of the stack. Pressing {Window} again brings SECOND back into view. The function of the {Window} key is somewhat different if you have created partial-screen windows, as you'll see in a few pages.

The {Services} Window Use command can also be used to shuffle the windows in a worksheet. Window Use immediately makes the window of your choice the current window. If all the windows are full-screen windows, the Window Use command effectively moves the selected window to the top of the stack.

When you issue the {Services} Window Use command, Symphony prompts you to supply the name of the window you want to use and presents a list of the window names in the current worksheet. You can select the window you want by pointing to its name in the list and pressing [Enter]. (Remember that you can display the entire list on the screen at once by pressing {Menu} or {Services} when Symphony displays the one-line list in the control panel.) Once you select the window name, Symphony moves the cell pointer into the specified window.

For example, if you issue the {Services} Window Use command from within the window SECOND, Symphony displays a list of windows in the current worksheet. Since only two windows—SECOND and MAIN—exist in the current worksheet, only two names appear in the list. To use MAIN, simply point to that name in the list and press [Enter]. Symphony instantly brings MAIN into view.

MANY WINDOWS, ONE WORKSPACE

When working with windows you must remember that Symphony has only one 256-column by 8192-row workspace and that every window you create views a part of that one workspace. No matter how different the view of the worksheet might be through the different types of windows you create, all windows view a single workspace.

In our example, both MAIN and SECOND display the upper-left corner of the worksheet—cells A1 to H20. Suppose that SECOND is at the top of the stack (in view). Move the cell pointer to cell A1 and enter the number 100. Now press {**Window**} to bring MAIN to the top of the stack. You see that the entry you made in the window SECOND also appears in the window MAIN.

Can you guess what would happen if you erased cell A1 from MAIN? Move the cell pointer to cell A1 and issue the {Menu} Erase command. Now press {Window} to bring SECOND into view. As you probably expected, the entry in cell A1, 100, is gone.

Remember—all windows look at the same worksheet. Any entry you make in one window becomes a part of that one worksheet and is visible through other windows.

WINDOW CHARACTERISTICS

Although every window looks at the same Symphony workspace, the view through those windows can be quite different. Several of Symphony's SHEET environment commands, including the Settings Width command, the Settings Title command, and the Settings Format command, affect only one window at a time rather than the entire workspace.

For example, suppose that from the window SECOND you issue the {**Menu**} **S**ettings **W**idth command and change the default column width to 5. The screen should now look like Figure 11.3. Next, press {Window} to bring MAIN into view. Notice that although MAIN displays the same part of the worksheet as SECOND, the width of the columns is still 9 in MAIN, as shown in Figure 11.4. Obviously, it is possible for the same column to have two different widths when viewed through two separate windows.

The same thing is true of the {Menu} Setting Format command. If your worksheet contains several windows, each of which has a different default format and each of which views the same part of the worksheet, the numbers in that part of the worksheet will have three different formats when viewed through the three windows. (If you are working along with the chapter, restore the width of the columns in SECOND to 9 by issuing the {**Menu**} **S**ettings **W**idth command from within SECOND before proceeding with the next section.)

MOVING THE WINDOW

As mentioned above, both MAIN and SECOND are full-screen windows that display the upper-left corner of the worksheet—the range A1 . . H20. As you have probably guessed, there is usually little reason to display exactly the same portion of the work-

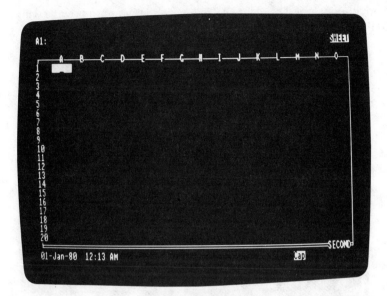

Figure 11.3

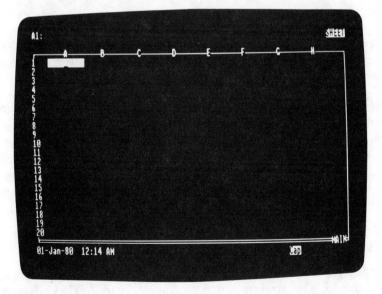

Figure 11.4

sheet. But there are many times when you'd like to be able to see two different parts of the worksheet through two separate windows.

Let's move the window SECOND so that it views an entirely different part of the worksheet. Press **{Window}** to bring SECOND to the top of the stack and press **[Ctrl]** →. The

screen should now look like Figure 11.5. Notice that you are now viewing the range
I1 .. P20 through SECOND.

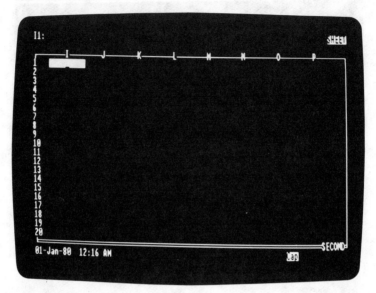

Figure 11.5

Now press {Window} to bring MAIN into view. Notice that MAIN is still viewing the
range A1 .. H20. In other words, the two windows are now viewing two different parts
of the worksheet.

To make the point even more clear, enter the number 100 in cell A1 through the window MAIN. Now press {**Window**} to bring SECOND into view. Since SECOND is viewing the range I1 .. P20, the entry in A1 is not visible in SECOND. Don't let this confuse
you, though. The only reason you can't see the entry on A1 is that SECOND is not positioned to see it. If you press [**Ctrl**] ← moving SECOND back to its original location, the
entry in cell A1 will come into view. (If you are working along with the chapter, use the
{**Menu**} Erase command to remove the number 100 from cell A1 before going on.)

CREATING A PARTIAL-SCREEN WINDOW

Let's create yet another window, this one named THIRD. First make sure MAIN is at
the top of the stack, because much of the following discussion depends on having the
windows in order.

To define this window, issue the {**Services**} Window Create command. Specify
THIRD as the window name and SHEET as the window type. Symphony should now
prompt you to specify the window size and location by displaying the entire screen in
inverse video.

Symphony is once again "guessing" that you want to create a full-screen window. If you press **[Enter]** in response to this prompt, Symphony will create THIRD as a full-screen window.

This time, however, you want to create a partial-screen window. Symphony allows you to create windows of any size and position those windows wherever you want on the screen. When Symphony highlights the entire screen, push the ← key a few times. Notice that the right edge of the inverse video block moves left each time you press ←. Likewise, if you press ↑, the bottom edge of the inverse video block will move up from the bottom of the worksheet. After you press ← five times and ↑ four times, your computer's screen should look something like Figure 11.6.

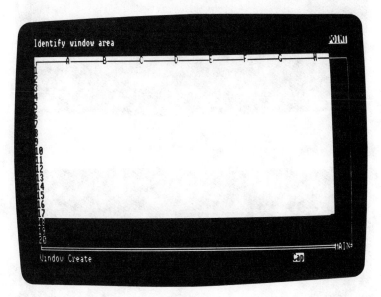

Figure 11.6

You may remember from Chapter 2 that the period key or the [Tab] key can be used to change the anchored corner of a range when pointing in Symphony. This same principle applies to defining windows. For example, while defining the range for THIRD, press the period key once to change the anchored corner of the window range from the lower-right corner to the lower-left corner. Now press → and notice that the left edge of the worksheet moves to the right each time you press the key.

Similarly, if you press the period key again, and then press ↓ a few times, the top edge of the window range moves down. Figure 11.7 shows the screen after the → key has been pressed 10 times and the ↓ key has been pressed 10 times.

You can, of course, use the cursor movement keys to expand or restrict the window. For example, if you press ↑ five times from the position shown in Figure 11.7, the screen will look like Figure 11.8.

The one absolute limitation on the size of a window is that it cannot exceed the size of the screen. A window can be as big as the entire screen, but no bigger.

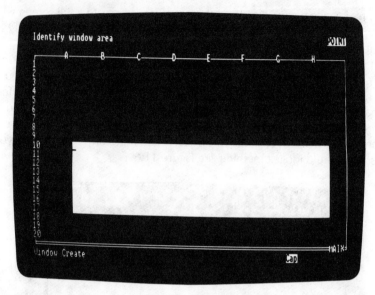

Figure 11.7

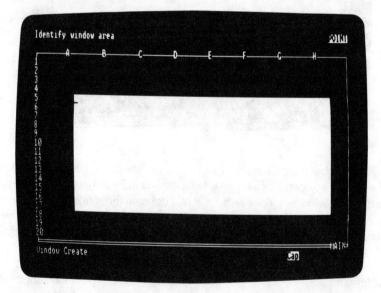

Figure 11.8

You can use any of the keys that move the cell pointer to move the edges of the window during the layout phase. Most of the keys perform as you would expect them to. For example, pressing **[Home]** moves the unanchored corner of the window range to the upper-left corner of the screen. However, the **[Pg Up]** and **[Pg Dn]** keys cause the unanchored corner of the range to move up and down only four rows at a time. Table 11.1 shows the effect of each of Symphony's cursor keys on the definition of windows.

Key	Effect
←	Moves unanchored corner one space left
→	Moves unanchored corner one space right
↑	Moves unanchored corner one row up
↓	Moves unanchored corner one row down
[Home]	Moves unanchored corner to upper-left corner
[End]→	Moves unanchored corner to right edge of screen
[End]←	Moves unanchored corner to left edge of screen
[End]↑	Moves unanchored corner to top edge of screen
[End]↓	Moves unanchored corner to bottom edge of screen
[Pg Up]	Moves unanchored corner up four rows
[Pg Dn]	Moves unanchored corner down four rows
[Ctrl]→	Moves unanchored corner right eight spaces
[Ctrl]←	Moves unanchored corner left eight spaces
[End][Home]	Moves unanchored corner to lower-right corner

Table 11.1

The Scroll Key

After reducing the size of the new window with the cursor-movement keys, you can use the [Scroll Lock] key to move the window to any location on the screen. For example, suppose that you have created the window range shown in Figure 11.8. You want to reposition this window so that the right edge of the window is at the right edge of the screen. To move the window, simply press [Scroll Lock] and →. Each time you press →, the inverse video block moves right one space. When you've pressed → several times, the window will be at the right edge of the screen, as shown in Figure 11.9.

You can use the [Scroll Lock] key to reposition any partial-screen window. However, you cannot move a window beyond the edge of the screen. When the window range reaches the right edge of the screen, it cannot be moved any further. Pressing → with the window range in the position shown in Figure 11.9 will not have any effect other than causing Symphony to beep.

If you think about it for a moment, you'll realize that the bigger the window you try to move, the less latitude you have in moving it. A window that nearly fills the screen can only be moved a few rows up or down and a few spaces to the left or right. A tiny window, on the other hand, can be moved great distances across the screen. A full-sized screen cannot be moved at all.

You can use any of the cursor-movement keys with [Scroll Lock] to reposition the window range. Once you press [Scroll Lock], the cursor keys retain their special effect until you press [Scroll Lock] again. Table 11.2 shows the effect of each cursor-movement key when it's used with [Scroll Lock].

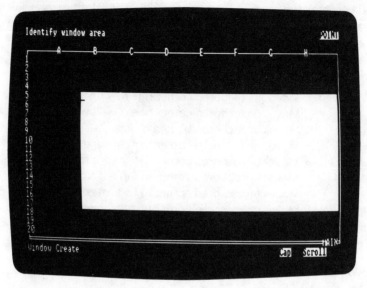

Figure 11.9

Key	Effect
←	Move window one space left
→	Move window one space right
↑	Move window one row up
↓	Move window one row down
[Home]	Move window to upper-left corner
[End]→	Move window to right edge of screen
[End]←	Move window to left edge of screen
[End]↑	Move window to top edge of screen
[End]↓	Move window to bottom edge of screen
[Pg Up]	Move window up four rows
[Pg Dn]	Move window down four rows
[Ctrl]→	Move window right eight spaces
[Ctrl]←	Move window left eight spaces
[End][Home]	Move window to lower-right corner

Table 11.2

Completing the Definition

If you press **[Enter]** after positioning the tentative window range as shown in Figure 11.9, THIRD will be a partial-screen window that appears as an island in the larger window MAIN (see Figure 11.10). THIRD will also be the active (or current) window, meaning that the cell pointer is positioned in THIRD.

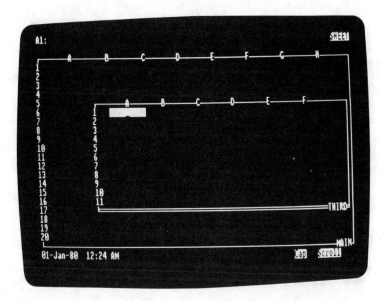

Figure 11.10

Notice that the bottom border of THIRD consists of two lines, while the bottom border of MAIN is a single line. Whenever two or more windows are in view at once, you can identify the active window by the two lines that form that window's lower border.

The {Zoom} Key

The {Zoom} key temporarily expands the current window to fill the screen. Pressing {**Zoom**} from within a partial-screen window temporarily turns the window into a full-screen window. Pressing {**Zoom**} a second time restores the window to its original size. The {Zoom} key has no effect on full-screen windows.

When you press {**Zoom**}, the legend Zoom appears at the bottom of your computer's screen. This message informs you that the current window has been expanded. The message disappears when the window is restored to its original size.

Let's look at an example of the {Zoom} key at work. Suppose you have created the window THIRD shown in Figure 11.10. You decide you want to temporarily expand this window to fill the screen. To expand the window, simply press {**Zoom**}. The window instantly expands to fill the screen, as shown in Figure 11.11. Notice that the Zoom message appears at the bottom of the screen. Also notice that the cell that appeared in the upper-left corner of the partial-screen window is in the upper-left corner of the expanded window.

To return this window to its original size, just press {**Zoom**} again. The screen will once again look like Figure 11.10.

The screen can also be returned to its original size by moving the cell pointer to another window. As soon as you move the cell pointer out of the window (either by

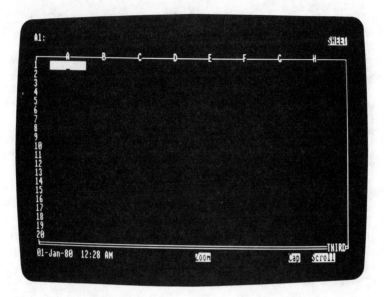

Figure 11.11

pressing {Window} or by issuing the Window Use command), Symphony returns the expanded window to its original size.

The {Zoom} key works on all five Symphony window types. A window that has been expanded with {Zoom} behaves just like any other full-screen window of the same type.

Creating a Window from within a Partial-Screen Window

Suppose you want to create a new window called FOURTH in the sample worksheet. Also suppose that the cell pointer happens to be in the partial-screen window THIRD when you issue the {Services} Window Create command. After you supply the name, FOURTH, and the type, SHEET, Symphony may surprise you. Notice that the inverse video block that marks the tentative size and location of the new window includes only the portion of the screen covered by THIRD, as shown in Figure 11.12.

Symphony always guesses that a new window will be the same size as the current window (the window the cell pointer is in when the Window Create command is issued). If the cell pointer is in a full-screen window, Symphony assumes the new window will be a full-screen window. If, however, the current window is a partial-screen window, Symphony guesses that the new window should be an identically sized and positioned partial-screen window. If you want the new window to be a full-screen window, you'll need to use the cursor-movement keys to expand the window size.

If you want to abort the creation of this new window, press [Esc] several times. If you press [Esc] from the position shown in Figure 11.12, Symphony returns you to the Type menu. Pressing [Esc] again returns you to the Name prompt, and pressing the key once more returns you to the main Window menu.

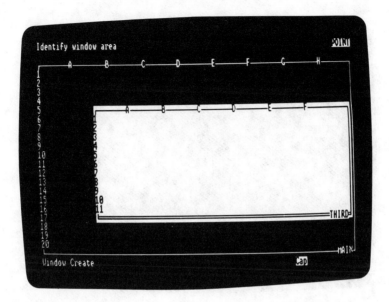

Figure 11.12

LAYOUT

The Window Layout command, one of the options on the main Window menu, lets you change the size or location of a window that has already been created. When you choose this option, Symphony displays the current window in inverse video and pauses while you move the window or change its size with the cursor keys. The keys used to modify a window at this stage are identical to the keys used to change the window's size and position in the creation process.

For example, suppose you want to change the layout of the window THIRD. Just issue the {**Services**} **W**indow **L**ayout command. The screen should once again look like Figure 11.9. From this point, you can use the cursor-movement keys to change the size and shape of the window. If you want to move the window to the left edge of the screen but maintain its size, press [**Scroll Lock**] and then ← several times. When the window reaches the left edge of the screen, press [**Enter**]. The worksheet should now look like the one in Figure 11.13.

PANE

The Window Pane command is used to divide one window into quarters or halves. The name for this command is derived from the way it divides one large window into smaller windows much like the windows in your house are divided into panes.

Continuing with our example, suppose the cell pointer is in the full-screen window SECOND and you want to divide SECOND into four equal windows. (If you need to, press {Window} to move SECOND to the top of the stack.) To divide this window, issue

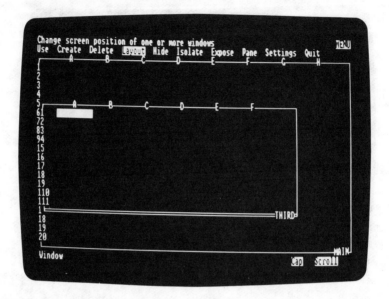

Figure 11.13

the **W**indow **P**ane command. The following menu appears:

Vertical-Split   Horizontal-Split   Both

Choosing the **B**oth option causes Symphony to split the window into four quarter-screen windows, as shown in Figure 11.14.

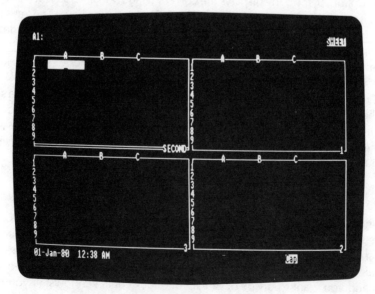

Figure 11.14

Notice that all four windows display the range A1 . . C9, the cells displayed in the upper-left corner of the original window, while the original window displayed the range A1 . . H20. Because the borders of all of the new windows consume space on the screen, the smaller windows created with Pane never exactly occupy one-half or one-quarter the size of the original window.

Also notice that while the window in the upper-left corner has retained the name SECOND, Symphony automatically assigns the names 1, 2, and 3 to the three new windows. Whenever you ask Symphony to create windows with Pane, the program begins numbering the windows at 1. The second window created by Symphony in any worksheet will be named 2, the third 3, and so on. If an existing window has already been given a numeric name, Symphony skips that number and assigns the new window the next number in line. There is no way to change the numbering scheme used by Symphony in the Pane command.

If you want to change the name Symphony has assigned, you can move the cell pointer to that window and issue the Window Settings Name command. You can then replace Symphony's numeric name for the window with a name that is more to your liking.

Although Pane is usually used to split full-screen windows, you can use the command to divide partial-screen windows as well. In fact, you can even use Pane to further divide a partial-screen window created with Pane. For example, if you move the cell pointer to the window named 2 and issue the Window Pane Both command, Symphony will divide this small window into four even smaller windows. Figure 11.15 shows this screen.

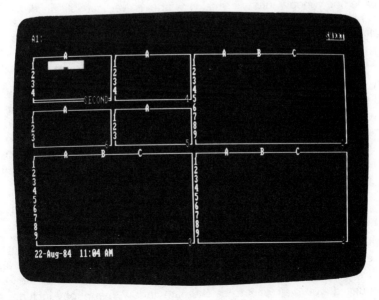

Figure 11.15

Notice that the top two new windows display four rows each, while the bottom windows display only three rows. Because the original window included nine rows, Symphony could not divide it precisely in half. When confronted with this choice, Symphony always makes the upper window(s) slightly larger.

The smallest window that can be created with the Window Pane command is a window one row deep by six spaces wide. However, there is no limit to the number of times you can divide a window with the Pane command. After the window has been divided enough times to reach the minimum size, Symphony simply creates two or four copies of the window each time you issue the Pane command. The new windows will be the same size as the original and will overlap on the screen.

The tiny windows created by Pane have some unusual characteristics. For example, you may remember that Symphony's standard column width is nine characters. This means that a standard column cannot be displayed in one of the tiny windows created by Pane. Symphony compensates for this problem by imposing an apparent width of five on columns displayed through these narrow windows. However, although the column appears to be five characters wide, a quick check of the {Menu} Width setting shows that Symphony has not actually adjusted the column width. In effect, in a very narrow window the Width setting is overridden by the width of the window.

By the way, there is no "Unpane" command in Symphony. The only way to reverse a Pane operation is to use Window Delete to erase all the panes except the pane with the name of the original window, and then to use the Layout command to expand the remaining window to full size. (The Window Delete command is discussed in a few pages.)

The other two options on the Pane menu, Vertical-Split and Horizontal-Split, are used to divide one window into two smaller windows. Vertical-Split divides a window vertically, creating two tall, narrow windows. Horizontal-Split divides the window horizontally.

The {Zoom} Key and Pane

Suppose you create a partial-screen window like the window SECOND in Figure 11.15 and then press the {Zoom} key to expand the window to fill the screen. Now, while the window is expanded, issue the Pane Both command to divide the window into four quarter-screen windows. The screen will now look like Figure 11.16. Now press {Zoom} again. Figure 11.17 shows the screen at this point. Notice that the window SECOND is returned to its original size, but that the new windows 7, 8, and 9 remain the same size and stay in the same position.

DELETING A WINDOW

There will be times when you will want to remove one or more windows from a worksheet. For example, while trying to debug a large worksheet you may create a special small window that displays the contents of a critical region of the worksheet. Once the sheet is debugged, you may want to delete that window. Symphony includes a command, Window Delete, that lets you do just that.

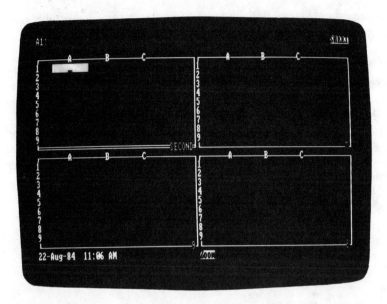

Figure 11.16

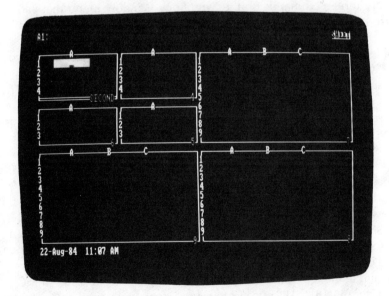

Figure 11.17

The worksheet shown in Figure 11.17 includes 12 separate windows: MAIN, SECOND, 1, 2, 3, 4, 5, 6, 7, 8, 9, and THIRD. Suppose you want to delete the window named 5 from this group. First issue the {**Services**} **W**indow **D**elete command. Symphony prompts you to supply the name of the window to be deleted and presents a list of all windows in the current worksheet. To select window 5 for deletion, either type **5** next to Symphony's prompt or point to the name 5 in the list and press **[Enter]**. Symphony immediately deletes the window.

Remember that deleting a window does not delete the contents of the worksheet that are displayed through that window. It simply reduces the number of portholes through which you can view the worksheet. However, as you'll see in later chapters, when you delete a COMM or DOC window you loose any special format settings that have been established in that window. Similarly, when you delete a FORM or GRAPH window, the connections that attach the window to a data base or graph definition on the worksheet are lost. (We'll cover the concept of attaching windows to graph and data base definitions in later sections.)

In Symphony, you can never delete the only window in a worksheet. If you attempt to delete the last window, Symphony will deliver the message "Cannot delete or hide only window".

Suppose you want to delete windows 2, 3, 4, 6, 7, 8, and 9 from this worksheet as well. Unfortunately, these extra windows must be deleted one at a time with the {Services} Window Delete command.

HIDING, EXPOSING, AND ISOLATING WINDOWS

There are three commands on the Symphony Window menu that allow you to emphasize or deemphasize certain windows. The commands are Hide, Isolate, and Expose.

The Hide command simply "hides" one of the windows in the stack. When you hide a window, Symphony will not allow you to move the cell pointer into that window or view the worksheet through that window. A hidden window seems to disappear from the stack.

When you issue the {Services} Window Hide command, Symphony prompts you to supply the name of the window to be hidden and displays a list of the window names in the current worksheet. You can choose the name of the window you wish to hide by pointing to the name in the list and pressing **[Enter]**. You cannot hide the only window in a worksheet.

Let's go back to Figure 11.10 to look at an example of the Hide command. (Figure 11.10 shows a partial-screen window, THIRD, and a full-screen window, MAIN. A third window, SECOND, lies behind MAIN.) To hide the window MAIN in Figure 11.10, issue the {Services} Window Hide command and choose MAIN from the list. As soon as the command is issued, MAIN disappears from the screen. THIRD, the partial-screen window, remains at the top of the stack, but it now appears as an island in SECOND, as shown in Figure 11.18. MAIN appears to have disappeared from the stack of windows. In fact, MAIN still exists. If you issue one of the window commands, such as Window Delete, MAIN is still included in the list of windows in the current worksheet. It is simply hidden.

You can expose a hidden window in one of two ways. First, you can issue the Window Expose command. Window Expose restores all hidden windows in one fell swoop. The

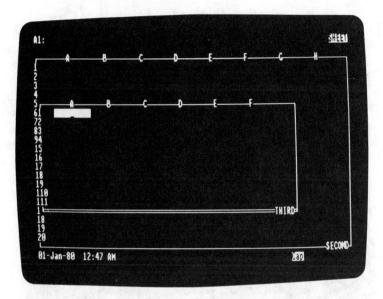

Figure 11.18

hidden windows are returned to the bottom of the stack. In the example, if you issue the Window Expose command from the position shown in Figure 11.18, MAIN reenters the stack behind the window SECOND. If you press {**Window**} once after exposing MAIN, THIRD disappears and SECOND is displayed as a full-screen window. Pressing {**Window**} again brings MAIN to the top of the stack, obscuring both SECOND and THIRD.

The other way to expose a hidden window is to issue the Window Use command. This method differs from the Window Expose command in two ways. First, the Window Use command restores only the hidden window you specify. Any other hidden windows in the worksheet remain hidden. Second, the Window Use command returns the hidden window to the top of the stack, while Window Expose returns it to the bottom of the stack.

The Isolate command is the contrapositive of the Hide command—it hides all windows *but* the current window. For example, if the cell pointer is in MAIN and you issue the {Services} Window Isolate command, all windows but MAIN disappear from the screen. This situation is illustrated in Figure 11.19.

If you press {**Window**} to try to jump to another window after you've issued the Isolate command, nothing will happen. Until you restore the hidden windows, Symphony behaves as though there is only one window in the worksheet.

You can restore the hidden windows by issuing the Window Expose command. This command restores all hidden windows. If you want to bring just one window into view, try the Window Use command.

You may wonder why you'd ever want to use the Hide and Isolate commands. Suppose you have built a worksheet that contains three windows, each of which displays a different part of a large spreadsheet. Suppose further that you need to make a change to the parts of the worksheet visible through the first two windows, MAIN and SECOND. In order to make this change, you need to switch back and forth between MAIN and SECOND several times. If you use the Window Hide command to hide THIRD, you'll be able to use the {Window} key to jump directly from SECOND to MAIN and from MAIN to SECOND without having to pass through THIRD.

Alternatively, suppose you have created a worksheet that contains two SHEET windows, a FORM window, a COMM window, and a DOC window. In the current work session, you plan to work in only the two SHEET windows. If you issue the Window Isolate command from within one of the SHEET windows, all windows but the one you're in will be hidden. If you then issue the Window Use command and specify the name of the other SHEET window, only the two SHEET windows will be visible.

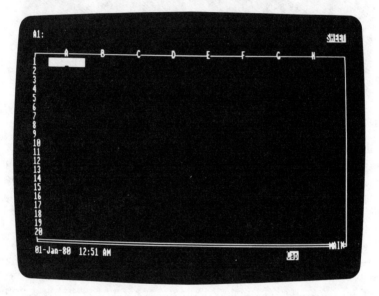

Figure 11.19

WINDOW SETTINGS

The Window Settings command allows you to control many of the characteristics of the windows you create. When you issue the Settings command, the menu and settings sheet shown at the beginning of the chapter (Figure 11.1) will appear on the screen.

Two of these settings options, Name and Type, should be familiar to you by now. The other options—Restrict, Borders, and Auto-Display—will be covered in the following sections.

Restrict

One of the most useful commands on the Window Settings menu is Restrict. With this command you can restrict the portion of the worksheet that can be viewed through a given window.

All windows have a restricted range. However, since the default Restrict range, A1 . . IV8192, specifies the entire worksheet, it doesn't restrict the movement of the window at all. The Restrict range doesn't become important until you define a range that actually imposes some limits on the movement of the window.

Suppose, for example, that you are looking at the worksheet through the full-screen window SECOND, which displays the range A1 . . H20. You want to restrict SECOND so that it will display only the part of the worksheet it is currently displaying. Issue the {**Services**} **W**indow **S**ettings **R**estrict command. The following menu appears in the control panel:

   Screen   Range   None

The Screen option defines a Restrict range for the current window that matches the range currently visible through that window. Since the window SECOND is positioned over the range A1 . . H20, selecting Screen creates the Restrict range you want.

Let's look at the effect of this restricted range. Use the → key to move the cell pointer from cell A1 to the right edge of the window. Notice that the cell pointer cannot move past cell H1 and that each time you try to move it beyond H1, Symphony beeps. Now press ↓ 20 times to move the cell pointer to cell H20. Again, Symphony will not let you move the cell pointer below this point.

Try as you may, you will not be able to move the cell pointer outside of the restricted range A1 . . H20 in the window SECOND. Once the Restrict range is defined, SECOND is "locked" into it.

To "unrestrict" a window, issue the {**Services**} **W**indow **S**ettings **R**estrict **N**one command. This setting returns the Restrict range to the default, A1 . . IV8192, and removes all restrictions on the window's movement.

The second option on the Restrict menu, Range, allows you to define a Restrict range that is larger than the range displayed through the current window. Returning to our example, suppose you wanted to restrict the window SECOND to the range A1 . . Z100. To make this change, issue the {**Services**} **W**indow **S**ettings **R**estrict command. Notice that Symphony immediately supplies the current Restrict range—A1 . . IV8192—in response to the prompt. Since you want to restrict the window to a somewhat smaller range, press **[Esc]** to unanchor the range supplied by Symphony, press the period key, move the cell pointer to cell Z100, and press **[Enter]**. Notice that the Restrict range setting in the Settings sheet is now A1 . . Z100.

To test this new restrict range, starting with the cell pointer in cell A1, press [Pg Dn] until the window shows the range A81 . . H100. Now press ↓ to move the cell pointer to the bottom of the window. Once the cell pointer is in cell A100, Symphony won't let you move it any farther. The same thing happens if you try to move the cell pointer to the right of column Z. Trying to move beyond the restricted range will only elicit a beep from Symphony.

Using Restrict Ranges

Restrict ranges can come in very handy in certain situations. For example, suppose you have created a worksheet that contains some very sensitive formulas you don't want anyone to see. You could group all of these formulas in an area to the right or below the active part of the worksheet, then use the Restrict command to prohibit the window or windows in that worksheet from viewing the sensitive material.

Restrict ranges are also useful for dividing a large worksheet into smaller, more manageable chunks. For example, suppose you have built a payroll worksheet that includes detailed payroll records for four employees as well as a summary of all payroll records. These five sections are arranged as follows:

John	A1 . . Z50
Mary	A51 . . Z100
Jane	A101 . . Z150
Sam	A151 . . Z200
Summary	A201 . . Z250

You want to create five separate windows in this worksheet, one for each employee and one for the summary section. These windows might be given the names of the employees: JOHN, MARY, JANE, and SAM. The summary window could be called SUMMARY. After you create the windows, use the **S**ettings **R**estrict command to restrict the range of each window to the range that contains data about that particular employee. For example, the window MARY should be restricted to the range A51 . . Z100 and the window JANE to the range A101 . . Z150.

Once all of this is complete, your payroll worksheet is divided into five windows and each window is restricted to viewing the records of one employee. Going back to our earlier example, these windows are like sheets of paper in a payroll ledger book. To jump from one employee's records to another, you need only press {**Window**} a few times. This same technique can be applied to nearly any large worksheet that can be meaningfully divided into sections.

Remember that restricting the range of the worksheet you can view through a window does not change the size of the worksheet. For example, if you are working in a worksheet with only one window, MAIN, and you restrict the range of that window to A1 . . H20, you will not be able to view entries located outside of that range. However, those entries are still very much a part of the worksheet. The worksheet still spans the range A1 . . IV8192, even though you can only view a portion of the worksheet through MAIN.

The Restrict Range command can also create a restricted range that is smaller than the entire range visible through the window. For example, suppose you are working in a full-screen window called MAIN, and that you are looking at the range A1 . . H20 through that window. Now you use the **S**ettings **R**estrict **R**ange command to assign the Restrict range A1 . . C3 to this window. Although you can still view the range A1 . . H20 through MAIN, the cell pointer cannot be moved outside of the range A1 . . C3. The range visible through the window is thus larger than the range you can actually access through the window.

The Restrict range you assign to a window is not affected by changes you make to the size of the window. Suppose you restrict the full-screen window named MAIN to the range A1 . . H20. At some later time, you use the Layout command to change MAIN to a partial-screen window. The Restrict range for MAIN remains A1 . . H20. Similarly, suppose you use the Restrict Screen command to restrict a partial-screen window to the range A1 . . C5 and then later use Layout to turn that window into a full-screen window. Again, the Restrict range remains A1 . . C5.

Restrict ranges are really only applicable to SHEET and DOC windows. Actually, the effect of a Restrict range on a DOC window is somewhat different than its effect on a SHEET window. The effect of the Restrict command on a DOC window will be covered later in the book.

Inserting and Deleting Partial Rows and Columns

One of the major limitations of 1-2-3 is that it does not allow the user to insert or delete partial rows and columns. Symphony overcomes this problem by offering versions of the cut-and-paste commands {Menu} Insert and {Menu} Delete that operate only on the Restrict range of a particular window.

Suppose you want to insert a new row *only* between columns A and C in a worksheet. You couldn't do this with 1-2-3, but you can with Symphony. First, set up a window that is restricted to the range A1 . . C5. Such a window is shown in Figure 11.20.

```
    -----A----------B----------C------    ------D------
 1        123                        |      987   |
 2        234                        |      876   |
 3        345                        |      765   |
 4        456                        |      654   |
 5                                   |      543   |
      ========================SECOND=              |
 7        789                                      |
 8        890                                      |
 9                                                 |
    -------------------------------------------MAIN-
```

Figure 11.20

Now move the cell pointer into cell A3 in window SECOND and issue the {**Menu**} Insert command. When the menu appears, select the **R**ows option. Symphony prompts you with the range A3 . . A3. Since you want to insert a row at row 3, you can accept Symphony's guess. Just push [**Enter**] to insert the new row. The worksheet will look like the one in Figure 11.21.

Notice that a new row has been added within the window SECOND, but that the cells in the visible portion of window MAIN have not been affected. The row has only been inserted between columns A and C, and it has not pushed down the contents of rows 7 and 8. The new row has affected only those rows and columns covered by the restricted window range.

If you press the {**Window**} key, you'll see that the new row has been added in the window MAIN as well, but only in the range A1 . . C5. Figure 11.22 shows this situation.

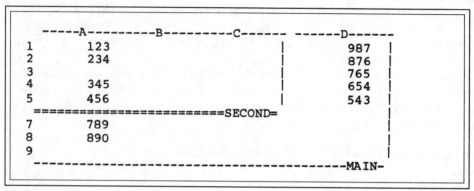

Figure 11.21

```
    -----A---------B---------C------- ------D------
  1       123                       |       987    |
  2       234                       |       876    |
  3                                 |       765    |
  4       345                       |       654    |
  5       456                       |       543    |
    ========================SECOND=               |
  7       789                                     |
  8       890                                     |
  9                                               |
    -------------------------------------------MAIN-
```

Figure 11.22

```
    -----A---------B---------C-------------D------
  1       123                              987    |
  2       234                              876    |
  3                                        765    |
  4       345                              654    |
  5       456                              543    |
  6                                               |
  7       789                                     |
  8       890                                     |
  9                                               |
    ========================================MAIN=
```

Going back to Figure 11.20, suppose you want to insert another row in the restricted window. If you repeat the {**Menu**} **I**nsert **R**ow command and specify the range A3 . . A3, Symphony returns the message

      Window full error

This occurs because cell A5, at the bottom edge of the window, contains a value that Symphony cannot push down without violating the limits of the window.

Looking again at Figure 11.20, suppose you want to insert a new column at the left edge of the worksheet. Move the cell pointer to cell A1 in the window SECOND and issue the {**Menu**} **I**nsert command. Choose the **C**olumns option from the Insert menu, and accept Symphony's prompted range, A1 . . A1, by pressing **[Enter].** The worksheet now looks like Figure 11.23.

As in the previous example, only the portion of the worksheet covered by the restricted range in window SECOND has been affected by the command. The entries in column D have not been shifted to the right by the addition of a new column, nor have the entries in cells A7 and A8.

The {Menu} Delete command also has the ability to delete partial rows and columns. For example, suppose you have set up the worksheet shown in Figure 11.24.

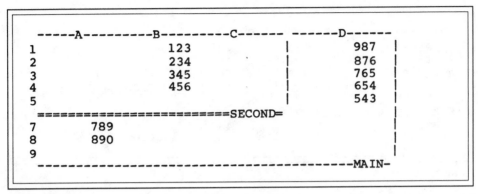

```
     -----A----------B---------C------  ------D------
  1                 123                |       987  |
  2                 234                |       876  |
  3                 345                |       765  |
  4                 456                |       654  |
  5                                    |       543  |
     ======================SECOND=             |
  7      789                                    |
  8      890                                    |
  9                                             |
     ---------------------------------------------MAIN-
```

Figure 11.23

```
     ------A---------B---------C---------D--------
  1 AAAAAA                    123       345      |
  2 BBBBBB                    234       456      |
  3 CCCCCC                    345       567      |
  4                                              |
  5 ABCDEF          987       654                |
  6 ZYXVUT          876       543                |
  7 FEDCBA          765       432                |
     =========================================MAIN=
```

Figure 11.24

Now suppose you want to adjust the worksheet so that the entries in cells C1 to D3 are located above the entries in cells B5 to C7. One way to do this would be to delete *only* cells B1, B2, and B3.

To delete these cells, first create a window SECOND that is restricted to the range A1 .. D3. Next, move the cell pointer to cell B1 in the window and issue the {**Menu**} **D**elete **C**olumn command. The range to delete is B1 .. B1. Since Symphony supplies this range automatically, you need only press [**Enter**] to accept that range and delete the column. At this stage, the window will look like Figure 11.25.

Notice that the range B1 .. B3 has been deleted from window SECOND. This partial column was deleted, but the visible portion of window MAIN was not affected by the command. If we now delete the window SECOND with the {**Services**} **W**indow **D**elete command, the worksheet looks like Figure 11.26.

As usual, Symphony adjusts any formulas affected by these commands. Remember that the Rows and Columns options insert and delete partial rows and columns only if your window has a restricted range. If the window is not restricted, these options have the same effect as the Global options.

Going back to Figure 11.20, suppose we use the {**Menu**} **I**nsert **G**lobal **R**ow command to insert a new row across the entire worksheet above row 3. Figure 11.27 shows the result.

```
     -----A---------B---------C---------D---------
   1 AAAAAA         123       345                  |
   2 BBBBBB         234       456                  |
   3 CCCCCC         345       567                  |
   ===============================================SECOND=
   5 ABCDEF         987       654                  |
   6 ZYXVUT         876       543                  |
   7 FEDCBA         765       432                  |
     -----------------------------------------MAIN-
```

Figure 11.25

```
     -----A---------B---------C---------D---------
   1 AAAAAA         123       345                   |
   2 BBBBBB         234       456                   |
   3 CCCCCC         345       567                   |
   4                                                |
   5 ABCDEF         987       654                   |
   6 ZYXVUT         876       543                   |
   7 FEDCBA         765       432                   |
     ===============================================MAIN=
```

Figure 11.26

```
     -----A---------B---------C------  ------D------
   1         123                      |       987   |
   2         234                      |       876   |
   3                                  |             |
   4         345                      |       765   |
   5         456                      |       654   |
     =========================SECOND=         543   |
   7                                                |
   8         789                                    |
   9         890                                    |
     --------------------------------------------MAIN-
```

Figure 11.27

There are several important differences between this worksheet and the one shown in Figure 11.21. First, notice that the new row has been inserted across the entire worksheet, affecting not only the cells in columns A through C but also column D (and all other columns). Second, notice that the contents of cells A7 and A8 have been pushed down so that they are now in rows 8 and 9.

The third effect of this command is not visible, but it is important. Remember that the Insert and Delete commands adjust any ranges that include the rows or columns being inserted. When the Global option is used, this includes a restricted window range. In the example above, then, the restricted range of window SECOND has been changed from A1 . . C5 to A1 . . C6.

Borders

The Window Settings Borders command is used to change the type of border that surrounds a window. This command has three options:

Standard   Line   None

The first choice, Standard, is the default setting. This option causes the current window to be displayed with the borders that are standard to the chosen type of window. For example, if the current window is a SHEET window, choosing Standard causes Symphony to display the window with column numbers at the top of the window and row numbers on the left edge of the window. If the current window is a DOC window, the top border will be the ruler line common to DOC windows.

The Line option replaces the standard borders with simple lines. This option can be used to create a special "display" window that is used only to display the results of a special section of the worksheet. However, Line has certain disadvantages. Because Line removes the column letters and row numbers from a SHEET window, it is easy to lose your bearings in a SHEET window that has line borders. The Line option really affects only SHEET windows. For FORM, COMM, and GRAPH windows, the standard border is made up of lines, so selecting Line does not substantially change the display.

The None option causes Symphony to display the window with no border at all. Windows with no borders can be very confusing. For one thing, a SHEET window without borders offers no visual clues to the location of the cell pointer. The only way to determine the location of the cell pointer is to read the cell location in the control panel.

If a nonbordered window is a partial-screen window, the problems are even worse. For example, suppose you have created the screen shown in Figure 11.13. The window THIRD in this example is a partial-screen island window. The window MAIN is a full-screen window. Now suppose you issue the Window Settings Borders None command from within THIRD. Figure 11.28 shows the screen after this command has been issued. Notice that THIRD has "disappeared" from the screen. Although the window still exists, you cannot see it. The cell pointer seems to be located in the window MAIN, even though it is really in THIRD.

Despite these cautions, there are some cases where the None option can be used to create a special screen display. Usually, however, the Borders None option should be used only when working with a worksheet that contains a single SHEET or DOC window, and unless you are very experienced with Symphony you should probably avoid it.

Auto-Display

The last option on the Window Settings menu, Auto-Display, is used to suppress the display of a window after a change is made to the worksheet. This command is most

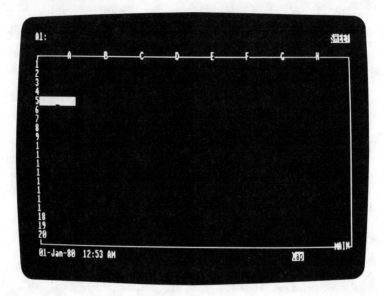

Figure 11.28

useful when you are working with GRAPH windows, but it's also useful with SHEET windows.

Consider this example. Suppose you have created the two windows, MAIN and SEC-OND, shown in Figure 11.29. Cell A1, visible through the window MAIN, contains the number 100. Cell C1, visible through SECOND, contains the formula

        C1: +A1

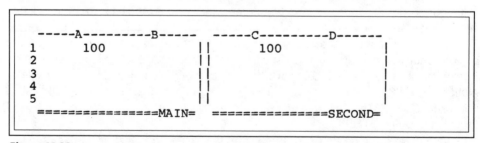

Figure 11.29

If you move the cell pointer to cell A1 in window MAIN and change the number in that cell to 200, the worksheet immediately changes to look like the one in Figure 11.30.

Now move the cell pointer to SECOND and issue the {Services} Window Settings Auto-Display command. Symphony prompts you with the message "Automatically redisplay window when worksheet changes?" and allows you to choose Yes or No. Choose No, which tells Symphony not to redraw the window after each change to the worksheet. Now move the cell pointer to cell A1 in window MAIN and change the entry in cell A1 to 100. The worksheet should now look like Figure 11.31.

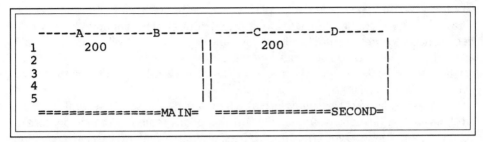

Figure 11.30

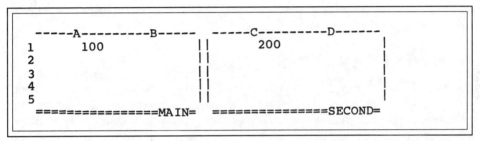

Figure 11.31

Notice that the value in cell C1 in the window SECOND apparently has not changed. It is important that you understand, however, that the value in cell C1 has, in fact, changed to 100; this change is not displayed through the window SECOND because we set Auto-Display for this window to No. Symphony signals that there is an outdated window in the worksheet by displaying the message "Draw" at the bottom of the screen.

If you move the cell pointer to cell A1 in MAIN and then press → twice, the worksheet will look like Figure 11.32.

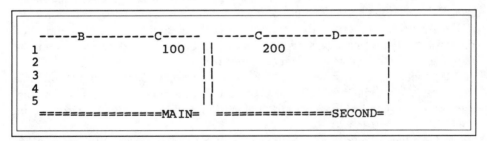

Figure 11.32

Notice that the apparent values in cell C1 in the two windows are different. Make sure you understand that this difference arises only because SECOND has not been redrawn since the change was made, not because the value in cell C1 is somehow different in the two windows.

There are three ways to bring SECOND up to date. You can force Symphony to redraw the window by issuing the **Window Use** command. If you jump to the window with the {**Window**} key you accomplish the same thing. Finally, you can use the {**Draw**} key. Pressing {**Draw**} tells Symphony to redraw all of the windows in the worksheet. Once you press {**Draw**}, all windows in the worksheet will be updated. But redrawing SECOND does not change the Auto-Display setting for the window. The only way to change the Auto-Display setting is to issue the Window Settings Auto-Display command.

The Auto-Display setting is most useful when you have created several different GRAPH windows on the same screen. Because Symphony requires a second or more to redraw a graph window, you could find yourself waiting several seconds each time you make a change to the worksheet. Setting Auto-Display to No in your GRAPH windows eliminates these unwanted delays. Because Auto-Display is so important to GRAPH windows, we'll cover the topic again in Chapter 13.

THE WINDOW TYPES

So far we have been working only with SHEET and (briefly) DOC windows. As you know, Symphony offers several other window types. It is important to understand that the different types of Symphony windows give you substantially different views of the worksheet. In the following discussion, we'll try to explain the differences between the five window types. Some of the concepts may be unclear, however, until you have a chance to read about the individual window types in detail later in the book. For now, just try to understand the basic points.

When viewed through a SHEET window, Symphony behaves like an electronic spreadsheet. SHEET windows offer the purest view of the worksheet, since only in this type of window do you see the column letters and row numbers that define the Symphony worksheet. For example, when you view the range A1 . . H20 through a SHEET window, you see the contents of the range A1 . . H20 on the screen.

DOC windows allow you to use Symphony as a word processor. Like SHEET windows, DOC windows provide a more-or-less accurate view of the worksheet. However, DOC windows do not display the row numbers and column letters, and they restrict your ability to change certain entries that you view through the window. DOC windows are discussed in more detail in Chapters 15 and 18.

FORM windows are special tools that help you create, modify, and use Symphony data bases. As the name implies, a FORM window is a special window that displays the structure and content of a data base through a form. FORM windows are discussed in detail in Chapters 19 and 20.

FORM windows offer an even less direct view of the worksheet. A FORM window displays only the contents of the data base entry range. If no such range has been defined, the FORM window is blank. You cannot move a FORM window around on the worksheet, and you cannot directly make a change to a cell entry, other than a data base entry, through a FORM window.

COMM windows allow you to access Symphony's communications capabilities. All of Symphony's telecommunications capabilites are accessed through the COMM {Menu} command. Like FORM windows, COMM windows are not true windows onto the worksheet. In fact, you might think of a COMM window as a special workspace all to itself, since nothing that you type in a COMM window will appear in the workspace. (If you are thinking that this violates the rule about there being only one workspace in Symphony, you are right. Although this seems confusing now, the concept should become more clear as you learn about COMM windows in Chapter 24.)

GRAPH windows allow you to view the graphs you create with Symphony's {Menu} Graph command. (Of course, you can only view graphics if you have a graphics monitor and interface card.) Because Symphony allows you to create several partial-screen GRAPH windows in a single worksheet, you can view several graphs at once in Symphony. Former users of 1-2-3 will recognize this as a major improvement. GRAPH windows are covered in more detail in Chapter 13.

Notice that all of the window types other than the SHEET window interpret the contents of the worksheet. For example, DOC windows restrict your access to certain entries. COMM and FORM windows display only specific types of information or ranges from the worksheet. GRAPH windows display only graphic representations of spreadsheet data. You might think of DOC, FORM, COMM, and GRAPH windows as being made of a special material that alters the view of the worksheet, much as polarized glass filters out certain kinds of light.

CREATING NON-SHEET WINDOWS

In general, the steps for creating a DOC, FORM, COMM, or GRAPH window are the same as those for creating a SHEET window: issue the {**Services**} **W**indow **C**reate command, select a name, select a type, and specify a size. The GRAPH and FORM windows require additional steps, covered in later chapters, to be fully functional.

Changing the Window Type

Suppose you want to change the window SECOND from a SHEET window to a DOC (word processing) window. There are several ways to do this.

First, you could issue the **W**indow **S**ettings **T**ype command, which brings the Type menu to the screen:

SHEET DOC GRAPH FORM COMM

Notice that this menu is identical to the Type menu that appeared when you first created the window. To change the type of SECOND, just select DOC from this menu and press Quit to exit from the Window command menu.

After the command is issued, the screen will look like the one in Figure 11.33. Notice that the numbers and letters that identify a SHEET window are now gone, having been replaced by the tab marks of a DOC window. Also notice that the prompt in the upper-right corner of the screen has changed from SHEET to DOC.

The window SECOND is now a DOC window. If you press {**Menu**}, the DOC environment command menu appears in the control panel. You can see from this that changing the type of a window can have a major impact on the display of the worksheet and on the effect of certain keys and commands.

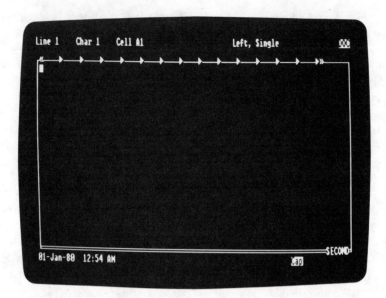

Line 1   Char 1   Cell A1   Left, Single

01-Jan-80 12:54 AM   SECOND

Figure 11.33

There is a quicker way to change a window type. Instead of using the Window command, you can just press {**Type**} from within SECOND and then select DOC from the Type menu. The result is the same as when you issued the {Services} Window Settings Type command, but much faster.

Be sure that you understand that changing the type of a window is not the same as creating a new window. For instance, before you converted the window SECOND from a SHEET window into a DOC window, your worksheet contained two windows, SECOND and MAIN. After the change was made, the worksheet still contained only two windows, SECOND and MAIN. The difference is that one of these windows is now a DOC window.

Of course, you could create a DOC window from scratch with the {Services} Window Create commmand. If you did this, your worksheet would contain three windows: the new DOC window plus the SHEET windows SECOND and MAIN.

Toggling Back and Forth

Suppose you have used the {Type} key to change SECOND from a SHEET window to a DOC window. Now you want to change SECOND back to a SHEET window. Although you could use the {Type} command to accomplish this change, there is an easier way. Just press {**Switch**}. Presto! SECOND is now a SHEET window. If you press {**Switch**} again, SECOND will become a DOC window again. In other words, the {Switch} command switches, or toggles, a window between two different window types.

The {Switch} key only works when you have first used the Settings command or the {Type} key to change the original type of a window. For example, if you press {**Switch**} from within the window MAIN, which is a SHEET window, nothing will happen. To change the window type of MAIN, you would have to press the **{Type}** key and specify the new window type. Once the window type of MAIN had been switched once, however, the {Switch} key can be used to toggle between window types. In the word processing section of this book (Chapters 15–18), you see why it is important to be able to switch a window from a DOC to a SHEET and back again.

CHANGING THE DEFAULT WINDOW TYPE

The Window option of the {Services} Configuration menu allows you to adjust the type and name of the default Symphony window. The default window is the window that appears when you first load Symphony into your computer.

The default window type is SHEET. Since the spreadsheet is the most heavily used element of Symphony, most Symphony users probably will find this default acceptable.

However, if you use Symphony more often as a word processor than as a spreadsheet, you may want to use the {Services} Configuration Window Type command to change the default window to type DOC. If you use the data base more often, you may want to set the default type to FORM. This command can also be used to set the default type to COMM or GRAPH.

The {Services} Configuration Window Name command allows you to change the default name that Symphony assigns to the first window that appears when you load Symphony. The window name appears in the lower-right corner of screen. The default name is MAIN.

As with the Type option, most Symphony users will never take advantage of this command. However, if for some reason you need to use a different name for the main window, this command can be very handy. One case where a different name might be appropriate is in a macro-driven custom application where you want each window name to convey a message to the user. In that case, the first window might be called "First" or "Main Menu."

PART
IV

GRAPHICS

CHAPTER TWELVE

CREATING GRAPHS

So far we've concentrated on Symphony's capabilities as an electronic spreadsheet. These, however, are just a part of the program's overall power. Symphony also allows you to create graphs that represent the data in your worksheets as pictures. Symphony offers six different kinds of graphs—line graphs, bar and stacked-bar charts, pie charts, XY charts (scatter charts), and high-low-close-open graphs. In addition, the program has commands that allow you to format and to print the graphs you create.

Former 1-2-3 users will find Symphony's graphics capabilites reasonably familiar, but will notice several new capabilities and a couple of tricky twists. For example, in Symphony it is possible to view more than one graph at a time on the same screen and to view one or more graphs at the same time you view text. Symphony also offers one new type of graph—the high-low-close-open graph—and one variation on an old type—the exploded pie chart—that will be unfamiliar to 1-2-3 users.

HOW SYMPHONY DISPLAYS GRAPHS

The way Symphony displays a graph depends on two factors: the number and type of monitors attached to your computer system and the choices you made about displaying graphics when you installed Symphony.

Obviously, if you do not have a monitor capable of displaying graphics, you will not be able to view the graphs Symphony can create. For example, if the only monitor attached to your computer is an IBM monochrome display attached to a normal IBM Print and Display Adapter, you will not be able to view graphs. However, even though you can't view your graphs on such a system, you can still create graphs that can be saved and printed. (This approach is awkward at best, however. Since you can't see your graphs as they are created, you can't be sure they are properly defined until after they are printed. You can easily waste a lot of time editing, printing, reediting, and reprinting graphs in this situation. My advice—if you want to work with graphs, get a graphics display.)

If you have one graphics monitor attached to your computer, you can view your graphs in one of two ways. First, you can instruct Symphony to display graphs on the screen at the same time text and numbers are visible. This is called the shared mode. Or you can tell Symphony to toggle back and forth between graphs and text/number displays. The choice between shared mode and toggle mode is made when you install Symphony.

I originally installed Symphony in the shared mode, because it is quite thrilling (especially for ex-1-2-3 users) to see both graphs and the spreadsheet on the screen at the same time. However, I quickly shifted to the toggle mode, because in the shared mode Symphony's screen can be sluggish. Unless you really need to see graphs on the screen at the same time as your spreadsheet, it's better to use the toggle mode.

If you have two monitors, one for text and one for graphics, Symphony will operate in the dual mode. In this mode, graphics will be displayed on the graphics monitor and text and numbers will be displayed on the nongraphics monitor. If you can afford it, this is the best way to view Symphony's graphics.

This chapter will assume you are working with a single graphics monitor installed in the toggle mode. In Chapter 13 we'll explore the differences between the toggle mode and the shared mode.

THE GRAPH COMMAND

Symphony's graphics capabilities are controlled by the Graph command on the SHEET window main menu. The following menu appears in the control panel after you issue the Graph command:

Preview 1st-Settings 2nd-Settings Image-Save Quit

The four options on this menu allow you to create, view, and save graphs. Ignoring the other commands for a bit, select the 1st-Settings command by typing 1. A new menu and the Graph 1st-Settings sheet appears on the screen, as shown in Figure 12.1.

```
 Switch to 2nd-Settings
 Switch Type Range Hue Format Data-Labels Legend Cancel Name Quit
 -------------------------------------------------------------------
 |   Type: Line
 | Range              Hue      Format     Data-Labels    Legend
 | X                  1
 | A                  2        Both
 | B                  3        Both
 | C                  4        Both
 | D                  5        Both
 | E                  6        Both
 | F                  7        Both
 |
 =====================================Graph 1st-Settings: Main=
```

Figure 12.1

Symphony offers so many graph options that two settings sheets are required to display them all. The Graph 2nd-Settings sheet can be reached in two different ways.

First, you may have noticed that 2nd-Settings was one of the choices on the main Graph menu. Selecting this option places you in the 2nd-Settings sheet. Alternatively, you can skip to the 2nd-settings sheet from the first using Switch, the first option on the 1st-Settings menu. Figure 12.2 shows the Graph 2nd-Settings sheet and menu. Notice that the first choice on this menu is also Switch. This choice moves you back into the 1st-Settings menu.

```
Switch to 1st-Settings
Switch  Titles  Y-Scale  X-Scale  Other  Name  Quit
---------------------------------------------------------------
|  Titles                                 Type: Line          |
|    First                      X Axis                        |
|    Second                     Y Axis                        |
|  Y-Scale               X-Scale              Other           |
|    Type     Automatic    Type    Automatic   Grid   None    |
|    Lower                 Lower                Hide   No      |
|    Upper                 Upper                Color  No      |
|    Format   G            Format  G            Skip   1       |
|    Exponent Automatic    Exponent Automatic   Origin 0       |
|    Width    9                                 Aspect 1       |
=========================================Graph 2nd-Settings: Main=
```

Figure 12.2

Building a Simple Graph

The best way to understand Symphony's graphics is to build a simple graph. For now, we'll assume we're working in a worksheet with no graph windows. Although this means that we can view graphs only with the Preview command, it also means that we avoid a few complexities that are better left to the section where we discuss graph windows in detail.

We want to build a simple line graph that shows the pattern of total sales growth for the year. We'll use the worksheet in Figure 12.3 as the basis for our graph.

```
      ------A-------B--------C--------D--------E--------F-----
  1  ============================================================
  2  Sales Forecast
  3  ============================================================
  4                     Qtr 1      Qtr 2     Qtr 3     Qtr 4
  5  Product 1          $76,123    $79,010   $83,167   $94,100
  6  Product 2          $21,549    $20,833   $19,984   $21,870
  7  Product 3          $17,354    $19,411   $25,683   $32,187
  8  Product 4          $10,932    $12,748   $17,983   $11,549
  9                     -------    -------   -------   -------
 10  Total Sales        $125,958  $132,002  $146,817  $159,706
 11  ============================================================MAIN=
```

Figure 12.3

Only two pieces of information are required to create a graph in Symphony: a graph Type and one data Range. Both the Type and the Range are specified from the 1st-Settings sheet. The Type menu looks like this:

Line Bar Stacked-Bar XY Pie High-Low-Close-Open

Since we want to build a line graph, we would select the Line option. (We'll cover the other options later in the chapter.) Since the Line type is the default, we could technically omit this step. However, it's good to get into the habit of specifying a graph Type for all graphs. After the choice of Type is made, Symphony returns us to the 1st-Settings menu.

The next step in building this graph is to use the Range option of the 1st-Settings menu to specify the range containing the data to be graphed. After you select the **R**ange option, the following menu appears:

X A B C D E F Quit

Choices A through F are used to specify data ranges for graphs. Since we're building a simple graph, we need to specify only one data range, the A range. To select this range, type **A.** Assuming that the cell pointer is in cell A1, Symphony prompts you with the message

A range: A1

The reference to cell A1 in this prompt is Symphony's guess at the correct A range. Symphony guessed A1 simply because the cell pointer was in this cell when the A command was issued. Had the cell pointer been in cell F5, the prompt would have been

A range: F5

Selecting a graph range is just like selecting the range for any other Symphony command or function. You can specify the range by typing the correct coordinates (either as a pair of cell references or as a named range) or by pointing to the correct range. In this example, we want to graph total sales for all four quarters, so our A range is C10 . . F10. After typing or pointing to this range, type Quit to return to the 1st-Settings menu. The screen should now look like Figure 12.4.

```
 Switch to 2nd-Settings
 Switch   Type   Range  Hue   Format   Data-Labels   Legend   Cancel   Name   Quit
 ------------------------------------------------------------------------------
 |       Type:    Line                                                          |
 | Range                  Hue   Format   Data-Labels            Legend          |
 |                                                                              |
 | X                      1                                                     |
 | A   C10..F10           2            Both                                     |
 | B                      3            Both                                     |
 | C                      4            Both                                     |
 | D                      5            Both                                     |
 | E                      6            Both                                     |
 | F                      7            Both                                     |
 |                                                                              |
 ============================================Graph 1st-Settings: Main=
```

Figure 12.4

That's it! Although we haven't seen it yet, our graph is now defined. To look at the graph, we would step back up to the Graph menu by typing Quit or by pressing **[Esc]** and selecting the **P**review option from this menu. Assuming we have a computer system with a graphics monitor, the graph shown in Figure 12.5 will now appear on the screen.

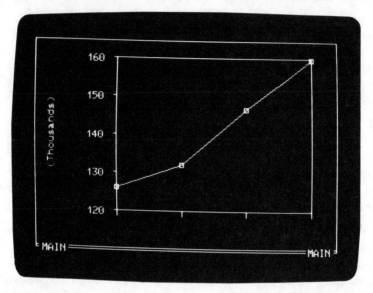

Figure 12.5

The Preview command temporarily converts the current window into a GRAPH window. While the window is converted, you can view your graph. Once you've seen enough, pressing **[Esc]** (or any other key) converts the current window back into a SHEET window.

Assuming you defined only one full-screen window, the Preview command causes the sample graph to fill the entire screen. (We'll discuss how to define GRAPH windows in Chapter 13.) The effect of the Preview command changes when you add more than one window to your screen. Whenever you issue the Preview command, the graph defined by the active graph settings sheet replaces the contents of the current window. If the window is a partial-screen window, the graph is displayed in only the part of the screen filled by the window.

If you have a single graphics monitor and have installed Symphony in the toggle mode, the contents of any SHEET, DOC, COMM, or FORM windows on the screen will disappear when you preview a graph from within a SHEET window. If you installed Symphony in the shared mode, the contents of the other windows will remain visible when the graph is previewed.

ENHANCING THE BASIC GRAPH

Although the graph you've just created presents exactly the information you want, it is very plain and lacks important information like titles and legends. As you might expect,

Symphony gives you the ability to format your graphs extensively. Many of these options are activated through the 2nd-Settings command.

Titles

The first enhancement we'll make to the basic graph is to add titles. Symphony allows you to add four titles: two at the top of the graph, one along the X axis, and one along the Y axis. To begin entering the titles, issue the Graph 2nd-Settings Titles command. The following menu appears:

First Second X-Axis Y-Axis

The First and Second options allow you to enter two lines of titles at the top of the graph. The X-Axis and Y-axis options let you enter titles that will appear along the two axes of the graph. Let's enter some titles in our example graph. Select the First option from the Titles menu. Symphony prompts you with the message

First Graph Title:

Type the label **Sales Forecast** in response to this prompt. This label will now appear at the very top of your graph. After you press **[Enter]** to lock in the title, Symphony returns you to the Titles menu. Select the Second option and enter the label **For the Current Year** in response to Symphony's prompt.

After these two titles are entered, press **[ESC]** twice to return to the Graph menu and use the Preview command to display the graph. Figure 12.6 shows the graph as it should appear on your screen.

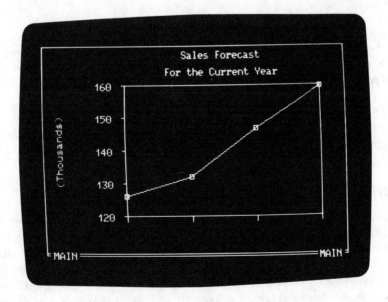

Figure 12.6

If you want to define titles for the X axis and Y axis as well, return to the Titles menu by issuing the **2**nd-Settings **T**itles command from the Graph menu. Select the **X**-Axis option and enter the label **Current Year.** For the **Y**-Axis option specify the label **Sales.** Once again, return to the Graph menu and issue the **P**review command. Your graph should look like Figure 12.7.

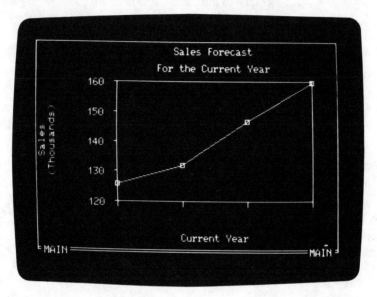

Figure 12.7

Although most of the time you'll probably type your graph titles, there is an alternative method of entering titles that can be more convenient. Suppose you want to reenter the first title in our sample graph. Issue the **G**raph **2**nd-Settings **T**itles **F**irst command, but instead of typing the title, enter the reference **\A2.** This reference tells Symphony to find the label that will be the first title of this graph in cell A2. If you Preview the graph again, the first title appears to be the same. But instead of being absolute, the title is now a reference to the contents of cell A2. If you change the entry in the cell, the title in the graph will also change. As we'll see in a few pages, this technique can also be used to define Legends.

X Labels

The next change we'll make to our basic graph is to add labels along the X axis. When we first defined the graph you may have been curious about the X option on the 1st-Settings Range menu. This choice is used to specify the range containing the labels or values you want to appear along the X axis.

For example, to add X labels to our sample graph, we would issue the **G**raph **1**st-Settings **R**ange command and select the **X** option. Symphony now prompts us to specify the range that contains the desired labels. Since each data point in our graph represents the total sales of our mythical company at the end of a quarter, we'll use the labels in row 4—Qtr 1, Qtr 2, and so on—as our X labels. Use Symphony's POINT mode to indicate the range C4 . . F4 and then press **[Enter]**. Press **[Esc]** twice to return to the main graph menu and issue the Preview command. Your graph should look like Figure 12.8. Notice the labels along the bottom of the graph.

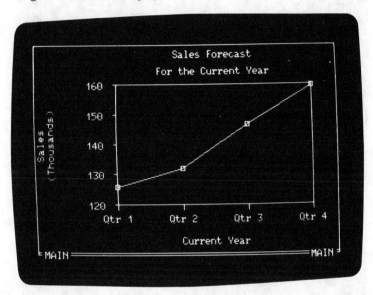

Figure 12.8

Although in our example the X range contained labels, the X range can include either values or labels. In fact, in XY graphs, the X range *must* contain values. (You'll learn more about XY graphs in a few pages.)

If the labels in the X range you define are very long, or if your data ranges contain more than just a few cells, the labels along the X axis can overlap. For example, Figure 12.9 shows the graph with the labels Quarter 1, Quarter 2, and so on substituted for the abbreviations you used earlier. Notice how difficult these labels are to read.

Skip

The Graph 2nd-Settings Other Skip command is used to help clean up the X axis of your graphs when it becomes too cluttered. This command allows you to specify a "skip factor" that suppresses some of the X labels. For example, if you want to clean up the graph in Figure 12.9, issue the **G**raph **2**nd-Settings **O**ther **S**kip command and set the skip factor at **2.** The resulting graph will look like Figure 12.10.

You can set the skip factor to be any whole number from 1 to 8192. This command is extremely handy; if you create very many Symphony graphs, you'll probably find yourself using it all the time.

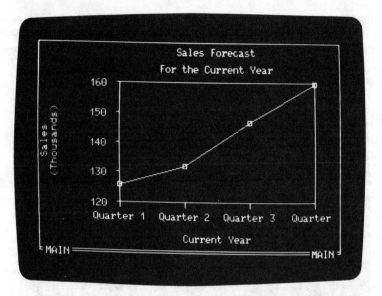

Figure 12.9

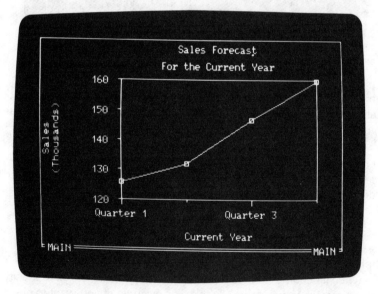

Figure 12.10

Formatting the Graph

Symphony also lets you control the display of each line in a line graph. Each line can be displayed in one of four different forms: lines only, symbols only, lines and symbols, and neither. The command that changes the format of a line graph is Graph 1st-Settings Format. When you issue this command, the following menu appears:

A B C D E F Quit

This menu lets you select the range you want to format. Since our example graph has only one range, select the A option. After the range is selected, this menu appears:

Lines Symbols Both Neither

This menu allows you to specify the format you desire for the selected range. The first choice, Lines, causes the graph to connect the data points with straight lines. The data points are represented by angles in the line. The Symbols choice displays each data point as a symbol, and the data points are not connected by lines. Table 12.1 shows the symbols associated with each data range.

Range	Symbol
A	■
B	+
C	{{ }}
D	▲
E	X
F	▼

Table 12.1

As you probably guessed, the Both option displays each data point as a symbol and connects these symbols with solid lines. Both is the default option, as you can see from the presence of lines and symbols on the graphs in the preceding figures. Finally, the Neither option completely hides the data range, showing neither symbols nor lines.

To test the Format option, select **Lines** from the **Format** menu, then press **[Esc]** twice to get back to the main Graph menu, and then choose **Preview.** Figure 12.11 shows the graph with range A formatted to display as a line only.

Most Symphony users find that the Lines or Both options are the most useful form for line graphs. The Symbols option is most commonly used to format XY graphs, as we'll see in a few pages. The Neither option isn't used very much. When it is used, it is in conjunction with the Data-Labels option.

If your graph had more than one range that you wanted to format, you'd have to repeat the command for each range you wanted to format. Since there are many times when you need to change the format of several data ranges in the graph at one time, it would have been nice if Lotus had added an Entire-Graph option to the Format menu.

Data-Labels

Symphony's Graph 1st-Settings Data-Labels command makes it possible to place labels near the data items in your graphs. In some graphics programs, this kind of label is known as a floating label.

The menu behind the Data-Labels command looks like this:

A B C D E F Quit

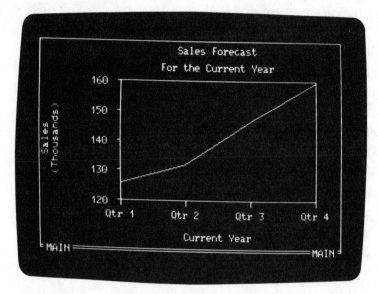

Figure 12.11

Symphony allows you to specify a different set of data labels for each range in your graph. When you select one of the ranges, Symphony prompts you to supply the range in the worksheet that contains the desired labels. Most of the time, the labels created with the Data-Labels command show the actual value of the data items in the range. This means that the Data-Labels range and the data range are the same range. For example, in our sample graph, the A range is C10 . . F10. Since we want the data labels to be the numbers in this range—$125,958, $132,002, and so on—our Data-Labels A range is also C10 . . F10. After this range is specified, Symphony displays a menu that asks you where you want the labels to appear relative to the data items:

Center Left Above Right Below

If you want the data labels to appear above their corresponding data points in the graph, select the **A**bove option from this menu. Figure 12.12 shows the graph with the data labels placed above the data items. If you decided to place the labels below the data points, the graph would look like Figure 12.13.

Don't be confused by the term data labels. Data labels can be, and usually are, values. The term *label* simply describes their function as labels for the data points in the graph. Of course, you can also use labels as data labels. If you do, though, be sure to keep the labels short to avoid having them overlap.

You can designate data labels for data ranges that are not defined, but these labels will not be displayed in the graph. For example, in our graph, Symphony would not display a set of Data-Labels attached to range B.

Be sure that if you change the A range for the graph you also change the A Data-Labels range. Otherwise, the data labels in the graph will not match the data on which the graph is based.

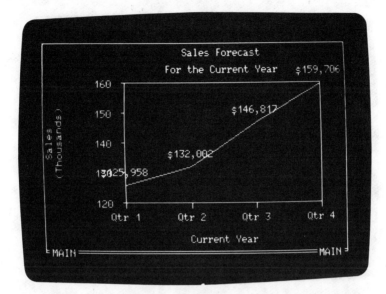

Figure 12.12

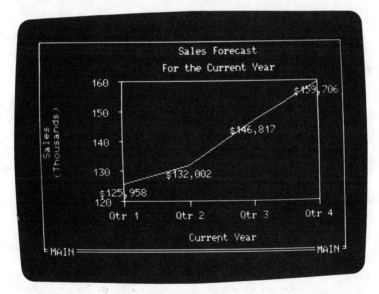

Figure 12.13

One clever use of data labels is to substitute the labels for the symbols in the graph. For example, suppose we used the Format Neither command to hide the lines and symbols in our sample graph, then changed the relative positioning of the data labels to Center. The graph would now look like Figure 12.14. Notice that the data labels in this graph are centered above the location of the data point for that range.

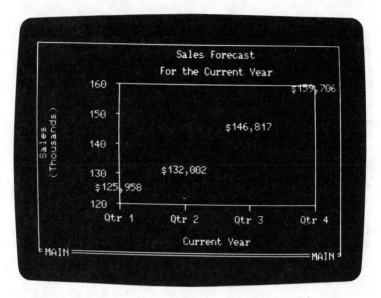

Figure 12.14

Although data labels are helpful, you don't want to overuse them. In graphs with more than one data range, it is nearly impossible to keep the data labels of one range from overlapping with the lines and symbols, and even the data labels, of another. This means that graphs with lots of data labels, or graphs with two or three data ranges and data labels, can be crowded and hard to understand.

Data labels can even be troublesome in simple graphs like the one in Figure 12.14. Notice that the first and last data labels in this graph overlap the left and right edges of the graph and make the graph unattractive. If you're working along with the chapter, remove the data labels with the Graph 1st-Settings Cancel Data-Labels A command.

Formatting the X and Y Axes

Graph 2nd-Settings X-Scale and Graph 2nd-Settings Y-Scale are two more of Symphony's graph formatting options. These commands give you the ability to control the layout and format of the X and Y axes.

Suppose you want to change the layout of the Y axis in your sample graph. First, issue the Graph 2nd-Settings Y-Scale command. The following menu appears:

    Type Format Exponent Width Quit

The Type option has three further options: Manual-Linear, Automatic-Linear, and Logarithmic. In the Automatic-Linear mode, Symphony lays out the Y axis automatically, determining the upper and lower limits of the axis for you. In the Manual-Linear mode, the user must specify the upper and lower limits for the selected axis.

The Type Option

Let's select the Manual-Linear option from the Type menu for our sample graph. After you select this option, Symphony prompts you to supply first the lower limit and then the upper limit for the Y-axis scale. The default for both limits is 0, so if you don't supply a new number, the graph will look like Figure 12.15.

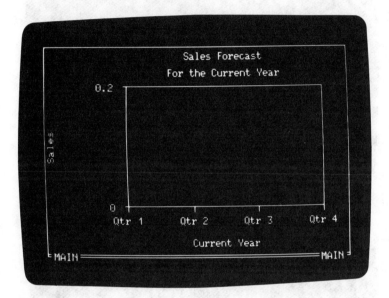

Figure 12.15

If you look at the graph in Figure 12.11, you'll see that Symphony has set the lower limit at 120,000. You want to set the lower limit at 0, so you need only press **[Enter]** to lock in the default value. Since the largest number in the data range is $159,706, be sure to enter a number greater than or equal to 160,000 when Symphony prompts for the upper limit. If you specified 160,000 as the upper limit, the sample graph would look like Figure 12.16.

Notice that the upper limit of the graph is 200,000, even though you manually set the Y-Scale upper limit to 160,000. Apparently, Symphony uses the upper limit you provide as a guideline, not as a strict limit. It might help you to think of the upper-limit setting as the value below which Symphony cannot place the graph's actual upper limit.

You can, by the way, use a negative number to define the lower limit. Figure 12.17 shows our sample graph with a lower limit of − 100,000.

The scale numbers that fall between the upper and lower limits are always supplied automatically by Symphony. Whether you use the Manual-Linear or Automatic-Linear methods of specifying the scale's limits, Symphony decides exactly how many intermediate numbers should be included and what those numbers should be.

Setting the limits for your graphs manually requires some care. You don't want to set limits that are either too far apart or too restrictive. Setting the ranges too far apart will

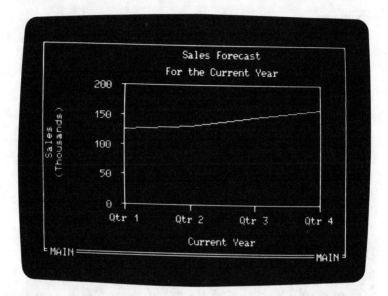

Figure 12.16

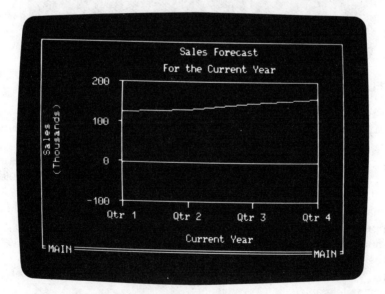

Figure 12.17

obscure the subtle ups and downs of your data. For example, Figure 12.18 shows our graph with a lower limit of −1,000,000 and an upper limit of 1,000,000. Setting the range too narrow squeezes the data too much, perhaps cutting some of the outlying data points from the graph.

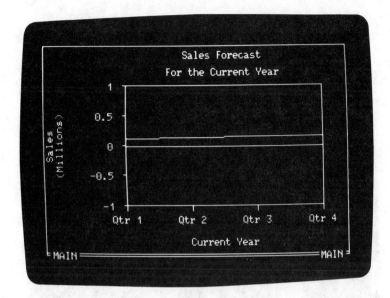

Figure 12.18

Another danger is that you will change the scale in such a way as to make your graph deceiving. In fact, Symphony is guilty of this crime quite often. For example, the automatic lower limit in Figure 12.11 is 120,000. If you placed this graph next to the one shown in Figure 12.16, you might think that the company whose sales are shown in Figure 12.16 was doing quite a bit better than our sample company. A closer look, however, reveals that these graphs show the same data, but that the lower limit in Figure 12.16 has been manually set to 0. The automatic lower limit of 120,000 in the original graph is a bit deceiving.

Probably the most important use of the Manual-Linear command is to force several different graphs to be displayed on a standard scale. Since in the Automatic-Linear mode Symphony sets the lower limit of the graph based on the data in the graph, Symphony may assign different lower limits to several graphs that are supposed to be comparable. By using the Manual-Linear command you can assign the same upper and lower limits to the Y scale on each graph.

The third option on the Type menu, Logarithmic, changes the Y scale from a linear to a logarithmic scale. This option is a response to the requests for a logarithmic graph by many engineers and scientists who used 1-2-3.

In a linear scale, each increment of measure represents a constant number of units. In a logarithmic scale, each increment of measure represents ten times as many units as the previous increment.

Logarithmic scales have very little application to the world of finance. If you don't use logarithms in your work, don't spend any time learning this command.

The Format Option

The second selection on the Y-Scale menu, Format, allows you to assign a format to the numbers along the Y axis. This command offers the same formats for the scale numbers that the SHEET environment {Menu} Format command offers for cells in the worksheet. (For more on these choices, see Chapter 5.)

Probably the most commonly used format for the scale numbers is Currency. If you issue the Graph 2nd-Settings Y-Scale Format command and select Currency with 2 decimal places, your graph will look like Figure 12.19.

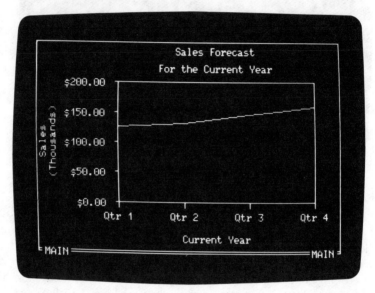

Figure 12.19

It is possible to format the scale numbers in a way Symphony cannot display. In the default mode, only nine spaces are available to display the entire scale number including decimal points, commas, and parentheses. If you used the Currency format with seven decimal places, your scale numbers would each be 12 characters long—for example, $100.0000000. Since this number won't fit in the allotted space, Symphony will display a series of asterisks. You may remember that Symphony handles numbers in the worksheet that are too wide to be displayed in a column in much the same way.

If you create a graph that has asterisks instead of the desired Y-axis labels, you can do one of three things to overcome the problem: change the format of the scale, change the scale exponent, or change the width of the space allotted to the scale.

Exponent

The Exponent option of the Y-Scale command is used to specify the exponent Symphony should use when displaying the numbers along the Y axis. Like the Type option, Exponent offers the option of letting Symphony decide the exponent for you (Automatic) or of setting the exponent yourself (Manual).

In the Automatic mode, Symphony chooses the exponent it feels best represents the numbers in the scale in the available space. In our earlier examples, an exponent of three causes the numbers on the scale to be divided by 1000 before being displayed. For example, the scale number 100,000 is shown as 100 in these figures. The exponent 3 also causes the legend (Thousands) to appear along the Y axis in the foregoing illustrations.

Symphony's choice of exponents is very predictable. Numbers between − 100 and 100 are displayed without exponents, numbers greater than − 1000 but less than 1000 are given an exponent of 2 and are shown with the legend (Hundreds), numbers greater than 1000 but less than 1,000,000 (or less than − 1000 and greater than − 1,000,000) are assigned an exponent of 3 and are shown with the legend (Thousands), and numbers greater than 1,000,000 (or smaller than − 1,000,000) are given an exponent of 6 and are shown with the legend (Millions).

The Manual option allows you to force Symphony to use an exponent of your choice when displaying the scale numbers. The legend along the Y axis will reveal the exponent you have selected. For example, choosing the exponent 4 should result in the legend (Numbers × 10E4). (One of the few bugs I am aware of in Symphony relates to this command. When you manually set the exponent to 4, the legend on the Y axis reads (Numbers × 1E4.) The legend 1E4 is meaningless, since 1E4 equals 1 × 1 × 1 × 1 or 1.) If you choose the exponents 3 or 6, the legend will read (Thousands) or (Millions), respectively.

You can use the Exponent command to overcome problems caused by formatting the scale numbers. For example, suppose you specified the Currency 2 format for a graph, and that decision made the numbers too wide to be displayed. You can make the number "narrower," and thus make it fit in the allotted space, by choosing a higher exponent. For example, choosing the exponent 4 would cause the number 100,000, which would be $100,000.00 in Currency 2 format, to be displayed as $10.00.

Changing the Width

If all else fails when you try to format the scale numbers, you can use the Width command to change the space in the graph allotted to the scale. Width is a very simple command. All you do after entering the command is specify the number of spaces you want set aside for the labels. You can choose any number from 1 to 40. The default is 9. Figure 12.20 shows the sample graph with a scale width of 20 characters.

Consider carefully setting the width too wide or too narrow. If the scale area is too narrow, it will be virtually impossible to fit your labels into the space alloted. If the space is too wide, your graph may be squeezed.

Choosing the Best Y-Scale

My favorite format for the Y axis in our graph calls for the exponent to be manually set to 0 and the width set to 15. When the exponent is 0, Symphony displays the scale numbers "as is." Setting the width to 15 leaves plenty of room for scale numbers up to 9,999,999, including decimals and formatting characters like the dollar sign and the comma. Figure 12.21 shows our sample graph formatted in this fashion.

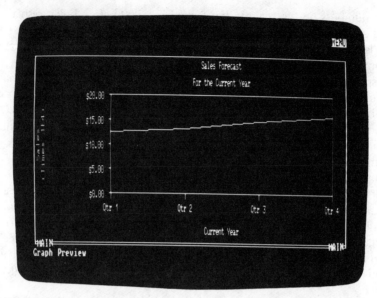

Figure 12.20

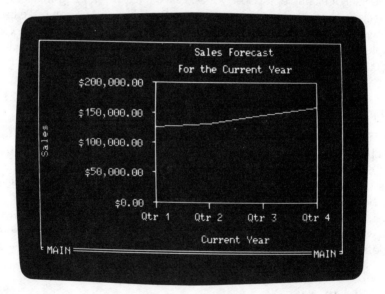

Figure 12.21

The X-Scale Command

The X-Scale command is very similar to the Y-Scale command, except, of course, that it controls the layout and format of the X axis. When you select the X-Scale option from the 2nd-Settings menu, the following menu appears:

Type   Format   Exponent   Quit

Notice that this menu is identical to the Y-Scale menu except that the Width option has been eliminated. The menus underlying each of these choices are also identical to those under the Y-Scale options.

The X-Scale Type Manual-Linear command can be used to set upper and lower limits for the X axis. This command is only effective, however, with XY graphs, since in all other types of graphs the numbers (if any) along the X axis are merely labels to the graph. We'll cover this concept better when we discuss XY graphs.

The Other Option

The Other option on the 2nd-Settings menu offers several other important formatting controls. The menu that lies behind this option looks like this:

Grid Hide Color Skip Origin Aspect

We'll cover the Color option in a few pages when we discuss graph hues. The Aspect command relates only to pie graphs, so we'll cover it when we discuss that graph type. Similarly, the Origin command relates only to bar charts. The other options can be applied to line graphs like our example, so we'll cover them here.

Adding a Grid

The Grid option makes it possible to superimpose a grid over a graph. The grid can consist of only horizontal lines or vertical lines, or it can be a true grid of both horizontal and vertical lines. To superimpose a grid over our graph, we would issue the Graph 2nd-Settings Other Grid command and select one of following choices:

Horizontal Vertical Both None

If we selected the option Both, our graph would look like Figure 12.22.

Grids in Symphony graphs are a mixed blessing. In some situations a grid can make a graph easier to read and understand. For example, horizontal grids are sometimes very useful in high-low-close-open graphs. On the other hand, grids can clutter your screen and make a graph nearly unreadable. My advice is that you use grids sparingly.

The Hide Option

As you'll see in the next chapter, if you try to display a Symphony graph in a small enough window, Symphony will drop the graph's scales and the titles in an effort to make the graph visible. The Hide command allows the user to do the same thing at his or her discretion. Try out the Hide command on your version of the sample graph. Your graph should look like Figure 12.23.

Before we go on, let's review the two settings sheets associated with this graph. If you've been following along with the text, your Graph 1st-Settings sheet should look like Figure 12.24, and your Graph 2nd-Settings sheet should look like Figure 12.25.

These settings sheets contain all of the ranges and other information we provided while creating and formatting the graph. You might think of the process of defining a

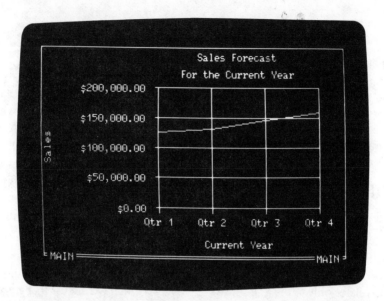

Figure 12.22

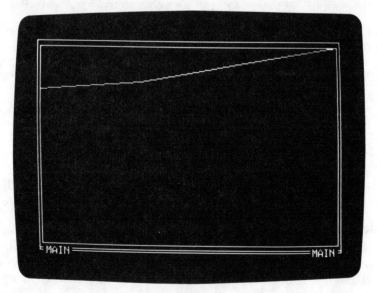

Figure 12.23

graph as you would of filling out a form. When the form is completely filled out, the graph is completely defined.

Making a Change

Suppose we decided to graph the trend of sales for Product 1 across the year instead of Total Sales. This change may be easier than you think. Simply issue the {**Menu**} **G**raph

```
Switch to 2nd-Settings
Switch Type Range Hue Format Data-Labels Legend Cancel Name Quit
------------------------------------------------------------------
|      Type:        Line                                         |
|   Range           Hue        Format      Data-Labels    Legend |
|                                                                |
|   X  C4..F4        1                                           |
|   A  C10..F10      2         Lines                             |
|   B                3         Both                              |
|   C                4         Both                              |
|   D                5         Both                              |
|   E                6         Both                              |
|   F                7         Both                              |
|                                                                |
|   =======================================Graph 1st-Settings: Main= |
```

Figure 12.24

```
Switch to 1st-Settings
Switch   Titles   Y-Scale   X-Scale   Other   Name   Quit
------------------------------------------------------------------
|   Titles                           Type: Line                  |
|     First     \A2               X Axis  Current Year           |
|     Second  For the Current Year  Y Axis  Sales                |
|   Y-Scale                  X-Scale              Other          |
|     Type     Manual          Type   Automatic   Grid   None    |
|     Lower    0               Lower              Hide   No      |
|     Upper    160000          Upper              Color  No      |
|     Format   C2              Format   G         Skip   1       |
|     Exponent 0               Exponent Automatic Origin 0       |
|     Width    15                                 Aspect 1       |
|   =======================================Graph 2nd-Settings: Main= |
```

Figure 12.25

1st-Settings command, and change the **A** Range from C10 . . F10 to C5 . . F5. To make this change, you must press **[Esc]** after Symphony shows you the current A range and then POINT to the new range with the cell pointer. After making these selections, type **Q**uit twice to return to the Graph menu and Preview to view your new graph. Figure 12.26 shows the graph as it should appear on your screen.

Notice that your new graph is identical to the old one in every respect except that it displays a new range. All of the other settings for this graph have remained the same. This example points out an important concept. Once you define a graph in Symphony, the program retains the settings for that graph until you turn off your computer or until you use the 1st-Settings Name Initial-Settings command to destroy the settings. This means that you can modify a graph that you have created as many times as you want. For example, you can change your new graph back to the original simply by issuing the {**Menu**} **G**raph **1**st-Settings **R**ange command and changing the **A** range to C10 . . F10.

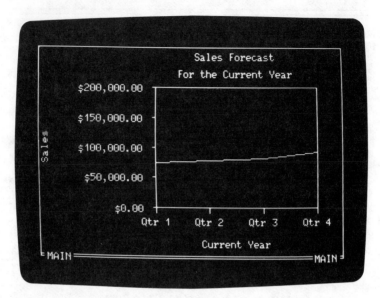

Figure 12.26

THE NAME COMMAND

In a couple of pages we'll move on to create some more Symphony graphs. At this point, however, we need to discuss the concept of graph settings sheet names. This can be a tricky concept, especially for Symphony users who are familiar with 1-2-3's /Graph Name command, so be sure to read the next few paragraphs carefully.

All Symphony graph settings sheets have names. Up to this point we have been working in a settings sheet named MAIN. MAIN is the default name for the first graph settings sheet in a Symphony worksheet.

It is important to remember that only one settings sheet can be active in the worksheet at any time. The active settings sheet is the sheet that will be affected by any and all graphics commands you issue. You can easily determine which sheet is active by issuing the Graph 1st-Settings command, which will bring the active settings sheet into view.

It is also important to remember that only one graph can be associated with any one settings sheet. If you decide to create a new graph using the settings sheet named MAIN, the act of creating that graph will destroy or modify the settings for your example graph. Since we want to build a new graph but don't want to lose the example graph quite yet, we need to create a second settings sheet.

The Name command on the Graph 1st-Settings menu lets you create, use, and delete graph settings sheets. You can create an unlimited number of settings sheets in a single worksheet. Symphony keeps a record of all the graph names you have created and remembers the settings that correspond to each name.

The Graph 1st-Settings Name menu looks like this:

Use   Create   Delete   Previous   Next   Initial-Settings   Reset   Quit

As we saw above, the default settings sheet name is MAIN. The settings sheet for our example graph has been assigned this name by Symphony. Because we want to create a new graph but want to preserve the work we have done so far, we need to create a new settings sheet. To create a new sheet, issue the Graph 1st-Settings Name command and choose the Create option. Symphony then asks you to provide the new name for this settings sheet and displays a list of all the named settings sheets on the default directory. In this example, only the name MAIN would appear.

To create a new settings sheet, simply type the new name—SECOND—and press [Enter]. Symphony immediately changes the name of the current settings sheet to SECOND. Of course, SECOND is just a sample name. You can specify any character string of up to 15 characters for your settings sheet names.

Let's be sure you understand what has happened here. When you issued the Create command, Symphony "created" a new graph settings sheet named SECOND. This new settings sheet is an exact clone of the settings sheet MAIN. In essence, we now have two copies of exactly the same settings sheet under two different names—MAIN and SECOND. SECOND is now the active graph settings sheet. MAIN is now in the background, so we can make changes to SECOND without affecting MAIN in any way.

Why did Symphony create SECOND as an exact clone of MAIN? Simply because MAIN was the current graph in the one window in our sample worksheet when we issued the Name Create command. Be sure you understand that Symphony always clones the current settings sheet, and not the settings sheet MAIN, when creating a new settings sheet. In other words, if you made some changes to SECOND and then issued the Name Create command again, creating a new settings sheet called THIRD, then THIRD would be an exact clone of SECOND.

In Symphony, the Name Create command is like a photocopier that produces an exact duplicate of the current settings sheet. The only difference between the photocopy and the original is that they have different names. The copy becomes the active settings sheet and can be manipulated by Symphony's Graph commands. The original settings sheet is "filed" in Symphony's list of Graph settings sheet names.

Note for 1-2-3 Users

If you are a former 1-2-3 user, you may be confused by Symphony's Name Create command. First, you are probably puzzled by the order of naming and creating graphs in Symphony. In 1-2-3, you first define a graph and then give it a name if you want to save it. In Symphony, where all graph settings sheets have names, you first create the name and then define the graph settings. The program creates the first name, MAIN, for you.

You are probably used to thinking about 1-2-3's Name Create command as a way to "save" a graph. When we created the graph name SECOND, you might have expected Symphony to store SECOND as a saved version of the current graph and retain MAIN as the active graph. In Symphony, however, it is better to think of the Name Create command as a way to create a new settings sheet. The old settings sheet isn't saved; it simply is replaced as the current settings sheet by the newly created sheet.

Don't let these differences confuse you. Just remember that in Symphony, every settings sheet has a name and only one settings sheet can be active at one time. To create a new graph while preserving your current settings you must therefore create the name for the new settings sheet.

Resetting the Current Settings

Typically, you wouldn't keep two copies of exactly the same graph settings sheet. For example, once you had created the new settings sheet called SECOND, you would usually reset or edit the settings in this sheet and then create a new graph. After this new graph was defined, you might create a new window called THIRD, and further modify the settings to create yet another graph.

If you want to completely erase the settings in SECOND, you would issue the 1st-Settings Name Initial-Settings command. Be careful! As soon as you issue this command, the settings in SECOND, including the graph Type and all Ranges, are restored to the defaults. In other words, the graph settings for SECOND are destroyed. Of course, these settings are still preserved in the settings sheet named MAIN.

The Graph 1st-Settings Cancel Command

An alternative to the Initial-Settings command is the Graph 1st-Settings Cancel command. Cancel is a bit more flexible than Initial-Settings because it allows you to cancel some parts of a graph settings sheet without completely resetting the settings. The Cancel menu looks like this:

> Entire-Row   Range   Format   Data-Labels   Legend   Hue

The Entire-Row option allows you to reset all settings that apply to a single data range. If you look at the 1st-Settings sheet, you'll see that the data for Range, Hue, Format, Data-Labels, and Legend for each of the six graph ranges are arranged in rows across the settings sheet. When you issue the Entire-Row command, the following menu appears:

> Graph   X   A   B   C   D   E   F   Quit

You can reset all of these settings for any of the data ranges individually by selecting A, B, C, D, E, or F, or for all the ranges at once by selecting the Graph option.

Notice that selecting Graph is not the same as using the Name Initial-Settings command. Initial-Settings resets every setting on *both* graph settings sheets. The Cancel Graph command just resets the data for ranges, hues, formats, data labels, and legends.

The other options on the Cancel menu allow you to reset only the ranges, formats, data labels, legends, or hues that have been defined in the current settings sheet. Each of these options allows you to reset the chosen setting range by range or for the entire graph at once. For example, if you selected the Range choice from the Cancel menu, you could reset the setting for range A, B, C, D, E, or F, or you could reset *all* of the data ranges in the graph.

Notes for 1-2-3 Users

1-2-3 users will notice that nearly twice as many keystrokes are required to reset a graph in Symphony than were required in 1-2-3. In 1-2-3, you could erase the current graph by issuing the /Graph Reset command. In Symphony, the required command is Menu Graph 1st-Settings Name Initial-Settings.

1-2-3 users beware: there is an important difference between Symphony's Name Use command and 1-2-3's version of the same command. In 1-2-3, if you used a graph and then destroyed it with /Graph Reset, you could restore it by reissuing the /Graph Name Use command. This protected your graphs from being accidentally destroyed.

In Symphony, on the other hand, if you use a settings sheet, then issue the Name Initial-Settings command, you destroy the settings in this sheet completely. No back-up copy remains.

If you want to test this assertion, simply issue the 1st-Settings Name Initial-Settings to initialize the settings in MAIN. Now issue the Name Use command and select MAIN from the list of names and try to Preview the graph. Notice that instead of showing you the graph, Symphony simply beeps at you. A quick look at the settings sheet explains why—the graph MAIN has no settings. They were destroyed when you issued the Initial-Settings command.

Think about the difference between 1-2-3 and Symphony in this way. In 1-2-3, a named graph was like a master copy of an important document. When you wanted to use the document, you made a copy of the original to work with (/Graph Name Use). If this copy was destroyed (/Graph Reset), you could easily retrieve the original and make a new copy (/Graph Name Use). In Symphony, however, when you use the graph (Menu Graph 1st-Settings Name Use), you actually use the original. If this graph is destroyed (Menu Graph 1st-Settings Name Initial-Settings), you destroy the only copy of the graph. There is nothing to fall back on.

This difference between the two programs is an unfortunate result of the overall design of Symphony's graphics. There is no way to protect your graphs from being destroyed accidentally.

Using a Settings Sheet

You can retrieve a settings sheet at any time simply by using the Graph 1st-Settings Name Use command and supplying the name of the graph you want to become the active graph settings sheet. Suppose that you wanted to retrieve the settings sheet MAIN. Simply issue the **Graph 1**st-Settings **N**ame **U**se command and select MAIN from the list of names offered by Symphony. When this command is issued, MAIN becomes the active settings sheet. SECOND is now in the background, waiting for future use. Any Graph commands you give will affect MAIN.

You can also retrieve a graph settings sheet with the **1**st-Settings **N**ame **P**revious or **N**ext commands. These commands simply step through the graph settings sheet names in the current worksheet one at a time. Previous moves you back to the graph settings sheet just before the current graph settings sheet in Symphony's list; Next moves you forward to the next graph in the list.

Deleting a Settings Sheet

The Graph 1st-Settings Name Delete command is used to delete a settings sheet. This command differs from the Initial-Settings command in that Initial-Settings erases the settings without destroying the sheet itself. Name Delete, on the other hand, actually destroys the settings sheet. After the **Name Delete** command is issued, both the settings and the settings sheet are gone. If, for example, you deleted the sheet SECOND, the name SECOND would disappear from the list of named settings sheets. If a GRAPH window was attached to SECOND, the window would be blank.

The Name Delete command can be used to delete any settings sheet in Symphony's list of sheets except the active sheet. If you try to delete the active settings sheet, Symphony displays the error message

Cannot delete the current settings sheet

Settings sheet names do more than just preserve graph settings for future use. Names make it possible to view several graphs on the screen at one time. We'll talk more about this use for settings sheet names in the next chapter.

SAVING A GRAPH

When you save a worksheet that contains graph settings sheets, all of the settings sheets are saved as a part of the worksheet. However, there is no way to save an individual graph in a form that can be recalled into the worksheet. The only way you can save an individual graph is to a file that can then only be used for printing the graph.

In Chapter 14 we'll examine Symphony's PrintGraph program. PrintGraph is used to create hardcopy versions of the graphs you build with the Graph command. However, since PrintGraph is a separate program in the Symphony system, you cannot directly access your Symphony graph definitions from PrintGraph. You must first save your graphs in special files, called .PIC files, which can be read by PrintGraph. .PIC files have only one purpose—to transfer graphs from Symphony to the PrintGraph program for printing. In fact, .PIC files can only be read by the PrintGraph program. You cannot recall a .PIC file into Symphony.

.PIC files are created with the **Graph Image-Save** command. When you issue this command, the graph defined by the active settings sheet is stored into a .PIC file. (These files are called .PIC files because they have the file name extension .PIC.)

Suppose you want to save our graph in a .PIC file for printing. Assuming that MAIN is the active settings sheet (if it isn't, use the **Graph 1st-Settings Name Use** command to activate it), just issue the **{Menu} Graph Image-Save** command. Symphony then presents a list of the .PIC files on the current disk and prompts you to supply a name for the graph you are saving. Since you are saving this graph for the first time, simply type an eight-character (or less) name like **GRAPH1** and press **[Enter]**. Remember not to include the suffix .PIC in the file name. After you press **[Enter]**, the active disk drive will whir for a few seconds as it saves the graph onto the disk.

Saving a graph into a .PIC file has absolutely no effect on the current graph settings in Symphony. If you look at your settings sheet, you can see that MAIN is still the active graph. If you issue the Preview command, MAIN will be drawn on your screen.

If the graph being saved is an updated version of a graph already stored on the disk, you can save the new version under the old name by pointing to that old name in the list of names provided by the command. This will save the new graph under the old name and destroy the old version of the file.

Remember that .PIC files are used only to transfer graphs between Symphony and the PrintGraph program. We'll use the graph we just saved to explore PrintGraph in Chapter 14, Printing Graphs.

ADDING A FEW RANGES

Suppose you decide that you want to create a graph that shows the trends for all four product lines, as well as for total sales, across the current year. This new graph will have five data ranges: one for each product line and one for total sales. Remember that six is the maximum number of ranges that can be included in a Symphony graph.

(If you are following along with the chapter, you may have deleted the settings sheet SECOND from your worksheet. Before going on, use the Graph 1st-Settings Name Create command to recreate the settings sheet SECOND. We'll use this sheet in the upcoming examples.)

Assuming that SECOND is the active settings sheet, you can create this new graph very easily. Issue the **M**enu **G**raph **1**st-Settings **R**ange command. Data range A is already defined as C10 . . F10, the range that includes the total sales numbers. Choose option **B** on the Range menu and point to the range C5 . . F5. Next, choose option **C** and point to the range C6 . . F6. Range **D** will be C7 . . F7, and range **E** will be C8 . . F8. After all five ranges are defined, type **Q**uit twice to return to the Graph menu, and then type **P**review to view the graph. If everything was properly defined, your graph should look like Figure 12.27.

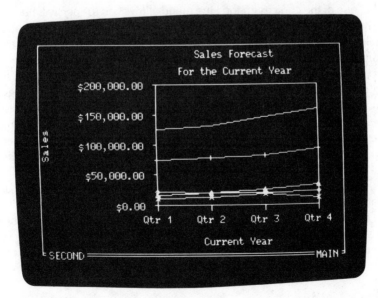

Figure 12.27

This graph is obviously not very easy to read. In the first place, the lines overlap so that it is difficult to follow one line from left to right across the graph. This problem is most acute if you are using a monochrome graphics display. The symbols used to distinguish one line from another are very hard to make out, especially when the lines are close together.

The Hue Option

Symphony automatically assigns a different hue to all six of the possible data ranges in a graph and to the X range. If you have color monitor, these hues cause the different data ranges in your graph to be displayed in different colors.

As you might expect, Symphony makes it possible to change the color of each data range. The Graph 1st-Settings Hue command is used to specify the color, or hue, that should be assigned to each data range. When this command is issued, the following menu appears:

X   A   B   C   D   E   F   Quit

Notice that like the Format command, the Hue command allows you to change the characteristics of each data range individually.

Suppose you want to change the hue of the A range in your graph. Your first step, after getting to the Hue menu, would be to select option A. The following menu appears:

1   2   3   4   5   6   7   None

Each number in this menu represents one of Symphony's hues. The default hue for the A range is 2, but you can select any of the seven choices as an alternative. Selecting None causes the line to disappear from the graph.

Notice that one of the choices on the Hue menu allows you to specify a hue for the X range. The hue you assign to the X range affects all elements of the graph except the data ranges and legends (if any), including the borders around the graph, the titles, the numbers and caption on the Y axis, and, of course, the numbers on the X axis.

The effect of the Hue command depends on the type of computer you have, the type of monitor connected to that computer, and on the setting of the 2nd-Settings Other Color command. The Color command offers two choices that control the display of hues. Choice 1, Yes, causes hues to be displayed as colors (if you have a color monitor) or as shades (if you have a monochrome monitor). Differences in shades are very hard to detect in line, high-low-close-open, and XY graphs. Shades do make a big difference in bar, stacked-bar, and pie charts, however.

Choice 2, No, causes hues to be displayed as crosshatches. Each hue results in a different crosshatch pattern. If you think about it for a second, you'll realize that it is impossible to use a crosshatch in a line, XY, or high-low-close-open graph, so this choice only affects bar, stacked-bar, and pie charts.

The Hue command has a different effect on pie charts than any other type of graph. We'll see how pie charts can be shaded and colored in a few pages.

Legends

Even if you have a color monitor and can tell the lines in Figure 12.27 apart by color, there is no way to tell which line represents which product. We therefore need to add legends to our graph that identify each line.

To add legends to this graph, issue the {**Menu**} **G**raph **1**st-Settings **L**egend command. As with many other graphic commands, the Legend command menu is simply a list of Symphony's six graphic data ranges.

   A B C D E F Quit

Symphony allows you to create a separate legend for each data range in your graph. For example, since data range A in our sample graph contains the total sales data, we might enter the label **Total** as the A-range legend. Since range B shows the results for product 1, the legend for that range might be **Product 1.** Similarly, the legend for range C would be **Product 2,** and so on. After all of the legends are entered, jump back up to the Graph menu and type Preview to view the graph. Your graph should look like Figure 12.28. Notice that each legend appears next to the symbol used to mark the line for that product in the graph.

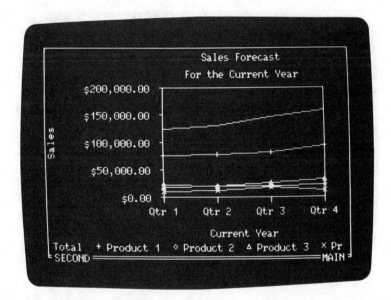

Figure 12.28

Symphony allows your legends to be up to 20 characters long. However, in a graph like our sample, your labels will probably need to be shorter than the maximum length. If your labels are too long to fit in the available space, they will overlap both edges of the screen. This means that the first few characters and the last few characters in the labels will not be visible. If you choose short labels where possible and abbreviate those that must be long, you'll nearly always be able to fit them into your graphs.

Since legends are used to distinguish one line or bar in a graph from another, they are usually only used in graphs that contain multiple ranges. You can define a legend for a line of a bar chart with a single range, but the legend really won't tell you anything. In multiple-range graphs, though, legends are indispensable.

BAR GRAPHS

The next type of graph is the bar graph. Bar graphs are similar to line graphs in that both are used to illustrate the trend of a set of data across time. Strictly speaking, line charts are preferable for plotting continuous data, where trend analysis is important, while bar charts are used to plot discrete data, where comparing two or more values is important. But in practice these two graph types are virtually interchangeable.

In fact, you can easily convert your first line graph, MAIN, into a bar chart. Issue the **G**raph **1**st-Settings **N**ame **U**se command to make MAIN the active settings sheet. Next, issue the Name Create command to create a new settings sheet named THIRD. This new settings sheet will be an exact copy of MAIN.

All you have to do to convert this line graph into a bar graph is issue the **{Menu}** **G**raph **1**st-Settings **T**ype **B**ar command. The graph should now look like Figure 12.29.

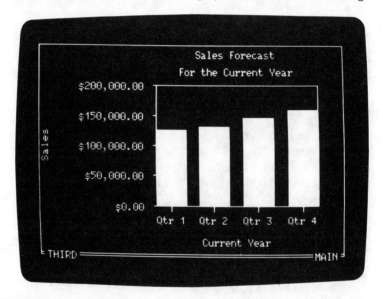

Figure 12.29

Be sure that you understand that this graph could also have been created from scratch by specifying a graph type, an A range, and any options that you desired. We chose to create the bar graph by converting the line graph only to save a few steps.

Even though the line and bar graphs are similar, there are a couple of important differences between this new graph and our line graph. First, the Format settings you selected for the line graph (Lines only, Symbols only, Both, Neither) have no effect on a bar graph.

On the other hand, the Hue settings, which were not too important in the line chart, make a difference with this new graph. If the 2nd-Settings Other Color setting is currently Yes, the bars in this graph will be a solid color. (Which color depends on the type of computer you are using. On an IBM PC, these bars will be white.) If the Color setting is No, the bars will be filled with crosshatching, as shown in Figure 12.30.

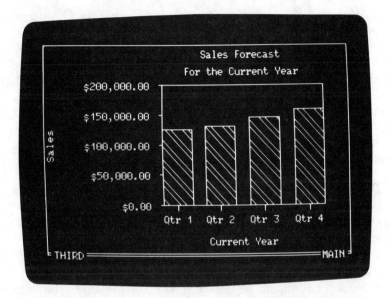

Figure 12.30

Of course, you can use the 1st-Settings Hue command to change the hue for any data range. Use this command to change the hue for data range A to 4, then return to the Graph menu and type Preview. Your graph should look like Figure 12.31.

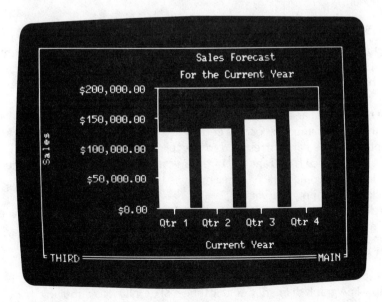

Figure 12.31

Another difference between line and bar graphs concerns the lower limit on the Y axis. In line graphs, the Y-scale lower limit is frequently not 0. This occurs because Symphony, in the Y-Scale Type Automatic mode, automatically selects the lower limit it "thinks" is best for the graph. In bar graphs, however, unless you tell it to do differently (we'll tell you how in the next section), Symphony always sets the lower limit to 0.

In fact, if you try to use the Menu Graph 2nd-Settings Y-Scale Type Manual-Linear command to set a lower limit that is greater than 0 for the Y axis of a bar graph, Symphony will ignore your setting. Symphony insists that the lower limit of a bar graph be less than or equal to 0. (If all of the data in the range being graphed is negative, Symphony insists that the upper limit of the Y scale be greater than or equal to 0.)

The Origin Command

However, there is a way around this obstacle. The 2nd-Settings Other Origin command, which allows you to control the location of the intersection of the X axis and the Y axis, only affects bar and stacked-bar graphs.

When you issue the {**Menu**} **G**raph **2**nd-Settings **O**ther **O**rigin command, Symphony prompts you for the Y value at which the X axis should intersect the Y axis. For example, suppose you issue this command and set the Origin value to 100000. The X axis will now intersect the Y axis at the value 100000 instead of 0. If you have set the Y-Scale Type setting to Automatic-Linear, the lower limit of the Y axis becomes 100,000 when you set the origin to 100,000.

I should now modify my statement about the lower and upper limits of the Y axis on a bar chart. Symphony insists only that the origin fall between the upper and lower Y-Scale limits of a bar graph. If you raise the origin to 100000, you can also set the Y-Scale lower limit to 100000.

Margins for Your Bar Charts

Take a look back at Figure 12.31. Do you see how the first and last bars in this graph are shoved against the left and right edges of the graph frame? You can overcome this problem by changing the 1st-Settings Range A from C10 . . F10 to B10 . . G10. Figure 12.32 shows the graph that results from this data range.

Notice how the left and right bars in this graph are now offset from the left and right edges of the graph frame. This occurs because Symphony is graphing six bars instead of the original four. The bars correspond to the cells in the A range: B10, C10, D10, E10, F10, and G10. Since cells B10 and G10 are blank, and thus have a value of 0, the first and last bars disappear from the face of the graph. So the graph appears to contain only four bars bracketed by empty margins.

This trick can be used on any Bar or Stacked-Bar chart to make the graph more attractive and more understandable.

Multiple-Bar Charts

It is also possible to build multiple-bar graphs in Symphony. In fact, you can convert the multiple-line graph defined in settings sheet SECOND into a multiple-bar chart just like we converted our simple line chart into a simple bar chart.

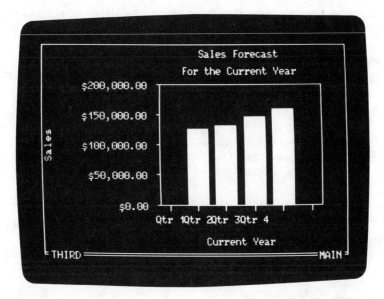

Figure 12.32

To make this conversion you must first retrieve the graph settings sheet for SECOND from the list of named settings sheets with the {**Menu**} **G**raph **1**st-Settings **N**ame **U**se command. Once SECOND is active, issue the **G**raph **1**st-Settings **T**ype **B**ar command to convert the graph to a bar chart. When you type **P**review to view this new graph, it should look like Figure 12.33.

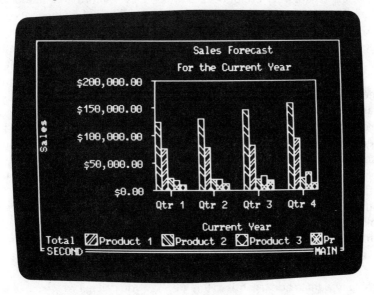

Figure 12.33

As you can see, when you ask Symphony to graph several data ranges on a bar chart, the program creates "sets" of bars at each point on the X axis. The bars in each group are arranged by range-letter order from left to right; that is, the A range is on the far left of each set, followed by the B range, and so on.

Notice also that the bars in each set are filled with a different shading or crosshatching pattern (or a different color, depending on your type of monitor). Our simple bar chart also used hues, but because there was only one data range in that graph, only one hue was used. The variations in hues make the graphs easier to understand. Of course, you can alter the Hue and Other Color commands to vary the display of this graph.

Notice that the legends we defined in SECOND are still in place in the multiple-bar chart. Each legend appears next to the shade or crosshatch pattern used to define the data range to which it applies.

The difference between multiple-bar and multiple-line charts is more significant than that between simple line and bar charts. Multiple-line graphs are good for depicting and comparing the trends of several different sets of data across time. Multiple-bar charts, on the other hand, are more useful for comparing the relationships of several data ranges at a given time or at several distinct times.

A STACKED-BAR GRAPH

Imagine now that you want to create another graph from the data in Figure 12.3. You want this graph to show the makeup of total sales for the four quarters. In other words, you want to build a stacked-bar chart where each bar is composed of four blocks—product 1 sales, product 2 sales, and so on. The full bar represents total sales.

Stacked-bar charts are very useful because they deliver information about both the trend of several data ranges across time and the relationship of the ranges at each point on the X axis.

Before beginning to create this graph, issue the **Graph 1**st-Settings **C**reate command to create a new settings sheet called FOURTH. Then, use the **Graph 1**st-Settings **N**ame **I**nitial-Settings command to reset this new graph settings sheet. Press **[Esc]** to back up through the menus until you reach 1st-Settings menu. Now select **T**ype and specify a Stacked-Bar chart. Press **Q**uit to return to the 1st-Settings menu.

Next, select the **R**ange option. Since there are four product lines in our sales forecast, we will specify four data ranges for the graph. The **A** range will cover the cells that contain data on product 1 sales, C5 . . F5. The **B** range will depict the product 2 sales data in cells C6 . . F6. Data range **C** is C7 . . F7, and range **D** is C8 . . F8. After the four data ranges are defined, type Quit once to return to the 1st-Settings menu.

Now you can use the Preview command to take a peek at the graph you've created. It should look like Figure 12.34.

Notice that Symphony has created four bars, and each bar is made up of smaller bars stacked together. The bottom section of each bar is the A range, the next is the B range, and so on.

You'll probably want to add legends to this graph so you can tell which set of bars represents which data set. To do this, you would issue the 1st-Settings Legends command

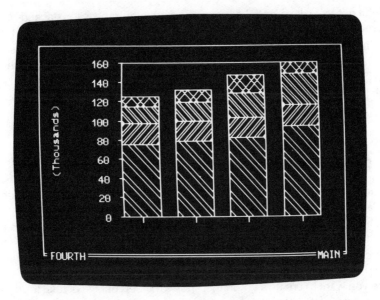

Figure 12.34

and enter a legend for each range. For example, the A-range legend might be **Product 1.** You could also add titles and X-Labels to the graph, and you might want to change the format of the Y-Scale. Figure 12.35 shows our stacked-bar chart with all of these options.

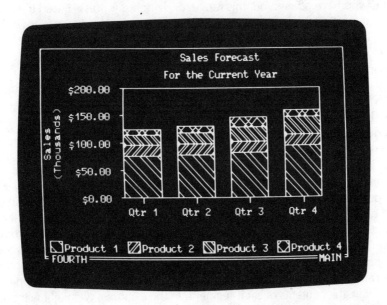

Figure 12.35

Be careful not to make a mistake when specifying the ranges for stacked-bar charts. Although bar graphs are used to show the component parts of some total (in the example, the portion of total sales accounted for by product 1, product 2, and so on), the range containing the actual total of the components should not be used when defining the graph. There is a very strong tendency on the part of some Symphony users (including myself from time to time) to use the total as one of the graph ranges in a stacked-bar chart.

A PIE CHART

Symphony's fourth type of graph is the pie chart. Pie charts and stacked-bar charts are closely related, because both show the component parts of some total amount. In a pie chart, each component of the total is a slice of the pie. The sum of the slices represents the sum of the components. The main difference between the two types of graphs is that pie charts can plot only a single set of data items at one time, while stacked-bar graphs can show several.

Suppose you want to create a graph that shows the percentage of total fourth-quarter sales accounted for by each product line. Begin by resetting the graph settings in MAIN with the Graph 1st-Settings Name Initial-Settings command. Select the Type command and then the Pie option.

Now you need to select the data range for this pie chart. Because pie charts can only graph one data range at a time, we need to specify only an A range to create this graph. Since we want to chart the components of quarter total sales, the **A** data range will be F5 . . F8. After you have pointed out this range for Symphony, press **[Enter]** to lock in the range and then **[Esc]** twice to return to the Graph menu. Use Preview to look at the graph, which is also shown in Figure 12.36.

As you look at this graph, notice that the graph contains four segments, one for each data item in the A range. The number of segments in a pie chart is controlled by the number of cells in the A range. For example, the range A1 . . A10 would always result in a pie chart with ten sections. A pie chart can have as many sections as you want. The only limitation on the number of segments is the resolution of your computer's screen and your graphics output device. A pie chart can also have just one section (although such a chart wouldn't tell you very much).

Notice also that Symphony has placed a percentage next to each segment in the graph. This number shows the ratio of the segment to the entire pie. Symphony also makes it possible to enter the actual value of each segment in the pie chart. To do this, you must create an X range for the graph that exactly overlaps the A range. For example, if you wanted to enter the actual values in the pie chart in our example, you would issue the {Menu} Graph 1st-Settings Range X command and specify the range F5 . . F8 as the X range. Figure 12.37 shows the graph that includes both the values and the percentages.

You can also define the X range to cover a range of labels. The labels will appear in the graph to define the contents of each segment. In the example, we might want the contents of cells A5 . . A8 to appear in the graph next to each segment. To accomplish this we

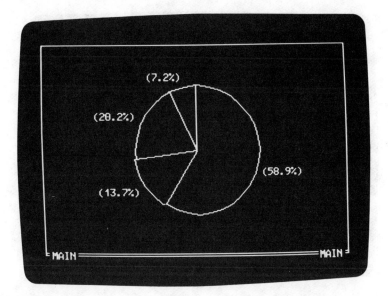

Figure 12.36

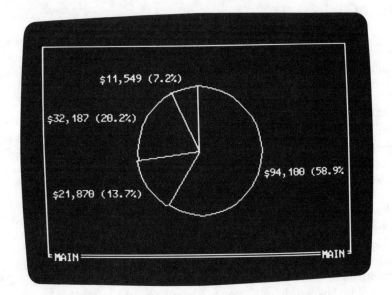

Figure 12.37

would change the **X** range from F5 . . F8 to A5 . . A8 using the **1st-Settings R**ange **X** command. Figure 12.38 shows a graph that includes labels. Unfortunately, there is no easy way to enter both the labels and the actual values into the graph.

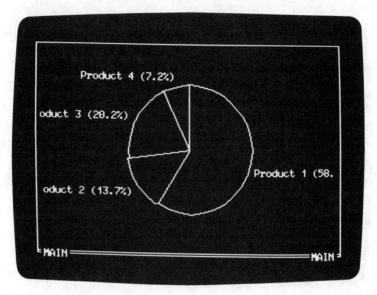

Figure 12.38

Pie Chart Options

Pie charts are in some ways the least complex of all of Symphony's graph types. Many of Symphony's graph options, like Grids, X- and Y-Scales, Legends, and Data-Labels have no application in pie charts. There are, however, a couple of interesting options that can be used with pie charts.

Exploded and Shaded Segments

One improvement of Symphony over 1-2-3 is the ability to "explode" one or more of the segments of a pie chart. Exploded segments are highlighted by being pulled out slightly from the center of the graph. The ability to explode pie charts is related to Symphony's method for shading the segments of a pie chart. The ability to shade a pie chart corrects one of the biggest complaints of 1-2-3 users about that program's pie charts.

Both shading and explosion are controlled by specifying a B range for the pie chart and entering special hue codes in that range. For example, suppose you used the {**Menu**} **G**raph 1st-Settings **R**ange **B** command to designate G5 . . G8 as the B range for our pie chart. If we don't enter any numbers in those cells, the graph will still look like it does in Figure 12.38. However, if we enter the number 1 in cell G5, the first segment of the pie will be shaded. If you enter a 2 in cell G6, the second segment will also be shaded.

As with all of Symphony's graphs, the exact effect of these hue codes depends on the type of monitor you have and on the status of the 2nd-Settings Other Color command. If you have a color monitor and set the Color command to On, the segments will appear in different colors. If the Color command is on but you have a monochrome display attached to a graphics adapter (as in a Compaq), the segments will be shaded. If the color option is off, the segments will contain different crosshatch patterns.

The B range is also used to designate those segments (if any) that you want to "explode." To explode a section, simply enter a number between 100 and 107 in the B range cell you want to explode. For example, to explode segment 1 in our example graph, enter the code 100 in cell G5.

The last digit in the explosion code controls the hue of the segment. For example, the code 100 is equivalent to the hue code 0, and 103 is equivalent to the hue code 3.

Figure 12.39 shows a graph with exploded and shaded sections. You can see how these features make the graph more dramatic and easier to understand.

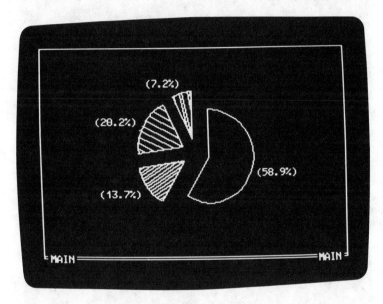

Figure 12.39

There are a couple of important things to notice about the B range. First notice that our B range is situated in the column next to the A range and includes the same number of cells as the A range. Although the B range can be located anywhere in the sheet you desire, and can include as many cells as you want, orienting it as we did will help you avoid a great deal of confusion.

If your B range includes fewer cells than the A range, only the segments that have a corresponding B range can be formatted. For example, if our B range in the example had been G5 .. G6, we would only have been able to format segments 1 and 2.

Aspect Ratio

Another new addition to Symphony's pie charts is the ability to change the aspect ratio of the graph. *Aspect ratio* is a complex term that describes the relationship between the height of a pie chart and its width. Symphony allows you to choose any aspect ratio from

.1 to 10. The default setting, 1, creates a perfect circle. Settings less than 1 flatten the pie chart. The graph in Figure 12.40 was drawn with an aspect ratio of .5. A ratio greater than 1 squeezes the graph, making it higher than it is wide. Figure 12.41 shows a graph that was drawn with an aspect ratio of 2.

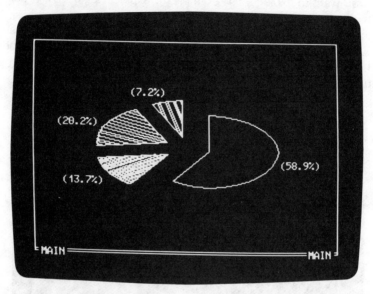

Figure 12.40

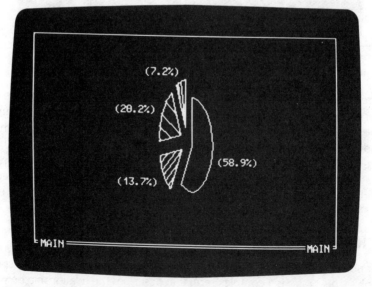

Figure 12.41

For the most part, aspect ratios below about .25 and above 3 result in graphs that are difficult to read. Smaller changes in the aspect ratio, however, can create some interesting variations on the standard pie chart.

Negative Amounts

One of the big problems with pie charts is that they cannot illustrate a set of numbers that includes negative numbers. (This is a fault of all pie charts, not just those created by Symphony. Think about it for a second—can you think of a way a negative segment could be illustrated on a pie chart?)

In Symphony, a segment that represents a negative number would be identical to a segment representing the corresponding positive number. For example, Figure 12.42 shows the pie chart that would result if you changed the entry in cell F5 from 94,100 to − 94,100. It is impossible to tell the difference between the two graphs.

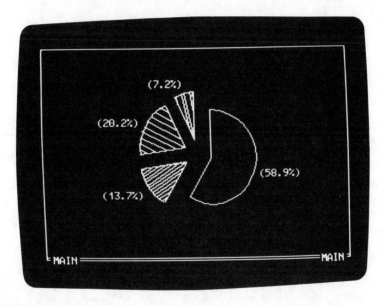

Figure 12.42

XY GRAPHS

XY graphs, sometimes called scatter diagrams, are used to show the relationship between two characteristics of a set of data. For example, you may have seen scatter plots that illustrate things like the relationship between age and annual income, or between annual income and the frequency of dining out, or between number of employees and the annual sales of several companies. Scatter plots are used widely by scientists and engineers, less commonly by business people.

Symphony's XY graphs are very much like the program's line graphs, with one important exception. In line graphs, as in all other Symphony graphs, the numbers along the X axis are just labels for the graph. In XY graphs, however, the numbers on the X axis are coordinates that help define the position of the points in the graph. For this reason, the XY graph is the only Symphony graph that requires three pieces of information: a graph Type, an A range, and an X range.

Figure 12.43 shows a simple worksheet that we'll use in building our XY graph. The figures in column A represent the weight of ten individuals. Column B shows the height of those individuals.

```
    -----A---------B---------C---------D---------
 1    Weight    Height                          |
 2       210       70                           |
 3       145       66                           |
 4       168       69                           |
 5       225       75                           |
 6       156       71                           |
 7       167       67                           |
 8       201       69                           |
 9       139       67                           |
10       183       74                           |
11       250       77                           |
12                                              |
    ======================================MAIN=
```

Figure 12.43

Before beginning to create the XY graph, use the {**Menu**} Graph 1st-Settings **N**ame **I**nitial **S**ettings command to clear the current settings sheet. Now issue the **T**ype **XY** command to select the correct type. Next, issue the **R**ange command, select the A option, and point to the range A2 . . A11. Then select the X option and specify the range B2 . . B11. Figure 12.44 shows the graph that results from these commands.

The numbers along the X axis in this graph represent the heights of the individuals in our group. The Y-axis numbers are the weights of these individuals. As you might expect, the graph shows a positive relationship between height and weight; that is, in general, as height increases, weight increases.

You're probably wondering about the spider web of lines in the graph. The lines exist because Symphony's default Format for XY graphs (and line graphs, as we saw earlier) is Both (Lines and Symbols). However, because the data points in XY graphs are usually not related, the lines in an XY graph are not very meaningful. For this reason, you'll nearly always want to use the Symbols format for your XY graphs. To change the format of this graph to Symbols, issue the 1st-Settings **F**ormat **A S**ymbols command. Figure 12.45 shows the graph without lines.

Notice also that in our sample graph, two individuals were 67 inches tall, so both of these points appear above the 67 point on our graph. An XY graph is the only Symphony graph where two data points can share the same X value. If you ponder it for a moment,

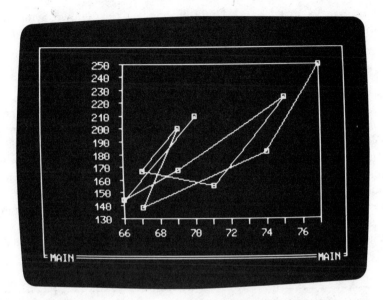

Figure 12.44

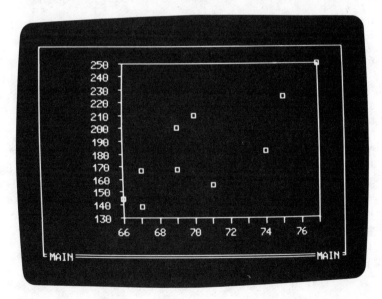

Figure 12.45

you'll realize that you cannot create a line graph that has two points "stacked" like these.

Many 1-2-3 users were hoping that Symphony would have the ability to plot a regression line on an XY graph. A regression line represents the mathematically computed trend suggested by the data points. A scatter plot that includes a regression line is easier to understand than one that does not. Unfortunately, Lotus let us down. Symphony does not have this ability.

HIGH-LOW-CLOSE-OPEN GRAPHS

The last of Symphony's graph types, High-Low-Close-Open, is the only graph type offered by Symphony that was not included in 1-2-3. A high-low-close-open graph is a very specialized graph used almost exclusively for tracking the activity in financial markets. However, this type of graph can be used to plot other data sets that, like stock-market data, require multiple readings within a time period. For example, a high-low graph could be used to plot the range of temperatures experienced in a given city across twelve months.

The example data we'll use to build a high-low-close-open graph is shown in Figure 12.46. This sample worksheet shows the high, low, closing, and opening prices for the stock of Integrated Software, Inc., a mythical rising star of the software industry.

```
      ------A---------B---------C---------D--------E------
  1   Stock: Integrated Software, Inc.                    |
  2     Date       High        Low      Close     Open    |
  3    6/25/84       58         54         57       55     |
  4    6/26/84       57         55         56       57     |
  5    6/27/84       56         54         54       56     |
  6    6/28/84       55         49         52       54     |
  7    6/29/84       54         49         54       52     |
  8                                                        |
      ==================================================MAIN=
```

Figure 12.46

Begin by initializing the settings sheet with the {**Menu**} Graph 1st-Settings Name Initial-Settings command. Issue the 1st-Settings Type command and select High-Low-Close-Open. Now you need to define four data ranges, one for the high values, one for the low values, one for the closing values, and one for the opening values. As shown in the following list, in high-low-close-open graphs the A range should always contain the high values, the B range the low values, the C range the closing values, and the D range the opening values.

Range	Values
A	High
B	Low
C	Close
D	Open

In our sample graph, the A range is B3 .. B7, the B range is C3 .. C7, the C range is D3 . . D7, and the D range is E3 .. E7. Figure 12.47 shows the graph that results from these settings.

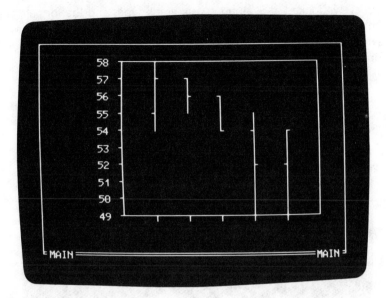

Figure 12.47

Interpreting a high-low-close-open graph can be tricky. As you can see, each day's activity is represented by a line. The top of the line is the daily high price, while the bottom is the low price. The opening price is represented by the small mark on the left side of the line, and the closing price by a similar mark to the right of the line. Long lines indicate wide daily variations in price, while short lines show that the price of the stock was relatively stable during that day.

Like pie charts, high-low-close-open charts can't use many of Symphony's formatting options. The 1st-Settings Format, 1st-Settings Data-Labels, and 1st-Settings Legends commands have no effect on this type of graph. Of course, you can add titles to a high-low-close-open chart, and you can format the Y-Scale and X-Scale. In fact, because Symphony tends to squeeze the top and bottom edges of high-low-close-open graphs, you'll nearly always want to specify manually the upper and lower limits of this type of graph. Figure 12.48 shows the sample high-low-close-open graph formatted in this way.

Although we used all four ranges in our sample graph, you can create graphs that show only the high value for a series of days, or only the high and low values, or the high, low, and closing values without the opening price. To create a high-only graph, you would select High-Low-Close-Open as the graph type but would specify only one data range (A). To create a high-low graph, you would specify an A range (the high values) and a B range (the low values). For example, to create a high-low graph from our sample data, you would specify B3 . . B7 as the A range and C3 . . C7 as the B range. Figure 12.49 shows this graph.

If you think about it for a minute, you'll realize that a high-low-close graph is essentially the same as a high-low-close-open graph in situations where the opening price on one day and the closing price on the next day are the same.

Now that we've looked at Symphony's six graph types and the formats and other graphic enhancements Symphony offers, we'll take a look at graph windows. Graph windows make it possible to display several different graphs on the screen of your computer at one time.

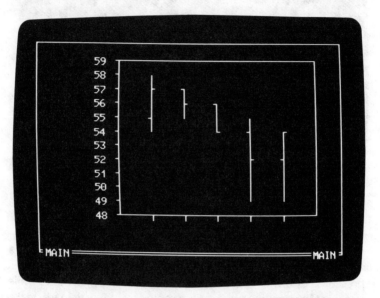

Figure 12.48

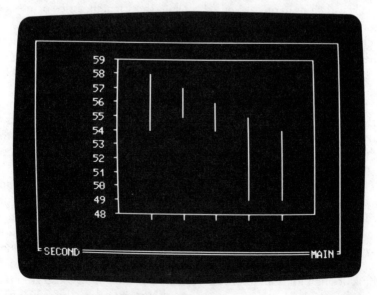

Figure 12.49

CHAPTER THIRTEEN
GRAPH WINDOWS

Up to this point, we have assumed that all graphs are created from within a SHEET window by using the {Menu} Graph command and that graphs can be viewed only one at a time by issuing the Preview command. But Symphony also allows you to set up one or more graphics windows and attach these windows to different graph settings, making it possible to have several active graphs at once.

The function of GRAPH windows depends greatly on the choices you made when installing Symphony. If you have a graphics monitor and have specified one of the install options that calls for text and graphics to share the monitor (the shared mode), Symphony allows you to set up one or more graphics windows, which makes it possible to view graphs at the same time as a SHEET or a DOC window.

If you installed Symphony in the toggle mode, you can still set up as many graph windows as you want, but you cannot display graphs and text on the screen at one time. When a graph window is displayed in the toggle mode, any windows containing text disappear from the screen. Similarly, when windows containing text are displayed, all GRAPH windows appear as blank space on the screen.

If you have two monitors, you probably installed Symphony in the dual mode. In this case, all graph windows appear only on your graph monitor and all text windows appear only on the text display.

In this chapter, we'll demonstrate the effect of each command in both the shared and toggle modes. But before we start fooling around with windows, we need to create two simple graphs. Issue the {**Services**} New command to reset the entire worksheet. Enter a few numbers in the range A1 .. C5, as shown in Figure 13.1. Next, issue the {**Menu**} Graph 1st-Settings command. Set the Type option to Bar and the Range A option to A1 .. A5. Press [Esc] twice to return to the Graph menu, and press Preview to view the sample graph, which should look like Figure 13.2.

Now issue the 1st-Settings Name Create command to create a new settings sheet named SECOND. Issue the 1st-Settings Name Initial-Settings command to reset the settings in this new sheet. Finally, use the 1st-Settings Type Line command and the 1st-Settings Range A command to a create a line graph from the data in B1 .. B5. This graph is shown in Figure 13.3.

```
    ------A---------B---------C---------D------
1        123        999       100                |
2        234        888       200                |
3        345        777       300                |
4        456        666       400                |
5        567        555       500                |
6                                                 |
    ======================================MAIN=
```

Figure 13.1

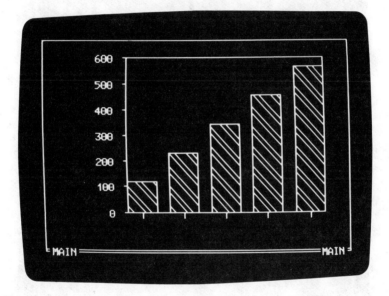

Figure 13.2

Our sheet now contains two graphs: one is a line graph defined by the settings sheet SECOND, and the other is a bar graph defined by the settings sheet MAIN. Although these graphs are trivially simple, they demonstrate the function of GRAPH windows.

CREATING A WINDOW

To create a graphics window, simply issue the {**Services**} **W**indow command. The Window menu appears in the control panel:

       Use   Create   Delete   Layout   Hide   Isolate   Expose   Pane   Settings   Quit

Choose the **C**reate option. Symphony then prompts you for the name of the new window. For now, just call the window PICTURE. Next, Symphony asks for the window type. Because we are setting up a graphics window, we'll choose GRAPH.

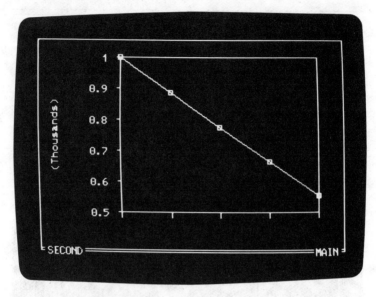

Figure 13.3

Now Symphony displays the entire screen in inverse video, as shown in Figure 13.4. At this point, you need to tell Symphony where on the screen you want this new window to be located. If you press [Enter], the new window PICTURE appears as a full-screen window. In the toggle mode you'll probably want full-screen graph windows, because they give you the best possible view of your graphs.

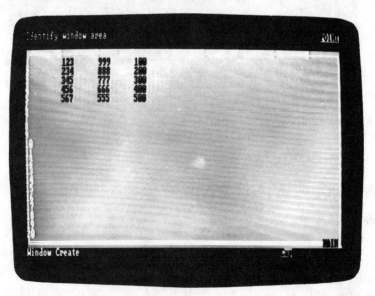

Figure 13.4

When working in the shared mode, however, you'll frequently want to create partial-screen GRAPH windows that can be overlaid on larger SHEET and DOC windows. Partial-screen GRAPH windows allow you to view both graph and text information at the same time on the screen.

The conventional location for partial-screen GRAPH windows is the bottom-right corner of the screen. If the graph to be displayed in the window is particularly wide, you might consider creating a window that spans the bottom of the screen. These are only suggestions, however. You can make your graph windows any size you want and place them anywhere on the screen you think best. Remember also that you can use the {Zoom} key to temporarily expand a partial-screen window into a full-screen window.

For an example, let's create a graph window that fills the bottom-right quarter of the screen. When Symphony prompts you for the range, press the period key twice. This shifts the "free" corner of the range from the lower-right corner to the upper-left corner. Now press the ↓ key ten times. The screen should now look like Figure 13.5. Next, press the → key 40 times. The screen should now look like Figure 13.6.

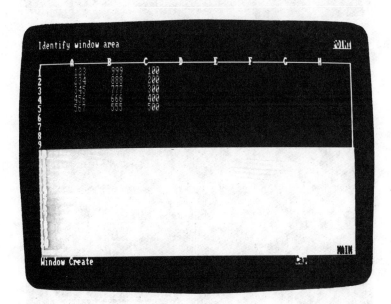

Figure 13.5

Press **[Enter]** to lock in the range you have specified. Symphony now displays the Window Settings menu in the control panel. For now, skip past this menu by pressing **Q**uit.

If your copy of Symphony is installed in the toggle mode, your screen should now be blank except for the new GRAPH window, as shown in Figure 13.7. If you have selected the shared mode, the new window overlaps the original window on your screen, as shown in Figure 13.8.

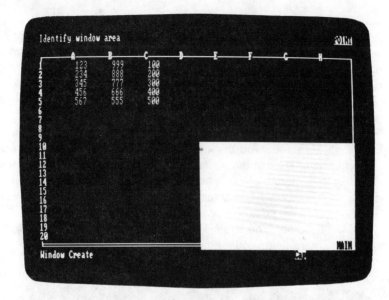

Figure 13.6

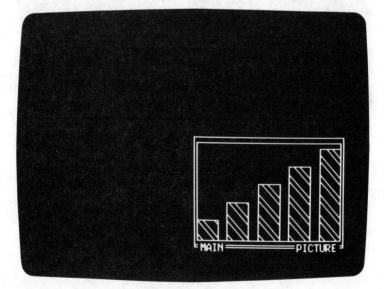

Figure 13.7

Notice that the new window displays the graph we just created and that the window name, PICTURE, appears in the lower-right corner of the window. The legend in the lower-left corner of the window should say MAIN. This legend indicates that this window is attached to the graph settings sheet named MAIN, which defines the graph displayed in the window.

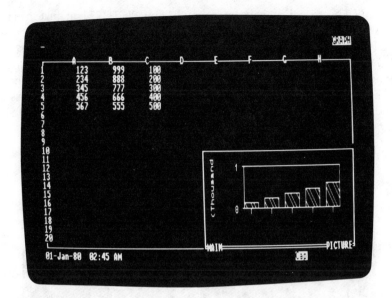

Figure 13.8

ATTACHING A WINDOW TO A SETTINGS SHEET

Every GRAPH window must be attached to a graph settings sheet. When we say that a window is attached to a graph, we mean that the window and the graph are linked so that the window always displays the attached graph. Although it is possible for one graph to be attached to two windows, it is not possible to attach two graphs to a single window at the same time.

Symphony automatically attaches new GRAPH windows to the settings sheet MAIN— even if MAIN is not the active settings sheet or if the name MAIN has been deleted. If MAIN is blank or has been deleted, Symphony will beep at you when the window is created (and every time you jump to it with the {Window} key), and the new window will be empty.

At times, of course, you'll want to display a graph other than MAIN through a GRAPH window. For example, if you want to display two different graphs on the screen at once, at least one of the two GRAPH windows needs to be attached to a settings sheet other than MAIN. You can easily attach any graphics window to any named graph, however, with the {Menu} Graph Attach command.

To attach a settings sheet to a GRAPH window, you must use the {Window} key to bring that window to the top of the stack and then issue the {Menu} **A**ttach command. Symphony then provides a menu of the graph settings sheet names in the worksheet. Usually, you'll select one of the names from this list. After you make a selection, the graph defined by the selected settings sheet appears in the GRAPH window.

For example, let's reattach the GRAPH window PICTURE in our example to our other graph settings sheet, SECOND. First, use the {**Window**} key to bring PICTURE to the top of the stack. (If you are in the toggle mode, you'll know PICTURE is at the top of the stack when you can see PICTURE and the SHEET window named MAIN has disappeared. In the shared mode, you'll know PICTURE is at the top when PICTURE seems to cover part of MAIN.) Issue the {**Menu**} Attach command and select SECOND from the list of available settings sheets. (If you are working in the shared mode, the GRAPH window PICTURE goes blank and the SHEET window MAIN appears while you are issuing the command.) Press **Quit** to leave the menu mode. The line graph defined by SECOND should now appear in the window PICTURE, as shown in Figure 13.9.

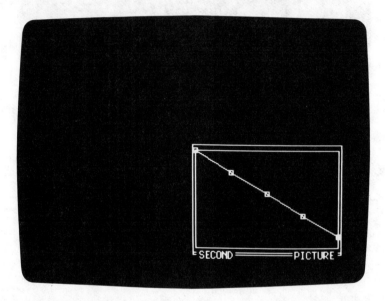

Figure 13.9

Attaching a Window to an Undefined Settings Sheet

It is possible to attach a GRAPH window to a nonexistent settings sheet by typing a new settings sheet name in response to the Attach command instead of choosing one of the names in the list provided by Symphony. In the previous example, for instance, if instead of selecting SECOND from the list you had supplied the settings sheet name THIRD in response to the Attach prompt, the window PICTURE would have been attached to a nonexistent settings sheet.

Any GRAPH window that is attached to a nonexistent settings sheet will be blank. In other words, attaching a settings sheet to a nonexistent settings sheet *does not force Symphony to create that settings sheet.* If you want to see a graph in the window, you must create a settings sheet and supply the necessary information.

The same thing happens if you use the Name Initial-Settings command to reset a settings sheet to which a GRAPH window is attached. If the settings for the current graph are incomplete, Symphony will beep whenever it attempts to display the window attached to that graph. Unless you plan to reattach the window to another graph, you'll probably want to use the Service Window Delete command to remove the window from the worksheet.

CREATING MORE WINDOWS

Suppose you wish to view both graphs in this worksheet—MAIN and SECOND—at the same time. To do this, you must define another GRAPH window. Begin by issuing the {**Services**} **W**indow **C**reate command and providing the name PICTURE2 for the new window. Orient PICTURE2 in the lower-left corner of the worksheet, making sure that it does not overlap the window named PICTURE. (Remember that the period key is used to move the anchored corner of the window range while you are defining the window.) If the two windows overlap, only one will be displayed at a time.

The new window PICTURE2 is automatically attached to the settings sheet MAIN. If all went well, your screen should now resemble Figure 13.10 (if Symphony is in the toggle mode) or Figure 13.11 (if Symphony is in the shared mode).

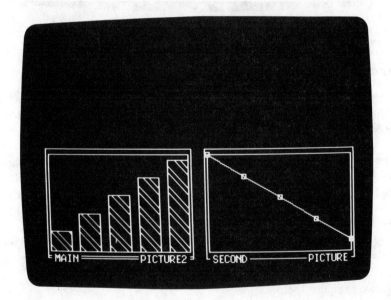

Figure 13.10

Now you can see why settings sheet names are so important. We used the names SECOND and MAIN to attach our two graphs to two separate windows. In Symphony, you can display two or more graphs at the same time by attaching the names of the settings sheets that define those graphs to two or more different windows. Former users of 1-2-3 will recognize this as a substantial improvement over that program's ability to display only one graph at a time.

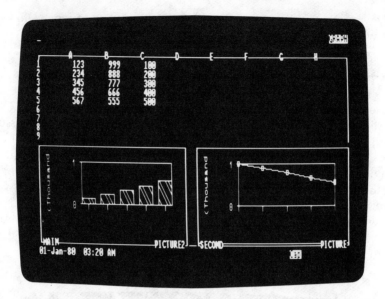

Figure 13.11

SHUFFLING THE WINDOWS

As you learned in Chapter 11, the {Window} key is used to shuffle the stack of windows in a worksheet. If you press {**Window**} from the window PICTURE2, the SHEET window MAIN should pop to the top of the window stack, and both graph windows should disappear. Figure 13.12 shows the worksheet in this condition.

Pressing {**Window**} again moves PICTURE to the top of the stack. If Symphony is in the toggle mode, MAIN disappears from the screen completely, and both PICTURE and PICTURE2 appear on the screen. If Symphony is in the shared mode, PICTURE overlaps the lower-right corner of MAIN, and PICTURE2 remains hidden. Figures 13.13 and 13.14 show the screen as it looks in both situations.

Pressing {**Window**} once more returns you to PICTURE2. If Symphony is in the toggle mode, this screen looks just like the one in Figure 13.13. In the shared mode, however, PICTURE2 and PICTURE both overlap MAIN at the bottom of the worksheet. This condition is shown in Figure 13.15.

DEFINING A GRAPH FROM WITHIN A GRAPH WINDOW

In the examples above, we created our graphs using the {Menu} Graph command from within a SHEET window. It is also possible, however, to define a graph from within a GRAPH window.

For example, suppose you have created a full-screen GRAPH window called PICTURE3 and that PICTURE3 is currently attached to the graph MAIN. Suppose further

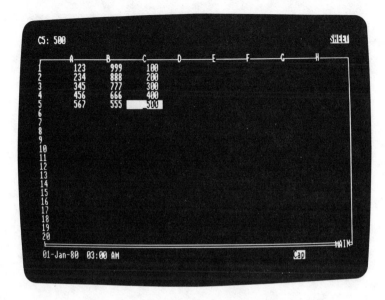

Figure 13.12

that you want to create a pie chart of the numbers in cells C1 . . C5. From within the GRAPH window PICTURE3, press {**Menu**}. The following menu appears:

       Attach   1st-Settings   2nd-Settings   Image-Save

Notice that this menu is very similar to the one that appears when you issue the {Menu} Graph command from within a SHEET window. In fact, the only difference

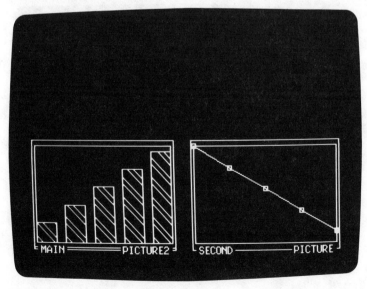

Figure 13.13

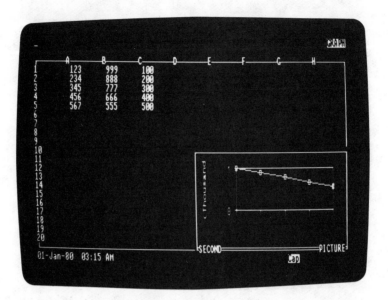

Figure 13.14

between the two menus is that the first choice on the GRAPH window menu is Attach and the first choice on the SHEET Graph menu is Preview. The Preview command can only be issued from the SHEET Graph menu. You cannot preview a graph from a GRAPH window.

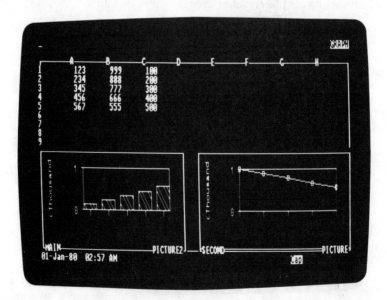

Figure 13.15

If you are working in the toggle mode, the GRAPH window PICTURE3 goes blank when you issue the {Menu} command. This occurs because in the toggle mode Symphony cannot display both the graph and the text on the screen at the same time. If you are in the shared mode, the graph remains on the screen.

Choose the 1st-Settings command from this menu. The 1st-Settings menu and the first page of the MAIN settings sheet then appear on the screen, as shown in Figure 13.16. Before you do anything else, issue the Name Create command, specifying **THIRD** as the name for the new settings sheet, and then issue the Name Initial-Settings command to initialize this new sheet.

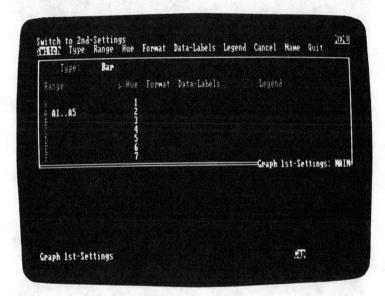

Figure 13.16

Next, issue the **T**ype command and select the **P**ie option to make our new graph a pie chart. Finally, select the **R**ange **A** option and point to the range C1 . . C5.

Although the graph THIRD is now defined, we're not quite finished. Press **[Esc]** or **Q**uit enough times to redisplay the GRAPH window PICTURE3. Figure 13.17 shows this window. Notice that PICTURE3 is still attached to the graph settings sheet MAIN. *Creating a graph from within a window does not automatically attach the window to the created graph.* In other words, although you created the graph THIRD from within the window PICTURE3, you must still attach PICTURE3 to THIRD if you want to view the graph through that window.

To attach PICTURE3 to THIRD, issue the {Menu} **A**ttach command from within PICTURE3 and specify THIRD as the settings sheet name to which you want to attach the window. After the window is attached to THIRD, the screen should look like Figure 13.18.

Although you can view several different graphs simultaneously on the screen, only one graph settings sheet is active in a given worksheet at any time. When we say that a

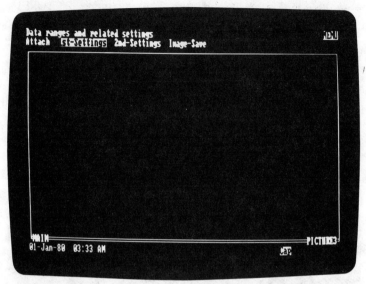

Figure 13.17

settings sheet is active, we mean that it is the sheet affected by any Graph commands you issue.

To see what we mean, press {**Window**} to bring the GRAPH window PICTURE2 to the top of the stack and issue the {**Menu**} 1st-Settings command. Notice that the active settings sheet in this window is THIRD, even though the window PICTURE2 is attached to the graph MAIN.

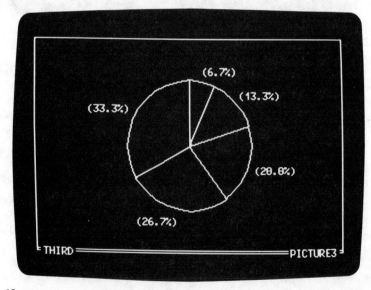

Figure 13.18

To test your understanding of this important concept, issue the **1**st-Settings **N**ame **U**se command from within PICTURE2 and make MAIN the active settings sheet. Now press {**Window**} to jump into the GRAPH window PICTURE. Remember that the graph SECOND is attached to window PICTURE. But if you press {**Menu**} 1st-Settings from within PICTURE, you'll see that the active graph settings sheet is MAIN.

This concept is very confusing to some Symphony users, but it needn't be. Just remember that only one settings sheet is active at any time, even though many different graphs can be viewed at different times through different windows.

WHAT-IF WITH GRAPHICS

Up to this point, we have been working with Graph windows that overlap the underlying SHEET window. In this configuration, the graphs disappear every time the SHEET window is brought to the top of the stack. However, it is possible to arrange the GRAPH and SHEET windows so that they do not overlap. If you are working in the shared mode and arrange the windows this way, you can keep your graphs in view while you are working in the SHEET window.

(The following discussion applies only to the shared mode. If you are using the toggle mode or the dual mode, skip to the next section.)

Before we demonstrate this feature, we must use the {**Services**} **W**indow **D**elete command to remove the GRAPH window **PICTURE3** from the worksheet; we won't need it in this example. Now issue the Window Use command to bring the SHEET window MAIN to the top of the stack.

Remember that MAIN is a full-screen SHEET window and that the GRAPH windows PICTURE and PICTURE2 overlap the bottom half of MAIN. We want to change the layout of the SHEET window so that it covers only the top half of the screen and is no longer overlapped by the two GRAPH windows. To change the layout of this window, issue the {**Services**} **W**indow **L**ayout command. Symphony then displays the entire screen in inverse video, as shown in Figure 13.19.

Now press ↑ ten times to change the layout from a full screen to a half screen. When you have the proper layout, press **[Enter]** and then **[Esc]** to return to the SHEET mode. The screen of your computer should now look like Figure 13.20.

Press {**Window**} to bring PICTURE onto the screen and again to bring PICTURE2 onto the screen. Figure 13.21 shows this configuration.

Now press {**Window**} once more to move the cell pointer to the window MAIN. If everything is set up correctly, the cell pointer should appear in SHEET, but the windows PICTURE and PICTURE2 should still be visible.

Move the cell pointer to cell A1 and enter the number 1000. As soon as you press **[Enter]**, both GRAPH windows (PICTURE and PICTURE2) should be redrawn immediately. The graph MAIN (in window PICTURE2) should change because cell A1 is a part of the A range for that graph. Now move to cell B2 and enter the number 1. Once again the graphs in PICTURE and PICTURE2 should be redrawn. This time the graph SECOND, which is displayed in the window PICTURE, should change.

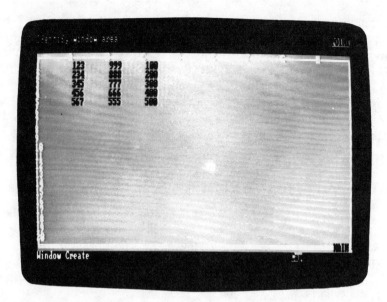

Figure 13.19

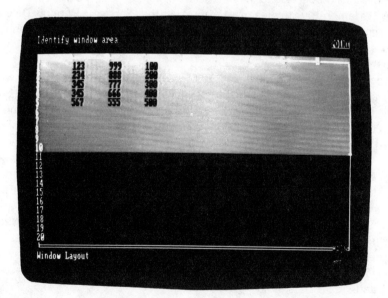

Figure 13.20

Because all three windows are visible at one time, you are able to make changes in the SHEET window and immediately see the effect of those changes on the two graphs. The ability to view a graph reflecting your changes to the sheet as soon as you make them is one of Symphony's most exciting capabilities. Because it is sometimes easier to

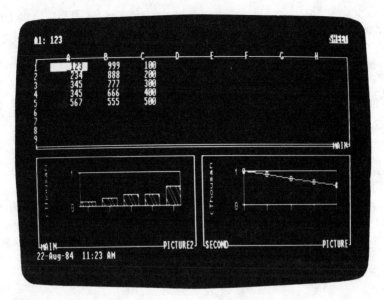

Figure 13.21

gauge the effect of a change in the worksheet from a graph than from a table of numbers, you might find yourself playing "what-if" games with Symphony's graphics—making changes to the worksheet and then letting Symphony's graphics show you the effect of those changes.

AUTO-DISPLAY

As you saw in the previous section, Symphony automatically redraws any visible graphs whenever you change the worksheet on which those graphs are based. If you want the graphs to be redrawn, this capability is very handy. Remember, though, that Symphony needs several seconds to draw a graph, so redrawing three or four graphs can waste ten seconds or more. If the change to the worksheet is minor (for example, if you merely correct a misspelling in a label and thus don't want the graphs to be redrawn), this delay can be extremely irritating.

Fortunately, Symphony offers a solution to this problem. You can use the {**Services**} **W**indow **S**ettings **A**uto-Display **No** command to instruct Symphony not to redraw a GRAPH window each time you change the underlying worksheet. The {Services] Window Settings Auto-Display No command is similar to the {Menu} Settings Recalculation Method Manual command, which instructs Symphony not to recalculate the sheet until the user tells it to do so.

Auto-Display is not a global command, so you must change the Auto-Display setting for each window in the worksheet individually. For example, to suppress automatic display of the window PICTURE, you press {Window} to move this window to the top of the stack and then issue the {Services} Window Settings Auto-Display No command. If you also want to suppress automatic display in the window PICTURE2, you issue the command again from within that window.

You can set Auto-Display to No for a SHEET window. However, there is no real reason to do so. In fact, setting Auto-Display to No for a SHEET window may cause the window to be "hidden" during the times you most wish to view it.

Once the Auto-Display setting in a window is set to No, the window is not redrawn until you specifically request Symphony to do so. When you issue the Auto-Display No command and make a change to the worksheet, the message DRAW appears at the bottom of the screen, indicating that the changes are not reflected in the graph.

There are two ways to redraw a graph when Auto-Display is set to No: moving its window to the top of the window stack with the {Window} key or pressing the {Draw} key. If you want to redraw one window while leaving the others unchanged, you can use the {Window} key of the {Services} Window Use command to bring that window to the top of the stack. However, the DRAW message remains visible until you press {Window} enough times to redraw all the windows. The other way to redraw a window is to press the manual redraw key {Draw}. When you press {Draw}, *all* visible graphs are immediately redrawn.

CHAPTER FOURTEEN
PRINTING GRAPHS

As we saw in Chapter 12, Symphony is capable of creating many different kinds of graphs. We also saw that Symphony offers a wide range of formatting commands. But Symphony cannot make printed copies of the graphs it creates. The job of printing graphs falls to the PrintGraph program.

The PrintGraph program is one part of Symphony that will be familiar to anyone who printed graphs created by 1-2-3. There is very little difference between the version of this program that works with 1-2-3 and the version that works with Symphony.

INSTALLING SYMPHONY FOR PRINTING GRAPHS

If you want to use the PrintGraph program to print the graphs you create in Symphony, you need to include one or more graphics device drivers in your driver set. If you don't expect to print graphs, you don't need to install a graphics device driver. Of course, if you need to use PrintGraph at some future time you can easily modify your driver set or create a new set that includes a graphics driver.

At the time this book went to print, Symphony offered drivers for more than 30 graphics output devices, including nearly every popular graphics printer and plotter. The chances are very good that your printer or plotter is included in the list. If for some reason your printer is not included in Symphony's list, don't panic. Lotus frequently adds new drivers to the library, so it is likely that your device will be covered soon. In addition, many printer and plotter manufacturers offer drivers for their printers that work with Symphony. You may be able to include one of these in your driver set.

The Install program allows you to include more than one graphics output device in a driver set. If, for example, you have both an Epson LQ-1500 graphics printer and an HP Plotter, you might include drivers for both of these devices in your driver set. If you do, you can use either device to print graphs; however, you can use only one graphics device at a time. The PrintGraph program includes a command that lets you choose which of the devices in the driver set you wish to use to print a given graph. For more information on the Install program, see Chapter 2.

ACCESSING PRINTGRAPH

The PrintGraph program is stored on the PrintGraph program disk. You can load PrintGraph directly from DOS by placing the PrintGraph disk in the default drive and typing **Pgraph** next to the DOS prompt (probably A> if your system uses floppy disks). You can also load PrintGraph through the Lotus Access System by typing **Access** next to the DOS prompt and then selecting PrintGraph from the Access System menu.

If you want to jump from Symphony into PrintGraph, you must first return either to the Access System menu or to the DOS prompt by issuing the {**Services**} **E**xit **Y**es command from within Symphony. If you entered Symphony directly from DOS, Symphony returns you to the DOS prompt when you exit the program. If you entered Symphony through the Access System, you return to the Access System menu when you leave Symphony.

If you have a hard disk, the PrintGraph program is probably stored on the same disk as Symphony. Before you try to enter PrintGraph from a hard disk, make sure you are in the correct subdirectory. For example, if your Symphony program files (including Print-Graph) are located on the subdirectory C:\Symphony, you need to issue the command

C>CD\Symphony

to jump into that subdirectory before you try to load PrintGraph.

After you load PrintGraph into your computer, the PrintGraph Settings sheet and menu appear on your screen, as shown in Figure 14.1.

```
Copyright 1982, 1983, 1984 Lotus Development Corp.  All Rights Reserved.   MENU
-------------------------------------------------------------------------------
Set graphic options
Image-Select  Settings  Go  Align  Page  Exit
===============================================================================
      GRAPH       IMAGE OPTIONS                      HARDWARE SETUP
      IMAGES      Size               Hue             Graphs Directory:
      SELECTED    Top        .395   1 Black            A:\
                  Left       .750   2 Black          Fonts Directory:
                  Width     6.500   3 Black            A:\
                  Height    4.691   4 Black          Interface:
                  Rotate     .000   5 Black            Parallel
                                    6 Black          Printer Type:
                  Font              7 Black
                  1  BLOCK1                          ACTION OPTIONS
                  2  BLOCK1                          Pause: No    Eject: No
```

Figure 14.1

SETTING UP PRINTGRAPH

If this is the first time you've worked with PrintGraph, you need to do some house-keeping before you actually print a graph. Before you can print anything, you must tell PrintGraph which disk drives contain your graph files and your font files, which graphics device should be used to print the graphs, which interface that device is connected to, and several other parameters.

All of these parameters are controlled by the Settings command on the PrintGraph menu. When you select Settings, the following menu appears:

Image   Hardware   Action   Save   Reset   Quit

The Image option is used to adjust the size, color, and other characteristics of the graphs being printed. Because this setting tends to vary from print session to print session while the other options remain more or less constant once they are set, we'll cover the other options first. The Image option will be discussed in a few pages.

Hardware

You use the Hardware option to tell PrintGraph which directory contains the graph and font files and which interface and graphics device to use when printing your graphs. The following menu appears when you select Hardware:

Graphs-Directory   Fonts-Directory   Interface   Printer   Quit

Graphs-Directory and Fonts-Directory

Graphs-Directory allows you to tell Symphony where to look for the graph files (.PIC files) that you want to print. Similarly, Fonts-Directory tells Symphony which directory contains the fonts you want to use. The fonts are located on the PrintGraph disk unless you copy them to another disk (which I don't recommend). If you have a computer with two floppy disk drives, you'll probably want to mount the PrintGraph disk in drive A and the disk containing your .PIC files in drive B. In this configuration, the Fonts-Directory should be A:\ and the Graphs-Directory B:\.

If you have a computer with a single floppy disk drive, both the Graphs-Directory and Fonts-Directory settings will be A:\. With this configuration, you need to switch disks whenever you print or preview a graph so that PrintGraph can read both the data and the font files.

If you have a hard disk (or if you create subdirectories on your floppy disks, which I strongly discourage), you also need to specify the subdirectory for these settings. For example, if your fonts are stored in the subdirectory Symphony on your hard disk, the Fonts-Directory setting would be C:\Symphony. If your graph files are stored on the subdirectory Symphony Files, the Files-Directory setting would be C:\Symphony\Files.

Printer

When you installed Symphony, you created a driver set that probably contained drivers for at least one graphics output device. If you didn't specify a graphics device driver when you installed Symphony, you'll need to modify your driver set to include such a driver before you can print graphs.

Because Install lets you include more than one graphics device driver in your driver set, PrintGraph includes a command, Settings Hardware Printer, that lets you select the device you want to use in a printing session. When you issue this command, a list of the available drivers appears on the screen, as shown in Figure 14.2.

Suppose you want to use the Epson LQ-1500 to print a graph. You point to this option in the list by pressing ↓ and select it by pressing the space bar. A crosshatch (#) appears next to the option you select, as shown in Figure 14.3. After you select the device, press [Enter] to return to the Hardware menu.

```
Copyright 1982, 1983, 1984 Lotus Development Corp.  All Rights Reserved.   POINT
--------------------------------------------------------------------------------
Select graph output device

================================================================================
        Type of Graphic Output
----------------------------------------  [Space] moves mark
    HP 7475A Plotter, 8.5 x 11 paper       [Enter] selects marked device
    Epson LQ-1500, density 2               [Escape] exits, ignoring changes
                                           [Home] goes to beginning of list
                                           [End] goes to end of list
                                           [Up] and [Down] move cursor
                                                List will scroll if cursor
                                                moved beyond top or bottom
```

Figure 14.2

```
Copyright 1982, 1983, 1984 Lotus Development Corp.  All Rights Reserved.   POINT
--------------------------------------------------------------------------------
Select graph output device

================================================================================
        Type of Graphic Output
----------------------------------------  [Space] moves mark
    HP 7475A Plotter, 8.5 x 11 paper       [Enter] selects marked device
  # Epson LQ-1500, density 2               [Escape] exits, ignoring changes
                                           [Home] goes to beginning of list
                                           [End] goes to end of list
                                           [Up] and [Down] move cursor
                                                List will scroll if cursor
                                                moved beyond top or bottom
```

Figure 14.3

Only one graphics output device can be active at a time. However, if you have more than one graphics device driver in your driver set, you can easily switch from one to another with the Hardware Printer command.

Interface

After you tell PrintGraph which device to use to print a graph, you must tell the program which interface that device is connected to. This command offers four options: Parallel, Serial, Second Parallel, and Second Serial.

The chances are good that your computer has only one parallel interface and that your graphics printer is attached to that interface. Most printers for the IBM PC and compatible computers use a parallel interface. Because PrintGraph's default interface is Parallel, you probably won't need to adjust this setting.

However, if you have a device that is attached to a serial interface (many plotters are serial devices) or if your graphics printer is attached to a second parallel interface, you need to adjust this setting.

In addition, if you are using a serial device you also need to specify a baud rate. The baud rate determines how fast information is sent from your computer to the printer. It is important to understand that the baud rate you select for sending data from your computer must match the baud rate at which your printer expects to receive the data. If you send data at 1200 baud to a printer that is expecting to receive data at 300 baud, the data will be garbled in transmission, ruining your printed graph. Symphony lets you choose baud rates from 110 to 19200. Most serial printers and plotters are configured to receive data at 1200 baud.

Action

Action is the last of the "permanent" PrintGraph settings. Use the Action option on the Settings menu when you want to print several graphs in one print session. This command controls the action taken by your printer before and after it prints a graph. Action offers only two options: Pause and Eject.

Setting Action Pause to Yes forces PrintGraph to pause before printing each graph, giving you time to feed new paper into the printer, change pens on the plotter, or make any other necessary adjustments. Using Pause ensures that you'll have time to set up your printer before each graph in the series is printed. The pause is signaled by an intermittent beep. After the needed adjustments have been made, press [Space bar] to begin printing.

If Action Pause is set to No, PrintGraph does not pause before printing each graph. If you plan to select graphs for printing one at a time, you'll probably want to set Action Pause to No.

If you want to print just one graph on each piece of paper, the Action Eject setting should be Yes. This setting forces Symphony to send a pagefeed command to the printer after each graph is printed. This setting is useful only when you fill your printer with continuous-form paper. If you use single-sheet paper, use the Action Pause command to stop printing long enough to feed another sheet of paper into the printer.

If you are using a plotter, Symphony prompts you to insert a new piece of paper in the plotter instead of automatically feeding a new sheet of paper (most plotters cannot feed new sheets of paper automatically). After you insert the new sheet, press **[Space bar]** to resume printing.

If Action Eject is set to No, PrintGraph does not send a pagefeed to the printer between graphs. In this configuration, PrintGraph can print several graphs on one sheet of paper. However, if PrintGraph determines that the entire graph does not fit in the space remaining on that sheet, the program automatically advances to the top of the next form before beginning the next graph.

Save

The settings for Printer, Interface, and Action are not likely to vary too much from print session to print session. In other words, most Symphony users always use the same graphics output device attached to the same interface as well as the same Action commands every time they print graphs.

Fortunately, once you've defined the Printer, Interface, and Action settings, you can save the Settings sheet for future use. Use the Settings Save command to save the current PrintGraph settings. Symphony immediately saves the current settings into the file

PGRAPH.CNF. Because the settings are always saved under this name, Symphony does not display a prompt before saving the file. Only the message

Writing configuration file

appears at the top of the screen. The file is saved onto the directory from which you loaded PrintGraph. If you are using a two-disk-drive system, this will probably be drive A. On a hard disk system, the file might be saved onto a subdirectory of drive C.

Each time you load PrintGraph into your computer, it searches the system directory for the file PGRAPH.CNF and loads the settings stored in the file into the PrintGraph Settings sheet. Of course, once the default settings have been retrieved, you can adjust any setting you want during a printing session. However, unless you save those new settings before exiting PrintGraph, they will be lost. The next time you load PrintGraph, the settings in PGRAPH.CNF will be the default.

Reset

The Settings Reset command returns all PrintGraph settings to the default settings. In other words, Reset restores the settings in the Settings sheet to the default settings in the Settings sheet in the file PGRAPH.CNF. This command is handy if you want to return quickly to the default after you have made a few settings adjustments to print a special file.

GETTING THE DATA

In Chapter 12 we created a simple line graph and saved that graph for printing under the name GRAPH1.PIC. We'll use that graph as our example in this chapter. If you worked along with the text in Chapter 12 and saved your own version of the file, you can work along with the text here.

The first selection on the PrintGraph menu, Image-Select, allows you to select one or more .PIC files for printing. When you issue the Image-Select command, Symphony displays a list of all the .PIC files stored on the current Graph directory, as shown in Figure 14.4.

```
Copyright 1982, 1983, 1984 Lotus Development Corp.  All Rights Reserved.   POINT
--------------------------------------------------------------------------------
Select graphs for output

================================================================================
   PICTURE      DATE      TIME      SIZE
  --------     ------    ------    ------        [Space] turns mark on and off
   GRAPH1     01-01-80   21:12      796          [Enter] selects marked pictures
   GRAPH2     01-01-80   21:12      796          [Escape] exits, ignoring selections
   GRAPH3     01-01-80   21:12      796          [Home] goes to beginning of list
                                                 [End] goes to end of list
                                                 [Up] and [Down] move the cursor
                                                      List will scroll if cursor
                                                      moved beyond top or bottom
                                                 [Draw] displays highlighted picture
```

Figure 14.4

You can select one or more graphs for printing by pressing ↓ or ↑ to point to the name(s) of the graphs you wish to print. To select a file, press [Space bar]. After you select a graph, a crosshatch (#) appears next to its name. Figure 14.5 shows how the computer screen looks after you select the file GRAPH1.

```
Copyright 1982, 1983, 1984 Lotus Development Corp.  All Rights Reserved.   POINT
--------------------------------------------------------------------------------
Select graphs for output

================================================================================
    PICTURE      DATE      TIME      SIZE
    --------------------------------------      [Space] turns mark on and off
 #  GRAPH1     01-01-80   21:12       796       [Enter] selects marked pictures
    GRAPH2     01-01-80   21:12       796       [Escape] exits, ignoring selections
    GRAPH3     01-01-80   21:12       796       [Home] goes to beginning of list
                                                [End] goes to end of list
                                                [Up] and [Down] move the cursor
                                                    List will scroll if cursor
                                                    moved beyond top or bottom
                                                [Draw] displays highlighted picture
```

Figure 14.5

If the current directory contains several .PIC files, you can select as many graphs as you wish. To select a second graph, you need only point to its name in the list and press [Space bar].

To change your mind about a selection, just move the cursor to the name of that .PIC file and press [Space bar] again. The crosshatch disappears, and the file will not be printed.

While in the Image-Select list, you might want to press the {Draw} key to display on the screen a preview of the graph currently being pointed to. Figure 14.6 shows a preview of the Graph GRAPH1. Notice that this graph does not look exactly like the graph we created and saved in Chapter 12. For example, the second title line in this preview is smaller than the first title line. When we created the graph in Symphony, these lines were the same size. Don't be alarmed by these differences; the preview graph is constructed using the fonts and other settings in the Settings sheet and shows an approximation of the graph as it will look when printed.

After you have selected all of the graphs you wish to print in the current session, press [Enter]. Symphony returns to the main PrintGraph menu and displays the name(s) of the selected graphs in the Settings sheet, as shown in Figure 14.7.

Image

PrintGraph gives you a great deal of control over the final appearance of your printed graphs. For example, you can control the size and orientation of the graph on the paper; the fonts used to print the Y-Scale numbers and any other titles, legends, or labels in the graph; and the colors (if any) assigned to each range in the graph. All of these parameters are controlled by the Settings Image command. The Settings Image menu looks like this:

Size   Font   Hue   Quit

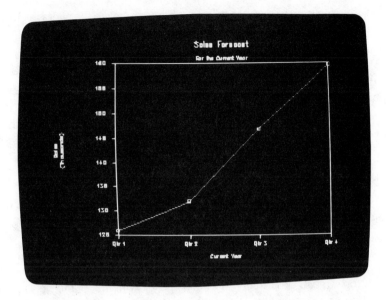

Figure 14.6

```
Copyright 1982, 1983, 1984 Lotus Development Corp.  All Rights Reserved.   MENU
-------------------------------------------------------------------------------
Select graphs for printing
Image-Select  Settings  Go  Align  Page  Exit
===============================================================================
        GRAPH      IMAGE OPTIONS                      HARDWARE SETUP
        IMAGES     Size                Hue            Graphs Directory:
        SELECTED   Top         .395    1 Black          B:\
           GRAPH1  Left        .750    2 Black        Fonts Directory:
                   Width      6.500    3 Black          A:\
                   Height     4.691    4 Black        Interface:
                   Rotate      .000    5 Black          Parallel
                                       6 Black        Printer Type:
                   Font                7 Black          Epson LQ/2
                    1  BLOCK1                         ACTION OPTIONS
                    2  BLOCK1                           Pause: No    Eject: No
```

Figure 14.7

Size

The Size option controls the size and orientation of printed graphs. This command offers the following options:

Full   Half   Manual   Quit

Full   The Full setting instructs Symphony to set the height and width of each printed graph so that it fills a standard 8½-by-11 inch sheet of paper. In addition, the Full option rotates graphs 90 degrees clockwise from the vertical, meaning that the Y-axis of the graph is printed horizontally and the X-axis is printed vertically. Because most graphs are wider (along the X-axis) than they are tall, Symphony can make the average graph larger if it is printed sideways, better filling the available space.

Half   The default setting, Half, prints graphs in an 8½-by-5½ inch space (approximately half of an 8½-by-11 inch sheet of paper). Half also sets Rotation to 0 degrees, meaning that the X axis is horizontal. Use the Half setting whenever you want to print two graphs on a single page.

Manual   As you probably guessed, the Manual option allows you to control the height, width, rotation, and other parameters manually. The Settings Image Manual menu looks like this:

> Left   Top   Height   Width   Rotation   Quit

The Left and Top options control the left and top margins that will be used when printing graphs. The default setting for the Left margin is .395 inches; the default Top margin is .75 inches.

Height and Width control the height and width of the graph. You can use these settings to make your printed graph as small or as large as you wish. Remember, though, that if the graph is too large to be printed on a single page, PrintGraph attempts to break the graph into two or more pieces. The results of PrintGraph's efforts are rarely satisfactory, so you're probably better off keeping your graphs on one page. On the other hand, although PrintGraph can print very small graphs, you are unlikely to be able to read them.

Changing the height and width can be tricky for several reasons. First, when the Image setting is Full or Half (implying that PrintGraph automatically sizes graphs to fit the available space), PrintGraph always sets the ratio between the height and width at 1 to 1.385. If the graph is 6 inches high, it will be 6 times 1.385, or 8.078, inches wide. If you decide to change the height or width of a graph, and you want to preserve the standard ratio of height to width, you need to make some calculations.

For example, if you want to create a graph that is 4 inches wide, and you want the graph to have the standard 1 to 1.385 ratio of height to width, you need to compute the correct height with the formula 4/1.385. Similarly, if you want to print a graph 3 inches high using the standard ratio, you need to compute the correct width with the formula 1.385 × 3.

The Rotation setting controls the orientation of the graph on the page. As you have seen, in the Full mode PrintGraph automatically prints graphs "sideways," rotated 90 degrees clockwise. In the Half mode the graph is not rotated at all. If you select the Manual sizing option, the Rotation command lets you control the rotation of your graphs.

Most of the time you'll want to use a rotation factor of 0 (X axis horizontal) or 90 (X axis vertical). Occasionally you'll want to use a factor of 180 to print the graph upside down or of 270 to print the graph sideways with the Y axis at the bottom of the graph.

If you decide to rotate a graph manually, you'll probably need to adjust your Height and Width settings. Height and Width are absolute measures; that is, the Height setting always controls the vertical dimension of the graph and the Width setting always controls the horizontal dimension. When rotation is 0, the Height setting controls the length of the Y axis and the Width setting controls the length of the X axis. If the graph is rotated 90 degrees, however, the Height setting controls the X axis (which is now vertical) and the Width setting controls the Y axis (which is now horizontal).

For example, if you set the Height to 6 and the Width to 8.070 (a standard ratio) and then rotate the graph 90 degrees, the X axis will be 6 inches long and the Y axis will be 8.07 inches long—an X/Y ratio of .74. To restore the proper proportions of the graph, you need to switch the Height and Width settings, changing Height to 8.07 and Width to 6.

If you select a rotation factor other than the right-angle factors 0, 90, 180, or 270, the axes of your graph are printed at angles to the edges of your paper. Unless you set the height and width very carefully, rotation factors other than 0, 90, 180, and 270 change your rectangular graphs to rhomboids and your circular pie graphs to ellipses. Unless you have a pressing need for a graph that is not square with your paper, I recommend that you avoid any nonright-angle rotation factors.

If you must use an odd rotation factor, you'll probably need to compute the height and width of your graphs using the ROTATE.WRK worksheet file that Lotus provides on the PrintGraph disk. This template automatically computes the correct Height and Width settings for a graph with a certain rotation and certain desired X-axis and Y-axis lengths. This template is explained thoroughly in the Symphony Reference Guide.

Using the size options   The Size settings can be used to print graphs in any size and at any location you want on the page. For example, suppose you had created and printed a document that filled three quarters of a printed page.

You want to print a graph in the remaining space. Let's assume that the empty rectangle begins 6.5 inches from the top of the page and 4 inches from the right margin. The rectangle itself is 4 inches wide by 4.5 inches high.

If you choose the Size Manual option and set the Rotation to 0, the Top margin to 7.5 inches, the Right margin to 4.5, the Width to 3, and the Height to 2.166 inches (calculated as 3/1.385) the graph will be printed in the rectangle. Assuming that the paper was properly aligned in the printer or plotter, a person reading the page probably wouldn't be able to tell that it had been printed in two operations.

Font

The next option on the Settings Image menu, Font, allows you to specify the font (typestyle) that you want PrintGraph to use when printing the titles, legends, data labels, and other text and numbers in the graph. Symphony offers 11 fonts: Bold1, Roman1, Italic1, Block1, Forum, Script, Lotus, Roman2, Script2, Italic2, and Block2 (the last four are simply bold versions of other fonts). For an illustration of all 11 fonts, see the Symphony Reference Guide.

PrintGraph allows you to use two different fonts in each graph. Font 1 is used in the first title line only. All other alphabetic and numeric charaters in the graph are printed in Font 2. Font 1 and Font 2 can be the same (in fact, if you do not define Font 2, PrintGraph automatically uses the same font for both) or different.

The default setting for Font 1 is Block1. If you don't want to use the default, simply issue the **Settings Image Font 1** command and point to one of the 11 font options in the list PrintGraph displays. To select the font, press **[Space bar]** and then **[Enter]** to return to the Image menu. Figure 14.8 shows the Font menu.

```
Copyright 1982, 1983, 1984 Lotus Development Corp.  All Rights Reserved.   POINT
-----------------------------------------------------------------------------
Select font 1


==============================================================================
            FONT NAME      SIZE
            ----------     ----
         #  BLOCK1         5737        [Space] moves mark
            BLOCK2         9300        [Enter] selects marked font
            BOLD           8624        [Escape] exits, ignoring changes
            FORUM          9727        [Home] goes to beginning of list
            ITALIC1        8949        [End] goes to end of list
            ITALIC2        11857       [Up] and [Down] move cursor
            LOTUS          8679            List will scroll if cursor
            ROMAN1         6863            moved beyond top or bottom
            ROMAN2         11847
            SCRIPT1        8132
            SCRIPT2        10367
```

Figure 14.8

Unless you have a very high quality printer or plotter, you should probably avoid the boldface fonts Block2, Roman2, Script2, and Italic2. These fonts are difficult to produce and probably will not look very good when printed by a standard graphics printer like the Epson FX-100.

Hue

If you have a color graphics printer or a plotter, PrintGraph will print color graphs. If, like me, you use a more mundane graphics device, you cannot print your graphs in color. In fact, if your graphics device is not a color printer or a plotter, you can't even use the Hue command. In other words, if you're going to use a black-and-white graphics printer, you might as well skip to the next section.

In Chapter 12 you learned that Symphony automatically assigns a different hue to each range in a graph and that you can define hues for the segments of a pie chart. You also saw that with the command sequence Symphony Graph 1st-Settings Hue, you can change the hue assigned to any range.

The PrintGraph Settings Image Hue command lets you assign a color to each of the hue codes in the graph you are printing. Suppose you are printing a graph that includes three data ranges: A, B, and C. These ranges have the default Symphony Hue settings: A is 2, B is 3, and C is 4. Now, in PrintGraph, you want to assign a color to each of these hues. Issue the **Settings Image Hue** command. The screen will look like Figure 14.9.

Notice that the device specified in this Settings sheet is the HP 7475A plotter, a color graphics device. If this device were not selected, PrintGraph would not allow us to change the color of each hue from the default, black.

Now select hue 1. The menu shown in Figure 14.10 now appears. You can select the color used to print any part of the graph that has been assigned hue code 1 simply by pointing to a color and pressing [Enter]. After choosing the color you wish for hue code 1, select hue codes 2 and 3 and repeat the process.

```
┌──────────────────────────────────────────────────────────────────────────┐
│ Copyright 1982, 1983, 1984 Lotus Development Corp. All Rights Reserved.  MENU │
│ ────────────────────────────────────────────────────────────────────────── │
│ Select color for Hue 1                                                       │
│ 1   2   3   4   5   6   7   Quit                                             │
│ ══════════════════════════════════════════════════════════════════════════ │
│      GRAPH        IMAGE OPTIONS              HARDWARE SETUP                   │
│      IMAGES       Size              Hue      Graphs Directory:                │
│      SELECTED     Top        .395   1 Black    B:\                            │
│         GRAPH1    Left       .750   2 Black  Fonts Directory:                 │
│                   Width     6.500   3 Black    A:\                            │
│                   Height    4.691   4 Black  Interface:                       │
│                   Rotate     .000   5 Black    Parallel                       │
│                                     6 Black  Printer Type:                    │
│                   Font              7 Black    HP 7475A, 8x11                  │
│                   1  BLOCK1                  ACTION OPTIONS                    │
│                   2  BLOCK1                  Pause: No   Eject: No             │
└──────────────────────────────────────────────────────────────────────────┘
```

Figure 14.9

```
┌──────────────────────────────────────────────────────────────────────────┐
│ Copyright 1982, 1983, 1984 Lotus Development Corp. All Rights Reserved.  MENU │
│ ────────────────────────────────────────────────────────────────────────── │
│ Output Hue 1 in Black color                                                  │
│ Black   Red   Green   Blue   Orange   Lime   Gold   Turquoise   Violet   Brown │
│ ══════════════════════════════════════════════════════════════════════════ │
│      GRAPH        IMAGE OPTIONS              HARDWARE SETUP                   │
│      IMAGES       Size              Hue      Graphs Directory:                │
│      SELECTED     Top        .395   1 Black    B:\                            │
│         GRAPH1    Left       .750   2 Black  Fonts Directory:                 │
│                   Width     6.500   3 Black    A:\                            │
│                   Height    4.691   4 Black  Interface:                       │
│                   Rotate     .000   5 Black    Parallel                       │
│                                     6 Black  Printer Type:                    │
│                   Font              7 Black    HP 7475A, 8x11                  │
│                   1  BLOCK1                  ACTION OPTIONS                    │
│                   2  BLOCK1                  Pause: No   Eject: No             │
└──────────────────────────────────────────────────────────────────────────┘
```

Figure 14.10

When you print the graph, PrintGraph uses the colors you have selected to print each hue in the graph. If the same hue code is used for several different ranges in the graph, all of these ranges appear in the same color.

Remember that in Symphony the X range also has a hue. The default hue for the X range is 1, so the color you assign to hue code 1 is used to print the X range and all of the labels and titles in the graph.

If you save your graph with the Color setting at No, each range in the graph is filled with crosshatches according to Symphony's pattern. If you wish, PrintGraph will print these crosshatches in color.

PrintGraph offers enough colors to print every range in your graph in a different shade. Remember, though, that the colors in the final printed graph are limited by the capabilities of your printer or plotter. If your printer can print only four colors, the printed graph will include only four colors.

PRINTING THE GRAPH

Once you have defined the size, hue, and font settings, you're ready to print. Before you begin, make sure there is paper in the printer or plotter and that the printer or plotter is attached and on line. Also before you begin, you should press Align to set Print-Graph's top-of-form counter.

When you are ready to print, press **Go**. PrintGraph first loads the fonts that you have selected for printing the selected graphs from the Fonts Directory. Because this process takes a few seconds, PrintGraph displays the message

> Loading Font A:\BLOCK1

and after a moment, the message

> Generating Picture B:\GRAPH1

Once the fonts are loaded, Symphony begins to print the graph. Graph printing is very slow, especially if you selected one of the double-, triple-, or quadruple-density options for your graphics output device. Be patient; the result is usually worth the wait.

If you selected the Eject Yes setting, Symphony ejects the page containing the printed graph when the printing is finished. Otherwise, you can use the Page command to eject the page containing the graph, or you can use the printer's controls to advance the paper. You can, of course, leave the paper alone and print another graph on the same page.

To print another graph, simply select that graph with the Image-Select command and make any desired changes to the settings. Before you print the second graph, be sure to press Align to reset Symphony's top-of-form counter. To print the new graph, just press **Go**.

If you choose more than one graph in a session, PrintGraph prints the graphs one by one in the order you selected them. You can tell the program to pause between each graph to allow you time to put another sheet of paper in the printer or plotter. However, you cannot change any of the PrintGraph settings between graphs. Each graph in the sequence is printed the same size and uses the same fonts and hues. If you want each graph to be formatted differently, you must select and print them one at a time.

A SAMPLE GRAPH

Figure 14.7 shows the settings sheet used to print GRAPH1. This graph was printed half size, with no hues and with the standard Block1 fonts. Figure 14.11 shows the printed graph.

Figure 14.12 shows a slightly modified settings sheet. In this case, the graph was printed full size using Forum for Font 1 and Block 1 for Font 2. The printed graph is shown in Figure 14.13.

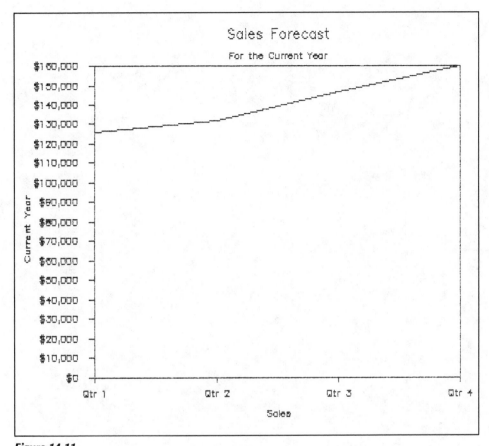

Figure 14.11

Copyright 1982, 1983, 1984 Lotus Development Corp. All Rights Reserved.   MENU
```
-------------------------------------------------------------------------
Select graphs for printing
Image-Select  Settings  Go  Align  Page  Exit
=========================================================================
       GRAPH      IMAGE OPTIONS                  HARDWARE SETUP
       IMAGES     Size              Hue          Graphs Directory:
       SELECTED   Top        .250   1 Black        B:\
          GRAPH1  Left       .500   2 Black      Fonts Directory:
                  Width     6.852   3 Black        A:\
                  Height    9.445   4 Black      Interface:
                  Rotate   90.000   5 Black        Parallel
                                    6 Black      Printer Type:
                  Font              7 Black        Epson LQ/2
                  1   FORUM                      ACTION OPTIONS
                  2   BLOCK1                       Pause: No    Eject: No
```

Figure 14.12

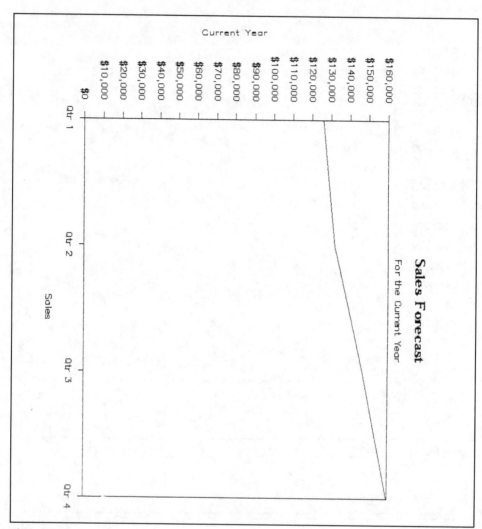

Figure 14.13

PART
V

WORD PROCESSING

CHAPTER FIFTEEN
BASIC EDITING AND FORMATTING

Up to this point, we've concentrated on Symphony's abilities as an electronic spreadsheet and business graphics program. This section of the book covers Symphony's third major capability, word processing.

Symphony's word processor has most of the capabilities of standalone word processing software. For example, Symphony has all of the editing features you would expect to find in a word processor, including the ability to insert, delete, erase, move, and copy characters, lines, and blocks of text. Symphony also allows you to embed special format characters to create underlined, boldface, italic, or other specially formatted text.

Symphony goes beyond the basics of word processing, however. For instance, it can number pages automatically, search for a string of characters and replace it with another, specially format an entire document or document sections, and store formats for reuse in later documents.

For users of 1-2-3 or the Symphony spreadsheet, the Symphony word processor has one tremendous advantage: it is easy to learn. If you are familiar with the general command structure of 1-2-3 or the Symphony SHEET environment, you can learn the basics of Symphony word processing without much effort. Another advantage is Symphony's ability to integrate word processing with the other functions of the program. For example, you can embed a spreadsheet in a document or send a document to another computer via the communications function.

Before you read further, you should become familiar with a couple of terms. In the DOC environment, the equivalent of the cell pointer is the *cursor*. The cursor (the blinking block on the screen) indicates where in a document you are working. It is similar to the cell pointer of the spreadsheet except that it is only one character wide.

In the DOC environment the word *column* refers to the cursor location on a line. (Note that the word has a different meaning in the SHEET environment.) On most computers, a full screen is 80 columns wide, with column 1 at the left edge of the screen and column 80 at the right edge of the screen.

GETTING INTO THE DOC ENVIRONMENT

When you first load Symphony, you see the worksheet through a familiar SHEET window. Before you can take advantage of Symphony's word processing capabilities, you must create a DOC window. You can do this in one of two ways: either by creating a whole new window or by converting the current window into a DOC window.

Assume that you have loaded Symphony into your computer and that you are looking at the worksheet through a SHEET window called MAIN. To convert MAIN into a DOC window, simply press the {**Type**} key. The Type menu, explained in Chapter 11, appears:

SHEET   DOC   GRAPH   FORM   COMM

To convert the current window into a DOC window, select DOC from the menu by typing **D** or by moving the pointer to the DOC option and pressing **[Enter].** You are now looking at the worksheet through a DOC window and thus are in Symphony's word processing environment. Figure 15.1 is a picture of the blank document worksheet.

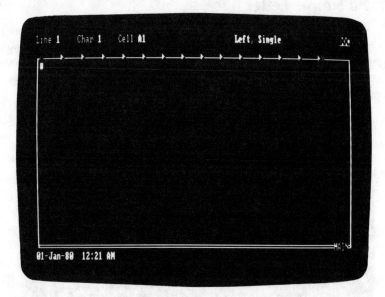

Figure 15.1

This window looks different from the familiar SHEET window. First, notice that the row numbers and the column letters you saw on the SHEET window are missing from the DOC window. Instead of showing column letters, the top border of a DOC window is a ruler line that indicates the default right margin, left margin, and tab settings. Also notice the small blinking cursor in the upper-left corner of the screen. The legend

Line 1   Char 1   Cell A1

in the upper-left corner of the screen identifies the current location of the cursor, in this case Line 1, Character 1 of the empty worksheet. We'll call this the *home position.* (Character 1 is what I refer to as Column 1, using the word *column* as explained above. I prefer column because it designates a position on the screen that may or may not contain text, while character seems to imply that there is a letter or number at that position. For example, a standard video display shows 80 columns per line, but a single line may contain only 20 characters.) Notice also the "Cell A1" near the center of the top line on the screen. This part of the legend is a clue to what you are really seeing when you look at the worksheet through a DOC window.

In the upper-right corner of the screen, you will see

Left, Single DOC

This tells you that the document you create on this worksheet will be flush left and single spaced. Both of these features will be explained later in this chapter. The "DOC" that appears in inverse video is, of course, an indication that you are working in the DOC environment.

Creating a Simple Letter

Once you are in the DOC environment, creating a letter or other document is just as simple as typing. You can begin typing from the home position or use the ↓ key to begin typing a few lines from the top. To get the feel of the word processor, you might want to enter the sample letter shown in Figures 15.2 and 15.3. Figure 15.2 shows the letter as it appears on the screen, and Figure 15.3 is the printed version of that letter.

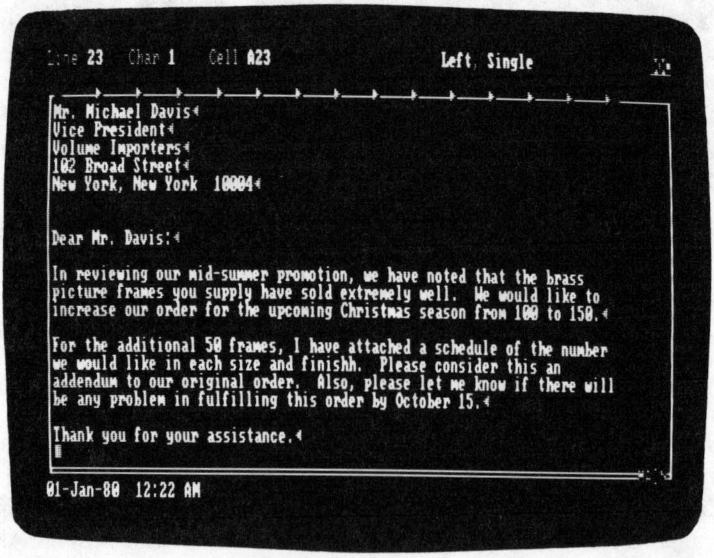

```
Line 23    Char 1    Cell A23                    Left, Single                 ::
   →    →    →    →    →    →    →    →    →    →    →    →    →    →    →
Mr. Michael Davis◄
Vice President◄
Volume Importers◄
102 Broad Street◄
New York, New York  10004◄


Dear Mr. Davis:◄

In reviewing our mid-summer promotion, we have noted that the brass
picture frames you supply have sold extremely well.  We would like to
increase our order for the upcoming Christmas season from 100 to 150.◄

For the additional 50 frames, I have attached a schedule of the number
we would like in each size and finishh.  Please consider this an
addendum to our original order.  Also, please let me know if there will
be any problem in fulfilling this order by October 15.◄

Thank you for your assistance.◄
█
```
01-Jan-80 12:22 AM

Figure 15.2

After you type each line in the address header at the top of this letter, you must press **[Enter]** to jump down to the next line. In the DOC environemnt, the [Enter] key is similar to the [Return] key on a typewriter.

However, there is no need to press [Enter] at the end of each typed line in the main body of the letter. Instead, Symphony automatically moves the cursor down a line and to the left whenever the text reaches the right margin, as indicated by the ruler line at the top of the window. In effect, Symphony divides your document into lines of approximately equal length. This capability is called *word wrap.*

```
August 22, 1984


Mr. Michael Davis
Vice President
Volume Importers
102 Broad Street
New York, New York  10004


Dear Mr. Davis:

In reviewing our mid-summer promotion, we have noted that the brass
picture frames you supply have sold extremely well.  We would like to
increase our order for the upcoming Christmas season from 100 to 150.

For the additional 50 frames, I have attached a schedule of the number
we would like in each size and finish.  Please consider this an
addendum to our original order.  Also, please let me know if there will
be any problem in fulfilling this order by October 15.

Thank you for your assistance.

Yours truly,



Ann Brown
Buyer
```

Figure 15.3

How Symphony Stores Documents

After creating the letter, use the {**Switch**} key to toggle the window MAIN from the DOC environment to the SHEET environment. Figure 15.4 shows MAIN as a SHEET window.

Obviously, the text you entered through the DOC window has been stored in the basic Symphony worksheet. In fact, Symphony stored every line in the document as long, left-aligned labels in column A of the worksheet. If you position the cell pointer at the beginning of the date line (cell A1), the control panel looks like this:

A1: 'August 22, 1984

Similarly, if you move the cell pointer to cell A13, the following message appears in the control panel:

A13: 'In reviewing our mid-summer promotion, we have noted that the brass

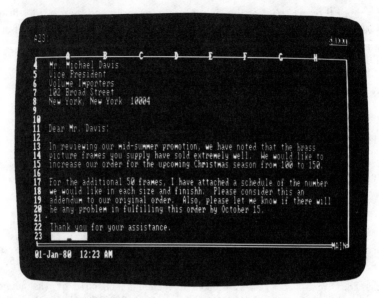

Figure 15.4

If you move the cursor to column B, the control panel is blank, indicating that there is no entry in column B. The reason is that Symphony treats the entire line of text as a long label in column A of the worksheet.

It is important that you understand this point, so we'll repeat it again: Any text you enter through a DOC window is stored as a long label in the left-most column of that DOC window—usually column A.

One disadvantage of the Symphony word processor is that the entire Symphony program and your entire worksheet are stored in RAM. This makes the word processor relatively slow when you are working with a document that is longer than 7 or 8 pages, and it makes it impossible to create documents longer than perhaps 25 or 30 pages (depending on the amount of memory in your computer).

To avoid this problem, you can split a long document into several shorter files. Symphony allows you to adjust page numbers so that page numbering is continuous from one file to another. This entire section on Symphony word processing was written with the Symphony word processor, using seven separate files.

There are some advantages to having the entire worksheet and the Symphony word processor stored in RAM, however. For example, rejustifying paragraphs is very fast, and, as you are creating text, there are no irritating pauses while the computer retrieves parts of the word processing program or the document from disk.

Managing Documents

There may be times when you'll create, edit, and print documents in Symphony without ever saving them into a .WRK file. For example, suppose you need to write a quick memo confirming your itinerary for an upcoming business trip. You might write the memo and print it, then use **{Services} N**ew to erase the worksheet without ever saving the memo.

However, sometimes you need to save your memos and other documents for future use. For example, suppose you are working on a long report that will take several days to write. You will certainly want to save the report to disk each night before you go home to avoid accidentally losing your work if the power fails or some friendly coworker decides to turn off your computer.

The general rules for saving and retrieving documents are identical to those for saving other worksheet files. These concepts are explained in detail in Chapter 10, so we'll cover them briefly here.

Saving a Document

To save a document, first create the document and then save the worksheet containing the document with the **{Services} F**ile **S**ave command. This creates a worksheet file containing the entire worksheet.

If the current worksheet contains more than just the document you want to save and you want to save the document into its own file, use the **{Services} F**ile **X**tract command to save only that portion of the worksheet containing the document. The extract range should be the entire range covered by the text in the document, not just the columns that actually contain the labels that make up the document. For example, suppose you have a document in lines 1 through 30 on your worksheet. Each line in the document is stored as a long label residing in column A. If you use the **F**ile **X**tract command to save this document, you cannot save cells A1 through A30 only. You must save all the cells that underlie the lines of text, so your Xtract range might be A1 through H30.

Retrieving a Document

When you are ready to reuse a saved document, begin with a blank DOC worksheet and press **{Services} F**ile **R**etrieve. Symphony prompts you with

> Name of file to retrieve:

Below this prompt you will see a menu of file names. You respond by typing the name of the file you want to retrieve next to the prompt or by pointing to the name of the file and then pressing **[Enter].**

Remember that the File Retrieve command automatically erases the entire contents of the current worksheet before it loads the file into the worksheet. If your worksheet already contains important information, you should use the **{Services} F**ile **C**ombine command to retrieve the document without erasing the contents of the worksheet. (For more on using the File Combine command, see Chapter 10.)

Once the document is loaded into the worksheet, you can edit it and add to it as you wish. If you want to resave the document again, simply repeat the **F**ile **S**ave or the **F**ile **X**tract command.

One very productive way to use a word processor is to store a standard document that can be reused in different variations. A common example of this is a contract that is virtually identical each time it is executed except for the names of the contracting parties and other details. Another common example is a standard letter, such as a sales letter, which is the same each time it is sent except for the name of the recipient and a personalized introduction. In these cases, you maintain a disk version of the standard documents and recall them into Symphony for editing each time you need to use them.

When you retrieve the standard version of a document in order to customize it for a particular use, make sure you save the custom version of the file under a new name when you are finished with the customizing steps. This will leave your standard document intact for the next time you want to create a custom document.

Doing a "Quick Save"

Because Symphony stores your entire document in RAM until you save it to disk, your Symphony documents are extremely vulnerable. If you accidentally kick your computer's electrical plug out of its socket, or if your building has a power failure, all of the work you have done since the last time you saved the document is lost.

Some word processors automatically save your work every so often, creating a backup of your work as you go along. Unfortunately, Symphony does not. We suggest that you use the {**Services**} **F**ile **S**ave command often as you are working on your document to create a disk backup. Then, if the power fails or your worksheet is destroyed for some other reason, you can simply reload the saved version and pick up where you left off.

The world's cheapest electrical line protection is a simple 60-minute kitchen timer. If you use the timer to remind you to save your work every 30 minutes or so, the most you will ever lose through a power problem is about 30 minutes of work.

GETTING AROUND A DOC WINDOW

From your experience with the SHEET mode, you already know that the arrow keys and certain other special keys allow you to move the cell pointer around the worksheet. Many of these keys have the same function in the DOC environment. The following summary will help you become adept at quick cursor movement. Mastering cursor movement will be of tremendous help as you begin to mark blocks of text you wish to move, copy, or erase.

Moving the Cursor Up and Down

Pressing the ↑ key once moves the cursor up a single line. The cursor remains in the same column as it moves up a line, whether the line contains text or is blank. (WordStar users may find Symphony's cursor movement one of the program's nicest features— WordStar doesn't allow you to move the cursor through blank lines unless you "create" those lines with carriage returns.) If you keep your finger on the ↑ key, the cursor moves up through the document continuously. The ↓ key works just like the ↑ key except that the cursor moves down instead of up.

Moving the Cursor to the Beginning or End of a Paragraph

To move to the beginning of the paragraph in which you are working, press the **[End]** key and then press ↑. Repeat this sequence if you want the cursor to jump to the beginning of the previous paragraph. To move to the end of a paragraph, press the **[End]** key and then press ↓. In response, the cursor moves to the carriage return or the first blank space after the last character in the paragraph. Repeat this sequence to move the cursor to the end of the next paragraph. If you have several blank spaces at the end of a paragraph, pressing the **[End]** key plus ↓ causes the cursor to move just beyond these blank spaces.

In moving the cursor paragraph by paragraph, it is helpful to know how Symphony defines paragraphs. Basically, Symphony treats any text that follows a paragraph delimiter as a new paragraph. Symphony recognizes the following as paragraph delimiters: a blank line, a format line, a page break, nontext cells, or a hard carriage return. You create hard carriage returns by pressing the **[Enter]** key. Do not confuse these with the carriage returns that Symphony automatically inserts at the end of each line when it wraps to the next line of text.

For example, each line in the address at the top of the letter in Figure 15.2 is treated as a separate paragraph because there is a hard carriage return at the end of each line. Therefore, if the cursor is on one of these address lines and you press **[End]** and then ↓, the cursor moves to the end of the line.

Moving the Cursor Up or Down Page by Page

Pressing the **[Pg Up]** or **[Pg Dn]** keys causes a new "page" of text to appear on your screen, with the cursor located on the center line of the screen. For example, if you are working with a full-screen window, 20 lines of text appear on the screen at one time. When you press the **[Pg Dn]** key from within this window, the 20 lines you were viewing are replaced with the next 20 lines of your document, and the cursor moves to the middle line of the screen. (Since there is no middle in 20 lines of text, the cursor moves to line 11 from the top of the screen.) If you continue to press the **[Pg Dn]** key when you reach the end of your document, Symphony brings up 20 new blank lines of the worksheet.

The [Pg Up] key works just like the [Pg Dn] key, except that your text moves up instead of down. If your document has fewer than 20 lines of text above the screen you are viewing when you press [Pg Up], Symphony brings all remaining lines into the screen.

The Lotus Symphony manuals say that [Pg Up] and [Pg Dn] cause the cursor to move up or down by 20 lines. This is not precisely true. What really happens when you press [Pg Up] or [Pg Dn] is that a new windowful of text appears on the screen. If you are working in a full-screen window, there will be 20 new lines on your screen. However, the cursor does not necessarily move 20 lines; it moves to the middle line of the new screen. Also, a window need not contain 20 lines. If you create a window of 15 lines, for instance, only 15 new lines appear on the screen when you press one of these keys, and the cursor moves to line 8, the middle.

Figures 15.5 and 15.6 illustrate the [Pg Dn] action in a full-screen window. Figure 15.5 shows the first 20 lines of a document with the cursor on line 5. Figure 15.6 shows the same document after [Pg Dn] is pressed. Notice that lines 21 to 40 are now visible in this window and that the cursor is on line 31. By the way, the cursor could have been on any

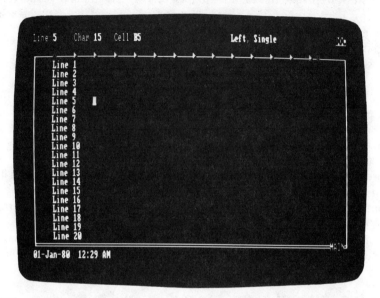

Figure 15.5

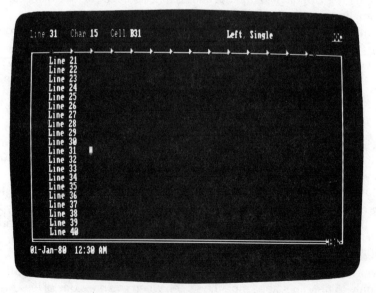

Figure 15.6

of the first 20 lines of the document in Figure 15.5 and still have moved to line 31 in Figure 15.6.

Moving the Cursor Left and Right

The ← and → keys move the cursor one character to the right or left. Holding either key down results in continuous movement right or left. When the cursor moves right and reaches the end of a line, it automatically wraps to the beginning of the line just below and continues moving right. Similarly, when the cursor moves left and reaches the beginning of a line, it jumps to the end of the line just above and continues moving left.

Moving the Cursor Word by Word

If you press the **[Ctrl]** key while pressing the → key, the cursor jumps to the blank space just before the next word to the right. Similarly, if you press the **[Ctrl]** key while pressing ←, the cursor jumps to the first character of the word to the left. If the cursor is in the middle of a word when you press **[Ctrl]** and the ← key, it jumps to the first character of that word.

If you keep holding down both the **[Ctrl]** key and either the ← or → key, the cursor moves from word to word continually. This word-by-word movement is called BIG LEFT and BIG RIGHT in the Lotus manuals. We prefer to refer to these movements as **[Ctrl]→** and **[Ctrl]←**.

Moving the Cursor to the Beginning or End of a Line

To move the cursor to the end of its line, press the **[End]** key and then press the → key. To move it to the beginning of a line, press the **[End]** key and then press the ← key. Note that repeating either of these sequences has no effect.

Moving the Cursor to the Beginning or End of a Document

To get to the beginning of your document, press the **[Home]** key. This moves the cursor to the top-left corner of your DOC window. If you began creating your document several lines down from the top of the window, pressing **[Home]** will not put the cursor on the first line of your document, but rather several lines above that, at the top edge of your window. To get to the end of your document, press **[End]**, then press **[Home]**. These keystrokes position the cursor on the blank space just past the last character in your document. If blank spaces are inserted at the end of your document, Symphony moves the cursor beyond these.

Positioning the Cursor with {Center}

You can use the {**Center**} key to place the cursor in the center of a blank line. To do this, put the cursor at the beginning of a blank line and press {**Center**}. The cursor moves to the point equidistant from the left and right margins. This procedure works only if the line on which you want to center the cursor is truly blank. If the line contains a few blank spaces, you must delete them before trying to center the cursor. To find out if a line contains blank spaces, change the Blanks Visible setting on the Format settings sheet to Yes.

The {Center} key can also be used to center a line of text. This will be explained later in this chapter.

Using [Scroll Lock] to View a Document

The [Scroll Lock] key allows you to view different parts of your document without moving the cursor. [Scroll Lock] is a toggle switch. When the scroll feature is turned on and you press any of the arrow keys, instead of the cursor moving through the text, the text itself moves. When the scroll feature is on, you see the word "Scroll" in a block at the lower-right corner of your screen.

For example, if you press **[Scroll Lock]** and then press ↑, the entire windowful of text moves down one line. The line at the bottom of the screen moves out of view and one new line at the top of the screen comes into view. Similarly, by pressing ↓ when **[Scroll Lock]** is on, you "pull" a line of text from the bottom of your screen into view and "push" the line at the top of the screen out of view.

If you continue to scroll text either up or down, the cursor remains on the same line until that line reaches the top or bottom of the screen. Then the cursor remains on the edge of the screen as text is scrolled through.

[Scroll Lock] also works with the → and ← keys. Pressing **[Scroll Lock]** and then the → key causes the 20 characters that are just off the right side of the window to come into view. At the same time, the text on the left edge of the screen is "pushed" out of view as more of the worksheet on the right is "pulled" into view, 20 characters at a time. While **[Scroll Lock]** is on, you can bring this text back into view by pressing the ← key.

[Scroll Lock] can be very useful in editing documents. For example, suppose you want to see a line that has just moved out of view at the top of your screen. Of course, you could move the cursor to the top of your screen and then press the ↑ key. But it's simpler to press the **[Scroll Lock]** key and then press the ↑ key. Similarly, if you have created a document with right margins that are wider than your screen, use **[Scroll Lock]** to view the part of your document that does not fit on the screen. [Scroll Lock] is also useful for viewing a spreadsheet, another document, or text created in a different part of the worksheet. (If you are working in a restricted window, Symphony will not allow you to scroll beyond the Restrict range. See Chapter 18 for a discussion of using windows in the DOC environment.)

Using the {Goto} Key

The {Goto} key gives you another way to move cursor in the DOC environment. After you press this key, Symphony responds with the prompt

Go to where?

You can then specify any one of the following: a line number, a printed-page/line-number combination, or a line marker.

{Goto} and a Line Number

If you specify a line number, Symphony moves the cursor to the first character on that line. For example, if you press {**Goto**} **3 [Enter]**, Symphony moves the cursor to the first character of the third line of your document.

{Goto} and a Printed Page

To specify a printed-page/line-number combination in response to the "Go to where?" prompt, type in the page number, followed by a comma and the line number. For example, if you want to go to the fifth line on the second printed page, press {**Goto**} **2,5 [Enter]**. This places the cursor on the first character of this line.

To jump to a specific line on a specific page, however, you must know how Symphony has divided the document into pages. As you learned in Chapter 9, it isn't always easy to tell exactly on which page a given line will fall because the length of a page depends on many variables. However, Symphony has a special key—{Where}—that provides this information.

Using {Where} with {Goto}

The {Where} key returns the number of the printed page and line where the cursor is currently located. In other words, if the cursor is in the fifth line of the third page of a document, pressing {**Where**} causes Symphony to display the message "Printed Page 3, Line 5."

You can use the {**Where**} key to identify the current cursor location prior to using the {**Goto**} key. Then, when you want to return to that location, use the {**Goto**} key again to seek out the current page and line number. The {Where} key is covered in more detail in Chapter 17.

{Goto} and a Line-Name Marker

If you specify a line name in response to the {Goto} prompt, Symphony moves the cursor to the first character in that line. Of course, in order for this to work, you must have assigned a name to at least one line in your document. You can name a simple line of text in your document by placing the cursor anywhere on that line and issuing the {**Menu**} Line-Marker command. Symphony gives you two choices: Assign or Remove. When you choose Assign, Symphony prompts you with the message

        Line-marker name:

You then type the name you wish to assign to the line and press **[Enter]**. Once the line is named, you can use that name in combination with the {Goto} key to move the cursor quickly to the named line. You'll learn more about naming lines in Chapter 16.

Assuming you have named a line, you can respond to the prompt

        Go to where?

by typing the name and pressing **[Enter].** For example, suppose you want to move the cursor to a line you have named MAX. Press the {**Goto**} key; when Symphony displays the prompt

        Go to where?

type the word **Max** and press **[Enter]**. Symphony then puts the cursor on the first character of the line.

Alternatively, after you see the prompt, you can press the {**Menu**} key to bring up a list of all the named lines in the document. Move the pointer through this list and press **[Enter]** when you are pointing to the name of the desired line. Again, Symphony moves the cursor to the first character of the line you specify.

SIMPLE EDITING

Once you begin using the Symphony word processor, you'll find you need to perform a few simple editing functions. This section explains these simple editing functions, including deleting incorrect characters and words, justifying text after it has been edited, and inserting new text and blank lines.

Deleting Characters and Words

You will probably want to correct typing errors you notice as you type a document. Often the most convenient way to do this is to use the [Backspace] or [Del] keys.

The [Backspace] Key

If you have just typed a word or a few characters that you want to change, use the **[Backspace]** key to delete the stray characters. Pressing the **[Backspace]** key causes the cursor to "back up" through the text you've just created, one character at a time, and delete each character. The first character deleted is the one to the left of the cursor.

For example, suppose as you are typing the third line of the letter in Figure 15.2, you accidentally type the word *our* twice. If you catch the error right after you make it, you can quickly delete the extra word by pressing the [Backspace] key.

The [Del] Key

To delete a character or a word that isn't the one you just typed, you can use the **[Del]** key. Suppose, again, you typed *our* twice in the third line of the letter but don't notice your mistake until you finish the paragraph. The third line of the letter would look like this:

increase our our order for the upcoming Christmas season from 100 to

Clearly, it would be impractical to backspace from the end of the paragraph to the error. Using the [Backspace] key would take too long and would delete text that is free of errors. Instead, use the arrow keys to move the cursor to either of the two *ours*. Then press the **[Del]** key and hold it down briefly to get rid of all the characters of the extra word. To keep the spacing between words correct, press the **[Del]** key until the cursor is on the first letter of the next word to the right.

For example, if you position the cursor on the *o* in the first occurrence of *our* and press **[Del],** the line will look like this:

increase ur our order for the upcoming Christmas season from 100 to

If you press [**Del**] again, the line will look like this:

> increase r our order for the upcoming Christmas season from 100 to

If you press [**Del**] twice more, the line will be correct.

Notice that the [Del] key doesn't move the cursor but rather "pulls" characters from the right "into" the cursor. The first character deleted is the one under the cursor when you first press [Del].

Justifying Text

The word justification describes text alignment and word spacing. Symphony offers four types of justification for text in a DOC window: Left, Even, Center, or None. The default Justification setting is Left, which causes each line of text to be positioned flush against the left margin. A document prepared with Left justification has an even left margin and a "ragged" right margin. We'll cover the other types of justification later in this chapter.

As you have seen, when you enter text in a document with a Left justification setting, Symphony automatically divides the text into lines of approximately equal length and automatically aligns the left margin. When you use the Even justification setting, Symphony automatically divides text at the end of each line but does not automatically justify it. You must press the {**Justify**} key when you use this setting. In the Center justification mode, Symphony will not automatically divide text at the end of each line, nor will it automatically center each line of text. You must press [**Enter**] at the end of each line and press the {**Justify**} key to center the text. When the justification setting is None, there is no automatic word wrap at the end of each line.

No matter what your justification setting is, Symphony does not automatically rejustify your document after you make corrections with [Del] or [Backspace] or if you insert additional text. If you want to rejustify the paragraph after you make a correction, press the {**Justify**} key. When you use the {Justify} key, the location of the cursor in a paragraph is insignificant. Even if the cursor is at the end of the paragraph, Symphony rejustifies the entire paragraph. (WordStar users may find this a nice change from the [Ctrl] B command, which justifies only that text between the cursor and the end of a paragraph.)

For example, notice that the sample line we used to demonstrate the [Del] key ends with the words "from 100 to", while the same line in the Figure 15.2 ends with the words "from 100 to 150." The difference is due to the repeated *our* in the example line, which forced Symphony to move the 150 and the period behind that number to the next line. To move those characters up to the proper line (and to adjust the justification of the rest of the paragraph), move the cursor to any location in the paragraph and press {**Justify**}. Symphony immediately rejustifies the entire paragraph. After justification, the line looks like this:

> increase our order for the Christmas season from 100 to 150.

In addition to using the {Justify} key, you can justify text in Symphony using the Justify command from the DOC command menu. The only difference between the Justify command and the {Justify} key is that the command allows you to justify either the paragraph you are working in or all text from the current paragraph through the end of your document. To invoke the Justify command, press {**Menu**} Justify. Symphony will then give you two choices: Paragraph and All-Remaining. If you select **P**aragraph, Symphony will justify the paragraph where the cursor is located (just as if you used the {Justify} key). If you select **A**ll-Remaining, Symphony will justify the paragraph where the cursor is located *and* all following text in the document window. We'll explain how to change Symphony's justification setting later in this chapter.

Inserting New Text

Symphony uses two basic conventions that determine how the text you enter from the keyboard affects the contents of a document: Insert and Overwrite. The default configuration is the Insert mode.

The Insert Mode

In the Insert mode, you can insert new text in the middle of old text without writing over the old text. If you omit some text from a line, you can use the arrow keys to move the cursor to the place where the omitted text belongs and type it in.

Going back to our example, let's suppose you left out the word *our* in the third line of the letter, as follows:

increase order for the upcoming Christmas season from 100 to 150.

To correct this, you could move the cursor to the *o* in order and type the first letter of the omitted word, *o*. The line will now look like this:

increase oorder for the upcoming Christmas season from 100 to 150.

If you complete the word *our* and type an additional space, the line will look like this:

increase our order for the upcoming Christmas season from 100 to 150.

As you insert text, you generally lose your paragraph justification. As soon as you insert more characters than a single line can hold, Symphony inserts a blank line just below and "pushes" part of the current line onto that blank line. All words to the right of the current cursor location (from the first word to the right of the cursor through the end of the line) are pushed onto the new blank line. Because Symphony breaks lines in such a strange way, you will almost always have to rejustify a paragraph after you insert text.

The Overwrite Mode

Alternatively, you can configure Symphony in the Overwrite mode. To do this, press the **[Insert]** key. This key acts as a toggle switch to change from Insert to Overwrite mode and back again. When Symphony is in Overwrite mode, "Ovr" appears in a highlighted block in the lower-right corner of the screen. In this mode, Symphony overwrites text already in the document with the text that you enter.

One way the Overwrite mode can be helpful is when you edit a series of numbers. For example, suppose you have created an outline with various points numbered 1 through 8. If you decide to insert a new point in the middle, you need to renumber each of the subsequent points. The fastest way to do this is to switch to the Overwrite mode and type the new numbers over the old.

When you use the Overwrite mode, Symphony's word wrap feature is turned off, so you must press **[Enter]** at the end of each line. If you do not press [Enter] when you approach the right margin, Symphony allows you to continue typing until you reach the right edge of your window's Restrict range or until the line you are typing is 240 characters long, the maximum line length in Symphony. (Windows and the 240-character limit on lines are explained in Chapter 18.)

Inserting and Removing Blank Lines

Suppose you want to insert a blank line in your document. One way to do this is to use the **[Enter]** key. Begin by checking to be sure that Symphony is in Insert rather than Overwrite mode. (If the legend "Ovr" does not appear at the lower-right corner of the screen, Symphony is in the Insert mode.) If Symphony is in the Overwrite mode, use the **[Ins]** key to return to the Insert mode.

Next, place the cursor at the beginning of the line before which you wish to insert a blank and press **[Enter].** A blank line appears, and the line with the cursor moves down. To insert additional blank lines, continue to press the **[Enter]** key.

You can also use the **{Split}** key to create new blank lines. However, you can use {Split} in both Overwrite and Insert modes. Just position the cursor at the beginning of the line before which you wish to insert a blank line and press **{Split}**.

To remove a blank line, place the cursor at the beginning of the blank line and press **[Del].** If the line does not disappear when you first press **[Del],** it probably contains one or more invisible spaces. (To see how many spaces are on a blank line, set **B**lanks Visible, on the Format Settings sheet, to **Y**es. See the section on Format Settings below.) To delete the blank line, you must delete all of the spaces in it first. Each time you press **[Del],** you remove one space. After you have deleted all of the spaces, press **[Del]** once more to remove the line.

EDITING LARGE BLOCKS

Symphony offers several special DOC environment commands that allow you to erase, move and copy text. These commands are a part of the DOC command menu, which is displayed when you press the {**Menu**} key. The DOC menu looks like this:

Copy Move Erase Search Replace Justify Format Page Line-Marker Quit

We have already explained the Justify command. The Copy, Move, and Erase commands are very important in editing larger blocks of text. These commands will be explained in the following section. We will also explain how to use the Format command to change the format settings of a document. The other commands—Search, Replace, Line-Marker, and Page—will be explained in the next chapter.

Blocking Text to Erase, Move, or Copy

To use the Erase, Move, or Copy commands, you need to mark the lines or blocks of text you wish to edit in this way. You indicate these ranges in the DOC environment much as you do in the SHEET environment. However, there are enough differences that I recommend you read the following section.

When you first issue the Erase, Copy, or Move commands, Symphony displays a prompt much like one of these:

Erase what block? 308,14 . . 308,14

Move FROM what block? 308,14 . . 308,14

Copy FROM what block? 308,14 . . 308,14

The numbers that follow the question indicate the range of text to be erased, moved, or copied. When this prompt first appears, the range given is simply the current cursor location (line number followed by the character number). For example, the lines above show that the cursor is on character 14 of line 308. By moving the cursor left, right, up, or down, you begin to expand the range to be erased, moved, or copied. The numbers on the prompt line change to reflect the expanding range. Marking a range in this manner is called "blocking text" or "marking a block of text."

In marking the block of text, you can use all the cursor-movement keys discussed previously. For example, if you want to block text word by word, use **[Ctrl]** and the arrow keys. Holding down the **[Ctrl]** key while pressing → causes the highlighted block to expand one word to the right. Similarly, holding down the **[Ctrl]** key while pressing the ← key causes the text block to expand one word to the left.

Blocking a Line or Part of a Line

To mark a block of text from the cursor location through the end of the line, press the **[End]** key, followed by the → key. Similarly, to block the text from the cursor location through the beginning of the line, press the **[End]** key and then press the ← key. (These procedures do not work on a single blank line.)

To block an entire line, place the cursor at the beginning of the line. After invoking the Erase, Move, or Copy command, press the **[End]** key and then press the → key. Another way to block an entire line is to position the cursor on the last character of the line before invoking the Erase, Copy, or Move command. Then press **[End]**, followed by the ← key to expand the block through the entire line.

I have suggested that you position the cursor at the beginning of a line before invoking the Erase, Copy, or Move command. You can, of course, change the initial position of the cursor after invoking a command. This is explained below in the section "Anchoring and Unanchoring the Cursor When Marking Text Blocks."

Blocking a Paragraph or Part of a Paragraph

To mark a block from the cursor location through the end of the current paragraph, press the **[End]** key and then press ↓. Similarly, to mark a block from the beginning of the paragraph through the cursor location, press **[End]** and then press ↑.

Blocking Other Ranges

When you use the ↓ key to mark a block of text, Symphony highlights text from the cursor location through the end of the line as well as part of the line just below. For example, if the cursor is on the tenth character of a line of text when you invoke the Erase, Move, or Copy commands and you then press the ↓ key, Symphony highlights a block from the cursor location through the end of the line and also highlights part of the line just below, from the beginning of the line through the tenth character. Figures 15.7 and 15.8 show you an example of this. As you continue to press the ↓ key, additional complete lines are highlighted.

Similarly, if the cursor is in the middle of a line and you press the ↑ key, Symphony highlights text from the cursor location through the beginning of the line and also part of the line just above. This is illustrated in Figures 15.9 and 15.10.

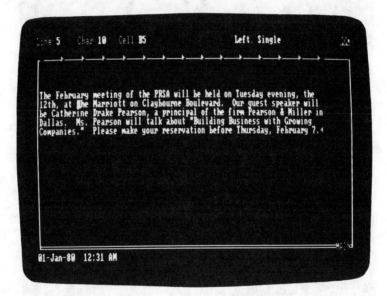

Figure 15.7

Blocking Text with [Pg Up] and [Pg Dn]

After invoking the Erase, Move, or Copy command, you can mark a large block of text by using the **[Pg Up]** or **[Pg Dn]** key. As was explained above, pressing [Pg Up] and [Pg Dn] produces different results each time you use them, depending on where the cursor is located when you press the key.

Pressing **[Pg Dn]** highlights the text from the cursor location through the last line of the window, plus half of the lines in the next window. For example, suppose you are working in a full-screen window (20 lines deep) and the cursor is positioned on the fifth line of the window. When you use **[Pg Dn]** to mark a block of text, Symphony highlights a block that extends from the cursor location through the last line of the window (16 lines) plus half of the next windowful of text (10 lines), a total of 26 lines. Had the cursor been positioned on line 14 of the window when you pressed **[Pg Dn],** the highlighted block would have included only 17 lines (7 lines of the current window plus 10 lines of the next window).

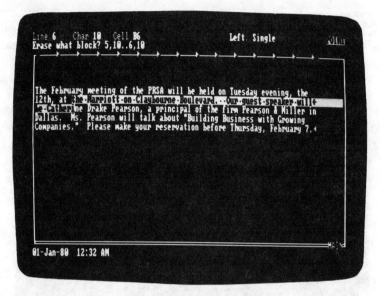

Figure 15.8

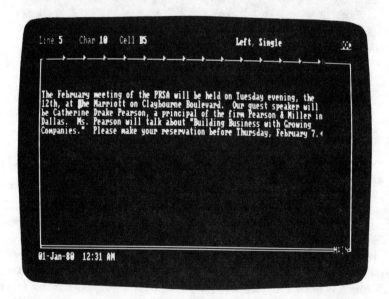

Figure 15.9

Suppose, however, that you are working in a window that is only 12 lines deep and that the cursor is on line 5. In this case, pressing **[Pg Dn]** marks a 14-line block of text (8 lines of the current window plus 6 lines, or half, of the next window).

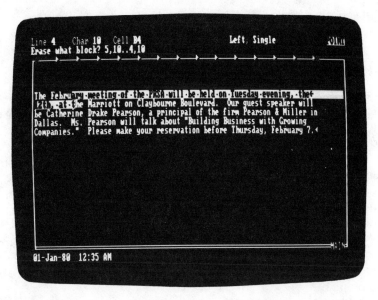

Figure 15.10

Pressing **[Pg Up]** highlights the text from the cursor location through the first line of the window plus half of the lines in the window just above. Again, suppose you are working in a full-screen window (20 lines deep). If the cursor is at the beginning of line 5 when you press **[Pg Up]**, the text highlighted includes the first 4 lines of the current screen plus 10 lines of the screen just above, or a total of 14 lines.

Blocking with the Next Occurrence of a Character

You can also mark blocks of text in Symphony by asking the program to highlight all of the text between the cursor location and the next occurrence of a specified character. For example, to mark a single sentence to be erased, moved, or copied, place the cursor at the beginning of the sentence. After invoking the Erase, Move, or Copy command, type a **period.** This causes the highlighted block to extend through the period at the end of the sentence. Typing another **period** highlights the next sentence as well. (Of course, if there is a period in the middle of the sentence, such as the period after an initial or a decimal point in a number, Symphony will highlight through this period rather than to the end of the sentence when you follow the procedure described above.)

Anchoring and Unanchoring the Cursor When Blocking Text

When you invoke the Erase, Copy, or Move command, the cursor is "anchored" at its current location. You can "unanchor" the cursor by pressing the **[Esc]** key. This allows you to move the cursor anywhere in the document before marking the range to be erased, moved, or copied. After you position the cursor where you wish, "reanchor" it by pressing **[Tab].** After reanchoring the cursor, you can begin to highlight text as explained above. Note that this is different from the SHEET environment, where [Esc] unanchors the cell pointer, but the period key reanchors it.

Now that you know how to mark blocks of text to be erased, moved, or copied, let's explore the Erase, Move, and Copy commands in detail.

Erasing a Line or More of Text

If you want to delete blocks of text that are longer than a few words or characters, it is not practical to use the [Backspace] or [Del] keys. The fastest way to delete a line or more of text is to use Symphony's Erase command.

After you issue the {**Menu**} **E**rase command, Symphony asks you to specify the range you want to erase. By moving the cursor, you can highlight the block of text you wish to erase. (See "Blocking Text," above.)

After you point to the appropriate range, simply press **[Enter]** and the block disappears. Symphony then closes up the space the erased text occupied and automatically rejustifies the paragraph.

For example, suppose you want to erase the line "This is an example of the Erase command" from the middle of the document shown in Figure 15.11. To erase this line, move the cursor to the first character of the sentence and press {**Menu**} **E**rase. Symphony will display the prompt

> **Erase what block?**

You respond by highlighting from the cursor location through the end of the sentence and pressing **[Enter].** Symphony will delete the sentence and close up the blank space it occupied. Figure 15.12 shows the document after the text has been erased.

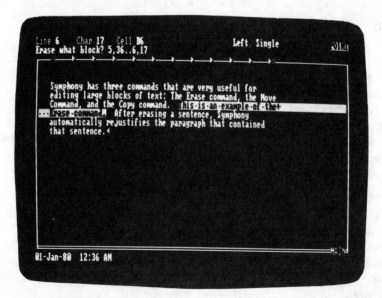

Figure 15.11

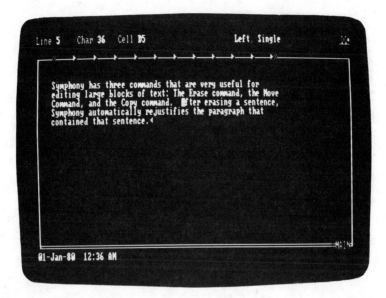

Line 5   Char 36   Cell D5   Left, Single

Symphony has three commands that are very useful for
editing large blocks of text: The Erase command, the Move
Command, and the Copy command. After erasing a sentence,
Symphony automatically rejustifies the paragraph that
contained that sentence.

01-Jan-80 12:36 AM

Figure 15.12

Symphony offers a shortcut for using the Erase command. In the DOC mode, the [F4] special function key is defined as the {**Erase**} key. Pressing this key has exactly the same effect as issuing the {**Menu**} Erase command.

SHEET Erase versus DOC Erase

If you are familiar with the SHEET environment Erase command, you might note that the DOC environment Erase command produces somewhat different results. When you use Erase in the SHEET environment to eliminate a cell entry, Symphony leaves a blank cell after you erase. In the DOC environment, however, Symphony closes up blank space after erasures. In fact, the DOC Erase command is really more like the SHEET Delete command, since SHEET Delete closes up the worksheet after deleting several rows or columns. (For more on the SHEET Erase and Delete commands, see Chapter 7, "Cut-and-Paste Commands.")

Copying Text

The Copy command lets you copy a block of text from one part of a document to another. For example, suppose you want to copy the text "This a test of the Copy command" from line 3 in Figure 15.13 to line 8 in the same example. Start by positioning the cursor at the beginning of the block you wish to copy.

Next, press the {**Menu**} key and select Copy from the DOC menu. Symphony will then ask

Copy FROM What Block?

Use the cursor to highlight the block of text you wish to copy. After marking the block,

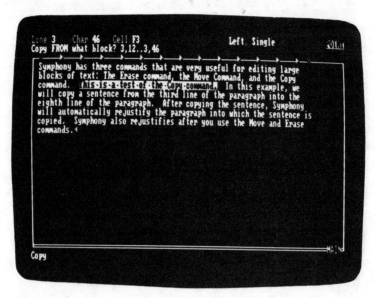

Line 3   Char 46   Cell F3   Left, Single
Copy FROM what block? 3,12..3,46

Symphony has three commands that are very useful for editing large
blocks of text: The Erase command, the Move Command, and the Copy
command. This is a test of the Copy command. In this example, we
will copy a sentence from the third line of the paragraph into the
eighth line of the paragraph. After copying the sentence, Symphony
will automatically rejustify the paragraph into which the sentence is
copied. Symphony also rejustifies after you use the Move and Erase
commands.

Copy

Figure 15.13

press the [**Enter**] key. Symphony then asks you to specify the range to copy to with the prompt

     Copy TO Where?

You respond by moving the cursor to the point where you want to copy the block and pressing [**Enter**]. In this example, you would move the cursor to the end of the paragraph, just past the word "commands.", and press [**Enter**].

After you follow this procedure, Symphony copies the block of text you indicated to the location you specified and automatically justifies the paragraph into which you copied. You may need to add or delete some spaces around the copied text after Symphony's automatic rejustification. Figure 15.14 shows the text after line 3 has been copied to line 8.

Note that when you use the cursor to show where you want the block copied, you do not have to show the entire range the copied text will occupy. Rather, you simply put the cursor where the first copied character will fall. In this regard, the DOC Copy command is like the SHEET Copy command.

SHEET Copy versus DOC Copy

Spreadsheet users might note one difference between the Copy command of the DOC environment and the Copy command of the SHEET environment. In the SHEET environment the Copy command causes the copied cells to overwrite any numbers or text on the worksheet at the Copy TO location. In the DOC environment, however, Symphony inserts the copied text at the location you specify. For example, for the Copy TO location, you could point to a single blank space between two sentences. Symphony inserts the text you wish to copy between these two sentences without overwriting any text.

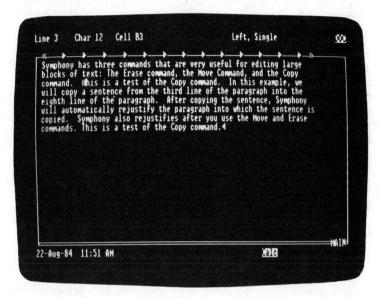

```
Line 3    Char 12    Cell B3              Left, Single          ▓▓▒

«——►——►——►——►——►——►——►——►——►——►——►——►——►——►——►—»
Symphony has three commands that are very useful for editing large
blocks of text: The Erase command, the Move Command, and the Copy
command. This is a test of the Copy command. In this example, we
will copy a sentence from the third line of the paragraph into the
eighth line of the paragraph. After copying the sentence, Symphony
will automatically rejustify the paragraph into which the sentence is
copied. Symphony also rejustifies after you use the Move and Erase
commands. This is a test of the Copy command.◄
```

```
22-Aug-84  11:51 AM                    CALC              MAIN
```

Figure 15.14

Moving Text

Use the {**Menu**} **M**ove command to move a block of text from one location in a document to another. To invoke the Move command, press the {**Menu**} key and select **M**ove. Symphony then asks you to supply the FROM range by displaying the prompt

>   Move FROM What Block?

Using the cursor, highlight the block of text you wish to move. After marking the block to be moved, press the [**Enter**] key. Symphony then asks

>   Move TO Where?

You respond by moving the cursor to the point where you want the block of text to be moved and pressing [**Enter**].

Note that when you use the cursor to show where you want the block of text moved, you do not have to show a range the moved text will occupy. Rather, you simply put the cursor where the first moved character will fall.

For instance, suppose you want to move the line "This is an example of the Move command" from line 4 in Figure 15.15 to line 6 in the same figure. To move this line, issue the {**Menu**} **M**ove command, then highlight the sentence to be moved and press [**Enter**]. Next, place the cursor at the position on line 6 where you want the sentence moved and press [**Enter**]. Symphony moves the text and automatically rejustifies the paragraph. Figure 15.16 shows the text after line 4 has been copied to line 6.

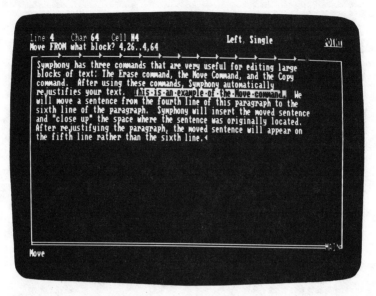

Figure 15.15

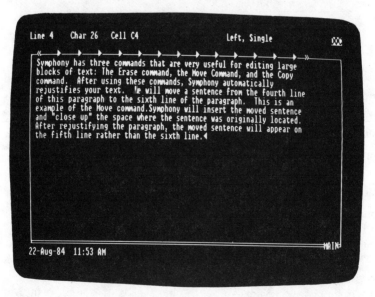

Figure 15.16

SHEET Move versus DOC Move

Again, spreadsheet users might note a difference between the Move command of the DOC environment and the Move command of the SHEET environment. In the SHEET environment, when you move a cell or a range of cells, Symphony "lifts" that cell or range out of one location in the worksheet and places it in another, leaving behind a blank cell or range. If the location to which you move the cell or range is not empty, the moved cell or range writes over the existing data or text.

In the DOC environment, by contrast, the Move command combines features of the Move, Insert, and Delete commands of the SHEET environment. When you move a word, for example, Symphony first "lifts" the word out of its location on the worksheet. It then deletes the space that word occupied. Next, Symphony inserts a space at the Move TO location on the worksheet. Finally, Symphony copies the word into this space.

BASIC DOCUMENT FORMATTING

The format of any document created with the Symphony word processor is controlled by several master settings, called Format settings. (The Lotus manuals refer to these as "Document settings.") These settings control the left and right margins, tabs, justification, spacing, and other characteristics of your documents.

Although these master Format settings control the overall document, you can alter the format of a portion or several portions of the document by using format lines. These are explained later in Chapter 16, "Advanced Editing and Formatting."

As we explained earlier in the chapter, the top border of a DOC window is a ruler line that shows the Left and Right Margin settings and the Tab settings. This line is a quick reference to some of the settings in the Format settings sheet. To view all of the default settings, issue the {**Menu**} **F**ormat **S**ettings command. The Format settings sheet and settings menu then appear on the screen.

Once you have called up the Format settings sheet, you can change any of the settings by selecting one of the settings shown at the top of Figure 15.17. For example, to change the left margin, choose the **L**eft option after giving the {**Menu**} **F**ormat **S**ettings commands. The following sections explain the Settings commands in detail.

Left Margin

The Left Margin setting controls the position of the left edge of your text on the screen. The default Left Margin setting is 1. This puts the left margin at the first space beyond the left edge of your DOC window, meaning that the first character of each line falls in the first column of your DOC window.

To change the left margin of your document, issue the {**Menu**} **F**ormat **S**ettings **L**eft command and specify the new left margin. The Left Margin setting can be any number from 1 to 240, but it must be less than the Right Margin setting. After you issue this command, the new left margin appears in the settings sheet, and the ruler line at the top of the screen reflects the new setting.

In addition, when you change the left margin of a document, Symphony automatically rejustifies all of the text in the document. For example, if you change the Left Margin setting from 1 to 4, a space three characters wide appears at the left edge of your window, and every line in the document shifts three spaces to the right.

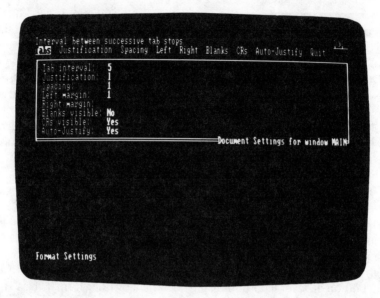

Figure 15.17

The Left Margin setting of the Format settings sheet, along with the Right Margin setting, determine how many characters can appear on each line of the screen. (This is explained in detail below.) The left margin of the final printed document (the space between the left edge of the page and the first character of each line), by contrast, is determined by the Left Margin of the Print settings sheet. See the section on Print settings and Format settings in Chapter 17.

Right Margin

The Right Margin setting determines the right margin of your documents. When you first see the Format settings sheet, the Right Margin setting is blank because Symphony's default Right Margin setting is determined by the right border of the window in which you're working.

In the default mode, the right margin falls at the last character of the last full column of the underlying spreadsheet that is visible through the window. For example, if you are working in a full-screen window, this default setting puts the right margin at column 72, assuming you have not changed the standard column-width settings of the underlying spreadsheet. (This is a tricky concept. The relationship between window size, column widths, and the default Right Margin setting is explained in detail in Chapter 18.)

To change the right margin, press the {**Menu**} key and issue the **Format Settings Right** command. In response, Symphony offers two options: Set or Reset. If you select **Set**, you can specify a number between 1 and 240 for the right margin. If you choose the **Reset** option, Symphony adjusts the right margin to the default setting, which is determined by the size of the window in which you are working.

The Right and Left Margin settings determine the maximum number of characters that can appear on a line of text. The first character of each line is at the left margin. The right margin determines where the last character of a line can fall (except when you set Justification to Center or None). For example, if you set the left margin at 3 and the right margin at 72, the first character of each line appears in column 3 of your screen. The last column where a character can appear is column 72. This means that the maximum number of characters that can appear on a line is 70.

If you changed the left margin of this same document to 1, the maximum line size would expand to 72 characters. If, however, you changed the right margin to 65, leaving the left margin at 3, the maximum line length would be 63. This can be summarized in a quick formula: The maximum number of characters on a line of text equals the Right Margin setting of the Format settings sheet minus the Left Margin setting plus one. In the last example, the maximum number of characters equals to $65 - 3 + 1$, or 63.

The Left and Right Margins of the Format settings sheet are not the final determinants of how the printed text will appear. When you print your document, you must specify Left and Right Margins in the Print settings sheet as well. These interact with the Left and Right Margins of the Format settings sheet to determine how the final printed document will look. Again, refer to the section on Print settings and Format settings in Chapter 17.

Tab Interval

The first selection on the Format settings sheet is Tabs. This setting controls the locations of tabs on each line of text. Tab settings are shown on the ruler line at the top of your DOC window with a ► symbol. A tab interval of 5 (the default setting) means that tabs are set every five spaces across a line, beginning in the sixth column from the left margin.

To change the tab interval, issue the {**Menu**} **F**ormat **S**ettings **T**ab command. The number you specify for the tab interval sets all the tabs for the document. For example, if the left margin is set at 1 and you specify a tab interval of 7, tabs will be set at columns 8, 15, 22, 29, and so on. Symphony lets you select any Tab Interval between 1 and 240.

Sometimes you may not want tabs evenly spaced across a line. To create variable tabs, insert a format line in your document. Using a format line to create variable tabs is discussed in Chapter 16.

To clear all the tab settings, use a Tab Interval setting equal to or greater than the right margin. For example, a document with a right margin of 70 and a tab interval of 75 would have no tab marks.

When the tab interval is set at 5 and the cursor is on the first character of a line, pressing **[Tab]** causes the cursor to jump to the sixth character position on the line. If you continue to press **[Tab]**, the cursor jumps to the eleventh position, the sixteenth position, and so on.

When you are in the Insert Mode, pressing [Tab] causes the cursor to insert spaces as it moves across the screen. For example, suppose you write a block-style paragraph and later decide you want to indent the first line. To do so, set the Tab Interval at 5, place the cursor on the beginning of the first line of the paragraph, and press **[Tab]**. This sequence "pushes" the first word of the line over by five spaces, or one tab interval. The rest of the line moves down one line, so you need to rejustify the paragraph by pressing {**Justify**}.

Justification Settings

The basic concept of justification should already be familiar to you. However, Symphony offers several justification options that are worth covering in detail.

The Justification setting determines how the text is aligned in relation to the left and right margins. Whenever you press the {**Justify**} key, invoke the Justify command, or whenever Symphony implements automatic justification, the text is reformatted according to the Justification setting of the Format settings sheet.

The Symphony word processor allows four different types of justification: Left, Even, Center, and None. Left Justification, the default, causes text to be aligned flush with the left margin and creates a ragged right margin. When Justification is set to Even, both the right and left margins of the text are flush, as they are in a newspaper column. As you enter text when Justification is set to Even, Symphony does not automatically justify the text. You must press the {**Justify**} key or use the Justify command from the Document menu to achieve Even Justification. When you do this, Symphony automatically inserts extra spaces between words to create even left and right margins.

Center Justification causes each line of text to be centered in the space between the left and right margins. When Justification is set to Center, Symphony does not center the line until you press the {**Justify**} key. In addition, with Center Justification, Symphony's automatic word wrap is turned off, so you must press [**Enter**] when you reach the end of a line in order to begin typing on the next line.

The last setting, No Justification (or None), allows text to remain on the screen exactly as you type it. Symphony neither changes the text position relative to the margins nor closes up extra spaces between words. When Justification is set to None, pressing the {**Justify**} key has no effect. Symphony's Auto-Justify capability (see below) is disabled by the Justification None setting.

In addition, the Justification None setting turns off Symphony's automatic word wrap, so you have to press [**Enter**] at the end of each line to move the cursor to the next line. This also means you can create lines of text that exceed the margins you have set. For these reasons, the None Justification setting is useful for creating tables or other text that you do not want to align with the margins. This is explained in the section on using format lines in Chapter 16.

Changing the Justification

To change a Justification setting, issue the {**Menu**} Format Settings Justification command and choose one of the options: **Left**, **Even**, **Center**, or **None**. As soon as the command is issued, Symphony immediately rejustifies the entire document, changing the justification of each line to match the new settings.

Justification Notes

If you change the Justification setting to Center and then decide to return to Left or Even Justification, Symphony does not rejustify the document fully. Symphony rejustifies all the lines in the document except the first line of each paragraph (remember that in Symphony a paragraph is any text that is set apart with a paragraph delimiter).

For example, suppose you create a letter with Justification set to Center. At the top of this letter, you type an address that looks like this:

> **Mr. A.L. Taggart**
> **4216 Winchester Street**
> **Houston, Texas 77005**

Symphony considers each line of this address as a separate one-line paragraph because each line ends with a hard carriage return. If you reset Justification to Left, the lines of this address are not rejustified automatically. To make these lines flush left, you must position the cursor on the first column of each line and press the **[Del]** key to delete the extra spaces until the line is flush with the left margin.

Justification Quirks

When your Justification setting is either Left or Even, Symphony observes two rather irritating format conventions. The first is that Symphony puts two spaces after most periods. You may or may not want two spaces separating your sentences, but you almost certainly do not want two spaces separating initials, for instance, T. S. Eliot. The second irritating convention is that with Left or Even Justification Symphony inserts only once space after colons, right quotation marks, right parentheses, numerals, and several other characters. Most style manuals recommend two blank spaces after a colon, so it is odd that Symphony doesn't automatically insert two spaces after a colon. In addition, if a sentence ends with a quotation mark, you may want two spaces, not one, before the start of the next sentence.

You can solve both of these problems by using the Replace feature. The section on using the Replace feature in Chapter 16 explains the solutions in detail.

Auto-Justify

The Auto-Justify setting determines whether Symphony rejustifies your text automatically after you make certain changes. When you set Auto-Justify to Yes, your document is automatically rejustified when you move, erase, or copy a block of text. If the setting is No, Symphony does not automatically rejustify after these block editing operations.

If the Auto-Justify setting is No and you want to rejustify a paragraph, you must use the {**Justify**} key. The only exception is that documents are automatically reformatted when you change the Left Margin, Right Margin, or Justification settings, even when the Auto-Justify setting is No.

To change the Auto-Justify setting, press the {**Menu**} key, issue the Format Settings Auto-Justify command and specify **Y**es or **N**o. Select **Q**uit to return to your working document. Auto-Justify is automatically disabled when you give the command sequence Format Settings Justification None. In other words, when you have a None Justification setting, there is no automatic rejustification after erasing, moving, or copying text.

No matter what the Auto-Justify setting is, Symphony does not rejustify automatically when you use the [Backspace] or [Del] keys to erase text nor when you insert text. After making these kinds of changes, you must press {**Justify**} to rejustify the text.

Spacing

The Spacing setting controls how many blank lines appear between each line of text in the printed document. Interestingly, even if you select double or triple spacing, your text appears on the computer screen single-spaced. Double and triple spacing become apparent only when you print the document.

To change the line spacing of a document, press the {**Menu**} key and select **Format Settings Spacing**. Then specify **1, 2,** or **3** for single, double, or triple spacing. Press **Q**uit to return to your working text.

When Spacing is set to 1 (single spacing, the default setting), no blank lines appear between lines of text unless you insert them manually with a carriage return.

When Spacing is set to 2 (double spacing), one blank line is inserted after each line of printed text. Also, with double spacing, each blank line you see on your screen (lines created with hard carriage returns or blank spaces) results in *three* blank lines in the printed document. I found this puzzling because I expected a single blank line to translate to only two blank lines in a double-spaced document. When Symphony creates a double-spaced document, however, it inserts a blank line after each line in the document, *including* each existing blank line. For example, assume you have inserted one blank line between the paragraphs of a single-spaced document. If you change the Spacing setting of this document to 2, Symphony inserts one blank line after the last line of the first paragraph and another blank line after the single blank line between the paragraphs. Thus, the printed document will have three blank lines between paragraphs.

Similarly, when Spacing is set to 3 (triple spacing), two blank lines are inserted after each line of printed text. Each blank line you see on your screen results in five blank lines on the printed document.

When you print a document, you will notice that there is a Spacing setting on the Print settings sheet. This does not affect the spacing of a printed document. Only the Spacing setting in the Format settings sheet determines the line spacing of the printed document. This concept is covered in more detail in Chapter 17.

Blanks Visible

This setting causes each space in a document to be displayed as a dot. A Blanks Visible setting of Yes is helpful if you are creating a table, outline, or other material in which relative spacing is critical.

To change the Blanks Visible setting, issue the {**Menu**} **Format Settings B**lanks command. Next, make the setting **Yes** or **No,** depending on your preference (the default Blanks Visible setting is No). If you change the setting to Yes, each blank space in your text is marked with a small dot.

Carriage Returns Visible

This setting allows you to display or suppress visible carriage returns. The default setting is Yes, which means you see a ◄ symbol at the location of each carriage return.

Technically, you do not see every carriage return in a document when the Carriage Returns Visible setting is Yes. Symphony inserts a carriage return at the end of each line of text, even when Automatic Word Wrap is set to On. These end-of-line carriage returns are never displayed, even when the Carriage Returns Visible setting is Yes. Similarly, a new line is created when the cursor is at the beginning of a line and you press [Enter], but the carriage return that created that line is not visible.

To remove the visible carriage returns, issue the {**Menu**} **F**ormat **S**ettings **C**arriage Returns Visible commmand and select **No**. *Advanced tip:* If you would like a visible indication of which blank lines in your text are created with carriage returns, set the Left Margin to 2 or greater and change the Blanks Visible setting to Yes. This causes the blank symbol (a small dot) to appear just to the left of each blank line you create with a carriage return.

Changing the Default Format Settings

In describing the format settings above, we mentioned a default setting for each one. For example, the default Left Margin setting is 1 and the default Justification setting is Left. These default settings are stored in the SYMPHONY.CNF file, along with the defaults for Symphony's other environments.

As you might expect, you can change one or more of these default settings with the {**Services**} **C**onfiguration **D**ocument command. This command causes the Configuration settings sheet and the following menu to appear on the screen:

Tabs   Justification   Spacing   Left   Right   Blanks   CRs   Auto-Justify   Quit

Notice that this menu is identical to the menu brought up by the {**Menu**} **F**ormat **S**ettings command. The {Services} Configuration Settings command lets you change the default for every DOC format setting.

To change one of the defaults, select from the menu the setting you wish to change. For example, to change the default tab interval setting, select **T**abs from the menu. Symphony responds with the message

Default tab interval: 5

You can change this default value by typing a new value and pressing **[Enter]**.

After making all desired default changes, press **Q**uit to go back to the Configuration menu. If you want to make the changes to the default settings permanent, use the {**Services**} **C**onfiguration **U**pdate command to rewrite the SYMPHONY.CNF file.

The SYMPHONY.CNF file and the {Services} Configuration command are covered in more detail in Chapter 30, Configuring Symphony.

Centering a Single Line of Text

Symphony is designed so that by pressing one key, {**Center**}, you can center a line of text between the left and right margins. To center a line of text, put the cursor anywhere on the line and press {**Center**}.

Apparently, Symphony is programmed so that the {Center} key has a permanent effect only on single, isolated lines. If you use the {Center} key to center a line or several lines that are part of a paragraph, the lines are centered only temporarily. When you press the {Justify} key, or when the paragraph is automatically rejustified after you erase, move, or copy text, the centered lines are rejustified along with the rest of the paragraph.

To keep a line permanently centered, separate it from surrounding text with a paragraph delimiter (a hard carriage return, a blank line, a page break, or nontext cells). For example, you can center a line embedded in a paragraph by putting a hard carriage return at the end of the line just above the line to be centered and at the end of the line to be centered. The delimiters cause Symphony to view this line as a separate paragraph, and the line remains centered whenever the rest of the paragraph is rejustified.

If you use {Center} to center a line of text, the centered line does not adjust automatically to new margin settings. If you want to center the line according to new margins, you must use the {**Center**} key again.

The {Center} key has no effect on text justified with the Even setting. If you want to center individual lines in a document with Even Justification, you must temporarily change the Justification setting to None, separate the line or lines to be centered from the rest of the document with a paragraph delimiter, and then use the {**Center**} key. After the line or lines are centered, you can return the document's Justification setting to Even. If you want to center more than a few lines, the easiest way is to use a format line. Format lines are explained in Chapter 16.

Special Format Codes

Symphony lets you embed special format codes in your documents that cause text to be printed underlined, boldfaced, superscripted, subscripted, and so on. All of Symphony's special text formats are achieved by typing **[Ctrl] B** (for "begin") before the text to be formatted, followed by one of Symphony's special format codes. Typing **[Ctrl] B** causes the symbol ▲ to appear on the screen. This symbol tells Symphony that a special format code follows.

At the end of the section to be formatted, type **[Ctrl] E** (for "end"). This causes a ▼ to appear on the screen. This symbol tells Symphony to discontinue the special formatting.

Except for the code embedded between the [Ctrl] B and the formatted text, the sequence is exactly the same for all of Symphony's special format codes. Figures 15.18 through 15.23 summarize Symphony's special format codes. They show how the format codes appear on your computer screen and display the printed results.

You should be aware that not all printers can generate specially formatted characters. Most printers can handle boldfacing and underlining, but many cannot print italic text, superscripts, or subscripts. Check your printer manual to see which of these formats your printer can display.

The format code you will probably use most frequently is the underline code, so this will be explained in detail below. I will also cover briefly the format code used to bold-face text.

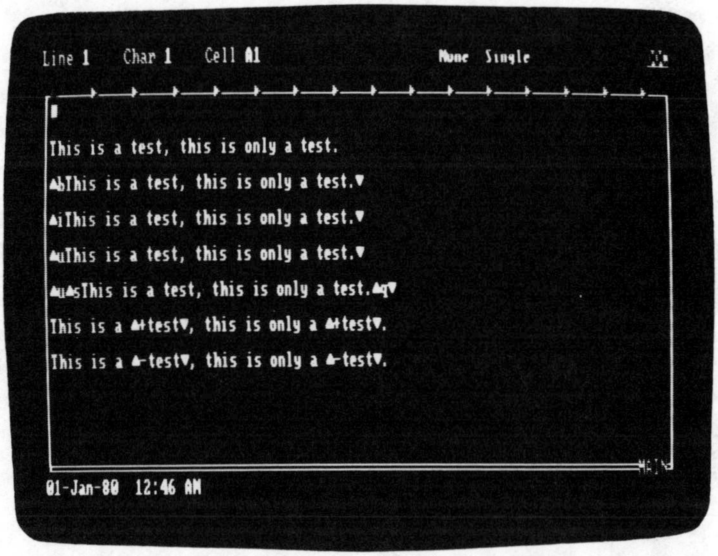

Figure 15.18

This is a test, this is only a test.   No Special Formatting

This is a test, this is only a test.   Bold

This is a test, this is only a test.   Italic

<u>This is a test, this is only a test.</u>   Underline

<u>This is a test, this is only a test.</u>   Underline with Spaces Underlined

This is a ᵗᵉˢᵗ, this is only a ᵗᵉˢᵗ.   Superscript

This is a test, this is only a test.   Subscript

Figure 15.19

Underlining Text

To show how Symphony's special format codes work, let's underline some text. Suppose you want to underline the title *Macbeth*. With Symphony in the Insert mode, place the cursor on the *M* and press **[Ctrl] BU.** A ▲ and a U appear before the *M*. This code tells Symphony that the special format is underlining and that it should begin under the next character in the line. Next, move the cursor to the blank space just past the *h* and type **[Ctrl] E.** A ▼ appears after the *h*. This symbol tells Symphony to stop underlining, beginning with the next character in the line. Of course, when the title *Macbeth* is printed, the two triangles and the U do not appear. Instead, Symphony uses these codes as instructions to underline the word *Macbeth*.

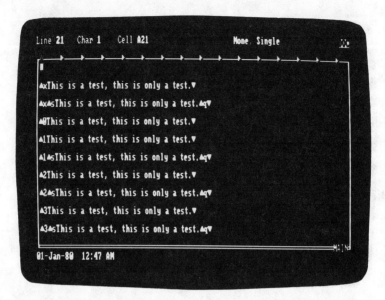

Figure 15.20

T̶h̶i̶s̶ ̶i̶s̶ ̶a̶ ̶t̶e̶s̶t̶,̶ ̶t̶h̶i̶s̶ ̶i̶s̶ ̶o̶n̶l̶y̶ ̶a̶ ̶t̶e̶s̶t̶.̶	Strike Through Characters
T̶h̶i̶s̶-̶i̶s̶-̶a̶-̶t̶e̶s̶t̶,̶-̶t̶h̶i̶s̶-̶i̶s̶-̶o̶n̶l̶y̶-̶a̶-̶t̶e̶s̶t̶.̶	Strike Through Characters Including Spaces
This is a test, this is only a test.	Bold Italic
This is a test, this is only a test.	Bold Underline
This is a test, this is only a test.	Bold Underline with Spaces Underlined
This is a test, this is only a test.	Bold Italic Underline
This is a test, this is only a test.	Bold Italic Underline with Spaces Underlined
This is a test, this is only a test.	Italic Underline
This is a test, this is only a test.	Italic Underline with Spaces Underlined

Figure 15.21

Figure 15.24 shows how the underline codes appear on the computer screen. Unfortunately, you cannot see the effect of special format codes until you print your document. The only way to identify the formatted portions of a document is to refer to the special codes that surround the formatted text.

We should note here that the Lotus manuals tell you to press {Compose} B A instead of [Ctrl] B and {Compose} E A instead of [Ctrl] E to generate the beginning and ending format codes. This method works, but I find it much easier to use the [Ctrl] key rather than the {Compose} key.

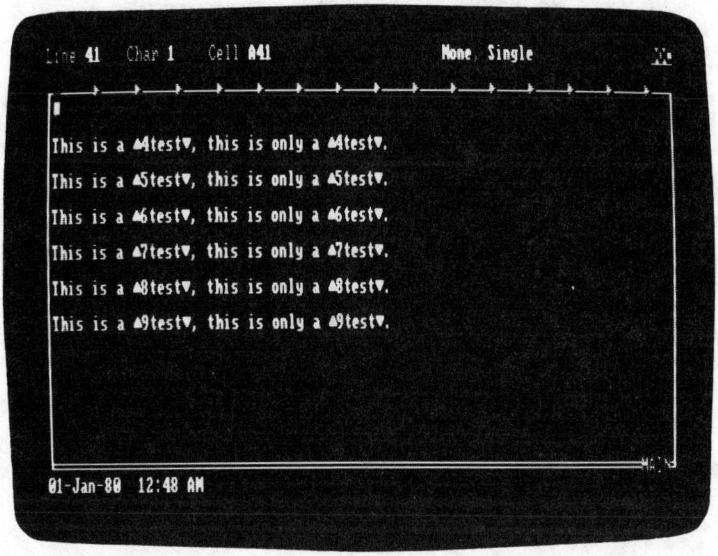

Figure 15.22

Figure 15.23

Underlining Spaces between Words

Symphony does not automatically underline blank spaces between words. To underline blank spaces, you must insert another code within the underline code. For example, suppose you want to underline the phrase "How to Lose Pounds and Inches While you Sleep!" You would place the cursor on the H and type **[Ctrl] BU.** Then you would move the cursor just past the exclamation point and type **[Ctrl] E.** This would cause the printed output to look like this:

How to Lose Pounds and Inches While You Sleep!

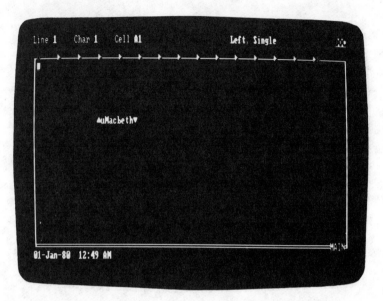

Line 1   Char 1   Cell A1   Left, Single

▲uMacbeth▼

01-Jan-80 12:49 AM

Figure 15.24

Now, suppose that in addition to underlining the words, you want to underline the spaces in the phrase "Pounds and Inches" so that the final printed result looks like this:

<u>How to Lose Pounds and Inches While You Sleep!</u>

To achieve this result, start with the normal underlining codes—**[Ctrl] BU** and **[Ctrl] E**—bracketing the entire phrase, as we explained above. Then move the cursor to the *P* of *Pounds.* Press **[Ctrl] BS** (for "start"). This causes the blank spaces as well as the words to be underlined. Now move the cursor to the blank space just past the word *Inches* and press **[Ctrl] BQ** (for "quit"). This tells the program to quit underlining blank spaces between words. After you go through these steps, your computer screen should look like Figure 15.25.

To summarize, if you want to underline spaces between words, type **[Ctrl] BS** after you have typed **[Ctrl] BU.** Whenever you want to stop underlining spaces, type **[Ctrl] BQ.** You do not *have* to type [Ctrl] BQ at any time. Once you have placed a [Ctrl] BS in your document, you can allow it to affect all subsequent underlining.

As you can see in Figures 15.18–15.23, [Ctrl] BS can be used with any of Symphony's underline codes (including regular underline, bold underline, and bold italic underline). [Ctrl] BS can also be used with the "strike-through" code ([Ctrl] BX) to cause Symphony to strike through spaces as well as characters.

One problem can occur when you use [Ctrl] BS to underline blanks between words. If the words you are underlining occupy more than one line, Symphony underlines the blanks in the left margin of the second line.

For example, in the two lines in Figure 15.26, the title, *The Economic Report of the President, 1984,* is split between two lines. Because we wanted to underline the entire

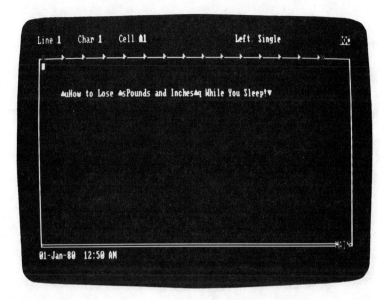

Figure 15.25

title including the spaces between words of the title, we put a **[Ctrl] BU** and the **[Ctrl] BS** at the beginning of the title. At the end of the title we put a **[Ctrl] E** to discontinue the underlining. Before printing these two lines of text, we changed the Left Margin setting to 10. The result of printing these two lines is shown in Figure 15.26.

Recommended reading for this course is <u>The Economic Report</u> <u>of the President, 1984</u>, available at the student bookstore.

Figure 15.26

As you can see, we managed to underline the entire title, including blank spaces, but we also ended up with a blank line ten spaces long in the left margin of the second line. To solve this problem, we moved the cursor to the end of the first line and inserted a **[Ctrl] BQ** after the word *Report*. This caused the underlining of blank spaces to stop. To begin underlining again, we inserted a **[Ctrl] BS** at the beginning of the second line, just before the word *of*. Figure 15.27 shows how these codes appear on the computer screen, and Figure 15.28 displays the printed results.

Creating a Blank Underline

To underline a series of blank spaces, simply use the underline key on your keyboard. It's not a good idea to create a blank underline by surrounding several blank spaces with the [Ctrl] BU, [Ctrl] BS, and [Ctrl] E sequences. Though these codes do create a blank underline, Symphony closes up the blank spaces between the control characters when it rejustifies.

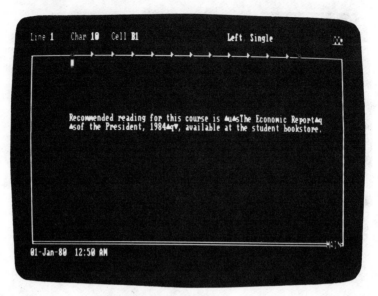

Line 1   Char 10   Cell B1   Left Single   W

Recommended reading for this course is ▲u▲sThe Economic Report▲q
▲sof the President, 1984▲q▼, available at the student bookstore.

01-Jan-80 12:50 AM

Figure 15.27

Recommended reading for this course is <u>The Economic Report
of the President, 1984</u>, available at the student bookstore.

Figure 15.28

Boldfacing Text

Another way to use Symphony's special format codes is for boldfacing text. For example, suppose you want to boldface the word "important" in a document. With Symphony in the insert mode, you would place the cursor on the letter i in this word and type **[Ctrl] B**, followed by **B**, the code for boldfacing. To stop boldfacing, place the cursor just past the last letter in the word and press **[Ctrl] E.** When the word "important" is printed, it will be boldfaced.

CHAPTER SIXTEEN
ADVANCED EDITING AND FORMATTING

In the previous chapter you learned about Symphony's basic word processing capabilities. In this chapter, we'll cover the program's advanced editing and formatting features. This chapter will tell you how to create, modify, and use format lines; how to store and reuse formats; how to use the {Indent} key; and how to use Symphony's Search and Replace commands.

FORMAT LINES

As we explained in Chapter 15, a document's overall format is controlled by several master settings on the Format Settings screen. However, Symphony allows you to assign special formats to sections of a document by embedding *format lines* in the document. For example, look at the printed text shown in Figure 16.1. Notice that the middle section of the document is single-spaced text indented from both the left and right margins.

To create the text pictured in Figure 16.1, we used these Format settings: Left Margin, 1, Right Margin, 70, and Spacing, 2. To create the indented section of single spaced text, we placed a format line just above and below the section. The first format line, placed just above the indented section, changes the Left Margin setting to 8, the Right Margin to 62, and the Spacing to 1. This format line also changes the Justification setting from Left to Even. The second format line, placed just below the indented section, resets all subsequent text to the original master settings.

Figure 16.2 shows the middle portion of the letter as it looks on the screen. Notice the format lines that are inserted before and after the indented section.

Mr. Paul Berry, Vice President of the Clinton Corporation, was the featured speaker at the annual Professional Marketing Managers chapter awards dinner. The topic of his address was "Encouraging Excellence in the People You Manage." He emphasized the importance of high expectations and well-defined goals for all people in an organization.

Mr. Berry also explained how a manager's primary job is to make sure that "the right things get done the right way." The only way to accomplish this, according to Berry, is to work through other people.

> In my thirty-plus years of experience, I have observed that the most successful managers are those people who know when to let their subordinates do the job. Of course, another word for this is delegation. This does not mean that a manager should not set goals and track the progress his people are making. As you can tell, I think it's critically important that people know what is expected of them. However, if you don't know when to get out of the way, you will severely limit the achievements of the people you manage--and in so doing, severely limit your effectiveness as a manager.

Mr. Berry also discussed the importance of allowing people to make mistakes, and using those mistakes as learning opportunities. "A good manager," said Berry, "has excellent communication with his or her subordinates. This alone will prevent many mistakes and make it much easier for people to correct problems and learn from them."

Mr. Berry is writing a book on motivation, entitled <u>Motivation Management</u>. The book will be published during 1985.

Figure 16.1

How to Create a Format Line

Now that you've seen how the finished product looks, let's go back and repeat the process of creating these format lines. Suppose you have entered only the portion of the text shown in Figure 16.3.

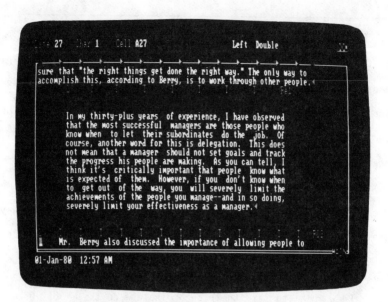

Figure 16.2

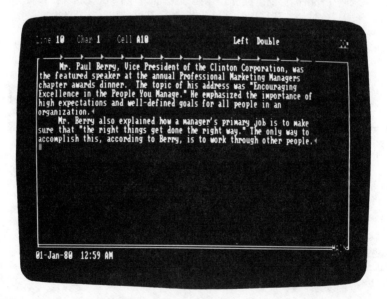

Figure 16.3

To create a format line, issue the {**Menu**} **F**ormat **C**reate command. Symphony responds with the question

Where should format line(s) be inserted?

Following this question, Symphony displays the line number of the current cursor location. If you press **[Enter],** a format line is inserted just above the line with the cursor. To put the format line somewhere else, move the cursor to where you want to insert the format line and then press **[Enter].**

To create the format line in the example, place the cursor one line below the last text line shown in Figure 16.3 and issue the **{Menu}** Format Create command. Then press **[Enter].** Figure 16.4 shows the result of those actions.

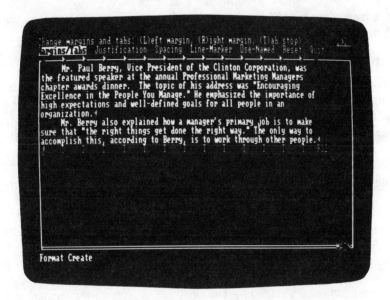

Figure 16.4

On a format line, the left and right margins are indicated by L and R, and each tab setting is indicated by a T. On the right edge of the format line, just past the right margin, you see two characters that indicate the justification and spacing for the format line. For example, the l2 at the end of the format line indicates that the Justification setting is Left and the Spacing setting is 2 (double-spacing).

The first format line you create in a document inherits the settings of the master Format settings sheet. Notice that the left and right margins and the tab settings in the new format line in the example match the master Format settings of the Format settings sheet, as indicated by the ruler line at the top of the window. Of course, Symphony allows you to change the settings in an existing format line.

Changing a Format Line

Notice the menu that appears at the top of the window in Figure 16.4.

Margins/Tabs Justification Spacing Line-Marker Use-Named Reset Quit

The commands in this menu allow you to change the characteristics of the format line. The Margins/Tabs command allows you to change the Left and Right margin settings and the Tab settings of the format line. The Justification command lets you change the Justification setting at the end of the format line. The third command, Spacing, allows you to change the Spacing setting.

The Line-Marker option lets you assign a name to the format line or remove a previously assigned name, and the Use-Named command allows you to use the settings of a named format line to define the settings of the current line.

Reset restores the master Format settings to the format line. The last option, Quit, returns you to your working document.

Assigning Margins and Tab Settings to a Format Line

To adjust the margins and tabs of a format line, select Margins/Tabs from the format line menu. After you make this selection, use the → and ← keys to move the cursor on the format line as you insert and delete tab intervals and adjust the margin settings.

To adjust the tabs and margins, you can also use the [Backspace] and [Del] keys to erase a tab setting or delete spaces between tabs. If you are working in the Insert mode, you can widen tab intervals or change the margins by pressing the space bar to insert spaces. If you change to Overwrite mode, you can write over the tab and margin settings to create new ones.

For example, suppose you want to modify the format line you created in the example. This format line has these settings: Left Margin, 1; Right Margin, 70; Tabs, 5; Justification, Left; and Spacing, 2. Now suppose you want to set the left margin at 8, make the right margin 62, create tabs every 6 spaces from the left margin, and change the spacing to 1.

Select Margins/Tabs from the format line menu and put the cursor at the beginning of the line, on the L. If you are in the Insert mode, you can press the **[Space bar]** seven times to move the Left Margin setting to column 8. The format line now looks like Figure 16.5.

Next, change to Overwrite mode by pressing the **[Ins]** key. Using the → key, move the cursor to the blank space just to the right of the new left margin. Now, using the **[Space bar]**, advance the cursor six spaces to the right and press **T.** This puts a tab six spaces to the right of the left margin. Using the [Space bar], repeat this sequence. Because you are in the Overwrite mode, the old tab settings are removed as you advance through the line with the [Space bar].

When you reach the column where you want to place the new right margin (column 62), type **R.** Now use the **[Del]** key to erase the part of the old format line that extends beyond your new right margin. Be sure to delete the old Right Margin setting as well.

After altering the Margin and Tab settings, press **[Enter].** The format line now looks like Figure 16.6. Symphony then returns you to the format line menu. You can make additional changes to the format line or return to your document by selecting Quit.

Specifying Justification for a Format Line

To change the Justification setting of a format line, select Justification from the format line menu. Symphony prompts you for one of four possible Justification settings: **Left,**

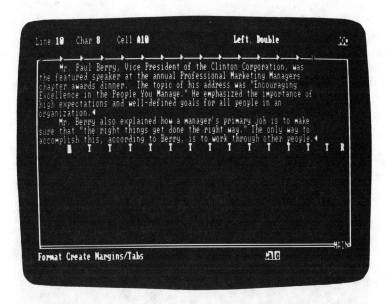

Figure 16.5

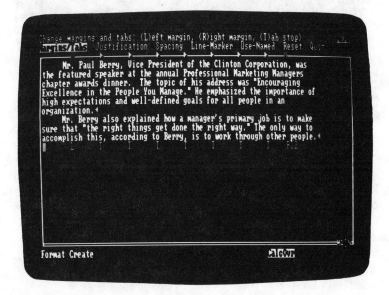

Figure 16.6

Even, **C**enter, or **N**one. Each of these Justification settings is explained in Chapter 15. Make a selection by pressing the first letter of the setting you want or by moving the pointer to your selection and pressing **[Enter].** The Justification setting you choose is indicated on the right edge of the format line by a lowercase letter: n for None, l for Left, e for Even, or c for Center.

In the example, we want to change the format of this section of the document from Left to Even. To make this change, issue the Justification command and choose the Even option. After you have specified the Justification setting, Symphony returns you to the format line menu. The worksheet now looks like Figure 16.7.

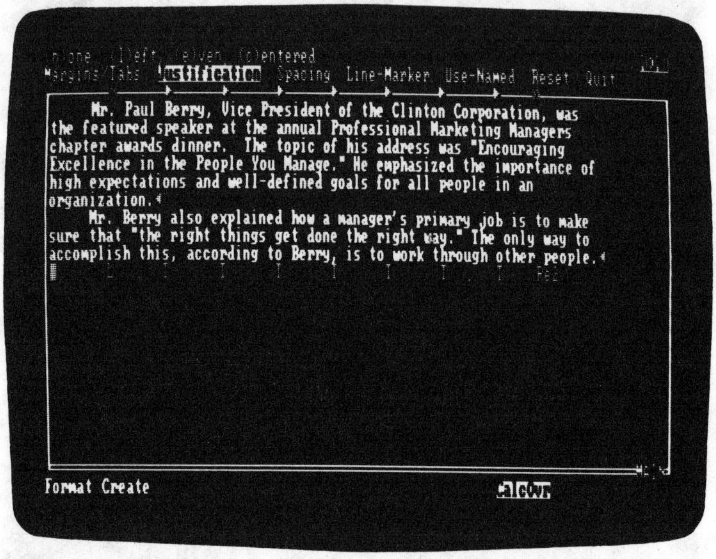

Figure 16.7

Specifying Line Spacing for a Format Line

To change the Spacing setting of a format line, select Spacing from the format line menu. Symphony responds by prompting you for one of three line spacings: 1 for single spacing, 2 for double spacing, or 3 for triple spacing. Make your spacing selection by pressing 1, 2, or 3 or by moving the pointer to your selection and pressing [Enter]. The spacing you choose is indicated on the right edge of the format line by a 1, 2, or 3 next to the Justification indicator.

For example, to change the Spacing setting in the new format line from 2 to 1, choose Spacing from the menu and select 1. After you have specified the Spacing setting, Symphony returns you to the format line menu. You can then make additional changes to the format line settings or return to your document by selecting Quit.

Naming a Format Line

After you create a format line, you may want to give it a name. By naming a format line, you make it possible to reuse the format line in the current document, in another document on the same worksheet, or in a document in a different worksheet file.

To name a format line, select **L**ine-Marker from the format line menu. Symphony then asks whether you want to assign or remove a name for the format line. If you select **A**ssign, Symphony displays the prompt

Name to assign:

Respond by typing the name you wish to assign to the format line. For example, to name the current format line, issue the **L**ine-Marker **A**ssign command and enter the name **INDENT.**

When giving a name to a format line, follow the rules for range names. The name can contain up to 15 letters or numerals. The name must not include spaces or punctuation marks. Symphony allows you to assign more than one name to a single format line.

However, if you give the new format line a name already used for another line, Symphony warns

Another line has this name; use the name here instead?

If you answer Yes, Symphony assigns the name of the other line to the new format line. The old line is no longer identified by that name. If you answer No, Symphony asks you to assign a new name.

You do not have to assign a name to a format line when you first create it. You'll see in a few pages how you can assign a name to an existing format line.

Creating the Second Format Line

After you finish changing the settings for the first format line, choose **Q**uit from the format line menu and begin typing the text shown in the indented section of the document. Notice that Symphony applies the settings in the format line to all of the text that comes after that line.

In the example, however, we want to indent only a small section of the document. To change the settings again (or to restore the settings stored in the Format settings sheet) you must create another format line in the document, after the indented section of text.

To create a second format line, simply position the cursor threee rows beneath the text and issue the **F**ormat **C**reate command. Symphony asks you where you want to place the new format line. To enter the line at the cursor location, simply press **[Enter].** Symphony then inserts the new format line at the current cursor location, as shown in Figure 16.8.

Resetting a Format Line to the Master Format Settings

Notice that the new format line is identical to the first format line. In fact, a new format line always has the same settings as the immediately preceding format line in the same document. If the new format line is the first format line in the document, Symphony assigns the settings stored in the Format settings sheet.

The Reset option is very useful if you want to restore the default settings after you create a specially formatted section. When you finish the specially formatted section, simply insert another format line. This format line has the same settings as the first format line. By using the Reset option, you can give it the settings of the master Format settings sheet.

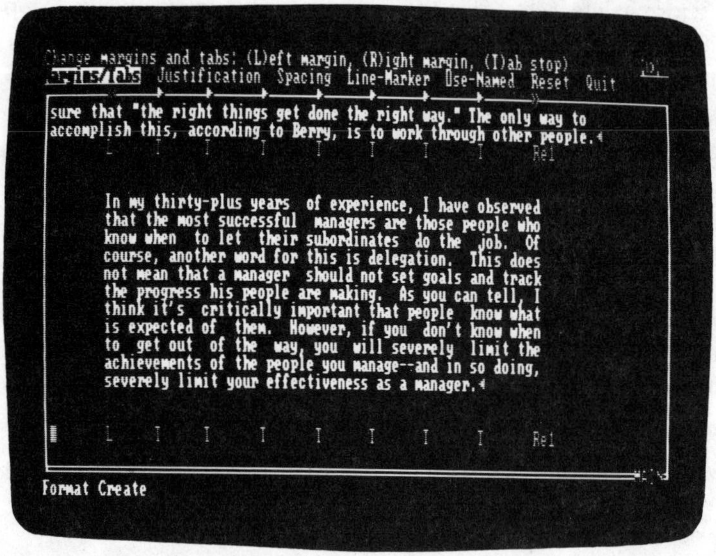

Figure 16.8

Suppose that you've created the second format line shown in Figure 16.8 and that this line has the same settings as the earlier format line. You, however, want to use the settings stored in the window's Format settings sheet. To reinstate those settings, select **R**eset from the format line menu. The format line immediately assumes the master Format settings for the document, as Figure 16.9 shows. This will cause all subsequent text to be formatted according to the master Format settings, leaving only one section with special formatting.

Creating Two Format Lines at Once

In the previous discussion, you saw how to create two different format lines in two separate operations. However, you can create two format lines with a single command. To do this, issue the {**Menu**} **F**ormat **C**reate command from the position shown in Figure 16.10. When you see the prompt

> Where should the format line(s) be inserted?

move the cursor to the line where the first format line is to be placed and press **[Tab]**. This anchors the cursor (indicated by a ← symbol at the left margin) and allows you to move to the location of the second format line.

As you move to the location of the next format line, Symphony highlights the block of text between the first format line and the cursor. When the cursor is on the line where you want to place the second format line, press **[Enter]**. This causes identical format lines to appear at both of the locations you specified. One format line will be on the line where the cursor was located when you pressed [Tab], and the other format line will be on the line where the cursor was located when you pressed [Enter]. The cursor is on the

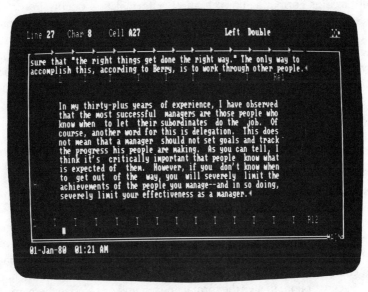

Figure 16.9

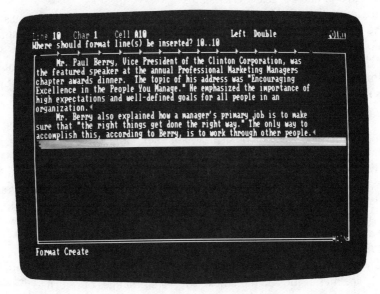

Figure 16.10

upper format line, and the format line menu appears in the control panel at the top of your screen.

Since both format lines were created at once, both lines have the same settings. If these are the first format lines in the document, both will have the same settings as the document's master Format settings. If another format line occurs in the document before these two new ones, the two new format lines will have settings identical to the preceding format line. Once the two lines are created, you can adjust the first line's settings using the same techniques explained above. Because you want the second format line to have the same settings as the master Format settings, you don't need to modify its settings. You can, however, change the settings of the second format line by placing the cursor on that line and issuing the {**Menu**} **F**ormat **E**dit command. The next section explains this command in detail.

Working with Existing Format Lines

Suppose that after you create a format line you decide to alter its settings. You can do so with the {**Menu**} **F**ormat **E**dit command. Editing an existing format line is exactly like changing the settings of a newly created format line. After issuing the {Menu} Format Edit command, Symphony gives you a menu of settings identical to the menu you see when you create a format line. To change the margins and tabs, select the **M**argins/Tabs option; to change the justification, select the **J**ustification option; to alter line spacing, select the **S**pacing option; to give the format line a name or remove the name of the format line, select **L**ine-Marker; to make the format line identical to another format line you have created and named, select **U**se-Named.

To edit a format line that does not have a name, first place the cursor on the format line or on the line just below. Then issue the {**Menu**} **F**ormat **E**dit **C**urrent command. This brings up the standard format line menu.

If, however, you want to edit a named format line, you can issue the {**Menu**} **F**ormat **E**dit **N**amed command when the cursor is at any location in the document. Symphony then displays the prompt

Format line to edit:

Below this prompt you see a menu of all line-marker names you have created, including the names of nonformat lines. You can move the pointer through this menu and press **[Enter]** when you reach the name of the format line you wish to edit. Alternatively, you can type the name of the format line you wish to edit on the prompt line. If you select a name that does not exist or if you choose the name of a nonformat line, Symphony displays an error message. After you supply the name of the format line you wish to edit and press **[Enter],** Symphony brings up the standard format line menu and moves the cursor to the named format line.

As soon as you make one change to the format line settings, Symphony returns you to the format line menu. You can then make additional changes or return to the document you are editing by selecting **Q**uit.

Naming an Existing Format Line

If you create a format line and decide later that you want to give it a name, you can do so in one of two ways. One way is to place the cursor on that line and issue the {**Menu**}

Line-Marker **A**ssign command. When you see the prompt

   Line-marker name:

type the name you wish to assign to that line. This is the same procedure you use to name a line of text (a nonformat line), as explained in Chapter 15. Alternatively, you can place the cursor on the format line you wish to name and issue the {**Menu**} **F**ormat **E**dit **C**urrent **L**ine-Marker **A**ssign command, then type the name you wish to assign to that line.

This brings up an interesting quirk in the Symphony word processing program. When you use the {Menu} Line-Marker Assign command to name a line, Symphony brings up a menu of all line names in the current worksheet (whether format lines or nonformat lines) at the same time that it prompts you to specify a line-marker name. This menu is useful if there are many named lines in your worksheet because it helps you avoid assigning a name you have already used.

Interestingly, you do *not* see this menu when you name a format line using {Menu} Format Edit Current Line-Marker Assign. If you are editing a format line that already has a name, Symphony shows you the current name of that line, but not the names of other lines in your worksheet. (Remember, Symphony lets you assign more than one name to a line.)

Removing a Format Line Name

To remove a format line name, press {**Menu**} **L**ine-Marker **R**emove. This brings up the prompt

   Line-marker to delete:

Below the prompt, you see a menu of all line-marker names in the current worksheet. To delete a line name, move the pointer through this menu until you reach the name you wish to remove and press **[Enter]**. Alternatively, you can type the name you wish to remove next to Symphony's prompt and press **[Enter]**.

Another way to remove a format line name is to place the cursor on the format line and issue the {**Menu**} **F**ormat **E**dit **C**urrent command. This brings up the standard format line menu. From this menu, select the **L**ine-Marker **R**emove option. Symphony then displays the prompt

   Name to remove:

Below this prompt you see the name or names currently assigned to this line. Respond to the prompt by pressing **[Enter]** when the pointer is on the line name you wish to remove or by typing the name you wish to remove next to the prompt. Since most lines have only one name, you can usually "un-name" a line simply by pressing **[Enter]** when Symphony prompts you for the name to delete.

A third way to remove a format line name is to assign that name to another line in the document. Because Symphony does not allow two lines to have the same name, the original line loses its name when you assign it to another.

Erasing, Moving, and Copying Format Lines

Format lines are like other lines in a document in that you can use Symphony's Erase, Move, and Copy commands to move them within a document or to erase them completely.

Erasing

Removing the name of a format line does not eliminate the format line itself. To delete a format line, place the cursor on the format line and press the {**Erase**} key. This causes the entire line to be highlighted. Pressing [**Enter**] deletes the line. Using {Erase} (or {Menu} Erase) is the only way to delete a format line. You cannot remove a format line using the [Del] or [Backspace] key.

Moving

You can use the DOC {**Menu**} Move command to move a format line from one location to another in a document. To move a format line, simply position the cursor on the first character of the format line and issue the {**Menu**} Move command. Symphony highlights the entire format line. If you want to move only the format line, press [**Enter**]. Next, point to the line where you want to move the format line and press [**Enter**]. Symphony then moves the format line to the new location.

You can use the Move command to move lines of text at the same time you move a format line. In fact, you frequently will move a format line at the same time you move the text that it formats. For example, if you want to move the indented block of text in the document in Figure 16.2, you would move not only the block of text but also the format lines. To do this, you would highlight the block of text and the two surrounding format lines in response to the "Move FROM what block?" prompt.

Copying

Suppose you've created a format line and you now want to use the line to format the text in another part of the document. For example, assume that you want to use the indented, single spaced format line you created previously to format another part of the document.

To copy a format line, position the cursor on the first character of the format line and issue the {**Menu**} Copy command. Symphony immediately highlights the entire format line. If you want to copy just the format line, press [**Enter**]. Next, position the cursor on the line where you want to move the format line and press [**Enter**]. Symphony copies the format line to the new location.

Creating Linked Format Lines

In addition to allowing you to copy a format line, Symphony allows you to link copies of a named format line to the original format line. When you create such linked copies, any changes you make to the settings in the named format line are duplicated in the linked copies.

To link a format line to an existing named format line, issue the {**Menu**} Format Use-Named command. Symphony then displays the prompt

Format line to use:

Below this prompt you see a menu of all the line-marker names you have assigned. This menu includes both named format lines and other named lines. From this menu, select the name of the format line you wish to use by placing the pointer on that name and pressing [**Enter**].

The format line that results from the Format Create Use-Named command does not look like a regular format line with margin and tab settings appearing on the screen. Instead, you see the name of the format line you've used, preceded by the symbol @. For example, if you decide to use the named format line INDENT to define this new format line, you see @INDENT at the position of the new format line. However, all the settings of the named format line INDENT apply to any text that follows the symbol @INDENT.

Figure 16.11 shows a DOC window in which the format line INDENT has been duplicated. The @INDENT on the screen marks the location of the duplicate.

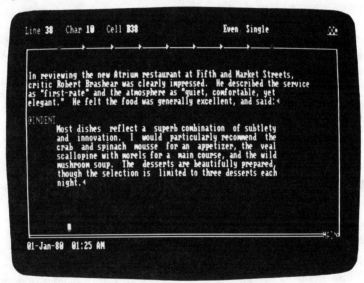

Figure 16.11

Whenever you edit a named format line, the changes you make also apply to all format lines that are linked to the original. For example, suppose a format line named STYLE has a Justification setting of I (Left). Suppose also that you have duplicated the STYLE format line twice in your document. If you change the Justification setting of STYLE from Left to Even, the Justification setting of each duplicate (@STYLE) line changes to Even also. This is evident because the text on the screen below each of the duplicate @STYLE lines is automatically rejustified after you change the Justification setting of the original STYLE line.

If you duplicate a named format line and then remove the name of the original format line, you break the link between the duplicates and the original. From that point on, any changes you make to the original format line are not reflected in the linked copies. In addition, when you move the cursor to the text below a linked copy of the format line, you will see a message at the top of your screen:

WARNING: Format line is invalid.

For example, suppose again that you have a document that contains a format line named STYLE and several linked copies (@STYLE). If you erase the original STYLE format line and then move the cursor to the text below one of the @STYLE copies, you will see the warning described above.

Symphony does not automatically rejustify the text below an invalid format line, so the text in the invalid region retains its current form until you use the {Justify} key or issue a command that causes automatic rejustification (Erase, Move, or Copy). After you use one of those commands, the text below the format line is rejustified according to the master Format settings or according to the format line (if there is one) immediately preceding the invalid format line.

You can reuse a named format line as often as you wish within a document. You can also create linked duplicates of a named format line in different documents and windows of the same worksheet. Furthermore, you can reuse a named format line in a different worksheet file by invoking the **File Combine** command (explained later in this chapter).

Editing a Linked Format Line

To edit a linked format line (let's call it @NAME), place the cursor on the word @NAME and press {**Menu**} **Format Edit Current**. This brings up the standard format line menu, which you can use to edit the format line.

When you edit a format line that is linked to named line (i.e., when you edit @NAME), you break the link with the original format line. After the line is edited, the @NAME representation on the screen is replaced with the standard format line indicator.

Examples of Using Format Lines

At the beginning of this chapter, we showed you how to use format lines to create an indented block of single-spaced text in a document. The following sections show further examples of how to use format lines to change the appearance of your documents.

Creating a Text Table within a Document

Figure 16.12 depicts a memo that contains a table of employee names. Before writing this memo, you should use the {Menu} Format Settings command to create the following master Format settings for this memo:

Justification: Left
Left Margin: 5
Right Margin: 76
Tabs: 5
Spacing: 1

```
May 10, 1985

TO:      Robert O. Grayson, President

FROM:    Jim Higgins, Personnel Manager

SUBJECT: Recipients of "Most Valued Employee" Award


After final review by the Division Managers, we have a list
of people who will receive the annual "Most Valued Employee"
award at the end of this month.  In addition to your official
announcement of the awards, we will publish some remarks from
each employee's supervisor in the next month's company
newsletter.

           Recipients of "Most Valued Employee" Award


   Name                 Position          Office   Years of Service

   Karen Smeltzer       Acctg. Supervisor  Dallas        8

   Donald Wright        Telephone Sales    Dallas        5

   Michelle Carruthers  Facilities Manager Austin        5

   Robert Berg          Research Scientist Austin        7

   Eugene Simon         Warehouse Clerk    Plainview     9

   Ann Shields          Secretary          Plainview    10


   If you would like any more information about these
   individuals, please let me know.  Naturally, they will not
   know of the award until you inform them personally.
```

Figure 16.12

After typing the first part of the memo, create a special format line by following these steps: First, place the cursor on the line where you want the table to begin and press {**Menu**} Format Create. Next, press [**Tab**], then move the cursor down four lines and press [**Enter**]. This creates two format lines with three blank lines between them. The table of names will occupy more than three lines, but you can insert as many lines as you need while you are creating the table. Both format lines initially have the master Format settings. After you create the two format lines, the cursor is on the upper format line and the format line menu is at the top of your screen.

Now select Margins/Tabs from the menu. You do not need to change the Left Margin setting in the example, but you must change the Right Margin setting to 78. In addition, you must place tabs at columns 27, 50, and 67. To make these changes, first use the → key to place the cursor in the blank space just to the right of the left margin indicator, L. Then press the [**Ins**] key to change to Overwrite mode and press the [**Space bar**] until you reach column 27. At space 27, type a **T.** By doing this, you write over the old Tab settings and create a new Tab setting at column 27.

To complete the changes, press the [**Space bar**] again until you reach column 50, type a **T,** then space over to column 67 and type another **T.** Finally, continue to press the [**Space bar**] until you reach column 78, the new right margin. Type an **R** to set the new right margin. Then press [**Enter**].

Now, select Justification from the format line menu. At the prompt, choose **None.** Then select **Quit** to return to your document. The None justification setting is used so the chart will remain on the screen exactly as you create it. If you create the chart using Left justification, Symphony will automatically close up extra spaces between words on the same line.

The first format line is now set so that you can create the table of names. You don't need to change the second format line, since its settings return the text to the original master Format settings.

To create the table, move the cursor to the first line below the top format line, type the heading and use the {**Center**} key to center it over the table. Next, create the body of the table. Generally, it is easier to type the body of the table before typing the subheadings (Name, Position, and so on).

After you complete the body, enter the subheadings. You can "eyeball" the location of each subheading as you create it. After positioning the subheadings in the table, go back to the first letter of the first subheading (Name) and insert the code for underlining ([**Ctrl**] **BU**). Then go to the space just beyond the last subheading and insert the code for discontinuing the underline ([**Ctrl**] **E**). Because underlining inserts extra characters on your screen, I suggest that you create the subheadings and position them exactly as you want before inserting the underline codes.

Creating an Indented Block of Text with Hanging Characters

Figure 16.13 depicts a letter with several blocks of indented text. Each block is numbered, with the numbers appearing to the left of the indented text. These numbers and the periods after them, are said to "hang" outside the text.

To create this block of text, first move the cursor to the line where you want the indented blocks of text to begin and issue the {**Menu**} Format Create command.

Next, press [**Tab**] to anchor the cursor, move the cursor down four lines, and press [**Enter**]. These actions create two format lines with three blank lines between them. Both format lines have the master Format settings. After you create the two format lines, the cursor is on the upper format line, and the format line menu is at the top of your screen.

Next, select Margins/Tabs from the menu. Then, with the document in the Insert mode, place the cursor on the left margin marker, L, and press the [**Space bar**] ten times. This causes the left margin to be indented. Then place the cursor on column 60 (the indented right margin), type an **R,** and press the [**Del**] key to remove the old format line that extends beyond this new right margin.

February 8, 1985

Mr. Donald E. Berg
4206 Brookfield Avenue
Atlanta, Georgia 30327

Dear Mr. Berg:

As someone who understands the lasting value of a superior work of
literature, you can appreciate the benefits offered by The Fine Book
Club. The Fine Book Club gives you the opportunity to build your
collection of literature with contemporary masterpieces and recognized
classics. Here are some of the unique benefits of membership in The
Fine Book Club:

   1. A selection of more than 3,500 literary
      masterpieces from which to choose. We very rarely
      discontinue a selection after it has been chosen
      for our catalog, so you can acquire the classics
      that your local bookstore no longer stocks.

   2. Every month, our panel of literary experts
      evaluates the merits of each new selection. These
      evaluations provide a summary of the book's story
      or content and specific details to help you decide
      whether or not you want to purchase the book.

   3. As a member of The Fine Book Club, you can
      purchase books at a savings of 20% to 45% off
      of normal retail price.

   4. There is no minimum purchase requirement. After
      you pay the annual membership fee of $35.00, you
      are eligible for all the Club's benefits--at no
      obligation.

I have enclosed a sample of one of our monthly brochures, describing and
evaluating some of our new selections.

Mr. Berg, if you would like to join The Fine Book Club, simply return
the enclosed Membership Reservation Form in the postage-free envelope
provided. We will be happy to bill you for your first year's dues.

I look forward to hearing from you soon.

Yours truly,

Margaret Smith

Figure 16.13

There is no need to change the Tab, Justification, or Spacing settings for this format
line. Also, you don't need to change the second format line, since this line will serve to
return the text to the original master Format settings.

Now you can begin typing the indented blocks of text with hanging numbers. First, place the cursor on the line where the first paragraph will begin. Press **[End]** ← to move the cursor beyond the indented left margin to the left edge of the window. Type the first hanging characters, that is, **1.,** then type the first block of text.

When you finish typing the first block, press the **{Justify}** key. This causes the paragraph to be aligned with the indented left margin, but the numeral and period hang outside the left margin with one trailing space. This same procedure should be used to create each of the numbered blocks of text shown in Figure 16.13.

To make this procedure work, you must end the hanging characters with one of the following separation characters:

.	(period)
*	(asterisk)
~	(tilde)
)	(right parenthesis)
>	(greater than sign)
=	(equals sign)
+	(plus)
−	(minus)
:	(colon)
]	(right bracket)

Hanging characters cannot include spaces except hard spaces (explained later in this chapter). In addition, the total number of hanging characters must be less than or equal to the number of spaces in the left margin, minus one. For example, if you set the left margin at 5, there are four spaces in the margin. This means that no more than three characters can hang outside an indented paragraph. In other words, in this case a two-digit number (plus a period) could hang outside the paragraph, but a three-digit number (plus a period) could not.

Creating Variable Tab Settings

The master Format settings for a document allow you to name a tab interval, but not specific tab locations. This is not very useful if you are creating a chart, outline, or another item that requires tabs that are not evenly spaced. To solve this problem, you can create a format line and place tabs on the format line wherever you need them.

For example, suppose you want to create a list of services like the one in Figure 16.14. You may want to experiment with the layout to decide exactly where you want to place the tabs. In the example, we decided to place tabs at columns 6, 10, and 13.

After deciding where to place the tabs, move the cursor to the top of the document and issue the **{Menu}** Format Create command. Next, select Margins/Tabs from the format line menu and put Symphony in Overwrite mode by pressing the **[Ins]** key. Then, use the [Space bar] to move the cursor to the column where you want to place the first tab (6 in our example). Type **T** to create the tab, then use the [Space bar] to move to the next tab location and type another **T.** Repeat this process until you create all the tabs you need. Because you are in Overwrite mode, pressing the [Space bar] will write over the

```
                    Services Provided by LCB Associates


HARDWARE SELECTION

        Personal Computers

        Multiuser Microcomputers

        Peripherals

                Printers
                Hard Disks
                Expansion Boards
                Monitors


SOFTWARE SELECTION

        Integrated Packages

        Word Processing Software

        Database Management Software

        Accounting Software

                General Ledger
                Payroll
                Inventory
                Accounts Receivable
                Accounts Payable


CUSTOMIZED PROGRAMMING

        Database Applications

        Accounting Systems

        Project Management


TRAINING ON ALL HARDWARE AND SOFTWARE PRODUCTS WE RECOMMEND
```

Figure 16.14

original tab settings as you create the new settings. When all your new tab settings are in place, return to your working text by selecting **Q**uit.

STORING FORMAT LINES AND FORMAT SETTINGS SHEETS

One advantage of word processing is that it gives you the ability to store and reuse particular document formats. If you are like most Symphony users, much of your work calls for only two or three basic types of documents. For example, you may write many letters that use the same format. This format reflects the design of your business stationery as well as standard format considerations such as margins, spacing, and justification. Rather than creating the Format and Print settings each time you type a letter, you can use stored settings.

Another stored format might be a chart or table that you use often. You can store a format line with a None Justification setting and all the tab settings you need to produce the chart. Use this format line each time you create the chart.

With Symphony, re-creating standard formats can be achieved by storing format lines, Format settings sheets, and Print settings sheets on disk.

Storing and Using a Format Settings Sheet

Suppose you want to create a Format settings sheet and a Print settings sheet you can use each time you write a business letter. To create these standard formats, start with a blank worksheet in the DOC environment. Issue the {**Menu**} **F**ormat **S**ettings command and change the format settings to be suitable for the letters you plan to write. For example, you might choose these settings: Left Margin, 10; Right Margin, 70; Justification, Left; and Spacing, 1.

Next, issue the {**Services**} **P**rint **S**ettings command and change the Print settings in this worksheet to be suitable for your business letters. In most cases, the most important settings on the Print settings sheet are the margins, Init-string, headers and footers (if you want them), and Page Wait. Use this last setting to tell Symphony to delay after each page that is printed so you can load another piece of stationery into the printer. (Chapter 17 explains how to adjust Symphony's print settings to print a document.)

After you create the Format settings and Print settings, store the blank worksheet by typing {**Services**} **F**ile **S**ave. When Symphony prompts you to name the file, you might want to choose a descriptive name, such as **LETTER**, that you can recognize quickly on your menu of file names.

After you create the LETTER file, each time you want to write a letter, simply press {**Services**} **F**ile **R**etrieve and choose the file **LETTER**. This brings up a blank worksheet with all the Format settings and Print settings in place. Use the blank worksheet to create your letter as you normally would.

If, after writing the letter, you want to save it on disk, do not use the file name LETTER. Reserve the name LETTER for a blank worksheet with Format settings and Print settings suitable for each new letter you write. If you store a letter you have created in the file LETTER, you won't be able to reuse the Format settings and Print settings of the file LETTER without also getting a worksheet that contains the letter you just created. For this reason, save the finished letter under a different name. (I use the last name of the recipient when I name a file containing a business letter.)

Storing and Using a Format Line

If you plan to reuse format lines, you might want to create a library file that contains nothing but named format lines. You can then use Symphony's File Combine Named-Range command to use any format line in the library when you write a document.

Creating a Library File

Creating a library file is as easy as defining a few format lines in a blank worksheet, naming each of the format lines, and saving the worksheet using the {**Services**} File **S**ave command. You might want to use a name like **LIBRARY** for this file.

Be sure to choose descriptive names when you name the format lines in your library file. You'll have to be able to remember the purpose of each line to retrieve one for use in another worksheet.

Using the Library File

Assume that you have created a separate file that contains only a collection of named format lines and that the name of the file is LIBRARY. Now suppose you are writing a document and want to use a format line stored in the library file. The name of the line you want to use is BILL. Begin by placing the cursor on the line of your document where you want the BILL format line to appear. If the document line you choose is blank, you can proceed. If the line contains text, however, press **[Enter]** or {**Split**} to insert a blank line and position the cursor on this blank line. If you do not create a blank line before copying a format line from another file, the format line will write over the line of text.

Next, press {**Services**} File Combine Copy. This tells Symphony that you want to copy part of a .WRK file into the current worksheet. When this command is issued, Symphony asks you if you want to copy the entire file or a named area. Select **N**amed-Area. This brings up the prompt

> Range or line-marker name:

Respond by typing the name of the format line you wish to use, **BILL,** and pressing **[Enter]**.

Symphony then asks you if you want to ignore or read range and line-marker names from the file. You can choose either option because this step has no effect when you use File Combine to combine a named area of a file into the current worksheet.

At the next prompt, Symphony asks you if you want to read Formulas or Values from the file. This step also has no effect because it does not apply to a document file; when you see this prompt, press **[Enter]**. Next you see the prompt

> Name of file to combine:

Below this prompt you see a menu of file names. Since the format line BILL is stored in the file LIBRARY, you should select **LIBRARY** from this list. After you complete this sequence, Symphony places the format line in your document on the line just above the cursor line.

Of course, you can combine a named format line from any .WRK file into the current worksheet. The source file can be any .WRK file that contains the desired line-marker name, and not just a special library file.

There are, however, some good reasons why you might want to keep a library of format lines in a separate file. Storing all of your format lines in one file allows you to delete some document files from your disk without deleting the format lines you want to keep and reuse. Additionally, you can copy the library file onto different disks so that the format lines are always easily accessible. If the format lines are scattered throughout several documents, you would have to copy all of those files to copy all of the format lines.

Updating the Library File

Suppose you are creating a document called SCRIPT that includes several format lines you want to store and use in other documents. Before saving these lines, be sure to assign each a name that has *not* already been used for one of the format lines in the library file. Next, save the SCRIPT file using the File Save command and clear your worksheet by pressing {**Services**} New and answering Yes to the prompt. Then, using {**Services**} File Retrieve, load the LIBRARY file into the worksheet. After that, press {**Services**} File Combine and follow the steps described above to copy the named format lines from the SCRIPT file into the LIBRARY file.

STORING AND USING LINES AND PARAGRAPHS OF TEXT

Symphony gives you the ability to save lines and blocks of text on disk for reuse in later documents. This ability can come in handy if you write a large number of similar letters or reports. For example, you may use several standard paragraphs in various sales letters. With the Symphony word processor, you can name each of these paragraphs and reuse them whenever appropriate.

Naming a Line

When you are in the DOC environment, you can name a line of text by placing the cursor on that line and issuing the {**Menu**} Line-Marker Assign command. Symphony then prompts you to type the name you wish to assign to the line. After you choose the name and press [**Enter**], the name of the line becomes a part of the document. Once you have saved the file, you can use the File Combine Copy command to retrieve the named line for use in another worksheet. (The steps for retrieving a regular line of text are identical to the steps for retrieving a named format line.)

Naming a Block

In the DOC environment, you can name only single lines of text; you cannot assign one name to a range of several lines or a paragraph. If you would like to assign a name to several lines, a paragraph, or several paragraphs, you need to switch temporarily to the SHEET environment and invoke the Range Name command.

Suppose you have just created a letter with a paragraph containing a brilliant sales pitch. Because you are sure you want to use the pitch in other letters, you decide to name and save the persuasive paragraph. Begin by placing the cursor on the first word of the paragraph. Then press {**Type**} and select **SHEET** to get into the spreadsheet environment. Where you saw a cursor in the DOC environment, you now see a cell pointer.

Once you are in the SHEET environment, issue the {**Menu**} **R**ange **N**ame **C**reate command. Symphony prompts you with the message

Range name:

You should respond by typing the name you wish to give the paragraph and pressing **[Enter]**. For our example, let's name the paragraph **PITCH.**

After you enter the range name, Symphony gives you the prompt

Specify range:

Respond by highlighting the lines that you want to include in the named range. In the example, let's highlight all the lines of the PITCH paragraph.

To highlight these lines, first press the period key to anchor the cell pointer. Then, move the cell pointer down until the last line of the paragraph is highlighted. Notice that you do not have to highlight entire lines in the paragraph. Symphony interprets each line in a document as a long label residing in column A. Therefore, moving the cell pointer only in column A is sufficient to specify that entire lines of the paragraph are in the named range.

After highlighting the paragraph you wish to name, press **[Enter].** This name is now part of the worksheet. When you save the worksheet in a disk file, you save the name of the paragraph as well.

You can use the **F**ile **C**ombine **C**opy command to retrieve a block of text into another worksheet. Be sure that the worksheet contains enough blank lines to accommodate the block you wish to transfer; otherwise, the combined block writes over the text in the current worksheet.

You might want to keep a special file of commonly used paragraphs and lines, like the file you use to store commonly used format lines. You can copy this file to different disks so that the paragraphs and lines are easily accessible no matter which disk you are working with.

INDENTATION

Symphony has a special {Indent} key you can use to indent the left margin of your text temporarily. You can use the {Indent} key only at the beginning of a paragraph; it will not work if you use it on a line other than the first line of a paragraph. Remember, Symphony treats anything that follows a paragraph delimiter as a new paragraph. Paragraph delimiters are: hard carriage returns, blank lines, format lines, and nontext cells.

The {Indent} key indents the first line of a paragraph and all subsequent text in that paragraph. Subsequent paragraphs are not indented unless you use the {Indent} key at the beginning of each one. You can use the {Indent} key either before or after you type the paragraph that you want to indent.

Suppose you have written the paragraph in Figure 16.15 and you decide you would like to indent the left edge of the paragraph 5 spaces. First, use **[End]**↑ to position the cursor on the first character of the paragraph. Be sure you are in Insert mode, then press the

[Space bar] four times so that the cursor and the first character of the paragraph are in the column just to the left of the column where you want the indented text to begin. In this example, you want the indented text to start in column 6, so you move the cursor to column 5, as shown in Figure 16.16. Now, press the {**Indent**} key. This will cause a → symbol to appear in column 5. To indent the entire paragraph, as shown in Figure 16.17, press the {**Justify**} key. Notice that the right margin does not change.

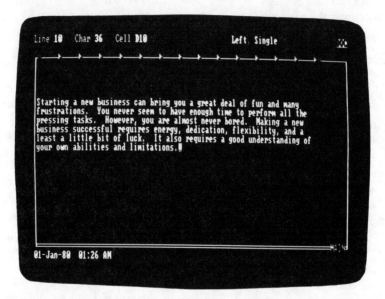

Figure 16.15

As another example, suppose you would like to indent a paragraph you are about to write. Before you begin typing, move the cursor to the column just before the column where you would like your indented text to begin. For instance, if you want your indented text to begin in column 6, place the cursor in column 5. Now press the {**Indent**} key and begin typing. Notice that no line after the first is automatically indented. You must press the {**Justify**} key to indent these.

Indentation works with both Left Justification and Even Justification settings. If your document has Center Justification, each indented line of text is centered between the indent column and the right margin. The {Indent} key does not work with the None Justification setting.

You can use the **[Del]** key to remove the indentation symbol from the beginning of a paragraph. When the → symbol is deleted, the entire paragraph, except for the first line, returns to the normal left margin when you press the {**Justify**} key. You must manually remove the extra spaces at the beginning of the first line after removing the indentation symbol.

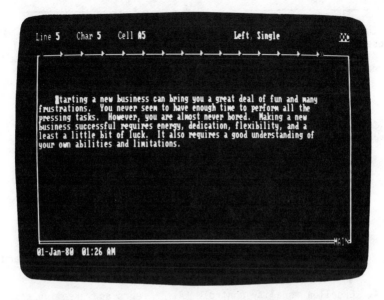

Figure 16.16

Using {Indent} with Hanging Characters

Suppose you would like to indent some text with hanging bullets or numbers, as shown in Figure 16.18. One way to accomplish this was explained above in the section on using format lines. Another way is to use the {Indent} key.

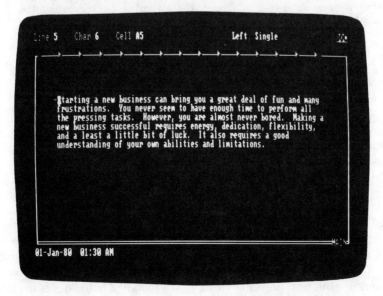

Figure 16.17

In the meeting of the Financial Group Directors, Mitch Stuart presented a summary of the report from Clark Consultants. Their findings show that the key factors in the success of Keeling Corporation are as follows:

1. A strong distribution system, based on excellent relationships with major distributors and wholesalers.

2. Superior performance from very knowledgeable sales personnel. Keeling has perhaps the most successful program of sales training and motivation in the industry. If we were to acquire this company, we would certainly adopt many parts of this program for the sales teams of our various divisions.

3. State-of-the-art inventory and receivables management, supported by a well-managed combination of centralized and distributed data processing.

4. Excellent quality control. A few years ago, Keeling's reputation was suffering because of high customer reject rates, especially on new products. It appears they have overcome this problem, and in fact, have earned a reputation for having some of the most consistently excellent product quality in the industry.

One of the potential problems of this company is a reputation for having very high prices. Though the consultants recommend that we continue the policy of high-end pricing, they believe there is room for some discounting, particularly if certain costs are brought into line. Both administrative overhead and materials costs appear to be far too high at this time. If these costs were properly controlled, several product lines could be discounted, with a net positive cash flow effect.

The attached pages contain detailed financial statements for the Keeling Corporation, as well as projections for the next five years' performance. The projections were prepared by Clark Consultants.

Figure 16.18

Figure 16.18 depicts part of a report with four indented points, each point numbered with a hanging numeral. To create the indented text of the example, move the cursor to column 4 and type the number 1 and the period after it. Then skip one space to the right and press {**Indent**}. Next, type the first point, beginning "A strong distribution system." After completing this text, press the {**Justify**} key to indent both lines of the first point. Then use **[Enter]** to skip down three lines. Again, move the cursor to column 4, type the number 2 and the period after it, skip one space, and press the {**Indent**} key to indent the second point. Follow this same procedure to indent each remaining point in the report.

SEARCHING

Like nearly every word processing program, Symphony has the ability to search through a document for a particular word or character sequence. In Symphony, you can search forward from the cursor location through the end of the document or backward from the cursor location to the beginning of the document. You can also replace the character or string you are searching for with another character or string.

To begin a search, issue the {**Menu**} **S**earch command. Symphony responds with the prompt

> **Search for what?**

You then type in the character, word, or words you want to search for (called the "search string") and press **[Enter]**. The maximum length of a search string is 50 characters, including spaces.

After you type the search string, Symphony gives you three choices: Forward, Backward, and Quit. If you want to search forward from the cursor location through the end of the document, point to **F**orward and press **[Enter]**. To search backward from the cursor location to the beginning of the document, point to **B**ackward and press **[Enter]**. If you want to abandon the search, choose **Q**uit.

When you choose Forward or Backward, the cursor moves in the direction you specify to the next occurrence of the search string. When the program finds the next occurrence of the search string, you are again given the options Forward, Backward, and Quit. If you choose **Q**uit, the search ends, and the cursor is positioned on the search string. You can then work at this location in the document.

If you want to continue the search, choose **F**orward or **B**ackward. Again, the cursor moves to the next occurrence of the search string.

When you reach the last occurrence of the search string in the document, your computer beeps and displays the message "String not found" in the lower left corner of the screen. You will also get this message when you first issue the Search command if the search string does not occur in your document.

The Search feature is helpful when you are editing a long document. Thanks to the Search command, you can go quickly to any place in your document. For example, suppose you are working on a 20-page report with numerous subheadings. When you reach the end of the document, you decide to edit the section of the document that is under the subheading, "Characteristics of a Good Test Market." This is a fairly lengthy subheading, but it is within the 50-character limit for a search string.

To go to the subheading quickly, press {**Menu**} **S**earch and then type in the subheading as the search string. Then specify **B**ackward as the direction of the search, since you are at the end of the document when you begin the search. When Symphony finds the subheading, it displays that section of the document in the window. If you want to work on this section of the document, select **Q**uit. The cursor is now at the subheading, and you can begin to edit this section of your report.

Symphony finds the search string you specify anywhere in the document, even if it falls in the middle of another word. For example, if your search string is *the,* Symphony finds occurrences in the words *then* and *other.* To avoid this kind of imprecise matching, include the entire word you are seeking, with one blank space in front and one behind, in your search string. Symphony recognizes one leading and one trailing blank space in a search string, but not more than one.

If you designate a search string in all lowercase letters, Symphony finds all occurrences of the word, whether in lowercase, capitals, or both. If the search string starts with a capital letter followed by lowercase letters, Symphony finds only those occurrences that start with a capital letter. If the string starts with a capital letter followed by a mixture of capitals and lowercase, Symphony finds all occurrences that match exactly and those occurrences in all capitals. If you specify a search string in all capital letters, Symphony finds only the occurrences in all capitals. Table 16.1 summarizes the way various search strings work in Symphony.

Search String	Occurrences Symphony Will Find
macintosh	macintosh, Macintosh, MacIntosh, MACINTOSH
Macintosh	Macintosh, MacIntosh, MACINTOSH
MacIntosh	MacIntosh, MACINTOSH
MACINTOSH	MACINTOSH

Table 16.1

Searching and Replacing

Symphony's Replace command allows you to find every occurrence of a character, word, or group of words and replace it with another.

One major difference between the Search feature and the Replace feature is that you can replace strings only when you move forward through a document, whereas you can search either forward or backward. Before starting a Replace procedure, be sure the cursor is in front of the part of the document you want to search. If you want to search the entire document, use **[Home]** to place the cursor at the beginning of the document before starting the Replace procedure.

To begin the Replace procedure, issue the **{Menu} R**eplace command. Symphony displays the prompt

Replace what?

You respond by typing the string of characters you wish to search for. This string is called the search string. The maximum length of a search string is 50 characters, including spaces.

After specifying the search string, press **[Enter].** Symphony then displays the prompt

Replace it with what?

You respond by typing the string of characters with which you want to replace the search string (called the replace string). After you specify this string, Symphony moves the cursor forward through the document until it reaches the first occurrence of the search string.

When Symphony finds the first occurrence of the search string, it offers five options: Once, Continue, Skip, All-Remaining, and Quit. If you want to replace only this occurrence of the search string, choose **O**nce. After making the first replacement, Symphony abandons the search and the cursor remains at this location until you move it.

To replace this occurrence of the search string and move to the next occurrence, choose **C**ontinue. Symphony makes the replacement and then jumps to the next occurrence of the search string.

If you do not want to replace this occurrence of the search string but want to look for other occurrences in the document, choose **S**kip. Symphony leaves this occurrence of the search string intact and jumps to the next occurrence.

If you want to replace this occurrence of the search string and all others in the document without pausing at each one, choose **A**ll-Remaining.

Finally, if you want to abandon the search without replacing this occurrence of the search string, choose **Q**uit. The cursor remains at the current occurrence until you move it.

Like the Search command, Replace finds the search string you designate wherever it falls in the document, even if it falls in the middle of another word. For example, if the search string is *the,* Symphony finds occurrences in the words *then* and *other.* Again, you can avoid imprecise matching by placing one blank space before the word you specify as the search string and another blank space after the search string. Imprecise matching can cause significant problems if you select All-Remaining during a Replace procedure. The Replace command also follows the same capitalization rules as Search does (see Table 16.1).

Replacing Double Blanks with Single Blanks

As we noted in Chapter 15, Symphony has the irritating convention of forcing two blank spaces after most periods, question marks, or exclamation points when you choose the Even or Left Justification setting. Because Symphony's Replace feature sees contiguous blank spaces as a single blank space, it is not possible to search for double blank spaces in order to replace them with single blank spaces.

Instead, follow these steps to change double blanks after periods to single blanks. After the document has been completed and justified Even or Left, move the cursor to the beginning of the document. Issue the {**Menu**} Format Settings Justification command and change the Justification setting to None. This prevents Symphony from reinstating the double blanks after you remove them.

Now issue the {**Menu**} **R**eplace command. In response to the first prompt

> **Replace what?**

type a period followed by a single blank space and then press **[Enter]**. In response to the second prompt

> **Replace it with what?**

type a period with no trailing blank space and press **[Enter]**.

After you specify the replace string Symphony searches for the first occurrence of the string ". " When it finds the first occurrence, use the All-Remaining command to replace all remaining occurrences in the document.

You can follow this same procedure to change double blanks after question marks or exclamation points to single blanks.

Replacing Single Blanks with Double Blanks

In addition to forcing double blank spaces after each period, Symphony has the annoying habit of forcing a single blank space after colons, parentheses, quotation marks, numbers, single quotation marks, ampersands, and several other characters. One way to solve this problem is to make one of the spaces after a colon (or other character) a hard space. (See below for an explanation of creating and using hard spaces.) However, this method is time-consuming and awkward. Alternatively, you could use the Replace command to find all occurrences of the string ":" (a colon with no leading or trailing blank spaces) and replace them with the string ": " (a colon with a single trailing blank space). After following this procedure, the single blank space after the colon that is *already* in the document will remain, making for a total of two blank spaces when you replace the colon with a colon plus one trailing blank. You can use the same procedure to change single blanks to double blanks after quotation marks, parentheses, or other characters.

Using Replace to Format all Occurrences of a Word

In Chapter 15, you learned about format codes that can be embedded in text to cause underlining, boldfacing, and other special formatting. You can use these format codes in a replace string to format all occurrences of a word or words in a document. For example, suppose you want to underline the words *Vanity Fair* every time they appear in a document. Start by pressing **[Home]** to move the cursor to the beginning of your document. Then issue the {**Menu**} Replace command. Specify **Vanity Fair** as the search string and press **[Enter]**. For the replace string, type **[Ctrl] BU** followed by the words **Vanity Fair.** Then type **[Ctrl] E** and press **[Enter]**. Symphony will then go through the normal Replace procedure, substituting the words with the special format codes (▲ U Vanity Fair ▼) for the occurrences of the unformatted words.

CORRECTING JUSTIFICATION PROBLEMS WITH HARD SPACES

A hard space is a special blank that cannot be eliminated when Symphony rejustifies text. To create a hard space, press {**Compose**} and then press the **[Space bar]** twice. This causes a dot to appear on the screen where you created the hard space. If you have used the Format settings to make all your blank spaces visible, hard spaces are indicated by a brighter dot than other spaces.

Using Hard Spaces to Create Extra Blanks in Your Text

You might want to use hard spaces in several situations. One, of course, is when you want to insert extra spaces in your text. When it justifies a paragraph written in Left, Even, or Center justification, Symphony automatically removes any extra spaces you inserted between words. If you want the extra spaces to remain in the document, you must make them hard spaces.

For example, suppose you want to type a title in all capital letters with double spaces between each word, for instance: THE MERCHANT OF VENICE. One space between each word can be a regular blank, but the second one must be created as a hard space.

Using Hard Spaces to Keep Words on the Same Line

Another practical use for the hard space is to keep Symphony from putting certain words on different lines when you want them always to appear on the same line in a document. This can be useful when blanks are a part of a long number, such as a Social Security number. For example, suppose you are creating a sentence that includes the Social Security number, 306 65 9144. To make sure that the number is never split between two lines of text, use a hard space to create the blanks between the three sections of the number. When two words or two numbers that are separated by a hard space occur at the end of a line, Symphony pushes both to the next line, if needed, instead of splitting them. In other words, if a hard space separates two words, Symphony treats them as a single word.

COMPOSING SPECIAL CHARACTERS

If addition to using the {Compose} key to create hard spaces, you can use this key to create certain characters that do not appear on most computer keyboards, such as a Greek pi, the British pound sign, and a plus/minus sign. These special characters are created by pressing {**Compose**} followed by a particular sequence of keystrokes. For example, to create the Greek letter pi, press {**Compose**} followed by the letters **pi**. In Appendix A of the Symphony Reference Manual you will find the correct sequence for creating more than 100 characters. It is worth pointing out that a separate {Compose} sequence is required to produce each combination of characters. For example, a separate sequence is used to produce an uppercase A with an acute accent versus a lowercase a with an acute accent.

Not all monitors can display all the special characters you can create with Symphony, and, of course, not all printers can print these special characters. You have to test your printer and monitor to see which characters they can display or print. Composing special characters is explained in more detail in Chapters 27 and 30.

CHAPTER SEVENTEEN
PRINTING DOCUMENTS

In Chapter 9 we covered Symphony's Print command in detail. Most of the concepts you learned in that chapter also apply to printing documents. However, there are some special considerations you must keep in mind when you print a document. This chapter explains these and gives you some tips and guidelines for printing a document created with Symphony's word processor.

The format of a printed document is determined by the interaction of the DOC Format settings sheet and the Print settings sheet. The DOC Format settings are explained in detail in Chapter 15, and the Print settings are explained in detail in Chapter 9. Some settings, such as right margin, left margin, and line spacing, appear on both the DOC Format settings sheet and the Print settings sheet. The interaction of these similar settings affects the appearance of your printed documents.

PRINTING A SIMPLE DOCUMENT

Before explaining the details of document printing, let's walk through a simple printing example. Suppose you have created a one-page letter like the one in Figure 17.1 and you want to print it. The first step is to load the letter into your current worksheet (if it's not already there), because Symphony cannot print a file directly from a disk.

Assuming the letter is loaded in your current worksheet and you are viewing it through a DOC window, issue the {**Services**} **P**rint command. This command brings up the following menu:

Go Line-Advance Page-Advance Align Settings Quit

Below this menu you will see a Print settings sheet. Each of the items on the Print settings sheet is explained in Chapter 9, but here we will explain more thoroughly the settings that apply particularly to printing a word processing document.

```
>>----->----->----->----->----->----->----->----->----->----->--<<---
|August 22, 1984                                                      |
|                                                                     |
|Mr. Michael Davis                                                    |
|Vice President                                                       |
|Volume Importers                                                     |
|102 Broad Street                                                     |
|New York, New York   10004                                           |
|                                                                     |
|                                                                     |
|Dear Mr. Davis:                                                      |
|                                                                     |
|In reviewing our midsummer promotion, we have noted that the brass   |
|picture frames you supply have sold extremely well.  We would like to|
|increase our order for the upcoming Christmas season from 100 to 150.|
|                                                                     |
|For the additional 50 frames, I have attached a schedule of the number|
|we would like in each size and finish.  Please consider this an      |
|addendum to our original order.  Also, please let me know if there will|
|be any problem in fulfilling this order by October 15.               |
|                                                                     |
|Thank you for your assistance.                                       |
|                                                                     |
|Yours truly,                                                         |
|                                                                     |
|                                                                     |
|                                                                     |
|Ann Brown                                                            |
|Buyer                                                                |
 =====================================================================:===MAIN=
```

Figure 17.1

If you have created a document using the default settings in the DOC Format settings sheet, you should be able to print that document without changing any of the Default settings on the Print settings sheet. To prepare to print the sample letter using the default settings, simply load your printer with paper and select **A**lign from the Print menu. This tells Symphony that the printer head is positioned at the top of a page of paper.

Select **G**o to print the letter. After the letter is printed, you still see the Print menu and Print settings on your screen. You can print the letter again by loading another sheet of paper into the printer and again selecting **A**lign and **G**o.

Notice that we didn't have to designate a Print Source range to print this simple document. You usually won't need to designate a Source range when printing documents. This topic will be addressed in detail in a few pages.

PRINT SETTINGS AND FORMAT SETTINGS

In the previous example you saw that you can print a document created with the default DOC Format settings without adjusting the Print settings. In most cases, however, you will change a few of the Format settings while preparing your document, so you'll have to change the Default settings on the Print settings sheet before you print your document.

Left Margin

The number of spaces in the left margin of a printed document is determined by *both* the Margins Left setting of the Print settings sheet and the Left Margin setting of the For- mat settings sheet. The formula for determining the number of spaces in the left margin of a printed document is Margins Left setting (from the Print settings sheet) + Left Margin setting (from the Format settings sheet) − 1. For example, if you have created a docu- ment with a Left Margin setting of 5, and you print that document using a Margins Left setting on the Print settings sheet of 4 (the default), the left margin of your printed docu- ment will be 8 spaces wide, and the first character of each line will be printed in the ninth column on the page.

To change the left margin setting, press {**Services**} **P**rint **S**ettings **M**argins **L**eft, and enter in the new left margin setting. The left margin setting can be any value from 1 to 240, but it must be less than the right margin setting of the Print settings sheet.

It is important to note that the actual width in inches of the left margin depends on the type of printer you use. If your printer is set to print pica characters (10 characters per inch), a left margin of 11 spaces will be slightly more than one inch wide. If your printer is set to print elite characters (12 characters per inch), a left margin of 11 spaces will be slightly less than one inch wide. Similarly, if you use compressed printing, your left margin will be reduced according to the size of the compressed characters.

Right Margin

The Margins Right setting on the Print settings sheet determines the last column on a page where a character can be printed. For example, the default right margin setting in the Print settings sheet is 76. This means that no characters can be printed on a page beyond column 76. (An 8$\frac{1}{2}$-by-11 piece of paper contains 85 columns of pica charac- ters and 101 columns of elite characters.)

To change the right margin setting, issue the {**Services**} **P**rint **S**ettings **M**argins **R**ight command and enter the new right margin setting. The right margin you choose should be greater than or equal to the sum of the Right Margin setting from the Format settings sheet plus the Margins Left setting from the Print settings sheet. If you do not set Margins Right at least equal to this sum, some characters will be truncated when you print the document. (If you have used format lines throughout your document, the Margins Right setting should be equal to or greater than the Margins Left setting of the Print settings sheet plus the largest right margin of any formatted section in the document.)

For example, assume you want to print the document described in the previous sec- tion. Remember that the Format settings sheet contains a Right Margin setting of 70 and a Left Margin setting of 4. Now suppose that you decide you want your printed document to have a left margin that is 10 spaces wide. To achieve this, you should set the Margins Left in your Print settings sheet equal to 7 (7 + 4 − 1 = 10). To make sure that no charac- ters are truncated in the printed report, the Margins Right setting of the Print settings sheet should be greater than or equal to 77 (7 + 70).

The default margins in both the Print settings sheet and the Format settings sheet are set so that no characters will be truncated when you print a document. This is one reason why you can print a document that uses the default DOC Format settings without making any changes to the default settings of the Print settings sheet. Recall that the default Left Margin setting in the Format settings sheet is 1 and the default Right Margin setting is 72.

Also recall that the default left and right margins in the Print settings sheet are 4 and 76. If you add the Right Margin setting from the Format settings sheet (72) to the Margins Left setting from the Print settings sheet (4), the sum is 76. This, of course, is equal to the default right margin setting of the Print settings sheet.

All of this sounds rather complicated, so let's summarize the steps you follow in setting the margins for a printed document:

1. Decide how many spaces you want in the left margin of your printed document. Then use the following formula to determine how to set the Margins Left setting on the Print settings sheet:

   Number of spaces in left margin = Left Margin setting (from Format settings sheet) + Margins Left setting (from Print settings sheet) − 1

2. Add the Margins Left setting from your Print settings sheet to the Right Margin setting from your Format Settings sheet. This sum tells you the minimum value for the Margins Right setting on the Print settings sheet. If you do not set Margins Right equal to or greater than this sum, Symphony will truncate some characters at the right edge of your document.

Spacing

The line spacing of your printed documents is determined exclusively by the Spacing setting in the DOC Format settings sheet. The Spacing setting in the Print settings sheet has no effect when a document is printed. For example, if you create a letter with a spacing setting of 1 (single spacing) in the Format settings sheet, and then print that document using a Print Settings Spacing setting of 2 (double spacing), the printed document will have single spacing.

Source

When you specify a Source range for printing, you are telling Symphony what part of your worksheet to print. Usually, you have to designate a Source range before you begin to print. However, if you issue the Print command from within a DOC window and you want to print the entire document, you do not need to specify a Source range. Symphony automatically prints the entire document displayed in the current DOC window. If you are printing from a restricted DOC window and you don't specify a Source, Symphony assumes that the Source range is equal to the window's Restrict range and prints all characters that appear in that range.

However, there may be times when you want to print only part of a document. In these cases, you can use the Source setting. For example, suppose you want to print only the first two paragraphs of the letter shown in Figure 17.1. These paragraphs begin on line 13 and end on line 20. We'll assume that the DOC window MAIN has a Restrict range of A1 . . I100.

To print these paragraphs, position the cursor on the first line of the first paragraph and issue the {**Services**} Print **S**ettings **S**ource **R**ange command. Symphony will highlight the first line of this paragraph. If you press the ↓ key, you can highlight additional lines of the paragraph to indicate that they are to be included in the range to be printed.

When highlighting the range to be printed, you can unanchor the cursor by pressing [**Esc**] and then reanchor the cursor by pressing [**Tab**]. For example, suppose you did not place the cursor on the first line of the first paragraph before issuing the {Services} Print Settings Source Range command. Since you want the cursor to be on the first line of the paragraph before you highlight the range, press [**Esc**] to unanchor the cursor and then move the cursor to the beginning of the paragraph. When you have positioned the cursor properly, press [**Tab**] to anchor the cursor on the first line. Symphony automatically highlights the entire line on which the cursor is located. Use the ↓ key to highlight the rest of the lines of the paragraph.

After highlighting the entire two paragraphs, press [**Enter**]. This will bring the Print settings sheet back into view. Notice that the Source setting is

>   Source: A13 . . I20

This tells you that the highlighted lines in your document are equivalent to the underlying range of spreadsheet cells that begins at cell A13 and has a lower right limit of cell I20.

If the window MAIN had an unrestricted range, the Source range in the settings sheet would be

>   Source A13 . . IV20

Notice that this range seems to extend all the way to column IV! In other words, there is no apparent limit on the right edge of the range. However, this is nothing to be alarmed about. The Print Settings Margins Right setting will keep Symphony from printing all of the columns in the Source range. Only as many characters as are allowed by the Print Settings Margins Right setting will appear on each line.

Whenever you print from a restricted DOC window, the Source range reflects the window's Restrict range. For example, suppose you have created a DOC window that is restricted to columns J through R of your worksheet. When you decide to print some text from this DOC window, you can use the standard command sequence to designate the Source range: {Services} Print Settings Source Range. Let's assume you highlight lines 1 through 15 of the text in this window. When you press [Enter], you see this on your Print settings sheet:

>   Source: J1 . . R15

As you can see, the top and bottom of the range to be printed are limited to the lines you highlighted, while the left and right edges of the range are limited by the Restrict range of the window in which you are working.

Start-Page and End-Page

If you use Symphony to create a lengthy document, there may be occasions when you want to print only certain pages of the document. For example, suppose you want to make changes on page 5 of a seven-page report. After making the changes, you don't necessarily have to reprint all seven pages of the document. Using the Start-Page and End-Page settings in the Print settings sheet, you can print out only page 5 or pages 5 through 7.

These settings can also be quite helpful when your printer runs out of paper or the paper gets misaligned or jammed in the printer in the middle of printing a long document. Using the Start-Page setting, you can avoid reprinting the entire document.

To use the Start-Page and End-Page settings, select Settings from the initial Print menu. This brings up another menu:

Page   Source   Destination   Init-String   Margins   Other   Name   Quit

Select **P**age **N**umber **S**tart-Page and type in the number of the first page in the document you want Symphony to print. For example, let's go back to the illustration above, where changes were made to page 5 of a seven-page report. Since you do not want to reprint the first four pages of the report, set Start-Page to 5 and press **[Enter]**. When you tell Symphony to begin printing, it will start with the fifth page of the document.

If you do not want to print any pages beyond page 5, set End-Page to 5 also. If, however, you want to print pages 5 through 7 of the report, you do not have to specify an End-Page. The default setting for End-Page is 999. You do not have to change this setting if your document is less than 999 pages, because Symphony automatically stops printing or feeding paper through your printer after the entire document has been printed.

The Start-Page and End-Page settings can be very tricky. If you plan to use them, I suggest you review the detailed discussion of these settings in Chapter 9.

Page Wait

If you are printing a document on noncontinuous paper (such as individual sheets of company letterhead), you will want to set the Page Wait setting to Yes before printing. When you set Page Wait to Yes, Symphony pauses after it has printed each page in the document to allow you to load a new piece of paper into your printer. Once the paper is loaded, you can resume printing by pressing any key. Since the default Page Wait setting is No, you must change this any time you have a document that is more than one page which you want to print on noncontinuous paper.

To change the Page Wait setting, select **S**ettings from the initial Print menu, then select **P**age **W**ait. Symphony will ask you, "Wait at end of page for paper change?" You respond by pointing to Yes and pressing [Enter].

Headers and Footers

Symphony allows you to place a header and/or footer on each page you print. A header or footer is simply a line of text that appears at the top or bottom of every page of a printed document. You can use the Header or Footer setting to number the pages in a document. Chapter 9 offers a complete explanation of how to create, adjust, and use headers and footers in Symphony.

CHAPTER EIGHTEEN
ADVANCED WORD PROCESSING TOPICS

Now that you've learned how to create, edit, and print a document using the Symphony word processor, you're ready to investigate some of the DOC environment's more advanced concepts. In this chapter, you'll learn more about how DOC windows behave. We'll show you how to set up more than one DOC window in a single worksheet and how to exchange information back and forth between DOC windows. Finally, you'll learn how to transfer information entered in the Symphony spreadsheet into a word processing document.

USING DOC WINDOWS

As you have seen, the key to Symphony's word processing capabilities is the program's DOC window. DOC windows allow you to view the worksheet as a word processing workspace, and such DOC environment commands as Search and Justify let you perform common word processing functions on the text you enter through a DOC window.

Up to this point, we have been working through a single DOC window named MAIN. This points out that you can do a great deal with Symphony's word processor without using its advanced windowing capability. However, sometimes windows are very useful in word processing. For example, by creating several windows you can switch among different parts of a long document quickly. Or you might use two or three DOC windows to create several individual documents in different parts of the worksheet. Symphony's windowing capabilities also make it possible to embed a table or section from a spreadsheet in the middle of a document.

This chapter focuses on some characteristics of DOC windows and on ways to use multiple windows to create documents. It also covers using a worksheet with both DOC and SHEET windows and moving data and text between the two kinds of windows. (For more on the basics of Symphony's windowing capabilities, see Chapter 11.)

Before beginning this discussion, we need to clarify one term that we use throughout the chapter. In Chapter 15, we introduced the word *column* to refer to one character space on the screen. This is its meaning in word processing. Because *column* is also part of Symphony's spreadsheet terminology, in this chapter we use the term *character column* to mean one character space (e.g., a standard monitor displays 80 character columns on a single line) and the term *column* to mean a standard spreadsheet column (e.g., columns A through M on a spreadsheet).

Review of Window Basics

Before discussing the use of windows in the DOC environment, let's review some basic facts about Symphony windows. (See Chapter 11 for a detailed explanation of Symphony windows.)

To create a new window, you issue the {**Services**} **W**indow **C**reate command. Symphony responds with the prompt

New window name:

Next to this prompt, type the name of the new window. Symphony then asks you to select the window type from this menu:

SHEET DOC GRAPH FORM COMM

If you want to create a DOC window, select **DOC** from this menu. After you select the appropriate type, Symphony asks you to identify the window area. If you want a full-screen window, simply press **[Enter]** in response to this prompt. If, however, you want to create a partial-screen window, use the arrow keys to change the size and layout of the window. Finally, Symphony brings up the Window Settings menu:

Name Type Restrict Borders Auto-Display Quit

You do not have to change any of these settings; you can simply press **[Esc]** and display the newly created window.

Before getting further into this discussion of windows, it is important to remember that Symphony has only one large workspace and that all windows give a view of that one workspace. In other words, windows are merely individual "frames" through which you view different parts of a single worksheet. The work you create in different windows all goes on the same worksheet.

The DOC Window MAIN

In Chapter 15 we created a DOC window called MAIN by changing the type of the SHEET window MAIN. Let's repeat that process. Begin by issuing the {**Services**} **N**ew **Y**es command to erase the entire worksheet. After the worksheet is cleared, Symphony positions the cell pointer in cell A1 in a SHEET window called MAIN. To convert this to a DOC window, press the {**Type**} key from within the SHEET window MAIN and select **DOC** from the Type menu.

After you create this window, enter the brief document shown in Figure 18.1 into the worksheet. We'll use this document in several of the following examples.

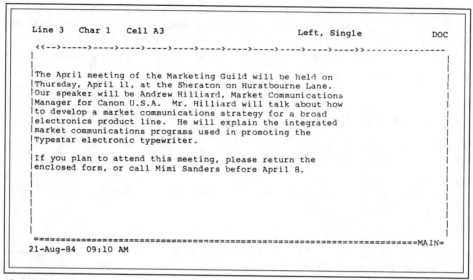

```
       Line 3   Char 1   Cell A3                    Left, Single        DOC

        <<-->----->----->----->----->----->----->----->----->----->----->>---------------
        |                                                                                |
        |The April meeting of the Marketing Guild will be held on                        |
        |Thursday, April 11, at the Sheraton on Hurstbourne Lane.                        |
        |Our speaker will be Andrew Hilliard, Market Communications                      |
        |Manager for Canon U.S.A.  Mr. Hilliard will talk about how                      |
        |to develop a market communications strategy for a broad                         |
        |electronics product line.  He will explain the integrated                       |
        |market communications programs used in promoting the                            |
        |Typestar electronic typewriter.                                                 |
        |                                                                                |
        |If you plan to attend this meeting, please return the                           |
        |enclosed form, or call Mimi Sanders before April 8.                             |
        |                                                                                |
        |                                                                                |
        |                                                                                |
        |                                                                                |
        |                                                                                |
        ==================================================================================MAIN=
        21-Aug-84  09:10 AM
```

Figure 18.1

How Symphony Stores Text in a Worksheet

To understand Symphony's DOC windows, you need to know how Symphony stores text in a worksheet. Symphony stores documents on the worksheet as a series of long labels that begin in column A (or in another column if the window has a Restrict range—more on that later).

You can prove this point by using the {**Switch**} key to change MAIN from a DOC window to a SHEET window. After you make the switch, the worksheet looks like Figure 18.2. If you position the cell pointer at the beginning of the first line of the first paragraph (Cell A3), the control panel looks like this:

A3: 'The April meeting of the Marketing Guild will be held on

If you move the cursor to column B, the control panel is blank, indicating that there is no entry in column B. The reason for this is that Symphony treats the entire line of text as a long label residing in column A of the worksheet (or in the left-most column of the window if the window's Restrict range does not include column A).

Using Two Windows to View a Document

An advantage of multiple DOC windows is that they let you view two or more sections of one long document through several different windows. For example, suppose you are working on a long report and you want to tie the final paragraphs of the report to the introduction. To make this easier, you can create a secondary window to view the introduction while you work in window MAIN to write the conclusion.

First, move the cursor so that you are viewing the introduction of the report through the window MAIN. Then issue the {**Services**} **W**indow **C**reate command to create a

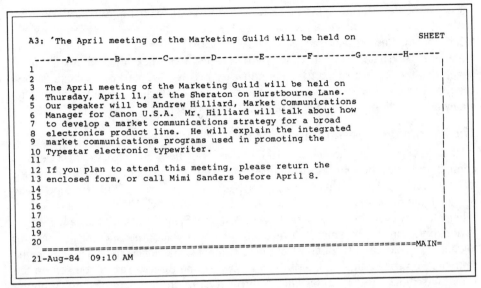

```
    A3: 'The April meeting of the Marketing Guild will be held on          SHEET

    ------A--------B--------C--------D--------E--------F--------G--------H------
 1                                                                              |
 2                                                                              |
 3   The April meeting of the Marketing Guild will be held on                   |
 4   Thursday, April 11, at the Sheraton on Hurstbourne Lane.                   |
 5   Our speaker will be Andrew Hilliard, Market Communications                 |
 6   Manager for Canon U.S.A.  Mr. Hilliard will talk about how                 |
 7   to develop a market communications strategy for a broad                    |
 8   electronics product line.  He will explain the integrated                  |
 9   market communications programs used in promoting the                       |
10   Typestar electronic typewriter.                                            |
11                                                                              |
12   If you plan to attend this meeting, please return the                      |
13   enclosed form, or call Mimi Sanders before April 8.                        |
14                                                                              |
15                                                                              |
16                                                                              |
17                                                                              |
18                                                                              |
19                                                                              |
20   ================================================================MAIN=
    21-Aug-84  09:10 AM
```

Figure 18.2

new window called INTRO and specify DOC as the window type. When Symphony asks you to define the window's layout, press **[Enter]** to make INTRO a full-screen window. You do not need to change any of the window settings, so you can select **Quit** when you see the Window Settings menu.

You are now in the window INTRO, viewing the introductory section of your report. To switch to the window MAIN, press the **{Window}** key. Because you were in the window MAIN when you created the window INTRO, MAIN also gives a view of the introductory section of your report. To move MAIN to the end of your report, press **[End]** **[Home]**.

You can now begin writing the conclusion to your report. Any time you wish to see the introduction, simply press the **{Window}** key to switch to the window INTRO.

Of course, you can view any part of your report through either INTRO or MAIN. For example, you may want to see another section in the report besides the introduction while you are writing the conclusion. To do this, use **{Window}** to bring INTRO into view on your screen and move the cursor so that INTRO is positioned over the section of your report you want to see. Pressing **{Window}** again puts you back in the window MAIN, which is still positioned over the end of the report.

Restrict Ranges for DOC Windows

A window's Restrict range is that part of the worksheet you are allowed to view and work in while you use that particular window. In general, when a window is unrestricted, there are no limitations on the areas of the worksheet you can view and work on through that window.

To view the Restrict setting for the DOC window MAIN, issue the {**Services**} **W**indow **S**ettings command from within MAIN. The Window settings sheet comes into view. Notice that the Restrict setting for MAIN is A1 . . IV8192. Since this Restrict range covers the entire worksheet, you can view any part of the worksheet through MAIN. (Also notice that the Restrict range for all window types is represented by the SHEET row-column coordinate system, rather than the DOC line-character system.) After viewing the Window settings, select **Q**uit to return to your worksheet.

The Automatic Restrict Range for DOC Windows

Now press {**Window**} to jump into INTRO and issue the {**Services**} **W**indow **S**ettings command. When the settings sheet comes into view, notice that the Restrict range for INTRO is A1 . . I8192. In other words, when Symphony created INTRO, it automatically restricted the range of this new window to columns A through I of the worksheet.

In fact, whenever you create a *new* DOC window, Symphony automatically restricts its horizontal range to columns A through I of the underlying spreadsheet. This translates to character columns 1 through 81 of the document worksheet. There is no automatic restriction on the vertical range of the window, so the Restrict range you see on the Window settings sheet includes lines 1 through 8192, the last line of the Symphony worksheet.

Symphony imposes this automatic range restriction even if you are viewing a part of the worksheet other than A1 . . H20 when you issue the {**Services**} **W**indow **C**reate command. In other words, unless you specify otherwise, Symphony puts the left edge of all created DOC windows in the first column of the worksheet.

To illustrate this concept, let's compare creating a DOC window to creating a SHEET window. Suppose that as you are building a large spreadsheet you decide to create a second window to view the right edge of the spreadsheet, which lies in columns O through V. To do this, move the cell pointer in the window MAIN to cell V1 so that you are viewing columns O through V on your screen. Then issue the {**Services**} **W**indow **C**reate command. After naming the window SECOND and setting the window type to SHEET, define it as a full-screen window.

You should now see the range O1 . . V20 through the window SECOND, and the cell pointer should be in cell V1. In other words, SECOND is displaying the portion of the worksheet you were looking at through MAIN when you defined SECOND. Unless you specify otherwise, this SHEET window is unrestricted; that is, its Restrict range on the Window settings sheet is A1 . . IV8192.

If you follow this same procedure to create a DOC window, the results are different. Assuming that MAIN is a SHEET window, scroll through your worksheet until the cursor is in cell V1. Next, create a DOC window by pressing {**Services**} **W**indow **C**reate. Choose SECOND as the window name, select DOC as the window type, and define it as a full-screen window.

After the window is created, you might expect it to display the range from character column 127 to character column 204 (the DOC equivalent of columns O through V). However, you will find that the window displays the range from line 1, character 4 through line 20, character 81. Because of the automatic range restriction, Symphony does not let you scroll beyond character column 81, which is the last character column in spreadsheet column I. In other words, when you create a new DOC window, Symphony automatically assigns the Restrict range A1 . . I8192 to that window and positions the new window so that it looks onto a portion of the Restrict range.

If you try to create the new document in this window, each line is entered as a long, left-aligned label in column A. The only way to prevent this is to specify a different Restrict range for the DOC window. You will learn you how to do this in the next section.

Trying to grasp the difference between the Restrict range of a window and the window area or window layout can be confusing. When you are creating a window, Symphony asks you to identify a window layout on the screen. When you do so, you specify only the size and shape of the window. You are *not* specifying a particular location on the worksheet that the window can view; this is determined by the Restrict range.

Restrictions on Unrestricted Windows

In the previous section, you saw that the Restrict range for the window MAIN is A1 . . IV8192. In other words, the DOC window MAIN is unrestricted. You may wonder why MAIN is unrestricted, since we just said that the Symphony automatically assigns the Restrict range A1 . . I8192 to all new DOC windows. The key is to remember that MAIN was not created as a new window with the {Services} Window Create command. Instead, you created it by changing the type of an already existing window. The automatic Restrict range applies only to DOC windows created with the Window Create command.

Even unrestricted DOC windows have certain limitations, however. When you are working in an unrestricted DOC window, Symphony does not allow you to create text beyond character column 240 of the worksheet. You can use the arrow keys to move the cursor anywhere in the worksheet, even to the far right edge. But once you move past character column 240, an asterisk appears at the top of your screen, indicating that the cursor is in "off-limits" territory. If you try to type a character or press the [Space bar], your computer beeps and fails to respond to your keystrokes.

This 240-character limit in a DOC window is due to the fact that Symphony considers each line of text as a long label residing in the left-most column of the window in which you are working. Because the maximum length for a label is 240 characters, including spaces, the maximum length of a line of text is also 240 characters.

Note that the 240-character limit on line length will occur in any DOC window even if its Restrict range is wider than 240 characters. For example, if you have a DOC window with a Restrict range of K1 through IV8192, you will be able to create a line of text that is 240 characters long, *beginning* at cell K1, the left edge of the Restrict range. You cannot create any text beyond character column 240 of this window.

Using a Second Window to Create a Document

Suppose that you want to create two separate DOC windows in one workspace and that in these two windows you want to create two distinct documents. For example, suppose you want to create one document in the range A1 . . I200 and the other in the range J1 . . R200.

In the previous section, you learned that Symphony automatically assigns the Restrict range A1 . . I8192 to any new DOC window created with the Window Create command. Because you want one of these two windows to display the range J1 . . R200, you must use the Window Settings Restrict command to change the Restrict range of the second window.

Restricting a Second DOC Window

Suppose that the current worksheet contains only one DOC window, MAIN, which has the Restrict range A1 . . IV8192. You want to create a second DOC window looking onto the range J1 . . R200. First, issue the {**Services**} **W**indow **C**reate command. Symphony prompts you to specify a name for the new window—let's use **NEW** in this example. After you supply the name, Symphony asks you to specify a window type. Since NEW is a DOC window, type **D**. Next, Symphony asks you to identify the window area. Initially, the entire screen will be highlighted as the window area. Assuming you want a full-screen view with this window, you can press **[Enter]** in response to this prompt.

Finally, Symphony displays the Window settings sheet and a menu of the settings at the top of the screen. Because you specified type DOC when you create the window, the initial Restrict setting is A1 . . I8192.

To change the Restrict setting, select the **R**estrict option from the Window Settings menu. Symphony then offers three choices: Screen, Range, or None. To define the new Restrict range, select **R**ange when you see the Restrict menu. After you do this, Symphony highlights the current Restrict range, A1 . . I8192, and pauses for you to adjust that range. If you press **[Esc]** to unanchor the range, the cell pointer jumps to cell A1. You can then use the arrow keys to move the cell pointer to cell J1, the upper-left cell of the range you wish to specify as the Restrict range for your window. Next, press **[Tab]** to anchor the cell pointer and then move the cell pointer to cell R1. Finally, press **[End]↓** to move the cell pointer to cell R8192 and press **[Enter]**. Notice that even though NEW is a DOC window, it looks like a SHEET window when you are specifying the Restrict range, with lettered columns across the top of the window and numbered rows down the side. In addition, you use a cell pointer instead of a cursor to define the Restrict range.

As an alternative, you can define the new Restrict range by typing its cell coordinates after issuing the **R**estrict **R**ange command. In the example, you could define the desired Restrict range simply by typing **[Esc]**, then **J1 . . R8192** when Symphony highlights the current Restrict range.

When this process is complete, the Restrict range in the Window settings sheet will be J1 . . R8192. Notice that although we plan to use only the range J1 . . R200 with this window, we extended the range all the way to the bottom of the worksheet. In general, when you specify the Restrict range for a DOC window, you should restrict only the left and right edges of the window and leave the top and bottom of the window unrestricted. This allows you to make a document you create in that window as long as you want.

Using the Second Window

With the cell pointer in NEW, press **[Home]**. The control panel should now look like this:

      Line 1   Char 1   Cell J1   Left, Single   DOC

Notice that the control panel claims that Line 1, Character 1, or the upper-left corner of the window, resides on cell J1 of the underlying spreadsheet. To test this claim, type the phrase "Are we really in cell J1?" on the first line of the window and then press {**Type**} SHEET to switch the window to a SHEET window. The screen should now look like Figure 18.3.

```
    -----J--------K--------L--------M--------N--------O----
  1 Are we really in cell J1?                              |
  2                                                         |
  3                                                         |
  4                                                         |
  5                                                         |
  6                                                         |
    ====================================================SECOND=
```

Figure 18.3

If the cell pointer indeed moved to cell J1, the control panel should look like this:

      J1: 'Are we really in cell J1?

Because you restricted the range of this new window to J1 . . R8192, any text you enter through this window becomes a long label in column J. In fact, *whenever you enter text into the worksheet through a DOC window, Symphony treats the text as a long label stored in the left-most column of the Restrict range for that window.* Since the left-most column of most DOC windows is column A, most documents in Symphony are entered as long labels in column A. However, if you supply a special Restrict range for a DOC window, any text entered through that window is stored as a long label in the left-most column of the Restrict range.

If you get rid of the automatic Restrict range and make the secondary DOC window unrestricted, Symphony forces any text you create in that window back to the first column in the worksheet—this will put that text in the same workspace as any text you have created in the MAIN window.

Restricting the Window MAIN

When you create more than one DOC window in a single worksheet, it is a good idea to restrict the ranges of *all* of the windows to a defined part of the worksheet. In the example, we should restrict the range of the window MAIN to A1 . . I8192. Otherwise, changes in MAIN may affect the contents of the window NEW, even though NEW is restricted.

For example, if MAIN is unrestricted and you erase lines 10 through 20 in the window, Symphony erases those same lines in the rest of the worksheet. In other words, by erasing lines 10 to 20 in MAIN you also erase lines 10 to 20 in NEW, unless MAIN is restricted.

Similarly, if you block several lines in MAIN to be moved or copied, Symphony moves or copies those same lines in parallel windows on the worksheet.

Thus, whenever you use a secondary window or windows to create a separate document in another part of your worksheet, you must specify unique Restrict ranges for all windows on the worksheet, including the MAIN window. If you don't, you will encounter an amazing variety of problems.

Figure 18.4 illustrates the overall layout of the worksheet containing the windows MAIN and NEW. Notice that these windows define parallel ranges in the worksheet.

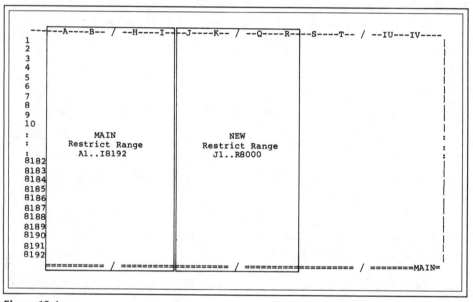

Figure 18.4

Format Settings of Second Windows

When you create a new DOC window, Symphony assigns the Format settings of the parent window to the new window. If the parent window is a DOC window with all the default Format settings, Symphony automatically assigns the default Format settings to the new window. Similarly, if the parent window is not a DOC window, the secondary DOC window will have the default DOC Format settings. (See Chapter 15 for a discussion of Symphony's DOC Format settings.)

Copying and Moving Text between Windows

If you do a great deal of word processing, you might want to use two or more DOC windows on your worksheet and move and copy text between these windows. For example, suppose you are creating a document in the DOC window MAIN and you decide you want to set aside a portion of the worksheet to jot down key paragraphs, sentences, or phrases you plan to incorporate in the document. To do this, create a secondary DOC window (called NOTES, perhaps) and restrict this window to a clear section of the worksheet. You should also restrict the range of the MAIN window. As you think of points or phrases you might want to include in your document, use the {**Window**} key to switch from MAIN to NOTES and jot down your ideas. Then use the **Copy** or **Move** command to move text from NOTES to MAIN. The fact that both MAIN and NOTES are restricted does not affect your ability to copy or move text between them.

To copy a paragraph from the NOTES window into the MAIN window, follow these steps: Begin in MAIN and press {**Menu**} Copy. When you see the prompt

> Copy FROM what block?

press the {**Window**} key. This moves the cursor into NOTES. Press [**Esc**] to unanchor the cursor and move it to the beginning of the paragraph you wish to copy. After marking the paragraph, press [**Enter**]. This brings up the prompt

> Copy TO where?

At the same time, Symphony moves back to MAIN, and the cursor returns to the position it occupied before you began the copy procedure. If you want to copy the paragraph at the current cursor location, press [**Enter**]. Otherwise, move the cursor to the desired location and press [**Enter**]. After the text is copied from the NOTES window into the MAIN window, Symphony will put you back in the NOTES window. To see how the paragraph looks after it has been copied into your document, you must press the {**Window**} key and go back to the MAIN window.

To move text from one window to another, follow this same procedure, selecting the Move command from the DOC window rather than the Copy command.

If you have more than two windows in your worksheet, you may need to press the {**Window**} key several times after you see the "Copy FROM what block?" (or the "Move FROM what block?") prompt in order to get to the window that has the text you wish to copy or move. When you press the {Window} key in the middle of a copy or move procedure, Symphony does not let you view non-DOC windows.

For example, suppose your current worksheet has five windows, including two DOC windows (MEMO and MAIN), one GRAPH window, one SHEET window, and one FORM window. Assume that you are working in MAIN and want to copy some text from MEMO into MAIN. After invoking the Copy command from within MAIN, press the {**Window**} key to move to another DOC window. MEMO comes into view. When you press {**Window**} again, MAIN comes back into view. In other words, Symphony allows you to view only DOC windows, skipping over the non-DOC windows entirely. You cannot invoke the Copy or Move command and then copy or move something from a non-DOC window into a DOC window.

In the example above, we suggest that you begin a Copy or Move procedure with the cursor in the window where you want to place the copied or moved text. Of course, you can also begin with the cursor in the window from which the text is to be moved or copied. In this case, you would use the {**Window**} key to move to another window after you have marked a block of text to be moved or copied and Symphony asks you to specify where the text is to be moved or copied.

Remember, however, that when you move or copy text from one window to another, you are only moving the text from one location on the worksheet to another. Using windows is just a handy way to separate two or more groups of text and to view different parts of the worksheet quickly. Copying or moving text from one window to another is really no different than copying or moving text within a single window.

Examples of Using Multiple DOC Windows

This section illustrates some ways to use multiple DOC windows. We cannot possibly cover every way to use multiple DOC windows, so these examples are designed just to give you some ideas.

Frequently Used Text in a Window

In Chapter 16, we suggested that you might want to keep a file of phrases and paragraphs that you use frequently in a variety of documents. If you create such a file, you can bring it into your worksheet and select the phrases or paragraphs you want to incorporate into a new document.

For example, suppose you are creating a proposal in MAIN and you want to incorporate some sections from an earlier proposal stored in a file named PROPOSE. Let's say you want to place this entire file in your current worksheet so you can review it and select parts to incorporate in your new proposal. To do this, first restrict your MAIN window by pressing {**Services**} **W**indow **S**ettings **R**estrict **R**ange [**Esc**] and entering the range **A1 . . I8000.** This restricts your MAIN window to the first nine columns of the worksheet and gives you 8000 lines (out of a possible 8192) to create the proposal.

Next, issue the {**Services**} **W**indow **C**reate command to create a new full-screen DOC window called SECOND. When the Window Settings menu is displayed, issue the **R**estrict **R**ange command and restrict this new window to the range **J1 . . R8000.** This Restrict range defines a window the same size as MAIN. You can place the PROPOSE file in this new window.

To place PROPOSE in the worksheet, first position the cursor in the upper-left corner of SECOND (cell J1). Then use the **F**ile **C**ombine **C**opy command to bring the PROPOSE file into this window. You can now use the {**Window**} key to switch between this proposal and the new proposal. When you decide to copy parts of the old proposal into the new proposal, simply follow the procedure outlined above for copying text between windows.

Outline in a Window

Another way to use multiple DOC windows is to create an outline in one window and then use another window to write the document based on that outline. For example, suppose you are writing a report and decide to outline it before you begin. Start by creating your outline in the DOC window MAIN. After you complete the outline, restrict the range of MAIN to A1 . . I8000. Then create a secondary DOC window in which to write the report.

Issue the {**Services**} **W**indow **C**reate command to create a new full-screen DOC window called REPORT. Next, use the **R**estrict **R**ange command to specify the range **J1 . . R8000** for this window.

Once the new window is created, you can write the report just as you would create any other document. However, when you want to refer to your outline, just press the {**Window**} key to display MAIN.

Explaining a Table in a Report

Multiple DOC windows are also useful when you must explain a long and complex table in a document. In order to write the explanation, you must keep referring to the numbers in the chart. A secondary DOC window helps you move quickly between the chart and the text that explains it.

Assume the whole document, including the chart, is in the MAIN window. You will also use MAIN to write the explanation. To create a secondary window containing only the chart, first move the cursor so that the chart is visible through MAIN. Then use the {**Services**} **W**indow **C**reate command to build a new full-screen DOC window called **CHART.** You don't need to change any of the window settings since you will use this window only to view a different part of the primary document in this worksheet.

After creating the CHART window, press {**Window**} to jump back into MAIN, then move MAIN so that it displays the part of your worksheet where you will write the explanation of the chart. As you write the explanation, you can quickly view the chart at any time by pressing the {**Window**} key. Pressing this key again moves you back into the MAIN window, and you can proceed writing your explanation.

Rewriting a Section of a Document

One of the main advantages of writing with a word processor is that it allows you to rewrite and revise easily. Symphony's windowing feature makes rewriting and revising text even easier. For instance, you can use a secondary window to rewrite a section of text while maintaining the original version of the text in your MAIN window.

For example, suppose you are creating a letter in MAIN. You decide you want to reword a couple of paragraphs, but you don't want to lose what you have already written. To do this, first restrict the MAIN window. Then issue the {**Services**} **W**indow **C**reate command to build a new full-screen DOC window named **REWRITE.** Use the **R**estrict **R**ange command to define **J1 . . R8000** as the range for this window.

After creating this window, press the {**Window**} key to switch back to MAIN. Now, use the **C**opy command to copy the paragraphs you want to reword into the part of the worksheet visible through REWRITE. (See above, "Copying and Moving Text between DOC Windows.") Finally, press {**Window**} to jump back to REWRITE and edit the paragraphs. While you are editing these paragraphs, you can press the {**Window**} key at any time to view the original wording of the paragraphs in the MAIN window. If you decide your new version is an improvement, use the **C**opy command to copy the new version from REWRITE into MAIN.

Defining the Right Margin in a DOC Window

Up to this point in this chapter we have been working with worksheets with column widths of 9, the default. However, sometimes you may need worksheets containing columns of various widths. Because the default right margin of a DOC window is determined by the widths of the columns in the underlying worksheet, it is important to understand the effect of the SHEET {Menu} Width command on your DOC windows.

As you know, the default right margin of a full-screen DOC window is 72. This default value will hold as long as the width of the columns on the underlying spreadsheet is 9. However, if you assign different widths to the underlying columns or if you change the layout of the DOC window, the DOC window's default right margin will be affected. Symphony sets this margin at the last character space in the right-most complete spreadsheet column visible through the window. Because this explanation is rather abstract, let's look at a couple of examples that clarify margin definitions.

Suppose you use the {**Menu**} Width **Set** command to set the width of column A in the SHEET window MAIN to 37 and the width of column B to 38 characters. Because a full-screen SHEET window is only 75 characters wide, these two columns span the window completely. Figure 18.5 shows a portion of the worksheet with only columns A and B.

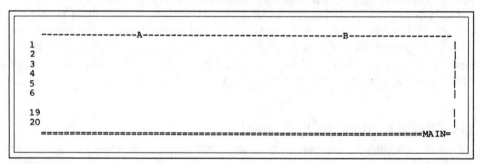

Figure 18.5

Now press {**Type**} and select **DOC** to convert MAIN into a DOC window. This window is shown in Figure 18.6.

Figure 18.6

The default right margin in this window is 75. Now press {**Switch**} to make MAIN a SHEET window again and issue the {**Menu**} **W**idth **S**et command to widen column B to 39 characters. Then move the cell pointer back into column A. The resulting worksheet is shown in Figure 18.7.

Figure 18.7

Notice that column B has disappeared from the screen. Because the new combined widths of columns A and B (76 characters) exceed the width of the window (75 characters), both columns cannot be displayed on the screen at once. The 38 spaces to the right of column A are a "dead zone." These spaces are neither in column A nor column B.

Now press {**Switch**} to turn MAIN back into a DOC window, as shown in Figure 18.8. Notice that the ruler line at the top of the window appears to span only a portion of the window. In fact, the Right Margin setting for this window is now 37. Notice that 37 is also the width of the only column visible through the window MAIN (when MAIN is a SHEET window). In other words, the right margin of this DOC window is the last character space within the last full spreadsheet column in the range underlying the DOC window—just as the rule predicted.

Figure 18.8

Let's assume we're in the position illustrated in Figures 18.5 and 18.6—columns A and B are 37 and 38 characters wide, respectively, and the right margin in the DOC window MAIN is 75. Now, from within MAIN, issue the {**Services**} **W**indow **L**ayout command. When Symphony prompts you to define the new layout for MAIN, press ← ten times to narrow the window by ten spaces and then press **[Enter]**. Select **Q**uit to return to the worksheet. Then press {**Switch**} to turn MAIN back into a SHEET window. The screen now looks like Figure 18.9.

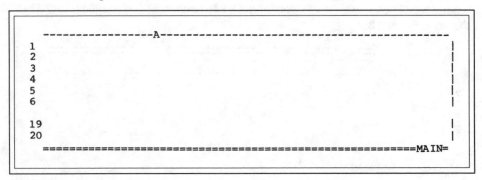

Figure 18.9

Once again, column B has disappeared from the screen. B disappeared because the new window width (65 characters) is too narrow to display both columns A and B at one time.

If you press {**Switch**} again to turn MAIN back into a DOC window, the screen looks like Figure 18.8. Once again, the right margin is 37, since 37 is the last character in the last column visible in MAIN.

In the example, we deliberately widened columns A and B to make the effects of changing the width of column B evident. But the principles demonstrated in this section also apply to changes in the widths of normal-sized columns. In fact, it is virtually impossible to change the width of a column in the Restrict range of a DOC window without affecting the right margin.

The only time this fairly complicated rule for setting the default right margin does not apply is when the width of the Restrict range is less than the width of the window layout. In that case, you see no Right Margin setting on your screen, though a Right Margin setting is stored with the other Format settings.

Overcoming Default Margins

Of course, you do not have to live with the strange default right margins that can result from changing the widths of the columns in the worksheet. You can use the {**Menu**} Format **S**ettings command to set a special right margin for any DOC window, including the windows in the example. For instance, if you issue the {**Menu**} Format **S**ettings **R**ight **S**et command from within the window shown in Figure 18.8, and set the right margin to 75 characters, the window changes to look like Figure 18.6. Notice that the ruler line at the top of this window is a full 75 characters wide.

INTEGRATING A SPREADSHEET AND A DOCUMENT

One of the main advantages of an integrated program like Symphony is that it lets you combine different types of data in a single report. In Symphony, it is possible integrate a table of numbers created in the SHEET mode into a document created with the word processor.

Before you attempt to combine spreadsheet data with documents, however, you need to understand how these two environments relate. You have learned that (1) the text you enter through a DOC window is stored as long spreadsheet labels in the left-most column of the DOC window's Restrict range, (2) the Restrict range of a DOC window is stated in rows and columns, and (3) the width of the columns in the range of the worksheet viewed through a DOC window affects the default right margin in that window. In this section, you'll learn how Symphony handles entries in the spreadsheet that are viewed through DOC windows.

An Example

To demonstrate how to combine a spreadsheet table into a document, let's look at a simple example. This example was created in a single Symphony worksheet.

Figure 18.10 shows a portion of simple memo created with the Symphony word processor. The document appears in the DOC window MAIN. (Assume MAIN is the only window in the worksheet.) The upper-left corner of MAIN is cell A1.

```
 <<----->----->----->----->----->----->----->----->----->----->----->---->>
|TO:        Les Porter                                                      |
|FROM:      Wayne Oliver                                                    |
|SUBJECT:   New Product Plan for "Handi-Tote"                               |
|                                                                           |
|I have completed my research and analysis for producing and marketing      |
|the new Handi-Tote carrying case and cooler.  The figures for the          |
|"most-likely" case of sales and costs are presented on the attached        |
|sheet.  The sales figures are based on studies performed by our            |
|marketing research department, as well as input from the sales force.      |
|Cost figures are derived from discussions with various suppliers as well    |
|as data from the controller's office.                                      |
|                                                                           |
|Here is a summary of these key figures:                                    |
|                                                                           |
|First-year sales:                                                          |
|                                                                           |
|First-year PAT:                                                            |
|                                                                           |
|My analysis assumes a manufacturing and marketing start-up at the          |
|beginning of 1985.  I expect this product will earn a healthy profit in    |
 =================================================================MAIN=
```

Figure 8.10

Notice that the memo includes two labels: "First-year sales:" and "First-year PAT:". No numbers, however, have been entered next to those labels. Now suppose you want to insert the appropriate sales numbers for these two years into the document.

The easiest way to insert these numbers in the document is to position the DOC mode cursor on the lines next to the labels and simply type in the numbers. When you enter the numbers this way, Symphony considers them part of a long label stored in column A of the worksheet. In other words, Symphony considers these numbers to be parts of labels, not values.

As long as you don't want to use the numbers as values, this method works. But suppose you want Symphony to treat these two numbers as values, so that you could refer to them by formulas elsewhere in the worksheet or use them in the arguments of spreadsheet functions.

To enter these numbers as values, first convert the window MAIN into a SHEET window by pressing {**Type**} and choosing **S**HEET from the Type menu. The window now looks like Figure 18.11.

```
     -----A--------B--------C--------D-------E--------F-------G--------H--------
 1   TO:        Les Porter                                                    |
 2   FROM:      Wayne Oliver                                                   |
 3   SUBJECT:   New Product Plan for "Handi-Tote"                              |
 4                                                                             |
 5   I have completed my research and analysis for producing and marketing    |
 6   the new Handi-Tote carrying case and cooler.  The figures for the        |
 7   "most-likely" case of sales and costs are presented on the attached      |
 8   sheet.  The sales figures are based on studies performed by our          |
 9   marketing research department, as well as input from the sales force.    |
10   Cost figures are derived from discussions with various suppliers as well |
11   as data from the controller's office.                                    |
12                                                                            |
13   Here is a summary of these key figures:                                  |
14                                                                            |
15   First-year sales:                                                        |
16                                                                           |
17   First-year PAT:                                                          |
18                                                                            |
19   My analysis assumes a manufacturing and marketing start-up at the        |
20   beginning of 1985.  I expect this product will earn a healthy profit in  |
     ====================================================================MAIN=
```

Figure 18.11

Next, move the cell pointer to cell C15 and enter the number 170622, the first-year sales estimate for this new product. Similarly, move to cell C17 and enter the number 25850, the estimate for first-year profit after tax (PAT). The worksheet now looks like Figure 18.12. Notice that you make these two entries just like any other spreadsheet entry. The fact that you are making the entries in the middle of a "document" makes no difference at all.

Finally, press {**Switch**} to change MAIN into a DOC window. Figure 18.13 shows the window at this point. Notice that the numbers 170622 and 25850 appear in the document next to the labels "First-year sales:" and "First-year PAT:".

If this trick surprises you, take a moment to consider what really happened here. It should be no surprise that the range A1 . . H20 is visible through MAIN whether MAIN is a SHEET window or a DOC window. You have simply made two entries through the SHEET window MAIN and viewed those entries through the DOC window MAIN.

If you are working along with the text, you can see that the entries in cells C15 and C17 appear dim when you view them through the DOC window. These two levels of brightness in the video display distinguish between the normal text of your document, which you can edit freely, and the spreadsheet entries, which are not subject to the usual document editing commands.

```
    -----A---------B--------C--------D-------E--------F-------G--------H---------
 1  TO:       Les Porter                                                        |
 2  FROM:     Wayne Oliver                                                       |
 3  SUBJECT:  New Product Plan for "Handi-Tote"                                  |
 4                                                                              |
 5  I have completed my research and analysis for producing and marketing       |
 6  the new Handi-Tote carrying case and cooler.  The figures for the           |
 7  "most-likely" case of sales and costs are presented on the attached         |
 8  sheet.  The sales figures are based on studies performed by our             |
 9  marketing research department, as well as input from the sales force.       |
10  Cost figures are derived from discussions with various suppliers as well    |
11  as data from the controller's office.                                       |
12                                                                              |
13  Here is a summary of these key figures:                                     |
14                                                                              |
15  First-year sales:  170662                                                   |
16                                                                              |
17  First-year PAT:      25850                                                  |
18                                                                              |
19  My analysis assumes a manufacturing and marketing start-up at the           |
20  beginning of 1985.  I expect this product will earn a healthy profit in     |
    ===============================================================MAIN=
```

Figure 18.12

```
    <<------>------>-----)----->-----)-----)-----)-----)----->-----)----->---->>
    | TO:       Les Porter                                                      |
    | FROM:     Wayne Oliver                                                     |
    | SUBJECT:  New Product Plan for "Handi-Tote"                                |
    |                                                                           |
    | I have completed my research and analysis for producing and marketing     |
    | the new Handi-Tote carrying case and cooler.  The figures for the         |
    | "most-likely" case of sales and costs are presented on the attached       |
    | sheet.  The sales figures are based on studies performed by our           |
    | marketing research department, as well as input from the sales force.     |
    | Cost figures are derived from discussions with various suppliers as well  |
    | as data from the controller's office.                                     |
    |                                                                           |
    | Here is a summary of these key figures:                                   |
    |                                                                           |
    | First-year sales:  170622                                                 |
    |                                                                           |
    | First-year PAT:      25850                                                |
    |                                                                           |
    | My analysis assumes a manufacturing and marketing start-up at the         |
    | beginning of 1985.  I expect this product will earn a healthy profit in   |
    ===============================================================MAIN=
```

Figure 18.13

Although Symphony allows you to view the entries in cells C15 and C17 through the DOC window, it does not allow you to edit these values. The entries in cells C15 and C17 are "off limits" while you are in the DOC environment. Symphony lets you know when you are in "off-limits" territory by displaying an asterisk at the top of your screen. For example, if you move the cursor to the number 170662 in the memo, you will see the asterisk at the top of your screen.

What exactly does it mean to say that the spreadsheet entries embedded in a document are "off limits"? Essentially, this means you cannot edit these entries through the DOC window by typing in new characters or deleting old characters using the [Del] or [Backspace] key. If you try to type characters in this part of the worksheet or press [Del], [Backspace], or the [Space bar], your computer beeps and there is no response on the screen.

The asterisk signaling "off limits" appears even before the cursor actually reaches the 1 in 170622 as you scroll across the line. In fact, you are in an "off-limits" section as soon as the cursor crosses into cell C15, even though the first few character columns in that cell are blank.

This should not surprise you. As you know, when Symphony is in the DOC mode, it treats all text and numbers as long labels in the left-most column of the window's Restrict range. In this case, all of the text in the document is entered as a left-justified label in column A. Because the entries in cells C15 and cells C17 are not a part of column A, you cannot edit them through the DOC window.

Even though you can't edit the spreadsheet figures in a document as you can normal text, you can easily use the {**Switch**} key to change the DOC window into a SHEET window and then alter previously "off-limits" material. For example, to change the entry in cell C15 from 170622 to 170623, use {**Switch**} to change MAIN into a **S**HEET window, move the cell pointer to cell C15, and make the change. In fact, you can always switch to a SHEET window and use the SHEET commands to operate on any cells in the worksheet, including the long labels that make up the memo.

The fact that the entries in cells C15 and C17 are values is not the main reason you cannot edit them through the DOC window. If you change MAIN back to a SHEET window and enter the label "ABCDEF" in cell C16 and then return to the DOC window, the label will also appear dim and you will not be able to edit it.

The only type of entry that you can make through a SHEET window and then edit in a DOC window is a left-aligned label in the first column of the Restrict range. In other words, if you enter the label "ABCDEF" in cell A16 of the SHEET window MAIN and then turn MAIN back into a DOC window, Symphony allows you to edit that label. If, however, you enter the number 1234 in cell A16, Symphony treats this entry like the ones in C15 and C17.

If you move the cursor beyond the number 170622 on the same line of the document, the asterisk remains in view at the top of the screen. If you try to make an entry in this part of the window, Symphony beeps and refuses to make the entry. In general, Symphony does not allow you to make an entry to the right of a spreadsheet entry through a DOC window. If you wish to make such an entry you must turn the window back into a SHEET window and make the entry as a SHEET label in a cell to the right of the old entry.

If you make a SHEET entry that overlaps text that already exists in the document, Symphony simply "hides" the part of the text that lies behind and to the right of the entry. For example, if you enter the number 12345 in cell D7 and then view the worksheet through a DOC window, the screen looks like Figure 18.14.

If you turn MAIN back into a SHEET window and then erase the entry in cell D7, then return MAIN to a DOC window, the text again appears normal.

```
<<------>----->----->----->----->----->----->----->----->----->----->--->>
| TO:      Les Porter                                                      |
| FROM:    Wayne Oliver                                                    |
| SUBJECT: New Product Plan for "Handi-Tote"                               |
|                                                                          |
| I have completed my research and analysis for producing and marketing   |
| the new Handi-Tote carrying case and cooler.  The figures for the        |
| "most-likely" case of sales        12345                                 |
| sheet.  The sales figures are based on studies performed by our          |
| marketing research department, as well as input from the sales force.    |
| Cost figures are derived from discussions with various suppliers as well |
| as data from the controller's office.                                    |
|                                                                          |
| Here is a summary of these key figures:                                  |
|                                                                          |
| First-year sales:  170622                                                |
|                                                                          |
| First-year PAT:     25850                                                |
|                                                                          |
| My analysis assumes a manufacturing and marketing start-up at the        |
| beginning of 1985.  I expect this product will earn a healthy profit in  |
| ==================================================================MAIN=   |
```

Figure 18.14

Justification

Any change in the document's Format settings has no effect on the "off-limits" characters. For example, if you change the default Justification from Left to Even, the spreadsheet figures remain exactly as you see them on your screen.

In fact, neither the {Justify} key nor the Justification setting has an effect on spreadsheet entries that you view through a DOC window. For example, suppose you enter three extra characters at the beginning of the phrase "First-year sales:" so that the worksheet looks like Figure 18.15.

```
<<------>----->----->----->----->----->----->----->----->----->----->--->>
| TO:      Les Porter                                                      |
| FROM:    Wayne Oliver                                                    |
| SUBJECT: New Product Plan for "Handi-Tote"                               |
|                                                                          |
| I have completed my research and analysis for producing and marketing   |
| the new Handi-Tote carrying case and cooler.  The figures for the        |
| "most-likely" case of sales and costs are presented on the attached      |
| sheet.  The sales figures are based on studies performed by our          |
| marketing research department, as well as input from the sales force.    |
| Cost figures are derived from discussions with various suppliers as well |
| as data from the controller's office.                                    |
|                                                                          |
| Here is a summary of these key figures:                                  |
|                                                                          |
| AAAFirst-year                                                            |
| sales:            170622                                                 |
|                                                                          |
| First-year PAT:    25850                                                 |
|                                                                          |
| My analysis assumes a manufacturing and marketing start-up at the        |
| ==================================================================MAIN=   |
```

Figure 18.15

First, notice that Symphony has shoved the entry in cell C15 (and a part of the line of text) down one row, to cell C16. This occurred because Symphony could not fit the extra three characters in the line without overwriting the spreadsheet entry. Because the Symphony will not overwrite a spreadsheet entry, the program inserted a new line in the document and moved the spreadsheet entry down into that line.

Suppose that you now delete the three extra characters and press {**Justify**}. The screen now looks like Figure 18.16.

```
<<----->----->----->----->----->----->----->----->----->----->---->>
|TO:        Les Porter                                                |
|FROM:      Wayne Oliver                                              |
|SUBJECT:   New Product Plan for "Handi-Tote"                         |
|                                                                     |
|I have completed my research and analysis for producing and marketing|
|the new Handi-Tote carrying case and cooler.  The figures for the    |
|"most-likely" case of sales and costs are presented on the attached  |
|sheet.  The sales figures are based on studies performed by our      |
|marketing research department, as well as input from the sales force.|
|Cost figures are derived from discussions with various suppliers as well|
|as data from the controller's office.                                |
|                                                                     |
|Here is a summary of these key figures:                              |
|                                                                     |
|First-year sales:                                                    |
|                    170622                                           |
|                                                                     |
|First-year PAT:      25850                                           |
|                                                                     |
|My analysis assumes a manufacturing and marketing start-up at the    |
=================================================================MAIN=
```

Figure 18.16

Notice that Symphony does not rejustify the spreadsheet entry. To move it back up to the correct position, you have to use Symphony's DOC or SHEET Move command.

Using the DOC Commands

Although you cannot insert text over a spreadsheet entry or use the [Del] or [Backspace] keys to edit these entries, you can use the DOC environment Copy, Erase, and Move commands to act on the "off-limits" spreadsheet labels and values. For example, if you want to erase the entry in cell C15 using the DOC Erase command, move the cursor to the entry and press the {**Erase**} key. Notice that Symphony automatically expands the cursor to cover the entire width (9 spaces) of cell C15 as soon as you issue the command. To erase the entry, just press [**Enter**].

You cannot erase part of a spreadsheet entry with the DOC Erase command. For example, you can't use the DOC Erase command to erase just the 1 in the number 170662. Of course, you can erase more than one spreadsheet entry at a time with the DOC Erase command, and you can erase both spreadsheet entries and DOC text at the same time.

Similarly, you can use the DOC Copy and Move commands to move a spreadsheet entry. As with the Erase command, you cannot copy or move a part of a spreadsheet entry; you must copy or move the entire entry. In every other regard, these commands work as usual.

The DOC environment Erase and Move commands do not affect spreadsheet entries exactly as those commands in the SHEET environment do. Of course, if you want to use the SHEET Move, Copy, or Erase commands to operate on spreadsheet entries, you can do so simply by switching to the SHEET mode and issuing the desired command. (See Chapter 15 for an explanation of the difference between using the Erase and Move commands in the DOC environment versus the SHEET environment.)

Linking Cells in the Document to the Spreadsheet

In the previous example, we entered the numbers 170662 and 25850 into cells C15 and C17 to complete the memo. This is not the only way to enter values into a document, however. You can also use formulas to link the cells in the document range to numbers stored elsewhere in the worksheet.

For example, suppose that the spreadsheet shown in Figure 18.17 is a part of the same worksheet as your memo. This spreadsheet is a five-year model projecting the sales and costs for a new product. Figure 18.18 is a graphic representation of the relative positions of the spreadsheet and the memo in the worksheet.

```
     -----A--------B--------C--------D-------E--------F-------G--------H--------
  31 Handi-Tote Product Plan, 1985 through 1989                                |
  32                                                                           |
  33 Unit Retail Price:   $19.95                                              |
  34 Average Discount        55%                                              |
  35                                                                           |
  36                              1985      1986      1987      1988      1989 |
  37                            ------    ------    ------    ------    ------ |
  38 Unit Sales                 15550     17105     18815     20697     22766 |
  39 Dollar Sales             $170,622 $187,685 $206,448 $227,098 $249,800   |
  40                                                                           |
  41 Costs of Goods Sold      $111,494 $122,643 $134,904 $148,397 $163,232   |
  42                            ------    ------    ------    ------    ------ |
  43 Gross Margin              $59,129   $65,042   $71,544   $78,700   $86,568 |
  44 Operating Expenses        $12,129   $12,864   $13,904   $15,676   $17,177 |
  45                            ------    ------    ------    ------    ------ |
  46 Profit Before Tax         $47,000   $52,178   $57,640   $63,024   $69,391 |
  47 Taxes          45%        $21,150   $23,480   $25,938   $28,361   $31,226 |
  48                            ------    ------    ------    ------    ------ |
  49 Profit After Tax          $25,850   $28,698   $31,702   $34,663   $38,165 |
  50                            ======    ======    ======    ======    ====== |
  =====================================================================MAIN=
```

Figure 18.17

Notice that the numbers 170662 and 25850 appear as calculated numbers in cells D39 and D49 of this spreadsheet. If you wish, you can complete the document by entering formulas in cells C15 and C17 that refer directly to the spreadsheet.

In general, if you are building a worksheet that includes both a spreadsheet and a document based on that spreadsheet, you should begin by creating the spreadsheet model for the projections starting at cell A1 and then, after you complete the spreadsheet, write the memo to explain the calculations below the spreadsheet itself. Although we've done it in the reverse order here, the example is still meaningful.

```
    -----A--------B--------C--------D-------E--------F-------G--------H-------
 1  TO:        Les Porter                                                     |
 2  FROM:      Wayne Oliver                                                   |
 3  SUBJECT:   New Product Plan for "Handi-Tote"                             |
 4                                                                            |
 5  I have completed my research and analysis for producing and marketing    |
 6  the new Handi-Tote carrying case and cooler.  The figures for the        |
 7  "most-likely" case of sales and costs are presented on the attached      |
 8  sheet.  The sales figures are based on studies performed by our          |
 9  marketing research department, as well as input from the sales force.    |
10  Cost figures are derived from discussions with various suppliers as well |
11  as data from the controller's office.                                    |
12                                                                            |
13  Here is a summary of these key figures:                                  |
14                                                                            |
15  First-year sales:                                                        |
16                                                                            |
17  First-year PAT:                                                          |
18                                                                            |
19  My analysis assumes a manufacturing and marketing start-up at the        |
20  beginning of 1985.  I expect this product will earn a healthy profit in  |
21                                                                            |
22                                                                            |
23                                                                            |
24                                                                            |
25                                                                            |
26                                                                            |
27                                                                            |
28                                                                            |
29                                                                            |
30                                                                            |
31  Handi-Tote Product Plan, 1985 through 1989                               |
32                                                                            |
33  Unit Retail Price:    $19.95                                             |
34  Average Discount      55%                                                |
35                                                                            |
36                       1985      1986      1987      1988      1989         |
37                      ------    ------    ------    ------    ------        |
38  Unit Sales          15550     17105     18815     20697     22766        |
39  Dollar Sales       $170,622  $187,685  $206,448  $227,098  $249,800      |
40                                                                            |
41  Costs of Goods Sold $111,494 $122,643  $134,904  $148,397  $163,232      |
42                      ------    ------    ------    ------    ------        |
43  Gross Margin        $59,129   $65,042   $71,544   $78,700   $86,568      |
44  Operating Expenses  $12,129   $12,864   $13,904   $15,676   $17,177      |
45                      ------    ------    ------    ------    ------        |
46  Profit Before Tax   $47,000   $52,178   $57,640   $63,024   $69,391      |
47  Taxes         45%   $21,150   $23,480   $25,938   $28,361   $31,226      |
48                      ------    ------    ------    ------    ------        |
49  Profit After Tax    $25,850   $28,698   $31,702   $34,663   $38,165      |
50                      ======    ======    ======    ======    ======       |
    =========================================================================MAIN=
```

Figure 18.18

Entering Formulas in the Document

Now let's use a formula to enter the Sales and PAT numbers in the memo. To do this, press {**Switch**} to change MAIN into a **S**HEET window and move the cell pointer to cell C15. Now simply enter the formula

> C15: +D39

in that cell. Next, move the cell pointer to cell C17 and enter the formula

> C17: +D49

Now, press {**Switch**} to convert MAIN back into a **DOC** window. Notice that once again the numbers appear next to the labels, as they did in Figure 18.14. However, this new version has at least one major advantage over the old. Suppose you decide to change the 1985 unit sales estimate for Handi-tote from 15550 to 20000. To make this change, switch MAIN to a SHEET window, move the cell pointer to cell D38, and enter the new number. Figure 18.19 shows the worksheet after this change has been made.

```
    -----A--------B--------C--------D-------E--------F-------G--------H--------
 31 Handi-Tote Product Plan, 1985 through 1989                                |
 32                                                                           |
 33 Unit Retail Price:   $19.95                                              |
 34 Average Discount         55%                                             |
 35                                                                           |
 36                            1985     1986     1987     1988     1989       |
 37                          ------   ------   ------   ------   ------       |
 38 Unit Sales               20000    17105    18815    20697    22766       |
 39 Dollar Sales          $219,450 $187,685 $206,448 $227,098 $249,800       |
 40                                                                           |
 41 Costs of Goods Sold   $143,400 $122,643 $134,904 $148,397 $163,232       |
 42                          ------   ------   ------   ------   ------       |
 43 Gross Margin            $76,050  $65,042  $71,544  $78,700  $86,568       |
 44 Operating Expenses      $12,129  $12,864  $13,904  $15,676  $17,177       |
 45                          ------   ------   ------   ------   ------       |
 46 Profit Before Tax       $63,921  $52,178  $57,640  $63,024  $69,391       |
 47 Taxes          45%      $28,764  $23,480  $25,938  $28,361  $31,226       |
 48                          ------   ------   ------   ------   ------       |
 49 Profit After Tax        $35,157  $28,698  $31,702  $34,663  $38,165       |
 50                          ======   ======   ======   ======   ======      |
    =================================================================MAIN=
```

Figure 18.19

Now switch the window back to DOC and move the cursor so that the two embedded numbers come into view. Notice that the two numbers embedded in the document match the new values in the spreadsheet. Like any other formula in Symphony, the values of these formulas automatically change when the cells referred to by the formulas change. The document is thus automatically updated when the spreadsheet is updated.

Because each figure embedded in the memo is linked to the original spreadsheet model with a formula, any changes to these numbers in the spreadsheet model are reflected in the memo figures as well. Remember that both the memo and the spreadsheet model are on the same worksheet; the fact that you generally view one through a DOC window and the other through a SHEET window does not affect your ability to link values in the memo to values in the spreadsheet.

In this example, we used formulas to embed values in the document. You can also use formulas to embed spreadsheet labels in a document. For example, suppose you wanted to place the label from cell A33 "Unit Retail Price:" in row 14 of your memo. To do this, press {**Switch**} to change MAIN to a **S**HEET window. Place the cell pointer on cell A14 and enter the formula

    A14: +A33

Next, enter the formula **+C33** in cell C14. The worksheet now looks like Figure 18.20.

Notice that the label "Unit Retail Price:" now appears in cell A14, and the number 19.95 appears in cell C14. If you decide to change the label in the spreadsheet, the change is made in the memo as well.

```
      ------A--------B--------C--------D-------E--------F-------G--------H--------
    1  TO:        Les Porter                                                     |
    2  FROM:      Wayne Oliver                                                    |
    3  SUBJECT:   New Product Plan for "Handi-Tote"                               |
    4                                                                             |
    5  I have completed my research and analysis for producing and marketing      |
    6  the new Handi-Tote carrying case and cooler.  The figures for the          |
    7  "most-likely" case of sales and costs are presented on the attached        |
    8  sheet.  The sales figures are based on studies performed by our            |
    9  marketing research department, as well as input from the sales force.      |
   10  Cost figures are derived from discussions with various suppliers as well   |
   11  as data from the controller's office.                                      |
   12                                                                             |
   13  Here is a summary of these key figures:                                    |
   14  Unit Retail Price:  19.95                                                  |
   15  First-year sales:   170662                                                 |
   16                                                                             |
   17  First-year PAT:     25850                                                  |
   18                                                                             |
   19  My analysis assumes a manufacturing and marketing start-up at the          |
   20  beginning of 1985.  I expect this product will earn a healthy profit in    |
       ====================================================================MAIN=
```

Figure 18.20

After you convert MAIN back into a DOC window, you may want to insert a line above and below the new line to improve the spacing of the document. If Symphony is in the Insert mode, you can insert these lines by pressing **[Enter].** Otherwise, you'll want to use the {**Split**} key.

The numbers in the memo remain linked to their original source in the spreadsheet even if you move them around in the document, insert rows of text above them, or erase one of the rows containing the spreadsheet values. For example, suppose that after you embed the spreadsheet figures, you decide to add another paragraph to the beginning of the memo. As you type this paragraph, all the embedded figures are "pushed down" several lines. But the numbers will not be affected because they remain tied to the original spreadsheet. Similarly, you can add lines of text between the lines where the figures appear and not affect the values.

Using Range Names

If you are working with a large spreadsheet and document, you may find it rather tedious to embed figures from the spreadsheet into the document. Each time you want to embed a figure, you must type + and then move the cell pointer across a wide expanse of the worksheet to point to the value you wish to embed.

You can use a shortcut for this procedure by giving range names to the spreadsheet figures that you want to embed in the memo. For example, you might want to name cell D39, which contains the first-year sales figure, FYSALES. Then, when you want to embed the first-year sales figure in the memo, you can use the formula

> C15: +FYSALES

in cell C15 of the memo.

Formatting Figures in a Document

After you embed figures into the memo, you will probably want to format each one. Notice that even though the figures were formatted in the original spreadsheet, they lose their format settings when they move into the memo. For example, the original first-year sales figure in the memo appears as 170662, with no dollar sign and no commas. This is because Symphony assigns formats to cell locations rather than numbers. Therefore, a number will have the format of the cell in which it resides.

To format the numbers in the memo, make sure MAIN is a SHEET window. Then position the cursor on C15 and issue the {**Menu**} Format Currency **0** command. Move the cell pointer to cell C17 and repeat the command.

Using Copy to Combine Spreadsheets and Documents

You can also use the SHEET mode Copy command to copy entries from a spreadsheet into a document. For example, to copy the number in cell D39 into the document, just position the cell pointer on cell D39 and issue the {**Menu**} Copy command. When Symphony asks you to provide the FROM range, just press **[Enter].** The TO range would be cell C15.

The Copy command is frequently not the best way to insert spreadsheet data into a document, however. For example, if you try to copy the formula in cell D39

> D39: +$C$33*$C$34*D38

into cell C15, the result is the formula

> C15: +$C$33*$C$34*C14

which would have the value 0. Because cell D39 contains a formula with a relative reference, the value that results from a copied version of the formulas is different from the value of the original.

In addition, when you copy a spreadsheet or part of a spreadsheet into a document, the copied numbers in a document are not tied to the numbers and formulas in the original spreadsheet. If you make changes in the original spreadsheet, the copied numbers in your document do not change accordingly.

When you copy part of a spreadsheet into a document, any spreadsheet labels in the left-most column of your document window become part of the document text. You can edit these labels using all the normal document editing features.

You can also copy several rows or columns of cells, or even an entire spreadsheet model, into a document. When you use Copy to integrate a spreadsheet and a document, it is important to check whether there is a blank space in the document large enough to hold the rows or columns of cells you want to copy. If there is not enough room for the cells, they may write over part of the document. To create extra blank lines in the document, put Symphony in the Insert mode and press the [Enter] key.

Using Separate Windows
to View a Spreadsheet and a Document

In the previous discussion, we used an example where a single window, the MAIN window, was used to view both the spreadsheet and the memo that contains embedded spreadsheet values. You can, of course, use separate windows on your worksheet to view a spreadsheet and a document without affecting your ability to embed spreadsheet values into the document or copy numbers and labels from the spreadsheet into the document. Remember, however, if you use separate windows to view a spreadsheet and a document, you should restrict both windows so changes in one window do not affect the other.

For example, suppose you have created the memo of the previous example in the MAIN window, and you create the spreadsheet in a second window called PROJECT. We will assume that the memo and the spreadsheet occupy the same positions on the worksheet as they did in the previous example. To embed the first-year sales figure from the spreadsheet into the memo, you would follow the same steps outlined previously. First, change MAIN into a SHEET window. Then position the cell pointer on cell C15 and type a +. Next, you can move the pointer into the spreadsheet to point to cell D39 and press [Enter]. Notice that the fact that both MAIN and PROJECT are restricted windows does not prevent you from moving the cell pointer freely from the range of the MAIN window into the range of PROJECT. Instead of pointing to cell D39, you could simply have typed in the entry

C15: +D39

You can also copy parts of the spreadsheet into the memo, even though the spreadsheet and the memo are created in separate windows. To do this, you must again change MAIN into a SHEET window and use the Copy command of the SHEET environment. Again, Symphony will let you move the cell pointer from one window's Restrict range into the range of another window to point to the cells you wish to copy.

Moving Text from a Document into a Spreadsheet

Finally, we should note that even though our discussion has focused on embedding spreadsheet values into a document, you can also embed text from a document into a spreadsheet. You can simply copy the text from the document into the spreadsheet, in which case any changes to the text in the document will not affect the copied text in the spreadsheet. Alternatively, you could use a formula to tie the text in the spreadsheet to the text in the original document. Remember, each line of text in a document is viewed as a label residing in column A or in the left-most column of the DOC window. Thus you could place the cell pointer on the line in your spreadsheet where you want the text to appear, type a +, then move the cell pointer to the beginning of the line of text in the document that you want to place in the spreadsheet (on column A), and finally press [Enter]. This will cause the line of text to appear in the spreadsheet. Any changes you make to the original line of text in your document will be reflected in the copied line that is now in your spreadsheet.

PART
VI

DATA BASE MANAGEMENT

CHAPTER NINETEEN
DATA BASE FUNDAMENTALS

Symphony's data base capabilities go far beyond those of conventional spreadsheet software, including Lotus 1-2-3. In the following chapters, we will explore all facets of data base management with Symphony. By the end of the section, you will be ready to use Symphony's data base features to accomplish tasks such as printing address labels from a list of addresses, printing form letters in which Symphony "fills in the blanks" with selected information stored in the data base, sorting the information in the data base into a useful order, extracting or highlighting information from the data base that meets the criteria you specify, and other such information-related tasks.

WHAT IS A DATA BASE?

Simply, a data base is a structured collection of information. A telephone directory is a common example of a data base containing thousands of entries. Each entry in the directory includes three pieces of information: a name, an address, and a telephone number. In data base terminology, the entries are called records. The pieces of information listed for each entry are referred to as fields. Thus, a telephone directory has thousands of records, each of which contains three fields of information: a name, an address, and a telephone number.

SYMPHONY DATA BASES: THE BASIC STRUCTURE

All Symphony data bases exist in the Symphony workspace. Information stored in a Symphony data base consists of cell entries (values and labels) just like those you've been working with throughout the book. The only difference between a Symphony data base and any other Symphony worksheet is that the entries in a data base must be entered in a special order.

All Symphony data bases have the same basic structure. Symphony can use only data that comply with this structure when it performs its numerous data base functions.

In a Symphony data base, each record is stored in a single row, and the individual fields of that record occupy single cells in that row. In fact, Symphony stores a data base in the same format you find in a telephone book. Just as each record occupies a single row in the Symphony spreadsheet, "John Jones 111 First Street 234-5678" is found on one line of the phone directory. Additional records are placed in individual rows beneath the first record. Similarly, each field of information in Symphony occupies a separate column in the worksheet, just as all phone numbers will be found in a single column of the phone directory. Take a look at the "telephone directory" in Figure 19.1 for an example of a Symphony data base.

```
         -------------A----------------------B-------------C--------
   1     Name                    Address           Phone           |
   2     John Jones              111 First Street  234-5678         |
   3     John Q. Public          222 Second Street 555-1212         |
   4     Jim Smith               333 Third Street  345-6789         |
   5     Mary Smith              123 First Street  876-5432         |
   6                                                                |
         =================================================MAIN=
```

Figure 19.1

A Symphony data base always has field names at the top of each field (column). In Figure 19.1, the field names are the labels Name, Address, and Phone in cells A1, B1, and C1. As we will explain later, these field names are Symphony's "key" to the records when it manipulates the information in the data base. The actual information (the records) must be placed in the columns beneath the field names.

Since the Symphony worksheet contains 8192 rows, and because the first row in every data base must contain the names of the fields in that data base, a Symphony data base has a theoretical maximum capacity of 8191 records. In fact, the real limit on the size of a data base is not the number of rows in the worksheet but the amount of memory in your computer. For example, I was only able to get 2458 records into a five-field Symphony data base in a computer with 512K of memory.

Using a Data Base

Information stored in a Symphony data base can be used for a variety of purposes. To explain some of these uses, let's continue with the telephone-book example. Suppose that you're given a telephone number, but you forget whom it belongs to. Symphony can rearrange your telephone data base so that the records are arranged in ascending numerical order based on the first digit of the telephone number. That is, the first entry in the telephone book would have the lowest number and the last entry the highest. Using this numeric directory, you can easily find the telephone number and look in the first field of the record for the name.

Alternatively, you can ask Symphony to find the number in question in the data base and display the name of the person corresponding to that number. Similarly, if you want to know how many people in your telephone data base have the last name of Smith, Symphony can count these for you or, better yet, print a listing of each of these records with the count at the bottom. You can even ask Symphony to find all people with the last name of Smith who live on First Street—or even the Smiths on First Street whose telephone number ends with the digit 3. You're probably getting the idea, but there is more.

If the zip code is included in a field of your telephone data base, Symphony can print all the records in the data base as address labels, or only the records containing the name Smith, or only the records with a 234 telephone exchange, or only the records containing 12345 or 12346 zip codes, or only the records for those people who live on First Street. Additionally, Symphony can print form letters to any of these sets of people, inserting their names into the proper spaces in the letters.

Furthermore, Symphony can calculate statistical information for various fields. It can count the number of entries in a field, finding the average, minimum, or maximum value of a field, or find the standard deviation of the entries in a field. These statistical functions can be restricted to a specific part of a field as well. For example, you can instruct Symphony to count the number of records with a phone number beginning with 234. Most of these statistical functions are probably not useful for the information in this telephone book example (for instance, who would want to know the average telephone number of the residents on a street?), but in many cases these functions are very valuable.

A Tale of Two Windows

Data base management within Symphony requires work in two types of windows: FORM windows and SHEET windows. In general, FORM windows are best suited to defining data bases, entering records into data bases, and editing records stored in data bases. SHEET windows are best suited for "using" the data once a data base has been defined and filled with records.

As you saw above, the actual contents of a Symphony data base reside in the worksheet and can be viewed through a SHEET window. From a SHEET window, you can use the query commands to manipulate the records in a data base to find or extract meaningful groupings of records from the data base. You can highlight or eliminate records in the data base that match predetermined criteria (the Find or Delete commands), copy selected records to another part of the worksheet (the Extract command), eliminate duplicate records from the data base (the Unique command), and introduce full lines of text into a data base (the Parse command). You can also use Symphony's Query Record-Sort to sort the entries stored in a data base. In this chapter and the next we'll cover Symphony's form windows in detail. We'll come back to these SHEET window commands in Chapter 21.

THE FORM WINDOW

A Symphony FORM window allows you to view the contents of a data base, one record at a time, through a specially designed Entry form.

The FORM window's menu of commands allows the user to generate a new data base, Entry form, and related ranges and to define and activate or deactivate use of specified criteria for selecting records. A FORM window can also be used to enter records into the data base, to retrieve records from the data base for viewing or editing, and to delete records from the data base. You can also use the FORM Record-Sort command to sort the records in a data base. Finally, you can generate a custom report from a FORM window, using the {Services} Print commands.

This chapter and the next will introduce you to a FORM window, explaining how it can be used to create a data base, enter information into the data base, and perform limited manipulations of the information in the data base. Advanced topics such as the modification of Entry forms and the printing of data base reports will be covered in Chapter 22.

Creating a FORM Window

You can create a FORM window in the same ways that you create other Symphony windows. In general, you'll want to begin creating a FORM window by positioning the cell pointer in a SHEET window. From this window, press {**Type**} and select the FORM option. This changes the SHEET window into a FORM window. Once you've done this, you can "toggle" between the two windows by pressing the {Switch} key. The {Switch} key is especially useful with FORM windows and data bases because you will be constantly switching back and forth between SHEET and FORM when working with your data base. Of course, you can also use the {Services} Window Create command to define a completely new window for the FORM. (For more on the creation of windows, see Chapter 11.)

When you first enter a FORM window, you will see a simple line border surrounding a blank screen. At the upper-left corner of the screen (outside of the border), you will see the message "(No definition range defined)". Ignore this message for now; we'll explain it in a few pages.

Generating an Entry Form

There are two different approaches you can take to creating a data base and Entry form in Symphony. The FORM Generate command is the easiest way. Generate uses specifications about the number, name, and type of the fields you want to include in a data base to create both a data base and the Entry form that you will use to access that data base. (Although they are closely related, an Entry form and a data base are two different things. The difference will become apparent as you read through this chapter.)

Of course, you can also create a data base manually through a SHEET window without ever using a FORM window. We'll cover this approach to building a data base in Chapter 21.

Specifying the Fields

Before Symphony can generate a form automatically, you must provide the field names that will be used in the data base and Entry form. These names can be entered into the worksheet through either a SHEET or a DOC window, but it's easier to do it from a SHEET window.

To begin defining the data base structure, move the cell pointer to a cell at the upper-left corner of a large blank area in the worksheet. In a blank worksheet, you'll generally start with the cell pointer in cell A1.

Starting with this cell, enter a name for each "blank" you want to appear on the form. For example, to create a simple address-book form, type the information in Figure 19.2 into cells A1 . . A5.

```
------A-----------------------B-----------
1  Name:L:25                              |
2  Street:L:25                            |
3  City:L:20                              |
4  State:L:2                              |
5  Zip:L:5                                |
6                                         |
   ==================================MAIN=
```

Figure 19.2

Each of these cells contains three pieces of information: a field name, a letter indicating the type of entry this field will contain, and a number indicating the maximum length of the entries in this field. These entries define the structure of the data base we're about to create.

Symphony uses the first part of each entry, the field name, to define the fields in the data base. The field name may be as long as you wish and may contain any alphabetic or numeric characters. You should not include spaces or the characters ? and * in your field names.

The second part of the entry is the field type. The field type is designated by a letter; in the example, the letter L designates each field as a label field. The other choices are N for number, D for date, T for time, or C for computed. The type definition for each field determines the way Symphony will interpret the entries you make into that field. If the type is Label, all entries to that field will be considered labels. We'll explain the concept of field type in detail in a few pages.

The numbers in each of the entries in the example specify the length of the "blank" Symphony will create for this field in the form and the width of the corresponding column in the data base. Notice that in the example we assigned relatively long field lengths (25 characters) to the Name and Street fields and a very short length (2) to the State field.

Only the field name portion of these definition entries is required. If you did not want to define a special type and length for each of these fields, you could have entered just the field names in cells A1 . . A5.

The Generate Command

To continue the form generation process, you must toggle back to a FORM window by pressing {**Switch**}. Next, press {**Menu**} to bring the FORM command menu into view:

Attach   Criteria   Initialize   Record-Sort   Generate   Settings

To begin the form generation process, issue the Generate command. Symphony displays the following message:

> **Select default field type:**
> **Label   Number   Date   Time   Computed**

The selection here determines how Symphony should interpret characters entered into the fields for which you have not specified a field type. In this case, you specified a field type for every field by including an L next to each field name in the range A1 . . A5, so your choice on this step doesn't matter. Since some response is required, however, simply press **[Enter]** to select Label.

If you had not specified a field type for each field when you defined the data base structure, you probably would have been more careful in making your decision. In many situations you'll want to choose a default field type other than Label.

Next, Symphony displays the prompt

> **Default field length: 9**

The number Symphony provides is the default column width for the current window, usually 9. The number you enter here determines the number of spaces in the "blank" for any field for which you have not specified a length.

As with the type, you have already specified a length for each field by including a number at the end of each field definition entry, so again this choice doesn't matter in this example. Simply press **[Enter]** to confirm the number Symphony has offered.

Symphony now proceeds to the next step, displaying the prompt

> **Name for Database settings sheet:**
> **MAIN**

Each FORM window must be attached to a data base settings sheet. As we will explore in detail later, a Symphony data base definition includes a number of related ranges, the boundaries of which must be specified and "tied together" in a central settings sheet. In the process of generating a form, Symphony defines and names these ranges. The settings sheet name you supply in this step will be used by Symphony to store the ranges created when generating the data base.

Since the data base settings sheet MAIN always exists in the worksheet, this name always appears in the list. If you have previously created other FORM settings sheets, their names will also be listed. Assuming this is your first Symphony data base, only the name MAIN appears in the list. To select this choice just press **[Enter].**

Next, Symphony moves you from the FORM window into the spreadsheet, placing the cell pointer on the cell it was last on when in the SHEET window. The prompt line reads

> **Range of field names:**

Use the arrow keys to move the cell pointer to the block of cells containing the field names—in this case, cells A1 . . A5. Starting at either A1 or A5, anchor the cell pointer by using the period or the [Tab] key, and use the arrow keys to highlight the entire block. Now press **[Enter].** Symphony returns to the FORM window, which now looks like Figure 19.3.

```
┌──────────────────────────────────────────────────────────────┐
│  Inserting Record 1        New Record                          │
│  Enter Name                                                    │
│  ----------------------------------------------------------    │
│ │ Name _____                            │   │
│ │ Street _____                      │   │
│ │ City _____                           │   │
│ │ State __                                                 │   │
│ │ Zip _____                                                │   │
│ │                                                          │   │
│  =MAIN=========================================MAIN=           │
└──────────────────────────────────────────────────────────────┘
```

Figure 19.3

As you can see, Symphony has automatically created this form in the FORM window MAIN. Notice that the field names you typed in cells A1 . . A5 in the worksheet appear in this form, with a "blank" following each name that is as long as the length you specified for that field. The name MAIN in the lower-right corner of this sheet indicates that this FORM window is named MAIN. The MAIN in the lower-left corner of the sheet indicates that this window is attached to the data base settings sheet named MAIN.

Although you can't tell this by looking at the FORM window, Symphony has also set up and defined the Database range, which will contain the data base itself, as well as a number of related ranges: the Criterion range, the Definition range, the Main Report and Above Report ranges, and the Entry range. All five of these additional ranges are stored in the worksheet and cannot be seen from a FORM window. We'll cover them in detail later in the chapter.

Entering Records into the Data Base

Now let's look at how the Entry form works. At the top of the form, the phrases "Inserting Record 1" and "New Record" indicate that you are in the Insert mode. This means that you are ready to fill this record for the first time. The cursor will be a single flashing underscore located immediately over the first underline next to the word Name. Since the prompt asks for a name, let's enter the name Mary Smith. The form will now look like Figure 19.4.

The cursor will be located after the "h" in Smith. To move to the next field within this record, simply press **[Enter]**. Mary Smith will now appear in dim letters, indicating that this entry is "locked in." The cell pointer is now located on the first space in the blank following the field name Street. Type in the street name and press **[Enter]**.

You can continue filling in the blanks in this fashion, ending with the Zip field. While typing entries into these blanks, the **[Backspace]** key may be used to erase the character to the left of the cursor, and the → and ← keys move the cursor between characters without erasing. The completed FORM window will look like Figure 19.5.

Note that pressing **[Enter]** after typing in 40222 moves the cursor back to the first space of the Name field. If you continue to press the [Enter], ↓, or → keys, the cursor will scroll through the five fields of Record 1. Similarly, the ↑ or ← keys will scroll the cursor

```
 Inserting Record 1      New Record
 Enter Name
-----------------------------------------------
| Name Mary Smith_____                    |
| Street _____          |
| City _____                    |
| State __                                     |
| Zip _____                                    |
|                                              |
 =MAIN==================================MAIN=
```

Figure 19.4

```
  Inserting Record 1      New Record
  Enter Zip
-----------------------------------------------
| Name Mary Smith_____                  |
| Street 111 First Street_____             |
| City Anytown_____                     |
| State KY                                     |
| Zip 40222                                    |
|                                              |
 =MAIN===================================MAIN=
```

Figure 19.5

through these fields in reverse order. You can use these keys to move to a field in the record that you need to revise prior to "inserting" the record into the data base. To revise a record once you've scrolled to it, press the [Edit] key. This returns the functions of the → and ← keys to their normal action—moving the cell pointer one space to the right or left on the current line.

You should not press [Backspace] or [Esc] when scrolling through the fields. Pressing [Backspace] will delete the contents of the current field, and pressing [Esc] will immediately erase all entries in the form.

Inserting the Record

After you have completed filling in Record 1 and have made any necessary modifications, you must instruct Symphony to insert the record into the data base by pressing **[Ins]**. Symphony automatically enters the record into the appropriate cells of the data base in the worksheet.

Immediately after inserting the record, Symphony displays an empty form on the screen and prompts you to begin filling in the next record. To complete this new record, just follow the same steps you used for the first record. You might want to practice entering records through a form by adding the following listings to the mailing list data base:

> John Doe
> 222 Second Street
> Mayberry
> NC
> 12345
>
> John Q. Public
> 333 Third Street
> Yourtown
> CA
> 11111
>
> Jane Smythe
> 123 Main Street
> Anytown
> MO
> 01010

The Edit Mode

Let's suppose that you have inserted four records into this data base, and you wish to go back and review these records for accuracy. Press the **[Pg Up]** key. This takes the cursor backwards through the data base, record by record. For instance, if you press the [Pg Up] key while you are viewing or working on Record 3, Record 2 will appear in the Entry form. In our example, the screen looks like Figure 19.6.

```
Editing Record 2 of 4
Enter Name
----------------------------------------------------
| Name John Doe_____                     |
| Street 222 Second Street_____                  |
| City Mayberry_____                         |
| State NC                                          |
| Zip 12345                                         |
|                                                   |
=MAIN==================================MAIN=
```

Figure 19.6

Notice that the message at the top of the screen has changed in two ways. First, the New Record indicator is no longer displayed. Second, the line

> **Inserting Record 3**

has been replaced by the message

> **Editing Record 2 of 4**

Both of these changes indicate that Symphony is now in the FORM Edit mode. Very simply, this means that you are viewing a record which has been created previously and is now stored in the data base. If you wish, Symphony will allow you to make changes to this record. For example, you could change the Name field of this record by moving to the Name blank in the form and retyping the name.

In the Edit mode, the [Ins] key inserts the current record into the data base, as it does in the Insert mode. However, instead of moving to the next record, the current record remains on the screen. To insert the current record and move to the next record while in the Edit mode, press the [Pg Dn] key. Similarly, to insert the current record and move back to the previous record, press the [Pg Up] key. Note that Symphony will not allow you to use the [Pg Dn] key while you're in the Insert mode.

The [Del] key also functions differently in the Edit mode. In the Insert mode your computer will beep when you press the [Del] key. But in the Edit mode this key can erase records from the data base. When you press the [Del] key, Symphony responds with the prompt

> Are you sure you want to delete this record?
> No   Yes

If you select Yes the record on the screen is permanently deleted and you are returned to the previous record. If you select No the current record is left intact and on the screen.

The [Esc] key is the third key that functions differently in the Edit mode. In the Insert mode, you can press [Esc] while typing in a field to erase the entry in that field. If you press [Esc] a second time you erase all of the entries in that record. Pressing [Esc] a third time returns you to the previous record.

In the Edit mode, pressing [Esc] while modifying a field of an existing record erases your modified entry. Pressing [Esc] a second time causes the original entry to reappear. Pressing [Esc] a third time restores all original values into the record. Experiment with these various keys in both modes so that you become comfortable with them and know what to expect.

THE WORKSHEET

At this point you have generated a form, used that form to enter records into a data base, and edited the records in that data base. But you haven't seen the data base or the other ranges Symphony has created. To do this, toggle to the SHEET window where these ranges are stored (use the {Switch} or {Type} keys). The worksheet will look like the one in Figure 19.7.

(This figure shows a range that is in fact too large to be displayed on the screen of most computers. Showing the whole range in the figure makes the following discussion easier to follow. If you're working along with the chapter, you'll need to scroll around the worksheet to view all the ranges.)

The entries in cells A1 . . A5 should look familiar. These are the field definitions you entered into the worksheet from a SHEET window at the start of the form generation process. Symphony has used the entries in these five cells to create all of the entries you

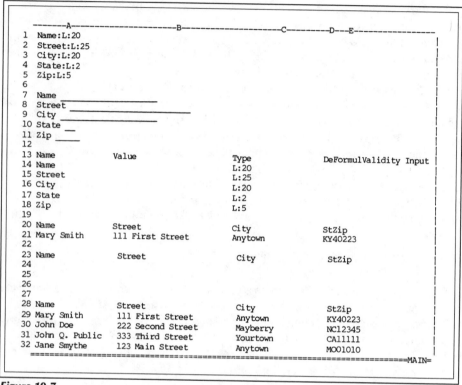

```
-------A----------------------B-------------------C---------D--E---------------
 1  Name:L:20
 2  Street:L:25
 3  City:L:20
 4  State:L:2
 5  Zip:L:5
 6
 7  Name _____
 8  Street _____
 9  City _____
10  State _____
11  Zip _____
12
13  Name            Value               Type            DeFormulValidity Input
14  Name                                L:20
15  Street                              L:25
16  City                                L:20
17  State                               L:2
18  Zip                                 L:5
19
20  Name            Street              City            StZip
21  Mary Smith      111 First Street    Anytown         KY40223
22
23  Name            Street              City            StZip
24
25
26
27
28  Name            Street              City            StZip
29  Mary Smith      111 First Street    Anytown         KY40223
30  John Doe        222 Second Street   Mayberry        NC12345
31  John Q. Public  333 Third Street    Yourtown        CA11111
32  Jane Smythe     123 Main Street     Anytown         MO01010
   ===================================================================MAIN=
```

Figure 19.7

see in this figure. The form generation process has also automatically defined a number of ranges that allow you to manipulate the data base.

The Database range and the Criterion range are used whether you are creating and using your data base from a SHEET window, from a FORM window, or from both. The Database range is simply the block of cells containing the actual data base. In the example, the Database range is A28 . . E32. The Criterion range gives Symphony the ability to select certain records from the data base, based on the contents of individual fields. In the example, this range is A23 . . E24.

The Entry range and the Definition range are only needed if you are using a FORM window to access the data base. The Entry range, A7 . . A11 in the example, shows the actual layout of the form we've been using. As you go through the chapter, remember that the blank form is not an ethereal creation of Symphony, but is in fact based on entries stored in cells of the worksheet.

The Definition range is the "gatekeeper" that links the form to the actual data base. The Definition range includes the length and type definitions for each field as well as other important information defining the structure of the data base. The Definition range in the example is A13 . . H18.

Two additional ranges, the Main Report range and the Above Report range, are used to structure the printing of reports that extract information from the data base.

Finally, although we cannot see it in the worksheet, Symphony creates a data base settings sheet, which lists the locations of all these ranges, effectively tying all the pieces together. We'll get to the settings sheet in the next chapter; first let's explore the ranges Symphony has generated.

The Database Range

The block of cells from A28 . . E32 in the example is the Database range. These cells contain the data base itself. The format of this data base conforms to Symphony's requirements: the names of the fields appear in adjacent cells in row 28, and the records appear in the rows immediately below these labels. Through the Generate process, Symphony has adjusted the widths of each of the columns in the Database range according to the field lengths specified in the entries in cells A1 . . A5.

When you press [Ins] or [Pg Dn] after you've entered a record into the Entry form, Symphony automatically places that record in the first empty row of the Database range. Simultaneously, Symphony expands the Database range to include this record and modifies the coordinates for this range in the data base settings sheet.

The distinction between the data base and the Database range is an important one. You intuitively recognize a data base as the field names and all the records that appear below these names. However, Symphony only recognizes as a data base those field names and records that are contained within the block of cells specified as the Database range. If you add a record to the data base from a SHEET window rather than from an Entry form, Symphony will not automatically expand the block of cells it has defined as the Database range. In this case, your data base would be larger than your Database range, and you would have to redefine the Database range manually. Symphony will only expand these ranges when you add information through a FORM window.

The Criterion Range

The Criterion range is the second most important range (after the Database range). It enables Symphony to select specific records from the data base. When data base commands such as Find, Extract, Unique, or Criteria Use are used, when data base reports are generated, or when data base functions are used, Symphony looks to the Criterion range to find out which records it should choose.

Like the Database range, the Criterion range must have a specific structure. This structure and the "rules" for the placement of criteria within this range are a bit more complex than those required for the Database range. We'll cover the Criterion range in the next chapter.

The Entry Range

You should immediately recognize the contents of the range A7 . . A11, which is called the Entry range. These cells contain the Entry form you see in the FORM window. As mentioned at the beginning of this section, the FORM window provides a view of only this very specific part of the worksheet. When looking through a FORM window, you are actually seeing the worksheet cells of the Entry range. As we will discuss later, you can change the appearance of the Entry form by editing the contents of these Entry range cells, from either a DOC or a SHEET window.

The Definition Range

Symphony has to have a way to "link" the Entry range to the Database range so that it can route the information typed into the FORM window to the appropriate cells in the data base. The Definition range is used to accomplish this task. In a sense, this range serves as the "traffic cop" for all information passing through the Entry form.

The Definition range must be eight columns wide and must contain the headers Name, Value, Type, Default, Formula, Validity, Input, and Prompt. (If you use the Generate command to define the data base, Symphony automatically creates these headers.)

The Definition range in the example is A13 . . H18. Because Symphony compressed several of the columns in this range when the data base was generated, not all of the Definition range can be seen in Figure 19.7. Figure 19.8 shows the full Definition range.

```
    ---A-------B--------C------D-------E---------F-------G------H----------
 13 Name      Value     Type   Default Formula   Validity Input Prompt     |
 14 Name                L:20                                    Enter NAME  |
 15 Street              L:25                                    Enter ADDRESS |
 16 City                L:20                                    Enter CITY  |
 17 State               L:2                                     Enter STATE |
 18 Zip                 L:5                                     Enter ZIP   |
    =================================================================MAIN=
```

Figure 19.8

Each field entry you "lock in" to the Entry form by pressing [Enter] is stored in the Definition range until you press [Ins]. Pressing [Ins] "dumps" the record into the data base itself. However, the function of the Definition range is not limited to simply accepting the entries you make and storing them into the data base. The Definition range also has the ability to test the validity of an entry and to reject the entry if it does not meet certain predefined conditions, to supply a predefined default value for a field, and to calculate the value of a field.

All information entered through a form eventually winds up in the Value column of a Definition range before it is dumped into the data base. When you press [Enter] after making an entry to a field in a form, Symphony first places the entry in the cell in the Input column that corresponds to that field. In most cases, Symphony immediately transfers the entry to the Value column and from there enters it into the data base.

However, if the current field includes a validity check, Symphony will test the information in the Value column before it accepts the entry. If the entry does not meet the validity test, Symphony rejects it, leaving the Value column blank.

If the current field is a computed field, the entry made to the Value column is the result of a calculation performed by Symphony. Alternatively, if you have defined a default value for the field, Symphony automatically enters the default value in the Value column.

The Definition range only serves a purpose when data is entered into the data base from a FORM window; this range has no control over data added directly to the data base from a SHEET window. If you prefer to construct and use a data base directly in the worksheet, neither the Definition range nor the Entry range need to be created.

Let's go through the columns of the Definition Range one-by-one. These columns will not be discussed in left-to-right order, but rather in the order in which Symphony uses these columns to process the information it routes to the Database range.

The Name Column

The first column in the Definition Range is headed Name. This column must contain the field names specified in the Entry range (shown in cells A7 . . A11 of our example worksheet). Symphony uses these names, common to the Entry, Database, and Definition ranges, as "keys" to connect information typed into the Entry range to the proper field in the data base.

The field names and the order of these names must match exactly the names and order of the Entry range. If they don't, Symphony will display the error message "Entry range/Definition range mismatch", and you won't be able to use the FORM window to enter records into the data base.

Additionally, all the entries in the Name column in the Definition range must be field names in the Database range. In the example, this means that the Database range must contain at least the Name, Street, City, State, and Zip fields, since these fields appear in the Definition range. The Database range may contain more field names than are included in the Definition range, but the opposite cannot be true. If a field name included in the Definition range is not a heading in the Database range, or if a blank row is included in the Definition range, Symphony will display the "Definition range/Database range mismatch" error message and will not allow records to be entered through the Entry form.

The Type Column

The third column in the Definition range is headed Type. Each entry in the Name column must have a corresponding entry in the Type column. The type of each field is determined by the type code you included when defining the form or by the default field type you selected in the process of generating the form.

The contents of each cell in this column include a letter, a colon, and a number. As explained previously, the letter, either L (label), N (number), D (date), T (time), or C (computed), specifies how Symphony will interpret each entry made through the FORM window. If L is specified for a certain field, any character typed into that blank in the entry form will be routed to the Database range as a label. For instance, if you type 1234 into the blank for City, Symphony enters 1234 preceded by ', ", or ^, indicating that this string is a label rather than a number.

An N in the Type column tells Symphony to treat all entries to this field as numbers which can then be manipulated with mathematical functions. Don't use N just because the entry might contain some numerical characters; many such entries should be labels. For instance, if you type the phone number 234-5678 into a number field, it would be entered into the data base as − 5444 because Symphony would subtract 5678 from 234.

Similarly, Symphony would not allow you to enter 111 First Street into a number field. When faced with a choice between specifying a number or a label field, a good rule of thumb is this: Unless the contents of the field are to be used for mathematical calculations, specify the type as label.

Specifying a D in the Type column tells Symphony to transform all entries in the field into a serial date format. All entries to this type of field must be in the form MM/DD/YY (full international date format). Similarly, the type T tells Symphony to transform the entry into a serial time format. Entries to T fields must be in the HH:MM:SS form. In both cases, these entries are stored as numbers in the data base.

The C type specifies that the contents of the field will be computed by Symphony based on the formula residing in the Formula column of the Definition range. Symphony will not allow you to make an entry into the "blank" in a form that corresponds to a computed field in the Definition range. Instead, Symphony displays the current calculated value for the field in the form. (You'll see how Symphony makes these calculations in a few pages.)

The number in the Type column following the letter and the colon (which is used only as a separator) specifies the field length. This is the maximum number of characters that can be entered into the field. In the example above, no more than 20 characters and spaces can be entered from the Entry form into the City field in the data base. When you type character 21, Symphony beeps, indicating that no more characters may be entered in that field of the record.

When choosing the length of a field, specify a number large enough to accommodate the longest entry you anticipate will be made to that field. Remember that the width of the column containing that field will be determined by the number you choose.

The Prompt Column

The eighth column in the Definition range contains the prompts Symphony displays in the upper-left corner of the screen when the user is entering data through a FORM window. When Symphony generates a form, it automatically creates a prompt for each field in the data base. These default prompts consist of the word "Enter" followed by the field name. For example, the prompt for the Name field in cell H14 is "Enter NAME".

You can modify the default prompts by simply editing the string supplied by Symphony or by entering a new string into the worksheet cell in the Prompt column corresponding to the desired field name. For example, to change the prompt for the Name field, move the cell pointer to cell H14 and enter the label

      Enter the name of this individual, please:

Like all labels, the prompt can be up to 240 characters long. However, prompts longer than about 50 characters are impractical.

The Input Column

The Input column is the seventh column of the Definition range. This column is used to store the information for each field of the record currently being entered through a FORM window. Once the field is entered it is "processed" and sent to the Value column.

It is best to think of this column as a "holding area" for information on its way to the Value column.

The Formula Column

Symphony uses the formulas entered into the cells of this column to convert the contents of the Input column into the values stored in the Value column. The values are then transferred to the data base itself. You can use this column to work on two types of fields: computed fields (C) and number fields (N).

If the field type is C (computed), you *must* specify a formula for that field. You must use a SHEET window to enter the formulas that correspond to computed fields into the appropriate cells in the Definition range. The formulas may refer to the contents of any cell in the Input or Value columns of the Definition range or to any other cell in the worksheet. If you define a field as computed but do not supply a formula for that field, Symphony will allow you to use the form containing the computed field, but it will not make any entries into the computed field in the data base.

The Definition range in Figure 19.9 shows an example of the Formula column at work. In this example, the formula corresponding to the field name TOTALHRS refers to the entries in the Value column for WEEK1HRS and WEEK2HRS.

```
     ---A-------B---------C------D-------E---------F-------G------H---------
 13 Name       Value     Type  Default Formula  Validity  Input Prompt      |
 14 NAME                 L:15                                  Enter NAME    |
 15 WEEK1HRS             N:2                                   Enter HOURS   |
 16 WEEK2HRS             N:2                                   Enter HOURS   |
 17 TOTALHRS             C:3           +B15+B16                              |
 18 PAY$                 C:6           +B17*J1                               |
     =============================================================MAIN=
```

Figure 19.9

If you enter 40 into the WEEK1HRS blank and 36 into the WEEK2HRS blank of the Entry form linked to this Definition range, these two numbers will appear in the Input column in cells G15 and G16. Since these fields are not C type fields, these numbers also would appear in the Value column in cells B15 and B16.

The formula in cell E17 tells Symphony that the value for the C type field TOTALHRS should be computed by adding the numbers entered in the WEEK1HRS field and the WEEK2HRS field. Symphony enters the result, 76, in cell B17. This is an example of an internally computed entry.

Cell E18 is an example of a computed field whose value depends on a cell outside of the Definition range. Let's assume that cell J1 contains the current hourly pay rate for your employees. After calculating cell B17, Symphony multiplies the value from cell J1 by the value in cell B17 and enters the product in cell B18.

You can use either a relative (+B17) or an absolute (+$B$17) reference when referring to cells outside of the Definition range. However, try to avoid making a reference to a cell that contains a formula, because Symphony does not automatically recalculate the worksheet as it updates the data base. This can lead to calculation based on "out-of-date" values.

You can also use formulas to manipulate the entries you make to number type fields. Consider this slightly modified version of the Definition range in Figure 19.10.

```
    ---A-------B--------C------D-------E---------F-------G------H---------
 13 Name      Value     Type   Default Formula   Validity  Input Prompt       |
 14 NAME                L:15                                      Enter NAME   |
 15 WEEK1HRS             N:2            +G15/10                   Enter HOURS  |
 16 WEEK2HRS             N:2            +G16/10                   Enter HOURS  |
 17 TOTALHRS            C:3            +B15+B16                                |
 18 PAY$               C:6            +B17*J1                                  |
    ===============================================================MAIN=
```

Figure 19.10

Cells E15 and E16 in this figure show how a formula can transform a numerical entry into another number. In this case the user makes an entry into a number field through the Entry form. However, before Symphony sends this entry to the Value column and then on to the Database range, it manipulates the number using the formulas in column E.

In the example, Symphony divides entries made to the fields WEEK1HRS and WEEK2HRS by 10 before entering the numbers in the Value column. This kind of formula might be useful to a company that keeps track of employee hours in terms of tenths of an hour. Each entry into the WEEK1HRS and WEEK2HRS fields needs to be in the form XX.X. To make the data entry process easier, you can instruct Symphony to divide all entries to these fields by 10. This way the person entering the figures can enter the figure 405 into the WEEK1HRS field of a record, and Symphony automatically transforms that entry in the number 40.5.

The Validity Column

The Validity column contains any formulas you want to use to verify that the contents of the Value column match a predefined criterion. As with the Formula column, you must enter the formulas in the Validity column manually through a SHEET window.

As you have seen, if the Formula column is blank, the entry in the Value column will equal the Input value or the Default value. In this case, the validity test will simply check the value you entered for that field. If the Formula column contains a formula, the validity check will test the result of that formula.

For instance, suppose you insert the formulas + B15 < = 40 and + B16 < = 40 into cells F15 and F16, respectively, so that the Definition range looks like Figure 19.11.

The entries in the Validity column instruct Symphony to check the entry in the Value column against the criteria that these entries must be less than or equal to 40. Because fields WEEK1HRS and WEEK2HRS are simple numeric fields, the validity checks test the entries you make to these fields. If the entries are less than or equal to 40, they pass the validity check and are accepted into the Value column. If the numbers are not less than or equal to 40, they will be rejected and the screen will display the message "Invalid field entry".

```
    ---A-------B--------C------D-------E--------F------G-----H--------
 13 Name       Value    Type  Default Formula  Validity Input Prompt      |
 14 NAME                L:15                                   Enter NAME  |
 15 WEEK1HRS             N:2                   +B15<=40        Enter HOURS |
 16 WEEK2HRS             N:2                   +B16<=40        Enter HOURS |
 17 TOTALHRS             C:3           +B15+B16                            |
 18 PAY$                 C:6           +B17*J1                             |
    =====================================================================MAIN=
```

Figure 19.11

Your validity tests can be very complex. For example, the test

$$@LEFT(B14,1) > = "A"\#AND\#@LEFT(B14,1) < = "K"$$

would check the left-most character of the input in cell B14. If that character was between A and K, the entry would pass the validation test. The name Jones would be accepted, but Smith would not.

The formulas in the validity check may contain functions and may refer to cells outside the Definition range. As with the Formula column, avoid referring to other cells that contain formulas when you're making an entry in the Validity column.

The Default Column

If you don't enter anything for a field through the Entry form, Symphony inserts the value in the Default column into the Database range. In fact, Symphony automatically displays this default value in each blank Entry form, where it remains until the user changes it. For example, look at cells D16, D17, and D18 in the Definition range in Figure 19.12. The corresponding blank Entry form looks like the one in Figure 19.13.

Symphony enters these default values into the Value column and then into the data base itself unless the user types another city, state, or zip code into the form.

Default values come in handy when certain fields in a data base generally have the same value. In the example above, if the mailing list was for customers of a retailer located in Anytown, USA, one would assume that the majority of its customers are located in the same town. Specifying the default value "Anytown" for the City field causes Symphony to enter that label automatically in the City field of any record for which a specific city name is not provided.

The Value Column

As you have seen, the Value column is the final "storage bin" for input that the Formula, Validity, and Default columns have processed. When you press [Ins] after entering a record through a form, Symphony transfers the entries stored in the Value column to the data base.

The information you see when you enter a record using a form is actually stored in the Value range. That is, the contents of the Value column is what you see filling the blanks in the Entry range.

As you can see, the Definition range is the "control center" for the entry of information into a data base through the FORM window. This range helps you customize the data base to meet your particular needs.

```
     ---A-------B--------C------D-------E---------F-------G------H----------
  13 Name      Value     Type   Default Formula Validity Input Prompt       |
  14 NAME                L:15                              Enter NAME        |
  15 STREET              L:20                              Enter STREET      |
  16 CITY                L:20   Anytown                    Enter CITY        |
  17 STATE               L:3    USA                        Enter STATE       |
  18 ZIP                 L:5    12345                      Enter ZIP         |
     ===============================================================MAIN=
```

Figure 19.12

```
     ----------------------------------------------------------
  |  NAME  _____                          |
  |  STREET _____                         |
  |  CITY Anytown_____                           |
  |  STATE USA_____                                |
  |   ZIP 12345                                              |
     =MAIN==================================MAIN=
```

Figure 19.13

The Report Ranges

The Main Report range and the Above Report range are the final ranges created by Symphony as a result of the Generate command. Symphony uses the Main Report range to supply the format for reports such as form letters, which incorporate the contents of selected records in the data base. Any time the contents of a data base need to be printed in a special format, or any time only the records meeting certain criteria are to be printed, the Main Report range must be identified.

The Main Report range occupies the row of cells from A21 . . E21 in Figure 19.7. Row 21 appears to contain a copy of the first record in the data base. However, Figure 19.14 shows the formulas that actually occupy these cells.

In the process of generating the form, Symphony assigns a range name to the first data cell of each field in the Database range. These names are based on the field names. For

```
     -------A----------------------B-------------------C--------D---E--
  19                                                                   |
  20  Name              Street              City              StZip    |
  21 +NAME              +STREET             +CITY             +STATE+ZIP|
  22                                                                    |
     ===============================================================MAIN=
```

Figure 19.14

example, in Figure 19.7, cell A29 is the range named NAME, cell B29 is the range named STREET, cell C29 is the range named CITY, and so forth.

Symphony defines the cells immediately above the Main Report range as the Above Report range. In this case the Above Report range is A20 . . E20. The labels in these cells will be printed once as a "header" whenever you instruct Symphony to print from a data base. The subject of printing data base reports will be discussed in detail in Chapter 22.

THE SETTINGS SHEET

Now that we've reviewed all the ranges that the Generate command creates, let's take a peek at the settings sheet that ties all these ranges together. To view the data base settings sheet MAIN, issue the {**Menu**} **S**ettings command from within the FORM window MAIN. The settings sheet shown in Figure 19.15 will appear on the screen.

```
                                                        MENU
    Basic Form Underscores Sort-Keys Report One-Record Name Cancel Quit
    ----------------------------------------------------------------
    |  Basic Ranges                      Report Ranges             |
    |     Database:      MAIN DB             Main:      MAIN MA     |
    |     Criterion:     MAIN CR             Above:     MAIN AB     |
    |     Output:                            Below:                 |
    |  Form Ranges                           Type:      Single      |
    |     Entry:         MAIN EN            Entry list:             |
    |     Definition:    MAIN DF            Input cell:             |
    |  Underscores:      Yes              One-Record: No            |
    |  Sort-Keys                                                    |
    |     1st-Key:                2nd-Key:              3rd-Key:    |
    |       Order:                  Order:               Order:     |
    |                                                               |
    ======================================Database Settings: MAIN=
```

Figure 19.15

Notice that all of the ranges discussed in the previous sections are defined in this settings sheet. Notice also that Symphony uses range names instead of simple cell references to define each of these ranges.

All of these settings are grouped by function. For instance, the settings that relate to all data base functions are grouped under the heading Basic Ranges. These include the Database range, the Criterion range, and the Output range. The two settings that are necessary only when working in a FORM window, the Entry range and Definition range, are grouped under the Form Ranges heading. The settings that affect the generation of data base reports are grouped under the Report Ranges heading.

Notice that the FORM Settings menu appears in the control panel above the settings sheet in Figure 19.15. These commands allow you to adjust the settings in the settings sheet. We'll cover them in detail in the following two chapters.

CHAPTER TWENTY
USING FORM WINDOWS

Now that we know how to define a data base, use an Entry form to enter records into that data base, and then edit those records, let's look at some of the ways we can work with the contents of a data base through a FORM window. Specifically, we will explore how to "browse" through the records in a data base, how to use the Criteria command to fill the cells of the Criterion range or search for records to display in the Entry form, how to delete and erase records from within the FORM window, how to sort records using the Record-Sort command, and how to modify, save, and activate the settings in the FORM settings sheet. This chapter will use the same example data base you saw in the last chapter.

BROWSING THROUGH RECORDS

Once you have created a data base and filled it with records, you may wish to "browse" through those records using a FORM window. This can be done in several ways. First, you can use the [Pg Dn] and [Pg Up] keys to scroll through the records in order. Each record is displayed through the Entry form in the FORM window. This method of reviewing records is simple and useful for finding particular records in small data bases. However, if your data base contains thousands of records, moving to a particular record in this way can be very time consuming.

The {Goto} key provides an easier way to move back and forth between distant records in a data base. To use this key, though, you must remember the record number of the record you want to see. Since remembering the numbers of all the records in a large data base is an almost Herculean task, this method of recall has only limited applications. Nonetheless, if you can remember the approximate location of a certain record, you can use this key to move quickly to an entry near the record you want, and you can use the [Pg Up] and [Pg Dn] keys to locate the exact record.

Using the {Goto} key from a FORM window is easy. First, press {**Goto**}. Symphony displays the following prompt:

Go to which record?

The number Symphony provides is the number of the record currently on the screen. To jump to a different record, simply type in the number of the record you want to go to and press [**Enter**]. Symphony displays that record in the FORM window.

SELECTING SPECIFIC RECORDS WITH CRITERIA USE

The FORM {Menu} Criteria Use command allows you to select and display specific records through a FORM window. The ability to select records that meet specified criteria is one of the most powerful capabilities of data base software.

Before Symphony can select a record, however, you must define the criteria that will be used to select that record or records.

Specifying Criteria

In the previous chapter, you were introduced briefly to the Criterion range. The Criterion range in the example developed in the previous chapter is A23 . . E24, as shown in Figure 20.1. This range was defined automatically by the Generate command. Notice that the Criterion range includes two rows. The first row includes the names of all of the fields in the data base. The second row is used to enter the criteria that will be used by the Criteria Use command to select particular records form the data base.

Thanks to the FORM {Menu} Criteria command, you can make entries into the cells of the Criterion range through the FORM window. You can also use the Criteria command to tell Symphony to display only the records in the FORM window that meet the criteria you have specified. First we'll cover entering criteria through an Entry form.

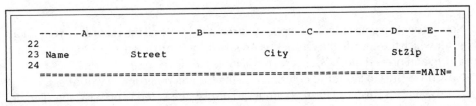

Figure 20.1

To explain this method, let's go back to our address-book data base. As a reminder, our data base contains the four records shown in Figure 20.2.

To begin entering the criteria, press {Menu} to go to the FORM command menu. The following menu appears on the screen:

Attach   Criteria   Initialize   Record-Sort   Generate   Settings

```
     -------A-------------------------B-------------------C---------D---E----
27                                                                         |
28 Name               Street                  City           StZip         |
29 Mary Smith         111 First Street        Anytown        KY40223       |
30 John Doe           222 Second Street       Mayberry       NC12345       |
31 John Q. Public     333 Third Street        Yourtown       CA11111       |
32 Jane Smythe        123 Main Street         Anytown        MO01010       |
   ========================================================================MAIN=
```

Figure 20.2

When you select the Criteria option from this menu, Symphony displays the following submenu:

   Use   Ignore   Edit

Since we are adding criteria to the Criterion range, select Edit. Symphony then displays the special form shown in Figure 20.3. The messages at the upper-left and upper-right corners of the screen confirm that you are entering information into the Criterion range instead of into the data base itself.

```
      Editing Criterion Record 1 of 1                    CRIT
      Enter Name
     ------------------------------------------------------------
   | Name _____                              |
   | Street _____                            |
   | City _____                              |
   | State ___                                                  |
   | Zip ____                                                   |
   |                                                            |
   =MAIN===========================================MAIN=
```

Figure 20.3

Now let's enter some criteria. Suppose you want to locate all the records in your data base for which the entry in the City field is Anytown. Type **Anytown** into the City blank in this form and press **[Enter]**. Your screen will look like Figure 20.4.

Now press **[Ins]** to insert this criterion into the Criteria range in the worksheet.

After you press **[Ins]**, the form continues to display the criteria you have specified. If you want to stop defining criteria, press **[Pg Up]**. Pressing [Pg Up] returns you to the normal FORM insert mode. Although you can't see it through the FORM window, the Criterion range now looks like Figure 20.5.

Using Criteria to Select Records

The Use command on the Criteria submenu instructs Symphony to display through the Entry form only those records that match the criteria in the Criterion range. This is a

```
  Editing Criteria Record 1 of 1                    CRIT
  Enter Street
 ------------------------------------------------------
 | Name _____                              |
 | Street _____                          |
 | City Anytown_____                            |
 | State __                                           |
 | Zip _____                                          |
 |                                                    |
  =MAIN=================================================MAIN=
```

Figure 20.4

```
     -------A-----------------------B--------------------C---------D---E--
  23 Name              Street              City             StZip  |
  24                                       Anytown                 |
  25                                                               |
     ===============================================================MAIN=
```

Figure 20.5

convenient way to locate a single record or a group of records from within a large data base. To clarify this concept, let's continue with the example above.

Press {**Menu**} to again reveal the FORM menu and select Criteria from this menu. The screen will now look like Figure 20.6.

```
  Select records using Criteria range          CRIT
  Use        Ignore       Edit
 ------------------------------------------------------
 | Name _____                              |
 | Street _____                          |
 | City _____                               |
 | State __                                           |
 | Zip _____                                          |
 |                                                    |
  =MAIN=================================================MAIN=
```

Figure 20.6

Notice that whatever is currently on the screen is replaced by a blank Entry form when you issue the command. This time, choose Use from the Criteria submenu. Symphony immediately displays the first record in the data base that matches the criteria you have defined. Continuing with the Criterion range shown in Figure 20.5, your screen will look like Figure 20.7.

```
  Editing Record 1 of 4 (Match 1 of 2)          CRIT
  Enter Name
 ---------------------------------------------------
| Name Mary Smith_____                            |
| Street 111 First Street_____                    |
| City Anytown_____                         |
| State KY                                          |
| Zip 40223                                         |
|                                                   |
  =MAIN=========================================MAIN=
```

Figure 20.7

The upper line of the control panel is unlike anything we've seen before. "Editing Record 1 of 4" tells you that you are in the Edit mode, reminding you to beware of the functions of the cursor-movement keys. "(Match 1 of 2)" tells you that two records in the data base match the criteria in the Criterion range, and that you are looking at the first of those records in the form. At this point, you can revise the contents of this record as you normally would in the Edit mode.

Pressing [Pg Dn] dumps this record back into the Database range and moves you to the next record that matches the criteria, as shown in Figure 20.8.

```
  Editing Record 4 of 4 (Match 2 of 2)          CRIT
  Enter Name
 ---------------------------------------------------
| Name Jane Smythe_____                           |
| Street 123 Main Street_____                     |
| City Anytown_____                         |
| State MO                                          |
| Zip 01010                                         |
|                                                   |
  =MAIN=========================================MAIN=
```

Figure 20.8

Notice that the legend at the top of this figure indicates that you are now editing Record 4 of 4 (the last record in the data base) and that this record is the second match of two matches. Again, you are free to edit this record in any way you wish. When you have finished viewing or editing the record, you can press [Pg Up] to return it to the data base and move back to the previous matching record. Pressing [Pg Dn] at this point would have no effect, since there are no more records that match the selection criteria.

As you can see, when you "activate" the criteria with the Use command, Symphony can bring into the Entry form only those records that match the criteria. In a sense, you are "locking out" of the FORM window all but a select group of the records in the data base.

This is an example of a simple, exact-match criteria. When you enter a plain word or number into a cell in the Criterion range and then issue the Criteria Use command (or one of Symphony's other data base commands), Symphony selects only the records in the data base for which the entry in the specified field matches exactly the word or number you've entered in the Criterion range.

The only exception to the "exact-match" rule is that Symphony forgives capitalization mismatches between the criteria you specify and the entries in the data base. For example, the criterion Anytown would match records from which the City field was Anytown, ANYTOWN, ANYtown and anytown. However, the criterion you specify must in every other way exactly match the entries in the data base field. Otherwise, Symphony will not select the desired records when you issue the Criteria Use command.

A Second Example

Suppose that in the example you want to make the criteria more restrictive. If, for instance, you want to locate all the records for which the City field is Anytown and the State field is KY, you need to modify the criteria record you just entered.

To make this change, you need to reissue the Criteria Edit command. When you issue the **Criteria Edit** command, Symphony displays the previously defined criteria in the form, so you see Anytown in the City field. To change the criteria, all you have to do is move to the State field and enter the proper string. In the example, you would enter the string KY in the State field and press **[Enter]**.

Once you've made the change, press **[Ins]** again to insert these criteria into the Criterion range. You should now see Anytown and KY in the City and State fields. The corresponding Criterion range now looks like Figure 20.9.

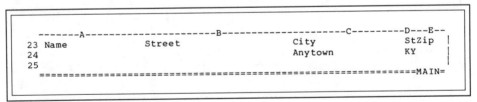

Figure 20.9

Again, once you've defined all the criteria you want, you need only press **[Pg Up]** to return to the normal FORM insert mode.

If you now issued the Criteria Use command, Symphony would look for only those records for which the City field was Anytown and the State field was KY. Since there is only one record in the database for which the city is Anytown and the state is KY, only one record will be found. Figure 20.10 shows this record as it would appear in the form.

This is an example of an AND criterion. When you make an entry in more than one cell in a given row of the Criterion range, Symphony combines those entries with a logical AND. In the example, the Criterion range tells Symphony to select only those

```
 _____
|  _____  |
| |  Editing Record 1 of 4 (Match 1 of 1)        CRIT  | |
| |  Enter Name                                        | |
| | ------------------------------------------------   | |
| | | Name Mary Smith_____                       |  | |
| | | Street 111 First Street_____              |  | |
| | | City Anytown_____                        |  | |
| | | State KY                                       |  | |
| | | Zip 40223                                      |  | |
| | |                                                |  | |
| |  =MAIN=====================================MAIN=   | |
| |_____| |
|_____|
```

Figure 20.10

records for which the City field is Anytown *and* the State field is KY. Only records that meet *both* criteria are selected.

In the example, we specified only two criteria, but we could have made entries into the Name, Street, and Zip fields as well. If we had done so, Symphony would have selected only those records for which the Name field matched the specified criteria *and* and Street field matched the specified criteria *and* so on. Each entry you add to the row makes the Criterion range more restrictive.

A Third Example

Suppose you want to create another set of criteria to select records from your data base for viewing through a FORM window. In this example, we'll enter two records into the Criterion range. Let's begin with the simple criteria defined in the previous example. If you issue the {Menu} Criteria Edit command from within the FORM window MAIN, the form will look like the one in Figure 20.11.

```
 _____
|  _____  |
| |  Editing Criterion Record 1 of 1             CRIT  | |
| |  Enter Street                                      | |
| | ------------------------------------------------   | |
| | | Name   _____                        |  | |
| | | Street _____             |  | |
| | | City Anytown_____                    |  | |
| | | State KY_____                        |  | |
| | | Zip  _____                                    |  | |
| | |                                                |  | |
| |  =MAIN=====================================MAIN=   | |
| |_____| |
|_____|
```

Figure 20.11

To define a second line in the Criterion range, press **[Pg Dn]**. Symphony advances you to Criteria Record 2, and your screen looks like the one in Figure 20.12.

Note that the message at the upper-left corner of the screen now says Inserting rather than Editing. This is because Symphony had already specified the Criterion range to

```
    Inserting Criterion Record 2                    CRIT
    Enter Name
   ------------------------------------------------------------
  |  Name _____                            |
  |  Street _____                      |
  |  City _____                         |
  |  State __                                             |
  |  Zip _____                                            |
  |                                                       |
   =MAIN===================================MAIN=
```

Figure 20.12

include the first row, row 24, which was blank. When we entered the first criterion, we were effectively editing a blank row. The second row is "uncharted territory," because it has not yet been included in the Criterion range, so here we are inserting rather than editing.

Suppose you wish to locate all people who live in Anytown, KY, as well as anyone living in California. To enter this criterion, simply advance to the State field, type **CA**, and press **[Enter].** Your screen will look like Figure 20.13.

```
    Inserting Criterion Record 2                    CRIT
    Enter State
   ------------------------------------------------------------
  |  Name _____                            |
  |  Street _____                      |
  |  City _____                         |
  |  State CA                                             |
  |  Zip _____                                            |
  |                                                       |
   =MAIN===================================MAIN=
```

Figure 20.13

After you press [Ins], the new record will be entered in the Criterion range, which will now look like Figure 20.14.

```
   --------A----------------------B--------------------C--------D---E--
   23 Name              Street            City              StZip  |
   24                                     Anytown           KY     |
   25                                                       CA     |
   =========================================================MAIN=
```

Figure 20.14

Now let's use these criteria. Press **{Switch}** to toggle MAIN back into a FORM window and issue the **{Menu}** Criteria Use command. When the command is completed, the screen will look almost identical to the one in Figure 20.7. To view the second matching record, press **[Pg Dn]**. The screen will now look like Figure 20.15.

```
 Editing Record 2 of 4 (Match 2 of 2)          CRIT
 Enter Name
 -----------------------------------------------------
| Name John Q. Public_____                            |
| Street 333 Third Street_____                    |
| City Yourtown_____                              |
| State CA_____                                   |
| Zip 11111                                            |
|                                                      |
 =MAIN=========================================MAIN=
```

Figure 20.15

Again, you can edit or delete this record if you wish. If you press **[Pg Dn]** at this point, Symphony beeps and continues to display this record, because no record farther down in the data base matches the criteria. Pressing **[Pg Up]** moves you to Record 1, which you just reviewed. If you press **[Pg Up]** a second time Symphony only beeps, since no record matching the criteria exists above this record.

This is an example of an OR criterion. When you expand the Criterion range to include more than one row, Symphony joins the criterion specified in each row with a logical OR. In the example, the Criterion range tells Symphony to select only those records for which the City field is Anytown and the State Field is KY, *or* for which the State field is CA.

Whenever you specify an OR criterion, Symphony selects records that match the criterion in either row. In the example, Record 1 was selected because it matches the entries in the first row of the Criterion range. Record 3 was selected because it matches the entries in the second row of the Criterion range.

More on Criterion Ranges

In the previous three examples, you have seen examples of Symphony's three main types of simple criteria: exact-match criteria, AND criteria (two or more entries in one row of the Criterion range) and OR criteria (two or more rows of entries in the Criterion range), However, there are a couple of topics left to cover before we go to the next section.

Blank Criterion Ranges

If you issue the Criteria Use command without making any entries in the Criterion range, Symphony shows you all of the records in the data base, since a blank in a

Criterion range is equivalent to a universal match. In other words, a blank cell under the Name field in the Criterion range matches the Name entry for all records in the data base, a blank cell under the City field matches the City entry for all records in the data base, and so on. As a general rule, it is not a good idea to leave blank rows in your Criterion ranges.

Wild Cards

Another feature of Symphony Criterion ranges worth mentioning at this point is the use of special characters. The three characters *, ?,and ˜ add a great deal of flexibility to Symphony criteria. Let's look at each of these briefly.

The ? is a "wild-card" character that can be used in place of any character in a label Criterion range entry. When you use a ?, Symphony matches any character in that position. For instance, if your Criterion range looked like Figure 20.16, Symphony would select any record whose Name field is Marten, Morton, etc.

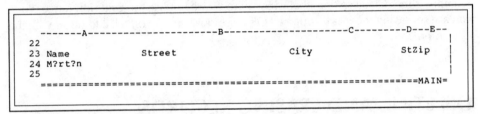

```
    -------A--------------------B------------------C--------D---E--
22                                                                |
23 Name             Street                City             StZip  |
24 M?rt?n                                                         |
25                                                                |
   ===============================================================MAIN=
```

Figure 20.16

Each question mark can match only a single character. This special wild-card character can be used only in a label entry. If you have specified the Zip field as a label field, as we did in the example, '6060? can be used to match any zip code from 60600 to 60609. However, you could not use this wild-card character if you had specified Zip as a number field, because you would be introducing a nonnumeric character into a number cell.

The second "wild-card" character is *. The asterisk can be used as a substitute for any number of characters at the end of a Criteria entry. For example, S* would match Smith, Smyth, Smythe, Stanley, Sidney, or any other collection of characters that begins with S (either upper- or lowercase). Symphony would match Sm* with Smith and Smythe, but not with Sidney.

You can place an * at the beginning or the middle of a word, but the characters following the * will be ignored. For instance, *y would match not only Smith and Smythe, but also Steve, Barbara, Michelle, and any other word or collection of characters imaginable. When used alone or followed by any letters, * is the equivalent of a blank criterion, or a universal match.

The final wild-card character is the ˜ . Placing this character in front of any character string in the Criterion range tells Symphony to choose anything *but* that character string. For instance, if you type ˜Anytown in the City field, you instruct Symphony to choose any record that does *not* have the entry Anytown in the City field. If you are preparing a mailing list and don't want to send anything to people in Chicago, you might use this criterion. As with ? and *, the ~ character can be used only in label fields.

You can use formulas and functions within the Criterion range to add more power and selectivity to Symphony's data base functions. These complex criteria will be discussed in Chapter 21. For now, let's take a look at the other ranges Symphony has created.

The Ignore Command

When you have finished reviewing the selected records allowed by the Criteria Use command, you must issue the Criteria Ignore command to return to the regular FORM insert mode. The Ignore command simply undoes what the Use command has done. In other words, Ignore instructs Symphony not to use the contents of the Criterion range when selecting records to display through the Entry form. Since Symphony ignores the criteria, every record can be displayed through the form.

Ignore is the default setting; that is, Symphony will not use the Criterion range when you are reviewing records through a FORM window unless you tell it to do so with the Use command.

DELETING AND ERASING RECORDS

There are two ways to erase a record through a FORM window. To delete the record entirely, you can press the **[Del]** key while reviewing the record in the FORM insert mode. If you want to erase the contents of all the fields in a record but retain the record itself, you can use the Initialize command on the FORM command menu. It's important to understand that these two processes are not identical.

Deleting a record removes that record from the data base entirely. If, for example, your data base consists of the four records shown in Figure 20.17 and you wish to remove the "John Doe" record, you must first bring that record into the FORM window. Either press the {Goto} key and specify the record number, if you remember it, or scroll through the records, with or without the aid of criteria, by using the [Pg Up] or [Pg Dn] keys. When the appropriate record appears in the Entry form, press **[Del]**.

```
    -------A-------------------------B-------------------------C---------D---E--
27                                                                              |
28 Name                 Street                  City                StZip       |
29 Mary  Smith          111 First Street        Anytown             KY40223     |
30 John  Doe            222 Second Street        Mayberry            NC12345     |
31 John  Q. Public      333 Third Street        Yourtown            CA11111     |
32 Jane  Smythe         123 Main Street         Anytown             MO01010     |
    ===========================================================================MAIN=
```

Figure 20.17

Symphony responds with the following question:

Are you sure you want to delete this record?
No   Yes

Selecting No simply returns you to the current record. Selecting Yes removes that record from the data base and returns you to the previous record. After the deletion, the data base looks like Figure 20.18. The "John Doe" record has been removed entirely from the data base, and the "John Q. Public" record has moved up to take its place.

```
       -------A---------------------B---------------------C---------D---E---
   27                                                                        |
   28  Name            Street                City           StZip            |
   29  Mary  Smith     111 First Street      Anytown        KY40223          |
   30  John Q. Public  333 Third Street      Yourtown       CA11111          |
   31  Jane Smythe     123 Main Street       Anytown        MO01010          |
       ===============================================================MAIN=
```

Figure 20.18

Initializing a record, by contrast, does not remove the record from the data base; it merely returns the contents of all the fields within that record to their default values. These are the values in the Default column in the Definition range. Since the Default column is usually blank, initializing a record generally erases all the fields in the record.

Initializing a record is also fairly simple. With the appropriate record in the FORM window, issue the {Menu} Initialize command. The spaces in the Entry form immediately return to their default values (usually blank), and Symphony places you in the Edit mode for that record. If you wish to retrieve the record you erased, you can press [Esc], undoing the action of the Initialize command. To finalize the process, press **[Pg Dn]** to dump the default fields into the data base. The result of the Initialize command is shown in Figure 20.19.

```
       -------A---------------------B---------------------C---------D--E---
   27                                                                       |
   28  Name            Street                City           StZip           |
   29  Mary  Smith     111 First Street      Anytown        KY40223         |
   30                                                                       |
   31  John Q. Public  333 Third Street      Yourtown       CA11111         |
   32  Jane Smythe     123 Main Street       Anytown        MO01010         |
       =============================================================MAIN=
```

Figure 20.19

The second record is still in the data base, but its fields have been erased. If you wish you can use the FORM insert mode to fill the fields of this record with new information.

The difference between deleting and initializing is important for a variety of reasons. First, keeping blank records in the data base uses up precious memory. If the record is deleted instead, the remaining records "fill in," and the total number of records is reduced. Second, when drawing information from the data base, especially when printing data base reports, these blanks will be treated as records, resulting, for instance, in the printing of blank address labels. My advice is this: use the Initialize command when you're editing a record you're going to replace and the [Del] key when you do not intend to replace the record.

SORTING RECORDS

The ability to rearrange the order of the records within a data base is a standard feature of most data base management software. Symphony enables you to sort the records within a data base from either a SHEET or a FORM window. The sort commands involved in both windows are essentially identical, so you may want to refer back to this section when we discuss the SHEET window Query functions in the next chapter.

Former users of 1-2-3 will note that sorting in Symphony is distinctly different than it is in 1-2-3. The 1-2-3 /Data Sort command sequence prompts you to specify a block of cells to be sorted. That block of cells does not have to be defined as a data base. (In fact, if that block of cells is in a data base format, you cannot include the field names at the top of each column as a part of the sort range.) This gives 1-2-3 users the flexibility to sort *any* block of data.

Symphony's sort commands are more restrictive. Only a block of cells defined as a Database range can be sorted, and it must, of course, be in the standard data base format and include the field names. I find this limitation inconvenient and unnecessarily restrictive.

Why Sort?

The sorting of data is useful for a multitude of purposes. For instance, you could arrange your address-book data base into zip-code order, making it possible to print address labels that can easily be separated into bundles by zip code. In another case, you might wish to arrange all of the randomly entered records in this data base into alphabetical order, to make each name easier to find on a printed list.

In other cases, you might wish to sort the records in a data base using more than one field. Each of these fields might be sorted in either ascending or descending order. For example, suppose that you are working with the following data base of your receivable accounts:

Company	Amount	Date
XYZ Inc.	$200.00	27-Feb-84
ABC Ltd.	$175.00	03-Jul-84
QRS Co.	$127.00	27-Feb-84
ABC Ltd.	$315.00	23-Nov-83
XYZ Inc.	$827.00	27-Feb-84
XYZ Inc.	$1,042.00	21-Dec-83

You might first be interested in listing these accounts by date, from oldest to newest, so that you can easily see which accounts have been outstanding for the longest time. For this, you sort the data base by Date in ascending order. The result looks like this:

Company	Amount	Date
ABC Ltd.	$315.00	23-Nov-83
XYZ Inc.	$1,042.00	21-Dec-83
XYZ Inc.	$200.00	27-Feb-84
QRS Co.	$127.00	27-Feb-84
XYZ Inc.	$827.00	27-Feb-84
ABC Ltd.	$175.00	03-Jul-84

Note that there are three accounts outstanding since February 27. It might be convenient to group the accounts in each "date group" by name, so that all of the accounts from the same company outstanding for the same amount of time appear together in the list. To do this, you do a secondary sort on the Name field while still doing the primary sort by Date. The result will look like this:

Company	Amount	Date
ABC Ltd.	$315.00	23-Nov-83
XYZ Inc.	$1,042.00	21-Dec-83
QRS Co.	$127.00	27-Feb-84
XYZ Inc.	$200.00	27-Feb-84
XYZ Inc.	$827.00	27-Feb-84
ABC Ltd.	$175.00	03-Jul-84

You can see that of the three accounts due since February 27, the QRS account is listed before the two XYZ accounts. You could also arrange the records so that the greatest amounts owed by the same company for the same period of time are listed first. If XYZ had several bills outstanding since February 27, you would probably want to collect the bill with the highest dollar amount first. To arrange the data base in this order, you could perform a tertiary sort using the Amount field. The result is as follows:

Company	Amount	Date
ABC Ltd.	$315.00	23-Nov-83
XYZ Inc.	$1,042.00	21-Dec-83
QRS Co.	$127.00	27-Feb-84
XYZ Inc.	$827.00	27-Feb-84
XYZ Inc.	$200.00	27-Feb-84
ABC Ltd.	$175.00	03-Jul-84

Now that we know what sorting is all about, let's explore how we can use Symphony to sort the records in a data base. We'll create a new data base similar to the accounts receivable example above. To do this, clear the worksheet with the {**Services**} New Yes keystroke sequence. Next, define a simple form and data base by entering the field names and specifications into the worksheet, as shown in Figure 20.20.

Next, switch to a FORM window with the {**Type**} FORM command and instruct Symphony to generate the data base by issuing the {**Menu**} Generate command. Simply press [**Enter**] in response to the prompts for the default length and type, and choose the name Accounts for the data base settings sheet. Pressing [**Enter**] one final time will reveal the newly created Entry form, which looks like the one in Figure 20.21.

```
     ------A--------------B----------C-----
   1 Company:L:15                          |
   2 Amount:N:10                           |
   3 Date:D:10                             |
     ==============================MAIN=
```

Figure 20.20

```
   ----------------------------------------------------------
   | Company  _____                              |
   | Amount  _____                                    |
   | Date  _____                                      |
   |                                                       |
   |                                                       |
   =ACCOUNTS=====================================MAIN=
```

Figure 20.21

After entering the six records from the example above into the data base through this form, press {**Switch**} to view the worksheet, which will look like Figure 20.22.

```
     ----A------------B----------C---------D--------E--------F----------
   1 Company:L:15                                                       |
   2 Amount:N:10                                                        |
   3 Date:D:10                                                          |
   4                                                                    |
   5 Company  _____                                          |
   6 Amount  _____                                                 |
   7 Date  _____                                                   |
   8                                                                    |
   9 Name          Value      Type      Default  Formula  Validity Input|
  10 Company       XYZ Inc.   L:15                                      |
  11 Amount            200 N:10                                         |
  12 Date          27-Feb-84 D:10                                       |
  13                                                                    |
  14 Company       Amount     Date                                      |
  15 XYZ, Inc.        200  27-Feb-84                                    |
  16                                                                    |
  17 Company       Amount     Date                                      |
  18                                                                    |
  19                                                                    |
  20                                                                    |
  21                                                                    |
  22 Company       Amount     Date                                      |
  23 XYZ Inc.         200       30739                                   |
  24 ABC Ltd.         175       30866                                   |
  25 QRS Co.          127       30739                                   |
  26 ABC Ltd.         315       30643                                   |
  27 XYZ Inc.         827       30739                                   |
  28 XYZ Inc.        1042       30671                                   |
  29                                                                    |
     ===========================================MAIN==
```

Figure 20.22

Now that you have set up this data base, you can use Symphony to sort the records. In the first part of this example, we will sort these records only on the basis of Date, from the oldest account to the newest. But before this can be done, we need to cover some basics.

Sorting Basics

The FORM Record-Sort command instructs Symphony to sort the records in the Database range. Before you can use Record-Sort, you must use the FORM {**Menu**} Settings command to define the order into which you want the data to be sorted. To view the FORM settings sheet, issue the {**Menu**} Settings command from within a FORM window. The FORM settings sheet and settings menu appear on the screen, as shown in Figure 20.23.

```
                                                               MENU
  Basic Form Underscores Sort-Keys Report One-Record Name Cancel Quit
 ---------------------------------------------------------------------
 | Basic Ranges                        Report Ranges                 |
 |   Database:      ACCOUNTS_DB          Main:      ACCOUNTS_MA       |
 |   Criterion:     ACCOUNTS_CR          Above:     ACCOUNTS_AB       |
 |   Output:                             Below:                       |
 | Form Ranges                           Type:      Single            |
 |   Entry:         ACCOUNTS_EN          Entry list:                 |
 |   Definition:    ACCOUNTS_DF          Input cell:                 |
 | Underscores:     Yes                One-Record: No                 |
 | Sort-Keys                                                          |
 |   1st-Key:              2nd-Key:            3rd-Key:               |
 |     Order:                Order:              Order:               |
 |                                                                    |
 ==========================================Database Settings: ACCOUNTS=
```

Figure 20.23

Remember that Symphony can only sort data in the cells currently defined as the Database range. Because you used the Generate command to create the data base and settings sheet, Symphony has defined the Database range and given it the name ACCOUNTS_DB. Since you entered records into the data base through a FORM window, Symphony has automatically expanded the Database range to A22 . . C28. The range name ACCOUNTS_DB applies to this entire range.

Let's look at the Sort-Keys settings at the bottom of the settings sheet. You use the Sort-Keys settings to tell Symphony which field to use as the basis for sorting the records in the Database range. These settings also indicate whether Symphony should sort in ascending or descending order.

When you select the Sort-Keys option from the Settings menu, the following submenu appears above the settings sheet:

> Column to determine the reordering of records
> 1st-Key   2nd-Key   3rd-Key

As you can see, Symphony can sort on up to three fields. Suppose you want to sort the data base so that it is arranged according to the age of each account, with the oldest accounts at the top of the data base and the newest accounts at the bottom. In other words, you want to sort the data base in ascending order based on the entries in the Date field.

To define Date as the primary sort key, select 1st-Key from the Sort-Keys menu. Symphony automatically switches to a SHEET window and prompts you to specify the data base field you want to use as the basis for sorting the records.

In this example you want the data base to be sorted according to the dates in column C. You can use any cell in column C to designate the primary key; the cell doesn't even have to be part of the Database range. For argument's sake, let's use C21, the cell just above the Date field head, as the key. Simply move the cell pointer to C21 and press **[Enter]**. After the primary key is defined, Symphony switches you back to the FORM window settings sheet, which now looks like Figure 20.24.

```
1st-Key column: A21              (A)scending or (D)escending: A
------------------------------------------------------------------
 Basic Ranges                     Report Ranges
    Database:     ACCOUNTS_DB         Main:      ACCOUNTS_MA
    Criterion:    ACCOUNTS_CR         Above:     ACCOUNTS_AB
    Output:                           Below:
 Form Ranges                          Type:        Single
    Entry:        ACCOUNTS_EN         Entry list:
    Definition:   ACCOUNTS_DF         Input cell:
 Underscores:     Yes              One-Record: No
 Sort-Keys
    1st-Key: C21..C21     2nd-Key:           3rd-Key:
      Order:                Order:             Order:

==================================Database Settings: ACCOUNTS=
```

Figure 20.24

Notice the message

> (A)scending or (D)escending: A

in the control panel of this figure. This message asks whether you want the records sorted in ascending or descending order. Assuming you've never sorted this data base before, the default selection is (A)scending, so an A appears at the end of the prompt.

In the example, you want to arrange the data base so that the oldest accounts are at the top of the list. If you select Ascending, the records with the lowest serial date numbers (the oldest accounts) will appear at the top of the list. Since Ascending is the default order, you need only press **[Enter]** to set the order to Ascending. At this point your Sort-Keys settings are recorded in the FORM settings sheet, which now looks like Figure 20.25.

The sort order is based on the first character of each entry in the field, with the second and subsequent characters used as "tie breakers." Obviously, if the first character in the field is a number, choosing an ascending sort order will arrange the records with the

```
1st, 2nd, 3rd                                              MENU
Basic Form Underscores Sort-Keys Report One-Record Name Cancel Quit
-------------------------------------------------------------------
| Basic Ranges                        Report Ranges                |
|   Database:      ACCOUNTS_DB           Main:      ACCOUNTS_MA     |
|   Criterion:     ACCOUNTS_CR           Above:     ACCOUNTS_AB     |
|   Output:                             Below:                     |
| Form Ranges                           Type:      Single          |
|   Entry:         ACCOUNTS_EN           Entry list:               |
|   Definition:    ACCOUNTS_DF           Input cell:               |
| Underscores:     Yes                One-Record: No               |
| Sort-Keys                                                        |
|   1st-Key: C21..C21    2nd-Key:             3rd-Key:             |
|     Order: Ascending      Order:              Order:            |
|                                                                  |
| ===================================Database Settings: ACCOUNTS=  |
```

Figure 20.25

lowest numbers first, and choosing a descending sort order will arrange the data base with the highest numbers first.

If the first letter of the field is a letter, an ascending sort will be in alphabetical order (A to Z), and a descending sort will be reverse alphabetical order (Z to A). When sorting on alphabetic fields, Symphony does not differentiate between upper- and lowercase letters.

If numbers and letters are mixed in the entries, the sort sequence is a bit more complex. The sort order in this case is determined by the Text Collating Driver that you specified when you installed Symphony. The standard sequence places empty cells before label cells, and labels before numeric cells. However, you can also specify the order so that blanks will appear before numbers which will appear before labels.

Changing the Sort-Keys Settings

To change any Sort-Keys settings, simply press Settings Sort-Keys and enter the new parameters in place of the existing ones. Symphony revises the settings sheet to reflect any changes. To erase a Sort-Keys setting without replacing it, you must choose the Cancel Sort-Keys command from the FORM command menu. This command erases the settings for all three of the sort keys, allowing you to start again from scratch.

Sorting the Data Base

Now that you have specified the Sort-Keys settings and Symphony has specified the Database range, you're ready to have Symphony actually sort the records. To sort the data base, select **Q**uit from the FORM Settings menu, followed by {**Menu**}. This again reveals the FORM command menu, which appears as follows:

Attach Criteria Initialize Record-Sort Generate Settings

Select **R**ecord-Sort from this menu. Symphony offers you two choices: Unique and All. Choosing Unique tells Symphony to sort the records and eliminate all duplicate records. This feature is useful for editing mailing lists, because it prevents one customer from receiving multiple pieces of correspondence.

A record must match another *exactly* to be eliminated. It is not enough for the Sort-Keys fields in the records to match; *every* field in two records must be identical for one of the records to be deleted. Extra spaces, letters, or even the substitution of a lowercase letter for a capital letter are enough for Symphony to consider the entry unique.

Choosing **All** instructs Symphony to sort every record in the Database range, whether or not these records are duplicates. This is the convention you will normally choose when sorting records.

To sort the example data base, select **All**. Symphony immediately sorts the records in the Database range and returns you to your previous position in the data base. If you were inserting or editing the third record in the data base prior to sorting, Symphony displays the third record after the data base is sorted. However, the record in that location probably will not be the same one that was there prior to the sort.

You may now scroll through the records in their new order or switch to a SHEET window to view several records at once. When viewed through a SHEET window, the data base will now look like Figure 20.26. If you were to view these records through a FORM window, they would scroll through the Entry form in this order.

```
-----A-------------B----------C--------D---------E--------F---
22  Company      Amount      Date                                |
23  ABC Ltd.        315       30643                              |
24  XYZ Inc.       1042       30671                              |
25  XYZ Inc.        200       30739                              |
26  QRS Co.         127       30739                              |
27  XYZ Inc.        827       30739                              |
28  ABC Ltd.        175       30866                              |
===========================================================MAIN=
```

Figure 20.26

If you wish to sort the records of this data base into an even more meaningful order, you may wish to designate a 2nd-Key and a 3rd-Key in addition to the primary key used above. You do this the same way you designated the primary key. This time, use the Company field as the secondary key so that the outstanding accounts from any given day will be grouped together by company name.

First use {**Switch**} to get back into the FORM window. After pressing {**Menu**}, issue the Settings Sort-Keys command. From the Sort-Keys menu choose 2nd-Key and position the cell pointer somewhere in the column that contains the Company field—for example, cell A21. Pressing [Enter] records this choice and returns you to the settings sheet, which looks like Figure 20.27.

Now we are ready to perform the sort. Press [**Esc**] to return to the FORM command menu, and select the Record-Sort All command. Symphony sorts the records in the data base according to your new specifications. The resulting data base looks like Figure 20.28 when you switch to a SHEET window.

To generate an even more specific sort, you may wish to designate a tertiary key for sorting. In this example, you might specify the Amount field as the 3rd-Key, causing the

```
1st, 2nd, 3rd                                                  MENU
Basic Form Underscores Sort-Keys Report One-Record Name Cancel Quit
  ------------------------------------------------------------------
 | Basic Ranges                          Report Ranges              |
 |   Database:        ACCOUNTS_DB          Main:      ACCOUNTS_MA    |
 |   Criterion:       ACCOUNTS_CR          Above:     ACCOUNTS_AB    |
 |   Output:                               Below:                   |
 | Form Ranges                             Type:      Single        |
 |   Entry:           ACCOUNTS_EN          Entry list:              |
 |   Definition:      ACCOUNTS_DF          Input cell:              |
 | Underscores:       Yes                One-Record: No             |
 | Sort-Keys                                                        |
 |   1st-Key: C21..C21    2nd-Key: A21..A21    3rd-Key:             |
 |     Order: Ascending     Order: Ascending     Order:            |
 |                                                                  |
  =====================================Database Settings: ACCOUNTS=
```

Figure 20.27

```
    -----A------------B----------C----------D--------E--------F--
 22 Company        Amount     Date                                |
 23 ABC Ltd.          315     30643                               |
 24 XYZ Inc.         1042     30671                               |
 25 QRS Co.           127     30739                               |
 26 XYZ Inc.          200     30739                               |
 27 XYZ Inc.          827     30739                               |
 28 ABC Ltd.          175     30866                               |
    ======================================================MAIN=
```

Figure 20.28

greatest amount owed by the same company for the same period of time to be listed before lesser amounts due since the same date.

To perform this triple sort, you must first go back to the data base settings sheet, select the 3rd-Key option from the Sort-Keys menu, and specify cell B21. Then choose Ascending as the sort order.

Now all you have to do is the actual sort. Press **[Esc]** to return to the FORM menu and the issue the **R**ecord-**S**ort **A**ll command. After the sort is completed, the data base should look like Figure 20.29.

WORKING WITH MULTIPLE SETTINGS SHEETS

In the previous section, you used three different sets of sort specifications to sort the records in your accounts receivable data base. Each time you wanted to sort the records in a different way, you used the FORM {Menu} Settings command to modify the Sort-Keys settings in the settings sheet named ACCOUNTS. When you finished, the ACCOUNTS setting sheet contained specifications for all three sort keys.

Suppose that you now want to go back and sort the records using only the first key, as you did in the first part of this example. One way to do this is to go back into the

```
    ----A------------B----------C----------D--------E-------F--
 22 Company          Amount      Date                           |
 23 ABC Ltd.            315        30643                         |
 24 XYZ Inc.           1042        30671                         |
 25 QRS Co.             127        30739                         |
 26 XYZ Inc.            827        30739                         |
 27 XYZ Inc.            200        30739                         |
 28 ABC Ltd.            175        30866                         |
    ==========================================================MAIN=
```

Figure 20.29

ACCOUNTS settings sheet and erase the 2nd-Key and 3rd-Key specifications. Then, if you again want to sort using all three keys, or specify a different 1st-Key or sort order, you can go into the ACCOUNTS settings sheet one more time and change the Sort-Keys specification.

You can see that it takes a lot of time to revise the ACCOUNTS settings sheet in this way each time you want to reuse a sort specification. Fortunately, Symphony allows you to create many different data base settings sheets in one Symphony worksheet. In this case, you might create three different settings sheets, one for each set of sort keys. This way, each time you want to sort the data base in a different order, you simply tell Symphony to sort using the settings sheet that contains the desired Sort-Keys settings. Let's see how this is done.

Creating a Second Settings Sheet

To create a second settings sheet, use the Settings Name Create command. Select Name from the FORM Settings menu to bring the following menu into view:

> Use   Create   Delete   Previous   Next   Initial-Settings   Reset   Quit

When you move the cursor to Create, Symphony displays the following message above the command menu:

> Create copy of this sheet under a new name

The Create command does just what this message says: it creates an exact copy of the settings sheet currently displayed in the FORM window, while retaining the original settings sheet with its original name. Once you've created this new settings sheet, you'll use the Settings commands to modify it. The result will be two different settings sheets that will sort the data base in different ways.

When you issue the Create command Symphony asks you to supply a name for the new settings sheet it is about to create, followed by a list of the names of previously created settings sheets. In this example, our screen will look like Figure 20.30.

Symphony will not allow you to select the name of an existing settings sheet as the name for the new settings sheet. If you attempt to do so, Symphony will beep and display the message "Name already exists". The list is provided simply as a reminder that these names have already been used.

```
 Name for new Database settings sheet:
 ACCOUNTS  MAIN
 -----------------------------------------------------------------
 | Basic Ranges                        Report Ranges             |
 |   Database:      ACCOUNTS_DB           Main:      ACCOUNTS_MA  |
 |   Criterion:     ACCOUNTS_CR           Above:     ACCOUNTS_AB  |
 |   Output:                              Below:                  |
 | Form Ranges                            Type:      Single       |
 |   Entry:         ACCOUNTS_EN          Entry list:              |
 |   Definition:    ACCOUNTS_DF          Input cell:              |
 | Underscores:     Yes                 One-Record: No            |
 | Sort-Keys                                                      |
 |   1st-Key: C21..C21    2nd-Key: A21..A21    3rd-Key: B21..B21  |
 |      Order: ASCENDING     Order: ASCENDING     Order: ASCENDING|
 |                                                                |
 |=====================================Database Settings:ACCOUNTS=|
```

Figure 20.30

Let's give the new settings sheet the name SORT2. Symphony immediately displays the settings sheet named SORT2 on the screen, as shown in Figure 20.31. Notice that SORT2 is an exact copy of ACCOUNTS. In fact, SORT2 is distinguishable from ACCOUNTS only by the word SORT2 in the lower-right corner of the sheet.

```
 -----------------------------------------------------------------
 | Basic Ranges                        Report Ranges             |
 |   Database:      ACCOUNTS_DB           Main:      ACCOUNTS_MA  |
 |   Criterion:     ACCOUNTS_CR           Above:     ACCOUNTS_AB  |
 |   Output:                              Below:                  |
 | Form Ranges                            Type:      Single       |
 |   Entry:         ACCOUNTS_EN          Entry list:              |
 |   Definition:    ACCOUNTS_DF          Input cell:              |
 | Underscores:     Yes                 One-Record: No            |
 | Sort-Keys                                                      |
 |   1st-Key: C21..C21    2nd-Key: A21..A21    3rd-Key: B21..B21  |
 |      Order: ASCENDING     Order: ASCENDING     Order: ASCENDING|
 |                                                                |
 |=====================================Database Settings:SORT2=   |
```

Figure 20.31

Modifying the New Settings Sheet

You can now modify the SORT2 settings sheet any way you wish. In this case, let's change the Sort-Keys settings so that this settings sheet instructs Symphony to sort the records in our accounts receivable data base into a simple ascending order based on the name of the company.

The process of changing the sort keys involves two steps. The first is to erase the current Sort-Keys settings in SORT2, and the second is to redefine the primary Sort-Keys setting, just as you did in the previous sort examples.

Erasing the Old Settings

To begin, let's get back to the FORM Settings menu. As you recall from our work with the sorting process, this menu looks like this:

> Basic Form Underscores Sort-Keys Report One-Record Name
> Cancel Quit

To erase the current Sort-Keys settings, select the Cancel command from this menu. Symphony gives you the following choices:

> Basic Form Sort-Keys Report All

These selections correspond to the major groupings of ranges in the FORM settings sheet. Choosing any of the options from this menu instructs Symphony to erase all of the specifications for that group from the settings sheet that is currently on the screen. For instance, selecting Basic erases the settings for the Database, Criterion, and Output ranges.

Because you want to erase all of the Sort-Keys settings, choose Sort-Keys from this menu. Symphony erases these settings, and the SORT2 settings sheet now looks like Figure 20.32.

```
----------------------------------------------------------------
|  Basic Ranges                      Report Ranges              |
|    Database:      ACCOUNTS_DB         Main:       ACCOUNTS_MA  |
|    Criterion:     ACCOUNTS_CR         Above:      ACCOUNTS_AB  |
|    Output:                            Below:                   |
|  Form Ranges                          Type:         Single     |
|    Entry:         ACCOUNTS_EN          Entry list:            |
|    Definition:    ACCOUNTS_DF          Input cell:            |
|  Underscores:     Yes               One-Record: No            |
|  Sort-Keys                                                     |
|    1st-Key:                2nd-Key:               3rd-Key:     |
|     Order:                  Order:                 Order:      |
|                                                                |
===============================================Database Settings:SORT2=
```

Figure 20.32

Defining New Settings

You can now redefine the 1st-Key setting by issuing the Sort-Keys 1st-Key command. Move the cell-pointer to cell A21 (or any other cell in column A) and press [Enter]. Then confirm Ascending order by pressing [Enter] once again.

Now you have two distinct settings sheets. These settings sheets are not stored as individual files on disk, as is the case with COMM configuration sheets. Instead, they are retained as a part of the worksheet file when you issue the {Services} File Save command.

Attaching the Settings Sheet to the Form Window

Now let's press Quit to leave the FORM Settings menu and return to the FORM window Ready mode. If you instruct Symphony to sort the records in the data base by issuing the {**Menu**} **R**ecord-Sort command, the order of the records will not change, because Symphony is still using the Sort-Keys settings contained in the ACCOUNTS settings sheet, not the new sort order specified by the SORT2 settings sheet. Creating a settings sheet does not automatically call that sheet into use.

To call the SORT2 settings sheet into service, you must issue the Attach command by selecting Attach from the FORM command menu. Symphony displays the following message, followed by an alphabetical listing of the names of all the settings sheets you have created:

> Name of data base/entry-form to attach:
> ACCOUNTS   MAIN   SORT2

The MAIN settings sheet is the default settings sheet. This sheet is always present in the worksheet unless you specifically delete it with the Settings Name Delete command. ACCOUNTS and SORT2 are the two settings sheets that you have been working with.

To attach SORT2 so that you can use the sort keys defined in that sheet, move the cursor to SORT2 and press [**Enter**]. Symphony immediately attaches SORT2 to the current FORM window and returns you to the Edit mode in the FORM window. Your screen should now look like Figure 20.33.

```
    Editing Record 1 of 6
    Enter Company
    ----------------------------------------------------------------
  |    Company ABC Ltd._____                                      |
  |    Amount 315_____                                              |
  |    Date 23-Nov-83_                                               |
  |                                                                  |
  |                                                                  |
    =SORT2==========================================================MAIN=
```

Figure 20.33

Notice that the word SORT2 now appears in the lower-left corner of the screen, just where ACCOUNTS appeared when we were using that settings sheet. The name in the lower-left corner of the window indicates the name of the settings sheet currently attached to the FORM window. The name of the FORM window (in this case, MAIN) appears at the right side of the bottom border.

Now when we issue the Record-Sort command, the records in the data base will be sorted into ascending alphabetical order, based on the Company field, as specified by the 1st-Key setting in the SORT2 settings sheet. If we press {**Switch**} to view the data base through a SHEET window, the screen will look like Figure 20.34.

Once we attach the settings sheet SORT2 to the FORM window MAIN, Symphony will look to the SORT2 settings sheet whenever any data base command is issued from within MAIN.

```
     -----A----------------B----------C------
 22  Company           Amount      Date           |
 23  ABC Ltd.             315         30643        |
 24  ABC Ltd.             175         30866        |
 25  QRS Co.              127         30739        |
 26  XYZ Inc.            1042         30671        |
 27  XYZ Inc.             827         30739        |
 28  XYZ Inc.             200         30739        |
     ===================================MAIN=
```

Figure 20.34

Only one settings sheet can be attached to a single FORM window at any one time, and this attached settings sheet remains attached until you attach a new one. You can attach a new settings sheet to a FORM window by issuing the Attach command or by issuing the Generate command to build another data base from within that FORM window.

Creating More Settings Sheets

Now that we have worked through an example of how to create and attach a new settings sheet, let's broaden our view of the applications for multiple settings sheets. Instead of having two settings sheets that differ only in the Sort-Keys settings, you can build settings sheets that define different Entry ranges and Definition ranges, different Criterion ranges, different Output ranges, or any combination of the above, still using the same Database range (and therefore the same data base). To make any of these changes, you simply follow the process that we demonstrated above to create, modify, and attach these new settings sheets.

For instance, suppose you decide to create separate settings sheets that share the same Database range but define different Criterion ranges. Each of these sheets allows you to view the records for only one company at a time through the FORM window.

The first step is to go back into the worksheet and create three Criterion ranges, all of which conform to the necessary row and column structure explained earlier in this chapter. To do this, use {Switch} to change the current window to a SHEET window and enter the three Criterion ranges in a group of empty cells. In this example, we'll enter the new criteria in column E, adjacent to the recently sorted data base, as shown in Figure 20.35.

Cells E22 . . E23 contain the criteria that select the ABC Ltd. records, cells E25 . . E26 contain the criteria that select the records for XYZ Inc., and cells E28 . . E29 contain the criteria that select the records for QRS Co.

Next, use **{Switch}** to get back to the FORM window to create three new settings sheets. Each of these new sheets will refer to one of the new Criterion ranges we created in the prior step. Since you want these settings sheets to be modifications of the ACCOUNTS sheet, you need to bring the ACCOUNTS settings sheet back to the screen.

```
     -----A---------------B----------C----------D----------E-----
  22 Company           Amount    Date                   Company    |
  23 ABC Ltd.             315      30643               ABC Ltd.    |
  24 ABC Ltd.             175      30866                           |
  25 QRS Co.              127      30739               Company     |
  26 XYZ Inc.            1042      30671               XYZ Inc.    |
  27 XYZ Inc.             827      30739                           |
  28 XYZ Inc.             200      30739               Company     |
  29                                                   QRS Co.     |
     ========================= : :=======================MAIN=
```

Figure 20.35

Then you can use the Create command to make an exact copy of this sheet. Remember that the Create command only copies the settings sheet currently on the screen, and that Symphony now displays SORT2 because you attached it to the FORM window in the previous example.

There are several ways to get Symphony to display the ACCOUNTS sheet. First, you could use the Attach command to bring ACCOUNTS back into active service. Alternatively, you could issue the Name Use, Previous, or Next commands to simply bring ACCOUNTS back into the display, without making it the active sheet.

Let's employ the Name Use command to temporarily bring the ACCOUNTS sheet back, without making it active. Starting from the FORM command menu, issue the Settings Name Use command. Symphony displays the names of all of the settings sheets you have created—in this case MAIN, ACCOUNTS, and SORT2.

To bring ACCOUNTS to the top of the stack, position the cursor on ACCOUNTS and press **[Enter].** Symphony immediately brings the ACCOUNTS settings sheet to the screen but does not attach it to the FORM window.

You can also use the Settings Name Previous command, which instructs Symphony to scroll in reverse alphabetical order through the collection of settings sheets you have created. Similarly, the Settings Name Next command scrolls the cursor forward through the catalog of settings sheets. Both commands have a wrap feature, so that when you reach either end of the list Symphony automatically loops back to the opposite end of the list.

Now that you have brought the ACCOUNTS settings sheet back onto the screen, make a copy of it under a new name, using the Settings Name Create command. Select the name ABC for this settings sheet, since it will refer to the criteria that will select the records for ABC Ltd.

Once ABC is created, use the Create command twice more to create two additional settings sheets named XYZ and QRS. You'll end up with six settings sheets in all, as follows:

ABC ACCOUNTS MAIN QRS SORT2 XYZ

ABC, QRS, and XYZ are all exact copies of ACCOUNTS. Now you need to modify each of these sheets so that each one refers to one of the Criteria ranges we created in the previous step.

Modifying the Settings Sheet

First let's modify XYZ, since it is the last sheet you created and is therefore still displayed on the screen. Select Basic from the FORM {Menu} Settings command menu. This command allows you to change the settings sheet specifications for any or all of the three Basic data base ranges: the Database range, the Criterion range, and the Output range.

To specify a Criterion range, choose Criterion from the Settings Basic menu. Symphony immediately displays the worksheet through the window MAIN and prompts you to specify the cells you want to define as the Criterion range in the settings sheet XYZ. Use the cursor-movement keys and the period to highlight the cells E25 . . E26, and then press [**Enter**]. Your screen will now look like Figure 20.36.

```
---------------------------------------------------------------
 Basic Ranges                        Report Ranges
   Database:       ACCOUNTS_DB          Main:        ACCOUNTS_MA
   Criterion:      E25..E26             Above:       ACCOUNTS_AB
   Output:                              Below:
 Form Ranges                           Type:        Single
   Entry:          ACCOUNTS_EN          Entry list:
   Definition:     ACCOUNTS_DF          Input cell:
 Underscores:      Yes                One-Record: No
 Sort-Keys
   1st-Key: C21..C21   2nd-Key: A21..A21    3rd-Key: B21..B21
     Order: Ascending    Order: Ascending     Order: Ascending

 =========================================Database Settings:XYZ=
```

Figure 20.36

You're now finished modifying the XYZ settings sheet. Repeat this process for QRS and ABC, first bringing each to the screen with the Name Use command and then using the Settings Basic command to redefine the Criterion ranges in both sheets. The Criterion range in sheet ABC should be E22 . . E23 and the Criterion range for sheet QRS should be E28 . . E29.

Using the Settings Sheet

You now have three new settings sheets, all addressing the same Database range and using the same Entry and Definition ranges, but each of which addresses a different Criterion range. You can now selectively attach any of these sheets to the FORM window so that you can view different subsets of the records in the data base through a common entry form.

To illustrate this concept, attach XYZ to your FORM window. First, select Quit to exit to the FORM command menu. Then select Attach, and specify the settings sheet XYZ. Your screen will look like Figure 20.37.

Notice that the Entry form has not changed in appearance, since the XYZ settings sheet has the same Entry range as the ACCOUNTS settings sheet you used earlier.

Now let's use the Criterion range specified in this settings sheet. Issue the Criteria Use command. Immediately, the screen will change to look like Figure 20.38. Now you can use the [**Pg Up**] and [**Pg Dn**] keys to scroll through the records for XYZ Inc.

```
 _____
|                                                        |
|   Editing Record 1 of 6                                |
|   Enter Company                                        |
|    ------------------------------------------------    |
|   | Company ABC Ltd._____                        |   |
|   | Amount 315_____                               |   |
|   | Date 23-Nov-83_                                |   |
|   |                                                |   |
|   |                                                |   |
|    =XYZ=========================================MAIN=   |
|_____|
```

Figure 20.37

```
 _____
|                                                        |
|   Editing Record 4 of 6 (Match 1 of 3)                 |
|   Enter Company                                        |
|    ------------------------------------------------    |
|   | Company XYZ Inc._____                        |   |
|   | Amount 1042_____                              |   |
|   | Date 21-Dec-83_                                |   |
|   |                                                |   |
|   |                                                |   |
|    =XYZ=========================================MAIN=   |
|_____|
```

Figure 20.38

If you want to review only the records for ABC Ltd., use the **{Menu}** Attach **ABC** command to make the ABC settings sheet active. Then issue the Criteria Use command. Only the records for ABC Ltd. will appear in the Entry form. As soon as you issue the Criteria Use command, the screen will look like Figure 20.39. You can also attach the settings sheet QRS to the FORM window, with similar results.

```
 _____
|                                                        |
|   Editing Record 1 of 6 (Match 1 of 2)                 |
|   Enter Company                                        |
|    ------------------------------------------------    |
|   | Company ABC Ltd._____                        |   |
|   | Amount 315_____                               |   |
|   | Date 23-Nov-83_                                |   |
|   |                                                |   |
|   |                                                |   |
|    =XYZ=========================================MAIN=   |
|_____|
```

Figure 20.39

Multiple FORM Windows

As a final step, let's look at the use of multiple settings sheets with multiple FORM windows. In the example above, you might want to switch between settings sheets faster than is possible with the Menu Attach command. You might also want to view the records for two or more companies at the same time through two or more FORM windows. To accomplish either objective, all you have to do is create multiple FORM windows, restrict their size to a partial screen, and attach a different settings sheet to each window. Please refer to Chapter 11 (Windows) for a more in-depth discussion on using multiple windows.

As you become better acquainted with Symphony data bases, you will discover many more reasons for creating multiple data base settings sheets and selectively attaching them to single or multiple FORM windows. We will approach this topic again in Chapter 22, when we create new settings sheets to print different data base reports.

OTHER SETTINGS SHEET MANAGEMENT COMMANDS

The FORM {Menu} Settings Name menu provides three additional commands to help you manage data base settings sheets: the Initial-Settings, Delete, and Reset commands.

Name Initial-Settings

The Name Initial-Settings command returns the settings of the sheet currently on the screen to their default values. It erases all ranges except the Underscores, Type, and One-Record settings, which return to their default values. The effect of this command is identical to the Cancel All sequence of keystrokes described earlier.

Name Delete

The Name Delete command does just what it says: it deletes any settings sheet you select. For instance, if you no longer want the SORT2 settings sheet, you can issue the Settings Name Delete command, pick SORT2 from the list Symphony presents, and press [Enter]. Once this command is issued, SORT2 is permanently deleted. There is no safety step in the Name Delete command, so exercise caution when using it. Symphony will not allow you to delete a settings sheet that is currently attached to a FORM window, nor will it allow you to delete the only settings sheet in the worksheet.

Name Reset

Reset is another powerful command that should be used with caution. Selecting Reset and confirming your choice with Yes deletes all the settings sheets you have created, leaving only a settings sheet named MAIN. Even though MAIN is not deleted, this command returns all the settings in MAIN to their default values.

The FORM {Menu} Settings command offers three more command which we have not yet discussed: Underscore, One-Record, and Report. The Report command controls Symphony's data base report-generating capabilities. We'll cover this command in detail in Chapter 22. The other two options are covered in the following sections.

Eliminating Underscores

The Underscores setting allows you to turn on or off the underlines that follow the field names in the Entry form. By default, Symphony displays these underlines according to the field length you specified when creating the form. I feel that these underlines are a great convenience, adding structure and clarity to the form. However, if you want the form to appear without these underlines, simply select Underlines No. With the underline feature off, there is no visual indication of the maximum length allowed for each field.

One-Record Data Bases

The final command on the FORM Settings menu is One-Record. When you select this setting, Symphony displays the following prompt:

Database restricted to single record?
No   Yes

Selecting No (the default setting) instructs Symphony to treat the data base normally. Selecting Yes tells Symphony to allow only a single entry in each field of the data base.

The One-Record Yes setting is useful when you wish to use an Entry form to enter information into a spreadsheet model. For example, suppose that you have created the simple income statement model shown in Figure 20.40. This model includes formulas that calculate the quarterly net income of your company when you input the sales and operating expenses for the period. These are the formulas contained in the cells in column B:

B1: (C0) + D20
B2: (C0) + B1 * 0.50
B4: (C0) + B1 − B2
B5: (C0) + E20
B7: (C0) + B4 − B5

Columns D and E in Figure 20.40 contain the structure of a simple data base that was created with the Generate command. The entries used to define the data base appear in cells D1 and D2.

Suppose you want to use the Entry form defined in cells D4 and D5 (and illustrated in Figure 20.41) to enter the sales and operating expenses figures into this worksheet. Begin by pressing {**Switch**} to transfer MAIN into a FORM window. Next, issue the {**Menu**} Settings One-Record Yes command.

To enter data into this worksheet, switch to a FORM window. You will see the simple form shown in Figure 20.41.

```
------------------A------------------B--------C--------D--------E----------
 1 Sales:                           $0         Sales:N:9                    |
 2 Cost of Goods Sold:              $0         Expenses:N:9                 |
 3                          --------                                        |
 4 Gross Margin:                    $0         Sales  _____              |
 5 Operating Expenses:              $0         Expenses _____            |
 6                          --------                                        |
 7 Net Income:                      $0         Name      Value      Type    |
 8                                             Sales                N:9      |
 9                                             Expenses             N:9      |
10                                                                          |
11                                             Sales     Expenses           |
12                                                  0           0           |
13                                                                          |
14                                             Sales     Expenses           |
   =========================================================================MAIN=
```

Figure 20.40

```
---------------------------------------------------------
| Sales  _____                                       |
| Expenses _____                                     |
|                                                       |
 =================================================MAIN=
```

Figure 20.41

To enter the correct numbers into the worksheet, simply type the sales figure into the Sales blank in the form, and the operating expenses figure into the Expenses blank. When you press **[Ins]**, the values will be inserted into the worksheet in cells D20 and E20, the first and only row of the data base.

Notice that the formulas in cells B1 and B5 refer to the cells in the simple data base. When the values you entered in the form are entered into the data base, cells B1 and B5 will "pull" these entries from the data base into the income statement. If you press {**Calc**}, Symphony will calculate the net income figure, as shown in Figure 20.42.

Because this data base has only one row, any additional records that you enter through the Entry form overwrite the record already in the data base. This means that the data base only includes the most recent values for sales and operating expenses.

Although this method of entering information into a spreadsheet model might seem cumbersome, it can save you a lot of time for large spreadsheet models, where the input variables are in distant sections of the spreadsheet, because it spares you the trouble of manually moving to distant sections of the worksheet to enter each number.

This ends our discussion of the basics of working in a Symphony FORM window. In the final chapter of this section, we will cover two advanced topics relating to the FORM window: How to modify the appearance of the Entry form and how to generate data base reports. First, however, we'll take a look at what we can do with a data base in a SHEET window.

```
    --------------A--------------------B--------C--------D---------E-------
 1  Sales:                       $50,000      Sales                        |
 2  Cost of Goods Sold:          $25,000      Expenses                     |
 3                               -------                                   |
 4  Gross Margin:                $25,000      Sales    _____           |
 5  Operating Expenses:          $10,000      Expenses _____           |
 6                               -------                                   |
 7  Net Income:                  $15,000      Name     Value               |
 8                                            Sales    50000               |
 9                                            Expenses 10000               |
10                                                                         |
11                                            Sales    Expenses            |
12                                            50000    10000               |
13                                                                         |
14                                            Sales    Expenses            |
15                                                                         |
16                                                                         |
17                                                                         |
18                                                                         |
19                                            Sales    Expenses            |
20                                            50000    10000               |
    ================================================================MAIN=
```

Figure 20.42

CHAPTER TWENTY ONE

DATA BASES AND SHEET WINDOWS

Although a FORM window provides a convenient way to insert records into a data base and view a limited number of those records, the SHEET environment is best suited for working with the information in the data base once it has been entered. In this chapter, we will explore the ways you can manipulate the information in a data base using the SHEET Query commands and data base statistical functions. At the end of the chapter, we'll consider Criterion ranges again, expanding on the knowledge you acquired in Chapter 20.

THE QUERY COMMANDS

Let's first take a look at the SHEET command menu, which becomes visible when you press {**Menu**} from within a SHEET window:

Copy Move Erase Insert Delete Width Format Range Graph Query Settings

In the earlier sections of this book, we explored all of these commands except Query. Now that we have a good background in Symphony data bases, the Query menu will look pretty familiar right from the start. To bring up the Query menu, select Query from the main SHEET menu:

Settings Find Extract Unique Delete Record-Sort Parse Quit

Selecting the first item, Settings, reveals a data base settings sheet similar to the ones you used in the FORM window. This duplication of function is merely a convenience, eliminating the necessity of switching to or creating a FORM window to change the data base settings if you are working with the data base exclusively from a SHEET window.

The sixth item on this menu, Record-Sort, should also look familiar to you. This command is identical to the Record-Sort command found in the FORM command menu. Rather than covering the command again in this chapter, we refer you to the discussion of Record-Sort in Chapter 20.

The Find command will look new to you, but its function is familiar. This command is the SHEET equivalent of the Criteria Use command sequence used in the FORM window. When you select Find, Symphony starts at the top of the data base and searches through the records one by one, stopping at and highlighting each record that matches the criteria which you have specified in the Criterion range. When you press the ↓ key, Symphony moves to the next record that matches those criteria, and so forth. This is very similar to the way that Symphony allows you to scroll to only those records that match the Criterion range when you select Criteria Use in the FORM window.

The Extract and Unique commands, which do not have exact equivalents in the FORM window, are two of Symphony's most useful data base commands. Briefly, the Extract command allows you to copy from the data base those records or parts of records that meet the criteria in the Criterion range and insert those copies into the part of the worksheet designated as the Output range. The Unique command is similar, but it detects duplicate entries in the records it selects and copies only one record of each duplicate set into the Output range.

Delete is a powerful editing command that is not available in the FORM window. This command instructs Symphony to remove from the data base every record that matches the criteria you have specified in the Criterion range.

These Extract, Query, Find, and Delete commands should be familiar to former users of Lotus 1-2-3. However, the last command on the Query menu, Parse, will be new to all Symphony users. The verb *to parse* means to break a sentence down into parts of speech. This "division into parts" is basically what Symphony's Parse command does. When you define a Parse range, Symphony takes the contents of the cells in that range and enters them into a data base through an Entry form. In so doing, it divides the lines of characters into pieces according to the field lengths in the Entry form and converts these characters into whatever type (number, label, date, or time) you have specified in the Definition range. This command is extremely useful for converting data received through a COMM window into a usable form. You will find a thorough example of this application in the last chapter of the COMM section (Chapter 27).

CREATING A DATA BASE

Before you can use the Query commands, you must first define a simple data base. Because you don't plan to use an Entry form to view this data base, there's no point in using the Generate command. We'll begin this example by developing a simple inventory data base. Start by entering the field names for this new data base in cells A7 . . C7. (By the way, you could begin building the data base at any convenient location in the worksheet, not just at A7.) Next, fill in the fields of the data base with some records, so that it looks like Figure 21.1.

Notice that this list meets all of Symphony's rules for a data base: each record occupies a row, each column is a field, the first cell in each column contains a label that serves as a field name, and there is no space between the field names and the first records in the data base.

All of the entries in the Item# field are labels, even though some are composed wholly of numeric characters. To make these entries labels instead of numbers, you must start the entries in the range A9 . . A12 and A14 . . A16 with a single quote ('). (Cells A8 and A13 begin with letters, so Symphony automatically intreprets them as labels.) Although

```
-----A----------B------------C-----------D------
7      Item#      Supplier      Quantity                     |
8    AZ27        XYZ Inc.            16                       |
9    16          ABC Ltd.            37                       |
10   185         XYZ Inc.             8                       |
11   37E         QRS Co.             43                       |
12   139XX       DEF Inc.            96                       |
13   AZ27        XYZ Inc.            27                       |
14   16          ABC Ltd.            37                       |
15   9D          ABC Ltd.            52                       |
16   185         DEF Inc.            74                       |
17                                                            |
     =========================================MAIN=
```

Figure 21.1

you can enter some of these entries as numbers and some as labels, it is generally prefer-able to have all the entries in the same field be the same type.

This illustrates one of the primary differences between entering records in a data base through a FORM window and entering records through a SHEET window. You may remember that when you entered records through an Entry form, Symphony checked each entry against the field type setting in the Definition range. If the field was a label field, all entries to that field were automatically interpreted as labels. However, when you enter records directly into the data base through a SHEET window, you must specify the type of each field in each record manually. One advantage of using a FORM window to enter data and criteria into a data base is that all entries made to a given field through an Entry form are automatically the same type.

Once you have created the data base, you need to construct a Criterion range. To build this range, simply enter the field names from the data base into a convenient range of cells. In this example, use cells A1 . . C1. Next, enter a simple criterion in the cell beneath the "Supplier" field name (cell B2). The criterion shown in Figure 21.2 will match any records from which the entry in the Supplier field is ABC Ltd.

By the way, Symphony forgives capitalization errors when you specify the field names in a Criterion range. For example, the field names Zip and ZIP are identical to Symphony. If the data base used the name ZIP and the Criterion range the name Zip, Symphony would accept these as the same field name.

THE QUERY SETTINGS COMMANDS

Even though these two ranges meet all of Symphony's rules for Criterion and Database ranges, they are not yet ready to be used by Symphony. Before you can use the Query commands on this data base, you must use the Settings commands to specify the loca-tions of these two ranges in a data base settings sheet. Until you do this, Symphony has no way of knowing that you intend to use these collections of cells as a Database and Criterion range.

```
       -----A----------B------------C----------D------
   1     Item#      Supplier    Quantity                 |
   2                ABC Ltd.                              |
   3                                                      |
   4                                                      |
   5                                                      |
   6                                                      |
   7     Item#      Supplier    Quantity                  |
   8   AZ27         XYZ Inc.         16                   |
   9   16           ABC Ltd.         37                   |
  10   185          XYZ Inc.          8                   |
  11   37E          QRS Co.          43                   |
  12   139XX        DEF Inc.         96                   |
  13   AZ27         XYZ Inc.         27                   |
  14   16           ABC Ltd.         37                   |
  15   9D           ABC Ltd.         52                   |
  16   185          DEF Inc.         74                   |
  17                                                      |
       ====================================MAIN=
```

Figure 21.2

The SHEET window Query Settings commands are identical to the Settings commands found in the FORM environment. You have already seen how to use the FORM Settings commands to modify a data base settings sheet that already exists. The SHEET settings commands can be used for exactly the same purpose. However, you can also use the SHEET Settings commands to define a brand-new data base from within a SHEET window.

To define these ranges for Symphony, issue the {Menu} Query Settings command. Assuming you are working in a fresh worksheet and no data base settings sheet has been defined previously, Symphony displays an "initialized" settings sheet, which looks like Figure 21.3.

```
                                                            MENU
   Basic Form Underscores Sort-Keys Report One-Record Name Cancel Quit
   -------------------------------------------------------------------
   | Basic Ranges                    Report Ranges                  |
   |   Database:                       Main:                        |
   |   Criterion:                      Above:                       |
   |   Output:                         Below:                       |
   | Form Ranges                       Type:        Single          |
   |   Entry:                           Entry list:                 |
   |   Definition:                      Input cell:                 |
   | Underscores:    Yes             One-Record: No                 |
   | Sort-Keys                                                      |
   |   1st-Key:              2nd-Key:              3rd-Key:         |
   |   Order:               Order:                Order:           |
   |                                                               |
   ================================Database Settings: MAIN=
```

Figure 21.3

To specify the Database range, select Basic from the Query Settings menu. Then choose Database and use the cursor-movement keys and the period key to highlight the entire block of cells from A7 to C16. Notice that this Database range includes the field names at the top of the data base. Press **[Enter]** to lock in this selection and get back to the Settings menu. Next, select Basic again, this time choosing Criterion from the sub-menu. Highlight the block of cells from A1 . . C2, and again press **[Enter].** Symphony now enters the data base and criteria you selected into the MAIN settings sheet as the Database range and Criterion range, as shown in Figure 21.4. Press Quit to return to the Query command menu.

```
                                                              MENU
   Basic Form Underscores Sort-Keys Report One-Record Name Cancel Quit
  --------------------------------------------------------------------
  |  Basic Ranges                      Report Ranges                 |
  |    Database:      A7..C16             Main:                       |
  |    Criterion:     A1..C2              Above:                      |
  |    Output:                            Below:                      |
  |  Form Ranges                          Type:        Single         |
  |    Entry:                             Entry list:                 |
  |    Definition:                        Input cell:                 |
  |  Underscores:     Yes               One-Record: No                |
  |  Sort-Keys                                                        |
  |    1st-Key:              2nd-Key:              3rd-Key:            |
  |     Order:                Order:                Order:             |
  |                                                                   |
  |  ===========================================Database Settings: MAIN=
```

Figure 21.4

Although the settings sheet in Figure 21.4 is pretty empty (especially when compared to the settings sheets we saw in the previous chapter), it contains enough information for Symphony to use the Query Find command. It is important to understand that when you define a data base through the SHEET window you usually don't need to define all the ranges that are included in the settings sheet. In fact, several of the ranges, like the Definition range and the Entry range, usually are needed only when you are working with a FORM window and thus will almost never be defined from within a SHEET window. In most cases, you need to define only three ranges when you set up a data base from within a SHEET window: the Database range, the Criterion range, and (sometimes) the Output range (we'll discuss this last range in a few pages).

In general, you're probably better off using the FORM Generate command to automatically create and define your data bases, even if you don't plan to use the FORM window to view the data. Setting up the ranges by hand is just too time consuming when Symphony has a tool that does the job for you.

Modifying the Database Range

You may recall from Chapter 19 that when you enter new records into a data base through a FORM window the Database range in the active data base settings sheet is automatically adjusted to include the new records. The same is not true when you enter records into a data base through a SHEET window. You must use the Query Settings Basic command to adjust the Database range manually.

For example, suppose you decide to enter a new record into the data base in Figure 21.1. You can always enter a record into a data base simply by positioning the cell pointer in the proper cells and typing the desired entries. Figure 21.5 shows the data base with this new record.

```
     -----A----------B------------C-----------D-----
  7    Item#       Supplier     Quantity                 |
  8  AZ27        XYZ Inc.            16                   |
  9  16          ABC Ltd.           37                   |
 10  185         XYZ Inc.            8                    |
 11  37E         QRS Co.            43                    |
 12  139XX       DEF Inc.           96                    |
 13  AZ27        XYZ Inc.           27                    |
 14  16          ABC Ltd.           37                    |
 15  9D          ABC Ltd.           52                    |
 16  185         DEF Inc.           74                    |
 17  Q563        QRS Co.           100                    |
 18                                                       |
     ========================================MAIN=
```

Figure 21.5

Although it appears that the new record is a part of the data base, Symphony still considers the Database range to be A7 . . C16. Because you entered the new record through a SHEET window rather than through a FORM window, Symphony did not automatically include this record in the data base. As far as Symphony is concerned, the new record is not a part of the data base because it lies outside of the Database range. You must issue the {Menu} Query Settings Basic Database command sequence to include this new record in the data base. When you issue the command, Symphony highlights the cells currently within the Database range. Using the cursor-movement keys, you can expand the highlighted area to cover the range A7 . . C17. Pressing [Enter] locks this new range into the settings sheet.

Modifying the Criterion Range

As with the Database range, when you make entries into the cells of the Criterion range from a SHEET window, you must use the Settings Basic Criterion command sequence to expand the Criterion range to include those new entries.

As you have seen, the structure of the Criterion range is similar to that of the Database range. In fact, the Criterion range created by the Generate command matches the structure of the Database range exactly. However, the Cirterion range does not have to match the Database range exactly. First, the Criterion range does not have to include all of the field names found in the Database range. In fact, the Criterion range must contain only one field name that appears in the data base. Second, if the Criterion range does contain more than one field name, the field names do not have to appear in the same order used in the Database range.

Since the fields included in the Criterion range can be a subset of the fields included in the Database range, you can also use the Settings Basic Criteria on command to limit the Criterion range to just one or two adjacent columns (fields).

The Name Use Command

The Query Settings Name Use command is quite different from the FORM Settings Name Use command. You may recall that when you were working through a FORM window the active data base settings sheet was the one attached to that window (with the Attach command). The FORM Settings Name Use command is used to bring a settings sheet into view so that it can be copied (with the Name Create command) or modified.

There is no Attach command on the Query menu, however. When working in a SHEET window, you use the Query Settings Name Use command instead. When you issue this command from within a SHEET window, the specified sheet becomes the active sheet, meaning that the settings in the selected sheet assume control of the various SHEET Query commands and the data base functions. In a way, the Query Settings Name Use command is the SHEET window's equivalent of the FORM window's Settings Attach command.

FINDING RECORDS IN A SHEET WINDOW

Now that you have defined the Database and Criterion ranges, you are ready to explore the Query commands. Let's begin with a familiar concept: selecting records that match specified criteria. You have already used the FORM window's Criteria Use command to select certain records that match specified criteria; the SHEET Query Find command accomplishes nearly the same purpose.

When you select Find from the Query command menu, Symphony moves the cell pointer to the first record in the Database range that matches the criteria in the Criterion range and expands the cell pointer to highlight all three fields of that record. In this example (Figure 21.6), Symphony moves the cell pointer to the second record in the data base, which is the first record that has ABC Ltd. in the Supplier field.

Pressing the ↓ key moves the highlighting to row 14. Pressing ↓ one more time moves the highlighting to row 15, which contains the third matching record. If you try to press ↓ one more time, Symphony will beep, indicating that row 15 contains the last record in the data base that matches the criteria.

You can use the ↑ key to scroll back up through these three records. For example, if the cell pointer is in row 15 and you press ↑, the cell pointer will move to row 14. If you press ↑ with the cell pointer on the first record in the data base that matches the criteria (row 9 in the example), Symphony will beep.

```
    -----A----------B-----------C-----------D------
  1     Item#       Supplier    Quantity               |
  2                 ABC Ltd.                            |
  3                                                     |
  4                                                     |
  5                                                     |
  6                                                     |
  7     Item#          Supplier    Quantity            |
  8   AZ27         XYZ Inc.             16              |
  9   16           ABC Ltd.            37              |
 10   185          XYZ Inc.             8              |
 11   37E          QRS Co.             43              |
 12   139XX        DEF Inc.            96              |
 13   AZ27         XYZ Inc.            27              |
 14   16           ABC Ltd.            37              |
 15   9D           ABC Ltd.            52              |
 16   185          DEF Inc.            74              |
 17   Q563         QRS Co.            100              |
      =========================================MAIN=
```

Figure 21.6

You can also use the [Home] and [End] keys with the Find command. Pressing [Home] moves the cell pointer to the first record in the data base, regardless of whether that record matches the criteria. Pressing [End] moves the cell pointer to the last record in the data base.

Once you have finished reviewing the matching records, you must press [Esc] or [Enter] to exit the Find mode and return to the Query menu. When you press one of these keys, the cell pointer returns to the cell it was in when you issued the Find command. Until you press one of these keys, you will not be allowed to issue any command or move the cell pointer outside the Database range.

As you can see, the Find command is similar in function to the FORM window's Criteria Use command. With both commands, Symphony displays only those records that match the stated criteria. There are a couple of important differences between the commands, however.

First, you cannot use the Find command to erase or edit a highlighted record. If you try to change a highlighted record while you're using the Find command, Symphony only beeps. With the Find command you can only *look* at the information in all the fields of a record. The FORM Criteria Use command, on the other hand, does allow you to make changes and even erase records that are displayed through the Entry form.

Second, when you use the Find command to look at records, you are looking at the data base itself in the worksheet, so you can see a screen full of records surrounding the record Symphony selects. In other words, the Find command allows you to view the record in context. With the FORM window's Criteria Use command, you can view only the record displayed through the Entry form.

EXTRACTING RECORDS FROM A DATA BASE

The Query Extract command is more powerful than the Query Find command, because it not only finds data base records that match a Criterion range but also pulls copies of these records to a separate section of the worksheet. Once you have extracted copies of these records, you can define them as a separate data base. Then you can use the Query commands, data base statistical functions, or even the {Services} Print commands with these selected records.

The Output Range

Before using the Extract command, we must define one additional range: the Output range. The Output range is the area of the worksheet to which Symphony copies the records that match the selected criteria.

There are some rules to keep in mind when you are creating the Output range. The first row in this range must contain at least one of the field names from the first row of the Database range defined on the current data base settings sheet. If you are using more than one field name, the names may appear in any order. If you want to copy the information in only one of the fields in the data base to the Output range, type only that field name.

You can use either lower- or uppercase letters for the Output range field names; Symphony treats them the same as long as the spelling is consistent. If you list the same field name more than once, Symphony recognizes only the first occurrence of the name in the Output range. Similarly, if you include a field name that is not contained within the current Database range, Symphony ignores that column when using the Output range.

Figure 21.7 shows the sample worksheet with the Output range field names in cells E1 and F1. The example shows two of the three field names from the data base in the Output range, in reversed order.

```
    ---A-----------B-----------C-----------D-----------E-----------F----
 1    Item#       Supplier    Quantity                 Quantity    Item#   |
 2                ABC Ltd.                                                  |
 3                                                                         |
 4                                                                         |
 5                                                                         |
 6                                                                         |
 7    Item#       Supplier    Quantity                                     |
 8  AZ27          XYZ Inc.          16                                     |
 9  16            ABC Ltd.          37                                     |
10  185           XYZ Inc.           8                                     |
11  37E           QRS Co.           43                                     |
12  139XX         DEF Inc.          96                                     |
13  AZ27          XYZ Inc.          27                                     |
14  16            ABC Ltd.          37                                     |
15  9D            ABC Ltd.          52                                     |
16  185           DEF Inc.          74                                     |
17  Q563          QRS Co.          100                                     |
    ============================================================MAIN=
```

Figure 21.7

Now you have to tell Symphony the location of the Output range. Issue the Settings Basic Output command and specify the range E1 . . F1. Symphony reflects these coordinates in the data base settings sheet, which looks like the one in Figure 21.8.

```
-----------------------------------------------------------------
| Basic Ranges                         Report Ranges            |
|    Database:      A7..C17                Main:                 |
|    Criterion:     A1..C2                 Above:                |
|    Output:        E1..F1                 Below:                |
| Form Ranges                              Type:      Single     |
|    Entry:                                Entry list:           |
|    Definition:                           Input cell:           |
| Underscores:      Yes                 One-Record: No           |
| Sort-Keys                                                      |
|    1st-Key:             2nd-Key:               3rd-Key:        |
|      Order:               Order:                 Order:        |
|                                                                |
| ==============================================Database Settings: MAIN= |
-----------------------------------------------------------------
```

Figure 21.8

Notice that you defined the Output range by specifying only the two cells containing the field names. In fact, you can either designate the Output range as the single row of cells containing the field names or as a block of cells containing the field names and several blank rows. For example, you could use the range E1 . . F3 to define the Output range in this example.

If you define the Output range as a multirow range of cells, you must be sure to include enough rows in the range to accommodate all the records that may be extracted from the main data base. If you do not provide enough room for the extracted data, Symphony delivers the message "Output range full" and aborts the extraction. If you see this message, press [Esc]. Notice that Symphony fills the Output range to capacity before it issues the error message.

If you designate the Output range as the single row containing the field names, Symphony assumes that the range extends downward from those cells all the way to the bottom of the worksheet. In other words, selecting a one-row data base frees you from any concern about whether the Output range is large enough to handle all the records the Extract command might put into it.

However, there is also a disadvantage in using one-row Output ranges. Every time you issue the Extract command, Symphony erases every cell in the Output range before it fills it again with the records that meet the criteria. If the Output range has been defined as a one-row range, Symphony erases every cell from that row to the bottom of the worksheet. If that range contains important data, you are out of luck. For this reason, always try to set up a one-row Output range in totally empty columns.

Extracting the Records

Now we are ready to test the Extract command. Simply issue the {**Menu**} **Q**uery **E**xtract command, and Symphony will copy the contents of the Quantity and Item#

fields for each of the records with the Supplier ABC Ltd into the Output range. The resulting worksheet is shown in Figure 21.9.

```
   ---A----------B----------C----------D----------E----------F----
 1      Item#     Supplier   Quantity            Quantity     Item#   |
 2                ABC Ltd.                                  37 16     |
 3                                                          37 16     |
 4                                                          52 9D     |
 5                                                                    |
 6                                                                    |
 7      Item#     Supplier   Quantity                                 |
 8  AZ27          XYZ Inc.          16                                |
 9  16            ABC Ltd.          37                                |
10  185           XYZ Inc.           8                                |
11  37E           QRS Co.           43                                |
12  139XX         DEF Inc.          96                                |
13  AZ27          XYZ Inc.          27                                |
14  16            ABC Ltd.          37                                |
15  9D            ABC Ltd.          52                                |
16  185           DEF Inc.          74                                |
17  Q563          QRS Co.          100                                |
18                                                                    |
   ================================================================MAIN=
```

Figure 21.9

Notice that Symphony copied the Quantity and Item# information in rows 9, 14, and 15 into cells E2 . . F4 in the Output range. Because only the Quantity and Item# fields are in the Output range, only the contents of these two fields are copied to the Output range. If, on the other hand, the Output range had been defined in the settings sheet as E1 . . G1, and if cell G1 contained the field name Supplier, the completed Output range would look like Figure 21.10.

```
   ----E----------F---------G-----
 1 Quantity     Item#     Supplier   |
 2         37 16           ABC Ltd.  |
 3         37 16           ABC Ltd.  |
 4         52 9D           ABC Ltd.  |
 5                                   |
   ============================MAIN=
```

Figure 21.10

If we had defined the Output range in the example as the block E1 . . F3, Symphony would not have been able to copy all of the matching records into the Output range. Instead, only the first two records would have been copied, and Symphony would have displayed the message "Output range full".

Suppose you want to repeat the first Extract operation using QRS Co. as the entry in the Criterion range instead of ABC Ltd. To perform this extraction, change the Criterion range by moving the cell pointer to cell B2 and entering the label **QRS Co.** Since the Database, Criterion, and Output ranges have already been defined, all you have left to do is issue the {**Menu**} **Q**uery **E**xtract command. Figure 21.11 shows the completed worksheet.

```
    ---A-----------B-----------C-----------D-----------E-----------F----
  1    Item#      Supplier    Quantity                 Quantity   Item#   |
  2               QRS Co.                                    43 37E       |
  3                                                         100 Q563      |
  4                                                                       |
  5                                                                       |
  6                                                                       |
  7    Item#      Supplier    Quantity                                    |
  8  AZ27         XYZ Inc.          16                                    |
  9  16           ABC Ltd.          37                                    |
 10  185          XYZ Inc.           8                                    |
 11  37E          QRS Co.           43                                    |
 12  139XX        DEF Inc.          96                                    |
 13  AZ27         XYZ Inc.          27                                    |
 14  16           ABC Ltd.          37                                    |
 15  9D           ABC Ltd.          52                                    |
 16  185          DEF Inc.          74                                    |
 17  Q563         QRS Co.          100                                    |
 18                                                                       |
    =============================================================MAIN=
```

Figure 21.11

Notice that cells E2 . . F3 contain the quantity and item number information from the two fields in the data base with the Supplier field QRS Co. Notice also that cells E4 and F4, which had contained the third entry from the previous extraction, are now blank. Remember that Symphony automatically erases the entire Output range immediately before it copies the matching records into that range. Since the Output range in the example is a one-row range, meaning that Symphony considers the Output range to extend from row 2 to row 8192, the Extract command erased every cell in this range.

Extracting Unique Records

The Unique command works essentially the same way as the Extract command, with one important exception. If two or more of the records that match the stated criteria are identical in all fields contained in the Output range, the Query Unique command inserts only one of those records into the Output range. In other words, the Unique command is a quick and convenient way to purge your data base of duplicate entries.

We'll use the worksheet shown in Figure 21.9 to demonstrate the Unique command. The Output range in this worksheet is E1 . . F1, the Criterion range is A1 . . C2, and the Database range is A7 . . C17. The Output range in this example contains the results of the first Extract demonstration. Remember that we don't have to erase the contents of this range before issuing the Unique command, because Symphony does it automatically once you issue the command.

To instruct Symphony to copy the specified fields of these unique records to the Output range, issue the {**Menu**} **Q**uery **U**nique command. Symphony first erases any existing contents in the Output range and then copies the records to this range. The resulting Output range looks like Figure 21.12.

```
  ------E----------F-----
1 Quantity    Item#      |
2         37 16          |
3         52 9D          |
4                        |
    =================MAIN=
```

Figure 21.12

Notice that although the records in rows 9 and 14 in the data base both match the specified criteria, Symphony inserts only one copy of the Quantity and Item# fields of these two records into the Output range.

Problems with Unique

In the previous example, it is possible that you accidentally entered the results of your inventory of item number 16 twice and that the Unique command caught and corrected the error. However, it is also possible that you had 37 of item number 16 from ABC Ltd. in one part of your warehouse and another 37 of these same parts in another area, so that these records are not really duplicates. In this case, the Unique command provides incorrect information.

An alternative to using Unique to eliminate duplicate entries from a data base is to use the Extract command to collect all the records of interest into the Output range, and then use the Record-Sort command to sort the extracted information so that all identical entries appear together. You can then scan the Output range and use the SHEET Erase and Delete commands to remove duplicate records from the data base. In this way you can view the multiple entries before you decide to delete them.

Remember that the Unique command affects only the records in the Database range that are identical in the fields specified in the Output range. In other words, with the Output range shown in Figure 21.9, which includes only the field names Item# and Quantity, the Unique command would select only one of the following two records, even though they clearly differ:

Item#	Supplier	Quantity	Date
16	ABC Inc.	37	11/24/83
16	ABC Inc.	37	7/02/84

One of the most useful applications for the Unique command is eliminating duplicate records in a mailing list. This can save money that would otherwise be wasted sending two pieces of mail to a single individual.

DELETING CRITERIA-MATCHING RECORDS

Another powerful data base management command available only in a SHEET window is Query Delete. This command gives you the ability to automatically delete from a data base all records that meet the criteria specified in the Criterion range.

There are a number of situations when this capability is quite useful. For instance, suppose that in the inventory example above, ABC Ltd. recalls all of item number 16 due to a manufacturing defect. You can use the Query Delete command to erase all appearances of this item. To do this, you must first redefine the Criterion range so that all records with 16 in the Item# field and ABC in the Supplier field will be selected. The appropriate Criterion range is shown in Figure 21.13. Because all of the entries in the Item# field are labels and not numbers, you must be sure that the entry in cell A2 is a label—either specify it as '16, "16, or ^16.

```
    ----A----------B----------C----------D----
1      Item#      Supplier   Quantity           |
2  16             ABC Ltd.                       |
3                                                |
   =====================================MAIN=
```

Figure 21.13

Now we are ready to delete these records from the data base. Since the Database and Criterion ranges are already defined (Query Delete does not use an Output range), all you must do to delete the records is issue the {**Menu**} **Q**uery **D**elete command. Symphony finds all the records that match the criteria, deletes them from the data base, and shifts the remaining entries to fill in the vacant spots. Symphony also adjusts the boundaries of the Database range to reflect this deletion. When the command is finished, the worksheet looks like the one in Figure 21.14.

```
    ----A---------B----------C----------D----
7   Item#      Supplier   Quantity           |
8   AZ27       XYZ Inc.        16            |
9   185        XYZ Inc.         8            |
10  37         QRS Co.         43            |
11  139XX      DEF Inc.        96            |
12  AZ27       XYZ Inc.        27            |
13  9D         ABC Ltd.        52            |
14  185        DEF Inc.        74            |
15  Q563       QRS Co.        100            |
16                                           |
17                                           |
   =====================================MAIN=
```

Figure 21.14

The command deleted two records from the data base and contracted the data base to fill in the spaces left by these deletions. A quick look at the data base settings sheet in Figure 21.15 shows that the Database range has also been contracted by 2 rows.

```
 ----------------------------------------------------------------
|  Basic Ranges                        Report Ranges            |
|     Database:       A7..C15              Main:                 |
|     Criterion:      A1..C2               Above:                |
|     Output:         D1..E1               Below:                |
|  Form Ranges                             Type:        Single   |
|     Entry:                               Entry list:           |
|     Definition:                          Input cell:           |
|  Underscores:       Yes                  One-Record: No        |
|  Sort-Keys                                                     |
|     1st-Key:               2nd-Key:              3rd-Key:      |
|       Order:                 Order:                Order:      |
|                                                                |
| ==========================================Database Settings: MAIN= |
 ----------------------------------------------------------------
```

Figure 21.15

Because Query Delete permanently erases all records that match the specified criteria, you should be extremely careful when using this command. I suggest that you use {Services} File Save to save your data base on disk before you use the Delete command. In addition, you should always double-check the boundaries and contents of the Criterion range prior to invoking this command. If you use the Query Delete command with an empty Criterion range (which matches all records), it will delete every record in the data base. If your Criterion range contains even a single totally blank row, all of the records in the data base will be deleted.

THE QUERY PARSE COMMAND

Up to this point, we have discussed data base functions that either have counterparts in the FORM window or are found in Lotus 1-2-3. The next command—Query Parse—doesn't fit into either of those categories, and it will take a bit of explaining and practice to master. Once you get the hang of it, though, the Query Parse command will prove to be very useful, especially for data communications applications.

Symphony has the ability to take any row of data in the worksheet and feed it into a data base, dividing that line of characters to fit into the columns of the data base. Using the Query Parse command, you can instruct Symphony to fill a data base, using almost any range of text in the worksheet. In effect, you can use Query Parse to divide long labels into smaller labels that can be entered in different columns in a data base.

As an example, suppose you have created the data shown in Figure 21.16 as a part of a document while working in a Symphony DOC window. As you recall, each line of a Symphony document is stored as a long label in a single column of the worksheet. For example, cell A9 contains the label

A9: '16 ABC Ltd. 37 12/24/83

You'd like to work with this information as a data base, but you can't right away, because the fields are not in separate columns of the worksheet. The Query Parse command takes care of this problem.

```
    --------------------A---------------------------B-----
 7  Item#       Supplier        Quantity     Date            |
 8  AZ27        XYZ Inc.              16  03/05/84            |
 9  16          ABC Ltd.             37  12/24/83            |
10  185         XYZ Inc.              8  11/02/83            |
11  37E         QRS Co.              43  06/30/84            |
12  139XX       DEF Inc.             96  07/02/84            |
    ===================================================MAIN=
```

Figure 21.16

First, you need to create a Definition range and a Database range and define them in a data base settings sheet. You can do this manually, but it is much more convenient to use the Generate command and let Symphony do the work.

To create the required data base, enter the field definitions shown in Figure 21.17 into cells A49 to A52. Notice that the data base defined by these entries includes fields for each of the segments in the long labels in Figure 21.16: Item#, Supplier, Quantity, and Date. In addition, notice that each of the fields has been assigned a specific type and length. I'll explain the importance of the type and length in a few pages.

```
    ---A-----------B-----------C------
49  Item#:L:9                           |
50  Supplier:L:15                       |
51  Quantity:N:8                        |
52  Date:D:9                            |
53                                      |
    =============================MAIN=
```

Figure 21.17

Use the FORM Generate command to create a data base, complete with Definition range and other related ranges. The result will be the data base shown in Figure 21.18.

Notice that the Definition range in Figure 21.18 (A59 . . F63) includes the length and type definitions you assigned to each field in the range A49 . . A52. These specifications are crucial to the Parse process.

Now you are ready to parse the data in your document into the data base. Switch back to a SHEET window and press {**Menu**}. Select Query from the SHEET command menu and then select Parse. Symphony asks you to supply the range to parse. Use the cursor-movement keys and the period key to highlight the range A8 . . A12. There is no need to highlight the field names along with the data. Symphony would disregard that row anyway.

In the example, the long labels fit entirely in the widened column A, so the range A8 . . A12 includes all of the data you want to parse. However, if the entries to be parsed spill over into other columns, you need to highlight all the columns the labels spill over into,

```
    -----A-----------B----------C--------D--------E--------F-------
 49 Item#:L:9                                                       |
 50 Supplier:L:15                                                   |
 51 Quantity:N:8                                                    |
 52 Date:D:9                                                        |
 53                                                                 |
 54 Item#   _____                                                 |
 55 Supplier _____                                                |
 56 Quantity _____                                          |
 57 Date    _____                                               |
 58                                                                 |
 59    Name      Value       Type      Default  Formula  Validity  |
 60 Item#                    L:9                                    |
 61 Supplier                 L:15                                   |
 62 Quantity                 N:8                                    |
 63 Date                     D:9                                    |
 64                                                                 |
 65 Item#     Supplier       QuantityDate                          |
 66                                                                 |
 67                                                                 |
 68 Item#     Supplier       QuantityDate                          |
 69                                                                 |
 70                                                                 |
 71                                                                 |
 72                                                                 |
 73 Item#     Supplier       QuantityDate                          |
 74                                                                 |
    ===========================================================MAIN=
```

Figure 21.18

not just the single column where they "start." Otherwise, Symphony truncates the data and the Parse operation will be unsuccessful.

After you have highlighted the Parse range and pressed [Enter], Symphony asks you to designate a Review range. This is where Symphony puts all the data it discards in the Parse process (such as the field names, if you include them in the Parse range.) You need to specify only one cell for the Review range. Symphony interprets this as the upper-left cell of the range, filling in the rows below and to the right with the discarded data. The Review range generally should be in an unused part of the worksheet. In this example, use the cell Z1 as the Review range.

Now when you press [Enter], Symphony proceeds to parse this data. Let's walk through the process step by step. Symphony operates on the first label in the Parse range first, which in this case is in cell A8:

A8: 'AZ27 XYZ Inc. 16 03/05/84

The Parse command divides this long label into smaller labels according to the length settings for each field in the Definition range. Since the first field in the Definition range, Item#, is 9 characters wide, Symphony chops off the first 9 characters of the long label in cell A7 and enters that label into the first row of the data base under the Item# header. The first 9 character include the characters AZ27 and 5 spaces.

Because the second field in the data base is 15 characters wide, Symphony splits off the next 15 characters from the long label and enters that segment into the data base under the field name Supplier. This segment includes the characters XYZ Inc. and 7 blank spaces.

As you can see in the Definition range, the next field in the data base, Quantity, is 8 characters wide. This means that Symphony enters the next 8 characters of the long label into the first row of the data base under the header Quantity. This third segment includes the characters 16 preceded by 6 empty spaces.

Finally, Symphony enters the next 9 characters into the data base under the header Date. This segment includes the characters 03/05/84 and one trailing space.

The Parse command also uses the Type setting for each field to determine what type of entry each of the segments should become when they enter the data base. For example, the type for the first field, Item#, is label, so the first segment will be entered in the data base as a label. The segments parsed into the field Supplier will also be entered as labels. However, the type of the Quantity field is number, so the segments parsed into this field will be treated as values by the data base. The label segment " 16" is thus converted into the number 16. Similarly, Symphony converts the date type segment "03/05/84 " into the date value 30746 (30746 is Symphony's representation for the date March 5, 1984.)

After processing this first label, Symphony continues with the remaining labels in the Parse range. When the last label has been parsed, the data base looks like Figure 21.19. Not only has the Parse command separated the long labels in the document into four distinct columns, it also converted those entries into the appropriate field type. As you can see, Symphony uses the parameters defined in the eight columns of the Definition range to divide these rows of data into segments of a specified type and length so that they could be entered into the data base.

```
    -----A-----------B----------C--------D------
73 Item#       Supplier       QuantityDate          |
74 AZ27        XYZ Inc.             16      30746    |
75 16          ABC Ltd.             37      30674    |
76 185         XYZ Inc.              8      30622    |
77 37E         QRS Co.              43      30863    |
78 139XX       DEF Inc.             96      30865    |
    =====================================MAIN=
```

Figure 21.19

For example, cell A74 contains the label

A74: 'AZ27

and cell C74 contains the value

C74: 16

In the example, you defined the widths of the columns in the data base to match exactly the lengths of the segments in the labels you wanted to parse. For this reason, the final data base contains all of the characters that were part of the original labels. Suppose you had set up the data base so that all of the fields were only 9 characters wide and then had parsed the label in cell A8 through that data base. The resulting data base would look like Figure 21.20.

```
    -----A--------B--------C--------D--------E------
 73 Item#      Supplier  Quantity Date              |
 74 AZ27       XYZ Inc.            16       3        |
 75 16         ABC Ltd.           37       3        |
 76 185        XYZ Inc.            8       3        |
 77 37E        QRS Co.            43       3        |
 78 139XX      DEF Inc.           96       3        |
    ========================================MAIN=
```

Figure 21.20

These are the contents of some of the cells in row 74 of this range:

    A74: 'AZ27
    B74: 'XYZ Inc.
    C74: '
    D74: ' 16 3

As you can see, using column widths that do not match the lengths of the segments in the long labels causes the Parse command to divide the labels in strange ways.

The Parse command is the only SHEET data base function that requires the definition of anything more than the three Basic Ranges: the Database range, the Criterion range, and the Output range. Before using the Query Parse command, you must create a Definition range in the data base settings sheet.

Because every piece of data being parsed passes through the Definition range, you can configure this range to insert default values, perform validity checks, and even perform calculations on the data being parsed. Refer to Chapter 19 for a complete explanation of the features of the Definition range.

One common application for the Query Parse command is the conversion of lines of text captured in a COMM window into a usable columnar structure and type. A detailed example of this application is presented in Chapter 25, Getting On Line with Symphony.

Spend some time working through this example and the Parse example in the COMM chapter so that you become familiar with the Parse process. Mastering this command will make your data base work simpler and will expand your ability to deal with information received in a COMM window.

DATA BASE STATISTICS

In addition to the Query commands, Symphony offers another set of tools that can be used to work on a data base in a SHEET window: data base statistical functions. These functions work exclusively on the contents of Symphony data bases.

Each data base statistical function has an equivalent regular function. For example, the function @DSUM is similar to the @SUM function. However, while regular functions operate on a range of cells in the worksheet, the data base functions operate on the contents of a specific field in selected records in a data base. For example, the @SUM function computes the sum of a range of cells in the worksheet, while the @DSUM function computes the sum of the entries in a single field for certain records of a data base.

Symphony offers seven data base statistical functions: @DAVG, @DCOUNT, @DSUM, @DMAX, @DMIN, @DVAR, and @DSTD. @DAVG calculates the mean value of the entries in a field of selected records in the data base. Similarly, the @DSTD function calculates the standard deviation, and @DVAR calculates the variance of the values in the specified field of the selected records. The @DMAX and @DMIN functions extract the highest or lowest values from a field of selected records. The @DSUM function adds all of the values of the selected fields, while the @DCOUNT function counts the number of nonblank cells.

Since you need a data base and a Criterion range before you can use these functions, use the Generate command to create a simple example. In adjacent empty cells in a single column, type the field specifications shown in Figure 21.21.

```
     -----A-----------B-----------C-------
 1 Date:D:9                               |
 2 Item:L:9                               |
 3 Number:N:9                             |
 4 Price:N:9                              |
 5 Total:N:9                              |
   ==============================MAIN=
```

Figure 21.21

Next, switch to a FORM window and use the Generate command to create the data base and related ranges. Use the name DFCN for the data base settings sheet. Finally, use the Entry form to enter the records shown in Figure 21.22 into the data base.

```
    ----A-----------B---------C---------D--------E----------F------
28 Date          Item     Number   Price    Total                 |
29      30468    widget      5      1.52      7.6                  |
30      30499    doodad      8      3.27     26.16                 |
31      30543    widget     17      1.86     31.62                 |
32      30586    widget     36      2.07     74.52                 |
33      30619    doodad      2      2.95      5.9                  |
34      30599    gizmo       1      2.50      2.5                  |
   ==================================================MAIN=
```

Figure 21.22

Next, you need to place criteria in the Criterion range. To do this, switch back to the FORM window, select Criteria Edit from the command menu, enter "widget" in the Item field, and press **[Ins]**. A switch back to the SHEET window reveals the contents of the Criterion range, shown in cells A23 . . E24 of Figure 21.23.

A look at the data base settings sheet shows us that the Database range (A28 . . E34) has been named DFCN_DB, and the Criterion range (A23 . . E24) has been named DFCN_CR. Remember these names; we will use them often with the @D functions.

```
    ----A----------B--------C--------D--------E--------F---
 23 Date         Item       Number   Price    Total          |
 24              widget                                       |
 25                                                           |
    =========================================================MAIN=
```

Figure 21.23

@DAVG

Now that the preliminaries are out of the way, let's use the @DAVG function to demonstrate the general format of these seven functions. Suppose you want to know the average price you paid per widget during the five-month period covered by your data base. The Criterion range specifies that only records with "widget" in the Item field will be selected. The @DAVG function does the rest. To compute this average, enter the following formula in cell F29:

F29: @DAVG(DFCN_DB,3,DFCN_CR)

This example shows the standard form of a data base function. The first part of the function is the function name—in this case @DAVG. The name is followed by the argument, which has three parts. The first part of the argument designates the Database range to be acted upon. In the example, we've used the range name, DFCN_DB, to designate the range. You could also specify this range by entering its coordinates: A28 . . E34.

The second part of the argument, 3, is called the offset. This term tells Symphony which field in the Database range you want the function to operate on. Choosing an offset can be confusing, because the left-most column of the data base is assigned an offset of 0, the second column has an offset of 1, and so on. In the example, you want to compute the average of the Price field. Although the Price field is the fourth column in the data base, its offset is 3.

The final part of the argument designates the Criterion range that Symphony should use in selecting the records. In our example this Criterion range is the one defined in the previous section, DFCN_CR.

When this function is entered into cell F29, Symphony calculates the value of the function and displays that value as a number in cell F29, as shown in Figure 21.24. This function averages the values from cells D29, D31, and D32, the Price fields of each of the records with the label widget in the Item field.

```
    ----A----------B--------C--------D--------E----------F------
 28 Date            Item    Number   Price    Total                    |
 29     30468  widget         5       1.52        7.6     1.816666 |
 30     30499  doodad         8       3.27       26.16             |
 31     30543  widget        17       1.86       31.62             |
 32     30586  widget        36       2.07       74.52             |
 33     30619  doodad         2       2.95        5.9              |
 34     30599  gizmo          1       2.50        2.5              |
        =========================================================MAIN=
```

Figure 21.24

@DCOUNT

The @DCOUNT function works in the same way. If you enter the function

> F30: @DCOUNT(DFCN_DB,0,DFCN_CR)

into any cell in the worksheet (we've selected F30 arbitrarily), Symphony displays the number 3, the number of entries in the data base that meet the criterion (the label widget in the Item field).

With @DCOUNT, it really doesn't matter which field the offset term refers to, as long as each record has an entry in every field. In other words, the function

> F30: @DCOUNT(DFCN_DB,3,DFCN_CR)

would also return the value 3.

@DCOUNT is useful for computing a quick count of the number of records in a data base that meet the specified criteria. For example, you can use @DCOUNT to find out how many accounts in an accounts receivable data base are over 90 days old, or how many employees in an employee data base are over 55 years old.

@DSUM

The @DSUM function simply adds up the values in the selected field of the records that match the criteria. If you enter the formula

> F31: @DSUM(DFCN_DB,4,DFCN_CR)

into cell F31, Symphony displays the number 113.74, which is the sum of the values in cells E29, E31, and E32.

@DSUM only functions correctly when the field referred to by the offset term is a number. If the field is a label field, the function returns 0, since @DSUM, like @SUM, assigns the value 0 to all labels. For example, the function

> F31: @DSUM(DFCN_DB,1,DFCN_CR)

returns the value 0, since the Item field of DFCN_DB contains only labels.

@DMAX and @DMIN

The @DMAX function selects the maximum value from the designated field of the selected records. For example, the function

      F32: @DMAX(DFCN_DB,3,DFCN_CR)

instructs Symphony to display in cell F32 the highest price you paid for a widget—the value 2.07.

Similarly, @DMIN returns the lowest value in the specified fields of the selected records. For example, the function

      F33: @DMIN(DFCN_DB,3,DFCN_CR)

returns the value 1.52. Like @DSUM, @DMAX and @DMIN assign the value 0 to labels. When these functions are applied to fields containing only labels, they return the value 0.

@DVAR and @DSTD

The last two data base statistical functions, @DVAR and @DSTD, compute the variance and standard deviation of the values in the specified field for the selected records. For example, the function

      F34: @DVAR(DFCN_DB,3,DFCN_CR)

returns the value 0.0513555, the variance of the three numbers 2.07, 1.52, and 1.86. Similarly, the function

      F35: @DSTD(DFCN_DB,3,DFCN_CR)

returns 0.2266, the standard deviation of the numbers 2.07, 1.52, and 1.86. For a general discussion of the meaning of variance and standard deviation, see the discussion of the @VAR and @STD functions in Chapter 4.

Data Base Function Notes

There are a couple of fine points you should keep in mind when using data base functions. First, remember that the offset term in an @D function can never exceed the number of columns in the Database range referred to by the function. For example, the function

      @DSUM(A1 . . C5,3,D1 . . E2)

would return the @ERR message, because the offset term, 3, tells the function to compute the sum of the *fourth* column of a Database range that includes only *three* columns: A, B, and C.

Another thing to remember about @D functions is that the Database range argument and the Criterion range argument in these functions do not have to refer to a data base or criteria range that is defined in a settings sheet. In the examples, we chose the ranges DFCN_DB and DFCN_CR for the data base and criteria terms of the function. These names refer to the data base defined in the previous section. However, we could have referred to any other data base in the worksheet, including a data base that is not defined in a settings sheet. Likewise, the Criterion range you use does not need to be defined in a data base settings sheet. However, the Criterion range you use must agree with the data base range referred to by that same function.

It is important that you understand that data base functions are like all other functions in that they exist as cell entries in the spreadsheet. You can enter an @D function in any part of a worksheet, not just near a data base.

Like all functions, data base functions are recalculated when you press {**Calc**}. If you want to recompute a data base statistical function using new criteria, you need change only the entries in the Criterion range and then press {**Calc**} to recalculate the worksheet.

ADVANCED CRITERIA

Now that you have learned about the SHEET Query commands and about data base statistical functions—it is appropriate to consider Criterion ranges and criteria again. In Chapter 20 you learned the basic structure and function of the Criterion range. That chapter covers the use of simple "exact-match" criteria, logical ANDs and ORs, and three special characters (?, *, and ˜). Beginning users of Symphony data bases will find these basics sufficient for most data base uses.

However, as you gain experience with Symphony's data base capabilities, you probably will run into situations in which these basic tools simply are not powerful enough to select exactly the records you desire. In this section, we will explore the use of more sophisticated criteria. The use of these advanced tools greatly expands the usefulness of your data bases.

In the following examples, we will use the inventory data base you created for the discussion of the data base functions, shown in Figure 21.22. The Criterion range that accompanies this data base occupies rows 23 and 24, with nothing yet specified in row 24.

Simple Formulas

First, let's take a look at how you can use simple formulas as criteria within the Criterion range. To do this, enter the simple formula

    C24: +C29>5

into cell C24 of the Criterion range. This formula tells Symphony to select only records for which the entry in the Number field is greater than 5.

If you use the Query Find command or any other criteria-dependent data base command at this point, Symphony selects only the second, third, and fourth records from the data base, since these are the only records whose value in the Number column is greater than 5.

Notice that this criterion refers to the first cell in the Number field of our data base. Whenever you use a formula in a Criterion range that refers to one of the fields in the data base, the formula should refer to the first record in the desired field. For example, suppose you want to select all of the records for which the value in the Date field is greater than 30500. Entering the formula

    A24: +A29>30500

in cell A24 does the trick. Notice that this formula refers to the first cell in the Date field.

Look at the Criterion range in the previous example. Notice that although the formula +C29>5 is in cell C24, Symphony displays the number 0 in this cell of the worksheet, as shown in Figure 21.25.

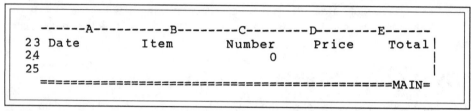

```
      ------A----------B--------C--------D--------E------
  23 Date          Item        Number     Price      Total|
  24                              0                        |
  25                                                       |
     =========================================-======MAIN=
```

Figure 21.25

This occurs because Symphony evaluates criteria formulas, like any other logical formula, as being either true or false. If the formula is false, Symphony displays a 0. If the logical formula is true, Symphony returns the value 1. In this case, since the current value in cell C29 is not greater than 5, Symphony evaluates the formula as false and displays a 0 in cell C24.

If the first data cell of a field has been given a name (Symphony does this automatically as a result of the Generate command), you can use that name as the cell reference in the formula. In this case, if cell C29 was named NUMBER, you could have entered the criterion

    C24: +NUMBER>5

in cell C24.

The easiest way to enter this criterion is to simply type +?>5 into the Number blank of the Entry form that accompanies this data base, as shown in Figure 21.26. (This figure shows the form as it looks before you press [Enter] to "lock in" the entry.)

```
    Editing Criterion Record 1 of 1
    Enter Number
    -----------------------------------------------
    |  Date     _____                            |
    |  Item     _____                            |
    |  Number   +?>5                               |
    |  Price    _____                            |
    |  Total    _____                            |
    |                                              |
    -----------------------------------------------
```

Figure 21.26

Symphony automatically interprets the ? as referring to the first cell of corresponding field in the data base. In fact, Symphony converts the ? into the proper cell reference as soon as you press [Enter] to "lock in" the entry, as shown in Figure 21.27. Unfortunately, this method of entering a complex criterion only works when you enter the criterion through a FORM window.

```
 Editing Criterion Record 1 of 1
 Enter Price
 -------------------------------------------
| Date    _____                         |
| Item    _____                         |
| Number  +NUMBER>5                         |
| Price   _____                         |
| Total   _____                         |
|                                           |
 -------------------------------------------
```

Figure 21.27

More Complex Formulas

You can use any of the logical operators ($>$, $<$, $=$, $<=$, or $>=$) to create different criteria. Also, instead of comparing the entries in a field of a data base to a fixed number, you may wish to compare them to the contents of a cell outside of the data base. For instance, suppose that you want to select records whose Price field value is less than or equal to the value of the contents of cell Q52. You can enter the following formula directly into cell D24 of the worksheet:

D24: +D29 < = $Q$52

Symphony compares the value of the Price field for each of the records in the data base to the current value of cell Q52. The entry in cell Q52 may be a number or a formula.

Be sure to use an absolute reference when referring to cells outside the data base. If you use a relative reference, Symphony will "move" the comparison cell as it goes down the list of records in the data base. For instance, if you had used the formula

D24: +D29 < = Q52

in the previous example, Symphony would use the formula +D30 < = Q53 as the criterion when evaluating the second record in the data base, +D31 < = Q54 when evaluating the third record in the data base, and so forth. The results would not be satisfactory at all.

You can also use simple formulas as criteria for label fields. For instance, if you want to select all records whose Item name begins with a letter greater than the letter "e", use this formula in cell B24:

B24: +B29 >"e"

In our example, Symphony would choose only the widgets and the gizmo, not the doodads.

Combining Formulas with #AND# and #OR

You can go even further by combining two simple formulas with logical ANDs or ORs. For instance, suppose you want to know which records have a value in the Number field between 7 and 35. This is a logical AND situation, which can be handled only by entering the following formula in cell C24:

C24: +C29>=7#AND#+C29<=35

Suppose you want to select all items whose value in the Price field is less than $2.00, as well as those items for which the Price value is greater than $3.00. You can designate this kind of logical OR criterion in two ways. First, you can use the Settings Basic Criteria command to expand the Criterion range to cover cells A23 . . E25 and then enter the formula

D24: +D29<2

in cell D24 and the formula

D25: +D29>3

in cell D25. You learned about this method in the earlier discussion of criteria basics.

Alternatively, you can keep the Criterion range at its original size and enter the following formula into cell D24:

D24: +D29<2#OR#+D29>3

The result of these two methods is identical. Either way, Symphony selects the first three records, with values of $1.52, $3.27, and $1.86 in their Price fields.

Using #NOT# in Criteria

Finally, just as you can negate simple label criteria by using the ˜ character, you can negate formulas by typing the characters #NOT# immediately in front of the formula. For instance, if you want to select all records whose value in the Total field is not greater than $10.00, you can type the following formula in cell E24:

E24: #NOT#+E29>10

Note that this has exactly the same effect as the formula +E29<=10. In both cases, Symphony will select only the first and last two records in the data base.

Remember that any of these formulas may be entered into the Criterion range either directly into the cells of the worksheet from a SHEET window or indirectly through an Entry form in a FORM window.

As you can see, even simple formulas can significantly increase the power of the Criterion range. However, there are still other types of criteria that we can use. These next examples will be a bit more complicated than the ones above, but they are not hard to master.

Using Functions as Criteria

Many of Symphony's regular functions are also useful tools for building criteria. First, let's use the @LENGTH function to specify the length of each record's entry in a particular field as the basis for selection. Continuing with our inventory data base, let's enter the following formula into cell B24:

B24: @LENGTH(+ B29) > 5

This criterion instructs Symphony to select only records whose entry in the Item field is longer than five characters. In this case, Symphony will not select the gizmo record, since the string "gizmo" has only five characters. However, since the strings "widget" and "doodad" have six characters each, Symphony will select all of the widget and doodad records.

To make criteria even more complex, you can combine two @LENGTH functions with a logical AND, like this:

B24: @LENGTH(+ B29) > 5#AND#@LENGTH(+ B29) < 7

This criterion tells Symphony to select records in the Item field with more than five but fewer than seven characters.

The @LEFT function can be used to select the left-most character or group of characters from within an entry as the basis for selection. For instance, you might want to select all of the records whose Item field has the first three characters "wid". To do this, enter the following formula in cell C24:

C24: @LEFT(D29,3) = "wid"

This tells Symphony to look for the left-most three characters for each record's Item entry and to select only those records in which these characters are "wid". Notice that this criterion is identical to the simpler wild-card criterion "wid*".

The other substring functions, @RIGHT, @MID, @FIND, and @EXACT, can also be used in Criterion ranges. All these functions work in essentially the same way as the @LEFT function, except that they operate on different parts of the string.

Using Dates as Criteria

You will often need to use dates as criteria for selecting records. The way you specify these criteria depends on whether you are entering them from a SHEET or a FORM window and whether you are specifying an exact match or using a formula.

The simplest way is to enter an exact-match criteria from a FORM window. In this case, you simply enter the date you want to match into the appropriate "blank" in the Entry form, in MM/DD/YY format. For example, if you want to select all the records that have a value of August 15, 1983 in the Date field, enter **8/15/83** into the Date blank of the Entry form associated with this data base.

If you specify that field as type D, Symphony automatically converts the entry into serial date format, as it does for the Date fields of the record entered into the data base through the form. In this case, when the criterion is used, Symphony searches for a value of 30543 in the Date field of each record.

If you wish to use a date criterion in a formula form, however, the situation is a bit more complicated. For instance, Symphony will not accept the entry + A29 < = 8/15/83 in the blank of an Entry form corresponding to a Date field type. In this case, you either must convert the date to serial date format yourself or use the @DATEVALUE function. This function converts dates from the MM/DD/YY format into the five-digit serial format Symphony uses.

For example, if you want Symphony to select all the records in our example data base that have a date of August 15, 1983 or earlier, enter the following formula directly into the Date blank of the Entry form:

+ ? < = @DATEVALUE("8/15/83")

Symphony automatically calculates the serial equivalent of 8/15/83 and enters the following formula into cell A24:

A24: + A29 < = 30543

Using this criterion, Symphony selects only the first three records from the data base, which have entries in the Date field equal to 30468, 30499, and 30543, respectively.

So far we have discussed entering date criteria only through a FORM window. Anytime you enter these criteria directly into the worksheet from a SHEET window, either as exact matches or inequalities, you'll need to use the @DATEVALUE function as we did above. For example, if you want to match all records that have a date of 8/15/83, enter the following formula directly into cell A24 of the worksheet:

A24: + A29 = @DATEVALUE("8/15/83")

Again, Symphony converts the MM/DD/YY date into a serial date format, which matches the entries in the Date field of our data base.

The tools presented here, combined with those in Chapter 20, are the building blocks you require to master the use of data base criteria. As you work with Symphony data bases, you will find ways to combine the concepts presented here to develop even more sophisticated Criterion ranges, making Symphony's data base management capabilities even more powerful.

CHAPTER TWENTY TWO
ADVANCED DATA BASE TOPICS

In this final chapter on Symphony data bases, we will explore two advanced topics: how to "customize" an Entry form and how to print various data base reports. These discussions draw upon Symphony data base principles covered in the previous three chapters, so before you attempt to follow these examples, make sure you feel comfortable with most of this previous material.

CUSTOMIZING AN ENTRY FORM

Although the Generate command provides a convenient way to set up a data base and related ranges, the standard Entry form is not always ideal for all applications. In this section, we will review how to modify the standard Entry form.

Remember that the Entry form that appears in the FORM window is an exact copy of the contents of the Entry range in the underlying worksheet. So to change this form, you must go to the worksheet and modify the contents of the block of cells defined as the Entry range. We'll again use our standard address-book data base example to clarify these concepts.

Briefly, let's review the results of the Generate command. In the example, you specified five fields, all designated as labels, with varying field lengths, as shown in Figure 22.1.

```
   -----A---------B---------C------
 1 Name:L:20                      |
 2 Street:L:25                    |
 3 City:L:20                      |
 4 State:L:2                      |
 5 Zip:L:5                        |
 6                                |
 7                                |
   ========================MAIN=
```

Figure 22.1

Using these entries as the range of field names, the Generate command produces a number of ranges in the worksheet, as well as a standard Entry form. The resulting Entry form is shown in Figure 22.2. The related worksheet containing the Entry range and part of the Definition range appears in Figure 22.3.

```
---------------------------------------------------
|   Name _____              |
|   Street _____        |
|   City _____            |
|   State __                                        |
|   Zip _____                                       |
|                                                   |
    =MAIN==================================MAIN=
```

Figure 22.2

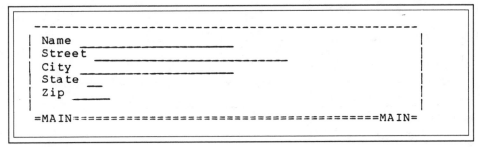

```
          ----------A---------------------B---------------------------C-----
    1    Name:L:20                                                            |
    2    Street:L:25                                                          |
    3    City:L:20                                                            |
    4    State:L:2                                                            |
    5    Zip:L:5                                                              |
    6                                                                         |
    7    Name _____                                           |
    8    Street _____                               |
    9    City _____                                          |
   10    State __                                                            |
   11    Zip _____                                                           |
   12                                                                         |
   13    Name                      Value                         Type         |
   14    Name                                                    L:20         |
   15    Street                                                  L:25         |
   16    City                                                    L:20         |
   17    State                                                   L:5          |
   18    Zip                                                     L:2          |
   19                                                                         |
         ====================================================================MAIN=
```

Figure 22.3

Now, suppose you want to modify the form in Figure 22.2 so that it looks like the form in Figure 22.4. At the beginning of Chapter 19, I stated that Symphony data base management is a "tale of two windows." Actually, it is a tale of three windows, since DOC windows are very useful for customizing Entry forms. Starting from the FORM window MAIN, switch to the DOC environment by pressing {Switch} and selecting DOC. Your screen should look like Figure 22.5. (In the remainder of this example, we will show only the part of this DOC window that displays the Entry range with which we will be working.)

Before making any changes to this range, select {**Menu**} **F**ormat **S**ettings **J**ustification **N**one. This prevents Symphony from automatically justifying each line, which can destroy the arrangement of the form you are trying to create.

```
--------------------------------------------------------------
| Name                    _____                    |
|         (Last, First)                                      |
|                                                            |
| Street  _____                      |
|                                                            |
|                                                            |
| City _____  State __ Zip _____         |
|                                                            |
|                                                            |
|                                                            |
| =MAIN==================================================MAIN=|
--------------------------------------------------------------
```

Figure 22.4

```
------------------------------------------------------------------
|                              Left, Single          DOC         |
| ---->---->---->---->---->---->---->---->---->---->---->---->----> |
| Name:L:20                                                      |
| Street:L:25                                                    |
| City:L:20                                                      |
| State:L:2                                                      |
| Zip:L:5                                                        |
|                                                                |
| Name  _____                                         |
| Street  _____                               |
| City _____                                 |
| State __                                                       |
| Zip _____                                                     |
|                                                                |
| Name                      Value                   Type         |
| Name                                              L:20         |
| Street                                            L:25         |
| City                                              L:20         |
| State                                             L:5          |
| Zip                                               L:2          |
| ===================================================MAIN=        |
------------------------------------------------------------------
```

Figure 22.5

To begin, position the cursor on the Z in Zip and issue the {**Menu**} Move command. Designate the FROM range by pressing the → key enough times to extend the cursor to cover the entire word Zip and the five underlines. Press [**Enter**] to lock in this range. Next, use the cursor-movement keys to position the cursor on the same line as the string "State ___". Be sure to leave at least one space between the last underline following State and the Z in Zip. When the cursor is properly positioned, press [**ENTER**]. This command will move the label "Zip _____" onto the same line as the label "State ___", as shown in Figure 22.6.

Next, let's move the State and Zip line up to a position beside the City field. Again, use the Move command, designating the entire 18-character string "State ___ Zip _____" as the FROM range. Now, point to the second space following the last underline in the string "City _____" and press **[Enter].** Your screen will look like Figure 22.7.

```
                                        None, Single              DOC

    ---> ----> ----> ----> ----> ----> ----> ----> ----> ----> ----> ----> ---->
   |                                                                         |
   |                                                                         |
   | Name _____                                            |
   | Street _____                                   |
   | City _____                                    |
   | State __ Zip _____                                                      |
   |                                                                         |
   |                                                                         |
   |                                                                         |
    ======================================================================MAIN=
```

Figure 22.6

```
                                        None, Single              DOC

    ---> ----> ----> ----> ----> ----> ----> ----> ----> ----> ----> ----> ---->
   |                                                                         |
   |                                                                         |
   | Name _____                                           |
   | Street _____                                   |
   | City _____ State __ Zip _____                         |
   |                                                                         |
   |                                                                         |
   |                                                                         |
    ======================================================================MAIN=
```

Figure 22.7

Next, let's get the proper spacing between these three lines. To do this, position the cursor on the space immediately following the last underline in the string "Name _____" and press **[Enter].** This adds a blank line between the Name line and the Street line. Similarly, place the cursor on the space immediately following the last underline in the string "Street _____" and press **[Enter]** two times. This creates two blank lines between the Street line and the City/State/Zip line. The result of these steps is shown in Figure 22.8.

The next step is to enter the label "(Last, First)" beneath the underline following Name. To do this, position the cursor on the first space of the line immediately below the Name line, and use the [Space] bar to move the cursor to a position under the underlines following Name. Then type **(Last, First),** followed by **[Enter].** Your screen will now look like Figure 22.9.

Figure 22.8

Figure 22.9

Now you're ready to switch back to the FORM window. To do so, press **{Switch}**. Instead of displaying your newly designed Entry form in the form window, Symphony greets you with this error message:

(Entry/Definition ranges mismatched)

This is because Symphony still defines the Entry range as the five cells A7 . . A11, while your new Entry form occupies the range A7 . . A13, as shown in Figure 22.10.

Remember that all of the field names in the Definition range must also be in the Entry range, and they must be in the same order in both ranges. The Definition range in this worksheet contains five field names: Name, Street, City, State, Zip. However, when Symphony looks in the range A7 . . A11, which it considers to be the Entry range, it sees only the field names Name and Street. Because the contents of the two ranges do not match, Symphony displays the error message.

To correct this situation you must go to the FORM settings sheet and modify the Entry range. First, issue the **{Menu}** **S**ettings **F**orm **E**ntry command. Use the cursor-movement keys to highlight the block of cells A7 . . A13, and press **[Enter].** Press **[Esc]** three times to get back to the FORM mode. Your screen will look like Figure 22.11. You are now ready to enter records into your data base using the new Entry form.

```
                                                              SHEET
        -----------------A-----------------------B------------------C-----
   7   Name _____
   8        (Last, First)                                                |
   9
   10 Street _____                                   |
   11
   12
   13 City _____  State __  Zip _____                    |
   14                                                                    |
       ==========================================================MAIN=
```

Figure 22.10

```
   Inserting Record 1      New Record                 FORM
   Enter Name
   ------------------------------------------------------------------
  | Name _____                                          |
  |        (Last, First)                                             |
  |                                                                  |
  | Street _____                                |
  |                                                                  |
  |                                                                  |
  | City _____  State __  Zip _____                 |
   =MAIN=====================================================MAIN=
```

Figure 22.11

Using these same techniques, you can create an endless variety of customized windows, either from scratch or as modifications of forms Symphony has generated, as long as you remember the following three rules:

1. The Entry range must contain every field name that the Definition range contains, and it cannot contain any field names not defined in the Definition range.
2. The order of the field names in the Entry range and the Definition range must match. Symphony reads the field names in the Entry range in order from left to right when more than one name appears on the same line.
3. The maximum number of characters (field names, spaces, and underlines) on any line may not exceed 78.

As you create customized Entry forms, you probably will want to save them in separate settings sheets following the guidelines presented in Chapter 20.

PRINTING DATA BASE REPORTS

One of the most convenient features of most data base management software is the ability to print customized reports using the information contained in the data base. Unlike 1-2-3, Symphony has the power to create such custom reports. In this section, we will explore three examples of Symphony's data base report capabilities: printing the data base, printing mailing labels, and printing form letters.

Printing the Data Base

First let's look at how to print a simple listing of the records in a data base, called a standard data base report. We will include a summary statistical function as a "footer" to the report.

The Report Ranges

Figure 22.12 shows the familiar address-book data base, and Figure 22.13 shows the settings sheet that accompanies this data base. As you recall, when you use the Generate command to create a data base Symphony automatically defines a number of related ranges, including two Report ranges, the Above Report range, and the Main Report range. Symphony does not, however, automatically create a Below Report range. You can see the Above Report range, named MAIN_AB, which occupies cells A20 . . E20, and the Main Report range, named MAIN_MA, which occupies cells A21 . . E21.

```
      -------A--------------------------B---------------------C----------D---E----
   7  Name     _____                                              |
   8  Street   _____                                       |
   9  City     _____                                              |
  10  State    __                                                                |
  11  Zip      _____                                                             |
  12                                                                             |
  13  Name             Value                        Type            DeFormula    |
  14  Name                                          L:20                         |
  15  Street                                        L:25                         |
  16  City                                          L:20                         |
  17  State                                         L:2                          |
  18  Zip                                           L:5                          |
  19                                                                             |
  20  Name             Street                       City            StZip        |
  21  Mary Smith       111 First Street             Anytown         KY40223      |
  22                                                                             |
  23  Name             Street                       City            StZip        |
  24                                                                             |
  25                                                                             |
  26                                                                             |
  27                                                                             |
  28  Name             Street                       City            StZip        |
  29  Mary Smith       111 First Street             Anytown         KY40223      |
  30  John Doe         222 Second Street            Mayberry        NC12345      |
  31  John Q. Public   333 Third Street             Yourtown        CA11111      |
  32  Jane Smythe      123 Main Street              Anytown         MO01010      |
      ========================================================================MAIN=
```

Figure 22.12

```
----------------------------------------------------------------
|                                                              |
|  Basic Ranges                     Report Ranges             |
|     Database:     MAIN_DB            Main:      MAIN_MA      |
|     Criterion:    MAIN_CR            Above:     MAIN_AB      |
|     Output:                         Below:                  |
|  Form Ranges                        Type:      Single       |
|     Entry:        MAIN_EN            Entry list:            |
|     Definition:   MAIN_DF            Input cell:            |
|  Underscores:     Yes             One-Record: No            |
|  Sort-Keys                                                  |
|     1st-Key:            2nd-Key:             3rd-Key:       |
|       Order:              Order:               Order:       |
|                                                              |
|  =====================================Database Settings: MAIN= |
----------------------------------------------------------------
```

Figure 22.13

The Report range settings on the FORM Settings sheet and the {Services} Print settings and commands control the printing of data base reports. The rules for generating data base reports are fairly straightforward.

The entries in row 21, which is the Main Report range or body of the report, appear to be labels, but they are really formulas that refer to the range names Symphony assigned to the entries in the first row of the data base. These are the formulas:

	A	B	C	D	E
21	+NAME	+STREET	+CITY	+STATE	+ZIP

The range names serve simply as a convenience; the contents of the cells in the Main Report range could just as well be +A29, +B29, +C29, +D29, and +E29. Any entries in the Main Report range that refer to a field of information must refer to the first data cell in that field either by name or by cell reference.

The entries in row 20, the Above Report range, are simply labels, which will be printed as the "header" of the report.

The third Report range is the Below Report range. This is like a footer, since it is always printed at the very bottom of a data base report. Let's add a Below Report range to this settings sheet. To do this enter the label

> A22: +"This report contains
> "&@STRING(@DCOUNT(MAIN_DB,0,MAIN_CR),0)&" records"

in an empty cell (in this example, we'll use cell A22). This entry concatenates the data base function @DCOUNT into a string of text. As explained in the previous chapter, @DCOUNT calculates the number of records in a data base.

Now you need to enter the location of this formula into the data base settings sheet. To do this, issue the {**Menu**} **Q**uery **S**ettings **R**eport **B**elow command. Now move the cellpointer to cell A22 and press [Enter]. The settings sheet will look like the one in Figure 22.14.

The Print Settings

Now that you have specified the Main, Above, and Below Report ranges, you are ready to print the report. The printing of all data base reports is controlled by the current

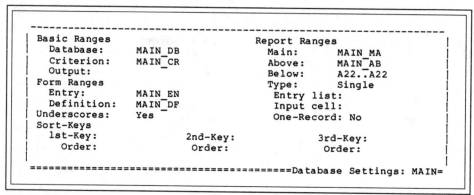

```
--------------------------------------------------------------
| Basic Ranges                      Report Ranges            |
|    Database:      MAIN_DB            Main:      MAIN_MA     |
|    Criterion:     MAIN_CR            Above:     MAIN_AB     |
|    Output:                          Below:     A22..A22    |
| Form Ranges                         Type:      Single      |
|    Entry:         MAIN_EN            Entry list:           |
|    Definition:    MAIN_DF            Input cell:           |
| Underscores:      Yes               One-Record: No         |
| Sort-Keys                                                  |
|    1st-Key:               2nd-Key:            3rd-Key:      |
|       Order:                 Order:              Order:    |
|                                                            |
| ========================================Database Settings: MAIN= |
--------------------------------------------------------------
```

Figure 22.14

Print settings sheet. We will not discuss all of the Print parameters here; if you need to refresh your memory, refer to Chapter 9, Printing. However, we will discuss two settings that are essential to the data base printing process: the Source setting and the Margins settings.

The Source Range   To begin the printing process, issue the {**Services**} **P**rint command. It is very important that you are in a FORM window when you press these keys. Otherwise, Symphony may truncate the lines of the report, printing only a single column of characters.

Next, choose Settings from the Print menu and select Source. Symphony displays the following choices:

>   Range Database Cancel

Since you want to print a report from a data base, select Database. Symphony responds with the prompt

>   Database settings sheet name:

This prompt is followed by a list of the names of every data base settings sheet in memory. Choose the settings sheet that has the report ranges you want to use. For this example, of course, you should choose MAIN. Symphony displays this choice in the Print settings sheet on the screen and returns you to the Print menu.

The Margin Settings   At this point, you should make sure that your margins are set wide enough to accommodate the data base you have specified. If you do not set the margins wide enough, each line of the report will overlap to the next line on the printed page, ruining the report.

When you use the Generate command, Symphony automatically sets the width of the columns of the Database range to be one space greater than the specified field length. For instance, since Symphony created the first field (Name) from the specification

>   Name:L:20

Symphony will set the width of column A at 21 spaces. To determine the total column width needed to print the report, add one to the specification for each field length, and add all of these figures together. For instance, if your field specifications are

> Name:L:20
> Street:L:25
> City:L:20
> State:L:2
> Zip:L:5

then here is your calculation:

$$20 + 1 = 21$$
$$25 + 1 = 26$$
$$20 + 1 = 21$$
$$2 + 1 = 3$$
$$5 + 1 = 6$$

77spaces

In the example, you need to set the right margin to 77 spaces beyond the left margin. To do this, select Margins from the Print settings menu, choose Right from the submenu, and enter a number equal to the left margin setting plus 77. For example, if the left margin setting is 4 (the default) the right margin setting should be 81. If your printer can print only an 80-character line, you can use either a Print Init-String to select compressed print or the {**Services**} Print Settings Margins Left command to set the left margin to 3 on the Print settings sheet.

Other settings   In addition to these two essential settings, you might wish to modify some of the other Print settings to create a "customized" Print settings sheet for this data base report. You probably should save these Print settings for future printings of this data base report (as the data base grows). Refer to Chapter 9 for a thorough discussion of this subject.

Printing the Report

Now that your Report ranges are specified in a data base settings sheet and your Print settings sheet refers to that data base settings sheet and specifies the proper margins, you are ready to print the report. First, press **[Esc]** to move to the main Print menu. Align the paper in your printer, select Align from the menu, and press Go. Symphony prints a report of your data base, which looks like the one in Figure 22.15.

```
Name                Street             City          StZip
Mary Smith          111 First Street   Anytown       KY40223
John Doe            222 Second Street  Mayberry      NC12345
John Q. Public      333 Third Street   Yourtown      CA11111
This report contains 3 records
```

Figure 22.15

As you can see, the Above Report range, which consists of the field names from the data base, is printed only once as a "header" for the report. The Main Report range, which consists of an individual record, has been printed three times, once for every record in the report that meets the criteria in the Criterion range. The Below Report range has been printed once at the bottom of the report.

Printing selected records   In our example the Criterion range is blank, so all the records were printed. If you specify any criteria in the cells of the Criterion range, as shown in Figure 22.16, Symphony prints only the records meeting these criteria. In our example, Symphony selects those records whose City field is Yourtown, as well as those records whose Name field begins with Mary. The resulting report looks like the one in Figure 22.17.

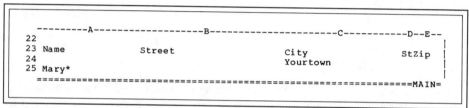

Figure 22.16

```
Name                Street                 City                 StZip
Mary Smith          111 First Street       Anytown              KY40223
John Q. Public      333 Third Street       Yourtown             CA11111
This report contains 2 records
```

Figure 22.17

Printing selected fields   If you want to limit the number of fields of information in the printed report, you can change the Main Report range to include only a subset of the fields in the data base. For example, if the Main Report range in the previous example is limited to the range A21 . . B21, the printed report would include only the fields Name and Street.

Printing Address Labels

The first example of a nonstandard report format is printing address labels from the address-book data base. Following this example, we will use Symphony's multiple-pass reporting capability to print these same labels grouped by zip code. For these examples, let's add some records to the data base so that our address-book data base looks like Figure 22.18.

Creating the Main Report Range

To print address labels, you need to change the printing arrangement of the fields from a row arrangement to a column arrangement. To do this, you must create a new Main Report range in the worksheet and specify this range in a data base settings sheet.

To begin, move to an area of the worksheet where you can find three empty, adjacent cells in a single column. For this example, we'll choose cells C1 . . C3, although almost

```
        -------A------------------B----------------------C-----------D---E--
28 Name              Street                 City                 StZip   |
29 Mary Smith        111 First Street       Anytown              KY40223 |
30 John Doe          222 Second Street      Mayberry             NC12345 |
31 John Q. Public    333 Third Street       Yourtown             CA11111 |
32 John Johnson      444 Fourth Street      Anytown              KY40223 |
33 Joe Clark         555 Fifth Street       Mytown               CA11111 |
34 Olde McDonald     Route 6                Mt. Pilot            NC12345 |
   ================================================================MAIN=
```

Figure 22.18

any block will do. We will enter simple formulas in these cells that refer to the cells of the first row of data in the Database range, just as Symphony did in cells A21 . . E21 of the standard Main Report range. The following formulas should be entered:

> C1: +NAME   or   C1: +A29
>
> C2: +STREET   or   C2: +B29
>
> C3: +CITY&", "&STATE&" "&ZIP   or   C3: +C29&", "&D29&" "&E29

Refer to Chapter 3 for an explanation of the use of the & operator and string arithmetic in general. After entering these formulas, the spreadsheet will look like Figure 22.19.

```
      -------A------------------------B--------------------C------------
1 Name:L:20                                 Mary Smith              |
2 Street:L:25                               111 First Street        |
3 City:L:20                                 Anytown, KY   40223     |
4 State:L:2                                                         |
5 Zip:L:5                                                           |
6                                                                   |
  ================================================================MAIN=
```

Figure 22.19

Note that the formulas in cells C1 . . C3 display as the labels to which they refer rather than the formulas themselves. This is exactly how the address labels will look when they are printed.

Changing the Data Base Settings

At this point, you ought to create a new settings sheet so that you can retain the settings sheet that contains the standard report ranges you used before. To begin this process, issue the {**Menu**} Query Settings Name Create command. Use a name like LABEL to describe the new data base settings sheet. Symphony makes an exact copy of the previous data base settings sheet (in this case the MAIN sheet that Symphony created through the Generate command), gives it the new name, and displays it on the screen.

Now we can modify this sheet so we can use it for printing labels, without losing the original settings in MAIN. The only modification that needs to be made in this case is to cancel the current Report ranges and then designate the cells C1 . . C6 as the Main

Report range. To do this, select Cancel from the Settings menu and select the **Report** option. Symphony will erase the entries MAIN_MA, MAIN_AB, and A22 . . A22 from the settings sheet.

To designate the block of cells C1 . . C6 as the new Main Report range, simply select Report from the Settings menu and choose the Main option. Symphony prompts you to supply a new Main Report range. Use the cursor-movement keys and the period key to highlight cells C1 . . C6. (In addition to the three information-containing cells, you should include three "blank" lines in the Main Report range, since most blank labels are 6 lines (1 inch) long. This will provide for proper spacing on the labels.) The settings sheet will now look like Figure 22.20.

```
--------------------------------------------------------------
|  Basic Ranges                        Report Ranges         |
|     Database:      MAIN DB              Main:       Cl..C6  |
|     Criterion:     MAIN CR              Above:              |
|     Output:                             Below:              |
|  Form Ranges                            Type:      Single   |
|     Entry:         MAIN EN              Entry list:         |
|     Definition:    MAIN DF              Input cell:         |
|  Underscores:      Yes               One-Record: No         |
|  Sort-Keys                                                  |
|     1st-Key:              2nd-Key:              3rd-Key:    |
|      Order:                Order:                Order:     |
|                                                             |
|  =====================================Database Settings: LABEL= |
--------------------------------------------------------------
```

Figure 22.20

Remember that this newly created sheet will not be active until you attach it to the FORM window with the Attach command. Once this is done, you are ready to move to the Print settings sheet.

Adjusting the Print Settings

As before, we must modify the Print settings sheet to refer to the newly created LABEL data base settings sheet. I suggest that you use the {**Services**} **P**rint **S**ettings **N**ame **C**reate command to create a new Print settings sheet before making these changes. After copying this old sheet under a new name (let's use LABEL again), issue the **S**ource **D**atabase command and specify **LABEL** as the data base settings sheet from which to print.

Since the labels will be printed on one continuous "spool," you should also use the **P**rint **S**ettings **P**age **B**reaks **N**o command sequence to prevent Symphony from inserting page breaks in the report.

Printing the Labels

At this point, you are ready to print the labels. Just insert and align the spool of blank labels into your printer, then select **A**lign and **G**o from the Print menu. Symphony prints each name and address on individual labels, as shown in Figure 22.21.

Because the Criterion range in this example is blank, all of the records were printed. Of course, if you make entries into the Criterion range, Symphony prints only the records that meet those criteria.

Multiple Passes

Symphony has the ability to print reports that separate the records in a data base into groups by a common characteristic. For instance, you can instruct Symphony to print address labels in groups by zip code. All you need to do is supply Symphony with a list of the zip codes for which you want labels printed. Then, when Symphony begins printing, it first prints labels for all of the records containing the first zip code in the group, then all of the records containing the second zip code, then the third, and so forth.

To begin, switch to a SHEET window and locate two convenient cells. Enter the zip codes you want Symphony to use when printing the labels into these cells. In Figure 22.22, we entered the zip code 11111 in cell C7 and the code 40223 in cell C8.

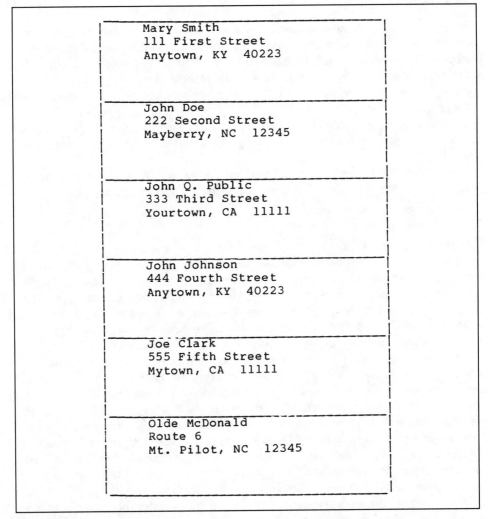

```
        Mary Smith
        111 First Street
        Anytown, KY   40223


        John Doe
        222 Second Street
        Mayberry, NC   12345


        John Q. Public
        333 Third Street
        Yourtown, CA   11111


        John Johnson
        444 Fourth Street
        Anytown, KY   40223


        Joe Clark
        555 Fifth Street
        Mytown, CA   11111


        Olde McDonald
        Route 6
        Mt. Pilot, NC   12345
```

Figure 22.21

```
--------A-----------------------B-------------------C----------D---E----
 1   Name:L:20                                John Q. Public              |
 2   Street:L:25                              333 Third Street            |
 3   City:L:20                                Yourtown, CA   11111         |
 4   State:L:2                                                            |
 5   Zip:L:5                                                              |
 6                                                                        |
 7   Name _____                 11111                       |
 8   Street _____         40223                       |
 9   City _____                                             |
10   State___                                                             |
11   Zip    ____                                                          |
     ==========================================================MAIN=
```

Figure 22.22

Since the zip codes in the data base are numeric labels and not numbers, you must enter the selected codes in cells C7 and C8 as labels by preceding the number with a label prefix— ', ", or ^. If you enter these codes as numbers, Symphony will be unable to match them to any of the entries in the Zip field of the data base.

You will recognize the entries in cells C1 . . C3 as the Main Report range we developed in the previous example.

To continue, use the {**Menu**} Query Settings Name Create command to create a new data base settings sheet for these new settings. Let's give this settings sheet the name GROUP.

Before you can print the report, you must modify the new settings sheet. From the Settings menu, issue the Report Type command. The following menu appears:

One pass for each item in Entry list
Single   Multiple

The default setting for Report Type is Single. Since you want Symphony to make a pass through all of the records in the data base for each zip code you specify, you should select Multiple from this menu. Symphony responds by switching you to the worksheet and asking you to specify the location of the Entry list. The Entry list is the list of zip codes in cells C7 and C8. Use the cursor-movement keys and the period key to highlight the contents of cells C7 . . C8. Symphony enters this range specification into the current data base settings sheet and then prompts you to designate an Input cell.

The Input cell is a cell in the Criterion range into which Symphony substitutes the values in the Entry list, one at a time, for each pass through the data base. In other words, the multiple report feature is based on the substitution of different criteria into a single cell of the Criterion range. In this case, specify cell E24 (the cell under the Zip header in the Criterion range) as the Input cell. (If this sounds familiar, it is because the process of printing a multiple-pass report is similar to that of processing a Range What-If table.)

Figure 22.23 shows the data base settings sheet you have created. Note that the Type has been changed to Multiple, and the coordinates for the Entry list and Input cell have been recorded in this data base settings sheet, which is called GROUP.

Before you print the report, you must modify the Print settings sheet to refer to this new data base settings sheet. Again, let's create a new Print settings sheet for these new

```
|-------------------------------------------------------------|
|  Basic Ranges                     Report Ranges             |
|     Database:      MAIN_DB           Main:       C1..C6      |
|     Criterion:     MAIN_CR           Above:                  |
|     Output:                          Below:                  |
|  Form Ranges                         Type:       Multiple    |
|     Entry:         MAIN_EN            Entry list: C7..C8      |
|     Definition:    MAIN_DF            Input cell: E24..E24    |
|  Underscores:      Yes               One-Record: No          |
|  Sort-Keys                                                   |
|     1st-Key:              2nd-Key:              3rd-Key:      |
|        Order:                Order:                Order:     |
|                                                              |
|  =====================================Database Settings: GROUP=|
```

Figure 22.23

settings. Issue the **{Services}** **P**rint **S**ettings **N**ame **C**reate command and specify a name such as GROUP. Next, select the **S**ource **D**atabase option from the Settings menu and choose GROUP from the choices Symphony presents. Finally, select Quit to exit from the Print Settings Menu.

Now we are ready to print the labels. Before printing, align the spool of labels in your printer, issue the Align command, and then choose Go. Symphony proceeds to print the labels by zip code group so that the labels appear as they do in Figure 22.24.

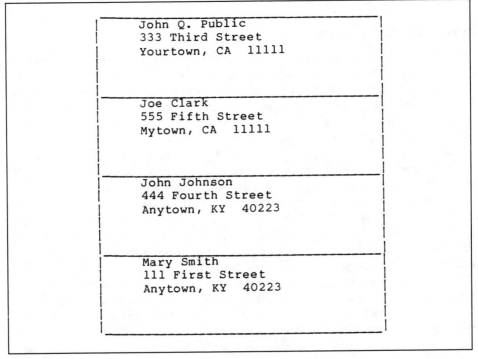

```
|-------------------------------------------|
|   John Q. Public                          |
|   333 Third Street                        |
|   Yourtown, CA   11111                     |
|                                           |
|-------------------------------------------|
|   Joe Clark                               |
|   555 Fifth Street                        |
|   Mytown, CA   11111                       |
|                                           |
|-------------------------------------------|
|   John Johnson                            |
|   444 Fourth Street                       |
|   Anytown, KY   40223                      |
|                                           |
|-------------------------------------------|
|   Mary Smith                              |
|   111 First Street                        |
|   Anytown, KY   40223                      |
|                                           |
|-------------------------------------------|
```

Figure 22.24

When you told Symphony to print the report, it actually printed two reports, back to back, one for each zip code in the Entry list. For the first report, Symphony used the Criterion range shown in Figure 22.25. This Criterion range selected the first two labels in Figure 22.24. For the second report, it used the Criterion range shown in Figure 22.26. This Criterion range selected the second of two records in the report in Figure 22.24.

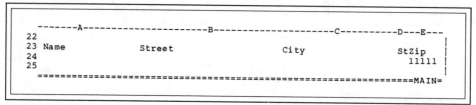

Figure 22.25

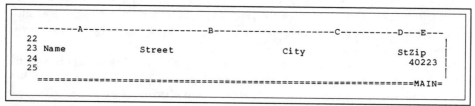

Figure 22.26

Printing a Form Letter

Since you've printed address labels, let's create a letter that Symphony can customize for each of the six people in our address-book data base. To create this letter, you need to use a DOC window. So that you can continue to toggle the window MAIN between the FORM and SHEET types, create a new window for your document by issuing the {**Services**} Window Create command. Assign the new window the name FORMLETTER and specify DOC as the window type. Press [**Esc**] to display this window.

Now type in the form letter shown in Figure 22.27. The parts of the letter enclosed in double braces are references to the fields of your address-book data base. You will replace these parts of the document in a few pages. Be sure to include four "hard spaces" (hard spaces are created by typing {Compose}[Space][Space]) before the reference to {{Name}} in the second line of the first paragraph, and four hard spaces following this reference. Also be sure to include the page break (::) at the bottom of the document. This marker tells Symphony to go to the top of the next page when it finishes printing one letter to begin printing the next one.

Once the letter has been typed, you must go back and replace the material in braces with references to the data base. Making these replacements is not as easy as it sounds, however. If you simply embed these references in lines of the document, Symphony interprets them as part of the document labels and not as formulas that refer to the data base. In order for Symphony to recognize these formulas, you must replace whole lines of the document with long string variables.

```
 ----------------------------------------------------------------
|                                                                |
|                                               {{current date}} |
|                                                                |
|                                                                |
| {{Name}}                                                       |
| {{Street}}                                                     |
| {{City}}, {{State}}  {{Zip code}}                              |
|                                                                |
|                                                                |
| Dear {{name}}:                                                 |
|                                                                |
|     We are sending this letter to inform you that you may be a winner in |
| the all-new TRANS-AMERICANA SWEEPSTAKES!  Yes, {{....name....}}, you and |
| the rest of your family could win up to $50,000 in cash!  Imagine what |
| you could do with that money - buy a car, a boat, or something for your |
| home at {{street}}!                                            |
|                                                                |
|     I know what you're thinking: "My chances of winning must be a |
| million to one.  I'll never win." But that's not true!  You are one of |
| only {{#}} people receiving this special announcement, so your chances of|
| winning are excellent!                                         |
|                                                                |
|     Don't pass up this opportunity to win!  Return the enclosed |
| registration card today!                                       |
| ::                                                             |
 ==================================================================FORMLETTER=
```

Figure 22.27

Let's switch to a SHEET window to replace the formula-containing lines of the document with string variables. To change the window type, press the {Type} key and select SHEET. You will now see your announcement in the familiar grid of the worksheet. Each line of the document is stored as a long label in the left-most cell of the sheet, in this case column A. Figure 22.28 shows the first ten lines of the document as they appear in a SHEET window.

```
    -------A-------------------------B-------------------C----------D---E----
 50                                                    {{current date}}     |
 51                                                                         |
 52                                                                         |
 53                                                                         |
 54 {{Name}}                                                                |
 55 {{Street}}                                                              |
 56 {{City}}, {{State}}  {{Zip code}}                                       |
 57                                                                         |
 58                                                                         |
 59 Dear {{name}}:                                                          |
    ==================================================================FORMLETTER=
```

Figure 22.28

First you must modify line 50, which will display the current date in the printed letters. Use the {**Menu**} Erase command to erase cell A50. (Remember that the characters {{current date}} are stored as a long label in cell A50).

Having done this, move the cell pointer to cell C50 and enter the function @NOW. Then use the {**Menu**} Format Date **1** command to display this cell in the DD-MMM-YY format so that the result of the @NOW function will be displayed and printed as a recognizable date. Assuming that you keep DOS up to date, the @NOW function will always return the current date.

Next, move the cursor to cell A54 and erase the contents of that cell. Replace the current entry with the formula + NAME, which refers to the first cell of the Name field in our address-book data base. Similarly, move to cell A55, erase the contents, and type + STREET. Then move to cell A56, erase the contents, and type the following:

+ CITY&", "&STATE&" "&ZIP

Notice that all of the formulas refer to cells in the first row of the data base. These are the same three formulas you used to print the address labels in the example above.

Next, move to cell A59 and type

+ "Dear "&NAME&":"

The resulting spreadsheet should look like the one in Figure 22.29. Notice that cells A54, A55, A56, and A59 display the contents of the first row of the data base.

```
   -------A---------------------B--------------------C---------D---E----
50                                                24-Jun-84          |
51                                                                   |
52                                                                   |
53                                                                   |
54 Mary Smith                                                        |
55 111 First Street                                                  |
56 Anytown, KY   40223                                               |
57                                                                   |
58                                                                   |
59 Dear John Q. Public:                                              |
   ================================================================FORMLETTER=
```

Figure 22.29

Now let's change line 13 of the document. Type the following in cell A63:

A63: + "the all-new TRANS-AMERICANA SWEEPSTAKES! Yes, "&NAME&", you and"

Next, move the cell pointer to cell A66 and type the following string:

A66: + "home at "&STREET&"!"

Cell A70 in the draft letter contains the label

A70: 'only {{#}} people receiving this special announcement, so your chances of

We need to replace the {{#}} term in this line with an @DCOUNT function that computes the total number of records in the data base. Unfortunately, you cannot insert the @DCOUNT function or any other @D function directly into any cell of the Main Report range. If you do include one of these functions in the Main Report range, Symphony disregards the boundaries of the Database range while printing the report and continues to print reports "ad infinitum."

For this reason, you must first enter the @DCOUNT function in another part of the worksheet; then use the @STRING function to convert the result of @DCOUNT into a string value; and finally concatenate the result of that @STRING function into the text in cell A70.

First move to an area of the worksheet where you have an empty cell. In this example, choose cell C10. Enter the following formula into cell C10:

C10: @DCOUNT(MAIN_DB,0,MAIN_CR)

This instructs Symphony to count the number of entries in the first field of the Database range, which is equivalent to the number of records in the data base.

Unfortunately, a value entry like the @DCOUNT function cannot be combined directly with a string. To concatenate this number onto a string, you must convert it into a label. To do this, use the @STRING function

@STRING($C$10,0)

This formula tells Symphony to take what it finds in cell C10 and convert it into a label with no decimal places. You must use an absolute reference when referring to this or any other cell outside of the Database range.

To combine this formula with a string, move to cell A70 and replace the long label with this:

A70: +"only "&@STRING($C$10,0)&" people receiving this special announcement, so your chances of"

Now switch back into a DOC window. Symphony has filled in the formulas with the appropriate fields of the first record of the data base, so that the document looks like Figure 22.30.

Pay special attention to the line in the document that begins "the all new TRANS-AMERICANA . . ." Remember that when you typed this line in the first draft of the document, you inserted eight "hard spaces" in the reference to the name field. Because the reference to the Name field is in the middle of a line of text, you need to reserve space for the maximum possible character length of this substitution, so that the printed line does not run off the right side of the page. By using the phrase {{ . . . . Name . . . . }} to represent this reference in the draft, you reserved enough space in this line for the longest possible entry.

You may wonder why, since the Name field is 20 characters wide, we "reserved" only 16 spaces in this line with the string {{ . . . . Name . . . . }}. In fact, this was a conscious decision. Although the Name field is 20 characters wide, the longest entry currently in that field (John Q. Public) is only 14 characters long. If we had reserved 20 spaces in the document for this field, at least six blank spaces would appear at the end of this line in every letter. In some letters, even more spaces would be appended to the line. The result would look awkward and "form-letterish." To avoid this problem, we reserved only enough spaces for the longest current entry, plus a couple of additional "insurance" spaces.

Getting the Settings Right

Figure 22.30 shows the letter you want Symphony to print six times, with each copy

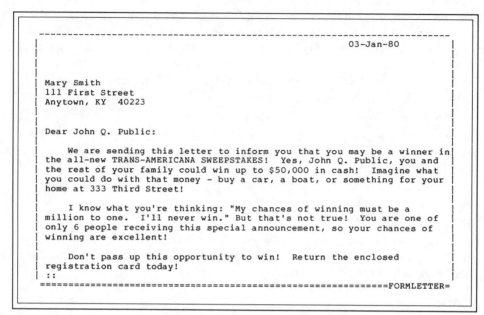

```
------------------------------------------------------------------
|                                                   03-Jan-80    |
|                                                                |
|                                                                |
| Mary Smith                                                     |
| 111 First Street                                               |
| Anytown, KY  40223                                             |
|                                                                |
|                                                                |
| Dear John Q. Public:                                           |
|                                                                |
|     We are sending this letter to inform you that you may be a winner in|
| the all-new TRANS-AMERICANA SWEEPSTAKES!  Yes, John Q. Public, you and |
| the rest of your family could win up to $50,000 in cash!  Imagine what |
| you could do with that money - buy a car, a boat, or something for your |
| home at 333 Third Street!                                      |
|                                                                |
|     I know what you're thinking: "My chances of winning must be a |
| million to one.  I'll never win." But that's not true!  You are one of |
| only 6 people receiving this special announcement, so your chances of |
| winning are excellent!                                         |
|                                                                |
|     Don't pass up this opportunity to win!  Return the enclosed |
| registration card today!                                       |
| ::                                                             |
|===============================================================FORMLETTER=
```

Figure 22.30

personalized for each of the six records in the data base. Before you can print it, however, you must designate the block of cells containing the letter as the Main Report range in a data base settings sheet. Create a new settings sheet, as you have in past examples, so that you can save all of your previous settings.

First recall an old settings sheet, MAIN, to the screen by issuing the {**Menu**} Settings Name Use command and specifying the name MAIN. You may recall that MAIN is the original settings sheet Symphony created when you used the Generate command to create the address-book data base. Again, make sure that you begin the printing process from a FORM window, or your text may be truncated.

Next, issue the Name Create command and supply a name for the settings sheet, such as FORMLETTER. To erase the existing Report range specifications, issue the Cancel Report command. To specify the newly created form letter as the new Main Report range, choose Report Main and use the cursor keys and the period key to highlight the cells A50 . . E74. Be sure to include every cell into which the lines of text spill over, even though every line is a long label stored only in column A. This designates the entire letter as the Main Report range. After doing this, your data base settings sheet will look like the one in Figure 22.31.

From the FORM window, press {**Services**} Print Settings to display the current Print settings sheet. Use the Name Create command sequence to create a new settings sheet and name it FORMLETTER. Next, using the Source Database commands, choose FORMLETTER as the data base settings sheet to be used for printing. Finally, use the Page and Margins commands to ensure that the page breaks are on and that the margins are correct for this letter.

```
-----------------------------------------------------------------
| Basic Ranges                       Report Ranges               |
|    Database:      MAIN_DB             Main:      A50..E74        |
|    Criterion:     MAIN_CR             Above:                    |
|    Output:                            Below:                    |
| Form Ranges                           Type:      Single         |
|    Entry:         MAIN_EN             Entry list:               |
|    Definition:    MAIN_DF            Input cell:                |
| Underscores:      Yes                One-Record: No             |
| Sort-Keys                                                       |
|    1st-Key:              2nd-Key:            3rd-Key:            |
|    Order:                Order:              Order:              |
|                                                                 |
| ============================================Database Settings: FORMLETTER= |
```

Figure 22.31

Now you are ready to print. Press **Q**uit to escape from the Print settings menu, align the paper in your printer, select **Align,** and then select **Go.** Symphony will proceed to print six customized form letters, each one containing the name and address of one of the people in your mailing list. Figure 22.32 shows one of these letters.

```
                                                    24-Jun-84



     Mary Smith
     111 First Street
     Anytown, KY  40223


     Dear Mary Smith:

          We are sending this letter to inform you that you may be a winner in
     the all-new TRANS-AMERICANA SWEEPSTAKES!  Yes, Mary Smith, you and
     the rest of your family could win up to $50,000 in cash!  Imagine what
     you could do with that money - buy a car, a boat, or something for your
     home at 111 First Street!

          I know what you're thinking: "My chances of winning must be a
     million to one. I'll never win." But that's not true!  You are one of
     only 6 people receiving this special announcement, so your chances of
     winning are excellent!

          Don't pass up this opportunity to win!  Return the enclosed
     registration card today!
```

Figure 22.32

Experiment with the examples presented above, as well as new applications of your own, to familiarize yourself with the intricacies of printing custom data base reports.

PART VII

COMMUNICATIONS

CHAPTER TWENTY THREE

A DATA COMMUNICATIONS PRIMER

In addition to having powerful spreadsheeting, data base management, word process-ing, and graphics capabilities, Symphony has the power to communicate with other computers. You can use Symphony's COMM capabilities to send information across telephone lines to computers anywhere in the world and to capture and store information that the program receives from these remote computers. Symphony can be used to connect with and receive information from services such as Dow Jones, CompuServe, and The Source, or it can be used to download information from a main frame computer into a worksheet range or a file. Symphony's COMM environ-ment opens up a new world for most users of integrated spreadsheet software: the world of data communications.

This five-chapter section of *Mastering Symphony* explains Symphony's data communi-cations capabilities. Because the subject of data communications is new to most users of integrated spreadsheet software, such as Lotus 1-2-3, this chapter begins with a discus-sion of the basics of data communications before moving on to discuss Symphony's data communications capabilities. This brief overview of data communications theory will help you understand the various commands used in the Symphony communications environment.

The next chapter deals with the COMM Settings sheet, explaining in detail each com-mand and setting necessary for getting Symphony to communicate with other computers. Chapter 24 draws upon the fundamentals presented in this chapter to explain the hows and whys of each command.

Chapter 25, Getting On Line with Symphony, explains how you can use Symphony to communicate with another computer. In that chapter you'll learn about the Phone com-mand, the Login command, and the Transmit-Range and Transmit-File commands.

Chapter 26 covers the how to's of communication between two computers using Symphony. That chapter is a quick guide through Symphony's communications settings. It summarizes the keystrokes necessary to configure Symphony's COMM settings for Symphony-to-Symphony communications.

The final chapter in this section addresses some advanced topics. The points in Chap-ter 27 may be of more interest to experienced users of Symphony communications than to beginners. That chapter shows you how to create and use custom character translation tables and how to configure a popular modem, the Hayes Smartmodem 1200, to take full advantage of Symphony's data communications capabilities, listing the proper modem switch settings to be used when working with Symphony. It ends with a few questions and answers covering special problems that may arise when using Symphony.

If you are new to the subject of data communications and are just starting out with Symphony, start at the beginning of this section and work your way through to the end, building your base of knowledge as you go along. If you are already knowledgeable about some of the basic topics, however, you may wish to skip the first chapter of this section. For example, experienced users of data communications software may wish to skip the fundamentals and concentrate on those parts that specifically address Symphony's communications capabilities.

DATA COMMUNICATIONS ESSENTIALS

Before any IBM PC or compatible microcomputer can communicate with another computer, both computers need the following three items: a **modem,** a **serial board** (including the RS-232 interface) and **communications software.** Let's begin by discussing the hardware needs: the modem and the serial board.

The Modem

A modem is a device that links the computer to the telephone line so that it can communicate with a remote computer. The term *modem* is a contraction of the terms that describe the two major functions of the device, **mo**dulation and **dem**odulation. Modulation is the process of converting the digital information (bits) stored in your computer's RAM into analog information (voice frequency signals) so that it can be transmitted via telephone lines. Demodulation is the process of converting voice frequency signals back into the binary information that the computer can use. In essence, this translation of information is the primary function of the modem. Modems vary in their location (internal versus external) and in their "bells and whistles," but this basic function is the same for all modems.

The Serial Board

A serial board is the second piece of hardware essential for data communications. In the simplest sense, the serial board is the physical connection between the computer and the modem. However, the serial board is far more than an adapter into which you plug your modem. To understand the full importance of the serial board, you must understand the way computers transmit information.

Within computers—from CPU to RAM to disk drives—information is usually transmitted in parallel form. Many printers also use the parallel communication convention. The term *parallel* means that the eight binary digits (bits), which represent one of the 256 characters (letters, numbers, or special characters) that the computer understands and uses, are transmitted from one location to another at the same time via eight different "wires." (The word *wire* is used loosely in this discussion to represent the electrical paths along which data is transmitted within a computer.) One bit travels down each wire, and all of the bits arrive at their destination at the same time. Thus, parallel communication involves the transfer of whole characters, or bytes, at one time. Parallel communication gets its name from the fact that the bits move from place to place on these parallel wires.

Serial communication involves the sequential transmission of binary digits. In other words, when information is transmitted serially, one bit follows another down a single wire to its destination. Data communications over telephone lines must be serial for the simple reason that most telephone lines contain only two wires: one for sending data and one for receiving data. Because parallel communication requires that eight bits be transmitted down eight wires at one time, there is no way to perform parallel communication across a two-wire telephone.

You can conceptualize the difference between parallel and serial communications by visualizing eight cars trying to cross a bridge. If the bridge has eight lanes, the automobiles can cross at once, using parallel lanes. When the bridge has only one lane, however, the eight cars must get in line, one after another, to cross and then get back into their eight lanes when they reach the other side.

Similarly, before data in parallel form can be communicated serially, it must be rearranged so that one bit follows another across the wire and then reassembled at the destination as an eight-bit byte. The rearrangement of data prior to transmission and the reassembly of data after receipt is the major function of a serial board.

Every serial board for IBM-compatible microcomputers uses a special interface, called an RS-232 interface, to actually send and receive data. The RS-232 interface is a more or less standard device for connecting modems and serial printers to computers.

The external part of the RS-232 interface is the 25-pin male connector (called a DB-25 connector) located at the back or side of your PC. The cable that links your computer to your modem should be attached to this connector. Don't confuse the male RS-232 connector with the female parallel connector, or printer port, that is standard on most PCs. These two connectors are completely different even though they look the same.

Because you just learned that serial communications involves individual bits of data transmitted one after another down a single wire, you may wonder why the serial board has 25 pins. In fact, only two of the pins on an RS-232 interface are actually used for data transmission. One of these pins is used to transmit data and the other to receive data. The other pins are used for related purposes, involving the sending of commands from the computer to the modem.

Successful data communications requires that each pin on your computer's RS-232 interface be connected to the correct pin on your modem's RS-232 interface. If you purchased your computer, modem, and Symphony from the same dealer, chances are that the cable provided will be correct for linking your computer and modem. However, this cable may not be correct for other purposes, such as directly connecting your computer to another without a modem. If you decide to connect your computer to another directly, ask your dealer for help in selecting the correct cable.

Your computer must have a serial board to use Symphony's COMM capabilities. Serial boards are often an integral part of RAM expansion boards for the IBM PC, such as those distributed by QUADRAM and AST. Since you probably bought a memory board for your computer before buying Symphony, you may very well have a serial board already. If you're not sure if your computer has a serial port, look for a 25-pin male DB-25 connector at the rear or side of your computer.

Data Communications Software

The third required ingredient for successful data communications is data communications software. Data communications software, such as Symphony, allows you to control the modem and the serial board and to specify the information that should be sent or received across the communications link. The parameters usually controlled by the communications software include character length, addition or deletion of parity bits, addition or deletion of stop bits, and control of the communication speed.

In addition to allowing you to control and configure the communications parameters, the communications software provides for the capture and display of data, transmission of data from files or RAM, storage, recall, and dialing of telephone numbers, and other functions. A complete discussion of Symphony's communications software features will be presented in the next section.

GENERAL TERMINOLOGY

The following sections discuss some of the general principles and terminology relating to data communications, specifically those aspects you'll be able to control when working with the COMM environment.

Asynchronous versus Synchronous Communication

Asynchronous and *synchronous* are terms that describe the timing of the transmission and receipt of communicated data. These terms describe systems by which the sending (originating) computer and the receiving (answering) computer extract meaningful bytes of information from the stream of serial data each sends or receives.

When information is transmitted by the *asynchronous* method, the sending computer adds special characters called *start bits* and *stop bits* to the data bits being sent across the communications link. As the eight-bit bytes are disassembled by the serial board for serial transmission, a start bit is added at the beginning of each byte and one or more stop bits are added at the end of each byte. These special bits "frame" each byte and thus divide the stream of data bits into meaningful eight-bit bytes. The receiving computer uses the start bits and stop bits to determine where a byte ends and a new byte begins. The IBM PC and most other microcomputers use asynchronous communication. Symphony communication is asynchronous.

The start bit is always a binary 0. This binary 0 is recognized as a change from the "resting" line-signal voltage representing a binary 1. This standard is set by Symphony and cannot be altered by you. Stop bits are binary 1s, which mark time until another start bit (binary 0) is transmitted.

Symphony allows the selection of one or two stop bits. As a rule of thumb, two stop bits are commonly used at speeds of 110 baud and below, while one stop bit is used at higher speeds. Because stop bits carry no useful information, it is common to use one stop bit when possible to avoid unnecessary waste of transmission time.

Synchronous communication describes a system of continuous data transmission in which blocks of data are transmitted without marking each transmitted byte with start and stop bits. Instead, the receiving computer uses an extremely accurate clock to divide the stream of data into individual bytes. Synchronous communication protocols are rarely used in microcomputer communications, although IBM main frames use this method exclusively. Because synchronous communication requires no extra start and stop bits, it is faster than asynchronous communication; however, the hardware and software necessary for this method are quite expensive.

Simplex, Half Duplex, and Full Duplex

Another important parameter in data communications is the "directionality" of the data transmission. In any data communications session, two computers are involved. The transmission of data can occur in one of three ways: in only one direction, in two directions but at different times, or in both directions at the same time.

The *simplex* configuration allows data transfer in only one direction. When the communications link is established, one computer is designated as the sender and the other as the receiver; the sender can only send and not receive data, and the receiver can only receive and not send data. This one-way communication has few applications in Symphony.

The *half-duplex* configuration is often used in microcomputer communications. Half-duplex communication allows each computer to be both a sender and receiver of data, but communication can occur in only one direction at a time. To clarify this point, let's go back to the automobile analogy. Picture several cars lined up at either end of a one-lane bridge. The cars can cross the bridge in only one direction at a time; thus, one or several cars from one end of the bridge traverse the span, then one or several cars cross in the other direction. Each end of the bridge is, at alternate times, both a sender and receiver of automobiles. If you think of the automobiles as data bits and the ends of the bridge as computers, you have a picture of half-duplex communications.

The *full-duplex* configuration is also commonly used in microcomputer communications applications, especially when connecting with services such as The Source, CompuServe, and Dow Jones. In the full-duplex mode, data transmission can occur in both directions at the same time. That is, each terminal can be both a sender and receiver of data simultaneously. Let's continue the previous analogy and suppose that the bridge has been widened to two lanes so that automobiles can cross in two directions at once. Similarly, in full-duplex communications, data can be sent and received by both computers at the same time.

Although in full-duplex mode both computers can "talk" at the same time, usually one computer talks while the other listens. The listening computer reflects, or echoes, the transmission it receives back to the sending computer, confirming the accuracy of the transmission. The sending computer thus sends and receives the same data at essentially the same time.

When using data communications, the configuration of the terminal that makes the call (the originating terminal) must match that of the terminal being contacted (the answering terminal). For example, if the answering terminal operates in a full-duplex mode, the sending terminal must also be set for full-duplex operation. Likewise, if the answering terminal is set for half-duplex operation, the sending terminal must also be set for half-duplex operation. Symphony uses the Echo command for this purpose.

Communications Speed

Another important data communications parameter is the speed of the transmission of data. The terms *baud rate* and *bits per second* describe the speed of data transmission. Although these terms are not necessarily interchangeable, Symphony uses both terms to mean the same thing, so you should simply think of the baud rate as the number of bits that are transmitted each second.

Most modems allow you to communicate at 110 or 300 baud, although some modems offer more options. At these speeds, the baud rate and the bit-per-second (BPS) rate are equal. A few advanced modems, like the Hayes Smartmodem 1200, let you transmit as many as 1200 BPS. Although many people call the Hayes 1200 and other similar devices 1200-baud modems, in fact they transmit at 1200 BPS but at only 600 baud.

Bits per second is simply a measurement of the number of bits that are transmitted across a data line in a second. Baud rate is defined as 1/(bit signal duration). At transmission speeds below 1200 BPS, the baud rate equals the BPS rate. However, a speed of 1200 BPS is equal to a baud rate of only 600 for the following reasons.

When communicating from 110 to 600 BPS, most modems represent binary 1s and 0s as different sound frequencies. This character-representation method is called *frequency shift keying.* Because only one tone is sent at a time, only one bit is transmitted at a time, and the baud rate is equal to the bits per second.

However, if the modem you use is capable of communicating at 1200 BPS, a different character-representation method, called *phase shifting,* is used, and bits are transmitted two at a time. Thus, at a speed of 1200 BPS, the baud rate is only 600 because two bits are sent during one signal duration.

It is crucial to successful communications that the transmission speeds of both terminals match. If one modem is transmitting at 1200 BPS and the other at 300 BPS, only meaningless gibberish will be sent between the terminals.

Character Length

Character length refers to the number of binary digits that the computer's serial board recognizes as a single character. Nearly every computer uses units called bytes to represent characters. These bytes are typically made up of eight bits, or binary digits. Each bit can have one of two states: 0 or 1. Given all of the possible combinations of 0s and 1s in eight bits, an eight-bit byte can represent a maximum of 256 characters.

Most computers use a standard character set, called the ASCII character set, to determine which codes represent which characters. The first 128 codes are completely standardized; that is, all computers use the same codes to represent the first 128 characters. This group of characters includes all of the alphabetic characters, the numeric characters, mathematical operators, and punctuation marks. Only seven bits are required to represent the first 128 characters in the ASCII character set.

The upper 128 codes, however, are far from standardized. In fact, almost every computer uses these codes to represent its own special set of characters. In Symphony, these upper 128 codes represent the characters in the Lotus International Character Set. Eight bits are required to represent the upper 128 characters.

Most communications software allows you to choose a character length of either seven or eight bits. If the information being transmitted includes only the characters represented by the first 128 ASCII codes, then the eighth bit does not need to be transmitted. In this event, the eighth bit can be replaced by a parity bit (which will be discussed in the next section). If the information to be transmitted includes characters represented by the upper 128 ASCII character set, the eight-bit character length must be chosen.

Parity Bits

A parity bit is an error-checking mechanism that is transmitted as the eighth bit when you select a seven-bit character length for data transmission. If the communications software used by the receiving computer has a parity-checking feature, the receiving computer can identify faulty incoming characters. Because the maximum allowable character length is eight bits and because the parity bit is included as one of those bits, parity can be used only if a seven-bit character length is specified.

Parity can be designated as odd or even. If odd parity is chosen, the communications software commands the serial board on the transmitting computer to count the number of binary 1s in the seven-bit character and then add a binary 1 or 0 as the eighth character to ensure that the sum of the eight binary digits is odd.

Conversely, if even parity is chosen, an eighth bit of 0 or 1 is attached to the seven-bit character to produce an even sum. The use of even parity to communicate with seven-bit characters is an accepted convention.

Parity should be set to match the requirements of the remote computer so it will recognize the characters sent by the IBM PC. However, few PC communications software packages, including Symphony, take advantage of the parity bit for error checking of received data.

The X-On/X-Off Protocol

Most communications programs use a communications buffer to store characters that have been received across the telephone lines but not processed. If the rate at which data is received into the buffer exceeds the rate at which this data can be processed by the receiving computer's communications software, the buffer will "overflow," and characters will be lost. To prevent such overflows, a mechanism must exist to turn the flow of data between the computers on and off.

X-On/X-Off refers to a standard communications protocol that controls the flow rate of data across the transmission line. Under X-On/X-Off protocol, the receiving computer issues an X-Off (ASCII 19, or [Ctrl] S) to the sending computer to notify it that the receiver's communications buffer is approaching capacity. The sending computer responds by temporarily suspending the transmission of information, which allows the receiving computer to "catch up." When the receiving computer's buffer has been emptied (when the data has been processed by the receiving communications software), the receiving computer issues an X-On command (ASCII 17, or [Ctrl] Q), signaling the sending computer to continue transmitting data. Symphony can support this mechanism in both the sending and receiving modes.

X-Modem Protocol

X-Modem refers to a commonly used, public domain, error-checking protocol. Under X-Modem protocol, information is transmitted and received in 128-byte blocks. After each block is received by the answering computer, the block is checked for accuracy of transmission through an algorithm that manipulates the sum of the binary digits in the block. Blocks of data that do not "check" are retransmitted until no error is detected. Symphony mandates the use of this protocol for disk-to-disk transfers.

MORE ON COMM

This chapter should have given you enough background in data communications to work with Symphony's COMM environment. For an in-depth study of this topic, consult either *Digital Communications Programming on the IBM PC* by David Schwaderer, published by Brady, or *Communications and Networking for the IBM PC* by Larry Jordan, published by Wiley and Sons.

In the next chapter, we'll look into the Symphony commands that control the communications parameters you just learned about.

CHAPTER TWENTY FOUR

SYMPHONY COMMUNICATIONS BASICS

Before you can use Symphony for data communications, you must install drivers that describe the communications hardware and protocol you will use. (The installation process is covered in detail in Chapter 2).

One of the last questions in the Install program asks whether you wish to install a modem driver on the program disk. Answer yes if you plan to use the communications feature of Symphony. The program then asks you to select from a menu of two possible modems: the Hayes Smartmodem or the Popcom X60. Select the appropriate device by typing its number. If you plan to use a different modem, consult Lotus or your dealer for external driver sets and additional instructions.

Next, the Install program asks you to specify which serial port to use during communication. If your computer has only one serial port, choose Option 1 (IBM or COMPAQ COM1 8250). If your machine has two ports, you can communicate through either of them. Remember, however, that you must connect your modem to the port specified in order for Symphony to communicate.

There is a third parameter relating to communications that you do not specify; rather, the Install program provides a default value. This parameter specifies the use of the X-Modem protocol for the disk-to-disk transfer of files.

You can view the settings for all of the Install options from within Symphony by choosing Option 2 (Display Selections in a Driver Set) from the Install program master menu.

ENTERING THE COMM ENVIRONMENT

As you have seen throughout this book, the default window in Symphony is a SHEET window. When Symphony is first loaded into your computer, you view the worksheet through a SHEET window named MAIN.

Changing the Window Type

The easiest way to enter a COMM environment from a SHEET window is to press {**Type**}. This action displays the Type menu in the control panel:

SHEET DOC GRAPH FORM COMM

To convert the current window to a COMM window, select **C**OMM from this menu. Figure 24.1 shows a full-screen COMM window named MAIN.

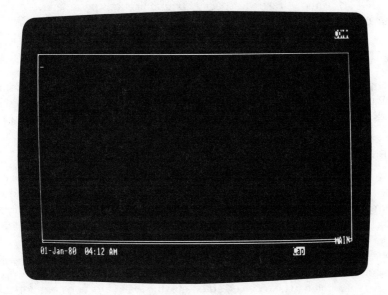

Figure 24.1

Once you have changed the window type to COMM, you can toggle the window back to its original type (probably SHEET) by pressing {Switch}.

Creating a New COMM Window

You can also enter a COMM environment by creating a completely new COMM window. This window can be as large or as small as you wish (within the limitations of your computer's display), and it can be positioned on the screen wherever you wish.

To create a new COMM window, issue the {**Services**} –**W**indow **C**reate command. At the prompt, enter the name of the new window. You may wish to use a name that specifies with whom you are communicating. For example, if you are going to log into The Source, you might name your window SOURCE.

Next, Symphony displays the Type menu and pauses while you choose a type for the new window. To create a COMM window, of course, you choose **C**OMM.

Now Symphony highlights the entire screen and pauses for you to size and position the new window. The default size is a full screen. If you want the new COMM window to fill the entire screen, just press [Enter]. For most communications applications, you will probably wish to use the whole screen.

If you want to make the window smaller than full size, use the arrow keys and the period key to expand or shrink the size of the window and to position it in the desired location on the screen.

Finally, press **[Esc]** to choose default values for the Window Settings menu that appears. (None of these settings have any meaning in the COMM environment.) You are now in a COMM window, ready to specify communications parameters and begin a communications session. (For more details on windows, see Chapter 11.)

THE COMM COMMAND MENU

Once you are in the COMM environment, pressing {**Menu**} displays the Command menu unique to the COMM environment. This menu and related submenus list all of the commands you will use when communicating with Symphony. This menu consists of six options:

Phone Login Transmit-Range File-Transfer Break Settings

The Phone command controls the majority of the telephone-related functions needed to communicate over telephone lines. The options behind the Phone command order the modem to dial, allow you to specify the number to dial, command the modem to answer or hang up, command the modem to answer an incoming call automatically, and enable or disable voice communication over the phone line.

The Login command instructs Symphony to send and receive a series of strings to a remote computer, as necessary to log onto that system. The prespecification of up to ten strings to be sent and ten to be received automates the log-in function common to many time-sharing host computer systems.

The Transmit-Range command instructs Symphony to send a range from the worksheet to a remote computer. Transmit-Range is an extremely useful command because it allows you to send data stored in your worksheet, including documents and spreadsheets, to another computer.

The File-Transfer command instructs the computer to either send or receive a file directly to or from the computer's disk drives.

The Break command instructs Symphony to transmit a Break signal (a sustained series of binary 0s) to the remote computer, instructing it to suspend the transmission of data. This command is not the same as the [Ctrl][Break] command recognized by Symphony, which can be used to interrupt the execution of various Symphony commands.

We'll cover each of these commands in more detail in this chapter and the next, but not in the order in which they appear on the COMM command menu. The next-to-last command on the menu, Settings, is covered first, because it is the most complex COMM mode command and the most essential to successful Symphony communications. Chapter 25 covers the rest of the COMM mode commands.

SETTINGS

The last command on the COMM command menu, Settings, is the most important communications command. The Settings command controls the COMM environment Settings sheet and allows you to specify values for the communications parameters discussed in Chapter 23. The Settings menu and COMM Settings sheet are shown in Figure 24.2.

```
Interface Phone Terminal Send Break Handshaking Capture Login Name Quit
----------------------------------------------------------------------
| Interface                 Terminal                  Send            |
|   Baud:        110         Screen:    Window          EOL:     \013  |
|   Parity:      None        Echo:      No             Delay:    0     |
|   Length:      7           Linefeed:  No             Response:       |
|   Stop bits:   1           Backspace: Backspace     Break:     60    |
| Phone                      Wrap:      Yes            Handshaking      |
|   Type:        Pulse       Delay:     0               Inbound:  Yes  |
|   Dial:        60          Translation:               Outbound: Yes  |
|   Answer:      15          (none)                    Capture         |
|   Number:                                             Range:    No   |
|                                                       Printer:  No   |
| ==========================================Communications Settings=   |
```

Figure 24.2

The fundamental rule in the world of data communications is that the communications parameters (settings) of two communicating computers must match exactly. The critical parameters include the baud rate, character length, number of parity bits, stop bits, full- versus half-duplex, special protocols (X-Modem or X-On/X-Off), end-of-line characters, and response characters.

The first corollary to this rule is that the originating computer (the one that places the phone call) must adjust its settings to match those of the computer it is contacting (the answering computer). On very rare occasions it is possible to establish successful communications between computers with mismatched communications parameters, but in nearly every case the settings must agree exactly.

The point to remember is this: before you attempt to contact another computer, determine (from published data, a phone call to the other operator, etc.) what communications settings the remote computer uses. Then adjust Symphony's communications settings to match these parameters. Unless this is done, contact and communication will be difficult, if not impossible.

Interface

The first choice on the COMM Settings menu is Interface. This selection allows you to change four parameters with which you should be familiar by now: baud rate, parity, character length, and stop bits.

Baud

The Baud command allows you to specify to the computer's serial board and modem the speed at which data transmission will occur. When you select **B**aud from the Interface menu, Symphony prompts you to select a number from 1 to 8. Each number represents a different communications speed, as shown in Table 24.1.

Menu Number	Baud Rate
1	110
2	150
3	300
4	600
5	1200
6	2400
7	4800
8	9600

Table 24.1

Select a baud rate by typing one of the numbers listed in the menu or pointing to one of the selections and pressing **[Enter]**. Remember that you can't select the baud rate directly; in other words, to set the baud rate to 300, you must type **3,** not 300.

The speed to select is determined by two factors. First, as stressed above, the selected speed must match the speed used by the remote computer. Services such as The Source, CompuServe, Newsnet, and Dow Jones use either 300 or 1200 baud. Most microcomputer modems also use either 300 or 1200 baud.

Second, your choice of the baud setting is constrained by the modem you use. For example, the Hayes 1200 Smartmodem operates at only three speeds: 110, 300, and 1200 bits per second (BPS). If you select any one of the other five choices in the Symphony menu, Symphony will be unable to communicate with the Hayes modem. When you select the **b**aud rate, make sure that you match the remote computer and the capabilities of your modem.

Parity

The Parity command allows you to specify whether the computer's serial board should add a parity bit to data being sent and subtract a parity bit from incoming information. As explained earlier, parity bits are a mechanism the receiving computer uses to check for transmission errors.

Symphony has the ability to add and subtract parity bits from transmitted data so that understandable information can be sent to and received from other computers that mandate the use of parity. Unlike some other communications software, however, Symphony cannot use the parity bit to check for errors in received information. This means that Symphony can communicate with remote computers that use parity, but it does not use the parity bits it receives to detect transmission errors.

If you want to adjust the parity setting, issue the {**Menu**} **S**ettings **I**nterface **P**arity command. Symphony then prompts you to choose a number from 1 to 3. The parity settings represented by each number are as follows:

Menu Number	Parity Setting
1	None
2	Odd
3	Even

(If you don't understand these options, take a moment to read the section on parity in Chapter 23.)

As with baud rate, the rule to follow when selecting parity is to choose the parity state used by the remote computer. In most circumstances, if a parity mismatch exists, received data are either rejected or unrecognizable.

To communicate with services such as The Source and Dow Jones, specify no parity. CompuServe operates with either even or no parity. Because most data communications programs for microcomputers do not use parity checking, a setting of 1 (none) is usually best for PC-to-PC communications.

Remember that parity (odd or even) can only be used if seven-bit character length is selected. If you select eight-bit length, Symphony simply ignores the parity command, resulting in no parity bit being added or subtracted.

Length

The Length command allows you to specify the number of bits which each transmitted or received character contains. As mentioned in Chapter 23, the standard ASCII character set includes ASCII codes from 0 to 127. This range of codes includes all of the most commonly used characters on the IBM PC, such as uppercase and lowercase letters, numbers, punctuation marks, and mathematical symbols. The next 128 codes stand for "special characters," which are represented by strings of eight bits. The special characters in the Lotus International Character Set are represented by the codes from 128 to 255.

If the data being transmitted contain some of the special characters represented by the upper 128 codes, you must use the eight-bit setting. If you try to transmit these special characters using a seven-bit character length, the eighth bit in each character will be truncated in transmission, erroneously changing these special characters into totally different seven-bit ASCII characters. If only the first 128 characters are transmitted, you may use the seven-bit setting.

If, on the other hand, you decide to add a parity bit to the outgoing characters, you must select a seven-bit character length. Because the parity bit is the eighth bit in a character, only seven data bits are allowed when parity is used.

To change the Length setting, select **L**ength from the Settings Interface menu. Symphony prompts you to select a number, 1 or 2—1 sets the length to seven bits and 2 sets the length to eight bits.

The same old rule applies to the selection of character length: select the character length used by the computer you are contacting. Character length mismatches usually result in the inability to receive characters or in the reception of different characters than were sent, due to the truncation of the eighth digit.

The Source, Newsnet, and Dow Jones all require that you use an eight-bit character length. You can access CompuServe using either seven- or eight-bit communications. Either seven- or eight-bit character lengths can be used in communications betweeen microcomputers. Remember, though, that if you choose a seven-bit length you cannot easily send characters represented by ASCII codes 128 to 255.

Stop Bits

The Stop Bits command allows you to specify the number of stop bits to be added to the end of each transmitted character. As explained in the preceding chapter, the start bit and stop bit(s) are transmitted by the originating computer before and after the character bits and the parity bit (if selected). These bits tell the receiving computer's serial board that a complete character has been received. The stop bit(s) and the start bit "frame" data characters communicated between computers.

The Settings Interface Stop Bits menu offers two options: 1 or 2. Selecting 1 instructs the serial board to add a single stop bit after each character in the data stream. Likewise, selecting 2 directs the serial board to add two stop bits after each character. You can make this selection by typing the appropriate number or by pointing to the desired choice and pressing [Enter].

As you would expect, you should specify the number of stop bits that the remote computer expects to receive. A good rule of thumb is to use two stop bits at baud rates of 110 or less and one stop bit at speeds greater than 110.

Phone

Phone is the next item on the COMM Settings menu. The Phone settings allow you to control telephone-related parameters, such as the type of phone being used, dial time, answer time, and the storage of phone numbers. Unlike the essential settings affected by the Interface command, these parameters are mostly convenience features. In most instances, successful communication can occur with no changes to the Phone commands.

Upon issuing the Settings Phone command from the COMM Settings menu, Symphony gives you four command choices:

Type Dial-Time Answer-Time Number

To avoid confusion, note the following point: the COMM {Menu} Settings Phone command is used to define values for Symphony's COMM Settings sheet (see Figure 24.2, earlier). The Symphony command that instructs the modem to dial is also Phone; however, this command is accessed from the main COMM command menu by typing {Menu} Phone. Even though they have the same name, these commands are entirely different.

Type

The Type command lets you tell Symphony whether you are using a pulse or tone telephone. You should select the type that matches the telephone line to which your modem is connected. If the line to which your modem is connected is a rotary line (evidenced by a dial on the face of the phone), you must select Pulse. If the line to which your modem is connected is a touch-tone line, select Tone. Nearly all business phones are tone phones, so most Symphony users will choose the Tone option.

If you wish, you may select the Pulse setting for use on your tone line. However, although this combination is compatible, pulse dialing is slower than tone dialing, so there is no real reason to make such a selection. The reverse is not possible; that is, you cannot select Tone if you have a pulse phone line.

Dial-Time

The second choice on the Settings Phone menu is Dial-Time. This command controls the amount of time Symphony allows for the modem to make a connection with another computer. In other words, this command lets you tell Symphony how long to wait after dialing the phone before it should "hang up" if no connection is made.

When you select **D**ial-Time, Symphony prompts you to type the number of seconds desired for this parameter. You can select any number of seconds between 0 and 32767. The default value for this setting, 60 seconds, is ideal in most cases, since it is sufficiently forgiving of a remote computer operator who is slow in answering the call manually and provides enough time for a remote computer with a multiline queue to answer your call. I can't imagine any circumstance in which the full 32767 seconds (9.1 hours) would be specified.

When commanded to dial, Symphony dials the telephone and waits the full period you specified, whether the line is "ringing," "busy," or "dead," unless a connection is made in that time. A long, unsuccessful dial attempt can be stopped by pressing **[Ctrl][Break]** simultaneously, after which pressing **[Esc]** returns you to the COMM window.

Answer-Time

The Answer-Time command is similar to the Dial-Time command. The number entered for this setting is the maximum amount of time that Symphony should spend attempting to establish a connection after the telephone is answered. The Answer-Time count does not start when the phone begins to ring, but rather when the modem answers (in the Autoanswer mode) or when the user answers with the Phone Answer Manual command.

As with Dial-Time, the Answer-Time setting must be between 0 and 32767 seconds. Again, the default setting of 15 seconds should be sufficient for most applications. If a connection is not made 15 seconds after the receiving modem answers the phone, one of the modems is probably not working properly.

Number

The final command on the Phone menu is Number. The Number command allows you to specify a default telephone number. This number is stored in the COMM Settings sheet and is automatically used whenever Symphony asks the modem to dial.

When this command is selected, Symphony prompts you to enter a telephone number. This number may have from 1 to 38 digits and may include area codes, special long-distance access codes for services such as Sprint or MCI, and international access codes, in addition to local telephone numbers.

The number should be entered as a long string of digits. For example, the number 15025551212 is Symphony's representation of the number 1-502-555-1212. You can add nonnumeric characters to this string, but Symphony ignores these when placing the call. For example, Symphony treats 555-1212 and 5551212 identically.

The only exception to this rule is the comma. Inserting a comma anywhere in the phone number causes the modem to delay for two seconds before dialing the next number. Multiple commas will cause dialing delays of four, six, eight, ten, or more seconds, at two seconds per comma.

The delay(s) introduced by comma(s) can be very useful. For instance, if the telephone system to which your modem is connected requires dialing certain numbers (such as 9 or 85) to access an outside line, you could include the access number(s) in the Number settings this way: 9,,5551212. The two commas cause the modem to delay four seconds while the outside line is reached.

In another case, you might wish to insert a pause after the modem dials your long-distance service access code, allowing time for a dial tone to be heard before the dialing sequence is completed. It is important to recognize that commas insert a predetermined time delay only; Symphony cannot be programmed to "listen" for a dial tone and then complete the call. Thus, it is wise to insert enough commas to allow for the maximum possible delay.

Terminal

The seven Settings Terminal commands allow you to "customize" your computer to emulate various standard terminals commonly used to access main frame computers. These commands allow you to alter the display of information (either received from another computer or locally echoed) in the COMM window. The Settings Terminal menu looks like this:

Screen Echo Linefeed Backspace Wrap Delay Translation

Four of these settings—Screen, Echo, Linefeed, and Wrap—have no effect on the way information is sent to other computers or to your modem. Rather, these four settings affect only how you see information on the screen of a COMM window. These commands control the size of the COMM window, the local echoing of data, the insertion of linefeeds, and the wrapping of text.

Screen

The **S**creen command allows you to alter the size of the COMM display. This command offers the choice between a full-screen COMM display or a window display. If you choose **F**ull-Screen, the borders of the COMM window disappear, and the total screen (80 characters wide by 24 lines deep) is available for the display of incoming data. **Win**dow tells Symphony to display received data inside the COMM window you are using.

Some remote computers may send your computer data arranged to fill an 80-by-24 screen. Because even the largest possible COMM window is smaller than 80 by 24, you'll need to use the Screen setting when communicating with these computers.

If the current COMM window is a partial-screen window, selecting **F**ull-Screen eliminates the window borders and expands the window to fill the screen. Figures 24.3 and 24.4 show the effect of the **F**ull-Screen command on a partial-screen window. Note that the effect of this command is similar to that of the {Zoom} key.

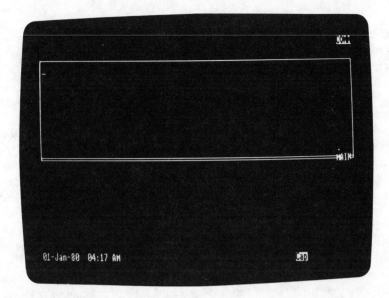

Figure 24.3

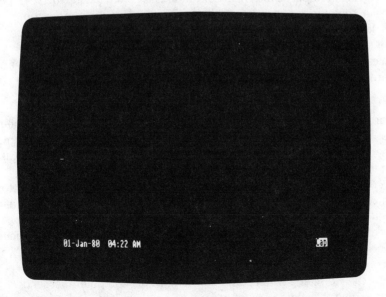

Figure 24.4

You cannot alter the size of the COMM window by using the Screen command. You can change the size and position of a window only by using the {Services} **W**indow **L**ayout command.

Echo

The Echo command adjusts Symphony for full-duplex or half-duplex communications by enabling or disabling local echo of transmitted characters.

As discussed in the previous chapter, computers that operate in a full-duplex mode usually return a copy of each received character to the sending computer. This is called "echoing" the signal. The echoed character is displayed on the screen of the sending computer, confirming that the character was properly received.

In half-duplex communication, the receiving computer does not echo a received character back to the sending computer. Because no character is echoed from the receiving computer, the screen of the sending computer does not display the characters being sent. In order for these characters to be displayed, the sending computer must echo the characters *locally,* that is, display on its screen the characters it is sending.

If the remote computer is operating in a full-duplex mode, you should select No in response to the Echo prompt. This setting instructs Symphony not to add a software-generated local echo of each character (which is not needed because the sending computer is providing the echo).

If you select Yes when communicating with a full-duplex system, double characters are displayed on the screen. If you see this effect during a communications session, simply press {Menu} Settings Terminal Echo No to turn off the locally produced echo.

If Symphony is communicating with a computer operating in a half-duplex mode, you should select Yes in response to the Echo prompt. This command instructs Symphony to echo to your computer's screen each character you send to the remote computer.

If you select No when communicating with a half-duplex system, your screen displays none of the characters you send out over the communications link. If, when you are communicating with a remote computer, the characters you type do not appear on your screen, press {Menu} Settings Terminal Echo Yes to enable the locally produced echo.

Linefeed

Many aspects of data communications are far from standardized. Among them is the character or characters used to mark the end of a line of transmitted data. Some computers send both a carriage return (ASCII 13, or [Ctrl] M) and a linefeed (ASCII 10, or [Crtl] J) at the end of each line. Others send only the carriage return.

When communicating with a remote computer that sends only a carriage return, the receiving computer must add a linefeed at the end of each line. Otherwise, each line of received text will overwrite the previous line.

A response of No to the Linefeed prompt tells Symphony not to issue a linefeed each time it receives a carriage return from the sending computer. Use this setting when the sending computer is supplying both a carriage return and a linefeed.

If you use the No setting when communicating with a computer that sends only carriage returns, then each time Symphony receives a carriage return, the cursor returns to the left border of the COMM window but remains on the same line. Any information that follows the carriage return overwrites the data already displayed on that line.

A response of Yes to the Linefeed prompt instructs Symphony to interpret a carriage return signal (ASCII 13) as a carriage return plus a linefeed character (ASCII 10), causing the cursor to move to the left border of the COMM window and then down one line. In essence, Symphony "translates" ASCII character 13 into (ASCII 13 + ASCII 10). Use this setting when communicating with computers that send only a carriage return instead of a carriage return plus linefeed.

For many applications, you'll want to change the Linefeed default setting of No to Yes. For instance, if you use the default setting of No when communicating with another computer using Symphony (which in the default mode sends only carriage returns and not linefeeds at the end of each transmitted line), each line of received data overwrites the previous line. Information typed on your keyboard and echoed locally suffers the same fate. Furthermore, if you capture the transmission into the worksheet (this concept is explained in Chapter 25), the same overwriting occurs, rendering the captured information useless. In this instance, you would set Echo to Yes to force a locally generated linefeed to accompany every carriage return.

However, if the remote computer is configured to send a carriage return plus a linefeed at the end of each line of text transmitted, you may wish to select the **No** option. In this situation, there is no need to have Symphony add another linefeed command. If you specify **Yes**, the text is double-spaced.

The Linefeed command controls only the interpretation of the carriage-return character when Symphony is receiving data. You can instruct Symphony to send both a carriage return and linefeed signal after transmitting a line of text by using the Settings Send End-of-Line setting. This command is discussed in a few pages.

Backspace

The **B**ackspace command (like the Delay and Translation commands, below) does more than merely affect the display of information. It defines the meaning of the [Backspace] key during data communications. This command offers two options: Backspace or Delete.

If **B**ackspace is selected, pressing the [Backspace] key in the COMM environment causes the cursor to move one space to the left. In this mode, the [Backspace] key is equivalent to the ← key.

If you choose the **D**elete option, pressing [Backspace] deletes the character at the current cell pointer location and moves the cursor one space to the right. This is equivalent to pressing the **[Del]** and → keys in the DOC environment.

Notice that neither setting for [Backspace] matches the normal function of this key in other Symphony windows. Usually, [Backspace] moves the cursor one space to the left and erases the character in that space. We find it disturbing that the familiar backspace-and-erase function of the [Backspace] key in other Symphony windows is not an option in the COMM environment.

A mismatch in this specification has no apparent effect on the transfer of ranges from the worksheet or from disk. However, during communication with a remote computer, the specification for this key by the sending computer determines the character the remote computer receives.

Wrap

Sometimes the lines of data you receive from a remote computer are too long to fit on one line of a COMM window. This is especially likely when you receive data through a partial-screen COMM window. The Settings Terminal Wrap command controls the automatic wraparound of received lines that are too long to fit on a single line of the COMM window.

If you choose the **No** option, lines of data received from the remote computer's keyboard or echoed from the local keyboard do not wrap around to the beginning of the next line when they reach the right border of the COMM window. Instead, the cursor remains lodged against the right margin, and no characters appear on the screen until [Enter] is pressed on either computer's keyboard.

Choosing the **Yes** option causes the characters received from a remote keyboard to wrap around to the next line, much as they do in a DOC environment. Because you usually want to see all of each line of transmitted data, in most cases you should select the **Yes** setting.

Figures 24.5 and 24.6 show two versions of a COMM window that is about 40 characters wide. In both cases, the sentence

This is the time for action; we dare not delay any longer.

has just been received. If Wrap is set to Yes, the window will look like Figure 24.5 after receiving the line. Notice that Symphony broke the line when it reached the edge of the window and wrapped it around to the next line. If Wrap is set to No, the window will look like Figure 24.6.

```
 ------------------------------------------
|This is the time for action; we dare no|
|t delay any longer                     |
|                                       |
|                                       |
|                                       |
 ===============================MAIN=
```

Figure 24.5

```
 -----------------------------------------
|This is the time for action; we dare no|
|                                       |
|                                       |
|                                       |
 ===============================MAIN=
```

Figure 24.6

The Wrap setting has no effect on the form of received data that is captured into a worksheet range or to the printer. For example, suppose you are working in a

40-character-wide COMM window and are receiving 80-character lines from the remote computer. If Wrap is set to No, only 40 of the 80 characters on each line appear in the COMM window. However, if this transmission is being captured to a range, the data are captured in one long line in the specified range, even though the COMM window does not display the data being received. Similarly, if Wrap is Yes, lines that wrap in the COMM window do not wrap in the Capture range.

Delay

The Settings Terminal Delay command instructs Symphony to insert a delay between each transmitted character during communication. These delays are in multiples of 1/128 second.

A delay between transmitted characters is useful when you send information to a computer that processes incoming information slowly. Inserting a delay allows the receiving computer time to process each character before receiving the next.

The default Delay setting of 0 is satisfactory for most applications. However, if experience shows that the remote computer needs more time to process characters, you can adjust the Delay setting to any integer up to 32,767 (4.26 minutes).

The use of a delay factor can substantially reduce the speed of communications. Thus, if a delay is specified when communicating at 1200 bits per second, the actual speed of character transmission is significantly less than 1200 BPS.

Translation

The Translation command instructs Symphony to use a specified translation table when sending or receiving information. You can use any one of the ten Lotus-developed national character replacement sets, or you can create and specify custom character code translation tables.

Most Symphony users will probably never need to use a translation table when communicating. For this reason, we'll skip over this topic for now and cover it later.

Send

Send is the fourth option on the COMM Settings menu. The three Send commands— End-of-Line, Delay, and Response—determine Symphony's behavior when sending the data in a range from the worksheet to another computer using the Transmit-Range command (covered in Chapter 25). These three commands determine which characters are sent at the end of a line of transmitted text, set a delay between transmission of successive lines of text, and instruct Symphony to wait for a response character from the remote computer before sending another line.

End-of-Line

When you select the End-of-Line command from the Send menu, Symphony prompts you to supply the string of characters it will *send* automatically at the end of each transmitted line. (The Terminal linefeed setting controls the way Symphony interprets *received* linefeeds.) The default value for this parameter is \m, which is a representation for [CTRL] M, the ASCII character for a carriage return. This means that in the default condition Symphony will send a carriage return at the end of each line of a transmitted range.

This default condition is ideal for most Symphony communications applications. However, if the computer receiving the transmitted information does not automatically insert a Linefeed character whenever a carriage return is received, the data received by the answering computer are overwritten in both the COMM screen and the Capture range.

For example, suppose that the receiving Symphony program has been set to not add a linefeed at the end of each received line (accomplished with the command sequence {Menu} Settings Terminal Linefeed No) and that the sending Symphony computer is set to send only a carriage return at the end of each line. When the sending computer transmits a range, every line in the transmitted range is received on one line of the receiving computer's screen and Capture range.

To correct this situation, the receiving computer operator could issue the command sequence {**Menu**} **S**ettings **T**erminal **L**inefeed **Y**es. Because an automatic linefeed is necessary when receiving or locally echoing keyboard communication, this is the best solution. Alternatively, you could set the sending Symphony program to send a linefeed character (\j) in addition to the carriage return at the end of each line by issuing the command {**Menu**} **S**ettings **S**end **E**nd-of-Line [**Esc**] **\m\j.** However, this setting causes double-spacing when you transmit a range to a computer set to add a linefeed to a received carriage return automatically.

Delay

The Send Delay command instructs Symphony to wait for a specified time after it transmits each *line* of a range before sending the next. This setting is useful if the remote computer processes incoming information slowly.

After selecting **D**elay from the Send menu, Symphony prompts you to specify the number of 1/128-second intervals to be inserted after each line. As with the Terminal Delay command, any number up to 32767 (4.26 minutes) may be selected. The default value of 0 is optimal in most situations.

Please note that the Settings Send Delay command sequence differs from the Terminal Delay command sequence in that Send Delay inserts a pause after each transmitted *line* in a range transmission, while Terminal Delay inserts a delay between each character in a transmission. However, these commands have a very similar function—to aid the receiving computer by allowing time for received data to be processed.

Response

The Settings Send Response command instructs Symphony to wait for a specified response character to be sent from the remote computer before sending each successive line of text from a range. This command provides a more sophisticated way than Send Delay to ensure that the receiving computer is ready to receive the next line before it is sent.

In response to Symphony's prompt, you may type any string of up to 240 characters. You can enter these codes either as a three-digit ASCII code preceded by a backslash (for example, \027) or as a single-character control code (for example, \O). Notice that these are the same as the printer Init-String codes.

The response string you specify should match the string the receiving computer sends when it is ready to receive data. In most cases, the default setting of \j ([Ctrl] J, or Line-feed) is *not* appropriate. In fact, most of the time no response character should be used. To erase this setting, issue the command {**Menu**} **S**ettings **S**end **R**esponse [**Esc**] [**Enter**]. Do not use a response character when two Symphony programs are communicating.

Break

The next option on the Settings menu is Break. In data communications, a break signal is a series of binary 0s sent to a remote computer. This series instructs it to suspend transmission or stop processing data. The Break setting defines the duration of the break signal Symphony should send when the COMM {Menu} Break command is issued.

The default setting of 60 milliseconds is appropriate for most applications. However, this setting should match the break signal duration expected by the receiving computer. To change the default setting, simply issue the {**Menu**} **S**ettings **S**end **B**reak command and supply the number desired. The Break setting can be any number up to 32767.

Handshaking

Handshaking is the sixth item on the Settings menu. The Handshaking command tells Symphony whether to use X-On/X-Off protocol when sending or receiving data. As explained in greater detail in Chapter 23, the receiving computer sends special signals that tell the sending computer to turn off the flow of data when the receiving computer's COMM buffer reaches capacity and to resume the flow when the buffer empties. Symphony can be set both to transmit and receive using X-On and X-Off signals.

When you select **H**andshaking from the Settings menu, you see the options Inbound or Outbound. The default condition for both Inbound (receiving) and Outbound (sending) is **Yes**, meaning that X-On/X-Off protocol is used.

To deactivate or reactivate the use of Inbound Handshaking (Symphony's ability to stop or restart sending data in response to a signal from the receiving computer), press **I**nbound, followed by **Y**es or **N**o. Similarly, to change Symphony's use of Outbound Handshaking (the ability to transmit a signal to instruct a remote computer to suspend the transmission of data), press **O**utbound, followed by **Y**es or **N**o.

In most situations, you will want Symphony to use both Inbound and Outbound handshaking. For example, you should use X-On/X-Off protocol for information transfers between two Symphony programs. However, some computers do not support X-On/X-Off protocol or use a modified protocol that is not compatible with Symphony's. When communicating with these computers, you will want to deactivate one or both of these settings.

It is important to understand the difference between the Send Delay, Terminal Delay, and Handshaking settings. The difference between delays and handshaking is like the difference between a stop sign and a traffic light at a busy intersection. Delays are like stop signs; they force every character (or every line, in the case of Send Delay) to delay for a specified time before being transmitted. Handshaking is like a traffic light; when the sending computer receives an X-On (the green light), characters move through the communications link without delay. When an X-Off is issued, character transfer stops for a moment, much as traffic stops at a red light.

Most of the time you won't need to use delays if the remote computer supports X-On/X-Off handshaking. However, at 1200 baud, you may need to specify a brief inter-character delay by using Terminal Delay. You may also need to specify a delay when communicating with computers that do not support X-On/X-Off handshaking.

Capture

The Settings Capture command allows you to designate a worksheet range as a Capture range. As its name implies, the Capture range "captures" incoming information in the worksheet. Once captured, you can manipulate the information with Symphony commands and use it in your spreadsheets and documents.

Because this command relates to the actual sending and receiving of data, and not to the preliminary settings needed to prepare Symphony for communication, it will be covered in Chapter 25.

Login

Many main frame computers and on-line services insist that you log on (or log in) to the system before gaining access to the information stored on that computer. To log in, you must type several phrases, or strings, usually including a password and a billing code.

Most communications software requires you to log on to a remote computer manually by typing the password, billing code, and other information at the keyboard. Symphony, however, lets you define a log-in sequence that can be sent automatically to the remote computer.

Because log-in sequences are closely related to dialing and connecting to a remote computer, we've covered them in detail in Chapter 25, Getting On Line with Symphony.

Name

Let's suppose you have fully configured Symphony to communicate with another computer by adjusting all of the COMM settings to match the settings of the remote computer exactly. After communicating with that machine, you issue the File Save command to save the worksheet, assuming that the COMM settings will be saved along with the other settings and all of the data in the worksheet.

Suppose that later you retrieve the file, issue the {Type} COMM command, and bring up the Settings sheet. You'll be in for a big surprise. All of the settings will be restored to the original default settings, and all of your settings will be destroyed. Note this well: *When you save a Symphony worksheet into a .WRK file, the COMM settings that were a part of the worksheet are not saved into the .WRK file. The next time you retrieve the file, the COMM settings will return to the default settings.*

All is not lost, however. Realizing that the creation of a COMM Settings sheet is a diffi-cult and time-consuming task, the developers of Symphony have made it possible to save and reuse any number of different COMM Settings sheets. These Settings sheets are stored in Communications Configuration Files (.CCF files).

.CCF files are created and accessed with the COMM {Menu} Settings Name com-mand. When you select Name from the COMM Settings menu, the following menu appears on the screen:

> Save Retrieve Erase Phone-and-Login

These commands allow you to create, destroy, and recall .CCF files, and to command Symphony to automatically dial the phone and begin a log-in sequence without any action on your part.

Save

The Save command lets you save the current COMM settings into a .CCF file.

When you select **S**ave, Symphony searches the system directory (the directory from which Symphony was loaded at the beginning of the current session, usually A:\) for existing .CCF files. If it finds one or more .CCF files, these are displayed in the control panel along with the prompt

> Configuration file name:

For example, assuming that the system directory was A:\ and that the disk in drive A contained three .CCF files, the control panel would look like this after the Name Save command is issued:

> Configuration File Name: A:\ * .CCF
>
> SYMPH.CCF SOURCE.CCF MAINFRAM.CCF

If you want to save the current COMM settings under one of the existing file names, just point to the name you want to use and press **[Enter].** Saving the current settings under an old name erases the settings previously stored in that file.

If you want to save the current settings under a new name, type the new name next to the prompt and press **[Enter].** In most cases, you'll want to save the new settings under a new name. The usual rules for file names (up to eight characters with no spaces or spe-cial characters) apply to .CCF files. You should not add the .CCF file name extension. Symphony will automatically supply the extension when you save the file.

Ideally, a .CCF file should match the requirements of each remote computer with which you communicate regularly, so that the laborious process of recreating a COMM Settings sheet will not be necessary prior to each communications session. For example, the previous example shows three .CCF files. The first is a Settings sheet for communicat-ing with another computer using Symphony; the second, a Settings sheet for communi-cating with The Source; and the third, a Settings sheet for communicating with the company main frame.

As we will discuss in later sections, once you have created a .CCF file, you can instruct Symphony to attach it to a worksheet file so that those COMM settings will be made current whenever that worksheet file is retrieved. You can also instruct Symphony to automatically load and use a designated .CCF file whenever Symphony is loaded into your computer.

Remember: once you have created a Settings sheet, the only way to save it is by creating a .CCF file. Simply saving the worksheet containing the settings is not enough.

Retrieving

When you want to communicate with a remote computer for which you have constructed a special .CCF file, you can retrieve the settings in the .CCF file into the COMM Settings sheet with the Name Retrieve command. The Name Retrieve command allows you to recall and make current a previously saved .CCF file.

To retrieve a .CCF file, issue the {**Menu**} **S**ettings **N**ame **R**etrieve command from within a COMM window. Symphony prompts you for the file to be retrieved:

> Configuration file name: A:\ * .CCF
>
> SYMPH.CCF SOURCE.CCF MAINFRAM.CCF

Notice that the Retrieve command is also displayed by a list of all the .CCF files on the system directory (the directory from which Symphony was loaded). To retrieve one of these files, point to its name in the list and press [Enter]. Symphony reads the .CCF file into the worksheet, replacing the current settings in the COMM Settings sheet with the settings contained in the file. The name of the retrieved .CCF file appears in the lower-right corner of the COMM Settings display to confirm the successful retrieval of the named .CCF file.

You can modify and resave a retrieved file using the Save command. For example, you might need to modify the Settings sheet named MAINFRAM.CCF if your password to the company main frame changes.

Unless you save the current settings before you retrieve the .CCF file, they will be destroyed. If the current settings are important, be sure to issue the Name Save command to store the settings in a file before you retrieve new settings.

This warning goes for the default settings, too. If you modify the default settings, or if you retrieve a .CCF file on top of the default settings, no command returns you to the defaults. Unless the default settings were saved to a .CCF file, the only way to restore those settings is to exit from Symphony and reenter the program.

Erase

The **E**rase command does just what it says: it instructs Symphony to erase the name and contents of the .CCF file you specify. As with the other Name commands, typing **E**rase from the Name menu causes Symphony to prompt you for the name of the file to be erased and to display a listing of the names of the .CCF files in the system directory. To erase a .CCF file, point to its name in the provided list and press **[Enter]**. Before erasing the selected file, Symphony asks, "Are you sure you want to erase this file?" A response of **Y**es permanently erases the file; **N**o returns the user to the Name command in the Settings submenu.

Because .CCF files use only about 1500 bytes of disk space, you can create and save many of these files without seriously affecting the capacity of your Symphony program disk.

Using a different directory   Of course, you can save, retrieve, and erase files from a directory other than the system directory if you so desire. For example, suppose the system directory is A:\, but you want to save a .CCF file under the name TEST.CCF on directory B:\. When you issue the Name Save command, the following message appears:

> Configuration File Name: A:\ * .CCF

To save the file on directory B:\, press **[Esc]** twice to erase Symphony's prompt and type **B:\TEST.CCF**. Symphony then saves the file on that directory.

Working with .CCF files   Two other command sequences affect the use of .CCF files. These commands, found in the {Services} command menu, affect the communications settings by attaching .CCF files to individual worksheets and specifying the default .CCF file to be made active when Symphony is first loaded into the computer.

Attaching a .CCF file to a worksheet   The command {Services} Settings Communications allows you to attach a .CCF file to an individual worksheet file, so that the attached .CCF file is loaded into the worksheet whenever that worksheet file is retrieved.

Suppose that you occasionally generate a report that contains information you receive from the Dow Jones service. The report is simply a form letter, into which you insert the opening, closing, high, and low prices for ten different securities. For the sake of convenience, you have created a worksheet file, named DOWJONES.WRK, which contains the form letter with a blank space for the stock information and the settings for a high-low-close-open graph.

In addition, you have created a .CCF file named DOWJONES.CCF containing the appropriate settings for communicating with the Dow Jones Service. This .CCF file designates a Capture range that matches the "blank spot" in your form letter. In this way, the stock price information is automatically inserted into the report, which is then ready for printing.

Instead of having to use the sequence COMM {Menu} Settings Name Retrieve DOWJONES.CCF to get into your worksheet whenever you wish to generate this report, you can use the {Services} Settings Communications command to attach the file DOWJONES.CCF to the worksheet DOWJONES.WRK.

To attach the file DOWJONES.CCF to the worksheet file DOWJONES.WRK, first retrieve the file DOWJONES.WRK into Symphony. Next, issue the **{Services} S**ettings Communications command. Symphony then prompts you to select **S**et or Cancel. These selections have the same effect as in the configuration discussion. You select **S**et, at which point Symphony displays the message

> Configuration file name: A:\ * .CCF
> DEFAULT.CCF SYMPHONY.CCF DOWJONES.CCF

To select the file DOWJONES.CCF, simply point to its name in the list and press [Enter].

When you save the worksheet file DOWJONES.WRK, the instructions to use DOWJONES.CCF as the default COMM settings for this worksheet are now saved with it. From that point on, whenever the worksheet file DOWJONES.WRK is retrieved, the settings in the .CCF file DOWJONES.CCF are loaded into the COMM Settings sheet.

It is important to remember that a .CCF file attached to a worksheet may be stored on a disk other than the one containing the worksheet. For example, the .CCF file may be on directory A:\ and the file on directory B:\. When the .WRK file is loaded, Symphony searches directory A:\ for the .CCF file. If that .CCF file is not on the disk, the .WRK file is still loaded. However, Symphony then displays the error message

> **Missing or Illegal .CCF file . . .**

and you must press the [Esc] key to make the worksheet appear on the screen.

Additionally, if disk drive A:\ is empty, the error message

> **Disk drive error**

appears at the bottom of the screen. Again, the .WRK file is retrieved, but it appears only after you press [Esc]. The point of these examples is that the disk containing your .CCF files should always be in drive A when you retrieve a worksheet file from any other drive.

Changing the default .CCF file   The command sequence {**Services**} Configuration Communications allows you to specify the .CCF file to be made active each time you load Symphony into the computer. If the majority of your data communications sessions involve talking to one particular remote computer, you'll probably want to designate the .CCF file containing those settings as "default" settings (that is, defaults custom-made by you), so that Symphony will always retrieve those settings when you load it into the computer.

For instance, suppose that nine times out of ten you communicate remotely with a computer that also uses Symphony. That computer is located in your company's office in Chicago. You have created a .CCF file that matches the parameters used by the computer in Chicago and have named that file CHISYM.CCF, which is stored on the Symphony Disk in drive A. So that you will not have to load that .CCF file into the worksheet manually every time you wish to connect with Chicago, you should make CHISYM.CCF the default file.

To change the default .CCF file, issue the {**Services**} Configuration Communications command. Symphony then prompts you to select **Set** (to establish a new default file) or **Cancel** (to cancel the previously specified default file). To establish CHISYM.CCF as the default, choose **Set**. Symphony then searches the system directory for all .CCF files that have been created and prompts you with

> **File name: A:\∗.CCF**

followed by a listing of the names of all the .CCF files on the disk. To install CHISYM.CCF as the default, simply point to the file name CHISYM.CCF in the list and press **[Enter].** At this point, drive A becomes active for approximately ten seconds as it loads CHICAGO-SYM.CCF into RAM. After that Symphony returns you to the {Services} menu.

However, CHISYM.CCF is not yet the default file. To complete the process, select Update from the {Services} Configuration menu and press [Enter]. Drive A again becomes active, time saving CHISYM.CCF as the default .CCF file. From this point on, the settings in CHISYM.CCF are used as the default settings whenever you create a COMM window.

Be sure not to confuse the {Services} Configuration Communications command, which defines the .CCF file to be used whenever Symphony is first loaded into the computer, with the {Services} Settings Communications command sequence discussed above. The .CCF file specified by the {Services} Settings Communications sequence is retrieved *only* when the specific worksheet to which it has been attached is retrieved into Symphony.

Phone-and-Login

The final Name command, Phone-and-Login, tells Symphony to retrieve a specified .CCF file, dial the telephone according to the Phone settings in that .CCF file, and then log in to the remote computer using the Login sequence contained in that file. In other words, this one command controls three ordinarily time-consuming functions.

The Phone-and-Login command is so useful and powerful that we wonder why it was "hidden" at the end of the Settings menu. This command should probably be a part of the COMM {Menu} Login menu. We'll cover the command where it belongs: in the next chapter with the discussion of the Login command.

Quit

As with most other Symphony menus, the final command on the Settings menu is Quit. Selecting **Quit** takes you back to the COMM mode, not back to the COMM menu, as you might expect. If you have revised the COMM settings and wish to get back to the COMM menu—perhaps to dial the phone—you must press **Quit** and then {Menu}.

Now that we have mastered the Settings command, let's look at the commands that actually tell Symphony to send and receive information.

CHAPTER TWENTY FIVE

GETTING ON-LINE WITH SYMPHONY

In the previous chapter you were introduced to all of the basic settings that affect data communications in Symphony. This chapter tells you how to communicate using Symphony. In the first part of the chapter, the Phone, Login, and Break COMM commands are explained. After that, all of Symphony's communications capabilities—transmitting a worksheet range, capturing data to the worksheet, and sending and receiving disk files—are covered in detail.

PHONE

The main function of the Phone command is to instruct the modem to dial the telephone and establish a connection with a remote computer. This command also controls the answering of incoming calls (either automatic or manual), terminates a connection, and allows voice communications (with certain modems).

The Phone command options work only with certain kinds of modems. For example, the Phone Call command is effective only if you use a direct-connect, autodial modem. If you have an acoustic modem, you must dial the number manually. Similarly, the Phone Wait-Mode command, which controls automatic answering of the phone by the modem, works only if your modem has autoanswer capability.

As mentioned in the discussion of the Phone settings, the Phone command tells Symphony to implement the settings in the Phone portion of the COMM Settings sheet. Please don't confuse these two commands; the Phone command draws information from the Phone settings.

You access the Phone command from the COMM environment menu by pressing {**Menu**} Phone. The following command options then appear at the top of the screen:

Call   Wait-Mode   Answer   Hangup   Data-Mode   Voice-Mode

Call

If you have a direct-connect, autodial modem, choosing **C**all tells the modem to dial the phone, using the Number, Dial-Time, and Phone type (tone or pulse) settings specified in the current COMM Settings sheet. When you select **C**all, Symphony displays the message

   Phone Number:

in the control panel. The prompt is followed by the phone number (if any) specified in the current Phone settings.

Pressing **[Enter]** confirms this number, and Symphony displays the message "Dialing . . ." in the upper-left corner of the screen as the modem dials and attempts to connect with the remote modem. Most modems allow you to hear the dialing of the phone number as confirmation that dialing is occurring.

Symphony continues a dial-and-connect attempt until it is successful or until the Dial-Time limit is reached. If the phone is answered within the Dial-Time, the modem squeals and Symphony displays the message "OnLine" in reverse video to confirm that a connection has been made. If a connection cannot be made, Symphony displays a "No Carrier" message.

Dialing will not occur if your modem cannot handle Symphony's **B**aud rate setting. For instance, the Hayes Smartmodem 1200 operates only at 110, 300, and 1200 baud. If Symphony's COMM settings are 150, 600, 2400, 4800, or 9600, Symphony cannot communicate with the modem, and dialing does not occur.

Wait-Mode

The Wait-Mode command instructs Symphony to set your modem in autoanswer mode. Your ability to use this feature and its default value depends on the modem you use. Some modems do not have the capability to answer incoming calls.

If your modem has autoanswer capability, Wait-Mode allows your modem to answer incoming telephone calls automatically. To enable the autoanswer feature, simply respond **Y**es after selecting **W**ait-**M**ode from the **P**hone menu. To disable the autoanswer capability, select **N**o.

Most modems have a software- and hardware-switchable autoanswer ability. If yours does, you can control this feature with the Wait-Mode command. However, you should set the modem's default setting (controlled by a switch on the front of the modem) to the state most often used.

For instance, if you use a Hayes Smartmodem 1200 and usually use the autoanswer feature, set the modem to this default condition by flipping up the #5 dip switch. This sets the modem to autoanswer every time you turn it on. On the rare occasions that you do not want this capability, turn it off by using Symphony's **P**hone **W**ait-**M**ode **N**o command sequence. Once this command is issued, autoanswer remains off until you either use the Yes command or turn off the modem.

If, on the other hand, you wish to answer manually in most situations, flip the #5 switch down. If you want to enable autoanswer occasionally, issue the **P**hone **W**ait-**M**ode **Y**es command.

The amount of time it takes Symphony to answer depends on your modem. When you use Symphony with a Hayes Smartmodem 1200, incoming calls are answered on the second ring.

Answer

The Answer command instructs the modem to answer an incoming call. This command is the manual alternative to Wait-Mode. If your modem cannot answer automatically, or if you have set the Wait-Mode command to No to prevent autoanswering, you must issue the **P**hone **A**nswer command to answer an incoming call manually.

An incoming call is indicated by a ringing signal generated by your modem's speaker and/or a display of the message "RING" in the COMM window. To answer, issue the command sequence {**Menu**} **P**hone **A**nswer. After this, the modem attempts to make a connection. The time it spends in this attempt is determined by the Answer-Time setting, discussed in the previous chapter.

While Symphony attempts to answer the phone, the message "Answering . . ." appears in the upper-left corner of the COMM window. If a connection is made, Symphony displays the message "OnLine" in reverse video at the bottom-center of the screen. If no connection is made within the time allowed by the Answer-Time setting, the "Answering . . ." message disappears, and a "No Carrier" message may appear in the COMM window (depending on the type of modem you are using).

If you are not in a COMM window when the phone begins to ring, you must first get to a COMM window and then issue the {**Menu**} **P**hone **A**nswer. Unfortunately, you may miss the phone call by going through this lengthy sequence. To avoid missing calls, either set up Symphony to answer incoming calls automatically or write a simple macro that automates the window changing and manual answer command sequence. Such a macro is demonstrated in the section of the book on macros.

Hangup

The Hangup command is self-explanatory; this command instructs the modem to break the telephone connection. To use this command, simply select **H**angup from the Phone command menu. When the connection is broken, "OnLine" disappears from the screen and your modem may display an "OK" in the COMM window, confirming the execution of the command.

Like the Answer command, the Hangup command cannot be used unless you are in a COMM window. Unfortunately, sometimes you may want to hang up yet not be able to reach the COMM menu. For example, you cannot reach the COMM menu easily when you are sending a range (Transmit-Range), sending a file from disk (File-Transfer Send), or receiving a file from disk (File-Transfer Receive). In each of these cases, you must press **[Ctrl][Break]** to stop the transfer or receipt of information and then press **[Esc]** and {**Menu**} **P**hone **H**angup to break the connection. The simultaneous use of the [Ctrl] and [Break] keys gets you out of most tight spots like these.

Data-Mode and Voice-Mode

The Data-Mode and Voice-Mode commands make it possible to toggle back and forth between the transmission of data signals and voice signals over the communications link. If your modem allows this switching, you can use these commands to suspend data communications temporarily and talk over the telephone line connecting the two modems.

These commands can be very handy. For example, suppose you have just transmitted a long file and want to be sure the receiving computer has captured it correctly before you break the connection. If your modem supports voice communications, both users could switch to Voice-Mode, pick up the receiver, and confirm that the file has been received. If you needed to, you could then switch back to data mode to retransmit all or part of the file.

The Hayes Smartmodem 1200 does not support this feature. To find out whether your modem does, consult your modem's operator's manual.

LOGIN

Many main frame computers and on-line services require you to "log in" to the answering system before you can access any information from that computer. For example, most time-sharing services, such as The Source, require you to give a password and a billing code before you can access information.

Most people who use these services are used to typing the log-in string by hand after the modem makes a connection with the service's main frame computer. Unfortunately, typing these required log-in strings and waiting for the computer to answer can waste a lot of time.

The Login settings allow you to define a log-in character sequence that Symphony sends to the remote computer at your command or automatically after a connection is established. Creating a predefined log-in sequence frees you of the tedium of typing it in yourself every time.

Like the Phone command, the Login settings are defined in the COMM Settings sheet under the Login option. The actual Login command instructs Symphony to implement the log-in sequence created and stored in the COMM Settings sheet. The next several sections discuss the Login settings defined in the COMM Settings Login sheet.

The Login Settings

Symphony lets you specify up to ten different log-in strings. The Login command also lets you specify the strings that Symphony should receive in response from the answering computer, as well as the number of times each string should be repeated if the proper response string is not received. This command also allows you to limit the time allotted to the log-in sequence.

After you select Login from the Settings menu, the menu and settings sheet shown in Figure 25.1 appear in the control panel. Notice that the Login settings sheet is separate from the main COMM Settings sheet and is displayed only when you select the Settings Login option.

```
    Maximum-Time Repeat-Time A B C D E F G H I J New Quit
    ------------------------------------------------------------
  |   Count       Send (maximum time 0)        Receive (repeat time 0)   |
  | A  1                                                                  |
  | B  1                                                                  |
  | C  1                                                                  |
  | D  1                                                                  |
  | E  1                                                                  |
  | F  1                                                                  |
  | G  1                                                                  |
  | H  1                                                                  |
  | I  1                                                                  |
  | J  1                                                                  |
    =================================================Login Settings=
```

Figure 25.1

Defining the Strings

A log-in sequence can include from one to ten different send/receive sequences. Each of the letters A through J represents one complete send/receive sequence. A send/receive sequence includes (1) the log-in string that Symphony should send to the answering computer, (2) the response string acknowledging the receipt of the log-in string by the answering computer, and (3) the number of times the log-in string should be repeated if the correct response string isn't received.

To begin building a log-in sequence you first select option A from the Settings Login menu. After this, the following menu appears:

Count   Send   Receive   Quit

The Count command controls the number of times Symphony should resend a log-in string if the appropriate receive string is not received. The Login Count setting can be any number from 1 to 100. Choosing the correct Count setting is a matter of experience. The Count you use for each send/receive sequence may vary. The timing of these retransmissions is governed by the Repeat-Time setting, which we'll cover in the next section.

The Send command controls the actual log-in string to be sent to the answering computer. This string can be up to 30 characters long and can include any characters, including the Symphony representations of control characters. Remember that Symphony can represent control characters in two ways: first, as three-digit ASCII codes preceded by a backslash and second, as single characters preceded by a backslash. For example, the linefeed character [Ctrl] J could be represented as \010 or \J.

The characters in the log-in string should match exactly the characters the answering computer expects to receive. If they do not, log-in will not be successful.

The Receive setting lets you specify the response string that Symphony should expect to receive from the remote computer to acknowledge the receipt of a log-in string. A response string is like a cue from the answering computer that tells Symphony that the previous log-in string has been received and accepted and that the next log-in string, if any, should now be transmitted.

When Symphony asks you to specify this string, enter the exact string that the remote computer will send to acknowledge receipt of a log-in string. This response string can be from 0 to 30 characters long.

If the response sent by the remote computer is different in even the smallest detail from the response string Symphony expects, Symphony assumes that the preceding log-in string was not properly received. Symphony therefore resubmits the log-in string, which is likely to void the log-in attempt.

Maximum-Time

The Maximum-Time setting specifies the maximum time (in seconds) Symphony should spend attempting to complete the log-in sequence. If the log-in is not successful after this time, Symphony returns you to the interior of the COMM window.

To set the Maximum-Time for a log-in sequence, simply issue the **S**ettings **L**ogin **M**aximum-Time command. Symphony then asks you to specify the maximum duration, in seconds, of a log-in attempt. The maximum time can be any number of seconds between 0 and 32767. After entering the correct number of seconds, press [Enter] to return to the Login submenu.

Remember that the Maximum-Time setting must be changed from its default value of 0 for a successful log-in. If the default is retained, the log-in sequence ends before it even starts! In general, it is better to specify a longer Maximum-Time setting than Symphony normally needs to complete the log-in sequence. Choose a relatively long Maximum-Time to prevent the program from cutting off the log-in attempt halfway through the sequence.

Repeat-Time

The Repeat-Time setting specifies how long Symphony should wait to receive the appropriate response string, after sending a log-in string. If the appropriate response string is not received after that time, Symphony either repeats the log-in string or terminates the log-in process.

As with Maximum-Time, the default Repeat-Time setting is 0. You must change this to log in successfully. If you don't, Symphony terminates the log-in as soon as the first Send string is transmitted.

When you issue the Repeat-Time command, Symphony asks you to specify the number of seconds it should wait before retransmitting a log-in string. As with most other COMM mode time settings, Repeat-Time must be a number between 0 and 32767. You should choose a Repeat-Time setting that is long enough to allow the computer being contacted to respond but does not cause an excessive delay. Typically, a setting of 15 to 30 seconds is sufficient.

Notice that Repeat-Time does not control the number of times the log-in string is transmitted. That is controlled by the Count setting, determined when the send/receive sequence itself is defined. Repeat-Time merely controls the time interval between each repetition.

The Repeat-Time setting works with the Count setting to limit the time allowed to send a log-in string. For example, suppose you set the Count for a given string to 4 and the Repeat-Time to 15 (seconds). After you send the string for the first time, Symphony waits 15 seconds to receive the correct response. If the response is not received within that time, Symphony repeats the log-in string three times, waiting 15 seconds each time. If the appropriate response is not received after those 60 seconds, the log-in sequence ends.

The Maximum-Time setting, on the other hand, limits the duration of the entire log-in process. For example, if the Maximum-Time setting in the previous example had been 30, Symphony would have repeated the log-in string only twice before abandoning the log-in attempt. In general, therefore, the Maximum-Time setting should be greater than the number of log-in strings times the Count for each string times the Repeat-Time.

An Example

Because the log-in process can be a bit confusing, let's step through the definition of a sample log-in sequence. Suppose the computer you want to reach requires you to provide a password and a billing code before you go on line. Your password is CESSNA and your billing code is AB1234. You want to include these two strings in an automatic log-in sequence.

Begin by issuing the {**Menu**} **S**ettings **L**ogin command and selecting the **A** option. Next, select **S**end from the menu and enter the string **\013,** the ASCII code for carriage return, in response to Symphony prompt. This carriage return doesn't convey any information; it merely "wakes up" the receiving computer. Although this string may not be required for all log-in sequences, in general, your log-in sequences should begin with a carriage return.

Next, select the Receive option. Symphony then prompts you to supply a Receive string. Let's assume that the receiving computer prompts you for your password with the message "Password:". If so, the Receive string for line A will be "Password:". Remember that this string must match the response message exactly; in other words, if the answering computer will send the response "Password:" (with a colon), then the Receive string "Password" will not work.

Once the A line is specified, press **Q**uit to return to the Login menu. To define the second line of the log-in sequence, select option **B** and **S**end and enter the string **CESSNA\013.** The first part of this string is the password, and the second part is the ASCII representation for carriage return. Most receiving computers require that you end all Send strings with carriage returns.

Choose Receive to enter the Receive string Symphony should look for. Let's assume that the receiving computer acknowledges the receipt of the password by prompting you with the message "Billing Code:" In this case, enter **Billing Code:** as the correct Receive string.

After you define the Receive string for line 2, return to the Login menu and select option **C** to define the third log-in string. The **S**end string for line 3 should be your billing code, **AB1234\013.**

Specifying the last Receive string can be tricky. In many cases, no Receive string is required for the last line in the sequence. However, sometimes you need to specify a last Receive string.

If we assume that a Receive string is required in our example, the best choice is probably the system prompt used by the receiving computer. Different computers use different system prompts, but some of the most common prompt characters are ?,], *, and >. Let's assume that the prompt of the receiving computer is the question mark. Because this is the character we should receive after the billing code is accepted, enter the character ? when Symphony prompts you for the correct Receive string.

Finally, you must change the Maximum-Time and Repeat-Time settings from their defaults of 0. Use the Maximum-Time command to change the maximum time setting to 30 and the Repeat-Time command to change the repeat time interval to 20.

That's it; the log-in sequence is now defined. Your Settings Login sheet should look like Figure 25.2.

```
  Maximum-Time Repeat-Time A B C D E F G H I J New Quit
  ------------------------------------------------------------
  |   Count      Send (maximum time 30)    Receive (repeat time 20) |
  | A 1          \013                       Password:               |
  | B 1          CESSNA\013                 Billing Code:           |
  | C 1          AB1234\013                 ?                       |
  | D 1                                                             |
  | E 1                                                             |
  | F 1                                                             |
  | G 1                                                             |
  | H 1                                                             |
  | I 1                                                             |
  | J 1                                                             |
  ===================================================Login Settings= |
```

Figure 25.2

Notice that we did not adjust the Count for any of the three lines in the sequence. In most cases, you will probably want to repeat each line at least twice before allowing Symphony to abandon the log-in attempt. To change the Count for any of the lines, simply choose the letter that represents that line from the Settings Login menu, then select the Count option.

New

The next option on the Login menu is New. This command resets the current Settings Login sheet to blanks, allowing you to create a new log-in sequence "from scratch." A safety step is included for this command; when you issue the Settings Login New command, Symphony asks, "Clear all login settings?" If you do want to eliminate the current log-in settings, type Yes; otherwise, type No to preserve them.

The Login Command

The Login command is one of two ways to start a log-in sequence. (The second, Phone-and-Login, is discussed in the next section.) Just as the Phone command instructs

Symphony to implement the settings specified in the Phone section of the current COMM Settings sheet, the Login command instructs Symphony to implement the log-in sequence created and stored in the Login section of the COMM Settings sheet.

When you select the Login command from the COMM command menu, Symphony displays the prompt

Log in beginning at what sequence?

followed by the choices A through J. These choices correlate with the send/receive sequence you created with the Settings Login commands.

Usually you'll choose to begin the log-in process with the A option. However, Symphony has the flexibility to begin the automated log-in sequence at any of ten steps. For example, if you select option B, Symphony skips the send/receive sequence stored under option A and goes immediately to the sequence stored under option B. After you select one of the options, the log-in process proceeds under the timing parameters you specified when defining the log-in sequence.

Once you issue the Login command, Symphony sends the log-in strings one by one. The log-in process continues until it is either successfully completed, until the Maximum-Time is exceeded, or until one of the individual log-in strings cannot be transmitted with the Repeat-Time.

Phone-and-Login

Phone-and-Login is the second way to begin a log-in sequence. The Name Phone-and-Login command instructs Symphony to retrieve a specified .CCF file, dial the telephone according to the Phone settings in that .CCF file, and then log in to the remote computer with the log-in sequence contained in that file. In other words, this one command controls three ordinarily time-consuming functions.

The Phone-and-Login command is so useful and powerful that I wonder why it was "hidden" at the end of the Settings menu. Because it is buried in the Settings Name menu, you must give the four-keystroke sequence {**Menu**} **S**ettings **N**ame **P**hone-and-Login to access the command. Had it been a part of the main COMM menu, or an option under the Login command, you could retrieve a Settings sheet, dial the phone, and log in to a remote computer with just a couple of keystrokes.

After you select **P**hone-and-Login, Symphony prompts you to choose the .CCF file to be used from a list of the .CCF file names on the default directory (usually A:\). Of course, you can instruct Symphony to retrieve the .CCF file from a directory other than the default.

After you select a file, Symphony retrieves it and instructs the modem to dial the number specified in the Phone section of that Settings sheet.

Next, the message "Dialing . . ." appears in the upper-left corner of the screen. After the modem signals that the connection is made, Symphony begins the log-in sequence specified by the Login settings in the .CCF file. The log-in process always begins with line A in the Settings Login sheet. During this process, the message "Logging in . . ." appears in the upper-left corner of the screen. After the log-in sequence is successful, the reverse-video message "OnLine" appears at the bottom center of the screen, and the communications session can begin.

An important word of caution: The Phone-and-Login command won't work if your modem continuously sends a carrier-detect signal to Symphony. As just mentioned, Symphony doesn't begin the log-in sequence until the modem signals that the connection is made. Usually, this signal, known as the carrier-detect signal, is not sent until communication has been established. However, some modems generate this signal continuously. Symphony interprets this situation as a completed connection, and it begins the log-in sequence even before it has finished dialing. Of course, the log-in attempt will fail.

BREAK

In the world of data communications, the Break command instructs your computer to send a prolonged series of binary 0s to the remote computer, signaling it to stop sending data and wait for further commands. When you issue the {**Menu**} **B**reak command, Symphony generates the break signal. The duration of the signal is determined by the Break settings value in the current Settings sheet (set by the {Menu} Settings Break command).

Of course, the Break command is useful only if the remote computer is configured to cease transmission upon the receipt of a break signal. Interestingly, Symphony itself does not respond to the break signal, even though it can generate such a signal. Because Symphony does not recognize the Break command, often the only way to interrupt Symphony-to-Symphony communications is by pressing the **[Ctrl][Break]** keys, followed by **[Esc]**. This brings the local computer back to the COMM window Ready mode, but has no direct effect on the remote computer.

SENDING AND RECEIVING DATA: AN OVERVIEW

The Symphony user can send data to and receive data from a remote computer in three ways. First, data typed at the keyboard can be transmitted through a COMM window to the remote computer. These characters appear on the screens of both the sending and receiving computers. This type of communications is useful for accessing on-line services and sending quick on-line messages to the operator of a remote computer.

Second, you can tell Symphony to transmit the contents of a range in the worksheet to another computer or to capture the contents of a communications session into a range. This type of communications is useful for sending and receiving long messages. For example, you might use Transmit Range to send a memo created in the DOC environment to a remote computer or to an electronic mail system. Similarly, you might capture information from an electronic mail system or from an on-line stock quote service to a range in the worksheet.

Third, Symphony can transmit a file stored on the disk to another computer's disk drive and can receive files to the disk. This capability allows you to send files created by Symphony (including .WRK files and .PIC files) as well as files created by any other program. File transfers are accomplished with the **F**ile-Transfer command.

Once a connection is established with another computer, communication from the keyboard is as simple as typing. It's just like typing a letter that appears on the computer screen of the addressee as you are typing it.

Transmitting a range is more complex. Range transfers are faster but more error prone and more difficult to receive than file transfers. Range transfers are covered in the next section.

Communication to and from a disk file is accurate but slow. Such file transfers use the X-Modem protocol, which transmits information in small, 128-byte blocks and includes an error-checking system. Only information transferred by the X-Modem protocol can be captured directly onto a disk with Symphony. These direct disk-to-disk transfers are discussed in detail in a later section.

TRANSMIT-RANGE

The Transmit-Range command is used to transfer a range in the current worksheet to a remote computer. The transmitted range can occupy any part of the worksheet, from one cell to the entire worksheet. The range is sent according to the parameters specified on the current COMM Send settings—End-of-Line, Delay, and Response—discussed in the preceding chapter.

Before you can transmit a range, you must make a connection with a remote computer. To establish a connection, both computers will have to agree on such settings as baud rate, parity, and character width. Once the settings agree, you can either use the Phone Dial command to initiate a call or the Phone Answer command to answer a call from the remote computer. When the connection is made, the message "OnLine" appears at the bottom of your screen.

To transmit a range of information from the underlying Symphony worksheet, simply issue the {**Menu**} Transmit-Range command from within a COMM window. Provided that you have not previously transmitted a range, Symphony responds with the prompt

Range to send: A1

The A1 in the prompt is simply Symphony's guess at the correct range to transmit. Because you rarely wish to transmit just the range A1, you need to specify the correct transmit range by pointing or by typing. Specifying a transmit range is, in fact, very similar to identifying a print range.

After the range has been specified, press [**Enter**]. Symphony responds by sending the range, echoing on your screen the characters as they are transmitted. When a range is transmitted, the information in that range is not erased from the RAM of the sending computer. In effect, Symphony copies the designated range and transmits the copy over the data link.

If you have previously specified a range, the range designation appears in the prompt. For example, if you previously transmitted the range I1 . . I400, the Transmit-Range prompt would look like this:

Range to Transmit: I1 . . I400

If you want to transmit this range again, simply press **[Enter]** to accept Symphony's prompt. If, on the other hand, you want to change the transmit range, press **[Esc]** to unanchor the prompt and then point to the range you want to transmit.

The most important thing to remember about the Transmit-Range command is that Symphony transmits a range of data as a series of long labels. For example, suppose you wanted to transmit the range A1 . . C2 from the worksheet in Figure 25.3.

```
     -----A----------B----------C----------D------
  1      1234       2345 AAAA                     |
  2      1111 BBBB            12345               |
  3                                               |
  4                                               |
  5                                               |
  6                                               |
     ===================================MAIN=
```

Figure 25.3

This range contains a mixture of values and labels. For example, cell A1 contains the value

        A1: 1234

and cell C2 contains the formula

        C2: (A1 * 10) + 5

To transmit this range, you would issue the COMM {**Menu**} Transmit-Range command and specify the range **A1 . . C2** as the range to be sent. If you are on line with another computer, simply press **[Enter]** to send the range. The first line would be sent as one long label, like this:

        1234   2345   AAAA

and the second as the long label

        1111   BBBB   12345

As you see, the Transmit-Range command strings together all of the entries in a row—values, labels, and formulas—into one long label. All values in the range are converted to labels and all formulas are converted into the text equivalent of their current values. Thus, a transmitted range is sent as a bunch of text, not as a worksheet. In a later section, we'll discuss ways to overcome this problem when transmitting a worksheet range from one computer using Symphony to a receiving Symphony worksheet.

Capture

In the previous chapter we mentioned the Settings Capture command, which tells Symphony to capture incoming data directly into a specified range in the worksheet or to a printer, or both.

You might often want to capture data to the worksheet. For example, you might download a group of stock quotes from an on-line service into a range of the sheet. Once captured, this data can be manipulated and analyzed. Similarly, you might capture a range transmitted from another Symphony worksheet. You can insert this captured data into the body of a report prepared in a DOC window or directly into certain cells of a current worksheet. Examples of direct capture are given later in this chapter.

Symphony can capture to a range or to a printer data received from a remote keyboard, echoed from the local keyboard, or sent from a range in another Symphony worksheet. However, data sent directly from a remote disk file cannot be captured in this manner; it can only be captured directly to disk. (Details of the capture of data to disk are discussed in a later section.)

Capture Range

To prepare Symphony to capture incoming data to a range in the Symphony worksheet, issue the **S**ettings **C**apture **R**ange command. In response, Symphony flashes to the underlying worksheet and prompts you to specify a capture range. You specify this range by pointing to or typing the coordinates of its upper-left and lower-right cells. The range may include any number of cells.

Once you specify a capture range, you can modify its boundaries but you can't eliminate it. However, you can turn the actual capturing of data to that range on and off with the {**Capture**} key or the **C**apture **C**ancel command. You can also erase the contents of the range with the **C**apture **E**rase command.

Capturing data to a range can be very tricky. In a few pages, we'll look at several examples of the Capture Range command at work.

Capture Printer

To prepare Symphony to send a copy of incoming information to your printer, simply issue the **S**ettings **C**apture **P**rinter command. Symphony is now set to capture the received data to the character printer specified when Symphony was installed (see Chapter 2 for a discussion of printer installation).

Controlling Capture

Specifying a capture range or choosing to capture incoming data to the printer automatically turns on the Capture function. The actual capturing of data (as opposed to the designation of a range or a printing device) is controlled in two ways.

First, the **S**ettings **C**apture **C**ancel command allows you to disable the recording of data to both the capture range and the printer, once a range and device have been specified. However, this command does not erase from the computer's memory the original designation of the capture range or the printing device.

Second, the {Capture} key is an on-off toggle that allows you to capture selectively—perhaps only the important parts of a communications session. The rest is lost as soon as it scrolls from the COMM window.

When you press the {**Capture**} key from within the COMM environment, you see the menu

Range Printer

If you select **P**rinter, Symphony asks, "Record terminal session on printer?" Selecting **Y**es causes incoming data to be captured to the printer; selecting **N**o disables capture to the printer.

Similarly, choosing **R**ange lets you turn capture to a predefined range on or off. As with the **P**rinter option, after you select **R**ange you have the choice of **Y**es or **N**o. **N**o turns off the capture of data to the range but does not eliminate the specification of the range. **Y**es enables the capture of data to that range. Remember that this key does not activate the capture of data to a range unless a range has been specified in the Settings sheet. This function merely turns the capture of data off or on once the capture range has been set.

Capture Erase

The Capture Erase command allows you to erase the contents of the capture range in the worksheet with a single keystroke. Capture Erase is a powerful command; use it carefully. Fortunately, after you issue the Capture Erase command, Symphony asks, "Are you sure you want to erase the contents?" before actually erasing the range.

Remember that Capture Erase does not reset the predefined capture range, but simply erases the contents of the capture range.

The Form of Captured Data

Information captured into the worksheet with Capture Range is always received as a series of labels. This applies not only to data received from another computer using Symphony's Transmit-Range command but also to data captured from on-line data bases, electronic mail systems, etc.

When you use the Capture Range command, Symphony uses the columns in the capture range to divide the incoming labels into smaller, cell-sized labels. When Symphony captures data to the worksheet, the transmitted lines of text are separated into columns according to the column widths of the receiving capture range, not the column widths of the sending worksheet. Unless the column widths in the capture range are set up properly, the captured information may be improperly divided.

For example, suppose you plan to transmit the range A1 . . C6 in the worksheet in Figure 25.4. This range is to be sent to a receiving Symphony worksheet capture range. Columns A, B, and C in this worksheet are 9, 12, and 40 characters wide, respectively.

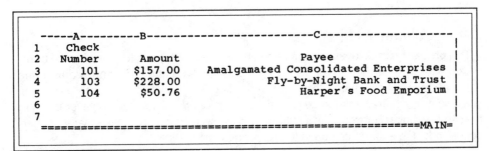

Figure 25.4

The Symphony computer receiving this information uses the Symphony default column width of nine characters for all columns in the capture range A1 . . G5. Figure 25.5 shows the result of the transmission.

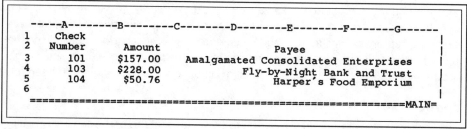

Figure 25.5

Because Transmit-Range converts all numbers and formulas into numeric labels before they are transmitted, cell A3 in this worksheet contains the label

> **A3: ' 101**

Similarly, cell B3 contains the label

> **B3: ' $157.**

cell C3 contains the label

> **C3: '00 Ama**

and cell D3 contains the label

> **D3: 'lgamated**

Notice that the value in cell B3 in the sending worksheet has been divided into two parts in the receiving worksheet. The first nine characters in the label are entered in cell B3 of the receiving worksheet. The last two characters in cell B3 of the sending worksheet are combined with the first three characters of cell C3 and appear in cell C3 of the receiving worksheet.

Notice also the entries in cells C3, C4, and C5 in the originating worksheet were broken up into a series of smaller labels in columns C, D, E, F, and G in the receiving worksheet.

Setting Column Widths

This problem can be overcome in one of two ways. First, prior to receiving the transmitted data, you can set up the receiving worksheet so that the column widths in the capture range exactly match those in the sending worksheet. If you do this, the long labels sent by the Transmit-Range command are properly divided into smaller labels in the capture range. For example, if column B in the receiving worksheet is made 12 characters wide, the entry in cell B3 in the receiving worksheet is

> **B3: ' $157.00**

Alternatively, you can define one column in the receiving range so that is wide enough to receive all of the data in each transmitted line. For example, if column A in the receiving worksheet is widened to 70 characters, then cell A3 in the receiving worksheet will contain the label

> A3: '   101 $157.00   **Amalgamated Consolidated Enterprises**

The second method is especially useful when you are capturing a document from one Symphony worksheet into another. Because documents in Symphony consist of sets of long, left-aligned labels, it is important that you receive documents as long, left-aligned labels.

For example, suppose you want to transmit the line

> A1: 'Now is the time for all good men to come to the aid

from one worksheet to another. If the label is received from a worksheet, where all of the columns have the standard column width of nine characters, the results are not satisfactory. Cell A1 would contain the label

> A1: 'Now is th

cell B1 would contain the label

> B1: 'e time fo

and so on. In this form, these labels cannot be edited in Symphony's DOC environment. However, if column A in the receiving sheet is expanded to 75 characters prior to transmission, the label in cell A1 will be:

> A1: 'Now is the time for all good men to come to the aid

This long, left-aligned label can now be edited in Symphony's DOC environment.

Converting Data to a Usable Form

Although adjusting the column widths in the receiving worksheet eliminates the problem of incorrectly divided labels, the data received are still in the form of labels and thus cannot be added, subtracted, manipulated by Symphony's mathematical functions, or used to build graphs. Fortunately, Symphony offers two methods for converting the received labels back to their original forms.

The @function conversion method   Let us begin by assuming that the information shown in Figure 25.6 has been sent from a remote Symphony program with the Transmit-Range command and has been captured, with the Capture Range command, into the worksheet of the receiving computer.

A close inspection reveals that all the entries in this worksheet are labels. For example, cell B3 contains the label

> B3: ' 11/24/83

and cell C3 contains the label

> C3: ' $327

```
     -----A--------B---------C--------D--------E--------
  1   Item     Purchase                                |
  2   Code       Date     Amount                       |
  3       C31  11/24/83     $327                        |
  4      AZ57  07/04/83     $563                        |
  5     QR354  10/06/83      $52                        |
  6       A27  06/18/84     $199                        |
  7      SC58  07/15/84      $76                        |
  8                                                     |
     ================================================MAIN=
```

Figure 25.6

Before you can use Symphony's date arithmetic capabilities to determine the time span between various purchases, or before you can use Symphony's mathematical capabilities to add the dollar amounts of the purchases, these labels must be converted back into dates and numbers that Symphony can understand.

Columns D, E, and F in Figure 25.7 are used to convert these labels back into numbers. First, use the SHEET {**Menu**} **M**ove command to move those cell entries that should remain as labels from the range A1 . . A7 To the range D1. Use the command again to move the entries from the range B1 . . C2 to the range E1. When these moves are completed, the spreadsheet should look like Figure 25.7.

```
     -----A--------B---------C--------D---------E---------F-------
  1                                  Item      Purchase          |
  2                                  Code        Date    Amount  |
  3            11/24/83     $327      C31                         |
  4            07/04/83     $563      AZ57                        |
  5            10/6/83       $52      QR354                       |
  6            06/18/84     $199      A27                         |
  7            07/15/84      $76      SC58                        |
     =============================================================MAIN=
```

Figure 25.7

Next, let's convert the dates in column B into the serial number representation familiar to Symphony. To do this, enter the function

> E3: @DATEVALUE(B3)

into cell E3 and then use the Copy command to copy this formula into cells E4 . . E7. The result should look like Figure 25.8.

Next, we can use the @VALUE function to convert the numerical labels in column C into values. To do this, enter the function

> F3: @VALUE(C3)

in cell F3 and then use the Copy command to copy this function into the range F4 . . F7. The resulting worksheet should look like Figure 25.9.

```
     ----A--------B---------C---------D---------E---------F------- |
  1                                    Item      Purchase           |
  2                                    Code      Date      Amount   |
  3              11/24/83    $327       C31       30644             |
  4              07/04/83    $563       AZ57      30501             |
  5              10/6/83      $52      QR354      30595             |
  6              06/18/84    $199       A27       30851             |
  7              07/15/84     $76      SC58       30878            |
     =====================================================MAIN= |
```

Figure 25.8

```
     ----A--------B---------C---------D---------E---------F------- |
  1                                    Item      Purchase           |
  2                                    Code      Date      Amount   |
  3              11/24/83    $327       C31       30644       327 |
  4              07/04/83    $563       AZ57      30501       563 |
  5              10/6/83      $52      QR354      30595        52 |
  6              06/18/84    $199       A27       30851       199 |
  7              07/15/84     $76      SC58       30878        76 |
     =====================================================MAIN= |
```

Figure 25.9

The numerical entries in column F are now values that Symphony can manipulate mathematically. You can also format the entries in columns E and F as you wish now. For example, you can display the serial dates in the range E3 . . E7 as dates by issuing the {**Menu**} **F**ormat **D**ate command, choosing the Date 1 (DD-MMM-YY) format, and specifying the format range E3 . . E7. To display the values in column F in currency format, simply issue the {**Menu**} **F**ormat **C**urrency **2** command. The worksheet should now look like Figure 25.10.

```
     ----A--------B---------C---------D---------E---------F------- |
  1                                    Item      Purchase           |
  2                                    Code      Date      Amount   |
  3              11/24/83    $327       C31     24-Nov-83  $327.00 |
  4              07/04/83    $563       AZ57    04-Jul-83  $563.00 |
  5              10/6/83      $52      QR354    06-Oct-83   $52.00 |
  6              06/18/84    $199       A27     18-Jun-84  $199.00 |
  7              07/15/84     $76      SC58     15-Jul-84   $76.00 |
     =====================================================MAIN= |
```

Figure 25.10

Finally, you should move the contents of the range D1 . . F7 into the single cell A1. This erases the labels created by the Transmit-Range command and returns the correct entries to the upper-left part of the worksheet. The final version of the worksheet should look like Figure 25.11.

```
    -----A--------B---------C---------D----
  1  Item     Purchase                     |
  2  Code        Date     Amount           |
  3  C31      24-Nov-83  $327.00           |
  4  AZ57     04-Jul-83  $563.00           |
  5  QR354    06-Oct-83   $52.00           |
  6  A27      18-Jun-84  $199.00           |
  7  SC58     15-Jul-84   $76.00           |
    ===================================MAIN=
```

Figure 25.11

The Query Parse conversion method   The second method that can be used to convert received data into a usable form involves the use of a FORM window and the Query Parse command. This method is useful whenever the captured data can be presented in data base form easily, even if the data are not technically going to be used to create a data base.

Transforming the received data with Query Parse requires that you first create a data base and a FORM window that matches the structure of the received data. Then you must "parse" the received data through the FORM into the data base.

Let's start with the worksheet in Figure 25.6. As explained in Chapter 19, you can define a data base and a data base form by entering the names of each field in the data base in consecutive cells of the worksheet. In addition to specifying a field name, you can also specify a field type and a field length.

We want to create a data base that accommodates the information in the sample worksheet. This data base should have three fields: Code, Date, and Amount. Each of these fields holds a different type of information. The Code field should contain labels (L); the Date field, dates (D); and the Amount field, numbers (N). These three fields have different widths: the Code field is 9 characters wide, the Date field is 12, and the Amount field is 9.

To set up the data base, enter the definitions for these fields in cells D1, D2, and D3 in the worksheet, as shown in Figure 25.12.

```
    -----A--------B---------C---------D---------E--------
  1  Item     Purchase              Code:L:9              |
  2  Code        Date     Amount    Date:D:12             |
  3        C31  11/24/83    $327     Amount:N:9            |
  4       AZ57  07/04/83    $563                           |
  5      QR354  10/06/83     $52                           |
  6        A27  06/18/84    $199                           |
  7       SC58  07/15/84     $76                           |
  8                                                        |
    ================================================MAIN=
```

Figure 25.12

To create a data base form and a data base from these entries, switch to a FORM window by pressing {**Type**} and selecting **F**orm. Your screen is now blank except for the message "(No Definition range defined)" in the upper-left corner and the word FORM in reverse video at the upper right. Now, issue the {**Menu**} **G**enerate command, selecting **L**abel as the default field type and 9 as the default field length. Next, press **[Enter]** to tell Symphony that the field names and parameters are contained in the current worksheet. Symphony then displays the spreadsheet and asks you to specify the range containing the field names. To define the range, press **[Esc],** move the cell indicator to cell D1, type a period to anchor the cell indicator, and press ↓ twice. This highlights the cells D1, D2, and D3. Finally, press **[Enter]** one final time, and your screen should look like Figure 25.13.

```
  ----------------------------------------------------------
  |                                                        |
  |     CODE     _____                                |
  |     DATE     _____                             |
  |     AMOUNT                                             |
  |              _____                                |
  |                                                        |
  |                                                        |
  |                                                        |
  ================================================MAIN=
```

Figure 25.13

Now that you have created this form, you can instruct Symphony to fill in the form automatically with the received data in cells A3 . . C7. First, though, switch back to a SHEET window by pressing {Switch}. Your screen should look like Figure 25.14.

Notice that Symphony has automatically built the data base you specified with the entries in cells D1, D2, and D3. The data base and all associated ranges were defined at the same time as the form in Figure 25.13 by the FORM Generate command. Most of the entries in columns D, E, and F are not important to the present discussion; the only important thing is that Symphony created the data base in the desired form. You are now ready to instruct Symphony to enter data into the data base through the form. (For more information on data bases and the FORM Generate command, see Chapter 19.)

To begin this next step issue the {**Menu**} **Q**uery **P**arse command. In response, Symphony asks you to specify the range to parse; in the example, the range is A3 . . C7, the part of the worksheet that contains the imported data. To define this range, press **[Esc],** move the cell indicator to cell A3, type a period to anchor the cell indicator, and move the cell indicator to cell C7, highlighting the entire block of labels. Now press **[Enter]** to lock in the range.

Next, Symphony asks you to supply a Review range. Simply position the cell pointer on any remote cell (we chose cell Z1) and again press **[Enter].**

Once the Parse and Review ranges have been defined, Symphony uses the labels in cells A3 through C7 and enters them into the data base through the FORM, converting

```
     -----A---------B---------C---------D---------E---------F-----
  1   Item    Purchase             Code:L:9                        |
  2   Code     Date      Amount  Date:D:12                         |
  3      C31 11/24/83     $327  Amount:N:9                         |
  4     AZ57 07/04/83     $563                                     |
  5    QR354 10/06/83      $52  Code _____                    |
  6      A27 06/18/84     $199  Date _____                    |
  7     SC58 07/15/84      $76  Amount _____                  |
  8                                                                |
  9                             Name        Value        Type      |
 10                             Code                      L:9       |
 11                             Date                      D:12      |
 12                             Amount                    N:9       |
 13                                                                |
 14                             Code        Date         Amount    |
 15                                      0   00-Jan-00        0     |
 16                                                                |
 17                             Code        Date         Amount    |
 18                                                                |
 19                                                                |
 20                                                                |
 21                                                                |
 22                             Code        Date         Amount    |
 23   =============================================================MAIN=
```

Figure 25.14

them into dates and numbers as indicated in the field definition. Figure 25.15 shows the result.

Let's take a close look at what happened. You first created a FORM and a data base with the FORM Generate command. You gave each field in the data base a particular type: Label, Number, or Date. Next, you asked Symphony to "parse" the data in cells A3 to C7 through this FORM into the data base. In the process of parsing the data, or reading it into the data base, the received data were automatically converted into the data types assigned to each field. For example, cell B3 in the worksheet in Figure 25.15 contains the label

B3: 11/24/83

but cell E23 contains the value

E23: 30644

the parsed version of that label and Symphony's serial date representation for the date November 24, 1983. Similarly, cell F24 contains the value 563, the parsed version of the label in cell C4.

Although Symphony entered the parsed entries in a data base, you are not limited to working with these entries in that form. Once the information is parsed, you can erase the data base definition, form, and other unnecessary parts of the worksheet. You can also copy or move the newly parsed entries to any locations on the worksheet.

As you can see, it is possible, though time-consuming, to convert the labels that are received through the Capture Range command back into values. These methods make it possible to download numeric data from an on-line data base or from your company's main frame computer and then convert that data into a form that Symphony can manipulate.

```
   -----A---------B---------C---------D---------E---------F-----
 1    Item    Purchase            Code:L:9                      |
 2    Code      Date     Amount   Date:D:12                     |
 3       C31 11/24/83      $327   Amount:N:9                     |
 4      AZ57 07/04/83      $563                                 |
 5     QR354 10/06/83       $52   Code _____                |
 6       A27 06/18/84      $199   Date _____        |
 7      SC58 07/15/84       $76   Amount _____        |
 8                                                              |
 9                                Value        Type      Default|
10                                       C31       L:9          |
11                                24-Nov-83       D:12          |
12                                22-Nov-00        N:9          |
13                                                              |
14                                Code      Date        Amount  |
15                                C31    24-Nov-83         327  |
16                                                              |
17                                Code      Date        Amount  |
18                                                              |
19                                                              |
20                                                              |
21                                                              |
22                                Code      Date        Amount  |
23                                C31          30644        327 |
24                                AZ57         30501        563 |
25                                QR354        30595         52 |
26                                A27          30851        199 |
27                                SC58         30878         76 |
      ===================================================MAIN=
```

Figure 25.15

FILE-TRANSFER

The File-Transfer command instructs Symphony to send a user-specified file directly from the computer's disk drive to a remote computer. Since File-Transfer always uses the X-Modem error-checking file-transfer protocol, transmission errors are greatly reduced. However, this method of transfer is significantly slower than the Transmit-Range method.

File-Transfer transmits files "as is," so the number-to-text conversion and column-width matching problems of Transmit-Range are eliminated. Once received, a worksheet file that is transmitted from one computer to another using File-Transfer can be immediately retrieved into the answering machine. Therefore, in spite of the speed disadvantage, File-Transfer is the method of choice for transmitting information from one Symphony computer to another.

Before attempting a file transfer, make sure that the Interface settings in the current Settings sheet or .CCF file are as follows:

Word-Length: 2 (8-characters)
Parity: 1 (None)
Stop-Bits: 1 (One)

These settings are required by the X-Modem protocol.

Send

To send a file, first select **File-Transfer** from the COMM menu and choose **Send** from the File-Transfer menu. In response, Symphony prompts you to specify the name of the file to be transferred and displays a list of the file names on the default drive. (The default drive can be changed with the {Services} Configuration File command.) You may select any file from the default drive by pointing and pressing **[Enter]** or by typing the file name. To select a file from another directory, type the directory designation (A:\, B:\, etc.) followed by the file name.

Once a file has been selected, Symphony displays the message

Sending file: FILENAME Waiting for connection . . .

while it waits for the remote computer to be readied for the receipt of the file. When both ends of the connection are ready, the file transfer begins. Symphony then displays the message

Sending file: FILENAME X bytes out of Y sent   Z errors corrected

In this message, X represents the number of bytes that have been transferred at any given time. Because the X-Modem protocol always transmits files in 128-byte chunks, X is always a multiple of 128. Y represents the total size of the file being sent. Z indicates the number of times that blocks of data had to be resent due to errors.

While the file is being transferred, the active disk drive switches on and off at regular intervals as each block of data is read. At the end of the transfer, the "Sending file" message disappears, and you return to the COMM window.

Receive

Receiving a file with Symphony is similar to sending a file. As when transmitting a file, it is critical that you set the character-length setting to 8, the Parity to No, and the Stop Bit setting to 1.

To receive the file, issue the **File-Transfer** command from the COMM menu, and then choose **Receive** from the **File-Transfer** menu. In response, Symphony displays the prompt

File to receive:

followed by a listing of the files currently on the disk in the default drive. You may select to receive the incoming files under one of the existing file names by pointing to the desired file name and pressing [Enter]. Remember that if you save the new file under an old file name, the previous contents of that file are destroyed.

If you want to save the incoming file under a new file name, just type that name next to the prompt and press **[Enter].** Most of the time you'll want to save the incoming file under the same name used by the sending computer. If you want, the sender can transmit the file name to you prior to sending the file using straight keyboard-to-screen communications.

Be sure that you do not simply press [Enter] as a response to the "File to receive:" prompt. Doing so causes the incoming file to erase and replace the first file in the list provided by Symphony.

If you are receiving a worksheet file, be sure to include the .WRK extension when providing the file name. If you supply this extension, Symphony's **{Services} F**ile **R**etrieve command displays the file name on the prompt line, with the other .WRK files, making the file easier to load. Of course, even if you do not add the .WRK suffix, the file is still a retrievable worksheet file.

After you specify a file name and press [Enter], Symphony displays the message

Receiving file: FILENAME.EXT   Waiting for connection . . .

as it waits for the remote computer to be readied to send the file. When both ends of the connection are ready, the file transfer sequence begins. During the transfer sequence, Symphony displays the message

Receiving file: FILENAME   X bytes received   Z errors corrected

In this prompt, X is the number of bytes that have been successfully received, and Z represents the number of times that blocks of data had to be retransmitted due to errors. Just as when you send a file, the active disk drive toggles on and off as the blocks of data are received. When the transfer is complete, Symphony returns to the COMM Ready mode.

Once the file has been transferred, it can be immediately retrieved (if a worksheet file) or imported (if an ASCII text file). For example, suppose a Symphony spreadsheet is received onto directory C:\Files\ under the name TEST.WRK. To retrieve this file, issue the **{Services} F**ile **R**etrieve command and specify TEST.WRK as the file to be retrieved. TEST.WRK is loaded into Symphony, with all labels, values, formulas, range names, etc. intact. In addition, all windows defined on the sending computer before the worksheet was saved are a part of the transferred worksheet.

The result of transferring a worksheet file from one computer using Symphony to another is essentially the same as inserting the disk from the sending computer into the receiving computer's disk drive and issuing the File Retrieve command.

ASCII text files can be imported into the worksheet using the File Import command, which is covered in detail in Chapter 10.

Please remember that Symphony can only capture information directly to a file by using the X-Modem protocol. If the computer with which you are communicating does not support this protocol (many main frames and minicomputers do not) then the only way to receive the contents of a file from the remote computer is to use a capture range. Similarly, the only way to send a file to a computer that cannot use X-Modem is to use File Retrieve or File Import to get the file into the worksheet and then send it using the Transmit-Range command.

CHAPTER TWENTY SIX

A SAMPLE
COMMUNICATIONS
SESSION

Now that we have explored in detail all of Symphony's Communications features, let's run through an example of how to set up Symphony to communicate with another computer using Symphony. This common application draws on the knowledge you gained in the previous two chapters. You can use it to test your comprehension of the previous material or simply as a quick recipe for successful communication between two Symphony programs.

If you are looking for the recipe for hooking your Symphony to another computer using Symphony, ignore the brief explanations of each keystroke and concentrate on the keystroke sequences. When you have time, go back and explore the first two sections of this chapter for a better understanding of Symphony's communications capabilities.

SETTINGS AND TIPS

Because Symphony's default COMM settings are not appropriate for Symphony-to-Symphony communication, you'll need to make a few changes with the {Menu} Settings command before communicating to another computer that uses Symphony. This section provides the correct settings, explains why each setting is necessary, and shows what happens if different settings are used. In addition, this section demonstrates some tricks that should make Symphony-to-Symphony communication much easier.

Interface

To communicate with another computer using Symphony, you should set the four interface settings as follows:

Baud:	1200, or as fast as your modem can handle
Parity:	None
Length:	8
Stop Bits:	2

Baud

The baud rate should be as high as your modem or the modem attached to the receiving computer allows. Remember that both modems must transmit at the same speed. If both computers have 1200 BPS modems, the baud rate should be set to 1200. If one computer has a 300-baud modem and the other a 1200 BPS modem, you'll need to use the slower speed.

In general, the faster the rate you choose, the less time you'll spend on line and the less money you'll spend on long-distance bills.

Parity

As explained in Chapter 23, Symphony cannot use parity bits as an error-checking device. For this reason, specifying either odd or even parity serves no useful purpose and prevents the use of eight-bit characters.

Length

Because many Symphony worksheets contain characters from the Lotus international character set that must be represented by eight-bit ASCII codes, a length of eight-bits should be used whenever possible in Symphony-to-Symphony communications. A character length of seven-bits may be specified only if seven-bit data are to be sent; however, because Symphony cannot use parity anyway, there is almost no reason to select a seven-bit length.

Stop Bits

I have found that the receiving Symphony computer tends to drop characters (resulting in garbled communications) when it receives a range of text sent from another Symphony computer at 1200 baud. This occurs both on a Compaq configured with a Quadram serial port and a Compaq configured with an AST serial port. For this reason, even though Symphony lets you select either one or two stop bits, I recommend the use of two stop bits for communication at 1200 baud. I also find it convenient to use two stop bits at lower speeds (110 and 300).

As an alternative to using two stop bits for 1200 baud communication, you can use the Terminal Delay setting to enable clear transmission. However, this setting slows the transmission of data significantly.

Configuring Interface Settings

To configure the Settings sheet with these settings, issue the following keystrokes:

Baud:	{**Menu**} Settings Interface **Baud 5**
Parity:	{**Menu**} Settings Interface **Parity 1**
Length:	{**Menu**} Settings Interface **Length 2**
Stop Bits:	{**Menu**} Settings Interface **Stop-Bits 2**

Phone

The four Phone settings should be set as follows:

Type:	Tone, if possible
Dial-Time:	60 (the default value)
Answer-Time:	15 (the default value)
Number:	User-specified

Type

Type should be set to Tone if you use a touch-tone phone and your modem supports tone dialing. If you have a Pulse system, indicated by a dial on the face of your phones, then the Pulse setting must be used. You can use the Pulse setting on either a rotary dial line or touch-tone line, but it is slower and therefore not recommended. If you do not have an autodial modem, this setting doesn't matter.

Dial-Time

The default value of 60 seconds for Dial-Time is adequate for most Symphony-modem pairs. This setting gives the remote system enough time to answer automatically, or the other user to answer manually, before the calling system hangs up. A setting greater than 60 seconds usually wastes time by forcing Symphony to "listen" to a busy signal or a ringing phone that no one answers.

Answer-Time

The default Answer-Time setting of 15 seconds is also sufficient for Symphony-to-Symphony communication. This setting allows plenty of time for the two modems to establish a connection without cutting off an attempt too early. If your modem cannot establish a connection with another Symphony system within 15 seconds of picking up the phone, then there is probably something wrong with one of the modems or with the telephone line.

Number

The Number setting should be set for the full phone number that you must dial to access the remote Symphony computer. Be sure to insert delays (in multiples of of two seconds) by including commas, where necessary, to handle outside line or long-distance service access code delays.

Configuring Phone Settings

To configure the Settings sheet with these settings, issue the following keystrokes:

Type:	{**Menu**} Settings **P**hone **T**ype **T**one
Dial-Time:	{**Menu**} Settings **P**hone **D**ial-Time **60**
Answer-Time:	{**Menu**} Settings **P**hone **A**nswer-Time **15**
Number:	{**Menu**} Settings **P**hone **N**umber (Number dialed)

Terminal

The seven Terminal settings should be set as follows:

Screen:	Window
Echo:	Yes
Linefeed:	Yes
Backspace:	Backspace
Wrap:	Yes
Delay:	0
Translation:	None

Screen

Although the choice of Screen or Window for the Screen setting isn't crucial to successful communication, we find it pleasing to view all data through a window when using Symphony. Using full-screen COMM windows can be very disorienting, especially to new Symphony users.

The two communicating Symphony programs do not have to agree on the Screen setting. In other words, you can transmit from a window to another Symphony user who will receive the data through a full screen.

Echo

Because the receiving Symphony does not automatically echo received characters back to the sending computer, transmitted characters must be locally echoed if they are to appear on the sender's screen. For this reason, you must change Echo from the default value of No before you communicate with another Symphony program.

Linefeeds

Because Symphony does not transmit a linefeed character every time a carriage return is sent, you must specify that the receiving Symphony insert a linefeed character every time it receives a carriage return. Otherwise, information transmitted from the keyboard or a range will overwrite previous lines, rendering the information unusable.

Backspace

Although the Backspace setting can be set for either Backspace or Delete (as long as the parameter is the same on both computers), we find it preferable to leave this setting at the default, Backspace. Remember, though, that neither the Backspace nor the Delete settings allow the [Backspace] key to function as it does in the SHEET and DOC environments.

Wrap

The default value of the Wrap setting, Yes, is the appropriate one for Symphony-to-Symphony communications as well as most other communications applications. If you select No, the cursor moves to the right edge of the screen as each line is received and does not return to the left edge of the next line until a carriage return signal is received from the sending computer.

Delay

The Delay default value of 0 is appropriate for Symphony-to-Symphony communications between most computers at speeds of less than 1200 baud. However, as mentioned in the discussion of stop bits, you'll probably want to slow down the receipt of data to a Symphony computer when operating at a baud rate of 1200. This can be accomplished by using two stop bits or by specifying a delay factor. Setting Delay to 1 introduces a 1/128 second delay between each transmitted character and should solve the garbled transmission problems. This setting slows communications significantly, however.

Translation

The Translation setting should remain at the default specification of None, unless special applications require that either a national replacement character set or a custom character code translation table be used. In any case, remember that both computers must use the same translation table, or some characters will be received incorrectly.

Configuring Terminal Settings

To configure the Settings sheet with these settings, issue the following keystrokes:

Screen:	{**Menu**} Settings Terminal **S**creen **W**indow
Echo:	{**Menu**} Settings Terminal **E**cho **Y**es
Linefeed:	{**Menu**} Settings Terminal **L**inefeed **Y**es
Backspace:	{**Menu**} Settings Terminal **B**ackspace **B**ackspace
Wrap:	{**Menu**} Settings Terminal **W**rap **Y**es
Delay:	{**Menu**} Settings Terminal **D**elay **[Esc] 0**
Translation:	{**Menu**} Settings Terminal **T**ranslation **D**efault

Send

The Send settings should be specified as follows to communicate from Symphony to Symphony:

End-of-Line:	\m
Delay:	0
Response:	(blank)

End-of-Line

The default value of \m (carriage return) for the End-of-Line setting is recommended for Symphony-to-Symphony communications for two reasons. First, unless a carriage return is automatically inserted at the end of a line of text being transmitted from a range, the data are received in one long string, up to 240 characters long, rather than in a column-formatted, readable form. Second, although a carriage return and a linefeed can be sent together as an End-of-Line string, this causes the received text to be double-spaced if the remote Symphony program is set to supply an automatic linefeed.

Delay

The Delay default value of 0 can be used at all baud rates, since most Symphony-hardware combinations can assimilate transmitted information as fast as Symphony can send it. Choosing a Delay greater than 0 causes unnecessary delays in the transmission of data.

Response

The Response setting should be changed from its default value of \j for most Symphony-to-Symphony applications. If the default setting is on, the sending computer waits until someone types [CTRL] J on the keyboard of the receiving computer before it sends the next line of text during a Transmit-Range operation—a wholly undesirable situation.

Configuring Send Settings

End-of-Line:	{**Menu**} Settings Send End-of-Line **m**
Delay:	{**Menu**} Settings Send Delay **0**
Response:	{**Menu**} Settings Send Response [**Backspace**][**Backspace**]

Break

Because Symphony can send but does not seem to respond to the Break command, the value specified for the Break setting does not matter in Symphony-to-Symphony communications. For the sake of convenience, this setting should be left at its default value of 60.

Handshaking

The Handshaking settings should be set as follows:

Inbound:	Yes
Outbound:	Yes

Because Symphony supports the X-On/X-Off handshaking protocol both as a sender and a receiver of data, use this valuable capability whenever you communicate with another Symphony program. Using this capability helps to ensure successful communication even at high baud rates.

Configuring Handshaking Settings

To configure the Settings sheet with these settings, issue the following keystrokes:

Inbound:	{**Menu**} Settings Handshaking Inbound Yes
Outbound:	{**Menu**} Settings Handshaking Outbound Yes

Name

Once you have completely defined the Settings sheet, save it under the name SYM-PHONY.CCF with the command sequence Settings Name Save. After going to all the trouble of creating the proper settings for Symphony-to-Symphony communications, you will certainly want to save these settings for future use. We suggest that you name this .CCF file SYMPHONY to remind you of its purpose.

Of course, once you save these settings as SYMPHONY.CCF you can use this name to retrieve the settings. For example, to retrieve the SYMPHONY.CCF file into the current worksheet, issue the command {**Menu**} Settings Name Retrieve.

Specifying the Default .CCF File

If Symphony-to-Symphony communication is your most common application, you will want to specify SYMPHONY.CCF as the default .CCF file. If you make SYMPHONY-.CCF the default file, it is retrieved automatically whenever you load Symphony into your computer. This saves you the trouble of going through the {**Menu**} Settings Name Retrieve FILENAME sequence every time you wish to use SYMPHONY.CCF.

To change the default .CCF file, type

{Services} Configuration Communication Set FILENAME [Enter] Update

CONNECTING AND TRANSMITTING DATA

Now that we have created and saved a COMM Settings sheet appropriate for Symphony-to-Symphony communications, let's use Symphony to connect and communicate with a remote Symphony-using computer.

First, you must get back into a COMM window if you are not already there. If a COMM window has already been created, you can press {**Window**} to jump to it, or you can press {**Type**} COMM to change the current window to a COMM window. After you change the current window to a COMM window, you can change it back to its previous type (probably a SHEET window) by pressing {**Switch**}.

Next, retrieve the .CCF file you created in the previous section by typing {**Menu**} Settings **N**ame **R**etrieve **SYMPHONY.CCF**. If the remote computer operator has also followed these steps, you are now ready to connect.

To make a phone call, first press the {Menu} key to reveal the COMM command menu. Select the first command, Phone. Select Call from the Phone menu. Confirm the default number by pressing [Enter], or type in a different number. At this point, Symphony instructs your modem to dial. Your COMM window will appear blank, with the message

Dialing . . .

at the top-right corner. Your modem will probably let you hear the ringing of the remote phone.

The **P**hone-and-**L**ogin command is useless for Symphony-to-Symphony communications, because no Login sequence is needed when contacting a Symphony computer. To dial the phone number stored in the settings sheet quickly, you can simply issue the {**Menu**} [**Enter**][**Enter**][**Enter**] command sequence.

To make the connection, the receiving Symphony computer either autoanswers (if the Wait-Mode setting is Yes) or the operator must manually answer using the {**Menu**} **P**hone **A**nswer command. Either way, the message

Answering . . .

appears at the top of the screen. With most modems, each audible ring from the modem is displayed in the COMM window as RING. When a successful connection is made within the allotted 60 seconds, the message "Online" appears in reverse video at the bottom of the screen.

Once the connection is made, you are ready to communicate. You can now communicate from keyboard to keyboard, transmit or receive a disk file, or transmit or receive a worksheet range. Let's start by communicating from the keyboard. You want to let the remote operator know that you wish to transmit a range of cells from the worksheet. To do this, simply type a message, such as

Good morning. Are you ready to receive the range which I will transmit?

Because Symphony is set to generate a local echo of all the characters you type, the phrase appears on your screen as well as on the screen of the receiving computer. Remember that the text, as it appears in both the sending and receiving COMM windows, wraps at the end of each line. Both COMM windows might look like Figure 26.1.

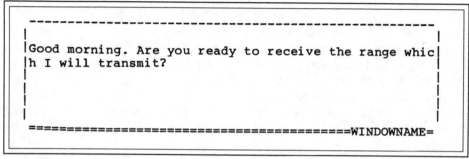

```
 -----------------------------------------------------
|                                                     |
|Good morning. Are you ready to receive the range whic|
|h I will transmit?                                   |
|                                                     |
|                                                     |
|                                                     |
|                                                     |
 ================================================WINDOWNAME=
```

Figure 26.1

At this point, the remote operator might respond

> First give me the column widths of the range you are transmitting, and the size of the range, in rows and columns.

Again, the message appears on both screens. The request of the remote computer's operator is very important because, to maintain the columnar integrity of the transmitted data, the widths of the columns in the Capture range of the receiving computer must be the same as those in the Transmit range of the sending computer. The remainder of the conversation might be

> The range is 3 columns, 10 rows. Column A width is 3, Column B is 9, and Column C is 5. Signal when you are ready to receive the range.

At this point, the remote operator specifies a Capture range (if this has not already been done) by issuing the {**Menu**} Settings Capture-Range command and specifying the appropriate cell coordinates. The selected range must be empty and should be large enough to capture the contents of the range to be transmitted. In addition, the remote operator will wish to modify the column widths of the columns in the Capture range to agree with the information you have transmitted. After doing this and ensuring that the Capture-to-Range feature is toggled on (using the [F4] key on the IBM PC), the remote operator might type

> Ready to receive. Transmit the range.

Upon receiving this message, you should tell Symphony to send the range. To do this, use the following keystrokes: {**Menu**} Transmit-Range **A1 . . C10 [Enter].** As Symphony sends the range, each line scrolls across the screen of both your computer and the receiving computer. Additionally, the range is captured as labels in the Capture range of the remote computer. The entire transfer takes only a few seconds.

After the transfer is completed, the remote operator may wish to save the transmitted range before further transmission takes place. He could then convert the received text into useful information at a later time by using either the @Value function or the Query Parse method. He can save the contents of the Capture range without having to break the connection by issuing the {**Services**} File Save command.

Now suppose you wish to continue this communications session by sending the remote computer a file from a disk. Again, you should communicate your intention to the remote operator through the keyboard. You might send the message

Next, I will send you a file from disk, which I have named EXAMPLE.WRK.

Upon receiving this message, the remote operator inserts the disk that will receive the file into the default disk drive. Next, he types the following sequence of keystrokes: {Menu} File-Transfer Receive **EXAMPLE.WRK.** The file can be received and saved under any file name, but I suggest receiver and sender always use the same file name. The .WRK suffix is optional. If you use the suffix, Symphony lists the file name when the {Services} File Retrieve command is used. At this point, the control panel displays the message

Receiving file: B:\EXAMPLE.WRK
Waiting for connection . . .

While the remote operator makes these preparations, prepare your computer to send the file with the {Menu} File-Transfer Send command. You can either type the name of the file or, more simply, choose the file name from the list provided by Symphony. At this point, your control panel looks like this:

Sending file: B:\EXAMPLE.WRK
Waiting for connection . . .

Soon after, your default drive becomes active, and the control panel displays the message

Sending file: B:\EXAMPLE.WRK
{{x}} bytes out of {{y}} sent {{z}} errors corrected

The receiving computer's control panel looks like this:

Receiving file: B:\EXAMPLE.WRK
{{x}} bytes received {{z}} errors corrected

During transmission, nothing appears inside the COMM window of either computer. The transfer of information is direct from disk to disk. When the process is complete, Symphony returns both sending and receiving computers to the COMM mode.

Before ending the communications session, you might want to notify the remote operator with a simple message typed from the keyboard, such as

Our work is done for today. Signing off.

At this point, simply type {Menu} Phone Hangup. Symphony then instructs your modem to break the connection. When this is done, the Online indicator at the bottom of the screen disappears, confirming the end of the session.

You should now be familiar with Symphony's COMM settings and commands and with the various types of communication Symphony can perform: range transfers, file transfers, and direct keyboard-to-keyboard communications.

Of course, you can use Symphony to communicate with a wide variety of computers, including computers that use communications software other than Symphony. Although the settings and procedures for communicating with these computers will differ from the examples given in this chapter, the basics are always the same. By applying the fundamentals learned in the last three chapters, you should have little trouble configuring Symphony to communicate with just about any other computer.

CHAPTER TWENTY SEVEN
ADVANCED COMMUNICATIONS TOPICS

This chapter covers some of the advanced topics relating to Symphony communications. Among the subjects discussed in this chapter are character translation tables, communications macros, and the modem-Symphony interface. If you are fairly new to communications and to Symphony, you should probably skip this chapter. This chapter covers none of the essentials you need to know to communicate with Symphony. If you are an advanced user, however, you might find some of this information interesting.

At the end of the chapter you'll find a set of questions and answers that might help you overcome special problems that may arise when you communicate with Symphony.

CHARACTER TRANSLATION

The command sequence Settings Terminal Translation instructs Symphony to use a specified translation table when sending or receiving information. You can use any one of ten Lotus-developed national character replacement sets, or you can create and specify custom character code translation tables.

You can command Symphony to use any of these translation tables by selecting Translation from the Settings Terminal menu. The Translation menu looks like this:

Default   National   Custom   Generate   Quit

Choosing the Default option instructs Symphony to use the default translation table. Usually the default table is the null table, which provides for no translation. Selecting this option cancels any prior selection of another translation set.

Selecting the National option presents you with ten options, labeled A to J. Each of these letter codes corresponds to a national character replacement set, as shown in Table 27.1. The choice of one of these letters instructs Symphony to use the corresponding national character replacement set.

The ten national character replacement sets provide a way to transmit foreign-language characters (which are eight-bit characters in the Lotus International Character Set) in a seven-bit format. These replacement sets allow you to transmit selected special

Selection	Language
A	Spanish
B	British
C	French-Canadian
D	Danish/Norwegian
E	Finnish
F	French
G	German
H	Swedish
I	Italian
J	Swiss

Table 27.1

eight-bit international characters even when you select a seven-bit character length. The replacement sets work by redefining the special eight-bit characters used in each international character set as infrequently used seven-bit characters, such as #, {, ¦, \, or [(these are all in the first 128 ASCII and Lotus characters).

For example, let's examine the translation scheme for communication with Great Britain. After a communications link using a seven-bit character length has been established between two Symphony COMM windows, one in New York and one in London, the computer operator in New York wants to send the simple message, "You owe me £20." All of the characters in this phrase, except the £ symbol, can be represented by seven-bit bytes. In Symphony, the £ symbol can be represented only by the eight-bit sequence 10100011 (ASCII character 163). This character cannot be correctly transmitted if seven-bit communication is used. Unless a translation table is used, the New Yorker might never get the money.

If both the sending computer and the receiving computer select the B (for British) national character replacement set, the transmission proceeds as follows. The computer in New York passes each character it transmits through the British translation table, which has no effect on the seven-bit characters; however, instead of sending 10100011, it sends 0100011 to represent the £ symbol. The seven-bit character 0100011, in the absence of a translation system, is displayed as # (ASCII character 35). This seven-bit character can be transmitted without any difficulty.

When the characters reach the computer in London, each passes through the "mirror image" of the translation table used by the computer in New York, which translates 0100011 back into 10100011. The result is that £ is displayed in the COMM window of the computer in London.

Unfortunately, there is a catch. Suppose that the computer operator in London sends the response, "I'll send you the £20 when you send the #5 widgets." Again, all transmitted characters pass through the translation tables. All seven-bit characters (including the #) pass through the table unaltered, but the £ is converted into a # prior to transmission. When this message is decoded by the Symphony program in New York, the following message appears in the COMM window: "I'll send you the £20 when you send the £5 widgets."

Notice that the translation table changed the # in the transmitted data line to a £. Whenever an infrequently used seven-bit character used by the translation table as a replacement character is included in a translated transmission, the eight-bit character is diplayed, even if the original meaning of the character was intended.

The other nine national replacement character sets function in the same way, but they have more replacement characters than the British set. Refer to the Symphony Reference Manual for a listing of these sets and the replacement characters that are used in each.

CUSTOM CHARACTER CODE TRANSLATION TABLES

The Translate Generate and Translate Custom commands make it possible to design and use "customized" translation tables. The Translate Generate option is used to create and save these custom character translation (.CTF) files, while the Translate Custom option instructs Symphony to use one of these .CTF files during communications sessions.

You can use custom character code translation tables in a variety of ways. For example, you could build custom tables for languages not included in the ten national sets provided by Symphony. Of course, the foreign characters you wish to translate must be contained in the Lotus International Character Set. Custom character sets cannot be used to create new characters, such as the characters in the Russian alphabet.

Alternately, custom translation tables may be created to transmit sensitive information, that is, to encode and decode this information. Such an encoded transmission, if intercepted by a party not privy to the code, appears hopelessly garbled. However, to the intended receiving computer using the same custom table, the transmission is perfectly clear. This second use of custom character translation tables may sound a bit "cloak and dagger," but it is useful when sensitive information is transmitted.

Before we explore how to create a custom translation table, let's take a brief look at how translation tables are structured. Symphony always uses a translation table when transmitting characters; however, unless you specify a custom table or a national table, Symphony uses a null character translation table, so called because it results in no translation of characters. Figure 27.1 shows some parts of the null table.

Every translation table has two columns; these columns may be any two adjacent columns in the worksheet. The first column is the encoding column; and the second is the decoding column. In this example, the encoding column is column A of the worksheet, and the decoding column is column B. The numbers to the far left are simply Symphony's row numbers. Every translation table occupies 256 rows, one row for each character in the Lotus International Character Set (the only set of characters Symphony uses). The table appears in the worksheet only when it is being created or modified; when used for a transmission, it cannot be viewed.

When Symphony transmits a character, it "looks up" in the translation table the code that should be used to send that character. For example, suppose you transmit an "a"

```
     -----A---------B-------
1            0           0     |
2            1           1     |
3            2           2     |
.            .           .     |
97          96          96     |
98          97          97     |
99          98          98     |
.            .           .     |
122        121         121     |
123        122         122     |
124        123         123     |
.            .           .     |
256        255         255     |
        ==================MAIN=
```

Figure 27.1

with the null table in effect. The ASCII code for "a" is 97; however, because the ASCII code starts with 0, "a" is the 98th ASCII character. Before transmitting the character, Symphony searches for the 98th entry in the encoding column of the translation table and sends the ASCII code it finds in that cell. In the null table, the 98th cell contains the code 97, the standard code for "a", so no translation occurs.

As we discussed previously, translation tables work by substituting one character for another. In the case of national character sets, this involves substituting a rarely used seven-bit character for an eight-bit character. However, in a custom table, any character may be substituted for any other, whether seven-bit or eight-bit. This substitution is effected by realigning the codes in the encoding and decoding columns of the translation table. Figure 27.2 shows an abbreviated example of a custom translation table. Notice that the codes 122 and 97 have been transposed in both columns in this table.

When transmitting data, Symphony uses a custom or national translation table in exactly the same way it uses a null table. For example, suppose the character "a" is transmitted using the table above. When transmitting this character, Symphony skips down to the 98th cell in the encoding column and sends the character it finds there. In this case, Symphony sends character 122, which represents the character "z".

When this character is received by a computer *using the same custom translation table,* Symphony searches down to the 123rd cell (character 122 is the 123rd character in the set) in the second (decoding) column and displays the character it finds there. In this case, character number 97, an "a", is displayed. However, a computer not using this translation table would display a "z".

Translation tables thus work by substituting one character for another prior to transmission, then resubstituting at the other end. As you can see, it is critical that both the sending and receiving computers use the same table. Otherwise, characters translated by the sending computer will not be properly retranslated by the receiving machine.

```
     -----A---------B-------
1            0            0  |
2            1            1  |
3            2            2  |
.            .            .  |
97          96           96  |
98         122          122  |
99          98           98  |
.            .            .  |
122        121          121  |
123         97           97  |
124        123          123  |
.            .            .  |
256        255          255  |
     ==================MAIN=
```

Figure 27.2

Creating a Custom Table

To create a custom translation table from a COMM window, issue the command {MENU} Settings Terminal Translation Generate. Symphony then displays the following submenu:

Current   Retrieve   Save

Selecting Current or Retrieve loads into the worksheet either the table currently being used or a previously created and saved table, if one exists. For the purposes of this example, we will choose Current. With the cursor on Current, Symphony displays the prompt

Place current translation table in worksheet

Pressing [Enter] to choose this command causes Symphony to display the worksheet and the prompt

Location for table:

At this point you specify the cell you wish to have as the upper-left corner of the translation table, either by pointing and pressing [Enter] or by typing the address of the cell. In this example, we'll specify cell A1. Remember that this table will occupy 2 columns and 256 rows and will overwrite any existing entries in those 512 cells; so plan your space carefully.

After the command is issued, Symphony loads a copy of the translation table currently being used into the worksheet. In most cases, the default or null table is used. It consists of two identical columns of cells filled with the numbers 1 to 256, in ascending order. After the command is issued, the worksheet should resemble Figure 27.1.

At this point, you may move from cell to cell, changing the entries to create the character substitutions you want. Remember to make the two columns identical so that incoming data are decoded in the same way that outgoing data are encoded. Look again at Figure 27.2 for an example of a table with a couple of characters switched.

Saving a Custom Table

After you have completed the modifications, you will want to save this table permanently in a .CTF file. To save the table, return to a COMM window and issue the command sequence {**MENU**} **S**ettings **T**erminal **T**ranslation **G**enerate **S**ave. Symphony then returns you to the worksheet and prompts you to specify the upper-left cell of the table to be saved. Move the cursor to the first cell of the table you just created and press [Enter]. In the example, this would be cell A1.

Next, Symphony asks you to specify a name for the file and displays a list of the .CTF files (if any) that are stored on the system directory (the system directory is the directory from which you loaded Symphony to begin the current work session). You can save the new file under any of these names, or you can create a new name for the file. Either way, try to save the file under a name that helps you remember the purpose of the file, such as AZ.CTF. You do not have to supply the .CTF extension; Symphony does it for you. Type the name (up to eight characters) and press [Enter]. Symphony then saves the file on the system disk and returns you to the Translation menu.

Attaching the .CTF File to a Worksheet

The creation of a translation table and a .CTF file does not automatically attach that table to the COMM window; that is, the table is not immediately used. To activate a table, you must use the **C**ustom command. This links the .CTF file to the current COMM settings sheet so that it is used in the current communications session. The link to the .CTF file can be saved with the Settings sheet in a .CCF file.

To link the table to the current COMM Settings sheet, select **C**ustom from the Translation menu. Symphony then displays the prompt

Translation file name: A:\ * .ctf

as well as a listing of the .CTF files on the system directory (we've assumed the system disk is A). Move the cursor to the name of the .CTF file you have just generated and saved, and press [Enter]. The file name appears under the word "Translation" in the COMM Settings sheet on the screen. The file name is used in future communications sessions.

You can create as many .CTF files as you want. Remember, though, that creating a .CTF file is not easy and that Symphony offers ten national character set translation tables that handle almost all international communications needs. Also remember that to be effective, a translation table must be copied: the transmitting computer uses one copy to send data, and a remote computer uses a copy to translate the data.

COMMUNICATIONS AND THE SYMPHONY COMMAND LANGUAGE

By now, you are beginning to realize just how many keystrokes are required to use the communication powers of Symphony. Thanks to the Symphony Command Language, though, you can create macros that automate complex keystroke sequences. Among the macros you might consider building are the following:

- A macro that automates the keystrokes necessary to answer an incoming call manually

- A macro that instructs Symphony to enter the COMM environment at a specified time, receive a File or range, and then hang up

- A macro that instructs Symphony to enter the COMM environment at a specified time, send information from a file or range, and then disconnect

You'll learn about macros and the Symphony Command Language in Chapter 28.

THE HAYES SMARTMODEM 1200 SETTINGS

For many Symphony users, the Hayes Smartmodem 1200 is the computer's hardware link to the outside world. This modem allows you to take advantage of all of Symphony's modem-related features, including 110, 300, and 1200 BPS communication. The following section discusses the proper dipswitch settings for the Hayes Smartmodem 1200 when it is used with Symphony's communications software.

Underneath the front panel of the Hayes Smartmodem 1200 are eight small dipswitches. Table 27.2 shows the function of each of these switches and the best setting for each when the Smartmodem is used with Symphony.

Switch 1	Forces data-terminal-ready signal	UP
Switch 2	English language translator	UP
Switch 3	Result codes sent to computer	DOWN
Switch 4	Echo command state characters	DOWN
Switch 5	Autoanswer capability	UP
Switch 6	Forces carrier-detect signal	UP
Switch 7	Single or multiline phone	UP
Switch 8	Enables command recognition	DOWN

Table 27.2

Switch 1, in the up position, does not force a data-terminal-ready (DTR) signal. The modem must receive a DTR signal before it can respond to commands, such as answering a phone call. Some communications software does not send this signal; in such cases, the modem must automatically generate this signal. Because the IBM PC sends this signal to the printer automatically whenever you turn on the computer's power, there is no need for the modem to generate the signal. The switch should therefore be set to the off (up) position.

Switch 2 controls the modem's ability to convert received result codes into English words. When the switch is in the up position, the modem is able to translate the signals it receives into English words, such as RING or NO CONNECTION.

Leaving switch 3 in the down position instructs the modem to send to the computer the result codes that switch 2 instructs it to generate. These codes are then displayed on the screen.

Switch 4 enables the modem to echo characters typed into the keyboard while Symphony is in the command state (that is, before the modem has connected with another modem). Because Symphony is usually set to provide its own local echo in both the command and on-line states, this echo ability should be disabled by flipping switch 4 to the down position.

Switch 5 was mentioned in the discussion of the Phone Wait-Mode command (Chapter 25). Because it is usually advantageous to have the modem answer incoming calls automatically, set switch 5 to the up position to activate this feature.

Switch 6 was mentioned in the discussion of the Phone-and-Login command in Chapter 25. This switch enables the modem to generate a carrier-detect signal automatically, even when the modem is not on line. A modem-generated carrier-detect signal can fool Symphony into thinking a connection has been made when in fact it has not, resulting in the premature start of the log-in phase of the Phone-and-Login command. This ability should be deactivated by flipping this switch to the up position.

Switch 7 indicates to the modem that a single-line telephone connection is being used. This switch should be set in the up position for the majority of applications.

Switch 8 should be left in the down position. This setting enables the modem to receive, recognize, and respond to the commands sent by Symphony, such as changing baud rate, deactivating the autoanswer capability, and hanging up the phone.

For further information on the Hayes Smartmodem 1200, consult the modem's operations manual. Information regarding the proper settings for other modems will also be found in their respective operations manuals.

QUESTIONS AND ANSWERS

The following section addresses some questions that might arise when you use Symphony's communications capabilities. These questions identify some "traps" that might ensnare you and give advice on ways to avoid these pitfalls.

Question: Suppose that my modem is set to answer the phone automatically. The current COMM Settings sheet specifies the entire worksheet as the capture range. I am working on an important spreadsheet in a SHEET window, and someone calls my modem. Will the modem automatically answer the phone, and if so, will any information that is sent before I can get a COMM window be captured into my worksheet, destroying all my work?

Answer: Although the modem automatically answers no matter where you are within Symphony (this is the beauty of an autoanswer feature) and any information transmitted to your computer will be captured, the captured information will not overwrite the information already in the worksheet. Symphony's Capture Range command instructs Symphony to capture information only into the *blank* cells of the specified capture range. Specifically, Symphony begins capturing data in the first cell after the last filled cell in the Capture range. This means that Symphony will capture data at the bottom of the worksheet, not on top of the spreadsheet you have created. Thanks to this feature, you should have no fear of setting your system to autoanswer.

One further point is important here. If your modem makes a connection and the serial board begins to receive data before you switch to a COMM window, the amount of data received is limited by the communications buffer on your computer's serial board. Thus, it is not always possible to receive data "passively" while you work in another window; data reception and capture cease when the COMM buffer reaches capacity. The capacity of most buffers is in the range of 500–1000 bytes.

Question: If I use the File-Transfer command to send a file from my disk drive to the disk drive of a remote computer, and if I have used the {Services} Settings Security Lock command to prevent alterations to any of the cells in the worksheet, will the received worksheet also be locked?

Answer: Yes. All of the special Symphony features you might put in a file, including windows, learn ranges, range names, cell protection, and locking, are transferred when the file is transmitted with File-Transfer. If the transmitted worksheet is locked, the receiving computer user would have to know the proper password before being able to alter the contents of the file.

Question: After having created a COMM window, I press {**Menu**} **S**ettings and see the default Settings sheet, labeled "Communications settings:" in the lower-right corner. I then use the command sequence **N**ame **R**etrieve to load a .CCF file. After using this Settings sheet, can I recall the default settings?

Answer: Unless you have used the {Settings} Name Save commands to save the default settings in a .CCF file, you cannot retrieve this Settings sheet unless you exit from Symphony and then reenter the program. When you enter the communications environment for the first time, issue the {Settings} Name Save command and specify the name DEFAULT.CCF for the default Settings sheet. Once the settings are saved in this file, you can use Name Retrieve to access them at any time from the COMM command menu.

Question: I am using an IBM PC with a Hayes Smartmodem 1200. My current COMM Settings sheet specifies a baud rate of 300. My modem answers a call and makes a connection. However, all I receive from the remote computer is gibberish, even though I am certain that my parity, character length, and stop bits settings match those of the other computer. What is the problem, and how do I solve it?

Answer: Apparently, the baud rate for which Symphony is specified does not match the baud rate your modem is using. Upon answering the phone, the Hayes Smartmodem 1200 adjusts itself to the baud rate used by the calling system, not the baud rate specified by your Symphony COMM Settings sheet. In this case, communications are garbled because the incoming call is at a baud rate of 1200, indicated by the HS (high-speed) light on the front panel of the modem, and Symphony has instructed your computer's serial board to expect 300-baud communications.

To correct this local baud-rate mismatch, use the {**Settings**} Interface **B**aud **5** command to tell your serial board to expect 1200-baud communications. Once this is done, communications will be clear. Even if you don't know what baud rate the other computer (and thus your modem) is using, you can find the right rate fairly easily. Since the Hayes operates only at 110, 300, or 1200 baud, the received call must be at one of those speeds. A 1200-baud reception is indicated by the light on the front panel of the modem. If this light is not on, try either 300 or 110 baud.

Question: Using Symphony and a Hayes Smartmodem 1200, I have made a connection with another computer. In the middle of the communications session, can I change to a different baud rate, assuming the remote computer makes the same change, and still maintain clear communications?

Answer: Maybe, depending on the exact situation. If the original connection was made at 1200 baud, a switch to either 110 or 300 baud would lead to a local computer-to-modem speed mismatch, and strange characters result. Similarly, if the call was made at either 110 or 300 and you switch to 1200 baud, communications will be garbled. However, a switch either way between 110 and 300 baud works.

This apparent contradiction results from the different method of communication used by the Hayes modem at medium (1200) and low (110 and 300) speeds. At 1200 baud, phase shifting is used. At 110 and 300 baud, frequency shifting is used. Apparently, as long as the specified baud-rate change remains within the same communication method, satisfactory communications result. However, I still recommend that the answering computer change its baud rate to match the caller's and that the originating computer not change the baud rate once the call has been placed.

PART VIII

ADVANCED TOPICS

CHAPTER TWENTY EIGHT

MACROS AND THE SYMPHONY COMMAND LANGUAGE

In Symphony, the word *macro* describes a special kind of computer program that runs entirely within the Symphony worksheet. In its most basic form, a Symphony macro is just a collection of keystrokes stored as a label in the worksheet. When you run a macro, Symphony reads the keystrokes stored in the macro just as it would read the keystrokes if you typed them from the keyboard. The keystrokes in the macro can instruct Symphony to enter labels or numbers in certain cells, to move the cell pointer, or to issue Symphony commands. In other words, macros can be thought of as an alternative to typing instructions from the keyboard. In fact, in the earliest version of 1-2-3, the macro capability was called the Typing Alternative.

Macros can be far more than just a simple collection of keystrokes, however. Symphony offers a whole series of commands—The Symphony Command Language—that can be used only in macros. The Symphony Command Language (or SCL) makes it possible to create sophisticated programs that completely automate the operation of the worksheet. For example, the {GetNumber} command allows you to prompt the user for a number and then automatically enter that number in the worksheet. The {Blank} command allows you to erase the contents of a range of cells automatically. The {MenuCall} and {MenuBranch} commands allow you to create custom menus that guide a user through your macro program. These commands allow you to create sophisticated programs inside the Symphony worksheet.

THE COMPLEXITY OF MACROS

Although macros are not difficult to create and use, many Symphony users (and 1-2-3 users before them) hesitate to get involved with macros and the SCL. This is unfortunate, because even relatively inexperienced Symphony users can find ways to use macros effectively.

Nevertheless, macros are not as easy to learn and use as some other parts of Symphony. Before you can be proficient with macros, you need to have a general understanding of Symphony commands and functions. For this reason, if you are just starting out with Symphony, it is a good idea to put off learning about macros until you feel comfortable with the other elements of the program. But remember—you don't need to know everything about every element of Symphony before you begin using macros.

Because macros are a type of computer program and the SCL is a programming language, experience with other programming languages will help you learn to use these capabilities of Symphony. If you have experience with other programs, the SCL may seem simple.

This chapter is not an introduction to programming theory. If you plan to use the SCL to create highly complex applications and you have little programming experience, I recommend that you first take the time to read some books about programming and get some practice with Symphony macros.

A SIMPLE MACRO

Figure 28.1 shows a simple macro that enters the labels Jan, Feb, and Mar in three adjacent cells. This macro is so simple that it is trivial, but it illustrates many of the concepts that are important in understanding macros.

```
-----AA--------AB-------AC-------AD-------AE----
1   Sample   Jan~                                    |
2            {Right}Feb~                              |
3            {Right}Mar~                              |
4   ============================================MAIN=
```

Figure 28.1

First, notice that the macro consists of three ordinary labels stored in worksheet cells—in this case, cells AB1, AB2, and AB3. If you were to move the cell pointer to any of these cells, the control panel would look like this:

>   AB1:   'Jan ~
>   AB2:   '{Right}Feb ~
>   AB3:   '{Right}Mar ~

Note that each of these labels begins with a label prefix. The prefixes simply indicate that the entries in cells AB1, AB2, and AB3 are label entries. Label prefixes are ignored by Symphony when it processes the macro.

Next, notice the word {Right} in the second and third lines of the macro. This word is Symphony's way of representing the → key in a macro. When Symphony encounters this symbol as it runs the macro, it moves the cell pointer one cell to the right.

Symphony's other cursor-movement keys and special function keys are also represented in this way. For example, the ↑ key is represented by the word {Up}. The [Pg Up] key is called {Pg Up} or {Big Up} when used in a macro. If you want to move the cell pointer more than one cell in a given direction, you can follow the name of the arrow key with a number. For example, {Down 5} would move the cell pointer down five cells. {Left 10} would move the cell pointer ten columns to the left.

All of Symphony's special function keys, like {Goto}, {Calc}, and {Edit}, are also enclosed in braces when used in a macro. Since this is the convention we've used for special function keys throughout the book, you should be fairly comfortable with it by now. Table 28.1 shows the representations for each of Symphony's special keys in macros.

Cell Pointer Movement Keys	Function Keys
{Right}	{Abs}
{Left}	{Calc}
{Up}	{Capture}
{Down}	{Center}
{Pg Up} or {Big Up}	{Draw}
{Pg Dn} or {Big Dn}	{Edit}
{Big Right}	{Erase}
{Big Left}	{Help}
{Tab}	{Indent}
{Goto}	{Learn}
{End}	{Justify}
{Home}	{Menu} or {M}
	{Services} or {S}
IBM PC Keys	{Split}
	{Switch}
{Delete}	{Type}
{Insert}	{User}
{Backspace} or {BS}	{Where}
{Break}	{Window}
{Escape} or {Esc}	{Zoom}

Table 28.1

The only keys that cannot be expressed in a macro are [Num Lock], [Scroll Lock], and [Caps Lock]. I don't know why Lotus has excluded these keys from macros. Finally, notice the tilde (~) at the end of each line in the macro. When used in a macro, this symbol represents the [Enter] key.

Naming the Macro

Before you can use a macro, you must name it. Once you've given it a name, you use a macro by pressing the {User} key and typing the name of the macro.

A macro name is just a range name assigned to the first cell in the macro. You can use the {**Menu**} **R**ange **N**ame **C**reate command to name your macros, or you can include that name in the worksheet as a label and use the {**Menu**} **R**ange Name Labels **R**ight command to name the macro. I prefer the second method.

For example, notice the label "Sample" in cell AA1. This label represents the name of the macro. Using the {Menu} Range Name Labels Right command, we assigned the range name Sample to cell AB1, the first cell in the macro. When we get ready to run this macro, we'll use this name to identify it.

Of course, you don't have to enter the name of the macro in a cell in the worksheet. You can just move the cell pointer to cell AB1 and issue the **R**ange Name **C**reate command to assign the name Sample to this macro. However, by including the name of the macro in the worksheet you provide a visual clue about the identity of the macro. If your worksheet contains several macros, these clues can help you remember which is which.

Former 1-2-3 users will recognize that Symphony offers a great deal more flexibility in the naming of macros than 1-2-3 did. In 1-2-3, all macros have to be named with a single letter preceded by a backslash. For example, the names \A, \B, and \Z are acceptable 1-2-3 macro names.

This convention can also be used to name macros in Symphony, but the new program allows you to assign any name up to 15 characters long to your macros, which gives you a few important advantages. First, in 1-2-3 you were limited to 26 macros in a given worksheet, because there are only 26 possible combinations of \ and a single letter. In Symphony, you can have hundreds of different macros in one worksheet. The number is limited only by the memory capacity of your computer. Second, in Symphony you can give your macros names that clearly explain what they do. For example, if you write a macro that changes the default worksheet format to Currency, you can call that macro WRK_FRMT_CURR. In 1-2-3, that macro could only have a one-letter name like \C.

If you want to, you can use the 1-2-3 macro naming convention and name your macros with a backslash (\) and a single letter. If you do this you execute the macro by typing [Alt] plus the one-character name. For example, to invoke a macro named \A, you would type [**Alt**]A. Former 1-2-3 users will recognize this as the way all macros were executed in that program.

The Symphony manual tells you to press the {Macro} key to invoke this kind of macro; unfortunately, the manual never tells you what the {Macro} key is. Apparently, on the IBM PC and Compaq computers {Macro} and [Alt] are the same key.

Symphony also allows you to create special macro names that consist of a backslash and a number from 1 to 10. These macros are executed by pressing {User} and then one of the ten function keys on the IBM PC keyboard. For example, if you create a macro named \3, you execute it by typing {**User**}[**F3**].

Saving Macros

After you have created a macro, you'll probably want to save it to disk so that it can be used again and again. Because macros are simply labels stored in cells in the worksheet, all you need to do to save a macro is save the worksheet in which it is stored.

Running the Macro

To see how this macro works, move the cell pointer to cell C3 and press {**User**}, type **Sample,** and press [**Enter**]. Notice that when you press {**User**} the legend User appears at the bottom-right corner of the screen. When you type the name Sample, the actual name of the macro replaces the legend User. Since the User legend is only four spaces wide, only four letters from the macro name are visible.

When you press [**Enter**], the macro begins to run. It enters the label Jan in cell C3, moves the cell pointer to the right, enters the label Feb in cell D3, moves right again, and then enters the label Mar in cell D3. While the macro is running, the legend Macro appears at the bottom of the screen. When the macro is complete, the cell pointer stops in cell D3 and the Macro indicator disappears. The finished worksheet looks like Figure 28.2.

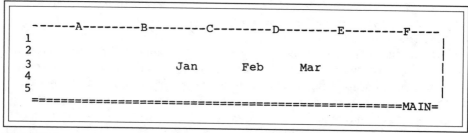

Figure 28.2

Let's walk through this process step by step. When you issued the {**User**} **Sample** *command and pressed* [**Enter**], Symphony immediately looked to the cell named Sample (AB1) for its first instruction. Since cell AB1 contains only a label, Symphony entered this label in cell C3. The tilde in cell AB1 tells Symphony to lock in the label.

If you think about it for a second, you'll realize that this line of the macro simply duplicates the action you would take to enter this label into a cell from the keyboard. If you were typing the label, you would type the three letters in the label and then press [Enter] to lock it into the cell.

After all of the keystrokes stored in cell AB1 are processed, the macro skips down to cell AB2 and begins to read the keystrokes stored there. This line tells the macro to move the cell pointer one cell to the right and to enter the label Feb in that cell. After the macro "presses" [Enter], it skips down to cell AB3, where it moves the cell pointer one more space to the right and enters the label Mar in cell E3.

Notice that Symphony ignored the label prefix character (') when it processed all three lines in the sample macro. Since Symphony expects that a macro will be stored as one or more labels in the worksheet, it always ignores the label prefix it encounters at the beginning of each line of a macro. However, if another label prefix is included in the cell, Symphony will use that prefix to align the following label. For example, if the above macro was modified slightly as shown in Figure 28.3, the results would look like Figure 28.4.

```
     -----AA-------AB-------AC-------AD-------AE----
1   Sample    ^Jan~                                |
2             {Right}^Feb~                          |
3             {Right}^Mar~                          |
4                                                   |
     ===========================================MAIN=
```

Figure 28.3

In Figure 28.3 we include the label prefix character ^ in front of the words Jan, Feb, and Mar in these three lines. For example, the entry in cell AB1 is

> **AB1:** '^Jan ~

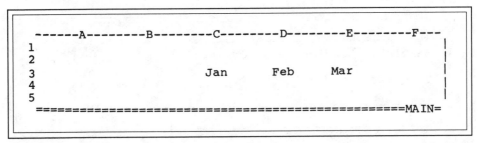

Figure 28.4

The first label prefix is the label prefix that determines the alignment of the label ^Jan ~ within the macro. When this macro runs, Symphony ignores this first label prefix. The second prefix, ^, is used by Symphony to determine the alignment of the label Jan when the macro enters it in a cell elsewhere in the worksheet.

Macro Structure

Notice that the sample macro in Figure 28.1 is laid out across three cells. In fact, the macro could just as easily have been written in one cell, as shown in Figure 28.5.

```
     -----AA-------AB-------AC-------AD-------AE----
1   Sample    ^Jan~{Right}^Feb~{Right}^Mar~         |
2                                                    |
3                                                    |
4                                                    |
     ===========================================MAIN=
```

Figure 28.5

The rules for structuring a macro are really quite simple. First, a macro can be stored in one or more text cells in a single column. Once a macro begins to run, it will continue to process every cell in the column until it either reaches a blank cell or a cell containing a value, an error occurs, or you issue the {Quit} command. Symphony always processes all of the keystrokes stored in one cell before it goes on to the next cell.

As a matter of convenience, I prefer to spread out my macros across several cells. First, doing so makes the macro easier to read and understand. Second, a long macro entered in a single cell is harder to edit and debug than the same macro spread out across several cells.

A MORE COMPLEX MACRO

As you probably expect, Symphony allows you to create macros that are far more useful than the previous trivial example. For example, consider the macro in Figure 28.6.

```
------AA-------AB-------AC-------AD-------AE----
1   Sample2   {Services}wcSECOND~s~q~                    |
2                                                        |
3                                                        |
4                                                        |
    ========================================MAIN=
```

Figure 28.6

This simple one-line macro creates a new full-screen SHEET window called SECOND. Notice that unlike the previous macro, this one contains a representation for a Symphony command: {**Services**} **W**indow **C**reate. When this macro is run (by typing {**User**} **Sample2 [Enter]**) Symphony immediately creates a new SHEET window.

This example illustrates another important macro convention. When you wish to include a Symphony command in a macro, the command should be represented by the first letter in every word of the command. The only exception is that you must spell out any special function keys and enclose them in braces. Thus the command {Services} Window Create is represented by {Services}wc.

I use lowercase letters to represent the first letter in each word of a command. This helps to distinguish the command from the words or names that follow. For example, if I had used uppercase letters to represent the command in the previous example, the macro would look like this:

{Services}WCSECOND ~ S ~ Q ~

Although Symphony would have no problem with this macro, I find it a lot harder to read. (Dick Andersen, author of the upcoming SYBEX book *Symphony Encore: Program Notes,* taught me this trick.)

Suppose you run the previous macro in a worksheet that already includes a window called SECOND. As you know, Symphony does not allow you to assign the name of an existing window to a new window. When the macro reaches the first " ~ " (which locks in the window name SECOND), it will stop, Symphony will beep, and the message

Name already exists

will appear at the bottom of the screen. You may remember that this message is the same one that you saw in the Chapter 11, "Windows." If you type [Esc] to acknowledge the error message, the macro will be terminated and Symphony will return to the SHEET mode.

The point here is that Symphony responds to command errors in macros in the same way it responds when the commands are typed from the keyboard. The only difference is that a command error that occurs in a macro terminates the macro.

You can include nearly every Symphony command in a macro. The only exceptions are commands like New and File Retrieve, which erase the entire worksheet. Since macros are stored in the worksheet, erasing the entire worksheet erases the macro.

Common Errors

Almost no computer program works the first time you try to run it, and macros are no exception. Once your macros pass a certain very basic level of complexity, you'll find that nearly every one includes a few errors that you must correct before it will perform properly.

There are a few common errors that seem to arise over and over in creating and using macros. By learning about these errors and watching for them in your macros, you can avoid lots of debugging time.

Misspellings and Typos

By far the most common source of errors in macros are simple misspellings and typographical errors. Macros are extremely literal and have no ability to infer the meaning of a slightly misspelled command. For example, you probably have no problem seeing that the command {Bracnh A1} is simply a misspelled attempt at the command {Branch A1}. If you saw the command {Bracnh A1} in this book, you would simply assume that we had made an error and would go on. Symphony, unfortunately, does not have the ability to infer the meaning of a misspelled command. When it sees the command {Bracnh A1}, it is completely baffled.

For this reason, you need to be very careful when creating your macros to make sure that every command is properly spelled. Still, some errors of this sort are bound to slip through. Since spelling errors are so common, when you see an error message, you should immediately check the macro to be sure that the error is not the result of a simple misspelling.

Omitting the Tilde

Another common error is the omission of the tilde (~) from a critical place in a macro. For example, in the macro shown in Figure 28.7, a tilde is missing after the window name SECOND. When this macro is run, Symphony assumes that you want the name of the new window to be SECONDs, and that the new window should be the "q" type. Since there is no "q" type window, this macro will not function properly.

```
   ----AA-------AB-------AC-------AD-------AE----
1  Sample2  {Services}wcSECONDs~q~              |
2                                               |
3                                               |
4                                               |
   =======================================MAIN=
```

Figure 28.7

Debugging Your Macros

The main tool that Symphony offers for debugging macros (correcting your errors) is the Step mode. To enter the Step mode, you press the {Step} key. When you press this key before executing a macro, the legend "Step" appears at the bottom of the screen. In the Step mode Symphony executes macros one character at a time. Before Symphony will process the next character, the user must press a key.

Macros run very fast; so fast, in fact, that it is virtually impossible to identify the precise location of an error, especially if the macro is more than a few lines long. The Step mode slows the processing of macros to a manageable pace so that you can identify the exact point at which an error occurred. Once you identify the error, you can easily remove it from the macro.

Editing a Macro

Editing a macro is no different from editing any other label entry. If you want to change a line in a macro, simply move the cell pointer to the cell containing that line and press {Edit}. You can then use the [Backspace] and [Del] keys to edit the macro.

You can also edit macros in the DOC environment. However, you should remember that while in a DOC window, you can only edit labels stored in the left-most column of that window's Restrict range. To edit a macro stored in column AB, you have to set up a special DOC window with the Restrict range AB1 . . IV8192.

Another Example

Figure 28.8 shows yet another example macro: a "quick print" macro that eliminates many of the steps that are required to print a worksheet.

This macro issues the {**Services**} **P**rint command, cancels the previous print source range (**S**ettings **S**ource **C**ancel), defines the new source range as the entire active area (**S**ource **R**ange {**Home**}.{**End**}{**Home**}), sets the destination to the printer (**D**estination **P**rinter), returns to the main Print menu, and prints the page.

Although this macro has some limitations (for example, it does not take into account the fact that the range you want to print in a worksheet and the active area of that worksheet are frequently very different), it represents several important techniques. First, this

```
    ------AA--------AB-------AC-------AD-------AE--------------------
  1 QP          {Services}p              Issue print command        |
  2              ssc                     Cancel source range         |
  3              sr{Home}.{End}{Home}~   Define new source range     |
  4              dp                      Set destination to printer  |
  5              qagq                    Print and quit              |
  6                                                                  |
    ==============================================================MAIN=
```

Figure 28.8

is an example of a macro that, once created, can save you many keystrokes each time you want to print a worksheet. In Symphony, just designating a print source range requires five keystrokes. The macro in Figure 28.8 reduces the entire printing process to only four keystrokes. If you decide to modify this macro to include commands that control the margins, page length, and other print settings, the time savings would be even greater.

You may have noticed that all of the sample macros in this chapter begin in cells AA1 and AB1. There are several reasons for this. First, by storing the macros in this part of the worksheet, you avoid having them interfere with the actual contents of the worksheet. Columns AA and AB are far enough to the right to be outside of the normal active areas, but they are not so far to the right that they waste large amounts of memory. Second, if you always place your macros in columns AA and AB, it will be easy to find and edit them should you need to. You always know that the first line of the first macro in any worksheet is in cell AB1.

You may also notice the labels in cells AE1 to AE5 in this worksheet. These labels describe the purpose and effect of each line in the macro. In programming jargon, these labels are called "internal documentation."

Whenever you create a macro that includes more than just a few keystrokes or one that you are likely to use only occasionally, I suggest that you include some internal documentation. This makes the purpose of each command much easier to understand.

THE LEARN MODE

As you might imagine, typing the macro in the previous example was a bit tedious. It would be far easier to create this kind of macro simply by issuing the desired commands and asking Symphony to record those commands in a range of cells. In fact, Symphony allows you to do just that with the Learn command. Once the commands are recorded, they are in the correct form to be named and used as a macro.

To activate the Learn mode, first issue the {Services} Settings command and select Learn from the Settings menu. (Why Lotus decided to put this command on this menu is beyond me.) Issuing the Learn command brings the following menu into view:

Range Erase Cancel No Yes Quit

When you issue the Range command, Symphony prompts you to specify the Learn range. The Learn range should be defined like any other range: simply point to the appropriate range with the cursor-movement keys, using the period key to anchor and unanchor the range as necessary.

The Learn range should be a single, partial column in the worksheet. I usually begin my Learn ranges at cell AB1 (or, if the worksheet already includes a macro, in a cell in column AB below the last line of the macro). It doesn't matter if the Learn range includes cells that contain entries. Symphony begins writing in the Learn range after the last cell that contains any entry. The Learn range should also be large enough to accommodate all of the keystrokes you plan to store. Suppose you define the Learn range in the example to be AB1 . . AB100.

When you are ready to activate the Learn mode, press {**Learn**}. As soon as you press it, the legend "Learn" appears at the bottom of the screen. Now simply issue the command you want to be recorded in the Learn range. In the example, begin by issuing the {**Services**} Print **S**ettings **S**ource **C**ancel command, followed by the **S**ource **R**ange command. Use the [Home], period, and [End][Home] keys to define the range, and press Quit to return to the MAIN menu. Since the command you are about to issue will not only be recorded into the Learn range but will also cause the contents of the current worksheet to be printed, make sure that your printer is attached to your computer and turned on, and that the paper is properly aligned in the printer.

Next, press **A**lign and **G**o. The document will now print. (If the worksheet is blank except for the macro in cells AB1 to AB5, the result of this printing operation will be strange.) Finally, press Quit to return to the SHEET mode.

Now press {Learn} again, followed by [Enter]. The worksheet should look like Figure 28.9.

```
  ------AA-------AB-------AC-------AD-------AE---------
1 QP         {Services}p                                |
2            ssc                                         |
3            sr{Home}.{End}{Home}~                       |
4            dp                                          |
5            qagq                                        |
6            {Services}psscsr{Home}.{End}{Home}~dpqagq   |
7                                                        |
  ==================================================MAIN=
```

Figure 28.9

The new macro is in cell AB6, immediately below the last line of the manually created macro. If you study these macros for a second, you'll realize that they are identical to one another. The only difference is that Symphony has created its own version of the macro in one cell, while we spread ours out across several cells.

The {Learn} key is a toggle switch. Once you have defined a Learn range, pressing {Learn} activates the Learn mode and pressing {Learn} a second time deactivates it.

The {Learn} key is in fact a substitute for the Yes and No commands on the Learn menu. Since the {Learn} key is so readily available, most users will never even bother with the Learn menu Yes and No commands.

One of the problems with the Learn mode is that, like macros in general, it is very literal. Every key you type while the Learn mode is activated will be recorded. If you make an error in typing the command you are recording and use [Esc] to recover from that error, both the erroneous keystroke and the {Esc} representation will appear in the Learn range.

Naturally, you can use the SHEET Edit mode or the DOC environment commands to edit a macro created in the Learn range. These commands make it possible to clean up a macro that contains errors or to divide a long macro into several parts.

Now that you've seen how the Learn mode works, let's consider the other Settings Learn commands briefly.

The Erase Command

The Learn Erase command erases the entire contents of the Learn range. This is a very powerful command, because it has the potential to erase hundreds of cells with a single keystroke. Fortunately, Lotus included a safety step in the Learn Erase command. When you issue the command, Symphony responds with the prompt

Erase contents of Learn range?

If you want to erase the Learn range, you can choose Yes; otherwise, choosing No preserves the contents of the range and returns you to the Learn menu.

Even with the safety step, you should be very careful when using the Erase command. You can erase a several-hundred-line macro in the Learn range in a flash with this command. Unless the macro is saved on disk, it will be lost forever. Therefore, after creating a macro or a segment of a macro in the Learn range, you should use the Copy command to copy those keystrokes out of the Learn range into another, safer part of the worksheet.

The Cancel Command

When you have created all of the macros that you expect you'll need in a worksheet, you can use the Learn Cancel command to cancel the Learn range designation. Note that this command does not erase the contents of the Learn range but merely erases the range definition in Symphony.

AUTOEXEC MACROS

Like 1-2-3, Symphony allows you to designate one macro in the worksheet as an autoexec macro. When you load a worksheet containing an autoexec macro, Symphony processes the macro immediately after the worksheet is loaded.

To designate a macro as an autoexec macro, issue the {**Services**} **S**ettings command and select the Auto-Execute option. Symphony then asks you whether you want to set or cancel the Auto-Execute setting. To create an autoexec macro, choose **S**et. Symphony then prompts you to identify the cell at which it should begin processing when the worksheet is loaded. You can identify this cell by supplying its name or column-row coordinates.

The autoexec macro setting is saved along with the worksheet when you issue the File Save command. To make the Auto-Execute setting permanent, you must save the worksheet after you define the setting. You can erase the Auto-Execute setting by issuing the {Services} Auto-Execute Cancel command.

THE SCL COMMANDS

So far we've looked at two types of macros. The first type consists simply of labels stored in cells, which the macro "types" into cells in another part of the worksheet. The second type of macro includes regular Symphony commands. But Symphony allows you to go even further in creating macros. It offers a special set of commands, collectively called the Symphony Command Language, that can be used only in macros. With these commands, Symphony has the power of a sophisticated higher-level programming language.

In most ways, the SCL is very similar to the 1-2-3 macro language. The basic structure of an SCL program is identical to that of 1-2-3 macro language programs. In fact, the main difference between the two languages is that Symphony does away with cryptic commands like /XG and /XN and replaces them with more meaningful English-language commands like {Branch} and {GetNumber}. Symphony also offers far more macro commands than 1-2-3 offers. The SCL contains more than a dozen new commands that have no parallel in the 1-2-3 macro language.

In all of my writings about 1-2-3, I advised people not to overextend that program's simple macro programming language. The new power of the SCL, however, turns Symphony's macro capability into a full-fledged programming language. I expect that many application developers will use Symphony and the SCL to write extremely sophisticated and complicated software. For the average Symphony user, though, the best macros are simple macros.

Commands with 1-2-3 Equivalents

The 1-2-3 macro language offers a number of commands that can be used to get information from the keyboard during the execution of a macro, to terminate a macro, or to build an if-then test into a macro. The SCL includes all of these commands; however, the name and form of the commands has changed a great deal. We'll look at these commands before we look at the commands that are unique to Symphony.

{?}

The simplest macro command is {?}. Former 1-2-3 users will feel right at home with this simple but powerful command, because in Symphony it works exactly as it did in 1-2-3.

The {?} command allows you to enter a label or a number in the cell containing the cell pointer while you are working within a macro. This command forces the macro to pause and wait while you make the desired entry. For example, Figure 28.10 shows an adaptation of a simple macro that has become a classic among 1-2-3 users.

```
     ------AA-------AB-------AC-------AD-------AE----
  1   Keypad    {?}~                                  |
  2             {Down}                                |
  3             {Branch AB1}~                         |
  4                                                   |
  5                                                   |
     =============================================MAIN=
```

Figure 28.10

This macro allows you to enter a column of numbers using the numeric keypad. As you know, the numeric keypad on the IBM PC cannot be used to enter numbers and move the cursor at the same time. This is a real barrier to Symphony users who are trained in the use of ten-key pads. This macro gets around the problem by automatically moving the cell pointer down one cell each time you make an entry and press **[Enter]**.

Before you execute this macro, position the cell pointer at the top of the column into which you want to enter some numbers and press **[Num Lock]** to toggle the numeric keypad into its numeric mode. To run the macro, press {**User**} **Keypad [Enter]**. As soon as the command is issued, Symphony pauses and waits for you to enter a number or label. As soon as you make the entry and press **[Enter],** Symphony moves the cell pointer down one cell and pauses again.

When you have entered the last number in the series, simply press **[Ctrl][Break]** to stop the macro and then press **[Num Lock]** to return the keypad to its cursor-movement function. Then reposition the cell pointer at the top of the next column of figures you want to enter, press **[Num Lock],** and reissue the macro.

Notice the braces in the {?} command. All SCL commands are enclosed in braces. You may recall that Symphony also uses braces to distinguish cursor-movement keys and special function keys in macros. This can lead to some confusion. About the only way to keep from becoming confused is to become thoroughly familiar with the names of all the special function keys, cursor-movement keys, and SCL commands.

{GetLabel} and {GetNumber}

{GetLabel} and {GetNumber} are two commands you are likely to use over and over. These commands allow for the prompted input of numbers or labels into Symphony during the execution of a macro. Former 1-2-3 users will recognize these commands as the equivalents of the /XN and /XL commands.

The forms of these functions are

> {GetLabel "prompt",location} ~
> {GetNumber "prompt",location} ~

To see how these commands work, create the simple macro shown in Figure 28.11.

```
    ------AA-------AB-------AC-------AD-------AE--------AF---------
  1  Input   {GetNumber "Please enter a number: ",A1}~            |
  2          {Quit}                                               |
  3                                                               |
  4                                                               |
    ===========================================================MAIN=
```

Figure 28.11

If you invoke this macro by typing **{User} Input [Enter],** Symphony immediately displays the prompt

      Please enter a number:

in the control panel and pauses while you enter a number. As you enter the number, it appears in the control panel. For example, if you enter the number 12345 in response to this prompt, the control panel looks like this:

      Please enter a number: 12345

If you make an error while entering the number, just press [Backspace] or ← and [Del] to make the needed correction.

Once you have typed the number correctly, you should press **[Enter].** Symphony stores the number in the destination, or target, cell specified in the second of the command's arguments. In the example, the number would be stored in cell A1.

There are a couple of things to keep in mind while you use {GetLabel} and {GetNumber}. First, notice that we included a tilde after the right brace at the end of the first line of this macro. This tilde is required. If you do not include it, Symphony will not enter the number you specify into the correct cell right away.

Also notice that the prompt in the {GetNumber} function must be enclosed in double quotes. This is absolutely essential. If you try to use a prompt that is not enclosed in quotes, Symphony will display the macro error message

      Macro: Illegal string in GETNUMBER

Finally, notice the space that follows the colon in the prompt in row 1. This space forces the number you type in response to this prompt to be separated from the colon by a space. If you did not include the space, the command line would look like this:

      Please enter a number:12345

just after you entered the number but before you pressed [Enter]. Although this space is not required, it helps make the prompt display more readable.

If you try to enter a label or even a string value in response to a {GetNumber} command, Symphony beeps and enters the @ERR message in the target cell. If you enter a function or a formula in response to the prompt, Symphony enters the current value of that function or formula in the target cell. For example, suppose you have created the simple macro shown in Figure 28.12. This macro prompts you to supply the current date and stores that date in a cell named DATE.

```
       ------AA--------AB-------AC-------AD-------AE--------AF---------
  1    Date        {GetNumber "Please enter the current date: ",DATE}~ |
  2                {Quit}                                               |
  3                                                                     |
  4                                                                     |
       ======================================================MAIN=
```

Figure 28.12

Suppose that you enter the function @NOW in response to this macro. When you press **[Enter],** Symphony translates the function into its current value and enters that value in the cell DATE. If, for example, you ran this macro on February 1, 1985, the value 31079 would be entered in cell DATE.

The {GetLabel} command works almost exactly like {GetNumber}, except, of course, that it is used to enter labels instead of numbers into the target cell. For example, the function shown in Figure 28.13 prompts you to supply a label and then stores that label in cell A1. Notice that this command conforms to the same rules (quotes around the prompt, space after the colon) that we explained in the previous section.

```
        ------AA--------AB-------AC-------AD-------AE--------
  1     Input       {GetLabel "Please enter a label: ",A1}~  |
  2                 {Quit}                                    |
  3                                                           |
  4                                                           |
        ======================================================MAIN=
```

Figure 28.13

If you supply a number in response to a {GetLabel} prompt, Symphony enters that number as a numeric string in the target cell. If you enter a function in response to {GetLabel}, Symphony enters the function name as a literal string in the target cell. For example, typing the function @NOW in response to the {GetLabel} prompt in Figure 28.13 results in the label

A1: '@NOW

{Get}

The {Get} command causes a macro to pause for the user to type a single keystroke. The keystroke is entered in the cell specified in the function's argument. For example, the command

{Get A1}

would cause Symphony to pause in the middle of a macro and wait for the user to type a keystroke. The keystroke can be a normal alphabetic or numeric character, or it can be a special Symphony key like {Calc} or [Pg Up].

Since {Get} makes no provision for a control panel prompt and can accept only a single character at a time, it is far less useful than its more powerful relatives {GetLabel} and {GetNumber}. In most cases, you'll want to use one of these commands instead of {Get} to accept characters from the keyboard.

There is, however, one clever use for {Get} that you'll probably be able to take advantage of in your macros. {Get} can be used to delay the execution of a macro while the user reads a message or reminder presented by the macro. When the message has been read, the user can type [Enter] and the macro will proceed.

{If}

Another commonly used SCL command with a parallel 1-2-3 command is {If}. The {If} command allows you to build logical tests into your macros. The form of this command is

{IF conditional test}

The {If} command tests the value of the conditional test in its argument. If the conditional test is false (value 0), the macro skips down one line and resumes processing with the first character on the line below the line containing the {If} command. If the conditional test is true (value 1), the macro continues to process beginning with the character immediately following the closing bracket in the {If} command.

For example, Figure 28.14 shows a macro that includes an {If} command. This macro requests the user to enter a number less than 500. The number that is entered is stored in cell A1. After you enter the number, the {If} command in the second line tests the value in cell A1 to ensure that it is less than 500. If the value in A1 *is* less than 500, the macro continues processing in cell AB2, which calls the subroutine Multiply (we'll talk about subroutines in a few pages). If, however, the value in cell A1 is *not* less than 500, the macro skips to cell AB3 and executes the commands stored there. These commands will cause Symphony to beep, erase cell A1, and branch back to cell AB1, repeating the request.

```
       ------AA--------AB-------AC-------AD-------AE-------AF--------AG----
   1  If_Test    {GetNumber "Please enter a number less than 500: ",A1}  |
   2             {If A1<500}{Multiply}~                                   |
   3             {Beep}{Blank A1}{Branch AB1}~                            |
   4                                                                      |
       ================================================================MAIN=
```

Figure 28.14

{Branch}

As you learned in the first example in this chapter, when Symphony processes a macro it begins with the cell to which the macro name has been assigned, processes all of the characters in the cell, skips to the next cell, processes all of the characters there, and so on. There are times, however, when you want the macro to "change directions" while it is running. The SCL includes the {Branch} command to allows you to direct the flow of your SCL programs. This command is Symphony's equivalent of the 1-2-3 /XG command.

{Branch} is frequently used in conjunction with an {If} command. For example, the macro shown in Figure 28.14 uses the {Branch} command to control the processing of a macro based on the result of the {If} command that comes immediately before it.

Figure 28.15 shows another example of the {Branch} command. This macro, which can be used in any worksheet that requires the current date to be correct, tests the value in a cell named DATE to be sure that it contains a value greater than 30682, the serial date representation of January 1, 1984.

```
      ------AA-------AB-------AC-------AD-------AE-------AF------
 1   Starter   {Calc}                                              |
 2             {If DATE>30682}{Branch AB10}~                        |
 3             {GetNumber "Please enter current date: ",DATE}~      |
 4             {Starter}~                                           |
 5                                                                  |
      ==================================================MAIN=
```

Figure 28.15

If the number in DATE is greater than 30682, the program branches to cell AB10, where it continues processing. Otherwise, the program requests the user to enter the current date, which is entered in cell DATE. The last line of the macro loops back to the cell named Starter, which is the first cell in the macro. In other words, this command causes the program to repeat itself, once again recalculating the worksheet and testing the entry in cell DATE. This loop will continue until a date greater than 30682 is entered in DATE.

Suppose that after you have built the macro shown in Figure 28.15, you decide to insert a row in the worksheet between rows 8 and 9. As you learned in Chapter 7, all of the entries in the rows below row 9—including the entry in cell AB10—will be shoved down one row as a result of this insertion. In other words, the entry in what was cell AB10 is now in cell AB11.

Now suppose that after inserting the row, you run the macro. When the command {Branch AB10} is processed, Symphony dutifully attempts to transfer control of the macro to cell AB10. However, it does not find the correct instruction in that cell. The instruction you want the macro to find is now in cell AB11, where it was moved as a result of the insertion.

Because macros are simply labels, cell references in macros are not adjusted when cells are moved or when rows and columns are inserted into or deleted from the worksheet.

Whenever you use cell references in {Branch} commands—or anywhere else in macros, for that matter—you run the risk of damaging the macro by inserting or deleting rows from the worksheet. One way to overcome this problem is to use range names instead of cell references in your macros. For example, suppose you assign the name

NEXT to cell A10 in your original worksheet and rewrite the macro in Figure 28.15 to look like the one in Figure 28.16.

```
     ------AA-------AB-------AC------AD------AE------AF------
  1  Starter  {Calc}                                          |
  2            {If DATE>30682}{Branch NEXT}~                   |
  3            {GetNumber "Please enter current date: ",DATE}~ |
  4            {Starter}~                                      |
  5                                                            |
     ========================================================MAIN=
```

Figure 28.16

Now suppose you use the Insert command to insert a row in the worksheet just as you did previously. Once again, the contents of cell AB10 are shifted to cell AB11 by the change. However, the range named NEXT is also shifted to cell AB11 when you insert the row. Since the macro refers to the range name, not to the cell reference, it can adjust to changes in the worksheet.

Subroutines

If you use the SCL a lot, there will be times when you'll find that the same simple task must be performed several times in a single macro. You can, of course, include the same lines of code in the macro several times, but there is a better way. Symphony allows you to create the frequently used code once and then call it into use every time you need it. This special kind of macro is called a subroutine.

You can invoke a subroutine (or any other macro, for that matter) from within another macro simply by including the name of the subroutine, enclosed in braces, in the first. For example, suppose you write a macro that enters several numbers in the worksheet and then assigns each of the numbers the Currency 2 format. Instead of writing the format routine several times, you can write it once and then call it as a subroutine each time you need to use it. Such a macro is illustrated in Figure 28.17.

```
     ------AA-------AB-------AC-------AD------AE-------AF----
  1  Num_Entry {?}~              Format   {Menu}fc2~~          |
  2            {Format}~                  {Return}~            |
  3            {?}~                                            |
  4            {Format}~                                       |
  5            {?}~                                            |
  6            {Format}~                                       |
  7                                                            |
     ========================================================MAIN=
```

Figure 28.17

When this macro is run, Symphony pauses and waits for you to enter a number. While Symphony is waiting, you can move the cell pointer to any location you wish before making an entry. After you make the entry, the macro "calls" the subroutine named Format and assigns the format Currency 2 to the cell in which you made the entry. When the format has been set, the subroutine returns the macro to cell AB3, the cell immediately after the cell that called the subroutine. Symphony again pauses and allows you to scroll about the worksheet before making an entry, then calls the subroutine again. The process repeats a total of three times.

The {Return} command instructs Symphony to resume processing the macro with the first character on the line after the line that called the subroutine. Notice that the {Return} command in cell AE2 is followed by a tilde. This character is required.

Former 1-2-3 users will recognize that the subroutine call and {Return} commands in Symphony are similar in function to the /XC and /XR commands in 1-2-3. However, Symphony commands offer a second level of sophistication that we will discuss at the end of this chapter.

{MenuBranch} and {MenuCall}

The 1-2-3 program gives the user the ability to create special menus. This tradition is carried on by Symphony's {MenuBranch} and {MenuCall} commands. These commands tell Symphony to process a custom menu stored in a specific location in the worksheet. {MenuBranch} tells Symphony to branch to the menu; it will not return you to the main program automatically. {MenuCall} calls a menu and allows you to return to the main program.

Probably the simplest use of custom menus is to ask simple yes-or-no questions of the user while the macro is processing. For example, consider the macro and menu in Figure 28.18.

Macro menus tend to be confusing for a couple of reasons. The most important of these is that the explanations that accompany the menus are nearly always too long to fit in a single column, and therefore usually run together, making the menu look like a mess. The menu in Figure 28.18 suffers from this problem. However, if you expand columns AC and AD, the menu will look like Figure 28.19.

When this macro is run (by pressing {**User**} **Save [Enter]**), the command in line 1 tells the macro to look for a macro menu that begins in cell AC3. When the program executes this menu, the control panel displays the message

> Save worksheet and exit
> Save Exit

with a standard menu cursor on the Save option. If you press → to move the cursor to the Exit option, the control panel will look like this:

> Exit without saving
> Save Exit

You can choose either of these options by pointing to the option name and pressing [Enter] or by typing the first letter in the option name. When you select an option, the macro continues to process in the cell beneath that option. If, for example, you select the Save option, Symphony executes the commands stored in cells AC5 and AC6, saving the current worksheet and exiting from Symphony.

```
  ------AA--------AB-------AC-------AD-------AE------AF
1  Save        {MenuBranch AC3}~
2
3                 Save            Exit
4                 Save worksheExit without  saving
5                 {Services}fs{Services}ey
6
  ===================================================MAIN=
```

Figure 28.18

```
  ------AA--------AB------------AC----------------AD---------
1  Save        {MenuBranch AC3}~
2
3                 Save                Exit
4                 Save worksheet and exit  Exit without  saving
5                 {Services}fs~y      {Services}ey
6                 {Services}ey
7
  ====================================================MENU=
```

Figure 28.19

Custom macro menus must follow a few simple rules. First, the options in the menu must be arranged in adjacent columns. The top cell of the left-most column in the menu is the cell used by the {MenuBranch} and {MenuCall} commands to identify the macro.

A menu can have as many as eight options, but no more. If the descriptions of the choices in the menu are all fairly long, you might be limited to even fewer choices, since the entire menu must be able to fit in one screen.

The cell to the right of the last choice in the menu must be blank. However, no blank columns are allowed within the menu. If you include a blank cell in the menu, Symphony ignores any choices to the right of that blank.

All of the options in the menu must begin with a different uppercase letter. If you use lowercase letters, Symphony allows you to make a choice from the menu by pointing to the desired choice and pressing [Enter], but not by typing the first letter in the choice you desire. If you start two choices with the same letter and then type that letter in response to the menu, Symphony always assumes that you mean to execute the option which appears first in the menu.

You must also include a description of each menu item in the second row of the menu. If you leave a cell in the second row blank, an error will result when the macro is executed. If you want to leave this row blank, you can get around this problem by creating a label consisting only of spaces in this row.

The difference between {MenuBranch} and {MenuCall} is similar to the difference between {Branch} and the macro subroutine capability. When you use the {MenuCall} command, the menu is accessed as a subroutine. A {Return} command in any of the options immediately returns the macro to the cell containing the {MenuCall} command. {MenuBranch}, on the other hand, redirects the flow of the program so that it is not possible to automatically return to the cell that branched to the menu.

The only exception to this rule is that if you press [Esc] while processing a menu, the macro will resume processing in the cell that branched to the menu. For example, consider the menu macro shown in Figure 28.20.

```
  ------AA--------AB-------------AC------------------AD---------
1  Save        {MenuBranch AC3}{Right 5}~                       |
2                                                                |
3                    Save                      Exit              |
4                    Save worksheet and exit   Exit without saving|
5                    {Services}fs~y            {Services}ey      |
6                    {Services}ey                                |
7                                                                |
  ==================================================================MENU=
```

Figure 28.20

Suppose you run this macro, bringing this menu to the screen:

> **Save worksheet and exit**
> **Save Exit**

Then you press **[Esc].** When you press [Esc], control of the macro is returned to cell AB1, and the instruction {Right 5} is processed, moving the cell pointer five spaces to the right.

Other Simple Macro Commands

Symphony offers several other macro commands that are less frequently used than the ones covered in the previous section. These commands, however, add a great deal of flexibility to the SCL.

{Beep}

The {Beep} command forces Symphony to emit a beep. In the macro

> {Goto}A1 ~
> {Calc}
> {Beep}{Beep}{Beep}

Symphony beeps three times after moving the cell pointer to cell A1 and recalculating the worksheet. The beeps alert the user that the recalculation has been completed.

The Symphony manual says that {Beep} accepts no argument. However, if you use a numeric argument between 1 and 4 with {Beep}, you can vary the duration and pitch of the beep. For example, the macro

> {Goto}A1 ~
> {Calc}
> {Beep 1}{Beep 2}{Beep 3}{Beep 4}

moves the cell pointer to cell A1, recalculates the sheet, and then emits four different beeps. Numbers higher than four also work, but there are apparently only four different tones, so tone 5 is the same as tone 1, tone 6 the same as tone 2, and so on.

{Blank}

The {Blank} command is identical to the SHEET Erase command. This command instructs Symphony to erase the contents of the cell or range you specify in the argument. For example, the macro line

{Blank A1 . . A5}

erases the contents of the range A1 . . A5. This line is equivalent to the line

{Menu}EA1 . . A5 ˜

except that the {Blank} command can be used from within any type of window to erase the contents of a worksheet range. The SHEET Erase command can, of course, only be used from within the SHEET environment. As an example, suppose you are in the middle of a communications macro and are working in a COMM window. Before receiving some data into a Capture range, you want the macro to erase the entire Capture range. Provided the Capture range has been given the name CAPTURE, the macro command

{Blank CAPTURE}

erases the entire range. Similarly, the command

{Blank MAIN_DB}

can be used to erase the contents of the Main Report range from within a macro even when you are viewing the worksheet through a FORM window.

{Wait}

The {Wait} command simply forces a macro to pause until the time specified in the argument is reached. While the macro pauses, the message Wait appears in the upper-right corner of the screen. For example, the macro segment

{Wait @TIME(11,15,00)}

causes the macro to pause until 11:15 AM. The {Wait} command simply compares the value in its argument to the current time in Symphony's internal clock. When the two numbers are equal, the {Wait} command releases its control of the macro.

It is important that you understand that the time in the {Wait} argument is an absolute time, not a relative time. In other words, the {Wait} command pauses until a specific time—such as 3:15 PM, August 20, 1984—is reached, not until a specific amount of time—such as 15 minutes—has passed.

If you want the macro to pause for a specific period of time—say, 30 seconds—the argument has to be more complex:

{Wait @NOW + @TIME(0,0,30)}

This command tells Symphony to wait until the time @NOW plus 30 seconds has arrived.

The {Wait} command can be used to "hold" the execution of a macro until a certain time has arrived. For example, suppose you write a macro that automatically calls your branch office in California each night to obtain the daily sales figures. You want to start this macro when you leave the office, but you don't want it to begin running until 11:01 PM. If you include the line

{Wait @TIME(23,01,00)}

at the top of the macro, the macro will wait until 11:01 PM before attempting to contact the branch office.

{Recalc} and {RecalcCol}

There are times when, in the middle of a macro, you need to recalculate the worksheet. However, you may find that the time required to update the entire worksheet is too long and delays the macro unnecessarily. In that event, you can use the macro commands {Recalc} and {RecalcCol} to recalculate any portion of the worksheet from a single cell to a range as big as the entire worksheet.

Suppose you're in the middle of a macro that controls the process of entering and printing invoices. As a part of the process, you ask Symphony to extend (multiply quantity times price) each line in each invoice. Suppose, however, the worksheet includes not only the simple invoice form but also a price list data base, a customer data base, etc., and thus requires several seconds to recalculate. Instead of using the {Calc} command to calculate each invoice prior to printing, you decide to use the macro command {Recalc} to recalculate just the small part of the worksheet that contains the invoice form.

The only difference between {Recalc} and {RecalcCol} is that the former recalculates the indicated range row by row, while the latter recalculates column by column. The differences between row-by-row and column-by-column recalculation are explained in more detail in Chapter 3. In most cases, the commands are interchangeable.

The ability to recompute only a portion of the worksheet is so potentially useful that I can't understand why Lotus decided to bury these commands in the SCL rather than include them on the {Menu} Settings Recalculation menu.

Environmental Commands

The SCL offers several commands that control some of the most basic aspects of macro processing, such as whether the [Break] key will abort a macro. These commands are usually used in a macro header—a group of lines that you use at the beginning of almost every macro. This group of commands includes {BreakOn}{BreakOff}, {WindowsOn}{WindowsOff}, {PanelOn}{PanelOff}, and {Indicate}.

{BreakOn} and {BreakOff} These two commands control the effect of the [Break] key on your macros. If you use the {BreakOn} command in a macro, you can terminate that macro by pressing [Break]. If you want to turn off the [Break] key, include the {BreakOff} command in your macro.

{WindowsOn} and {WindowsOff} The {WindowsOff} command allows you to "freeze" the screen of your computer during the execution of a macro. This keeps the screen from flashing and flickering as the macro moves the cell pointer around the screen and issues commands. {WindowsOn} restores the screen to normal operation.

{WindowsOff} is like the {Services} Windows Settings Auto-Display command but is more comprehensive than that command. When you include the {WindowsOff} command in a macro, all of the windows are frozen until the {WindowsOn} command is issued.

These commands should always be paired in a macro. In other words, whenever you use {WindowsOff} to freeze the screen, you should use {WindowsOn} later in the macro to reactivate the screen.

{PanelOn} and {PanelOff}   These commands control the redisplay of the control panel while a macro is executing. The default is {PanelOn}, which means that the control panel is active during the execution of the macro. If you issue the {PanelOff} command, the control panel is frozen and does not display any of the commands that are issued by the macro.

{PanelOn} and {PanelOff} are very similar in function to {WindowsOn} and {WindowsOff} and are frequently used in conjunction with them. When the {WindowsOff} and {PanelOff} commands are used together, the screen is completely frozen. If you create macros that are used by other people, the {PanelOff} command can be used both as a security tool and as a way to avoid confusion.

{Indicate}   {Indicate} is a clever command that allows you to replace the mode indicator in the upper-right corner of the screen with an indicator of your choosing. For example, suppose you write a complex SCL program that manages your company's accounts receivable. When you execute this macro, you might want the mode indicator to read ACCRV. The line

> {Indicate ACCRV}

does the trick. The argument of the {Indicator} command must be a literal string. If you try to use a cell reference, the cell reference ends up as the indicator. For example, the command

> {Indicate +A5}

would result in the mode indicator +A5.

The string in the argument of an {Indicate} function can be as long as you wish, but only the first five characters will be used. If the string is shorter than five characters, Symphony automatically places the indicator flush right on the screen. To center or otherwise align a short string, you must include preceding and trailing spaces and enclose the entire string in quotes. For example, to center the simple label A, issue the command

> {Indicate " A "}

The mode indicator you select with the {Indicate} command remains in effect (even after the macro has finished running) until you deliberately reset it or until you erase the worksheet with the New command. If you want to return control of the mode indicator to Symphony, simply include the {Indicate} command, without an argument, in the macro.

Advanced Commands

Several of the commands in the SCL are included primarily for professional programmers who plan to develop applications using Symphony. For example, the {Put} command has very little application for most Symphony users, nor does the {Look} command. However, these commands are very important to Symphony users who plan to create sophisticated macro programs, and you might find ways to use some of them in even simple macros.

{For}

Symphony users who are experienced with BASIC or nearly any other programming language will recognize the {For} command. {For} allows you to specify the number of times you want to repeat a given procedure. The form of this command is

> {For counter location,start number,stop number,step number,starting location}

Let's look at a simple example of the {For} command at work. The autoexec macro shown in Figure 28.21 forces the user to correctly enter a password before it allows him to access the worksheet. The {For} loop in this macro allows the user three tries at entering the password correctly.

```
    ------AA--------AB-------AC------AD---------------------
 1  Password  {BreakOff}                                          |
 2            {For COUNTER,1,4,1,AB5}~                            |
 3            {Let COUNTER,0}~{Services}ey                        |
 4                                                                |
 5            {GetLabel "Please enter the password: ",AD1}~       |
 6            {If AD1="cessna"#OR#AD1="CESSNA"}{BreakOn}{Quit}     |
 7            {Return}~                                           |
    =====================================================MAIN=
```

Figure 28.21

The first line of this macro disables the [Break] key. This line prevents the user from simply overriding the password macro by typing [Ctrl][Break].

Line 2 contains the {For} command. This command says: Repeat the subroutine that begins at cell AB5 until the value in the cell named COUNTER is 4. Start the counter at 1, and increment the counter by 1 each time this command is repeated.

COUNTER can be any cell in the worksheet. We could just as easily have referred to COUNTER by using a cell reference like +AC15 instead of the range name COUNTER. You don't need to make any entry to this cell; Symphony does all the work for you.

The subroutine that begins at cell AB5 simply requests the user to enter the password, stores the entered string in cell AD1, and then tests the string in AD1 against the correct password, cessna. Notice that the macro allows the user to enter the password in either uppercase or lowercase letters. If the string matches the password, the macro sets the

[Break] key on and issues the {Quit} command, allowing the user access to the worksheet. Otherwise, the {Return} command in line 7 returns the macro to cell AB2, where the {For} command increments the number in COUNTER by 1 and recalls the subroutine, giving the user another chance to enter the correct password.

When the value in COUNTER is 4 (the stop value specified in the {For} command), meaning that the user has had three tries to enter the correct password and has failed to get it right, the {For} loop is broken and the macro executes the commands in row 3. These commands reset the value in COUNTER to 0 and issue the Exit Yes command.

{Let}

The {Let} command allows you to assign a value to a cell without actually moving the cell pointer to that cell and without using the Copy command. For example, the command

   {Let A1,20} ˜

assigns the value 20 to cell A1. If cell D11 contained the number 20, the command

   {Let A1,D11} ˜

would also assign the value 20 to cell A1.

If the first argument in the {Let} command is a multicell range name, Symphony enters the value specified in the second argument into the upper-left corner of the named range. For example, if the name TEST applies to the range A1 . . C3, the command

   {Let TEST,20} ˜

enters the number 20 in cell A1.

There are two special forms to the {Let} command that allow you to specify the type of an entry as you assign that entry to a cell. For example, the command

   {Let A1,20:string} ˜

enters the *label* '20 in cell A1. Similarly, the command

   {Let A1, + "test":value} ˜

enters the string value 'test in cell A1.

If you don't supply one of the two qualifiers, Symphony first attempts to evaluate the expression as either a label or a number. If it cannot determine whether the entry should be a label or a value, it enters the characters in the argument into the target cell as a label.

{Put}

The {Put} command allows you to store a value or a label in a particular location with a predefined range. This command can be used to create index tables from within a macro. The {Put} command has the form

   {Put range,column offset,row offset,expression} ˜

The first argument, the range, describes a multicell range in the worksheet. The column-offset and row-offset terms describe a location within that range. The expression is the value or label you want to enter in the defined cell.

The only way to understand {Put} is to watch it work. Suppose you create the one-line macro

{Put A1 . . C5,1,1,100} ˜

The first term of this macro describes the {Put} range, A1 . . C5. The next two numbers tell Symphony that the target cell within this range has a column offset of 1 and a row off-set of 1. As with many of Symphony's functions, the first column and row in the specified range have an offset of 0, so the cell with the offset 1,1 is cell B2. When this macro runs, it enters the number 100 into cell B2.

You can also use cell references to describe the column-offset, row-offset, and expression terms in a {Put} command. For example, if cell D1 contains the number 1, cell D2 the number 3, and cell D3 the number 50, the macro command

{Put A1 . . C5,D1,D2,D3} ˜

would enter the number 50 in cell B4, the cell in the range A1 . . C5 with a column offset of 1 and a row offset of 3. In fact, you'll probably use cell references more often than constants to define the target ranges and coordinates in your {Put} commands.

You can also use {Put} to enter a label into a specified cell in a range. For example, the command

{Put A1 . . C5,2,2,Test}

enters the label Test in cell C3. If, however, Test was an active range name in the current worksheet, this command would enter the contents of the cell Test into cell C3.

If the column-offset or row-offset term in the {Put} command exceeds the number of columns or rows in the range, the command results in the error message

Illegal offset in PUT

{Contents}

The {Contents} command is a specialized form of the {Let} command. {Contents} allows you to create a *string value* in one cell that represents the current contents of another cell, and to specify a special format for the resulting copy. The form of this command is

{Contents destination,source,width,format code}

The destination argument indicates the cell into which you want to transfer an entry, and the source argument specifies the current location of that entry. The last two terms, width and format code, are optional. The width option should actually be called length, since it determines the maximum length of the entry in the destination. The format code option allows you to assign a special format to the entry in the destination cell.

Let's consider an example of the {Contents} command at work. Suppose cell A10 contains the value 12345 and you want to use the {Contents} command to transfer that number to cell A11. The macro command

{Contents A11,A10} ˜

does the trick. After you issue this command, cell A11 will contain the string

A11: '12345

Similarly, if cell A10 contains the label

A10: 'This is a test

the command

{Contents A11,A10} ˜

transfers the label into cell A11.

The effect of the width argument varies depending on whether the entry being transferred is a value or a label. If the entry is a label that is longer than the specified width, the destination cell will contain only the number of characters from that label specified by the width term. In the previous example, the command

{Contents A11,A10,2} ˜

enters the label 'Th in cell A11.

If, on the other hand, the source cell contains a number, the result of a restrictive width term is less predictable. For example, if cell A10 contains the number 1234567, the command

{Contents A11,A10,3}

causes the worksheet to look like Figure 28.22.

```
 --------A--------B--------C--------D----
 9                                        |
 10   1234567                             |
 11 ***                                   |
 12                                       |
 ================================MAIN=
```

Figure 28.22

Cell A11 in this worksheet contains the label '***. However, if you change the width setting to 7, as in the command

{Contents A11,A10,7}

the worksheet will look like Figure 28.23. Cell A11 in this worksheet contains the label '1E+06. Finally, specifying a width of 8 results in the worksheet shown in Figure 28.24.

The format code term allows you to assign a format to the numeric string that results from the {Contents} command. A complete list of all of the format codes can be found in the Symphony Reference Manual.

```
       -------A--------B--------C--------D----
 9                                            |
10    1234567                                 |
11   1E+06                                    |
12                                            |
      ================================MAIN=
```

Figure 28.23

```
       -------A--------B--------C--------D----
 9                                            |
10    1234567                                 |
11   1234567                                  |
12                                            |
      ================================MAIN=
```

Figure 28.24

If you specify a format code in the {Contents} command, you must also specify a width. Choosing a width term that matches the default column width—generally 9—is usually a safe bet.

{OnError}

The {OnError} command is used to trap errors that may occur while the macro is running. This command prevents accidental errors from stopping the execution of an otherwise correct macro.

The form of the {OnError} command is

{OnError branch location,message location}

The first argument in the command is the branch location. This argument tells Symphony where to resume processing after an error occurs. The second argument, the message location, tells Symphony where to display the message describing the error that has occurred.

For example, suppose you create a macro that uses the File Combine command to retrieve a file from disk into the current worksheet. Suppose also that when you run this macro, the file SECOND is not in the current directory, so Symphony returns the error message "File does not exist". If the macro does not include the {OnError} command, this error causes the macro to abort. Because the macro includes an {OnError} command, however, Symphony branches to the cell specified by the branch location argument, enters the error message in the message location, and continues processing the macro.

It is important that you realize that {OnError} cannot be used to debug macros, but only to trap general errors that occur while a macro is being processed. In fact, the {OnError} command does not even recognize macro errors; it only traps common errors like File Not Found, Memory Full, etc.

{Look}

The {Look} command "peeks" at the keyboard to see if you have typed any characters since the macro began executing. If a character has been typed, Symphony will accept it into the designated cell. The macro does not pause to get this character.

{Look} only reads the first character in the keyboard buffer. In other words, if you type three or four characters while the macro is running, only the first one appears in the designated cell.

The {Look} command provides a way to terminate a macro without pressing [Break]. For example, the macro in Figure 28.25 is a perpetual loop that will run until you press any key. As soon as you press a key, the macro stops.

```
-------AA--------AB--------AC--------AD----
1            {Look QUIT}~                    |
2            {IF QUIT<>""}{Quit}             |
3            {Return}~                       |
4                                            |
===================================MAIN==
```

Figure 28.25

Telecommunications Macros

The SCL includes two special commands that are used exclusively when you are attempting to communicate over the phone lines with another computer: {Phone} and {Handshake}.

{Phone}   The {Phone} command does just what you would expect—it causes Symphony to dial the phone. In that regard, this command is very similar to the COMM mode Phone Call command. The special benefit of the {Phone} command, however, is that it allows you to dial without being in a COMM window. For example, the command

{Phone 15025551212}

causes Symphony to dial the number 1-502-555-1212, even if the current window is a DOC or SHEET window.

The argument in a {Phone} command should include the number to be called or a reference to a cell containing that number. The argument must include only numbers; Symphony will ignore any other characters except the comma, T, and P.

Each comma in the number causes Symphony to pause for two seconds. These pauses can be used to delay the dialing while waiting for an outside line or for your long-distance service to answer. For example, the command

{Phone 9,,5025551212}

first dials a 9 (presumedly to access an outside line) and then pauses for four seconds to allow the outside line to open up.

You can include the letter P or T in the argument of this command to tell Symphony whether it should use the Pulse or Tone convention while dialing the phone. For example, to instruct Symphony to dial the number in the previous example using the Pulse convention, change the command to look like this:

{Phone P9,,5025551212}

You can set up an autodialing system with this command. Suppose all of your commonly used phone numbers are stored in a data base in a Symphony worksheet. You can define a macro that extracts the number you want to dial from your data base and enters it into a particular cell. It then issues the {Phone} command to dial that number without ever leaving the SHEET environment.

Naturally, the {Phone} command assumes that a modem is properly attached to your computer and that Symphony has been installed to use the modem. If not, the command will not work properly.

If the {Phone} command fails to make a connection, the macro continues to process in the cell containing the {Phone} command. If a connection is made, the macro skips to the cell below the {Phone} command and continues processing there.

{Handshake}   The {Handshake} command allows you to exchange a single line message with a remote computer. The command has the form

{Handshake "send string","receive string",seconds,capture range}

The send string is the string you want to transmit to another computer. This string can be up to 240 characters long. The receive string is the string you expect from the remote computer as an acknowledgement that the send string has been received. Both the send string and the receive string must be enclosed in double quotes, and both must be literal strings (not references to cells containing strings).

The seconds argument specifies the number of seconds you want Symphony to wait after sending the send string to receive the receive string.

The last term, capture range, is optional. If you supply a capture range, Symphony records any information received from the remote computer *prior to the receipt of the receive string.*

When you use the {Handshake} command in a macro, the command sends the send string to the remote computer and waits the number of seconds you specify in the seconds argument to receive the receive string. If the receive string is received within the allotted time, the macro continues with the first character in the cell following the cell that contains the {Handshake} command. Otherwise, the macro continues with the next character in the cell that contains the {Handshake} command.

The {Handshake} command has two applications. First, it can be used to transmit a log-in sequence to a remote computer. In this application, {Handshake} is very much like the COMM {Menu} Login command. The other use for {Handshake} is to receive large blocks of information from a remote computer. When used in this way, the {Handshake} command is similar to the COMM {Menu} Settings Capture Range command.

Overall, the {Handshake} command is a real puzzler. Since the COMM environment {Menu} Login command accomplishes exactly the same purpose as the {Handshake} macro command, I wonder why Lotus bothered to include both in the program. The name of the command is also confusing. You may remember that in Chapter 23, I defined handshaking as a means of coordinating the communication between two computers. The macro {Handshake} command has absolutely nothing to do with coordinating communications between computers, and I wonder why Lotus chose the name {Handshake} for this command.

More on Subroutines

Earlier in the chapter you learned about subroutines and saw a simple example of a subroutine that formats cells in different parts of the worksheet. This section examines Symphony's ability to pass variables to a subroutine.

The best way to explain this capability is to create a simple example. Figure 28.26 shows a macro that includes a subroutine call and passes two values to the subroutine.

```
      ------AA-------AB-------AC-------AD-------AE-------AF--------AG----
  1    Main    {Multiply A1,A2}                                          |
  2            {Let A3,AE3}                                              |
  3            {Multiply A4,A5}                                         |
  4            {Let A6,AE3}                                             |
  5                               Multiply {Define AE1:value,AE2:value} |
  6                                        {Let AE3,+AE1*AE2}~          |
  7                                        {Return}                     |
  8                                                                     |
       ==============================================================MAIN=
```

Figure 28.26

Notice that cells in column AB refer to cells in column A. Figure 28.27 shows that part of the same worksheet.

```
      ------A---------B---------C---------D-----
  1        50                                   |
  2         2                                   |
  3                                             |
  4        25                                   |
  5         5                                   |
  6                                             |
       ==================================MAIN=
```

Figure 28.27

Let's walk through this macro step by step. Line 1 of the macro calls the subroutine Multiply, which begins in cell AE5. Notice that the first line also includes the cell references A1 and A2. This subroutine call will "pass" the values in cells A1 and A2 (50 and 2) to the subroutine.

The first line of the subroutine defines the cells into which the passed values will be entered. In this case, the defined cells are AE1 and AE2, so the value 50 is entered in cell

AE1 and the value 2 is entered in AE2. The {Define} command tells Symphony to store the values passed by the subroutine call into the cells referred to in the define statement. Notice that in the example we specifically defined cells AE1 and AE2 as value cells. If we had not done this, the data items would have been entered as labels ('50 and '2).

The next line of the subroutine assigns the value of +AE1*AE2, 100, to cell AE3. In other words, this line multiplies the two values that were passed to the subroutine and enters the product in cell AE3. The final line of the subroutine returns control of the macro to the main program in cell AB2.

The command in cell AB2 tells Symphony to transfer the value from cell AE3, 100, to cell A3.

The third line of the macro calls the Multiply subroutine again and passes the values in cells A4 and A5—25 and 5—to the subroutine. Once again, the subroutine defines cells AE1 and AE2 and stores the passed values in those cells; computes the product of the passed values, 125, and assigns that value to cell AE3; and returns control to the main macro. The last line of the main macro assigns the new value in cell AE3, 125, to cell A6. When the entire macro is completed, the worksheet will look like Figure 28.28.

```
      ------A--------B--------C--------D-----
1             50                              |
2              2                              |
3            100                              |
4             25                              |
5              5                              |
6            125                              |
      ================================MAIN=
```

Figure 28.28

Let's take a step back to see the big picture. The subroutine defined here multiplies any two numbers you pass to it and stores the result of that computation in a known location, cell AE3. From there, the result can be passed to any location in the worksheet using the {Let} command. This subroutine can thus be used to multiply any two numbers stored anywhere in the worksheet.

The first line of a subroutine to which you pass information must always contain the {Define} command. The number of cells defined in a subroutine must always match the number of data items that are passed to the subroutine. Otherwise, Symphony returns the macro error

> Macro: Too many arguments in DEFINE

or

> Macro: Missing argument in DEFINE

You can, of course, also pass labels to a subroutine. If you do this, be sure that the type specification in the {Define} command is label.

In this chapter you've learned the basics about macros and the SCL. We've just barely scratched the surface of this powerful and exciting facet of Symphony, though. What you have learned here should be considered a foundation from which you can build your knowledge of macros and the SCL. The more you work with macros, the more you'll learn about them.

CHAPTER TWENTY NINE

ADD-IN PROGRAMS

One characteristic most successful personal computers have in common is "open architecture": These computers all have expansion slots that accommodate special boards, which increase the capabilities of the machines. To make sure that there would be boards to fill those slots, the manufacturers of these "open" computers published the technical specifications of the software so that expansion board manufacturers could understand the details of the computer. Open architecture helped make the Apple II and the IBM PC the most popular computers ever.

With Symphony, Lotus has brought the concept of open architecture to software. Lotus designed Symphony to be an "open" software system, meaning that it is possible for third-party software developers (and for Lotus) to develop add-in programs you can "plug" into Symphony. These add-in programs appear to be an integral part of the Symphony program.

So far, there are only two add-in programs available for Symphony—DOS.APP and TUTORIAL.APP. TUTORIAL.APP is the tutorial program that Lotus provides with Symphony. You probably used this tutorial when you were first getting acquainted with Symphony. DOS.APP is a terrific program that allows you to exit from Symphony to use a DOS command or function and then return at precisely the same point from which you departed.

Many other add-ins are being developed, including a spelling checker for the Symphony word processor, an advanced graphics package, and a personal calendar and reminder program.

THE ADD-IN COMMANDS

Add-in programs are controlled by the {Services} Application command. When you issue this command, the following menu appears:

Attach   Detach   Invoke   Clear   Quit

Attach

The first command is {Services} Application Attach, which allows you to attach an add-in program to Symphony. When you issue this command, Symphony prompts you for the name of the application you want to attach and presents a list of the applications files on the system directory.

Symphony always assumes that the applications programs are stored on the system directory, the directory from which you loaded Symphony. If you are using a floppy-disk system, the system directory is probably on drive A. If you are using a hard-disk system, the system directory is on drive C, where Symphony is stored.

The two add-ins provided with Symphony are stored on the Help and Tutorial disk, along with the file SYMPHONY.DYN. The SYMPHONY.DYN file *must* be on the system directory the first time you attach an application. This means that most of the time you'll need to replace the Symphony program disk with the Help and Tutorial disk (or another disk that contains SYMPHONY.DYN) before you attempt to attach any applications. Since it is a good idea to have the Help disk in the system directory anyway, and since the Help disk has over 200,000 bytes of free space, I recommend that you use the Help disk to store all applications you use with Symphony.

The main limitation on the number of applications you can attach at any one time is the amount of memory in your PC. The program DOS.APP consumes about 3100 bytes of memory. If you have only the minimum amount of memory required to use Symphony (320K), losing even a little bit of RAM can make a big difference. Future .APP programs are likely to consume far more memory. In general, if you have a relatively limited amount of RAM, your ability to load and use applications is restricted. Even if you have more memory, remember that you can't use memory taken up by attached applications for worksheet entries.

Suppose, for example, that you want to attach the program DOS.APP to Symphony. If you have a two-drive system, begin by replacing the Symphony program disk in drive A with the Help and Tutorial disk. Next, issue the {**Services**} Application Attach command. Symphony responds by prompting you for the name of the application you wish to attach and displays the list of .APP files on the system drive. Simply point to the name DOS.APP in the list and press [**Enter**]. The disk in drive A will spin for a few seconds. When the "Wait" message disappears, the application is attached.

You cannot attach an application that is currently attached. If you try to do so, Symphony responds with the error message "Add-in already attached".

Invoke

After you attach an application with the Application Attach command, you can invoke (execute) it with the Application Invoke command. When you issue this command, Symphony provides a list of the currently *attached* applications (not the applications on the disk) and asks you to select the one you wish to invoke. You must choose a program name from the list provided by Symphony.

For example, suppose you have attached the application DOS.APP and now want to execute this program. After you issue the {**Services**} Application Invoke command,

Symphony prompts you to supply the name of the application you want to invoke and displays a list of the attached applications. Because you have attached only one application, there will be only one name on the list. Choose the application DOS.APP by pointing to its name in the (one-name) list and pressing [Enter] or by typing DOS next to Symphony's prompt. Symphony executes the application after you select the name.

Notice that running an add-in application is always a two-step process. You must first attach the application and then invoke it. If you try to use the Invoke command when no applications are attached, Symphony beeps and refuses to proceed with the command. It's too bad that Symphony does not offer a run command that both attaches and invokes an application, much as the COMM environment Phone-and-Login command automatically dials and logs in to a remote computer.

Detach and Clear

Symphony offers two commands that let you detach an attached application. The first, Detach, lets you detach a single attached application. The other command, Clear, detaches all applications that are currently attached.

When you use the Detach command, Symphony prompts you for the name of the application to be detached and presents a list of the currently attached applications. To detach one of these, simply point to its name in the list and press [Enter]. There is no further warning; once you press [Enter], the application is detached.

The Clear command, by contrast, detaches all applications. Clear gives no warning; as soon as you type Clear, all applications are removed from memory.

Detaching an application frees the memory that was allocated to that application, allowing you to increase the size of your worksheet. If you have a limited amount of memory, I recommend that you immediately detach any application after you use it to keep memory waste to a minimum. In addition, whenever you see the message "Low memory", check to be sure that no applications are attached. If they are, use the Detach or Clear commands to detach them.

USING DOS.APP

Let's walk through a simple example of add-ins at work. Suppose that you have been using Symphony for several hours and want to save your work onto disk. However, you can't find a blank formatted disk, and the worksheet is too large to save on one of your other disks. With some programs you'd be out of luck, but not with Symphony. You can use DOS.APP to format the new disk without losing any of your work.

Assuming that DOS.APP is attached, you should begin by invoking the program. When the Invoke command is issued, the prompt

Press [Return] or enter program name:

appears in the control panel. This prompt gives you two choices. If you press **[Enter]**, you simply drop out of Symphony into DOS. The Symphony worksheet disappears from your screen and the DOS prompt (probably A> or C>) appears. Once the DOS prompt appears, you can issue any DOS command you want. In the example, you would issue the Format command. When Format is finished, you simply type **Exit** to return to the Symphony worksheet. If all goes well, the worksheet should be exactly as you left it.

If the disk in the system drive (usually A or C) does not contain DOS, Symphony beeps and delivers the message "Program not found".

If the system directory contains an AUTOEXEC.BAT file, DOS.APP executes this file before it returns you to the system prompt. Be careful! I've lost a couple of worksheets as a result of using DOS.APP to exit from Symphony into a disk with an AUTOEXEC.BAT file.

If you wish, you could enter the name of a specific program you want to run in response to Symphony's prompt. In the example, you could supply the name of the DOS utility you want to use, Format. Symphony then searches the system directory for that program. If the program is found, DOS.APP runs it automatically. Otherwise, the message "Program not found" is displayed.

If DOS.APP finds the requested program on the directory, the program is executed. As soon as the program is finished, you return automatically to the Symphony worksheet.

By the way, you are not limited to using DOS.APP to run DOS utility programs. In fact, provided your system has sufficient memory, you can run programs like WordStar and dBASE II using DOS.APP. My advice, though, is to be extremely careful when running a program like WordStar with Symphony in the background. Although I have done this successfully several times, I have also run into unexplained problems occasionally. In general, you should always save your worksheet before invoking DOS.APP.

CHAPTER THIRTY
CONFIGURING SYMPHONY

A 1-2-3 command, /Worksheet Global Default, allows the user to change some of the program's default settings. At the time 1-2-3 was introduced, it offered more flexibility in this area than any other program. Symphony, however, far outstrips 1-2-3 in this area.

It seems as if Symphony gives you the ability to change every one of its default settings. In fact, the program is so flexible that it is easy to become confused when changing the defaults. Because you don't need these commands to use Symphony, the beginning user is better off ignoring the Configuration options and making do with the program's default offerings.

For this reason, I left the discussion of these commands until near the end of the book. If you're still feeling your way through Symphony, I suggest that you skip this chapter for now and read it when you have a bit more experience.

The Configuration command is one of the options on Symphony's {Services} menu. To access this command, press {Services} and then choose the Configuration option. The Configuration command controls a settings sheet, which appears under the Configuration menu after you issue the command, as shown in Figure 30.1.

```
 File Printer Communications Document Window Help Auto Update Other Quit
 --------------------------------------------------------------------
| File:       B:\           Document              Window             |
| Printer:                   Tab-interval:  5       Type: SHEET       |
|   Type:     1              Justification: n       Name:             |
|   Auto-LF:  No             Spacing:       1          MAIN           |
|   Wait:     No             Left margin:   1       Help: Removable   |
|   Margins                  Right margin:          Auto Worksheet:   |
|     Left: 4     Top: 2     Blanks Visible: No                       |
|    Right: 76 Bottom: 2     CRs Visible:    Yes    Clock on Screen:  |
|   Page-length: 66          Auto-justify:   Yes       International  |
|   Init-String:                                    File Translation: |
| Communications name:                                               |
| ============================================Configuration Settings= |
```

Figure 30.1

You can see that this settings sheet controls a wide range of default settings, including settings relating to file management, printing, word processing, windows, and help. We'll go through these choices one by one.

FILE

As you have seen many times by now, each time you issue one of Symphony's {Services} File commands (such as File Retrieve or File Erase), the program displays a list of all of the files of a given type (usually .WRK) on the default directory. The Configuration File option gives you the power to change the default directory. Former users of 1-2-3 can see that this command is very similar to 1-2-3's /Worksheet Default Directory command.

Unless you use this command to make a change, the default directory is A:\. This means that whenever you issue a File command, Symphony displays a list of the files on directory A:\.

If you have a one-drive system, you'll probably want to keep this default. If, however, you have a two-drive system, you'll probably want to change the default to B:\. Making this change allows you to keep the system disk or help disk in drive A and the disk containing your files in drive B.

If you have a hard disk, you have even more options. You'll probably want to create a separate directory on your hard disk just for your .WRK files. You might call this directory

C:\SYMPH\FILES

In this case, you should change the default so that Symphony looks in this subdirectory for your files.

Although you can create subdirectories on floppy disks, I advise against it. It's hard enough keeping up with your disks without having to remember all of the subdirectories on each disk. You'll probably end up wasting a lot of time searching for files that are hidden away in subdirectories. If you want to divide your files, create a separate disk for each group of files: one for budgets, one for forecasts, one for employee records, etc.

If you change the default from A:\ to a blank, Symphony assumes that the directory that was active when you entered Symphony is the default. Usually, the active drive is the one that contains your Symphony program disk. However, this is not always the case. If your Symphony disk is in drive A and the prompt on your screen is B>, you can enter Symphony and allow B to remain the default drive by typing

B>A:Symphony

The {Services} Configuration File command is confusingly similar to the {Services} File Directory command. Both commands allow you to change the default drive. The only difference between them is that changes made with the {Services} Configuration File command can be made permanent, while changes made with {Services} File Directory are only temporary. As you will learn later, you can use the Update option of the Configuration menu to "lock in," or make permanent, changes made through the {Services} Configuration File command. Changes to the default made with the {Services} File Directory command are temporary; they are retained only until you leave Symphony.

PRINTER

If you have upgraded from 1-2-3 to Symphony, you already know how to configure 1-2-3 to handle a wide range of printer parameters. Symphony offers the same level of flexibility in this area, thanks to the Printer option of the Configuration command.

After you issue the Printer command, the following menu appears:

Type   Auto-LF   Wait   Margins   Page-Length   Init-String   Quit

The Type option lets you specify the interface through which Symphony should print. Because most printers for the IBM PC and PC-compatible printers use a parallel interface, the default Type is Parallel. If you have a serial printer (many letter-quality printers use a serial interface), you should select the second choice from the Type menu, Serial.

The Type command allows you to specify a second parallel or a second serial interface as well. Most users don't have more than one of each type of interface, so these options are not used very much. If, however, you have more than one parallel or serial interface and use the primary interface for another device, you can use this command to access your secondary interfaces.

The next option on the Printer menu, Auto-LF, lets you tell Symphony whether the printer should insert a linefeed after each line. The default Auto-LF setting is No. This command is required because some printers automatically issue a linefeed at the end of each line while others do not. If the printer does not issue linefeeds, then Symphony must do so, or the entire report would be printed on a single line. Similarly, if both the printer and Symphony issued linefeeds, there would be an unwanted blank line after every line of text.

If you're not sure whether your printer issues linefeeds automatically, you can ask your dealer. If the dealer doesn't know, perform this simple test: Print some text with Auto-LF set to No. Does the report look right, or does the printer keep printing on one line? If everything is OK, then your printer issues linefeeds by itself, and the Auto-LF setting is correct. If the report is printed on one line, Symphony needs to control the linefeeds. If so, you should set Auto-LF to Yes.

The remaining options on the {Services} Configuration Printer menu are used to set the default margins, page length, and other print parameters. The options on this menu correspond exactly to many of the options on the {Services} Print menu. Unless you make specific changes to these settings with {Services} Print commands, Symphony uses the {Settings} Configuration defaults every time you print.

The difference between the {Services} Configuration Print command and the {Services} Print command is that changes made with Configuration can be made permanent, while changes made with the Print command are only temporary.

COMMUNICATIONS

Use the Communications option on the {Services} Configuration menu to specify the name of the communications configuration file that should be loaded at the start of each Symphony session. Communications configuration files (.CCF files) are discussed in Chapters 24–27.

DOCUMENT

The Document option on the Configuration menu lets you change the default settings of Symphony's word processing parameters. This command is covered in depth in the word processing section (Chapters 15–18).

HELP

If your computer system uses floppy disks, sometimes you'll want to have a disk other than the Help disk (the disk containing the file Symphony.HLP) in the default drive. For example, if you have a one-drive system, you may be using the only available drive for saving and loading files. If you need to use Help, you have to put the Help disk in the drive before you press {Help}.

The Configuration Help command lets you tell Symphony whether the Help disk is permanently resident or not. This command has two options: Instant and Removable. The first option, Instant, is the default. When Help is configured to be Instant, Symphony expects the Help disk to be in the default drive. In this mode, the first time you press {Help} during a Symphony work session, Symphony opens the Symphony.HLP file and keeps it open until you exit from Symphony. Because the file stays open, the program can access Help very quickly.

If, however, you want to remove the Help disk from the drive, you should use the other option, Removable. When you select this mode, Symphony closes the Symphony-.HLP file after each time you use Help and reopens the file again when you next press {Help}. Because Symphony closes the Symphony.HLP file, accessing Help takes longer in the Removable mode than in the Instant mode.

If you have a two-drive computer system and have taken our advice to change the default drive to B, keeping the Help disk in drive A, you can use the Instant option. You can also use Instant if you have a hard-disk system and have copied the Symphony.HLP file onto the hard disk. Otherwise, I suggest that you use the Removable option to prevent accidentally damaging the Symphony.HLP file.

Never use the Instant option when you plan to remove the Help disk from the system drive. Removing the disk after selecting the Instant option can lead to serious problems with the Help command.

One problem with this command is that both options require the Help disk to be in the default drive when you press the {Help} key. Even if you have selected the Removable option, Symphony beeps at you and no Help appears if the Help disk is not in the drive when you press {Help}. I think a prompt like "Insert Help disk in drive A" would be useful, especially in the Removable mode.

WINDOW

The Window option of the Configuration menu allows you to adjust the type and name of the default Symphony window. The default window appears when you first load Symphony into your computer. This option was covered in detail in Chapter 11.

AUTO

The Auto option on the Configuration menu allows you to specify the name of a file to be loaded automatically every time Symphony is loaded. The file specified must be a worksheet (.WRK) file. You provide only the name of the file; Symphony automatically assumes the extension .WRK.

If you specify an Auto file, as soon as you load Symphony, it searches the default disk drive for the name of the file. If the file is found, Symphony automatically retrieves it to the workspace. If the file is not found, Symphony displays the error message

File not found

If the Auto file contains an autoexec macro, that macro runs automatically when you load the file. For more information on autoexec macros, see Chapter 28.

You can use the Auto command to "hide" Symphony from the users of your applications. If you create an application program that includes an autoexec macro and then configure Symphony to load your file automatically, Symphony takes the user straight through the loading of the application and right to the application menu. The user doesn't need to know anything about loading files or executing macros to use your application.

OTHER

The Other option on the Configuration menu is a catch-all that includes commands for changing the default settings of some Symphony formats, adjusting the clock in the lower-left corner of the screen, creating translation tables, and specifying the name of autoload and autoinvoke add-in programs. When you issue this command by typing {Services} Configuration Other, the following menu appears:

Clock   File-Translation   International   Application

Let's examine these options one at a time.

Clock

This option allows you to alter the format of the system date and time display in the lower-left corner of the worksheet. The command has two choices: Standard and International. The default is Standard, which causes the date and time to be displayed in the form

18-Jun-84 11:54 AM

You might recognize this format from Chapter 6 as a combination of date format 1 (DD-MMM-YY) and time format 2 (HH:MM AM/PM). Most users find this format satisfactory and never need to use this command.

If you want the system date and time to be displayed in international format, however, use the second option, International. This option causes the system date to be displayed in the form

06/18/84 11:54

which is a combination of date format 4 (DD/MM/YY) and time format 4 (HH:MM). Notice that the message AM is not used in this format. You may recall from Chapter 6 that in international time format a 24-hour clock is used, so 11:54 AM is displayed as 11:54 and 11:54 PM is displayed as 23:54.

The third option of the Configuration Other Clock command, None, lets you suppress the display of the system date and time altogether. Use this command if you don't want the system date and time to be displayed.

File-Translation

With this command, you can define a default custom translation table to be used when communicating text files between machines. This option has already been covered in Chapter 27 in the communications section.

International

The International option of the Configuration Other command allows you to change the default conventions for the Punctuation, Currency, and Date and Time formats. The International command controls yet another of Symphony's setting sheets, called the International Settings sheet. This sheet and the International menu are shown in Figure 30.2.

```
  Punctuation Currency Date Time Quit
  ----------------------------------------------------------------
  | Punctuation: A              Date Format 4: A (MM/DD/YY)       |
  |         Period Dot                                           |
  |       Argument Comma        Time Format 3: D (HHhMMmSSs)     |
  |       Thousands Comma                                        |
  |                                                             |
  | Currency Sign: $            (Prefix)                        |
  |                                                             |
  ==========================================International Settings=
```

Figure 30.2

This settings sheet shows the current status of the Punctuation, Currency, and Time and Date formats. You can vary all of these using the International command.

Punctuation

Symphony uses punctuation marks in three different ways: (1) as decimal points in numbers; (2) to separate hundreds from thousands, thousands from millions, and so on in formatted numbers; and (3) as separators in function arguments. The Punctuation option of the {Services} Configuration Other International command allows you to select the characters for each of these uses.

The Punctuation command offers eight choices, as shown in Table 30.1. Notice that each option specifies the characters used for the decimal point, argument separator, and hundreds/thousands separator. For example, option A instructs Symphony to use a period for the decimal place, a comma for the argument separator, and a comma for the hundreds/thousands divider. By limiting the number of choices, Lotus has prevented users from accidentally choosing the same character for both the argument separator and the decimal point.

Option		Thousands/Decimal	Argument
A	(.,,)	123,456.78	@HLOOKUP(A1,A2 . . C6,1)
B	(,..)	123.456,78	@HLOOKUP(A1.A2 . . C6.1)
C	(.;,)	123,456.78	@HLOOKUP(A1;A2 . . C6;1)
D	(,;.)	123.456,78	@HLOOKUP(A1;A2 . . C6;1)
E	(.,)	123 456.78	@HLOOKUP(A1,A2 . . C6,1)
F	(,.)	123 456,78	@HLOOKUP(A1.A2 . . C6.1)
G	(.;)	123 456.78	@HLOOKUP(A1;A2 . . C6;1)
H	(,;)	123 456,78	@HLOOKUP(A1;A2 . . C6;1)

Table 30.1

There is one exception to these conventions. The argument separator can always be a semicolon, no matter which option you select. For example, Symphony accepts the function @HLOOKUP(A1;A2 . . C6;1) even if you had selected option A (.,,), B (,. .), E (.,) or F (,.).

Since the default option, A (.,,), is by far the most commonly used, most people (other than international users) will probably never need to use this command. Still, it is nice to know that Symphony gives you the flexibility to make the decision.

Currency

One of the most interesting differences between 1-2-3 and Symphony is that Symphony lets you change the default currency symbol from a dollar sign to the symbol for the British pound, the symbol for pesetas, the symbol for Dutch guilder, and the symbol for yen. This is accomplished with the Services Configuration Other International Currency command. This command also allows you to change the currency symbol from a prefix ($123,456) to a suffix (123,456$).

Although you can use any string of up to 15 characters as the currency symbol, it is likely to be a single character. In fact, most users will probably never change the symbol from its default, $, or its default position, prefix. There are exceptions to this rule, however. Suppose that in some specialized worksheet you wanted your currency numbers to be displayed like this:

123,456 U.S. Dollars

In this case, the string " U.S. Dollars" replaces the simple symbol $. To make this change, select the Currency option from the International menu. If you had not changed the currency sign before, the command line would display the message

Currency Sign: $

To make the change, press [Backspace] to erase the $ symbol and type the new currency symbol: U.S. Dollars. Be sure to include a space before the U. After you make this entry, the program asks you whether the new currency sign should be a prefix or a suffix. Since you want the new symbol to be a suffix, point to Suffix and press [Enter].

You way be wondering how it is possible to use foreign currency signs when these characters don't show up on most keyboards. In fact, these characters can be used only because Symphony and the Lotus International Character Set allow you to create them.

To create a new currency symbol, you must use the {Compose} key. {Compose} is a strange key; when you press it, nothing seems to happen. But in reality {Compose} sends a message to Symphony, telling it that a multicharacter description of a single special character is coming. Symphony accepts the defining characters and then generates the special character. For example, to create the symbol £, you must press the keys

{Compose} L = [Enter]

Table 30.2 shows the {Compose} codes that create the other Symphony currency symbols.

British pound	**L =** or **L-** or **l-** or **l =**
Yen	**Y =** or **Y-** or **y-** or **y =**
Dutch Guilder	**ff**
Peseta	**PT** or **pt** or **Pt**

Table 30.2

There are some unfortunate limits to Symphony's ability to display foreign currency symbols. First, it is not possible for more than one symbol to be active at one time. In other words, it is not possible to use £ and $ in different cells of a single worksheet. Symphony users who deal in multiple currencies may find this limitation irritating.

Remember that in Chapter 2 we explained that Symphony allows you to start a numeric entry with the currency symbol $. As you might expect, if you change the default currency symbol, you can also use the new symbol to start a numeric entry as long as the new symbol is a prefix and not a suffix. For example, if you change the default currency symbol to £, you could begin a numeric entry by typing {**Compose**} **L = .** If the default currency symbol location was Suffix, however, you could not use the symbol £ (or any other currency symbol) to start an entry.

Date and Time

The other two options of the International command allow you to change the form of the international date and time formats. You may remember from Chapter 6 that the default form of these formats are:

Date format 4	Full international	MM/DD/YY
Date format 5	Partial international	MM/DD
Time format 3	Full international	HH:MM:SS (24 Hour)
Time format 4	Partial international	HH:MM (24 Hour)

The Configuration Other International Date command offers four options for the International Date format:

Option	Full International	Partial International
A	MM/DD/YY	MM/DD
B	DD/MM/YY	DD/MM
C	DD.MM.YY	DD.MM
D	YY-MM-DD	MM-DD

The first option is the default.

If you wish to use a format other than the default, issue the Configuration Other International Date command and point to the format you wish to use. As you point, the display in the first line of the control panel shows you exactly how date formats 4 and 5 will look, given the option you selected. For example, if you point to choice C, the control panel displays

> Format D4 will be: DD.MM.YY Format D5 will be DD.MM
> A (MM/DD/YY) B (DD/MM/YY) C (DD.MM.YY) D YY-MM-DD

If you point to option D, the control panel displays

> Format D4 will be: YY-MM-DD Format D5 will be MM-DD
> A (MM/DD/YY) B (DD/MM/YY) C (DD.MM.YY) D YY-MM-DD

When you change the default international date format, you also change the explanatory lines that appear in the control panel when you issue the {Menu} Format Date command. For example, in the default mode, this is how the control panel looks after you issue the {Menu} Format Date command and point to option 5 (Partial international).

> Currently configured: MM/DD
> 1 (DD-MMM-YY) 2 (DD-MMM) 3 (MMM-YY) 4 (Full Intn'l) 5 (Partial Intn'l)

However, if you change the international format to choice B (DD/MM/YY), reissue the Format Date command, and point to option 5, the control panel displays

> Currently configured: DD/MM
> 1 (DD-MMM-YY) 2 (DD-MMM) 3 (MMM-YY) 4 (Full Intn'l) 5 (Partial Intn'l)¢

Notice that the explanatory message has changed in the second version.

The option A international format (MM/DD/YY) is my favorite date format for a couple of reasons. First, I generally prefer the international formats to the standard formats because the international formats use only eight characters to express a full date and thus fit in a standard column, while the standard format (DD-MMM-YY) requires a wider column. I prefer MM/DD/YY to DD/MM/YY because this is the form I use to date letters and forms.

The Time format option works in the same way to alter the international time formats. This command also offers four choices, as shown below.

Option	Full International	Partial International
A	HH:MM:SS	HH:MM
B	HH.MM.SS	HH.MM

C	HH,MM,SS	HH,SS
D	HHhMMmSSs	HHhMMm

Like the Date option, the Time option shows you the effect a change will have as you issue the command. For example, if you issue the {Services} Configuration Other International Time command and point to option D, the control panel displays

Format T3 will be: HHhMMmSSs Format T4 will be: HHhMMm
A (HH:MM:SS) B (HH.MM.SS) C (HH,MM,SS) D (HHhMMmSSs)

Option D may be a bit puzzling at first, but it really makes a lot of sense. The time 12:15:33 PM is shown as 12h15m33s in format option D. Notice that, because of the trailing *s,* this format is one character wider than the others and thus requires a wider column.

You can get into trouble with the @DATEVALUE and @TIMEVALUE functions if you choose one of the optional international date or time formats. For example, suppose you enter the label "11/15/84" in cell A1 and the function

A2: @DATEVALUE(A1)

in cell A2. As long as the default international date format is in effect, this function works properly, returning the number 31001, Symphony's date value for November 15, 1984. However, if you use the {Services} Configuration Other International Date command to change the default form to YY-MM-DD (option D), the function returns the @ERR message because the string in cell A1 does not conform to one of the current date formats. If you change the international date format back to MM/DD/YY, or if you edit the contents of cell A1 and put them in the form "84-11-15," the function once again works properly.

The same problem can occur with @TIMEVALUE. Assume that cell A1 contains the string "13:11:33" and that cell A2 contains the function

A2: @TIMEVALUE(A1)

As long as the default international format is in effect, the function in A2 works perfectly. If you change the default format to selection D (HHhMMmSSs), though, the function fails because the string in cell A1 is not in a recognizable form.

Remember—the arguments of the functions @DATEVALUE and @TIMEVALUE must conform to one of the date or time formats in effect in the worksheet. If the argument is a date or time string in international form, make sure that the form of the string matches the currently active date or time format.

There is one final point about the International Time and International Date commands. Remember that the Clock option of the {Services} Configuration Other command can be used to switch the clock in the lower-left corner of the Symphony display from its default form to an international form. Since the international form is a combination of date format 4 and time format 3, the International Time and International Date commands affect the display of the clock.

UPDATE

To make the changes you have made to Symphony's configuration permanent, use the

Update option. Update rewrites the file SYMPHONY.CNF, storing your new defaults so Symphony can use them over and over.

If you don't use the Update option, the changes you have made remain in effect only until you exit from Symphony. If you exit without updating the SYMPHONY.CNF file, Symphony returns to the configuration that was in effect when you loaded it the last time.

Interestingly, Symphony does not offer you a choice (Update the .CNF File? Yes or No) before it updates the .CNF file, as it does with most other disk operations. Once you press Update from the Configuration menu, the new settings replace the old ones. Be careful—with the Update command you can easily destroy a configuration file that took a long time to create.

INDEX

When Problems with Symphony Occur, the Solution is at Your Fingertips

SYMPHONY ENCORE:
Program Notes
by Dick Anderson and Barbara Anderson

This new book is designed to help the Symphony user over the rough spots. Organized like a travel guide, the book takes the reader through each of Symphony's functions. It offers solutions to potential problems and practical suggestions for improving efficiency. Learn to combine different techniques to achieve effects you might not have thought possible. This is a life-saving reference guide that no Symphony user will want to be without!

ISBN: 0-89588-247-7   450 pages

Selections from The SYBEX Library

Introduction to Computers

OVERCOMING COMPUTER FEAR
by Jeff Berner
112 pp., illustr., Ref. 0-145
This easy-going introduction to computers helps you separate the facts from the myths.

INTRODUCTION TO WORD PROCESSING
by Hal Glatzer
205 pp., 140 illustr., Ref. 0-076
Explains in plain language what a word processor can do, how it improves productivity, how to use a word processor and how to buy one wisely.

PARENTS, KIDS, AND COMPUTERS
by Lynne Alper and Meg Holmberg
145 pp., illustr., Ref. 0-151
This book answers your questions about the educational possibilities of home computers.

THE SYBEX GUIDE TO FAMILY COMPUTERS UNDER $200
by Doug Mosher
160 pp., illustr., Ref. 0-149
Find out what these inexpensive machines can do for you and your family. "If you're just getting started . . . this is the book to read before you buy."—Richard O'Reilly, Los Angeles newspaper columnist

PORTABLE COMPUTERS
by Sheldon Crop and Doug Mosher
128 pp., illustr., Ref. 0-144
"This book provides a clear and concise introduction to the expanding new world of personal computers."—Mark Powelson, Editor, *San Francisco Focus Magazine*

PROTECTING YOUR COMPUTER
by Rodnay Zaks
214 pp., 100 illustr., Ref. 0-239
The correct way to handle and care for all elements of a computer system, including what to do when something doesn't work.

YOUR FIRST COMPUTER
by Rodnay Zaks
258 pp., 150 illustr., Ref. 0-142
The most popular introduction to small computers and their peripherals: what they do and how to buy one.

THE SYBEX PERSONAL COMPUTER DICTIONARY
120 pp., Ref. 0-199
All the definitions and acronyms of microcomputer jargon defined in a handy pocket-sized edition. Includes translations of the most popular terms into ten languages.

PROFIT FROM COMPUTER INFORMATION SERVICES
by Frederick Williams
200 pp., illustr., Ref. 0-213
Highly readable and interspersed with case studies, this book covers available services, their cost, and potential benefits.

Computer Books for Kids

THE COMPUTER ABC'S
by Daniel Le Noury and Rodnay Zaks
64 pp., illustr., Ref. 0-167
This beautifully illustrated, colorful book for parents and children takes you alphabetically through the world of computers, explaining each concept in simple language.

THE LIGHTYEAR EXCUSE: A COMPUTER SPACE ADVENTURE
by Richard Ramella
144 pp., illustr., Ref. 0-222
This children's science fiction tale uses type-in computer programs to involve the young reader in the story.

MONICA THE COMPUTER MOUSE
by Donna Bearden, illustrated by Brad W. Foster
64 pp., illustr., Hardcover, Ref. 0-214
Lavishly illustrated in color, this book tells the story of Monica the mouse, as she travels around to learn about several different kids of computers and the jobs they can do. For ages 5–8.

POWER UP! KIDS' GUIDE TO THE APPLE IIe® /IIc™
by Marty DeJonghe and Caroline Earhart
200 pp., illustr., Ref. 0-212
Colorful illustrations and a friendly robot highlight this guide to the Apple IIe/IIc for kids 8–11.

BANK STREET WRITING WITH YOUR APPLE®
by Stanley Schatt, Ph.D. and Jane Abrams Schatt, M.A.
150 pp., illustr., Ref. 0-189
These engaging exercises show children aged 10–13 how to use Bank Street Writer for fun, profit, and school work.

POWER UP! KIDS' GUIDE TO THE COMMODORE 64™
by Marty DeJonghe and Caroline Earhart
192 pp., illustr., Ref. 0-188
Colorful illustrations and a friendly robot highlight this guide to the Commodore 64 for kids 8–11.

EXPLORING WITH DR. LOGO™
by James H. Muller
200 pp., illustr., Ref. 0-183
This comprehensive introduction to Digital Research's version of the Logo language is presented with illustrations and an intriguing story line.

Humor

COMPUTER CRAZY
by Daniel Le Noury
100 pp., illustr., Ref. 0-173
No matter how you feel about computers, these cartoons will have you laughing about them.

MOTHER GOOSE YOUR COMPUTER: A GROWNUP'S GARDEN OF SILICON SATIRE
by Paul Panish and Anna Belle Panish, illustrated by Terry Small
96 pp., illustr., Ref. 0-198
This richly illustrated hardcover book uses parodies of familiar Mother Goose rhymes to satirize the world of high technology.

CONFESSIONS OF AN INFOMANIAC
by Elizabeth M. Ferrarini
215 pp., Ref. 0-186
This is one woman's tongue-in-cheek revelations of her pursuit of men, money, and machines. Learn about the many shopping services, information banks, and electronic dating bulletin boards available by computer.

Special Interest

COMPUTER POWER FOR YOUR LAW OFFICE
by Daniel Remer
142 pp., Ref. 0-109
How to use computers to reach peak productivity in your law office, simply and inexpensively.

THE COLLEGE STUDENT'S PERSONAL COMPUTER HANDBOOK
by Bryan Pfaffenberger
210 pp., illustr., Ref. 0-170
This friendly guide will aid students in selecting a computer system for college study, managing information in a college course, and writing research papers.

CELESTIAL BASIC
by Eric Burgess
300 pp., 65 illustr., Ref. 0-087
A collection of BASIC programs that rapidly complete the chores of typical astronomical computations. It's like having a planetarium in your own home! Displays apparent movement of stars, planets and meteor showers.

COMPUTER POWER FOR YOUR ACCOUNTING FIRM
by James Morgan, C.P.A.
250 pp., illustr., Ref. 0-164
This book is a convenient source of information about computerizing your accounting office, with an emphasis on hardware and software options.

COMPUTER POWER FOR THE BUSINESS WOMAN
by Barbara Deane
250 pp., illustr., Ref. 0-184
Computers can enhance your career and increase your effectiveness on the job. Lear how professional women use computers in business, law, medicine, education, and the arts.

COMPUTER POWER FOR PHYSICIANS
by John M. Allswang, Ph.D.
Assisted by Jon I. Isenberg, M.D.
and Michael H. Weiss, M.D.
225 pp., illustr., Ref. 0-197
Here is a comprehensive introduction to all the issues a doctor encounters when buying and using a computer system. Includes reviews of medical software.

PERSONAL COMPUTERS AND SPECIAL NEEDS
by Frank G. Bowe
175 pp., illustr., Ref. 0-193
Learn how people are overcoming problems with hearing, vision, mobility, and learning, through the use of computer technology.

ESPIONAGE IN THE SILICON VALLEY
by John D. Halamka
200 pp., illustr., Ref. 0-225
Discover the behind-the-scenes stories of famous high-tech spy cases you've seen in the headlines.

ASTROLOGY ON YOUR PERSONAL COMPUTER
by Hank Friedman
225 pp., illustr., Ref. 0-226
An invaluable aid for astrologers who want to streamline their calculation and data management chores with the right combination of hardware and software.

Computer Specific

Apple II—Macintosh

THE EASY GUIDE TO YOUR APPLE II®
by Joseph Kascmer
147 pp., illustr., Ref. 0-122
A friendly introduction to the Apple II, II plus and the IIe.

BASIC EXERCISES FOR THE APPLE®
by J.P. Lamoitier
250 pp., 90 illustr., Ref. 0-084
Teaches Applesoft BASIC through actual practice, using graduated exercises drawn from everyday applications.

THE APPLE II® BASIC HANDBOOK
by Douglas Hergert
250 pp., illustr., Ref. 0-115
A complete listing with descriptions and instructive examples of each of the Apple II BASIC keywords and functions. A handy reference guide, organized like a dictionary.

APPLE II® BASIC PROGRAMS IN MINUTES
by Stanley R. Trost
150 pp., illustr., Ref. 0-121
A collection of ready-to-run programs for financial calculations, investment analysis, record keeping, and many more home and office applications. These programs can be entered on your Apple II plus or IIe in minutes!

YOUR FIRST APPLE II® PROGRAM

by Rodnay Zaks

182 pp., illustr., Ref. 0-136

This fully illustrated, easy-to-use introduction to Applesoft BASIC programming will have the reader programming in a matter of hours.

THE APPLE® CONNECTION

by James W. Coffron

264 pp., 120 illustr., Ref. 0-085

Teaches elementary interfacing and BASIC programming of the Apple for connection to external devices and household appliances.

THE APPLE IIc™: A PRACTICAL GUIDE

by Thomas Blackadar

175 pp., illustr., Ref. 0-241

Learn all you need to know about the Apple IIc! This jargon-free companion gives you a guided tour of Apple's new machine.

THE BEST OF EDUCATIONAL SOFTWARE FOR APPLE II® COMPUTERS

by Gary G. Bitter, Ph.D. and Kay Gore

300 pp., Ref. 0-206

Here is a handy guide for parents and an invaluable reference for educators who must make decisions about software purchases.

APPLE II® FREE SOFTWARE

by Gary Phillips

250 pp., Ref. 0-200

This is a complete guide to locating and selecting free software for your particular application needs.

YOUR SECOND APPLE II® PROGRAM

by Gary Lippman

250 pp., illustr., Ref. 0-208

The many colorful illustrations in this book make it a delight for children and fun for adults who are mastering programming on any of the Apple II line of computers, including the new IIc.

THE EASY GUIDE TO YOUR MACINTOSH™

by Joseph Caggiano

280 pp., illustr., Ref. 0-216

This easy-to-read guide takes you all the way from set-up to more advanced activities such as using Macwrite, Macpaint, and Multiplan.

THE COMPLETE GUIDE TO YOUR MACINTOSH™

by Joseph Caggiano and Roy Robinson

350 pp., illustr., Ref. 0-204

This is an in-depth guide to the Macintosh, ideal for the intermediate and advanced user.

MACINTOSH™ FOR COLLEGE STUDENTS

by Bryan Pfaffenberger

250 pp., illustr., Ref. 0-227

Find out how to give yourself an edge in the race to get papers in on time and prepare for exams. This book covers everything you need to know about how to use the Macintosh for college study.

Atari

YOUR FIRST ATARI® PROGRAM

by Rodnay Zaks

182 pp., illustr., Ref. 0-130

This fully illustrated, easy-to-use introduction to ATARI BASIC programming will have the reader programming in a matter of hours.

BASIC EXERCISES FOR THE ATARI®

by J.P. Lamoitier

251 pp., illustr., Ref. 0-101

Teaches ATARI BASIC through actual practice, using graduated exercises drawn from everyday applications.

THE EASY GUIDE TO YOUR ATARI® 600XL/800XL

by Thomas Blackadar

175 pp., illustr., Ref. 0-125

This jargon-free companion will help you get started on the right foot with your new 600XL or 800XL ATARI computer.

ATARI® BASIC PROGRAMS IN MINUTES

by Stanley R. Trost

170 pp., illustr., Ref. 0-143

You can use this practical set of programs without any prior knowledge of BASIC! Application examples are taken from a wide variety of fields, including business, home management, and real estate.

YOUR SECOND ATARI® PROGRAM

by Gary Lippman

250 pp., illustr., Ref. 0-232

The many colorful illustrations in this book make it a delight for children and fun for adults who are mastering BASIC programming on the ATARI 400, 800, or XL series computers.

Coleco

WORD PROCESSING WITH YOUR COLECO ADAM™

by Carole Jelen Alden

140 pp., illustr., Ref. 0-182

This is an in-depth tutorial covering the word processing system of the Adam.

THE EASY GUIDE TO YOUR COLECO ADAM™

by Thomas Blackadar

175 pp., illustr., Ref. 0-181

This quick reference guide shows you how to get started on your Coleco Adam using a minimum of technical jargon.

Commodore 64/VIC-20

THE BEST OF COMMODORE 64™ SOFTWARE

by Thomas Blackadar

150 pp., illustr., Ref. 0-194

Save yourself time and frustration with this buyer's guide to Commodore 64 software. Find the best game, music, education, and home management programs on the market today.

THE BEST OF VIC-20™ SOFTWARE

by Thomas Blackadar

150 pp., illustr., Ref. 0-139

Save yourself time and frustration with this buyer's guide to VIC-20 software. Find the best game, music, education, and home management programs on the market today.

THE COMMODORE 64™/VIC-20™ BASIC HANDBOOK

by Douglas Hergert

144 pp., illustr., Ref. 0-116

A complete listing with descriptions and instructive examples of each of the Commodore 64 BASIC keywords and functions. A handy reference guide, organized like a dictionary.

THE EASY GUIDE TO YOUR COMMODORE 64™

by Joseph Kascmer

126 pp., illustr., Ref. 0-126

A friendly introduction to the Commodore 64.

YOUR FIRST VIC-20™ PROGRAM

by Rodnay Zaks

182 pp., illustr., Ref. 0-129

This fully illustrated, easy-to-use introduction to VIC-20 BASIC programming will have the reader programming in a matter of hours.

THE VIC-20™ CONNECTION

by James W. Coffron

260 pp., 120 illustr., Ref. 0-128

Teaches elementary interfacing and BASIC programming of the VIC-20 for connection to external devices and household appliances.

YOUR FIRST COMMODORE 64™ PROGRAM

by Rodnay Zaks

182 pp., illustr., Ref. 0-172

You can learn to write simple programs without any prior knowledge of mathematics or computers! Guided by colorful illustrations and step-by-step instructions, you'll be constructing programs within an hour or two.

COMMODORE 64™ BASIC PROGRAMS IN MINUTES

by Stanley R. Trost

170 pp., illustr., Ref. 0-154

Here is a practical set of programs for

business, finance, real estate, data analysis, record keeping, and educational applications.

GRAPHICS GUIDE TO THE COMMODORE 64™
by Charles Platt
261 pp., illustr., Ref. 0-138

This easy-to-understand book will appeal to anyone who wants to master the Commodore 64's powerful graphics features.

THE BEST OF EDUCATIONAL SOFTWARE FOR THE COMMODORE 64
by Gary G. Bitter, Ph.D. and Kay Gore
250 pp., Ref. 0-223

Here is a handy guide for parents and an indispensable reference for educators who must make decisions about software purchases for the Commodore 64.

COMMODORE 64™ FREE SOFTWARE
by Gary Phillips
300 pp., Ref. 0-201

Find out what "free software" is all about and how to find the specific programs you need.

YOUR SECOND COMMODORE 64™ PROGRAM
by Gary Lippman
240 pp., illustr., Ref. 0-152

A sequel to *Your First Commodore 64 Program*, this book follows the same patient, detailed approach and brings you to the next level of programming skill.

THE COMMODORE 64™ CONNECTION
by James W. Coffron
250 pp., illustr., Ref. 0-192

Learn to control lights, electricity, burglar alarm systems, and other non-computer devices with your Commodore 64.

PARENTS, KIDS, AND THE COMMODORE 64™
by Lynne Alper and Meg Holmberg
110 pp., illustr., Ref. 0-234

This book answers parents' questions about the educational possibilities of the Commodore 64.

CP/M Systems

THE CP/M® HANDBOOK
by Rodnay Zaks
320 pp., 100 illustr., Ref 0-048

An indispensable reference and guide to CP/M—the most widely-used operating system for small computers.

MASTERING CP/M®
by Alan R. Miller
398 pp., illustr., Ref. 0-068

For advanced CP/M users or systems programmers who want maximum use of the CP/M operating system . . . takes up where our *CP/M Handbook* leaves off.

THE BEST OF CP/M® SOFTWARE
by John D. Halamka
250 pp., Ref. 0-100

This book reviews tried-and-tested, commercially available software for your CP/M system.

THE CP/M PLUS™ HANDBOOK
by Alan R. Miller
250 pp., illustr., Ref. 0-158

This guide is easy for beginners to understand, yet contains valuable information for advanced users of CP/M Plus (Version 3).

INSTANT CP/M:® A KEYSTROKE GUIDE
by Robert Levine
250 pp., illustr., Ref. 0-132

This novice's guide includes a complete explanation of terms and commands, showing how they appear on the screen and what they do—a quick, foolproof way to gain proficiency with CP/M.

IBM PC and Compatibles

THE ABC'S OF THE IBM® PC
by Joan Lasselle and Carol Ramsay
143 pp., illustr., Ref. 0-102

This book will take you through the first crucial steps in learning to use the IBM PC.

THE BEST OF IBM® PC SOFTWARE

by Stanley R. Trost

351 pp., Ref. 0-104

Separates the wheat from the chaff in the world of IBM PC software. Tells you what to expect from the best available IBM PC programs.

THE IBM® PC-DOS HANDBOOK

by Richard Allen King

296 pp., Ref. 0-103

Explains the PC disk operating system. Get the most out of your PC by adapting its capabilities to your specific needs.

BUSINESS GRAPHICS FOR THE IBM® PC

by Nelson Ford

259 pp., illustr., Ref. 0-124

Ready-to-run programs for creating line graphs, multiple bar graphs, pie charts, and more. An ideal way to use your PC's business capabilities!

THE IBM® PC CONNECTION

by James W. Coffron

264 pp., illustr., Ref. 0-127

Teaches elementary interfacing and BASIC programming of the IBM PC for connection to external devices and household appliances.

BASIC EXERCISES FOR THE IBM® PERSONAL COMPUTER

by J.P. Lamoitier

252 pp., 90 illustr., Ref. 0-088

Teaches IBM BASIC through actual practice, using graduated exercises drawn from everyday applications.

USEFUL BASIC PROGRAMS FOR THE IBM® PC

by Stanley R. Trost

144 pp., illustr., Ref. 0-111

This collection of programs takes full advantage of the interactive capabilities of your IBM Personal Computer. Financial calculations, investment analysis, record keeping, and math practice—made easier on your IBM PC.

YOUR FIRST IBM® PC PROGRAM

by Rodnay Zaks

182 pp., illustr., Ref. 0-171

This well-illustrated book makes programming easy for children and adults.

DATA FILE PROGRAMMING ON YOUR IBM® PC

by Alan Simpson

219 pp., illustr., Ref. 0-146

This book provides instructions and examples for managing data files in BASIC. Programming design and development are extensively discussed.

SELECTING THE RIGHT DATA BASE SOFTWARE FOR THE IBM® PC

SELECTING THE RIGHT WORD PROCESSING SOFTWARE FOR THE IBM® PC

SELECTING THE RIGHT SPREADSHEET SOFTWARE FOR THE IBM® PC

by Kathleen McHugh and Veronica Corchado

100 pp., illustr., Ref. 0-174, 0-177, 0-178

This series on selecting the right business software offers the busy professional concise, informative reviews of the best available software packages.

THE MS™-DOS HANDBOOK

by Richard Allen King

320 pp., illustr., Ref. 0-185

The differences between the various versions and manufacturer's implementations of MS-DOS are covered in a clear, straightforward manner. Tables, maps, and numerous examples make this the most complete book on MS-DOS available.

IBM® PC SPREADSHEETS TO GRAPHICS

by Douglas Hergert

250 pp., illustr., Ref. 0-163

This book will supply you with all the tools you need to produce many kinds of business-oriented graphs directly from your spreadsheet data.

YOUR SECOND IBM® PC/PCjr™ PROGRAM

by Gary Lippman

250 pp., illustr., Ref. 0-210

The many colorful illustrations in this book

make it a delight for children and fun for adults who are mastering BASIC programming on the IBM PC or PC*jr.*

ESSENTIAL PC-DOS
by Myril and Susan Shaw
300 pp., illustr., Ref. 0-176
Whether you work with the IBM PC, XT, PC*jr,* or the portable PC, this book will be invaluable both for learning PC-DOS and for later reference.

LOCAL AREA NETWORKS FOR THE IBM® PC/XT
by Sheldon Crop
225 pp., illustr., Ref. 0-243
Learn what local area networks are all about and how to use them effectively. This book reviews existing local area networks, including the latest from IBM and AT&T.

IBM PCjr

IBM® PC*jr*™ BASIC PROGRAMS IN MINUTES
by Stanley R. Trost
175 pp., illustr., Ref. 0-205
Here is a practical set of BASIC programs for business, financial, real estate, data analysis, record keeping, and educational applications, ready to enter on your PC*jr.*

THE COMPLETE GUIDE TO YOUR IBM® PC*jr*™
by Douglas Herbert
625 pp., illustr., Ref. 0-179
Learn to master the new hardware and DOS features that IBM has introduced with the PC*jr.* A fold-out reference poster is included.

THE EASY GUIDE TO YOUR IBM® PC*jr*™
by Thomas Blackadar
175 pp., illustr., Ref. 0-217
This jargon-free companion is designed to give you a practical working knowledge of your machine—no prior knowledge of computers or programming is needed.

BASIC EXERCISES FOR THE IBM® PC*jr*™
by J.P. Lamoitier
250 pp., illustr., Ref. 0-218
PC*jr* BASIC is easy when you learn by doing! The graduated exercises in this book were chosen for their educational value and application to a variety of fields.

TI 99/4A

THE BEST OF TI 99/4A™ CARTRIDGES
by Thomas Blackadar
150 pp., illustr., Ref. 0-137
Save yourself time and frustration when buying TI 99/4A software. This buyer's guide gives an overview of the best available programs, with information on how to set up the computer to run them.

YOUR FIRST TI 99/4A™ PROGRAM
by Rodnay Zaks
182 pp., illustr., Ref. 0-157
Colorfully illustrated, this book concentrates on the essentials of programming in a clear, entertaining fashion.

Timex

YOUR TIMEX/SINCLAIR 1000® AND ZX81™
by Douglas Hergert
159 pp., illustr., Ref. 0-099
This book explains the set-up, operation, and capabilities of the Timex/Sinclair 1000 and ZX81. Covers how to interface peripheral devices and introduces BASIC programming.

THE TIMEX/SINCLAIR 1000® BASIC HANDBOOK
by Douglas Hergert
170 pp., illustr., Ref. 0-113
This complete alphabetical listing with explanations and examples of each word in the T/S 1000 BASIC vocabulary will allow you quick, error-free programming of your T/S 1000.

TIMEX/SINCLAIR 1000® BASIC PROGRAMS IN MINUTES
by Stanley R. Trost
150 pp., illustr., Ref. 0-119
A collection of ready-to-run programs for financial calculations, investment analysis, record keeping, and many more home and office applications. These programs can be entered on your T/S 1000 in minutes!

MORE USES FOR YOUR TIMEX/SINCLAIR 1000®
Astronomy on Your Computer
by Eric Burgess and Howard J. Burgess
176 pp., illustr., Ref. 0-112
Ready-to-run programs that turn your TV into a planetarium.

TRS-80

THE RADIO SHACK® NOTEBOOK COMPUTER
by Orson Kellogg
118 pp., illustr., Ref. 0-150
Whether you already have the Radio Shack Model 100 notebook computer or are interested in buying one, this book will clearly explain what it can do for you.

YOUR COLOR COMPUTER
by Doug Mosher
350 pp., illustr., Ref. 0-097
Patience and humor guide the reader through purchasing, setting up, programming, and using the Radio Shack TRS-80 Color Computer. A complete introduction.

Software Specific

Spreadsheets

VISICALC® FOR SCIENCE AND ENGINEERING
by Stanley R. Trost and Charles Pomernacki
203 pp., illustr., Ref. 0-096
More than 50 programs for solving technical problems in science and engineering. Applications range from math and statistics to electrical and electronic engineering.

DOING BUSINESS WITH MULTIPLAN™
by Richard Allen King and Stanley R. Trost
250 pp., illustr., Ref. 0-148
This book will show you how using Multiplan can be nearly as easy as learning to use a pocket calculator. It presents a collection of templates for business applications.

MASTERING VISICALC®
by Douglas Hergert
217 pp., 140 illustr., Ref. 0-090
Explains how to use the VisiCalc "electronic spreadsheet" functions and provides examples of each. Makes using this powerful program simple.

DOING BUSINESS WITH VISICALC®
by Stanley R. Trost
260 pp., illustr., Ref. 0-086
Presents accounting and management planning applications—from financial statements to master budgets; from pricing models to investment strategies.

DOING BUSINESS WITH SUPERCALC™
by Stanley R. Trost
248 pp., illustr., Ref. 0-095
Presents accounting and management planning applications—from financial statements to master budgets; from pricing models to investment strategies.

MULTIPLAN™ ON THE COMMODORE 64™
by Richard Allen King
260 pp., illustr., Ref. 0-231
This clear, straighforward guide will give you a firm grasp on Multiplan's functions, as well as provide a collection of useful template programs.

Word Processing

INTRODUCTION TO WORDSTAR®
by Arthur Naiman
202 pp., 30 illustr., Ref. 0-134

Makes it easy to learn WordStar, a powerful word processing program for personal computers.

PRACTICAL WORDSTAR® USES
by Julie Anne Arca
303 pp., illustr., Ref. 0-107
Pick your most time-consuming office tasks and this book will show you how to streamline them with WordStar.

THE FOOLPROOF GUIDE TO SCRIPSIT™ WORD PROCESSING
by Jeff Berner
179 pp., illustr., Ref. 0-098
Everything you need to know about SCRIPSIT—from starting out, to mastering document editing. This user-friendly guide is written in plain English, with a touch of wit.

THE COMPLETE GUIDE TO MULTIMATE™
by Carol Holcomb Dreger
250 pp., illustr., Ref. 0-229
A concise introduction to the many practical applications of this powerful word processing program.

THE THINKTANK™ BOOK
by Jonathan Kamin
200 pp., illustr., Ref. 0-224
Learn how the ThinkTank program can help you organize your thoughts, plans, and activities.

Data Base Management Systems

UNDERSTANDING dBASE II™
by Alan Simpson
260 pp., illustr., Ref. 0-147
Learn programming techniques for mailing label systems, bookkeeping, and data management, as well as ways to interface dBASE II with other software systems.

DOING BUSINESS WITH dBASE II™
by Stanley R. Trost
250 pp., illustr., Ref. 0-160
Learn to use dBASE II for accounts

receivable, recording business income and expenses, keeping personal records and mailing lists, and much more.

Integrated Software

INTRODUCTION TO INFOSTAR™
by Julie Anne Arca and Charles F. Pirro
275 pp., illustr., Ref. 0-108
This book gives you an overview of InfoStar, including DataStar and ReportStar, WordStar, MailMerge, and SuperSort. Hands-on exercises take you step-by-step through real life business applications.

DOING BUSINESS WITH 1-2-3™
by Stanley R. Trost
250 pp., illustr., Ref. 0-159
If you are a business professional using the 1-2-3 software package, you will find the spreadsheet and graphics models provided in this book easy to use "as is" in everyday business situations.

THE ABC'S OF 1-2-3™
by Chris Gilbert and Laurie Williams
225 pp., illustr., Ref. 0-168
For those new to the LOTUS 1-2-3 program, this book offers step-by-step instructions in mastering its spreadsheet, data base, and graphing capabilities.

MASTERING APPLEWORKS™
by Elna Tymes
250 pp., illustr., Ref. 0-240
Here is a business-oriented introduction to AppleWorks, the new integrated software package from Apple. No experience with computers is assumed.

Languages

BASIC

YOUR FIRST BASIC PROGRAM
by Rodnay Zaks
182 pp., illustr. in color, Ref. 0-092
A "how-to-program" book for the first time computer user, aged 8 to 88.

FIFTY BASIC EXERCISES
by J. P. Lamoitier
232 pp., 90 illustr., Ref. 0-056
Teaches BASIC through actual practice, using graduated exercises drawn from everyday applications. Programs written in Microsoft BASIC.

INSIDE BASIC GAMES
by Richard Mateosian
348 pp., 120 illustr., Ref. 0-055
Teaches interactive BASIC programming through games. Games are written in Microsoft BASIC and run on the TRS-80, Apple II and PET/CBM.

BASIC FOR BUSINESS
by Douglas Hergert
224 pp., 15 illustr., Ref. 0-080
A logically organized, no-nonsense introduction to BASIC programming for business applications. Includes many fully-explained accounting programs, and shows you how to write your own.

EXECUTIVE PLANNING WITH BASIC
by X. T. Bui
196 pp., 19 illustr., Ref. 0-083
An important collection of business management decision models in BASIC, including inventory management (EOQ), critical path analysis and PERT, financial ratio analysis, portfolio management, and much more.

BASIC PROGRAMS FOR SCIENTISTS AND ENGINEERS
by Alan R. Miller
318 pp., 120 illustr., Ref. 0-073
This book from the "Programs for Scientists and Engineers" series provides a library of problem-solving programs while developing the reader's proficiency in BASIC.

Pascal

INTRODUCTION TO PASCAL (Including UCSD Pascal™)
by Rodnay Zaks
420 pp., 130 illustr., Ref. 0-066
A step-by-step introduction for anyone who wants to learn the Pascal language.

Describes UCSD and Standard Pascals. No technical background is assumed.

THE PASCAL HANDBOOK
by Jacques Tiberghien
486 pp., 270 illustr., Ref. 0-053
A dictionary of the Pascal language, defining every reserved word, operator, procedure, and function found in all major versions of Pascal.

APPLE® PASCAL GAMES
by Douglas Hergert and Joseph T. Kalash
372 pp., 40 illustr., Ref. 0-074
A collection of the most popular computer games in Pascal, challenging the reader not only to play but to investigate how games are implemented on the computer.

PASCAL PROGRAMS FOR SCIENTISTS AND ENGINEERS
by Alan R. Miller
374 pp., 120 illustr., Ref. 0-058
A comprehensive collection of frequently used algorithms for scientific and technical applications, programmed in Pascal. Includes programs for curve-fitting, integrals, statistical techniques, and more.

DOING BUSINESS WITH PASCAL
by Richard Hergert and Douglas Hergert
371 pp., illustr., Ref. 0-091
Practical tips for using Pascal programming in business. Covers design considerations, language extensions, and applications examples.

Other Languages

FORTRAN PROGRAMS FOR SCIENTISTS AND ENGINEERS
by Alan R. Miller
280 pp., 120 illustr., Ref. 0-082
This book from the "Programs for Scientists and Engineers" series provides a library of problem-solving programs while developing the reader's proficiency in FORTRAN.

A MICROPROGRAMMED APL IMPLEMENTATION
by Rodnay Zaks
350 pp., Ref. 0-005

An expert-level text presenting the complete conceptual analysis and design of an APL interpreter, and actual listing of the microcode.

UNDERSTANDING C
by Bruce H. Hunter
320 pp., Ref 0-123
Explains how to program in powerful C language for a variety of applications. Some programming experience assumed.

FIFTY PASCAL PROGRAMS
by Bruce H. Hunter
338 pp., illustr., Ref. 0-110
More than just a collection of useful programs! Structured programming techniques are emphasized and concepts such as data type creation and array manipulation are clearly illustrated.

Technical

Assembly Language

PROGRAMMING THE 6502
by Rodnay Zaks
386 pp., 160 illustr., Ref. 0-135
Assembly language programming for the 6502, from basic concepts to advanced data structures.

6502 APPLICATIONS
by Rodnay Zaks
278 pp., 200 illustr., Ref. 0-015
Real-life application techniques: the input/output book for the 6502.

ADVANCED 6502 PROGRAMMING
by Rodnay Zaks
292 pp., 140 illustr., Ref. 0-089
Third in the 6502 series. Teaches more advanced programming techniques, using games as a framework for learning.

PROGRAMMING THE Z80®
by Rodnay Zaks
624 pp., 200 illustr., Ref. 0-069
A complete course in programming the Z80 microprocessor and a thorough introduction to assembly language.

Z80® APPLICATIONS
by James W. Coffron
288 pp., illustr., Ref. 0-094
Covers techniques and applications for using peripheral devices with a Z80 based system.

PROGRAMMING THE 6809
by Rodnay Zaks and William Labiak
362 pp., 150 illustr., Ref. 0-078
This book explains how to program the 6809 microprocessor in assembly language. No prior programming knowledge required.

PROGRAMMING THE Z8000®
by Richard Mateosian
298 pp., 124 illustr., Ref. 0-032
How to program the Z8000 16-bit microprocessor. Includes a description of the architecture and function of the Z8000 and its family of support chips.

PROGRAMMING THE 8086™/8088™
by James W. Coffron
300 pp., illustr., Ref. 0-120
This book explains how to program the 8086 and 8088 microprocessors in assembly language. No prior programming knowledge required.

8086™/8088™ APPLICATIONS
by James W. Coffron
250 pp., illustr., Ref. 0-191
Learn to use the 8086/8088 microprocessor with peripheral devices for a variety of systems applications.

PROGRAMMING THE 68000™
by Steve Williams
250 pp., illustr., Ref. 0-133
This book introduces you to microprocessor operation, writing application programs, and the basics of I/O programming. Especially helpful for owners of the Apple Macintosh or Lisa.

Hardware

FROM CHIPS TO SYSTEMS: AN INTRODUCTION TO MICROPROCESSORS
by Rodnay Zaks
552 pp., 400 illustr., Ref. 0-063

A simple and comprehensive introduction to microprocessors from both a hardware and software standpoint: what they are, how they operate, how to assemble them into a complete system.

MICROPROCESSOR INTERFACING TECHNIQUES
by Rodnay Zaks and Austin Lesea
456 pp., 400 illustr., Ref. 0-029
Complete hardware and software interfacing techniques, including D to A conversion, peripherals, bus standards and troubleshooting.

THE RS-232 SOLUTION
by Joe Campbell
194 pp., illustr., Ref. 0-140
Finally, a book that will show you how to correctly interface your computer to any RS-232-C peripheral.

USING CASSETTE RECORDERS WITH COMPUTERS
by Rick Cook
175 pp., illustr., Ref. 0-169
Whatever your computer or application, you will find this book helpful in explaining details of cassette care and maintenance.

MASTERING SERIAL COMMUNICATIONS
by Joe Campbell
250 pp., illustr., Ref. 0-180

This sequel to *The RS-232 Solution* guides the reader to mastery of more complex interfacing techniques.

MICROPROCESSOR INTERFACING TECHNIQUES: VOLUME II
by James W. Coffron and Bill Harmon
300 pp., illustr., Ref. 0-196
Engineers, technicians, and hobbyists will find this an invaluable guide to 16-bit interfacing techniques.

Operating Systems

REAL WORLD UNIX™
by John D. Halamka
209 pp., Ref. 0-093
This book is written for the beginning and intermediate UNIX user in a practical, straightforward manner, with specific instructions given for many business applications.

INTRODUCTION TO THE UCSD p-SYSTEM™
by Charles W. Grant and Jon Butah
300 pp., 10 illustr., Ref. 0-061
A simple, clear introduction to the UCSD Pascal Operating System for beginners through experienced programmers.

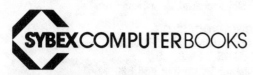

SYBEX COMPUTER BOOKS

are different.

Here is why . . .

At SYBEX, each book is designed with you in mind. Every manuscript is carefully selected and supervised by our editors, who are themselves computer experts. We publish the best authors, whose technical expertise is matched by an ability to write clearly and to communicate effectively. Programs are thoroughly tested for accuracy by our technical staff. Our computerized production department goes to great lengths to make sure that each book is well-designed.

In the pursuit of timeliness, SYBEX has achieved many publishing firsts. SYBEX was among the first to integrate personal computers used by authors and staff into the publishing process. SYBEX was the first to publish books on the CP/M operating system, microprocessor interfacing techniques, word processing, and many more topics.

Expertise in computers and dedication to the highest quality product have made SYBEX a world leader in computer book publishing. Translated into fourteen languages, SYBEX books have helped millions of people around the world to get the most from their computers. We hope we have helped you, too.

For a complete catalog of our publications:

SYBEX, Inc. 2344 Sixth Street, Berkeley, California 94710
Tel: (415) 848-8233   Telex: 336311